SCIENCE INTERACTIONS

Course 3

GLENCOE

Macmillan/McGraw-Hill

New York, New York   Columbus, Ohio   Mission Hills, California   Peoria, Illinois

Science Interactions

Student Edition

Teacher Wraparound Edition

Teacher Classroom Resource Package

Laboratory Manual: SE

Laboratory Manual: TE

Study Guide: SE

Study Guide: TE

Transparency Package

Computer Test Bank

Spanish Resources

Science and Technology Videodisc Series

Science and Technology Videodisc Teacher Guide

Send all inquiries to:

GLENCOE DIVISION
Macmillan/McGraw-Hill
936 Eastwind Drive
Westerville, OH 43081

ISBN 0-02-826106-2

Printed in the United States of America

2 3 4 5 6 7 8 9 - RRD-W - 00 99 98 97 96 95 94 93 92

Authors

Bill Aldridge, M.S.
Executive Director
National Science Teachers Association
Washington, DC

Russell Aiuto, Ph.D.
Director of Research and Development
Scope, Sequence, and Coordination
National Science Teachers Association
Washington, DC

Jack Ballinger, Ed.D.
Professor of Chemistry
St. Louis Community College at
    Florissant Valley
St. Louis, MO

Anne Barefoot, A.G.C.
Physics and Chemistry Teacher
Whiteville High School
Hallsboro, NC

Linda Crow, Ed.D.
Assistant Professor
Baylor College of Medicine
Houston, TX

Ralph M. Feather, Jr., M.Ed.
Science Department Chairperson
Derry Area School District
Derry, PA

Albert Kaskel, M.Ed.
Biology Teacher
Evanston Township High School
Evanston, IL

Craig Kramer, M.A.
Physics Teacher
Bexley High School
Bexley, OH

Edward Ortleb, A.G.C.
Science Lead Supervisor
St. Louis Board of Education
St. Louis, MO

Susan Snyder, M.S.
Earth Science Teacher
Jones Middle School
Upper Arlington, OH

Paul W. Zitzewitz, Ph.D.
Professor of Physics
University of Michigan-Dearborn
Dearborn, MI

Consultants

CHEMISTRY

Richard J. Merrill
Director, Project Physical Science
Associate Director, Institute for
  Chemical Education
University of California
Berkeley, California

Robert Walter Parry, Ph.D.
Dist. Professor of Chemistry
University of Utah
Salt Lake City, Utah

EARTH SCIENCE

Janifer Mayden
Aerospace Education Specialist
NASA
Washington, DC

James B. Phipps, Ph.D.
Professor of Geology and
  Oceanography
Gray's Harbor College
Aberdeen, Washington

LIFE SCIENCE

Mary D. Coyne, Ph.D.
Professor of Biological Sciences
Wellesley College
Wellesley, Massachusetts

Joe Wiliam Crim, Ph.D.
Associate Professor of Zoology
University of Georgia
Athens, Georgia

Kathleen A. Fleiszar, Ph.D.
Professor of Biology
Kennesaw State College
Marietta, Georgia

David G. Futch, Ph.D.
Associate Professor Biology
San Diego State University
San Diego, California

PHYSICS

Karen L. Johnston, Ph.D.
Professor of Physics
North Carolina State University
Raleigh, North Carolina

Eugen Merzbacher, Ph.D.
Kenan Professor of Physics, Emeritus
University of North Carolina
Chapel Hill, North Carolina

MIDDLE SCHOOL SCIENCE

Thomas Custer
Coordinator of Science
Anne Arundel County
Ellicot City, Maryland

Gerald Garner
LA Unified
Van Nuys, California

Garland E. Johnson
Science and Education Consultant
Fresno, California

SAFETY

Robert Tatz, Ph.D.
Instructional Lab Supervisor
Department of Chemistry
The Ohio State University
Columbus, Ohio

READING

Barbara Pettegrew, Ph.D.
Director of Reading/Study Center
Assistant Professor of Education
Otterbein College
Westerville, Ohio

MULTICULTURAL

Carol Mitchell
Science Supervisor
Omaha Public Schools
Omaha, Nebraska

Karen L. Muir, Ph.D.
Department of Social and Behavioral
  Sciences
Columbus State Community College
Columbus, Ohio

LEP

Harold Frederick Robertson, Jr.
Science Resource Teacher
LAUSD Science Materials Center
Van Nuys, California

Ross M. Arnold
Magnet School Coordinator
Van Nuys Junior High
Van Nuys, California

Linda E. Heckenberg
Director, Eisenhower Program
Van Nuys, California

Barbara Sitzman
Chatsworth High School
Tarzana, California

COOPERATIVE LEARNING

Linda Lundgren
Bear Creek High School
Lakewood, Colorado

SPECIAL FEATURES

Timothy Heron, Ph.D.
Professor
Department of Educational Services
  and Research
The Ohio State University
Columbus, Ohio

Reviewers

Assunta Black
Life Science Teacher
Lindenhurst Junior High
Lindenhurst, New York

Jayne Brown
7th Grade Science Teacher
Valley Springs Middle School
Arden, North Carolina

Mitchell Kyle Carver, Sr.
Science Department Chairperson
Reynolds Middle School
Asheville, North Carolina

James Cowden
Science Teacher Specialist
Chicago Public Schools
Chicago, Illinois

Gloria M. Dobry
Departmental Science Teacher
Gunsaulus Academy
Chicago, Illinois

Daniel H. Domenigoni
Science Department Chairperson
Milwaukie Junior High
Milwaukie, Oregon

Cheryl B. Domineau
Science Department Chairperson
Vero Beach Junior High
Vero Beach, Florida

Alex Domkowski
Physics Teacher
Saint Mary's Hall
San Antonio, Texas

Nancy Donohue
General Science Teacher
Emerson Junior High
Yonkers, New York

Nancy Ann Drain
Teacher
Bell Junior High School
San Diego, California

Nancy Prevatte Dunlap
7th Grade Science Teacher
Central Middle School
Whiteville, North Carolina

Susan Falk
Science Teacher
Los Cerritos Intermediate School
Thousand Oaks, California

Laraine O. Franze
Life Science Teacher
Greenwood Lakes Middle School
Lake Mary, Florida

John A. George
Science Department Chairperson
Rivera Middle School
Miami, Florida

Corless Horne Goode
Teacher
New Hope School
Rutherfordton, North Carolina

Raymond Pat Hadd
Science Department Chairperson
Richbourg Middle School
Crestview, Florida

Karen Sue Hewitt
Teacher
Coldspring High School
Coldspring, Texas

Barbara D. Johnson
Life Science Teacher
Deep Creek Junior High School
Chesapeake, Virginia

Thomas E. Johnson
Life Science Teacher
Western Branch Junior High School
Chesapeake, Virginia

James R. Kimsey
Lead Science Instructor/ Department
  Head
Plaza Park Middle School
Evansville, Indiana

Lonnie L. Lewis
Science Department Chairperson
Ramona Junior High School
Chino, California

William T. Martin
8th Grade General Science Teacher
Atkins Middle School
Winston-Salem, North Carolina

Vito Charles Mazzini, Jr.
Science Department Chairperson
H. D. McMillan Middle School
Miami, Florida

George Graham Ohmer
Teacher
Clay Junior High School
Carmel, Indiana

Chuck Porrazzo
Science Department Chairperson
CJHS 145
New York City, New York

Allan G. Reisberg
6th Grade Teacher
Abraham Lincoln
Chicago, Illinois

Steven F. Rinck
Supervisor of Science
Pasco County School Board
Land O'Lakes, Florida

Ouida E. Thomas
Life Science Teacher
B. F. Terry High School
Rosenberg, Texas

Mary Coggins White
Science Department Chairperson
Sequoia Intermediate School
Newbury Park, California

Nedra A. Williams
Science Department Chairperson
Los Cerritos Intermediate School
Thousand Oaks, California

Contents

UNIT 2   ATOMS AND MOLECULES   123

UNIT 3   OUR FLUID ENVIRONMENT   251

UNIT 4 CHANGES IN LIFE AND EARTH OVER TIME

415

Appendices 661

Skill Handbook 679

Glossary 694

Index 698

Introducing Science Interactions

If you've ever seen a magician perform, you know there is some truth to the expression "The hand is quicker than the eye." Whether it's pulling rabbits from a hat or "sawing" someone in half, you can be sure that what you think you see is not what is really happening.

Most of us delight in puzzling over the magician's sleight of hand—we wonder how on Earth we were fooled. Too often, we simply applaud and walk away, still puzzled.

Yes, the hand is quicker than the eye. But the brain is quicker than the hand. And a brain that understands and applies science principles can figure out all sorts of "mysteries," from magic tricks to puzzling occurrences in the world around us.

Making Sense of the World

The need to make sense of the world is not new. Since the beginning of time, figuring out the "why" behind the "what" has occupied human minds. But because their observations were limited and they did not always explore questions in an orderly way, ancient people often thought that natural occurrences were the work of magic or "the gods."

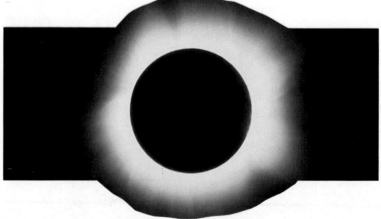

Solar eclipses were terrifying events for some ancient peoples—the sun disappeared from the sky as if it had been swallowed by a giant sky creature.

Mayans of Central America made careful observations of planets and stars from this ancient observatory. Some of their knowledge allowed them to make amazingly accurate calculations.

For example, some ancient people believed a comet was a signal that the gods were angry. Some believed that pregnancy occurred when women visited certain powerful places or ate certain kinds of foods. The Vikings explained lightning by saying that it flashed when Thor, the god of thunder, threw his magic golden hammer to Earth.

Some beliefs of the ancients were founded on fear and superstition, but others were founded on observed facts. Science principles make use of orderly methods that help show a connection between what you see happening and what causes it to happen. As our knowledge increases, finding connections often means looking at a topic in life science through the eyes of a chemist and physicist as well.

As part of understanding science, you will learn to compare, contrast, and sort information, and interpret and apply what you learn. In this process, you will train yourself to become a keen observer and a critical thinker—a person who is not easily fooled.

Earth's rotation caused these star streaks made on film exposed for several hours at a modern observatory.

Hat Tricks

Now, let's take a trial run at applying some of the ideas you'll learn in Science Interactions. Imagine you and your friends are seated front row center at a magic show. You yawn, expecting only hat tricks, but the magician announces his first two tricks will defy accepted principles of science. You quickly sit up and take notice!

He begins by holding up an ordinary paper cup and a table knife. Sweeping them grandly before the audience, he tips the cup forward to show it's empty. Moments later, the knife hangs suspended sideways from the bottom of the cup. You can't—and—shouldn't believe your eyes! You know that gravity should pull the knife clattering to the stage. Something else is holding the knife up, but what? What explanation or hypothesis can you form about what you have observed?

While you are thinking about how you would duplicate his first trick, the magician is already getting ready for the second one. He holds up two books, a flat piece of ordinary glass the size of a window pane, and two small, flat, green paper frogs. He lays the books flat and about six inches apart on an empty card table. He puts the paper frogs between the books and shouts that he will bring them to life!

The magician then remarks that the glass is dirty and begins rubbing it briskly with a bright silk scarf. Sure enough, when he lays the glass over the books, the frogs jump up and briefly hang onto the glass!

Solving Magic Tricks

You know from your own experience that paper frogs cannot be turned into live ones. How did the magician make them jump? And how did he "defy gravity" by suspending the knife? You can solve these puzzles for yourself by analyzing exactly what the magician did, making your own hypotheses about how each trick was done, and testing them by doing the tricks yourself.

▮▮▮ FIND OUT! ▮▮▮

How can you explain the magic tricks?

Try to figure out how the magician did one of his tricks and try to perform one of the tricks.

Did you come up with reasonable scientific explanations for the magician's tricks? Did you discover that magnets and static electricity are part of the answers? You'll learn more about these in Chapters 1 and 2. After you read those chapters, maybe you can come up with some different methods for doing the tricks.

The processes you used to observe and analyze the magician's actions are similar to the scientific processes you will follow to learn more about such puzzling occurrences as the reasons for severe weather (Chapter 9), why magnets can appear to float on a pencil (Chapter 2), and how blood clots form (Chapter 13).

In science class this year, you will read about, observe, analyze, investigate, and discover explanations for these and hundreds of other "mysteries of science." As you will see, learning and doing science can be fun.

D o you like to run? If so, you know the simple, heart-pounding joy that comes from having your arms and legs move you in perfect rhythm across Earth. Although it looks simple, running is based on a number of scientific principles. In fact—whether you're running around a track, baking brownies, or reading a book—life science, chemistry, Earth science, and physics are an essential part of your everyday life. You'll discover this for yourself in *Science Interactions*. It features lively narrative and exciting hands-on activities to help you observe, understand, and apply important science principles that affect you each day.

Getting Started

What's going on in this photo? You can be sure it's more than meets the eye! Each chapter begins with a thought-provoking EXPLORE! activity to get you involved with science right off the bat. Intriguing pictures and **Did You Ever Wonder?** questions whet your curiosity about what each chapter holds. Read the opener to Chapter 13 to find out how the movement of blood can be compared to a ride on a water slide.

DID YOU EVER WONDER . . .

Why your blood is red?

Why blood doesn't just keep flowing from your body when you cut yourself?

Why most people get mumps, measles, chicken pox, and some other childhood diseases only once during their lifetime?

You'll find the answers to these questions as you read this chapter.

Chapter 13

Blood: Transport and Protection

Imagine you could shrink yourself to the size of the period at the end of this sentence and go sailing through your body's blood vessels. Riding down a water slide is similar to the twisting and turning travels of a blood cell inside a blood vessel. At this very moment, blood pumping through your blood vessels behaves very much like the water that rapidly propels you through a narrow passageway in the waterslide. Just as rushing water surrounds and carries you along, solid particles move in a liquid through your arteries and veins propelled by the beating of your heart.

In this chapter, you will learn about the liquid and solid parts that make up your blood. You will also come to understand how your blood acts as a natural defense system to protect your body from disease.

EXPLORE!

How much blood is in your body right now?

Generally, blood makes up about eight percent of your body's total mass. Figure out your total body mass by multiplying your weight in pounds by 0.45. This will give you your body weight in kilograms. After you calculate your body weight, you will then have to find eight percent of that figure. The answer will be your body's mass of blood in kilograms.

385

Learning Science Requires Using Your Mind and All Your Senses

Each lesson in *Science Interactions* involves you in a range of experiences that make use of all your senses. As an active player in the science-learning process, you will discover new ways to view the world around you. You will learn to be a critical observer of events and processes. You will find out how to think critically, conduct careful experiments, and draw reasonable conclusions.

The text reading will support and enhance your self-discovery of science principles with real-life examples from your home, school or community. It will challenge you to think in new ways, and help you connect the new things you are learning.

EXPLORE! FIND OUT! INVESTIGATE!

When you see these words in *Science Interactions*, you'll know it's time to use your hands and your mind to discover for yourself how and why things work the way they do.

Scientists try to answer these questions by observing, predicting, and experimenting. You will be doing the same thing when you do the EXPLORE! FIND OUT! and INVESTIGATE! activities. As you do each of these activities, you will need to make careful observations, collect and analyze data, and make conclusions. When experiments don't turn out the way you think they should, remember that scientists often learn as much from experiments that fail as from experiments that always work as planned.

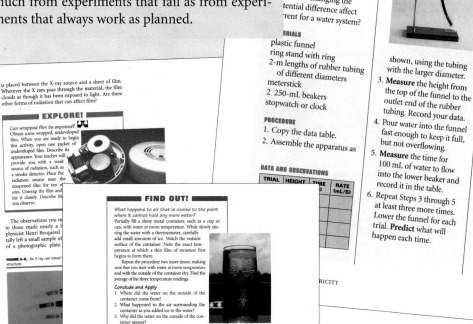

INVESTIGATE!

1-2 POTENTIAL DIFFERENCE AND CURRENT

You know that increasing resistance decreases current through a circuit. A water model will show how changes in potential difference affect the current.

PROBLEM

How does changing the potential difference affect current for a water system?

MATERIALS

plastic funnel
ring stand with ring
2-m lengths of rubber tubing of different diameters
meterstick
2 250-mL beakers
stopwatch or clock

PROCEDURE

1. Copy the data table.
2. Assemble the apparatus as shown, using the tubing with the larger diameter.
3. **Measure** the height from the top of the funnel to the outlet end of the rubber tubing. Record your data.
4. Pour water into the funnel fast enough to keep it full, but not overflowing.
5. **Measure** the time for 100 mL of water to flow into the lower beaker and record it in the table.
6. Repeat Steps 3 through 5 at least three more times. Lower the funnel for each trial. **Predict** what will happen each time.
7. Replace the tubing with tubing of a smaller diameter. Repeat Steps 3 through 6. What do you **observe**?

ANALYZE

1. The model compares water moving due to gravity with electrical charges moving due to potential difference, or voltage. Which trial corresponds to a circuit with the highest voltage?
2. If the voltage is increased, what happens to the current?
3. What effect does the diameter of the tube have on the rate of water flow?
4. **Compare** the effect of funnel height on the rate of water flow.

CONCLUDE AND APPLY

5. What electrical property do the hose diameters represent?
6. **Going Further:** If the smaller diameter hose corresponds to a greater electric resistance, what do you think will happen to the electric current if the voltage stays constant, but the resistance is increased?

DATA AND OBSERVATIONS

TRIAL	HEIGHT	TIME	RATE (mL/S)

...RICITY

is placed between the X-ray source and a sheet of film. Wherever the X rays pass through the material, the film clouds as though it has been exposed to light. Are there other forms of radiation that can affect film?

EXPLORE!

Can wrapped film be exposed?

Obtain some wrapped, undeveloped film. When you are ready to begin this activity, open one packet of undeveloped film. Describe its appearance. Your teacher will provide you with a weak source of radiation, such as a smoke detector. Place the radiation source near the unopened film for ten minutes. Unwrap the film and examine it closely. Describe what you observe.

The observations you m... to those made nearly a h... physicist Henri Becquerel... tally left a small sample of... of a photographic plate.

FIGURE 5-5. An X ray can travel... structure.

FIND OUT!

What happens to air that is cooled to the point where it cannot hold any more water?

Partially fill a shiny metal container, such as a cup or can, with water at room temperature. While slowly stirring the water with a thermometer, carefully add small amounts of ice. Watch the outside surface of the container. Note the exact temperature at which a thin film of moisture first begins to form there.

Repeat the procedure two more times, making sure that you start with water at room temperature and with the outside of the container dry. Find the average of the three temperature readings.

Conclude and Apply

1. Where did the water on the outside of the container come from?
2. What happened to the air surrounding the container as you added ice to the water?
3. Why did the water on the outside of the container appear?

When the relative humidity of air reaches 100 percent, the air is holding all the moisture it possibly can at that temperature. When this happens, the air is **saturated**. As you saw in the Find Out activity, when the temperature of the air around the container was cooled to the point of...

everything about a magnetic material? For [...]
most of the time one paper clip has little or n[...]
tion for other paper clips. Yet, sometimes when [...]
clip is near a magnet, the clip itself acts like a m[...]

MAKING MAGNETS

Let's use our theory of atomic magnets t[...]
how a material like the paper clip can be made [...]
ic. Suppose that, ordinarily, the atomic ma[...]
every which way. Figure 2[...]
diagram of this arrangem[...]
suppose that large number [...]
ic magnets line up in one [...]
Each cluster of aligned at[...]
contain billions of atomic magnets
all working together. If most of the
magnetic domains in the sample line up, as shown in
Figure 2-6(b), they would reinforce each other's magnetic fields. Then the material would produce large
magnetic effects.

You've already made a temporary magnet, one that
works only in the presence of a magnetic field. From what
you know about magnetic domains, do you think you can
make a permanent magnet?

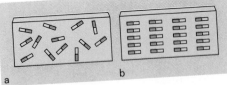

FIGURE 2-6. Domains in unmagnetized materials are randomly oriented (a); domains in magnetized materials are aligned (b).

How do we know?

Is there any observable evidence that magnetic atoms exist?

Yes. A fine powder of iron oxide, also known as rust, can be spread over a smooth surface of a magnetized metal. It's a little like placing iron filings around a bar magnet. The powder will collect along the boundaries between neighboring clusters of magnetic atoms. These clusters are called domains. The boundaries are visible under a microscope and can be photographed. These outlines allow us to observe the way magnetic atoms interact with each other.

SKILLBUILDER

INTERPRETING SCIENTIFIC ILLUSTRATIONS

The thermostat that controls a furnace works a little like the side-by-side straws. In Figure 8-5, what happens as the loop in the

Expanding Your View

At the end of each chapter, you'll find a variety of **Expanding Your View** articles that will help you understand and appreciate the important role of science in school, at home, and in society.

The types of articles will vary in each chapter, but will always begin with **A Closer Look**—an in-depth look at one of the topics you studied in the chapter. The second article will explore how ideas from one science area relate to or are useful in a different science area.

Other articles will present ideas on several of the following topics:

- Science connections to art, history, literature, and geography.
- New and everyday technology applications.
- The impact of science on society.
- Teenagers actively involved in some field of science.

At the end of each article, you'll be asked to answer questions, do an activity, or maybe research the topic further.

Throughout each chapter, you'll have plenty of chances to review and apply new ideas and skills. In this way, science will become a more natural part of your everyday vocabulary and experience.

Check Your Understanding will reinforce the key ideas of each section you study.

Reviewing Main Ideas near the end of the chapter uses words and pictures to help you pull together the main ideas of the chapter.

Chapter Review—the last two pages of every chapter—is loaded with options for reviewing and connecting ideas, thinking critically and solving problems.

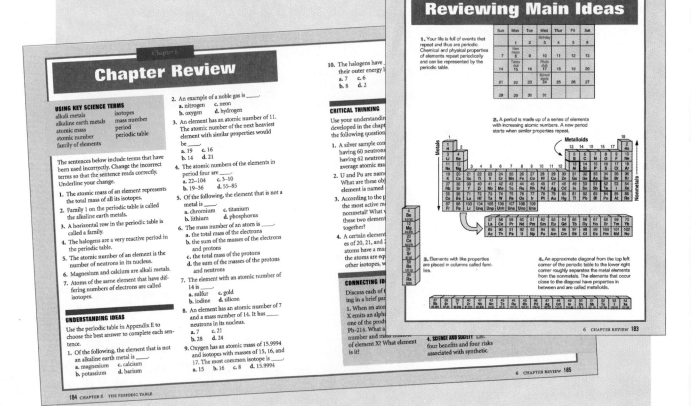

Looking Back
Looking Ahead

Looking Back and **Looking Ahead** are what you'll be doing when you come to the blue and red pages that separate one unit from another. The **Looking Back** page will help you focus on the big ideas from units you've already studied. The **Looking Ahead** page will pre-pare you for the next unit you are about to study.

Now that you've completed this quick tour of your textbook, it is time to begin the first unit. To find out what's coming up in Unit One, read the **Looking Ahead** page on your right.

TRY IT

A magnet, like those often found on refrigerators, is an inexpensive, common item. Bring it near the stove and you can feel the force of the magnet. The magnet is attracted to the stove or refrigerator, but it is not attracted to the side of a soft drink can. Both of these items are made of metal, but why does the magnet act differently? What happens when the magnet is brought close to items such as paper clips, aluminum soft drink can tops, paper, and rubber bands? Try it and see if your predictions were correct. Based on your observations, can you make a general statement about why a magnet does what it does? Using the materials that were attracted by the magnet, place a sheet of paper between the magnet and materials. Do you notice any difference in the way the magnet works? After you've learned more about magnets, try this activity again and see if your predictions change or your explanations were correct.

UNIT 1 ELECTRICITY AND MAGNETISM

CONTENTS

UNIT FOCUS

In Unit 1, you will be working with electricity and magnetism. As you study this unit, you'll learn the many different ways in which you use electrical energy each day. When you toast bread, pop popcorn in the microwave oven, or simply use a can opener, you are using electrical energy. In a kitchen, you might see notes held on the refrigerator by magnets. You will learn how special properties of a magnet enable it to stick to certain metallic surfaces. When you see sunlight or a rainbow, you are observing visible electromagnetic waves, and if your skin darkens after a sunny day, you are experiencing the effects of invisible electromagnetic waves.

DID YOU EVER WONDER . . .

What static cling is?

What makes electric eels electric?

Where is the safest place to be during an electrical storm?

You'll find the answers to these questions as you read this chapter.

Electricity

A bright light and the crash of thunder awaken you one night. You watch through your window as an electrical storm moves across the sky. Bright white bolts of lightning flash and then streak outward like cracks in broken glass. You're suddenly glad for the safety of your room as you sense the energy in lightning—energy that can start fires, split trees, and knock out the electrical power.

What causes this energy and draws it from the sky to Earth? And does the same form of energy light lamps and heat toasters? In this chapter, you will learn about a form of energy that we take very much for granted. Without this form of energy, our lives would be very different. It would not be as easy to cook food, clean our clothes, or entertain ourselves. This form of energy affects every aspect of our lives. Less than a hundred years ago, this energy was a new and mysterious novelty. The energy is electricity, and its story is fascinating.

EXPLORE!

Can a comb pick up paper?
Take a small plastic comb and hold it over several tiny scraps of paper. Does anything happen? Now hold a piece of dry, wool cloth in one hand and brush the comb along it several times with the other hand. Then hold the comb over the scraps of paper. What happens? How can the comb produce a force that can overcome gravity? Why does the paper jump to the comb after brushing with wool? What did the rubbing of the wool do to the comb?

1-1 Forces and Electrical Charges

OBJECTIVES

In this section, you will
- observe the force caused by electrical charges;
- demonstrate the two kinds of electrical charges.

KEY SCIENCE TERMS

electrical charge
unlike charges
like charges

FIGURE 1-1. Thales and Gilbert both used amber to produce electrical charges. In this case, the charged amber was able to attract pieces of paper.

STATIC ELECTRICITY

The scene is Ancient Greece around 600 B.C.E. A man named Thales is rubbing a piece of amber with some cloth. When he sets down the amber, small objects are attracted to it. Over two thousand years later, around 1570, an Englishman named William Gilbert repeats the same experiment. He calls the effects he sees *electricity* after the Greek word for amber. The type of electricity that Thales and Gilbert experimented with is called static electricity, which means it does not move.

After you rubbed the comb on the cloth in the Explore, the comb attracted the tiny scraps of paper. You repeated the experiment done by Thales and Gilbert and saw the effect of static electricity. Perhaps you've gotten a shock from touching a doorknob after walking on a carpet. You might even have seen a spark jump. These are the effects of static electricity. Lightning is a spectacular result of static electricity. You can explore the effects of static electricity by doing a very simple experiment.

FIND OUT!

Do electric charges interact?

Take a roll of removable cellophane tape. Fold over about 5 mm on the end of the tape for a handle. Then tear off a strip 8 to 10 cm long. Stick the strip on a dry, smooth surface, such as your desktop. Make a second strip of tape in the same way and stick it on top of the first tape. Now quickly pull both pieces off the desk and pull them apart. Then bring the tapes close together. Now make two new strips of tape, but this time press each one onto the desk. Then pull them off and bring the two strips close together.

Conclude and Apply

1. What happened when you brought the first pair of tapes close together? What happened when you brought the second pair together?

2. What did you do that might have caused the two different reactions?

3. Did the second pair of tapes push apart more when they were closer together or farther apart? When was the force between them stronger?

When you pulled the strips of tape from the desk, you caused them to have an **electrical charge**. By sticking one strip on top of the other, you treated the two strips differently. They received **unlike charges**.

You charged the strips of tape the same way by preparing them in the same way. When the strips were both stuck to the desk, you charged them alike, giving them **like charges**.

In the Find Out, you observed that when the strips were treated differently and therefore received unlike charges, they attracted each other. When both strips were treated the same and therefore received the same charge, they repelled. These observations are summarized in Figure 1-2 and in a fundamental law of electricity: Like charges repel and unlike charges attract. The Investigate will help you identify these charges.

FIGURE 1-2. When charges are brought together, opposite charges attract and like charges repel.

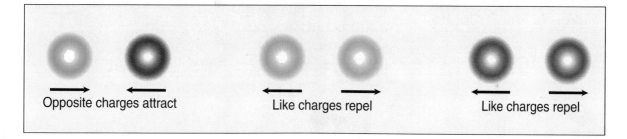

Opposite charges attract   Like charges repel   Like charges repel

1-1
IDENTIFYING CHARGES

Electric charges can be detected using strips of tape similar to the ones you used in the Explore activity.

PROBLEM
How can charges be detected?

MATERIALS
cellophane-tape charge detectors
objects made of plastic, glass, and ceramic
fabrics such as wool, silk, cotton, and fur
plastic bags and wrap

PROCEDURE
1. Make a data table, like the one shown. List the fabrics and objects that you plan to use.
2. Using what you learned in the Explore, make two strips of tape with unlike charges. Label the strip of

DATA AND OBSERVATIONS

OBJECTS	WOOL	SILK
Glass test tube		
Plastic comb		
Plastic spoon		

tape stuck to the desk B(ottom) and the strip stuck to the other strip of tape T(op).
3. Rub one of the objects on one of the fabrics.
4. Now bring the object near the tape charge detectors and **observe** what happens. If an object repels the B tape and attracts the T tape, it must be charged the same as the B tape and opposite of the T tape.
5. Record your results. Indicate if any object attracts both tapes.
6. Repeat Steps 3 and 4 for each object and each fabric.
7. **Identify** the combination of objects and fabrics that produced the charge with the strongest force.

8. With a plastic bag covering your hand, hold the fabric and rub the object.
9. Bring the fabric near the tapes to identify its charge. Then bring the object near the tapes to identify its charge.

ANALYZE
1. How many different kinds of charge did you produce?
2. **Compare** the charges on the object and the fabric. Are they alike or different?
3. Was there any material that did not become charged? If so, **identify** the material.

CONCLUDE AND APPLY
4. List two examples where rubbing the object results in a charge.
5. Explain why clothes often cling together after being tumble dried.
6. **Going Further:** A plastic comb is rubbed with a piece of wool and is suspended from a string. What will happen if a glass object that has been rubbed with silk is brought near the first comb?

The results of many experiments show that only two types of charges exist. In 1734, a French scientist named Charles Du Fay theorized that there were two types of electricity, which he called vitreous and resinous. He also stated that these electricities repel similar charges and attract opposite kinds.

You know Benjamin Franklin as one of the signers of the Declaration of Independence, but Franklin was also a scientific pioneer in electricity. Franklin didn't accept Du Fay's work of two types of electricity. Franklin believed that there was only one type of electricity. Franklin called an excess of electrical charge positive (+). He called an absence of charge negative (−).

We still follow his example and call electrical charges positive and negative. The charges on materials like vinyl, hard rubber, and silk are negative. Charges on fur, glass, and wool are positive. Can you devise a model for matter in which uncharged objects can still be composed of electric charges?

FIGURE 1-3. Benjamin Franklin was a pioneer in the study of electricity.

As Thales and Gilbert discovered, static electricity is everywhere. You often see its effects when you comb your hair, when you walk across a carpet, and in the sky during a thunderstorm. Static charges are motionless. This is where we get the name *static*. Static charges have some interesting uses. But for work to be accomplished, electric charges must move. In the next section, you will learn that an electric charge can move from one point to another, thereby setting the stage for putting electricity to work.

Check Your Understanding

1. As you move two charged cello tapes closer together, do the forces between them become greater or smaller?
2. If you rub hard rubber with a piece of wool, what charge is on the rubber?
3. **APPLY:** Explain why, after combing, your hair is sometimes attracted to your comb.

1-2 Electrical Charge Carriers

OBJECTIVES

In this section, you will

- distinguish electrical conductors from insulators;
- describe how a charged object attracts an uncharged one;
- demonstrate a variety of effects of static electricity.

KEY SCIENCE TERMS

insulator

conductor

ELECTRICAL CHARGES

In the last section, you observed that electrical charges may be positive (+) or negative (−). It was also hinted that electrical charges must move to do work. What type of material do we use to move charges from point to point? Do all materials move charges in the same way? Do electrical charges stay put on some materials? You can answer this question with a simple exploration.

FIND OUT!

Do electrical charges stay put?
Charge a plastic comb by rubbing one end of it with a piece of wool while holding it by the other end. Bring it close to a tape charge detector. Now, with your finger, touch the comb on the end you charged. Bring the comb near the charge detector again.

Conclude and Apply
1. What happened the first time you brought the comb near the charge detector?
2. What happened the second time you brought the comb to the charge detector?
3. What happened to the electrical charge?

In the previous activity, you observed that the comb held a charge until you touched the charged end. Why didn't the charge leave the comb when you were touching the uncharged end? Electrical charges don't move freely from one place to another through some materials. This type of material is called an **insulator**. The charge you put on the comb was at the end. Holding on to the opposite

FIGURE 1-4. Many types of metals are used for conductors. The metal used in these wires is copper.

end of the comb had no effect on the charge. The charge did not move through the comb because it was made of plastic. Plastic, such as the comb used in the activity, along with rubber, glass, wood, and ceramics are examples of insulators. Knowing this, can you explain why people who work with power lines wear heavy rubber gloves?

If you charge certain other materials, the charge can easily move anywhere through that material. Such a material is called a **conductor**. Metals such as copper, aluminum, and steel are good conductors. Gold and silver are among the best conductors but are very expensive. Even your body is a conductor, which is why the charge left the comb after you touched it. Your body provided a path for the charge to travel along. Let's look at an example of how charges move through the conductor.

DID YOU KNOW?

A safe place to be during an electrical storm is *inside* a steel-topped automobile. The car's metallic body serves as a large conducting shell. If lightning were to hit the car, the electricity would be quickly conducted around the outer surface and to the ground. This means that standing *outside*, touching the car, is one of the least safe places to be during the storm.

EXPLORE!

Do conductors hold a charge?

Place a balloon that has been given a negative charge by being rubbed with wool near a few small scraps of aluminum foil. The scraps should be no larger than the nail on your little finger. Is the foil attracted to the negatively charged balloon? Now try the same experiment with the positively charged wool. Is the result the same? Can you explain why?

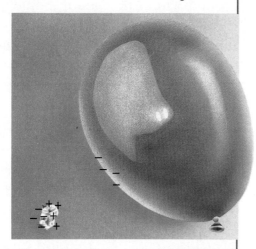

The Explore illustrates one example of the effects of static electricity. You observed that static charges do indeed move. A simple model of moving charges can explain the observations you just made. When you bring the negatively charged balloon near the uncharged bits of aluminum foil, the negative charges in the foil are pushed away from the balloon. The positive charges in the foil are attracted to the balloon. Since the positive charges in the foil are closer to the balloon, they are more strongly attracted than the more distant negative charges are repelled. The bits of foil experience a net attractive force. An object with no net charge can be attracted to both positively and negatively charged objects. You've observed that like charges repel and unlike charges attract. You have also seen that charges can move through a conductor.

There are many other ways that static charges move. Perhaps the most awesome charge is lightning. Charges build up on clouds when moving air currents in a storm cause charged particles to move around within the clouds. Sometimes the charged particles become separated to form areas of positive and negative charge, as shown in Figure 1-5. Lightning is actually a very large discharge of static electricity between clouds or between the cloud and Earth. Heat from the discharge expands the air in the cloud very rapidly and more air rushes into this area of lower pressure. This movement produces the sound we know as thunder.

Static electricity often builds up on airplanes as they move through the air. This static charge must be conducted away by the ground crew before refueling. They use a wire conductor from the plane to the ground. This prevents a possible explosion caused by a spark jumping from the plane to the fuel nozzle.

FIGURE 1-5. Charges build up in clouds to produce lightning.

Static electricity builds up on many different things. There are also machines that generate static electricity. The device shown in Figure 1-6 is called a Van de Graaff generator. This machine separates charges and stores one type on the sphere and the other on the base. These stored charges are nothing more than large accumulations of static charge. When a person touches the sphere, the charge is carried through his or her body, including hair. The charged hairs repel each other, flying straight out. The Van de Graaff generator can produce large sparks and light a fluorescent lamp.

Lightning is a more impressive example of the spark that jumps from your finger to a doorknob after you've built up a static charge. Static charges can be useful. Photocopiers and electric spray painters make use of the forces between electric charges.

SKILLBUILDER

DETERMINING CAUSE AND EFFECT
You have two balloons, each with an equal positive charge. You bring the first one up to cellophane tape charge detectors and the pieces of tape repel. Why? You bring the second balloon near the charge detectors and the tapes repel even further. Why? If you need help, refer to the **Skill Handbook** on page 685.

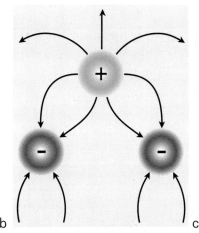

a   b   c

FIGURE 1-6. The Van de Graaff generator (a) transfers charge to the base and the sphere. Diagram (b) shows how this is accomplished and diagram (c) shows why the charged hair stands on end.

Check Your Understanding

1. If a charged object touches the end of an insulator, what happens to the charge put on the insulator? What happens on a conductor?
2. How does a charged object attract a small piece of an uncharged conductor?
3. List three examples of how static charges are built up and describe the visible effects of the charges.
4. **APPLY:** Why is it safe to be inside a metal enclosure during an electrical storm?

1-3 Making Electricity Flow

OBJECTIVES

In this section, you will

- state the function of a battery in a circuit;
- light a bulb using a battery;
- explain the effect of resistance on the current in a circuit.

KEY SCIENCE TERMS

potential difference
circuit
current
resistance

ELECTRICAL ENERGY

During a thunderstorm, the discharge of the static charge jumping from cloud to cloud or striking Earth produces a flash of light. Charges moving in air produce a brief flash of light. Could you light a lamp this way? Probably not. The spark occurs for only an instant. A lamp needs a continuous flow of charge to stay lit.

How can a continuous flow of charge be maintained? One way to answer this question is to think about what makes water flow. We can use a kind of comparison called an analogy as a model for the movement of electric charge. This model is shown in Figure 1-7. Because of gravity, pumps must do work to lift water above ground level. Once the water has been lifted, it has stored, or potential, energy. Because the water has potential energy, it can turn the water wheel and do work as it returns to ground level.

We can use the water analogy as a model for electricity. Due to the attractive electrical force between unlike charges, it takes work to separate them. These separated charges also have a form of potential energy. It's called electric potential energy. When the separated charges are provided with a conducting path, they will recombine. In doing so, the electric potential energy can be converted into other forms of energy, such as heat, light, and sound. That's what happens when a spark jumps from your finger to the doorknob and produces light and a crackling sound.

The electric potential energy is the total stored energy of all the charges. The change in total energy divided by the total charge is called the electric potential difference, or simply

FIGURE 1-7. Water being pumped into a reservoir creates potential energy to turn waterwheel.

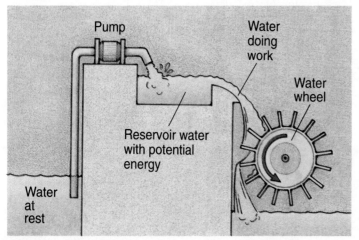

Pump

Water doing work

Water wheel

Reservoir water with potential energy

Water at rest

potential difference. The potential difference is measured in volts (V) and, therefore, is also called voltage.

Let's go back to our water analogy again. Water will not flow on a flat surface, a surface of constant gravitational potential. Water flow will occur only if there is a *difference* in potential between two parts of a system. One way to keep water flowing continuously down a hill is to use a pump to return water to the top. The pump maintains a potential difference.

In the same way, charge will flow only if there is a difference in electric potential. To keep charge flowing continuously, there must be a way of maintaining a potential difference. This is done with a charge pump, such as a battery. The next activity will help you understand how a charge flows.

FIND OUT!

How does charge flow from a battery through a light bulb?

Try to connect a battery, bulb, and two wires to light the bulb as shown. Remember, charges must flow out of one battery terminal, through the wire, and into one terminal of the bulb. Charges must also flow out of the other terminal of the bulb, through the wire, and back into the second terminal of the battery. **CAUTION:** *If a connecting wire gets hot, you don't have the wires connected properly. Immediately disconnect one end of the wire from the battery and try another connection.*

Conclude and Apply

1. Draw a picture of the battery, bulb, and wires. Trace the flow of charges in your drawing.
2. Using the analogy with water, explain how electric current flows along this path.

How do we know?

Is an object a conductor or an insulator?

A circuit containing a battery and a bulb can be used to test whether or not an object is a conductor or insulator. Just disconnect one wire from the battery. Connect the wire to one end of the object being tested and touch the other end to the battery. If the lamp lights, the object is a conductor.

When you made the battery light the bulb, you created a complete path through which charge flowed. Such a complete, or closed, path is called a **circuit**. When charges move through the lamp, their electrical potential energy is converted into thermal energy and light. Chemical action in the battery maintains the potential difference needed to keep the charges flowing. If it were not for the battery, the charges could not be given a potential difference and would stop moving.

The rate at which charges flow through the battery, lamp, and wires is called electric current. The amount of electric **current** can be defined as the amount of charge divided by the time interval it takes to pass a point. You can measure current using an instrument called an ammeter. Consider what happens when you turn the switch on a three-way lamp. When the switch is off, the lamp is dark because no current flows. When the switch is turned to the lowest setting, the current is small. At the medium setting, the lamp is brighter and the current is greater. When the lamp is the brightest, the current is the greatest. Thus, the greater the amount of current flowing, the brighter the lamp.

What makes the bulb light? Look at Figure 1-8. The bulb contains a thin wire called a filament. The filament is designed to become hot enough to give off some light and heat when a current passes through it. As a result, the electric charges lose electric potential energy in the filament of the lamp. This electric potential energy is converted into thermal energy and light.

You know that metals like copper, aluminum, silver, and gold are all good conductors. The filament in the light bulb is a metal wire called tungsten. It, too, is a conductor. But all conductors offer resistance to the flow of charge. Even gold and silver have some resistance to the flow of charges. The tungsten filament offers resistance to the flow of charge. The **resistance** of a material is a measure of how much potential a charge loses when moving through the material. Good conductors have low resistances. The wires in your home and in the circuit you constructed have very little resistance. A lamp filament and a wire in a toaster have high resistances. Much of the electrical potential energy is converted into light and heat.

FIGURE 1-8. A cutaway view of an incandescent light bulb shows the filament wire.

Filament

What is the relationship between resistance and current? You can find out for yourself using a battery and three small lamps.

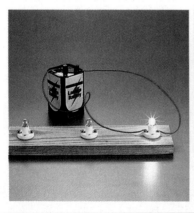
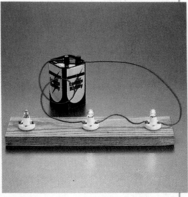
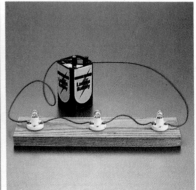
Each time you added a bulb, you decreased the brightness of the bulbs. You could infer that less current flowed when the bulbs were less bright. You can see that when the potential difference remains the same, the current decreases as the resistance—more light bulbs— increases.

FIGURE 1-9. In a series circuit, if the potential remains the same and the resistance increases, the current decreases.

Instead of moving static charges, you have seen the dynamic motion created by an electrical circuit. A simple circuit needs three things: a source of potential difference, a complete path, and a resistance. These three things are the basis of the science of electronics. Your television, your portable tape player, or your computer work because of these simple circuits. Without the basic circuits, electricity doesn't move, and therefore, work doesn't get done. But there is still more to learn. In the next section, we will study the properties of resistance, current, and voltage and how they apply to a circuit.

Check Your Understanding

1. Draw a circuit using a 6-V battery and a bulb that would cause the bulb to glow.
2. What happens to the potential energy of the charges between the terminals of a 6-V battery in the circuit you just drew? What happens to the potential when the charges pass through the bulb?
3. **APPLY:** Suppose you replaced the bulb in the circuit you drew in Question 1 with one of higher resistance. Describe the change in the current through the bulb. How would the new bulb's brightness compare with that of the bulb you replaced?

1-4 Resistance, Current, and Voltage

POTENTIAL DIFFERENCE AND CURRENT

As you saw earlier, a battery in a circuit acts like a pump in a water system. It increases the potential energy of electrical charges. The larger the battery's voltage, the greater the difference in potential across the battery's terminals. Consider a circuit containing a battery and bulb. A chemical reaction causes an increase in potential across the battery. There is an equal decrease in potential across the bulb. In the same way, there is a loss in potential energy of water flowing through rapids or over a waterfall to a lower level.

If a pump lifts water to an even higher level, the water will have to fall back a larger distance. Similarly, if a battery with a higher voltage is used, the potential drop across the bulb will be greater. How will this affect the current? We can investigate this with another water model.

OBJECTIVES

In this section, you will
- control the amount of current, in a circuit;
- list the variables that determine electrical resistance.

FIGURE 1-10. Water stored in this tower has potential energy and can do work.

I N V E S T I G A T E !

You know that increasing resistance decreases current through a circuit. A water model will show how changes in potential difference affect the current.

PROBLEM

How does changing the potential difference affect current for a water system?

MATERIALS

plastic funnel
ring stand with ring
2-m lengths of rubber tubing of different diameters
meterstick
2 250-mL beakers
stopwatch or clock

PROCEDURE

1. Copy the data table.
2. Assemble the apparatus as

DATA AND OBSERVATIONS

TRIAL	HEIGHT (cm)	TIME (s)	RATE (mL/S)
1			
2			
3			
4			

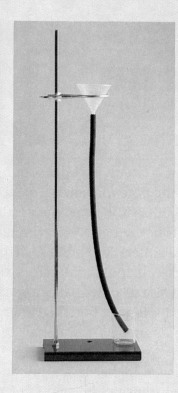

shown, using the tubing with the larger diameter.
3. **Measure** the height from the top of the funnel to the outlet end of the rubber tubing. Record your data.
4. Pour water into the funnel fast enough to keep it full, but not overflowing.
5. **Measure** the time for 100 mL of water to flow into the lower beaker and record it in the table.
6. Repeat Steps 3 through 5 at least three more times. Lower the funnel for each trial. **Predict** what will happen each time.

7. Replace the tubing with tubing of a smaller diameter. Repeat Steps 3 through 6. What do you **observe**?

ANALYZE

1. The model compares water moving due to gravity with electrical charges moving due to potential difference, or voltage. **W**hich trial corresponds to a circuit with the highest voltage?
2. If the voltage is increased, what happens to the current?
3. What effect does the diameter of the tube have on the rate of water flow?
4. **Compare** the effect of funnel height on the rate of water flow.

CONCLUDE AND APPLY

5. What electrical property do the hose diameters represent?
6. **Going Further:** If the smaller diameter hose corresponds to a greater electric resistance, what do you think will happen to the electric current if the voltage stays constant, but the resistance is increased?

The Investigate you just completed illustrates a basic principle of electricity. With a constant voltage, increasing the resistance will decrease the current. As you observed in the previous section, using a model is an important tool for drawing conclusions about various properties. You can compare the results from the Investigate you just performed by using a real circuit containing batteries and light bulbs.

FIND OUT!

How does increasing voltage affect current?

To find out, you will need two 6-V batteries, two bulbs rated at 6 volts, and connecting wires. Make a complete circuit with the two bulbs and one battery as shown. Observe the brightness of the bulbs. Now disconnect the bulbs from the first battery and connect the second 6-V battery with the first. That is, connect the negative (–) terminal on one battery to the positive (+) terminal of the other. The set of two batteries now has a positive (+) terminal and a negative (–) terminal that have no wires attached. Connect a bulb to each terminal and connect the bulbs together. Refer to the picture to make sure you connected everything properly. Notice the brightness of the bulbs.

Conclude and Apply

How does the brightness in the first circuit compare to the brightness in the second circuit? Why?

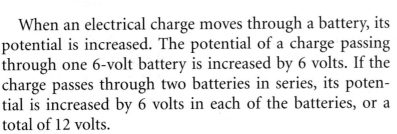

When an electrical charge moves through a battery, its potential is increased. The potential of a charge passing through one 6-volt battery is increased by 6 volts. If the charge passes through two batteries in series, its potential is increased by 6 volts in each of the batteries, or a total of 12 volts.

You've seen that as potential difference increases, current increases, and as resistance increases, current decreases.

The relationship among current, resistance, and potential difference can be made more quantitative by using

MAKING AND INTERPRETING GRAPHS

When you purchase wire, you specify the gauge, a number between 0000 and 40. The higher the gauge, the thinner the wire. The table gives the diameter and the resistance of a 1-km length of wire.

Use the information to find out how wire resistance depends on size. Make a graph with resistance on the vertical axis and wire diameter on the horizontal axis. If you need help, refer to the **Skill Handbook** on page 682.

GAUGE NO.	DIAMETER (MM)	RESISTANCE OF 1KM (Ω)
000	11.7	0.2
6	4.1	1.3
12	2.1	5.2
18	1.0	21.0
22	0.6	53.0

measurements. We can say that current is equal to the potential difference per unit of resistance, or the amount of voltage per unit of resistance. The relationship can be expressed mathematically:

$$\text{current (amperes)} = \frac{\text{potential difference (volts)}}{\text{resistance (ohms)}}.$$

In the study of electricity, I is used to represent current, V is used to represent potential difference or voltage, and R is used to represent resistance. Using the letters instead of the words, this equation can be stated as

$$I = V/R.$$

You can see from this equation that current (I) and potential difference (V) are directly related. As the potential difference increases, the current increases.

Resistance (R) and current are inversely related. As the resistance increases, the current decreases.

Current is measured in amperes (A), potential difference in volts (V), and resistance in ohms (Ω). We can now find the current in a circuit if we know the voltage and resistance.

When you plug an appliance into an outlet in your home, you complete a circuit. The potential difference at the outlet is usually 120 V. To see how the resistance of an appliance controls current, look at the following example.

EXAMPLE PROBLEM: Calculating Current

Problem Statement: If a light bulb with a resistance of 150 Ω is connected to a 120-Volt electrical outlet, what is the current in the bulb?

Known: $R=150\,\Omega$, $V=120$ V

Unknown: I

Equation to Use: $I=V/R$

Solution: $I=V/R = 120$ V $/ 150\,\Omega =0.80$ A

What would the current be if resistance were 200 Ω?

How does the manufacturer of a lamp control the resistance? A very thin tungsten wire is used in all incandescent light bulbs. When it is heated to a high enough temperature, it gives off light but does not melt. The resistance of the tungsten wire determines the brightness level of the lamp. The more loops in the filament, the longer the wire and the greater the resistance. If the wire length is increased, the resistance is increased. Would the lamp be brighter with a high resistance or a low resistance?

Carbon may be used to explore the effect of length on resistance. A common lead pencil is made from graphite, a form of carbon.

FIND OUT!

How does the length of a conductor affect its resistance?

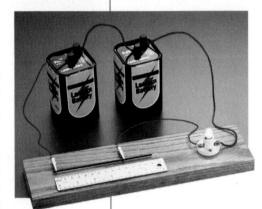

You will need two 6-V batteries, a lamp with socket, a long thick piece of pencil lead, a centimeter ruler, and three wires with clips. Lay the pencil lead alongside the ruler. Connect the two 6-V batteries as shown. Use a wire with clips on both ends to connect the unused positive (+) terminal of one battery to one end of the pencil lead. Connect one wire from the lamp to the unused negative (−) terminal of the other battery. A wire connected to the other lamp terminal will be touched to the pencil lead.

Touch the wire from the lamp to the pencil lead at a point farthest away from the end connected to the battery. What happened? Slide the wire up the pencil toward the end. Note any changes.

Conclude and Apply

1. What happened when you decreased the length of the pencil lead connections?
2. What happened to the current when you decreased the length of the pencil lead connections?
3. What conclusions can you draw about the resistance of the lead?

Many experiments have shown that the resistance of a metal wire depends on the length of the wire. When you increase the length of the conductor, you increase the resistance. The wire thickness will also affect resistance. Think back to the water model. The thinner hose offered the

How did the ohm get its name?

Georg Simon Ohm (1787–1854), a German scientist, studied the relationship between the current flowing through a metal and the potential difference across it. He found that the ratio of potential difference to current is resistance.

$$\frac{\text{potential difference}}{\text{current}} = \text{resistance}$$

Ohm found that for a wide range of metals, the resistance did not depend on the current or on the size or direction of the potential difference. Today we call the unit of resistance the ohm.

greater resistance to the water flow. The larger diameter hose offered less resistance to water flow. The same occurs in electricity. The larger the diameter of the conductor, the smaller the resistance. Thus a short, thick wire has a lower resistance, while a long, thin one has a higher resistance.

The resistance of a wire also depends on the material from which it is made. Low-resistance wire is used to carry current long distances with little loss in potential energy. High-resistance wire is useful in appliances such as toasters, lamps, and hair dryers where the electric potential energy is changed into thermal energy and light.

You have discovered that there is more to electricity than simply plugging something into a wall outlet. Batteries are a source of potential energy waiting to do work in a flashlight or tape player. The lights in lamps or the wires in ovens use the properties of resistance, voltage, and current to light your home or cook your meals. In fact, almost every part of your life is affected by electricity.

Check Your Understanding

1. A high-intensity lamp supplies 24 V to each of two bulbs. One bulb is bright, the other dim. Through which bulb is the current larger? Which bulb has the higher resistance?

2. A piece of carbon, resistance 18Ω, is connected to a 12-V battery. Find the current in the carbon. What would be the current if a 6-V battery were used?

3. **APPLY:** A length of wire is cut in half, forming two shorter wires. How does the resistance of each half compare to that of the original wire? If the two short wires are placed side by side and twisted together, how does the resistance of the combination compare to the resistance of one short wire?

IIIIIIIIEXPANDING YOUR VIEWIIIIIIIII

CONTENTS

A **CLOSER** LOOK

WHAT CAUSES LIGHTNING?

When you see city lights, you are seeing electrical energy under control. When you see lightning shatter the sky, you see electricity that is out of control. The charges in lightning lose 100 million volts of potential difference, causing a temperature that ranges from 15,000 to 33,000°C—hotter than the surface of the sun!

What causes the violent discharge of electrical energy in lightning? It starts very simply with the particles in a rain cloud. Lighter particles of water in the cloud collide with heavy particles, such as hail. During the collision, the heavy particles gain negative charges from the lighter particles and become negatively charged. Since the lighter particles lose negative charges, they become positively charged. The heavier, negative particles fall to the bottom of the cloud. The lighter, positive particles drift up to the top of the cloud.

Because the bottom of the cloud is negatively charged, it repels negative charges on the ground beneath it. This causes the ground to become positively charged.

Lightning begins with a weak, downward discharge in which large numbers of negative

WHAT DO YOU THINK?

Buildings, particularly farm buildings in open areas, have lightning rods atop their roofs. How are these rods used? How can these rods help avoid a fire due to lightning?

charges flow toward the ground. This is followed immediately by a return stroke from the ground to the cloud along the same path.

The shorter the distance from the ground to the cloud, the easier it is for the electrical discharge to take place. It's not a good idea to run under a tree during an electrical storm. The lightning seeks the shortest path to the ground, and the tree provides that path.

People can sometimes have a warning of a nearby lightning strike. They feel their skin tingling and their hair standing on end. A person in this situation should fall to the ground to avoid being struck by a lightning bolt.

LIFE SCIENCE CONNECTION

STUNNING EELS

Does it seem strange that a fish like the electric eel has electricity? All animals —even you—have electrical activity in your body. For example, your muscles move because of electrical potential. However, some fish, like the South American eels, have organs that produce high voltage. Electric eels use the voltage to stun their prey, and to fend off predators who tend to avoid the eel's electrical impulses.

of their body apparently are able to withstand the impulses without a fatty layer.

The electric eel is positively charged at the head and negatively charged at the tail. The tail, which makes up four-fifths of the 6-foot-long fish, has three pairs of electric organs made of more than 5000 electroplates arranged like the cells in a storage battery. An eel can produce a shock of about 500 volts at a current of 2 amperes. While the electric charge can be released in a fraction of a second, an eel may need nearly an hour to recharge its batteries. By the way, an electic eel is not an eel at all. It's a fresh water fish related to carp and minnows.

The voltage in an electric eel is large enough to kill an animal as large as a man or horse. When an animal is stunned by a high voltage, it stops breathing and drowns. Usually the electricity from electric eels stuns small prey, such as fish or frogs.

Many scientists have tried to find out why electric eels do not electrocute themselves. One theory is that the brain and heart of electric eels are packed in a fatty tissue that protects these two vital organs from the strong electrical impulses. The other organs

WHAT DO YOU THINK?

Besides the electric eel, other animals that live in water—the electric ray, for example— use electric impulses to stun their prey.

1. Why do you think water animals use electricity in this way, while animals that live on land do not?

2. Why might it matter where the electrical impulses enter the body of an electric eel's prey?

SCIENCE AND SOCIETY

RECYCLING BATTERIES

What is as small as a button and very dangerous to the environment? The answer is the kind of battery you find in watches and cameras. These cells make up 25 percent of the hazardous wastes that come from households. The tiny button batteries may have as much as 1.1 grams of mercury, a metal that can cause birth defects and even brain and kidney damage. Even one battery in six tons of garbage has more mercury than is allowed by government standards.

If the garbage is dumped in landfills, the mercury can leak into the groundwater and be taken up by plants, which are

then eaten by animals and people!

What can be done? If people used rechargeable batteries, fewer toxic metals would be in the environment. Nickel-cadmium batteries can be recharged. They cost three times more than ordinary batteries but last 40 times longer, so they

are more economical in the long run.

Recycling is also a solution to the problem. Jewelry stores usually accept button batteries, which they turn in at recycling centers. At present, however, only 23 states require stores to accept old batteries for recycling.

In 1983, the citizens of Tokyo discovered that the mercury given off by one incinerator was 30 times higher than the amount declared safe by the World

Health Organization. They insisted that local facilities separate batteries from the garbage before it was incinerated.

In Austria, some recycling plants use an experimental process to remove the mercury and zinc from old batteries. These two metals are then recycled. The rest of the battery can be used in the manufacture of new batteries.

In Denmark, authorities have placed a refund surcharge on batteries. A consumer who returns a used battery gets the money back.

Each year in the United States, 25 million household batteries are used. In spite of the danger of the toxic metals in batteries, the Environmental Protection Agency does not yet have regulations for the disposal of batteries.

WHAT DO YOU THINK?

What can you and your family do to reduce the amount of lead, mercury, and cadmium in the environment? How can you make others aware of the dangers of these metals?

TECHNOLOGY CONNECTION

LATIMER'S LIGHT

Ever since Thomas Edison patented the light bulb, people have been trying to improve it.

One of the first to improve the light bulb was Lewis Howard Latimer. Latimer, a self-taught draftsman, worked for Alexander Graham Bell in the 1870s. Latimer's ability to draw detailed diagrams of complex electrical devices was invaluable. He drew the plans for Bell that resulted in the 1876 patent of the telephone.

Latimer first became associated with Thomas Edison when Edison patented the first incandescent bulb in 1879. Latimer set about making it better. His improved method for securing the carbon filament to metal wires inside the vacuum bulb was patented in 1881. Latimer continued to work on the incandescent bulb and in 1882 received what he considered his most important patent. He improved the process for producing the carbon filaments used in light bulbs.

Latimer was the only African American invited to join the Edison Pioneers, a group of scientists and inventors who worked for Edison. He was asked to supervise the installation of electrical streetlights in New York City, Philadelphia, and London.

Consumer
CONNECTION

MAKING A BETTER LIGHT BULB

The thin filament you see glowing in a light bulb is made of tungsten—a metal that doesn't melt until it gets extremely hot. Instead, it glows as electricity passes through it. Some tungsten particles get so hot they turn into a gas. As a gas, the tungsten leaves the area of the filament and adheres to the glass bulb.

In newer bulbs krypton may be used. A krypton bulb stays relatively cool because krypton is a poor conductor of heat. Fewer particles of the filament are lost by turning into gaseous tungsten. This makes the light bulb last longer.

A smaller-sized bulb filled with krypton can provide the same amount of light as a larger bulb, as shown in the picture. Since a smaller bulb uses less power, a light bulb with krypton reduces the electric power consumed.

YOU TRY IT!

Observe halogen and krypton light bulbs in class. Notice the differences in how the light bulbs shine. Which bulb would you prefer to use? Explain the reasons for your choice.

*H*istory
C O N N E C T I O N

BEN FRANKLIN'S EXPERIMENT

In addition to being a great statesman, Benjamin Franklin was one of the outstanding scientists of the eighteenth century. Franklin thought of electricity as a fluid. Remember, it wasn't until the twentieth century that we realized matter was made up of electrically charged particles. Franklin's experiments with electricity were some of the best done in the infant science of electricity. Franklin found that electricity wasn't created when glass was rubbed with silk. He explained that the electrical properties already present were merely transferred from one object to another by rubbing.

In Franklin's time, many scientists thought that there were two kinds of electricity—positive and negative. Franklin hypothesized that there was one kind of electricity but that sometimes matter had a positive *or* negative charge. This depended on whether it possessed too much "electrical fluid" or too little.

WHAT DO YOU THINK?

Franklin's knowledge about electricity was acknowledged around the world. At the request of a group of people in Paris, he wrote a paper describing what he judged to be the safest spot during an electrical storm. His selection was a hammock—a freely swinging bed—suspended by silk cords. What do you think made Franklin choose that as the place that would least likely be struck by lightning?

Once, Franklin and his son flew a kite during an electrical storm to prove that lightning is a form of electricity. (His experiment with lightning was extremely dangerous and should never be copied! Franklin was lucky he wasn't killed.) Franklin also invented the lightning rod. A lightning rod is a metal rod installed on the top of a building. A wire leads to another metal rod that is buried in the ground a meter from the building. At this distance the lightning rod can conduct lightning to the ground safely.

TEENS *in* SCIENCE

OVERCOMING OBSTACLES

Nineteen-year-old Sieu Ngo was able to overcome much difficulty in his life and went on to complete an award-winning science project in electrochemistry.

Sieu Ngo is of Chinese origin. Most of his family lives in Vietnam. He immigrated to America when he was just seven years old. It was not an easy journey. Sieu was held in a refugee camp in Malaysia for more than nine months. The overcrowded camp was even more uncomfortable for Sieu because he had chicken pox!

Finally settling in Oklahoma, Sieu began working and attending high school. "I worked in a gas station from 11PM to 7AM." With school beginning at 8AM, Sieu was exhausted most mornings. Sometimes he became discouraged.

Once Sieu even thought about giving up his science interests. "One night I was cleaning the refreshment stand. I was thinking about the kids I would be competing against. As I cleaned, I imagined them at home working on their computers or studying. What chance did I have? I almost quit."

But Sieu Ngo's hard work and dedication had not gone unnoticed. His science teacher believed in the young man. In fact, he invited Sieu to live with his family until Sieu's project was complete.

This was just the break that Sieu needed. With more time and energy to devote, he made great strides on the project. "I spent a lot of nights in the computer lab. I was still

WHAT DO YOU THINK?

Sieu Ngo describes life as a mathematical equation. What do you think he means?

working all night, but this time for myself, for something I believed in."

It was a race right up to the deadline. In fact, Sieu's classmates helped him finish mounting his displays on the bus ride to the competition.

Despite many obstacles, Sieu Ngo's project has earned him a good deal of respect. He also won a full scholarship to the University of Oklahoma where he studies chemical engineering. "To me, life is one big mathematical equation. The amount of hardship in a person's life is equal to the amount of personal good. I am optimistic that life is fair."

Reviewing Main Ideas

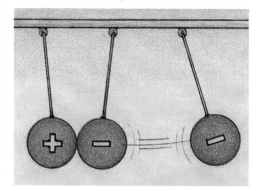

1. In static electricity there are two kinds of charges, positive and negative. Like charges repel and the unlike charges attract.

2. Electric charges can move easily through conductors but not through insulators.

3. The total stored energy of all the charges is called electric potential energy.

4. The three requirements of a circuit are a complete path, potential difference, and resistance. Resistance depends on the material of the conductor, as well as the length and thickness.

Chapter Review

USING KEY SCIENCE TERMS

circuit

conductor

current

electrical charge

insulator

like charges

potential difference

resistance

unlike charges

Use one of the terms to complete each sentence.

1. Two electrically charged objects that repel each other have ____.
2. Electric charges flow only when the ____ is continuous or unbroken.
3. Electric charges flow best through a ____.
4. The flow of electric charge is called ____.
5. Two electrically charged objects attract each other because they have ____.
6. A drop in potential when current goes through a bulb is due to ____.
7. A rubber glove prevents shock to exposed wires because it is a/an ____.
8. If you receive a shock upon touching a doorknob, it means your body has ____.
9. If the current through a bulb increases, the ____ must have increased.

UNDERSTANDING IDEAS

Answer the following questions.

1. What are the names for the two types of electrical charge?

2. You observe that a very large voltage produces only a small current in a circuit. What do you conclude about the resistance in the circuit?
3. Would you connect a battery to a bulb with a thick or thin wire if you did not want the wire to become hot? Why?
4. Should a long extension cord needed to carry high currents be made of thick or thin wires? Why?
5. What type of charge would you use to attract a positive charge?
6. What would happen if you disconnected one terminal of a battery in a circuit?
7. Why is your hair attracted to your comb after you comb it?
8. What causes the crackle you hear when you pull two pieces of clothing apart that have just come out of the dryer?
9. Why can separated charges be used to do work?

CRITICAL THINKING

Use your understanding of the concepts developed in the chapter to answer each of the following questions.

1. Why does a person's hair stand on end when the person becomes charged with static electricity?
2. A bird can sit on a single power line wire without harm. Why? What would happen if the bird were to touch another wire at the same time?

3. Signs often say "Danger—High Voltage." Why don't they say "Danger—High Current"?

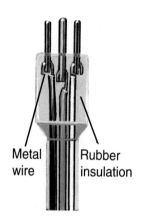

Metal wire   Rubber insulation

4. Electrical cords attached to a household appliance are constructed as shown in the diagram. Can you explain why they are made this way?

5. How does turning a dimmer light switch adjust current flow?

6. If a circuit containing 1 meter of wire and three light bulbs were changed to 0.75 meter of wire and two light bulbs, what would happen to the current if the power supply were kept the same?

PROBLEM SOLVING

Read the following problem and discuss your answers in a brief paragraph.

You are playing with your friends in a field. Suddenly, there is a bright flash of light. You know that a thunderstorm is coming and you had better take shelter. Nearby there is a metal building, a car, and a tree. Which would be safe places to wait out the storm? Why? Which would be the most hazardous? Why?

CONNECTING IDEAS

Discuss each of the following in a brief paragraph.

1. After you receive a shock from a doorknob, touching it a second time probably will not produce a second shock. Why? What could you do to give yourself a second shock?

2. Many times a car will not start if one of its battery terminals is covered with corrosion. Why won't the car start? How could it be fixed?

3. A CLOSER LOOK Describe the role negatively charged particles play in lightning.

4. HISTORY CONNECTION What major change did Franklin's experiments make in scientists' hypothesis of electricity?

5. SCIENCE AND SOCIETY What are two actions that you can take to decrease the hazard caused by discarded batteries?

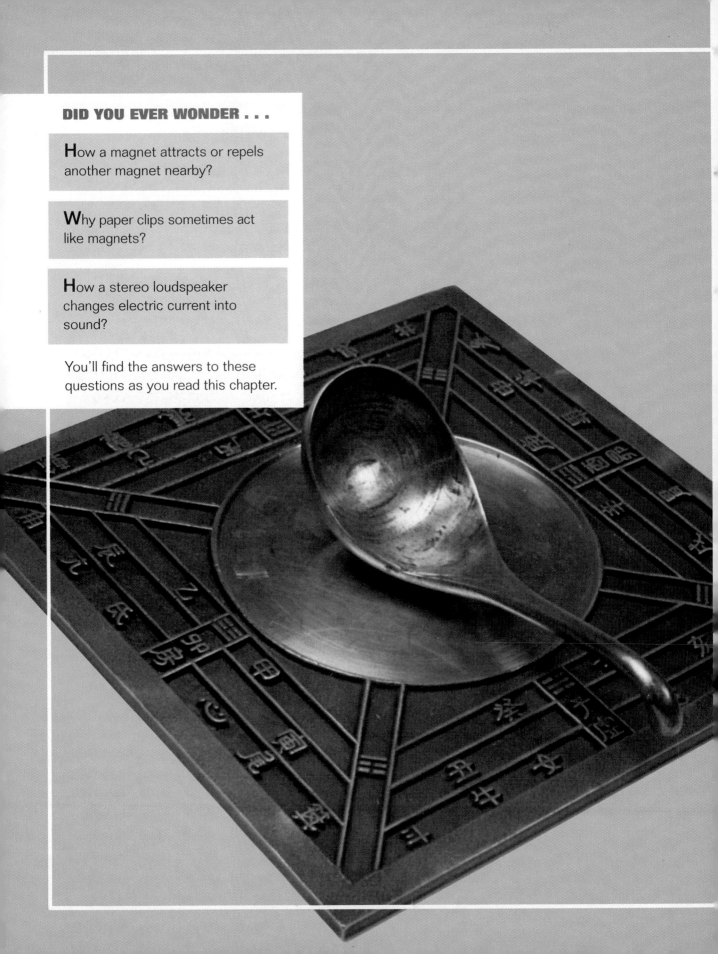

DID YOU EVER WONDER . . .

How a magnet attracts or repels another magnet nearby?

Why paper clips sometimes act like magnets?

How a stereo loudspeaker changes electric current into sound?

You'll find the answers to these questions as you read this chapter.

Magnetism

Remember playing with toy magnets as a child? Perhaps you could make a metal fish leap toward metal bait. There was something magical about a piece of iron suddenly leaping off the floor and flying into the air. Equally wonderful was a magnetic mouse skittering just ahead of the cat's extended magnetic paw. Suddenly, the paw would rise and snap at the mouse. How? And what about the mysterious behavior of a compass? A needle, jiggling on a pin to find its balance, swings back and forth a dozen times. Every time it stops moving, it's aligned north and south. Why? What causes it to turn? Why does it always point the same direction when it stops?

The actions of the toys and the compass seem mysterious. They don't match our ideas of the way things work. We can't see what's happening, what's making the objects move. Although we can't see magnetism, we can figure out how it works only by observing its effects. You can observe these effects while doing the activities in this chapter. And you may find that magnets play an important role in your daily life.

EXPLORE!

How are magnets used in your home and at school?

Some magnets in your home may keep doors closed. Others may keep game pieces on a board. Look for examples of magnets at home and at school. Make a list of their uses.

2-1 Forces and Fields

OBJECTIVES

In this section, you will
- describe the forces magnets produce;
- identify the north and south poles of a magnet;
- explain the role of magnetic fields.

KEY SCIENCE TERMS

magnetic poles
magnetic field

FORCES AT WORK

Besides being fun and intriguing toys, magnets play many useful roles in everyday life. Some uses are obvious. Magnets hold notes to your refrigerator or keep cabinet doors shut. But for other uses, magnets are hidden in places you might not suspect. There are magnets as fine as powder storing images and sounds on videotape and information on computer disks. There are magnets in telephones, television sets, and radios. Some of these magnets change electric currents into sounds. Some do other jobs. Magnets are all around you. You can begin to understand how magnets work by making some simple observations.

EXPLORE!

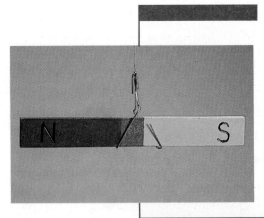

Can you make your own compass? Hang a bar magnet by a thread, as shown. When the magnet stops swinging, record the direction of the bar. Turn the magnet slightly and then let go, allowing it to turn by itself. What happens? Hang the magnet in another place. When it stops moving, what direction does it point?

You've just repeated an observation that was first made by ancient Chinese more than two thousand years ago. The Chinese had observed that a type of black rock, now called lodestone or magnetite, could attract pieces of iron. They also saw that if the lodestone was suspended by a thread and allowed to turn freely, it always came to rest in the same north-south direction. A free-moving lodestone was the first magnetic compass. Chinese traders and soldiers often placed a piece of lodestone on a piece of floating wood or bamboo to make a compass. By the end of the twelfth century, European sailors and explorers were using compasses to help guide their voyages.

Recall that one end of your suspended bar magnet always pointed north while the other end always pointed south. When a magnet is allowed to turn freely, the two ends of the magnet that point north-south are called the **magnetic poles.** The end pointing north is called the north-seeking pole or just the north pole. Is one pole of a bar magnet different from the other? Remember that by just looking at a magnet we might not be able to directly observe any differences between the north and south poles. We have to rely on observing how the magnet acts or interacts with other magnets and materials.

FIGURE 2-1. The Chinese made the first compass out of magnetite and bamboo.

FIND OUT!

How do magnetic poles interact?

Place a piece of tape or a dot of paint on the pole of your magnet that points north. Hang a second magnet more than 50 cm away from the first magnet. After the second magnet stops moving, mark its north pole. Then bring the north pole of the second magnet near the north pole of the first, as shown in the figure. What happens? Bring the south poles of the magnets together. What happens? Try bringing the north pole of one magnet near the south pole of the other. What happens this time? Observe what happens as you move one magnet away from the other.

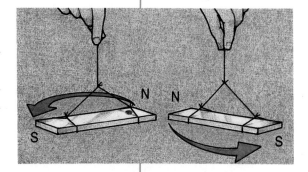

Conclude and Apply
1. How do like poles of magnets interact?
2. How do the unlike poles of magnets interact?
3. Does distance affect the way magnets interact?

As you can see, the poles of a magnet act differently from each other. Two north poles repel each other. Two south poles also repel each other. But a north pole and a south pole attract each other. Make up a law that summa-

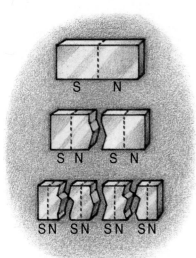

FIGURE 2-2. When a magnet is broken, each piece will have a north and south pole.

rizes your observations. The distance between the magnets also affects how they react to each other. As the poles are moved closer together, the force between them becomes greater. The behavior of magnetic poles may remind you of the behavior of electric charges you studied earlier.

Can a magnet have a single pole? Take a breakable bar magnet and identify its north and south poles. Now break the magnet in half. What happens? You will get two complete magnets. Each magnet will have its own north and south poles. Look at Figure 2-2. No matter how many times you break a magnet, you are left with more complete magnets. Despite many attemps, no one has ever been able to find an isolated magnetic pole.

REVEALING MAGNETIC FORCES

You know that a force acts between magnetic poles. But you've seen only its effects on other magnets—attraction or repulsion. What is the effect of a magnet on the region around it?

EXPLORE!

Can you map a magnet's force?
Place a bar magnet on a table and cover it with a sheet of paper, as shown. Now sprinkle iron filings onto the paper and gently tap it. Observe the pattern that results. Near the center of another piece of paper, sketch the position of the magnet and label the north and south poles. Then sketch the pattern of filings. Use the paper and filings to do two more maps. First place

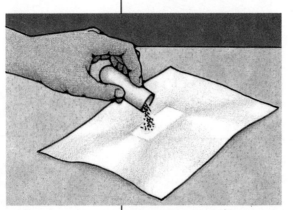

the like poles of two magnets opposite each other and keep them about 2 cm apart. Map the patterns made by these magnets as they repel each other. Then place the unlike poles of the magnets opposite each other and map the pattern as the magnets attract each other. How do the patterns differ?

Each filing that you sprinkled over the magnet acted like a tiny bar magnet. The filings lined up in the region near the magnet in much the same way a compass needle lines up with Earth. The patterns of filings form lines around the magnet, as shown in Figure 2-3(a). Notice that the lines are closest together near the poles of the magnet. You saw earlier that the force is strongest near the magnet's poles. The closer the lines of force, the stronger the force. The lines are farthest apart where the force is weakest. The region around a magnet where the magnetic force acts is called a **magnetic field.**

Figure 2-3(b) shows how the magnetic field acts between like poles of two magnets. The field lines from each of these poles bend away from the pole of the other magnet. When you bring unlike poles near each other, as in Figure 2-3(c), the filings line up to reveal that the magnetic field links the two poles.

The previous activity can help you explain the behavior of one magnet in the presence of another magnet. You've observed evidence of a magnetic field and the interaction between the magnetic poles. But how do you explain the behavior of the single magnet suspended in a compass? What causes the magnet to point north and south? It seems as if Earth itself has a magnetic field. By looking at the direction of the compasses placed all over the world, we can make a field map for Earth in the same way you did using filings and a bar magnet. When this is done, we get a pattern like the one in Figure 2-4. Compare the pattern around Earth to the one the iron filings made around a single bar magnet.

FIGURE 2-3. Iron filings form lines around single magnet (a); lines bend away from poles (b); lines link two poles (c).

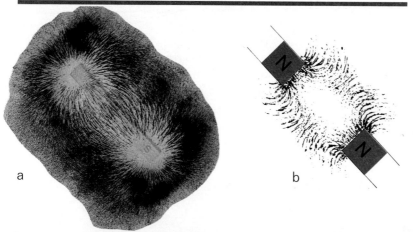

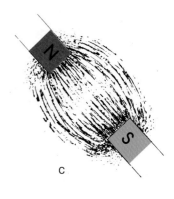

a

b

c

DID YOU KNOW?

Earth's magnetic field has flip-flopped, north and south, at least 171 times. One way scientists know this is by the direction of magnetized rock on the sea floor.

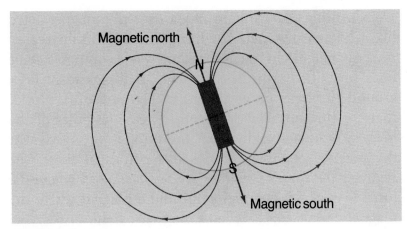

FIGURE 2-4. Earth acts as if it were a giant magnet.

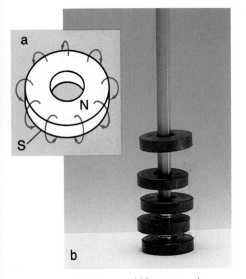

FIGURE 2-5. Where are the poles of the doughnut-shaped magnets on a pencil?

Your experience with magnetic toys, refrigerator magnets, and magnetic compasses showed you that magnets acted differently than other materials. Now you've started to understand the behavior of magnets. You've seen that every magnet has two kinds of poles—north and south. Like poles repel each other and unlike poles attract each other. You've seen that the poles are the part of the magnet where its force is strongest. You've mapped the region around the magnet, where the magnetic forces act, and identified it as the magnetic field of the magnet. The field can be represented by magnetic field lines. Earth has a magnetic field that resembles the field of a large bar magnet. You'll use this knowledge to explain some of the more puzzling magnetic behavior you'll see in the next section.

Check Your Understanding

1. Figure 2-5(a) shows the field around a doughnut-shaped magnet. Where are this magnet's poles? How would you identify the magnet's north and south poles?

2. Figure 2-5(b) shows five doughnut-shaped magnets on a pencil. Suppose the lower pole on the bottom magnet is the north pole. Identify both poles on each of the four magnets.

3. What is the relationship between the magnetic force and the magnetic field?

4. **APPLY:** If a magnetic compass needle points north, what is the actual polarity of Earth's northern pole? Explain.

2-2 Magnets

MAGNETIC ATTRACTION

In the previous section, you observed that there are magnetic fields around Earth and around bar magnets. And you know that if you break a magnet, you get two smaller magnets. What is a magnet? Can you make a magnet?

The iron nail you magnetized is only a temporary magnet. Its magnetism was caused by the presence of a strong magnetic field. Magnetism that occurs only in the presence of a magnetic field is called **induced magnetism.** The iron nail developed magnetic poles while it was touching the magnet. When you removed the nail from the magnetic field, the nail's poles soon disappeared. Why was it possible to make a magnet? Would a piece of plastic or an aluminum nail act this way? Try it!

From these activities you might hypothesize that the magnetism of materials depends on the kind of atom of which they are made. For the materials attracted to the bar magnet, such as those made of iron, cobalt, and nickel, our hypothesis would suggest that their atoms have tiny magnetic fields. Therefore, the atoms can act like magnets. Can this atomic magnet model explain everything about a magnetic material? For instance, most of the time one paper clip has little or no attraction for other paper clips. Yet, sometimes when a paper clip is near a magnet, the clip itself acts like a magnet!

MAKING MAGNETS

Let's use our model of atomic magnets to explain how a material like the paper clip can be made magnetic. Suppose that, ordinarily, the atomic magnets face every which way. Figure 2-6(a) is a diagram of this arrangement. Now suppose that large numbers of atomic magnets line up in one direction. Each cluster of aligned atoms might contain billions of atomic magnets all working together. If most of the magnetic domains in the sample line up, as shown in Figure 2-6(b), they would reinforce each other's magnetic fields. Then the material would produce large magnetic effects.

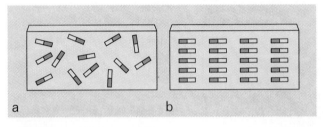

FIGURE 2-6. Domains in unmagnetized materials are randomly oriented (a); domains in magnetized materials are aligned (b).

You've already made a temporary magnet, one that works only in the presence of a magnetic field. From what you know about magnetic domains, do you think you can make a permanent magnet?

How do we know?

Is there any observable evidence that magnetic domains exist?

Yes. A fine powder of iron oxide, also known as rust, can be spread over a smooth surface of a magnetized metal. It's a little like placing iron filings around a bar magnet. The powder will collect along the boundaries between neighboring clusters of magnetic domains. The boundaries are visible under a microscope and can be photographed. These outlines allow us to observe the way magnetic domains interact with each other.

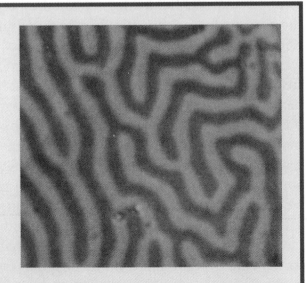

Can you make a permanent magnet?

Stroke a sewing needle along the length of a bar magnet about 50 times in one direction. Gently tap the needle while it's in the magnet's field. Remove the bar magnet. Test your needle to see if it's a magnet. Does the needle pick up paper clips and other small metal objects? Count how many paper clips, end to end, you can pick up with your new magnet. Explain how this magnet was created, using the model of magnetic domains.

Next, put the needle you just magnetized into an empty plastic bottle. Shake it hard about 100 times. Does the needle still attract the small metal objects? How many paper clips, end to end, can your magnet pick up now? You may need to shake more, but eventually the needle will lose its magnetism.

Conclude and Apply

1. Use domain model to explain how the steel needle lost its magnetism.
2. Make another steel needle magnet and heat it. What happens to the magnetism? Explain how heating destroys magnetism.

Some materials are noticeably influenced by magnetic fields—they become magnets themselves. Materials that can be made into permanent magnets are most useful. Most magnets are made of an alloy of aluminum, nickel, and cobalt. The ALNICO (ALuminum, NIckel, and CObalt) magnets retain their magnetism for a long time. Alloys made of different amounts of these metals differ somewhat in hardness and brittleness, but each can be made into a **permanent magnet**.

The temporary and permanent magnets you've observed have been made of magnetic materials. Is a magnetic material necessary to have a magnet?

SKILLBUILDER

OBSERVING AND INFERRING
A group of students must identify the poles of three magnets. Each end of each magnet is a different color. The students suspend one magnet. It rotates until its red end points north and its silver end points south. For the second magnet, they find that the green end repels the red end, but the yellow end attracts the red. Then the students place a blue/pink magnet next to the red/silver magnet. Both the blue end and the pink end attract the red end. How should the students label the green/yellow magnet? What can they conclude about the blue/pink magnet? If you need help, refer to the **Skill Handbook** on page 684.

2-1 MAKING A MAGNET

Suppose that you could make a magnet without using any magnetic materials. In the following activity, you will make such a magnet.

PROBLEM

How do you use an electric current to make a magnet?

MATERIALS

1 m, 22-gauge insulated wire
  scissors
large iron nail
drinking straw to fit over
  nail, cut to length of nail
3 D batteries
paper clips

PROCEDURE

1. Copy the data table.
2. Strip 1 cm of insulation from each end of the wire.
3. Slip the straw over the nail. Wrap the wire tightly around the straw for 30 turns. Leave about 5 mm of nail exposed at each end.
4. Connect one bare end of the wire to a terminal of the battery. Hold the second end of the wire against the other terminal. At the same time, touch the nail to a pile of paper clips, as shown.
5. Lift the nail while keeping the loose end of the wire on the battery terminal.
6. Record the number of paper clips the electromagnet picks up.
7. Connect the second battery with the first in series. **Predict** how the magnet will change.
8. Repeat Steps 4 through 6. Then connect the third battery with the others and repeat the same steps.
9. Add 15 more turns of wire to the magnet.
10. **Predict** how the magnet will change. Repeat Steps 4 through 6 and 8. Remove turns of wire until only 15 remain. Repeat the same steps.
11. Slide the nail out of the straw. **Predict** how the magnet will change. Record the number of paper clips you can pick up with your straw magnet now. Use all three batteries.

ANALYZE

1. How does the number of batteries affect the strength of the magnet?
2. How does the number of turns of wire affect the strength of the magnet?

CONCLUDE AND APPLY

3. How does the strength of the magnetic field depend on the current?

DATA AND OBSERVATIONS

NUMBER OF BATTERIES	NUMBER OF WIRE TURNS	NUMBER OF PAPER CLIPS
	15	
1	30	
	45	
	15	
2	30	
	45	
	15	
3	30	
	45	

You have seen that it's possible to make a magnet out of nothing more than a current-carrying wire. Such a magnet is called an **electromagnet.**

Hans Christian Oersted, a Danish physicist, was one of the first people to discover that electricity could produce a magnet. He put a magnetic compass near a current-carrying wire. When there was a current, the movement of the needle indicated the presence of a magnetic field. When the current was reversed, the compass rotated in the opposite direction. Oersted did a similar activity as a classroom demonstration.

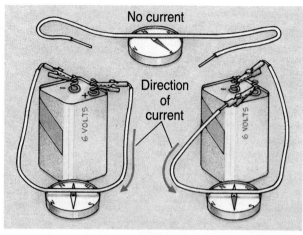

FIGURE 2-7. Oersted showed that there was a magnetic field whenever a current moved through the wire.

ELECTROMAGNETS AT WORK

You use an electromagnet whenever you listen to a record or a tape recording, talk on a telephone, ring an electric doorbell, or dry your hair with an electric dryer. Electromagnets are useful because their magnetism can be turned on and off and because they can produce magnetic fields that are stronger than the fields produced by most permanent magnets. As Figure 2-8 shows, a powerful electromagnet on the hook of a crane

FIGURE 2-8. Electromagnets are used to lift heavy loads.

can pick up huge loads of scrap metal when electric current flows through the magnet. When the scrap metal is over the desired place, the current is switched off and the scrap drops. One of the more exciting uses for electromagnets is in Maglev transportations. Maglevs are literally trains that fly. The force that levitates the trains is supplied by electromagnets.

FORMULATING MODELS AND OBSERVING AND INFERRING

There is a rule for determining the direction of the magnetic field around a current-carrying wire when the direction of the current is known. In the case of a straight wire, you would grasp the conductor in your right hand, as shown. The thumb would extend in the direction of the current. The fingers would then encircle the wire in the direction of the magnetic field.

The diagram shows the direction of the current in a coil. What direction is the magnetic field? If you need help, refer to the **Skill Handbook** on pages 684 and 692.

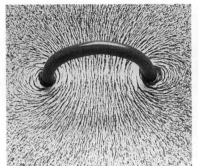
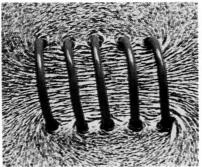

FIGURE 2-9. Current flowing through the wires of an electromagnet produces a strong magnetic field.

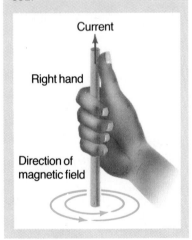

Current

Right hand

Direction of magnetic field

When you allowed current to flow through the wire of your electromagnet, as shown in Figure 2-9, the current created a magnetic field. You increased the strength of the magnet by increasing the number of batteries and by increasing the number of turns of wire. You also found that the field of the coil was stronger when the nail was inside the coil. Can you use the model of magnetic domains to account for the increased strength an electromagnet has on an iron core? The field produced by the coil will line up the magnetic domains in the iron. This adds additional strength to the field produced by the coil of wire.

In this section, you've thought of a magnet as a collection of tiny bar magnets, most of which are lined up in the same direction. You've made magnets that lasted for a minute or two and magnets that were more permanent. And you produced a magnetic field without using magnetic materials. In the next section, you'll use magnetism to change electricity into sound.

Check Your Understanding

1. Why are certain materials affected by magnets while others are not?
2. Describe how you would make a permanent magnet out of a paper clip.
3. Compare and contrast an electromagnet with a permanent magnet.
4. Using magnetic domains, explain how and why a permanent magnet can lose its magnetism.
5. **APPLY:** You leave a box of paper clips on top of your T.V. When you go to use them, you find they are stuck together. What might you infer about the T.V.?

2-3 Effects of Magnetic Fields

MAGNETISM AND ELECTRIC CURRENTS

In the last activity, you saw that an electric current can create a magnetic field. But what about the reverse situation? What effect does a magnetic field have on a static electric charge or on a current?

OBJECTIVES

In this section, you will
- demonstrate the effects of magnetic fields on wires carrying electric currents;
- explain how loudspeakers and electric motors work.

KEY SCIENCE TERMS

loudspeaker
electric motor

EXPLORE!

Does a magnetic field exert force on a charge?
First, you will need to make a pair of oppositely charged transparent-tape charge detectors. Fold to make a handle. Then tear off an 8 to 12 cm long strip. Stick the strip on a dry, smooth surface, such as your desktop. Make a second strip of tape in the same way and stick it on top of the first tape. Now quickly pull both pieces off the desk and pull them apart. Recall from

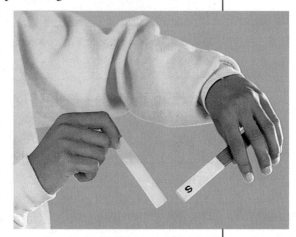

Chapter 1 that this produces a static charge. Bring one pole of a bar magnet near one tape and then near the other. What happens? (Remember that an uncharged conductor, such as your finger, will attract both tapes, so if both tapes move, make sure that you are not observing this effect.)

You might have predicted that a magnetic field would not exert force on a static electric charge. After all, a static charge does not create a magnetic field. Might a magnetic field affect moving charges?

Does a magnetic field exert force on a current?
For this activity, you'll need a 6 V battery, a length of thin, very flexible copper wire, and a bar magnet. First, bring the magnet near the wire and observe what happens. Next, connect one end of the wire to one terminal of the battery. Place the wire near the magnet and then touch the free end of the wire to the other pole of the battery. What happens? Reverse the direction of the magnet and repeat the experiment. Also try reversing the connections between the wire and the battery.

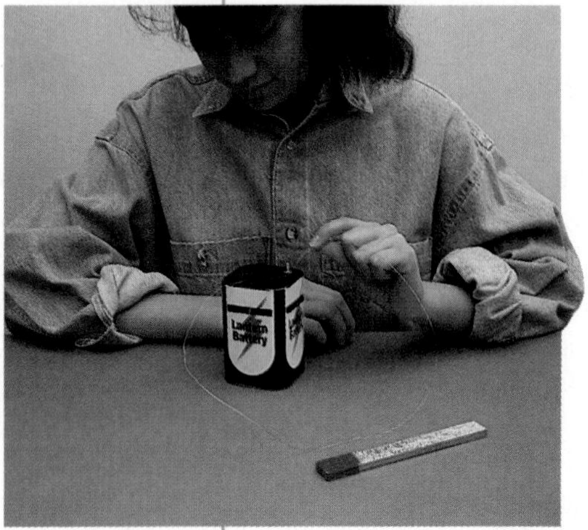

Conclude and Apply
How did the magnetic field affect the wire?

You can see that a magnetic field does exert force on a wire in which current is flowing. When you placed the current-carrying wire near the magnet, the magnet pushed the wire one way or the other. The magnet's field exerted force at right angles to the wire. The direction depended on which end of the magnet you brought near the wire. The direction of the force could also be reversed by reversing the current direction.

The relationship between magnetism and electricity is becoming more obvious. Now, how can it be used?

CHANGING CURRENT INTO SOUND

Here's one use you enjoy every day. Your radio or stereo runs on electricity. You may use batteries or a wall outlet, but either method produces electric current. What comes out of your radio or stereo? Electric current? No, what comes out are voices and music. The following activity will help explain what goes on inside the radio.

FIGURE 2-10. Your stereo turns electric current into sound.

How does electricity turn into sound?

You'll need a radio that has only an earphone jack, but no speaker; an earphone plug with wires attached; a small but powerful permanent magnet; 60 cm of insulated wire; a paper drinking cup; and glue. Assemble the cup, wire, and earphone plug, as shown in the figure. In the middle of the length of wire, make a coil of 10 turns, each about 1 cm in diameter. Use the glue to fix the coil to the bottom of the drinking cup. Strip the ends of the wire and connect them to the wires of the earphone plug. Insert the plug into the earphone jack and turn on the radio. Now hold the magnet very close to the coil of wire.

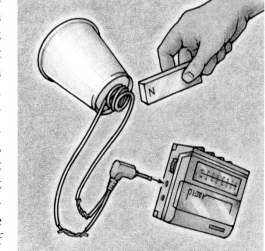

Conclude and Apply
1. What happens?
2. Why do you think this happens?

Do this activity for a minute or so. You'll notice that the force between the wire and the magnet changes whenever the output of the radio changes.

The radio sends a current through the wire. When you bring the magnet near the coil, a force pushes the coil either into or out of the magnetic field. The motion of the coil causes the cup to vibrate, creating sound waves. Remember, the radio output is only current. What you've observed is electric energy being changed into sound energy. You've built a loudspeaker. A **loudspeaker** changes variations in electric current into sound waves.

CURRENTS AT WORK

The coil in the loudspeaker vibrated because of the interaction between the electric current and a magnetic field. Can we use that interaction in other ways? Let's investigate.

2-2
MAKE AN ELECTRIC MOTOR

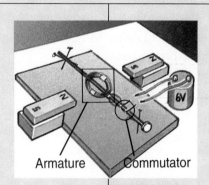

Armature   Commutator

When you made the paper-cup loudspeaker, you used magnetism to change electric energy into sound energy. In this activity, you'll use magnets to change electric potential energy into mechanical kinetic energy.

PROBLEM
How can you change electric energy into motion?

MATERIALS
22-gauge insulated wire
masking tape
fine sandpaper
steel knitting needle
wooden board (20 x 10 cm)
4 nails
2 bar magnets
2 wooden blocks
16-gauge insulated wire
6-V battery

PROCEDURE
1. Strip the insulation from 4 cm of each end of the 22-gauge wire.
2. Form a coil of at least 30 turns by winding the 22-gauge wire around a cylinder, such as a battery. Slide the coil off the cylin-

der and tape the turns of wire together. Leave about 4 cm of each end uncoiled.
3. Insert the knitting needle through the coil. Try to have an equal number of turns on each side of the needle, as shown in the diagram. This part of the motor is the armature. Tape each of the wire's bare ends to the needle. This part of the motor is the commutator.
4. Mount the needle on the crossed nails, as shown.
5. Tape a magnet to each block, as shown. Place the magnets on either side of the coil-needle assembly, the north pole of one magnet facing the coil and the south pole of the other magnet facing it.
6. Take two lengths of 16-gauge wire, strip one end of each, and connect it to one terminal of the battery. Strip 4 cm of insulation from the loose end of each wire.

7. Holding only the insulated part of each wire, as shown, brush the wire connected to the battery against the bare wires of the commutator. **Observe** what happens to the armature.

ANALYZE
1. **Observe** that the armature is designed so that the current through it turns on and off as the armature rotates. How could you test it to see if it is working?
2. Is there any position of the coil that makes it easier to start it spinning? Why would you **hypothesize** that this is true?

CONCLUDE AND APPLY
3. The electric motor operates on three basic principles. What are they?
4. **Going Further:** Would the motor work if you replaced the armature with a permanent magnet? Explain.

In making the motor, you see a practical application of the interaction between magnetism and electricity. Air conditioners, vacuum cleaners, and washing machines use electric motors. An **electric motor** uses an electromagnet to change electric energy into mechanical energy, which can be used to do work. Can you think of other uses for electric motors?

Electric devices that use batteries use direct current (DC). Direct current travels in only one direction. However, most electric appliances use alternating current (AC). Alternating current, the current from an ordinary wall outlet, reverses its direction in a regular pattern. The alternating current in your home changes direction 120 times a second and is sometimes called 60-cycle current.

In an electric motor, as the current flows through the coil, the force produced is at right angles to the magnetic field. This produces an upward force on one side of the coil and a downward force on the other, making the armature move. When the armature becomes vertical, the current changes direction, and the current running through the loop reverses and the force produced is once again at right angles to the magnetic field.

In this section, you've seen that magnetic fields can affect the direction of electric current. This interaction can be used in devices such as loudspeakers and electric motors. In the next section, you'll find out about still other useful roles that magnets play.

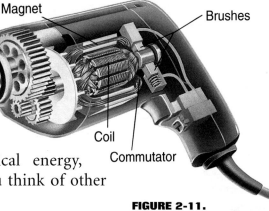

Magnet · Brushes · Coil · Commutator

FIGURE 2-11.
Motors in common appliances such as the power drill use alternating currents.

Check Your Understanding

1. In what direction must the magnetic field be in a coil of a loudspeaker to make the coil vibrate?
2. Why do electric motors contain both a permanent magnet and an electromagnet?
3. **APPLY:** In what direction—with respect to a magnetic field—would you run a wire carrying a current, so that the force on it due to the field is zero?

2-4 Producing Electric Current

OBJECTIVES

In this section, you will

- demonstrate the ability of a changing magnetic field to produce an electric current;
- describe the working principles behind electric generators;
- explain the operation of transformers.

KEY SCIENCE TERMS

induced current
electric generator
transformer

MAGNETISM AND ELECTRIC CURRENT

When you made the electromagnet in the last section, you found evidence that an electric current could produce magnetism. Once again, think about the reverse situation. Can magnetism produce electricity? The American scientist Joseph Henry and the British scientist Michael Faraday independently discovered that it could be done. How?

FIND OUT!

Does a moving magnet produce a current?

You'll need 4 m of 22-gauge insulated wire, a strong bar magnet, and a galvanometer. A galvanometer is an instrument used to detect electric current. This instrument gives a zero reading when no current is moving through it. If the pointer moves left or right from zero, there must be a current in the wire. Form the wire into a coil wide enough to allow the magnet to pass easily through it. Attach the ends of the wire to the terminals of the galvanometer. Observe what the galvanometer's pointer does when you do each of the following things: 1) Push the magnet into the coil. 2) Hold the magnet still inside the coil. 3) Pull the magnet out from the coil. 4) Hold the magnet still just outside the coil. 5) Move the magnet back and forth inside the coil.

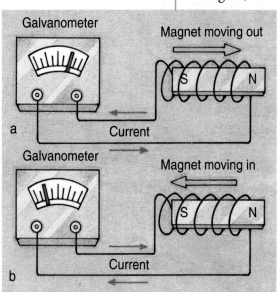

Galvanometer — Magnet moving out — S N — a — Current

Galvanometer — Magnet moving in — S N — b — Current

Conclude and Apply
1. Did the magnet produce a current?
2. When the direction of the magnetic field changed, what happened to the current?

When you move the magnet into the coil, the pointer moves as shown in the Part (a) portion of the Find Out figure. This indicates that a current has been induced, or created, in the wire. When you move the magnet in the opposite direction, the pointer moves in the opposite direction as well. See Part (b) of the Find Out figure. The current has changed direction. When you move the magnet back and forth in the coil, the current keeps changing its direction of flow through the wire. This is an alternating current. Suppose that the magnet didn't move, but the coil moved back and forth along the magnet. What would happen? Current also flows through the wire if you move the coil along the magnet. As you saw, whether the coil or the magnet moves makes no difference. It's the motion of one in relation to the other that matters. When either the magnet or the coil is moving, a changing magnetic field is produced. The magnetic field, in turn, induces a current in the coil. An electric current produced by using a magnet is an **induced current.**

GENERATING CURRENT

Induced current has made it possible for every home and business to receive electric energy from a central source. The current commonly used is produced by electric generators.

An **electric generator** changes kinetic energy of rotation into electric energy. A basic generator, as shown in Figure 2-12, is little more than a loop of wire rotating in a magnetic field. A similar system generates electric energy on a larger scale at power plants as you've learned previously.

CHANGING CURRENTS

Power companies use transformers to ensure the proper voltage for the circuits of lights, home appliances, and other electric equipment in your home. Transformers also enable power companies to transmit alternating current to their users easily and efficiently. A

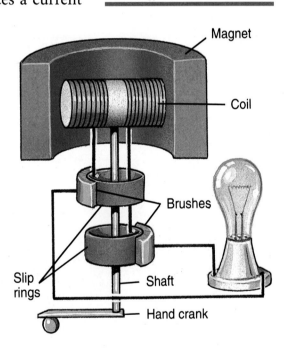

FIGURE 2-12. Electric generators change the kinetic energy of rotation into electrical energy.

Magnet

Coil

Brushes

Slip rings

Shaft

Hand crank

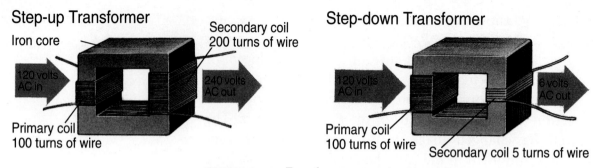

Step-up Transformer

Iron core

Secondary coil
200 turns of wire

120 volts
AC in

240 volts
AC out

Primary coil
100 turns of wire

Step-down Transformer

120 volts
AC in

6 volts
AC out

Primary coil
100 turns of wire

Secondary coil 5 turns of wire

FIGURE 2-13. Transformers can change voltage.

transformer can raise or lower the voltage. Look at Figure 2-13. Step-up transformers raise the voltage to a level that allows the electrical energy to travel long distances with little loss. When the energy reaches the area where it will be used, step-down transformers there lower the voltage to the level needed. Like generators, transformers work by inducing currents.

In this section, you've learned that an induced current results when a magnetic field is changed in a coil. The field can be changed by moving either the magnet or the coil. Electric generators induce current by rotating a coil in a magnetic field.

Now look back on this chapter. You started with simple toys that seemed to work by magic. Having reached the end of this chapter, you know enough about magnetism to make your own magnetic toys. You've made magnets, using a battery, wires, and a nail. You've made a loudspeaker, which might allow you to hear music while you work. You've even built a simple electric motor that could do work. You did all this because you've investigated the mysteries surrounding magnets!

Check Your Understanding

1. Describe three ways in which a current can be induced in a circuit.
2. How is a generator like a motor? How is it different?

3. **APPLY:** Small generators are often attached to bicycle wheels to light the headlight. Describe how this might work.

EXPANDING YOUR VIEW

CONTENTS

A CLOSER LOOK

HOW CAN YOU MAKE A TRANSFORMER?

You know that a transformer transmits electric energy from a source to a user, changing the voltage in the process. Construct your own transformer.

Insert a large nail in a soda straw that has been cut to the same length as the nail. Wrap 30 turns of 32-gauge wire in a tight compact coil at one end of the straw. Make a coil at the other end that has 120 turns. Use sandpaper to remove the insulating coating from the ends of the wire.

Connect the ends of the 30-turn coil to a low-voltage AC power supply. This will be the source of the voltage your transformer will

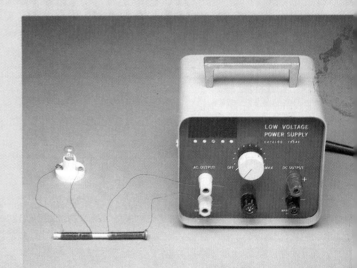

WHAT DO YOU THINK?

Repeat the activity you just completed without placing the iron nail inside the straw. Record your observations. Then place several other items, such as a paper clip, a pencil lead, and a string, inside the straw. What happens? Use your knowledge of magnetism, magnetic fields, and electric fields to explain your observations.

change. Connect the ends of the 120-turn wire to the light bulb, the user to which your transformer will transmit electricity. **CAUTION:** *The nail may become hot.* Observe how brightly the light bulb glows. Now reverse the position of the coils—connect the 120-turn coil to the power supply and the 30-turn coil to the light bulb. How brightly does the bulb glow in this arrangement?

Transformers are generally called step-up transformers or step-down transformers. Use your observations to determine which time your coil-wrapped straw acted like a step-up transformer. Explain your choice.

EARTH SCIENCE
CONNECTION

VAN ALLEN BELTS

You make use of Earth's magnetic field every time you find direction with a compass. You can see in the drawing how Earth's huge magnetic field extends far out in space. The field acts as an umbrella that protects us from the shower of high-energy charged particles from space. These particles could cause cancer and genetic damage in living things.

When the first artificial satellites were launched into space, scientists discovered a previously unknown region of charged particles in space near Earth. These particles are different from the high-energy charged particles mentioned before. Dr. James Van Allen of the University of Iowa proposed the theory that the particles the satellite detected come from the solar wind that streams outward from the sun. He hypothesized that charged particles from the sun interact with the umbrella of Earth's magnetic field. Van Allen said that the force due to Earth's magnetic field makes the particles move in circles around the field lines. You can see a model in the drawing of how the particles are trapped in regions above Earth's equator. These regions are now called Van Allen Belts in honor of the scientist who first explained them.

Occasionally, storms on the sun send larger than usual numbers of particles toward Earth, and the Van Allen Belts become over-crowded. The excess particles are pushed along Earth's magnetic field lines toward the north and south magnetic poles. There the particles interact with gases high in the atmosphere, creating spectacular displays known as the northern and southern lights, as shown in the photo above.

Intense solar storms can disrupt the Van Allen Belts. The storms on the sun can lead to changes on Earth, such as interference with radio reception, surges in power lines, and more visible northern and southern lights. Write a story for the newspaper explaining such happenings as these as if they occurred in your area. Mention Dr. Van Allen.

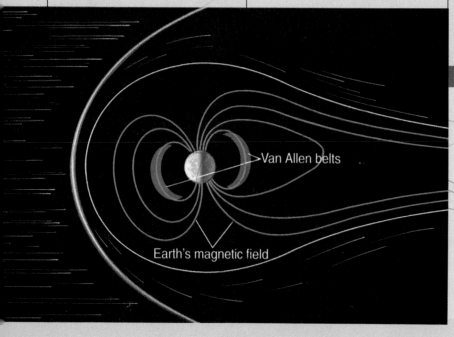

Van Allen belts

Earth's magnetic field

SCIENCE AND SOCIETY

HIGH-TECH HEALTH CARE

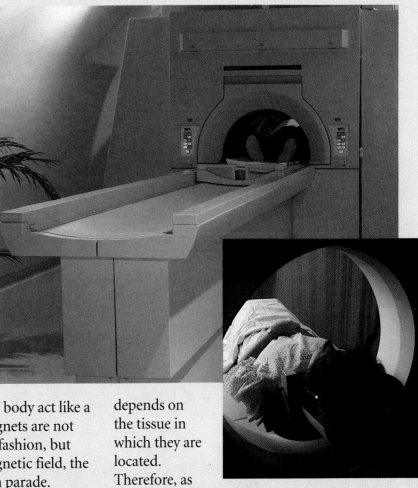

Several new technologies allow doctors to produce images of what is inside the human body without using X rays. One of the most common is called Magnetic Resonance Imaging (MRI). The machine consists of a large coil that creates a strong magnetic field. MRI works because the positively charged particles at the center of each atom making up the body act like a tiny bar magnet. These bar magnets are not usually lined up in any orderly fashion, but when subjected to a strong magnetic field, the magnets line up like soldiers on parade.

An electromagnetic wave is created in the region of the organ being studied. The rest of the body is protected by a shield. If the wave has exactly the correct frequency, it can cause the tiny magnets to flip over. The flipping requires energy—the more magnets flipped, the more energy required.

The frequency needed to flip the magnets depends on the tissue in which they are located. Therefore, as the frequency of the wave is varied, first one type of tissue absorbs energy, then another type. Cancerous tissue absorbs energy at a different frequency than normal tissue. A computer creates a three-dimensional image from the results.

Being able to distinguish between a cancerous and a normal tissue while it is still inside a patient's body, without surgery, is a great breakthrough. With MRI, doctors can watch blood coursing through a patient's blood vessels. They have also been able to watch the swelling caused by arthritis shrink when medicine is applied to a swollen knee.

As wonderful as these advances in medical science are, they do not come cheaply. An

CAREER CONNECTION

MRI technicians must be able to operate imaging equipment. They also need to use probes to measure the magnetic field strength. A period of specialized training is required. MRI technicians work in hospitals and medical schools.

MRI machine is very expensive and hard to maintain. The machine must be protected from the surrounding area in case magnetic materials, which could upset the strong magnetic field, are present. Even a lawn mower being run outside the hospital could affect the machine. On the other hand, the powerful magnets could affect other equipment in the hospital, causing it to malfunction.

The cost of running the MRI is also high. Its superconducting magnets must be kept cool, or they lose their magnetism. The cooling is done by liquid helium. To keep a constant supply of supercool helium for a machine can cost about $100,000 a year.

Some people say hospitals shouldn't pur-chase costly equipment, such as that needed for MRI. They say such purchases make the bill for ordinary medical care much higher than it should be. These people think MRI machines should be limited to only a few hospitals. What do you think? Would your opinion change if someone in your family needed to be diagnosed with MRI?

YOU TRY IT!

Call or visit a hospital in your area that has MRI. Find out how much the machine cost to purchase and how much it costs to maintain. Inquire about the source of the funds for these expenses.

History
CONNECTION

GRANVILLE T. WOODS

The communications industry owes much to Granville T. Woods. In 1881, the young African-American inventor used one of the most important applications of electromagnets in recent history to design a new telephone transmitter. It produced a much more distinct sound and was able to carry a voice over much greater distances than other transmitters because he made use of an alternating current. To produce the current, Woods used a thin metal disk that vibrated back and forth in response to the sound waves produced by a voice. When the disk vibrates one way, it presses against a box filled with tiny grains of carbon that conduct electricity. When it bends the other way, the grains no longer touch, and electrical conduction is poor. This bending back and forth produces an alternating current that is sent by wires to a telephone receiver.

An electromagnet in the receiver pushes and pulls a similar metal disk. The use of the electromagnet was important because it allowed the metal disk in the receiver to vibrate at the same frequency as the metal disk in the transmitter, thus producing amazing clarity of sound.

YOU TRY IT!

Compare and contrast Woods' telephone transmitter with a modern one. How are they similar? How are they different?

HOW IT WORKS

TELEVISION PICTURE TUBE

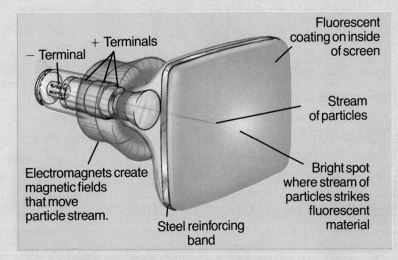

- Terminal
+ Terminals
Fluorescent coating on inside of screen
Stream of particles
Bright spot where stream of particles strikes fluorescent material
Electromagnets create magnetic fields that move particle stream.
Steel reinforcing band

Suppose you are watching an exciting football game on TV. When you see the action, you wonder how your favorite players appear on your television screen. Part of the answer lies in the magnetic and electric fields produced in the picture tube of your set.

Look at the illustration. At one end of the picture tube is the rectangular glass screen where you can watch the game. Inside the television set, video or picture signals are received. These signals are sent through the air on radio waves from the broadcasting station.

YOU TRY IT!

Closed-circuit television lets you watch what is happening in another part of the building. Find out how this works. From what you have learned about television, write an article that explains how closed-circuit TV works at your school or in a building lobby.

A wire in the tube heats up when you turn on your TV. The heated wire sends a stream of particles toward the screen. The television screen is coated with a fluorescent material that absorbs electrical energy from the stream of particles. It changes the electrical energy to light. The more charged particles that hit a spot, the brighter the light. In this way, a picture of what is happening at a distance is "painted" on your screen with varying colors and intensities.

When your TV is tuned in, the signals from the TV station are processsed in the TV set, and vary the stream of particles. The number of particles then corresponds to the picture that is being broadcast.

The particles are moved across the television screen by two varying magnetic fields. One field moves the stream of particles up and down. The other field moves the stream left and right. This movement allows the stream of charged particles to sweep across the entire screen. In one-thirtieth of a second, a total of 535 lines of light resulting from the particles cover the glass tube. A full, smoothly moving picture results.

TECHNOLOGY CONNECTION

MAGLEV TRAINS

Imagine riding on a train that floats through the air without making a sound! This may soon be more than a flight of fancy. The model train in the photo is a MagLev train. MagLev is short for magnetic levitation. When something is levitated, it is suspended in the air.

A MagLev train is an improvement over an ordinary train that rolls along on railway tracks. The clackety-clack you hear as this kind of train moves forward is caused by the contact of the wheels with the track. Ordinary trains waste a great deal of energy doing work against friction. The very fastest of ordinary trains travel 370 kilometers per hour.

One kind of MagLev train

has magnets on the bottom of the train. These magnets are repelled by the magnets in the guideway along which the train travels. The force of repulsion keeps the train about 10 centimeters above the ground. Another kind of MagLev train has magnets along its top side. These magnets are attracted to other magnets along a rail above the train. The rest of the train hangs free.

Both kinds of MagLev trains move forward because of the force of a series of propulsion magnets. These are spaced about a meter apart along the entire guideway. Electricity to each electromagnet is turned on and off in succession to exert a constant forward pull on the train.

The United States, Japan, and Germany are working on models of MagLevs. One Japanese prototype can already travel at a speed of almost 650 kilometers per hour. At that rate, you could travel from Chicago to Washington, D.C., in a little over an hour!

YOU TRY IT!

Draw up a simple plan in which you show the magnetic field that keeps a train suspended in the air and the magnetic field that propels the train forward along the guideway.

Reviewing Main Ideas

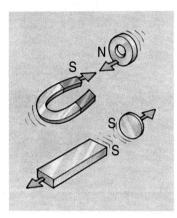

1. Magnets have two poles, the places where the magnetic field is strongest. Like poles repel each other; unlike poles attract each other.

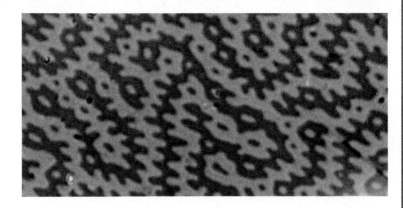

2. Some atoms themselves are magnets. In an unmagnetized substance, the atomic magnets point in random directions, but in a magnetized substance, they line up.

3. A magnetic field is a region where magnetic forces act.

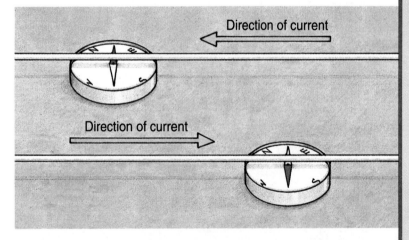

Direction of current

Direction of current

4. An electric current creates a magnetic field, making electro-magnets and electric motors possible.

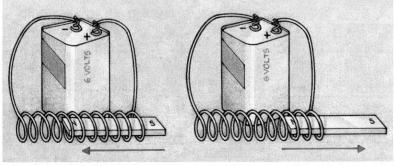

5. In an electric generator, a changing magnetic field induces an electric current. Transformers step up or step down a voltage.

Chapter Review

USING KEY SCIENCE TERMS

electric generator   loudspeaker
electric motor   magnetic field
electromagnet   magnetic pole
induced current   permanent magnet
induced magnetism   transformer

An analogy is a relationship between two pairs of words generally written in the following manner: a:b::c:d. The symbol : is read "is to," and the symbol :: is read "as." For example, cat:animal::rose:plant is read "cat is to animal as rose is to plant." In the analogies that follow, a word is missing. Complete each analogy by providing the missing word from the list above.

1. induced magnetism : electromagnet :: induced current : _____

2. electrical energy : electric generator :: mechanical energy: _____

Using the list above, replace the underlined words with the correct key science term.

3. Iron filings on paper can be used to reveal <u>a region in which magnetic forces act</u>.

4. Doorbells use <u>a current-carrying coil</u> to make a hammer strike a bell or chime.

5. A galvanometer can be used to detect <u>electric charges set in motion by a magnetic field</u>.

6. In most communities, electric current is produced by <u>a device that turns a coil through a magnetic field</u>.

UNDERSTANDING IDEAS

Choose the best answer to complete each sentence.

1. Current will be induced if a _____.
   a. current flows through a coil
   b. circuit is connected to a battery
   c. magnet moves in a coil
   d. motor runs a device

2. A current in one circuit can induce a current in another circuit when _____.
   a. both circuits are in a constant magnetic field
   b. the current in the first circuit is changing
   c. the current in the first circuit is constant
   d. the magnetic field created by the first circuit is at right angles to Earth's magnetic field

3. The direction of an induced current in a coil can be changed by _____.
   a. using a coil with more loops
   b. reversing the poles of a magnet moved through it
   c. passing a stronger magnet through it
   d. passing a weaker magnet through it

Complete each sentence.

4. An electric motor uses an electromagnet to change electric energy into _____.

5. The _____ in a motor reverses the current the electromagnet's coil receives just before its poles line up with the opposite poles of the permanent magnet.

6. When a coil of wire cuts through a magnetic field, it produces an _____ in the wire.

CRITICAL THINKING

Use your understanding of the concepts developed in the chapter to answer each of the following questions.

1. If a coil of wire were placed between these magnets, and a current passed through the wire, would the coil move? Explain.

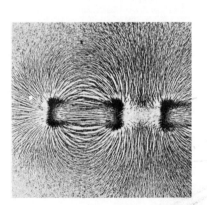

2. Is the magnetic pole in Earth's northern hemisphere like the north or south pole of a bar magnet? How do you know?

3. Explain how you could use Earth's magnetic field to help you magnetize a piece of iron.

4. A wire carrying an electric current has a magnetic field around it, but a metal sphere that has a static electric charge doesn't produce a magnetic field. What do these facts suggest about the relationship between magnetism and electricity?

5. Why will a magnet attract a nail to either of its poles but attract another magnet to only one of its poles?

PROBLEM SOLVING

Read the following problem and discuss your answer in a brief paragraph.

Abdul has a small motor that requires 12 V of electricity. He is building a transformer to change the 110 V from the wall outlet to 12 V. If the input coil has 800 turns, how many turns will the output coil have?

CONNECTING IDEAS

Discuss each of the following in a brief paragraph.

1. In what ways are magnetic poles like electric charges? How are they different?

2. **A CLOSER LOOK** How would you build a transformer to change 12 V to 60 V?

3. **EARTH SCIENCE CONNECTION** How are the Van Allen radiation belts produced?

4. **TECHNOLOGY CONNECTION** Why do MagLev trains use less energy than conventional trains?

5. **SCIENCE AND SOCIETY** Describe the role of the elctromagnet in an MRI machine. How does this magnet allow doctors to see different tissues in the body?

DID YOU EVER WONDER . . .

What it means to blow a fuse?

How a portable radio or calculator can be so small?

How your electric bill is determined each month?

You'll find the answers to these questions as you read this chapter.

Electrical Applications

Your pizza is hot, your favorite song is on the stereo, and your blown-dry hair looks great. You're all ready for a party with a few friends. How did you accomplish all this in such a short amount of time? With a flick of a few switches?

Consider what you are really doing when you flick these few switches in your home. You're controlling electricity so that you can use it just when you want it. Not only do you control just when you use the electrical energy in your home, you also can control exactly how much energy you use. You cooked the pizza at 400° for 12 minutes, you dried your hair on high for 15 minutes, and perhaps you turned up the volume of your stereo for dancing the whole evening. Electricity helps make life pretty simple, convenient, and even fun, doesn't it?

You're about to discover how electricity works to enable you to control it with a flick of a switch, and how electric energy is supplied and measured to provide you with these conveniences.

EXPLORE!

How many forms of useful energy does electricity provide for you?
Take a walk through your house and count the number of switches and wall outlets, and all of the appliances, lights, and other electrical devices connected or plugged into them. Classify each according to the kind of energy provided. How many provide heat, light, movement? Other?

3-1 Common Electrical Circuits

OBJECTIVES

In this section, you will

- draw circuit diagrams for series and parallel circuits;
- describe the role of the fuse or circuit breaker in household circuits.

KEY SCIENCE TERMS

series circuit
parallel circuit
circuit breaker

TWO KINDS OF CIRCUITS

Look around your home. It is probably full of appliances and other electrical devices that rely on circuits to supply electricity where you need it. These circuits include a voltage source, a conductor, and one or more devices that convert electricity into other forms of energy. You may recall that an electrical circuit is a closed path through which charges can flow. You'll find out now that an electrical circuit may be given a different name depending on the number of paths the charges can take in the circuit.

Series Circuits

In Chapter 1, you made an electrical circuit that would light a lamp. Your circuit had the three parts needed in all electrical circuits: (1) a conducting path, (2) a battery or power supply that produces the potential difference or voltage, and (3) a resistance. In that circuit, there was only one path for the current—from the battery, through the wires and lamp, and back to the battery. A circuit that has only one path is called a **series circuit**. Series circuits are found in all devices that can be turned off and on with switches, such as toasters, radios, flashlights, or your TV.

Do you remember what happened when you disconnected a wire from the battery? The lamps went out because without a complete circuit, the current could not flow. If the current stops in one part of a series circuit, it stops everywhere.

Because you want to be able to turn lamps off and on, you need a way to open and close the circuit—a switch. A switch is a device that opens or closes a circuit. When the switch is closed, current can flow. When it is open, there is no conducting path, and the current stops. In Figure

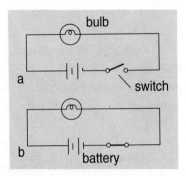

FIGURE 3-1. This schematic diagram of a series circuit shows a switch open/light off (a) and a switch closed/light on (b).

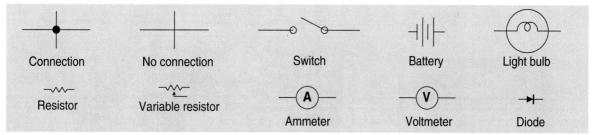

FIGURE 3-2. A circuit diagram is very easy to draw when you use these symbols.

Connection	No connection	Switch	Battery	Light bulb
Resistor	Variable resistor	Ammeter	Voltmeter	Diode

3-1(a), the switch is open, and there is no current. In Figure 3-1(b), the switch is closed. There is a complete circuit, and current flows. Figure 3-2 shows the symbols used to draw circuit diagrams. We'll use these symbols from now on as we draw circuits.

In your home, an electrical outlet replaces the battery as the source of potential difference. The outlet receives energy from a generator that is operated by the power company. Can you imagine how inconvenient it would be to run every electrical device in your home with batteries? Do you think you could find a battery large enough to heat an oven or run a washing machine?

How can you get electricity from the wall outlet to your stove to warm up your pizza? Easy! Turn on the electric stove. Getting sound out of your stereo or warm air out of your hair dryer requires only that you turn them on. In doing so, you close the switch that completes the circuit. Each switch must be in series with the appliance it controls. Closing the switch completes the circuit, and opening the switch interrupts it. You can see in Figure 3-3(a) that in a toaster, the switch must be in series with its heating coil. Switches are always connected in series with the appliances they control. But what kinds of circuits supply electricity to your wall outlets for all your appliances, electronic gadgets, video games, and lights? You'll discover more about circuits as you investigate how they work.

FIGURE 3-3. Raising and lowering the toaster handles opens and closes the series circuit in your toaster (a). Appliances are wired in circuits that allow them to be turned off and on separately (b).

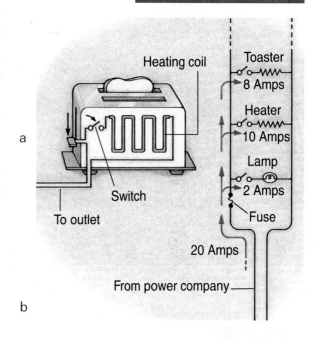

a

b

3-1 SERIES AND PARALLEL CIRCUITS

In this investigation, you will construct series and parallel electrical circuits and observe their different characteristics.

PROBLEM
How are series and parallel circuits different?

MATERIALS
3 6-V light bulbs
3 sockets to fit bulbs
1 6-V battery
wire connectors

PROCEDURE
1. Draw a series circuit, using the symbols from Figure 3-2, with three light bulbs, a 6-V battery, and wire connectors. Label each part.
2. Use the sockets, battery, and wire to build the circuit. Does it look like the drawing?
3. **Observe** what happens as you screw a bulb into a socket. Add a second bulb with socket to the circuit, then a third. What happens?
4. Unscrew the bulbs one at a time. **Observe** what happens.

a

b

5. Now change the circuit so that the lamps are connected as shown in the illustration.
6. Draw a diagram of this circuit using the symbols from Figure 3-2. This will be a parallel circuit.
7. Repeat Steps 3 and 4.

ANALYZE
1. When one bulb is removed from a series circuit, what happens to the circuit?
2. When one bulb is removed from a parallel circuit, what happens to the circuit?

3. In which circuit are the bulbs brighter? Is there more current flowing through each bulb in the parallel circuit? Why do you think so?

CONCLUDE AND APPLY
4. **Predict** where, in a parallel circuit, you would place a switch to control only a single light. Where would you place it to control all the lights?
5. What can you **infer** about whether or not your house lights are connected in series or parallel?
6. **Going Further:** Would you **conclude** that a power company wires all the homes in a neighborhood in series? Explain.

Parallel Circuits

Are all the lights in your home wired in series with each other? When you turn off one light, do all the others go off? Probably not. The current through one lamp doesn't depend on the current through the others. A circuit that operates this way is called a **parallel circuit**.

In the Investigate, you found that in parallel circuits, the electrical current from the battery flows through several paths instead of only one, as it does in the series circuit. You also observed that three bulbs in a parallel circuit were brighter than the same three bulbs in the series circuit. Why is that?

In a series circuit, the potential difference across all the bulbs together equals the voltage of the power supply or battery. If, for example, you have 100 similar bulbs in series on a string of holiday lights plugged into a 120-V wall outlet, each bulb has 1.2 volts across it. With a 6-V battery and 3 bulbs, each bulb would have 2 volts across it. You can see then, that in a series circuit, the more bulbs or lights you have, the dimmer each becomes.

In a parallel circuit, each bulb is connected directly across the battery so each bulb gets a full 6 volts. What controls the current through each bulb and thus its brightness? Recall from Chapter 1 that in a simple circuit,

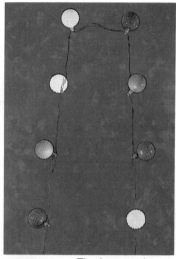

FIGURE 3-4. The box reads "When one burns out, the rest stay lit." Are the bulbs in parallel or series?

FIGURE 3-5. A household circuit is a complex combination of parallel circuits.

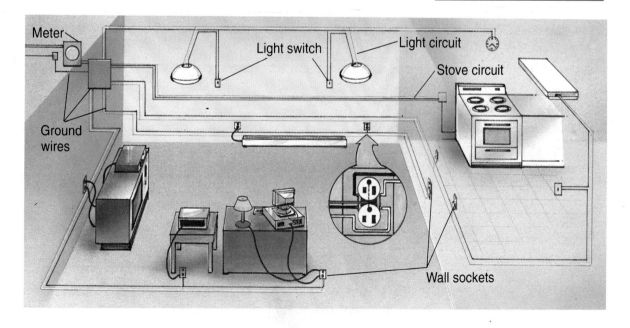

Meter

Light switch

Light circuit

Stove circuit

Ground wires

Wall sockets

a

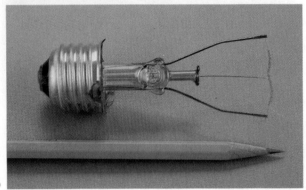

b

FIGURE 3-6. The thin tungsten filament (b) has more resistance than the thick copper wire (a). Which wire can carry more current without getting hot?

current depends on resistance. Current flowing through each bulb is equal to the voltage of the power supply divided by the resistance of the bulb. When you turn on a light in your home, the brightness of the other lights doesn't change. The current through one light does not depend on the current through the others, because your lights are in a parallel circuit.

The parallel circuits in your home may contain not only lamps, but a television, stove, and computer, as shown on Figure 3-5. The resistance of each appliance is different, and therefore, the current through each is different. As you use more lamps and appliances, you increase the total amount of current flowing through the wires in your home.

But how does the current you use get to your house or apartment? The next time you're outside, look at the electrical wires leading to your home. Are they the size of a lamp cord or a toaster cord? Figure 3-6(a) shows a wire of this type. Compare it with the filament wire from a light bulb. What do you notice?

The copper wire that brings electricity to your house first passes through a meter that records how much electrical energy is used. From there it goes to a metal box where it is connected to several parallel circuits. Each of these parallel circuits connects to some wall outlets in your house.

You know that the thin tungsten wire in a light bulb gets hot as electrical current goes through it. The wires that carry the electricity to the lamp are much thicker and made of copper, so their resistance is low, and they will not become too hot. The copper wires in appliances are also thick for the same reason. The wires in the metal box that supply the current to several wall outlets are even thicker, so they can safely carry even more current. However, if any of the wires in your home carry too much current, they can become hot enough to cause a fire. How can such a situation be prevented?

EXPLORE!

How can you prevent overheating in wires?

Strip the coating from the ends of two 15-cm lengths of #18 plastic-coated copper wire. Attach one end of each wire to a different terminal of a 6-V battery. **CAUTION**: *In the next step, the wire will become hot enough to cause a burn if touched.* Using a pliers to hold one wire, briefly touch the unattached end of the wire to the unattached end of the other wire. What happens? Why does the plastic coating melt? Cut a 5-cm × 2-cm piece of aluminum foil and secure the foil to a wood block with thumbtacks, as shown. Twist one wire from the battery around one thumbtack. Now use pliers to touch the other wire from the battery to the other thumbtack. Be careful! Heat will be produced, and precautions should be taken. Did the foil break the circuit before the coating started to melt?

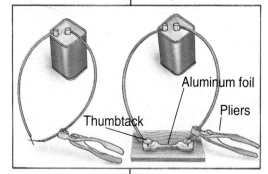

Aluminum foil

Pliers

Thumbtack

FUSES AND CIRCUIT BREAKERS

In the Explore, the strip of aluminum foil melted. This broke the circuit so that no more electricity flowed, and the wire was protected from overheating. The foil in this circuit acted as a fuse.

A fuse contains a small strip of metal that melts at a certain temperature. As you turn on more and more appliances in a parallel circuit, the current flowing into that circuit and through the fuse increases. When the current reaches the level for which the fuse is rated, the fuse metal melts, breaking the circuit. The fuse blows.

Different fuses melt at different levels of current. The type of fuse you select should depend on the thickness of the wiring in your home. Most wiring is designed to carry 15 amps safely. This means you should use a 15-amp fuse. If you use a 30-amp fuse, the wires may get dangerously hot before the fuse melts.

When fuses melt, they must be replaced. This is often inconvenient. Newer wiring for homes and buildings uses

DID YOU KNOW?

In the late 1870s, Thomas Edison attempted to find a light-bulb filament that would give lots of light with little current. This required a filament with high resistance. He and his workers tried over 1600 different materials, including paper, cloth, fishline, and even human hair. Modern light bulbs contain a fine tungsten filament that gives more light and lasts longer because it is a high resistance metal with a high melting point.

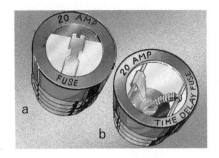

FIGURE 3-7. Fuse (a) blows at 20 amps. Fuse (b) allows a brief overload, as occurs when starting a motor. The circuit breaker (c) eliminates the need for keeping fuses on hand.

FIGURE 3-8. Plugging many appliances into the same outlet can cause wiring to overheat.

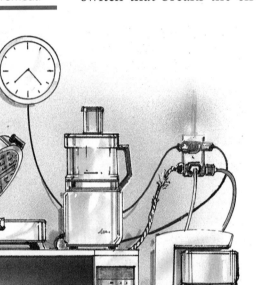

circuit breakers. Instead of a piece of metal that melts, a **circuit breaker** contains a metal strip that bends as it is heated. When the strip bends far enough, it activates a switch that breaks the circuit. Once you have turned off everything on the circuit, all you have to do is flip the switch to close the circuit again.

The next time you go through your home turning on the lights, the stove, and the TV or stereo, stop for a minute and think how your life might be without electrical energy at your fingertips. The wires and circuits bringing electrical energy to your home are designed with built-in protectors to provide you with all the electrical energy you need at the flick of a switch.

Check Your Understanding

1. Use symbols to draw a circuit containing a battery, an open switch, and two bulbs—all in series.
2. Draw a circuit containing a battery and two bulbs in parallel. Where would a switch be placed in this circuit to control both bulbs?
3. Why do you need to turn off every item in a circuit once the fuse or the circuit breaker has stopped the current flow?
4. **APPLY:** Before circuit breakers were widely used, people would sometimes replace a blown-out fuse with a coin. Why was this a very dangerous practice?

3-2 The Small World of Electronics

SEMICONDUCTORS

If you were to look inside your pocket radio or calculator, you would find it filled with tiny parts that control the movement of the electrical current. These take the place of large glass tubes that made old radios and TVs very big and bulky. You may still see a few of these tubes inside a very old TV set.

The microscopic circuits in TV games, hand-held calculators, and even wristwatch-sized televisions were made possible by research on materials called semiconductors. A **semiconductor** is a material that conducts current better than insulators, but not as well as a conductor. The elements selenium, germanium, and silicon, often combined with other elements, are three important semiconductors.

You know from Chapter 1 that electricity involves the movement of charges. We can best understand how semiconductors work by using a model. Figure 3-10 shows an arrangement for a game of musical chairs. There are four sets of three chairs (circles) and, as you can see, each chair contains a student (dots). The students represent negative charges. In order for a current to flow, the negative

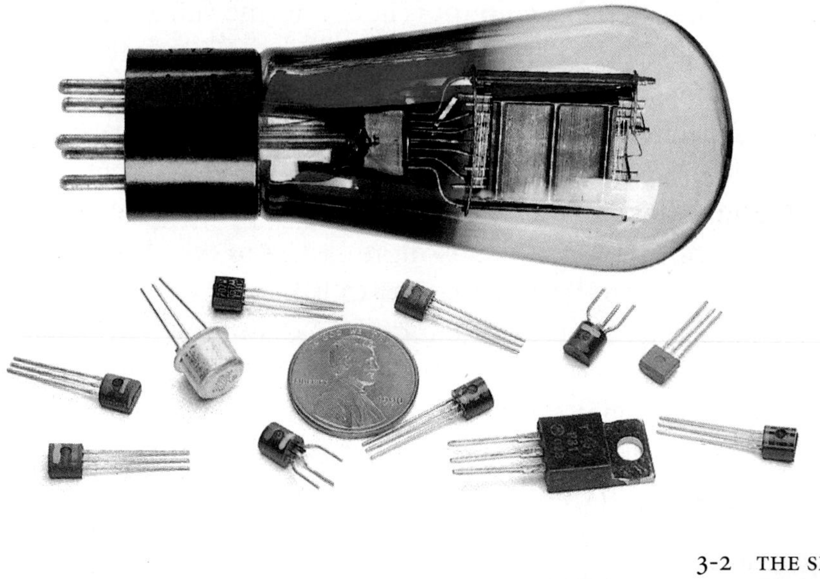

OBJECTIVES

In this section, you will

- describe how a diode allows current to flow in one direction only;
- discuss the uses of transistors and integrated circuits in modern electronics.

KEY SCIENCE TERMS

semiconductor
diode
transistor

FIGURE 3-9. Compare the size of this old radio tube with the tiny semiconductor devices that have replaced it.

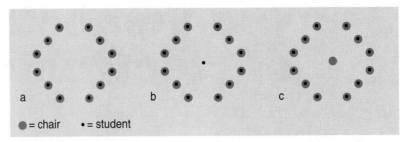

a   b   c

● = chair   • = student

FIGURE 3-10. Adding a chair or a student increases the chance that a student can move to an empty chair.

SKILLBUILDER

COMPARING AND CONTRASTING
Compare and contrast n-type and p-type semiconductors. Discuss how they are made, the elements used in each, and how they are used. If you need help, refer to the **Skill Handbook** on page 685.

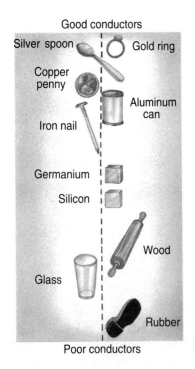

Good conductors

Silver spoon

Gold ring

Copper penny

Aluminum can

Iron nail

Germanium

Silicon

Wood

Glass

Rubber

Poor conductors

FIGURE 3-11. Semiconductors fall between good conductors and poor conductors.

charges must move from one chair to another. The problem is, there are no empty chairs. On a given signal, one student from each set of chairs may choose to leave his or her chair to look for another empty chair. Sometimes there is one and sometimes there isn't. At any rate, the game certainly doesn't proceed like a regular game of musical chairs. How can we increase the chance that a student can move to a different chair?

In Figure 3-10(b) and 3-10(c), you see two possibilities. One possibility is that an additional student is added to the game. The second possibility is that an additional chair is added. This time, when the signal comes, there is an increased chance that one or more of the students will be able to move to a different chair.

A semiconductor, such as silicon, is much like the first model. Although negative charges can move within it, it doesn't happen very easily. When a tiny amount of another element, such as arsenic, is added to the silicon, it's like adding another student, another free negative charge. When the element gallium is added to the silicon, it's like adding another chair. Adding small amounts of other elements, or impurities, to a semiconductor is called doping. Arsenic-doped silicon is called an n-type (negative-type) semiconductor because it has more free negative charges. Gallium-doped silicon is called a p-type (positive-type) semiconductor. It contains more spaces to which negative charges can go. These spaces are called holes. Adding only a few atoms of arsenic or gallium per million atoms of silicon can increase the conductivity by a factor of 1000 or more.

A radio relies on semiconductors to work. Radios and tape players require direct current (DC). Direct current always flows in one direction.

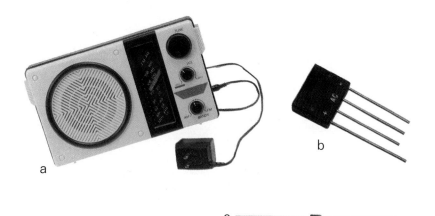

FIGURE 3-12. The tape player (a) requires current that flows in one direction. Diodes (b and c) are rectifiers that change alternating current into direct current.

The current from a wall socket is called alternating current (AC) because the direction of current flow changes back and forth 60 times a second. It would be like having the terminals of a battery switch from positive to negative. Because the radios and tape players require direct current, there must be a way to change AC to DC.

AC TO DC

Imagine that one end of a semiconductor has been doped n-type (free negative charges) and the other has been doped p-type (extra holes). A semiconductor that has been doped in this way is called a pn-diode. If this device is hooked up to a battery as in Figure 3-13(a), you can see that the free negative charges try to move to the positive terminal and the negative charges from the battery move to fill the holes. Once this has happened, the diode has very high resistance, and no current flows through the circuit.

On the other hand, if the diode is hooked up as shown in Figure 3-13(b), the negative charges move from the battery into the diode, across the diode to fill the holes and out of the holes to return to the battery. There is a continuous path for the negative charges to follow and a current continues to flow.

A **diode** permits current flow in only one direction. When an alternating current is put through a diode, the current can pass through the diode only when the current is flowing as it is in Figure 3-13(b). A device such as a diode converts AC to DC and is called a rectifier (REHK tuh fy uhr). In the next Investigate, you'll test how diodes control the direction of current flow.

FIGURE 3-13. Negative charges from the battery fill holes in a pn-diode. No current flows (a). If the diode is connected in the opposite direction, negative charges and holes recombine. Current flows (b).

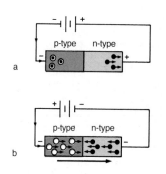

3-2
DIODES AND CIRCUITS

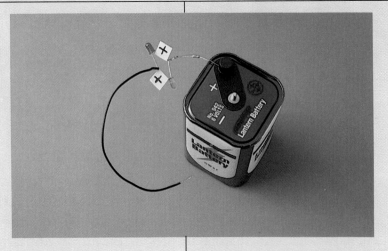

LEDs (light-emitting diodes) are semiconductor devices that light up when a current passes through them. This special property allows you to use them as signal lights to indicate the direction of current flowing in circuits.

PROBLEM
How do diodes control currents?

MATERIALS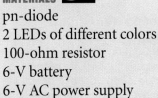
pn-diode
2 LEDs of different colors
100-ohm resistor
6-V battery
6-V AC power supply
wire connectors

PROCEDURE
1. Attach the resistor to one of the LEDs. Connect the free wire of the resistor to one battery terminal and the free wire of the LED to the other terminal. If the LED doesn't light, reverse the connections.
2. Mark the end of the LED closest to the positive terminal with a plus sign.
3. Repeat with the second LED.

4. Place the LEDs so that the positive end of one is opposite the negative end of the other. Twist together the wires of both ends of the LEDs so that the positive wire from one LED is connected to the negative wire of the other. Attach the resistor to one set of the wires.
5. Connect the ends of the wires to the opposite poles of the battery. Notice the color of the LED that lights. Reverse the connections and **observe** the LEDs.
6. Now connect the ends to the terminals of a 6-V AC power supply. Turn it on and **observe** the LEDs. Record the results.
7. Place the pn-diode in the circuit in series. **Observe** the LEDs.

8. Reverse the pn-diode. Notice the response of the LEDs.

ANALYZE
1. How do the LEDs allow you to **infer** that the battery produces direct current?
2. The resistance of a pn-diode is very high in one direction and low in the other. What observation showed that this is true?

CONCLUDE AND APPLY
3. **Draw** circuit **diagrams** of Steps 6 and 7. Use arrows to show how the diode controls the pathway taken by the current.
4. **Going Further**: Design a device using a pn-diode and a light bulb that can be used to determine which pole of a battery is positive.

The investigation showed that the pn-diode allowed an electric current to travel only in one direction, changing AC to DC. How else can this property be used?

TRANSISTORS

You've probably seen advertisements for transistor radios. In fact, you probably own a transistor radio. A **transistor** consists of a region of one type of doped semiconductor sandwiched between layers of the opposite type. For example, an npn-transistor is made with n-type regions on both sides of a very thin p-type region.

Transistors are frequently used to amplify or increase the power of electric signals. The signal coming into a radio or TV is a constantly changing voltage that represents sound, a picture, or other information. The electric signal is often very weak and must be amplified before it can cause a speaker to vibrate or a picture to appear on the television tube. A transistor, teamed up with a power supply such as a battery, is used to amplify the signal. Figure 3-14 shows how a transistor is used to amplify sound entering through a microphone.

Transistors are very efficient—that is, they use little energy. They are inexpensive, and their size makes such things as miniature TVs and tiny hearing aids possible.

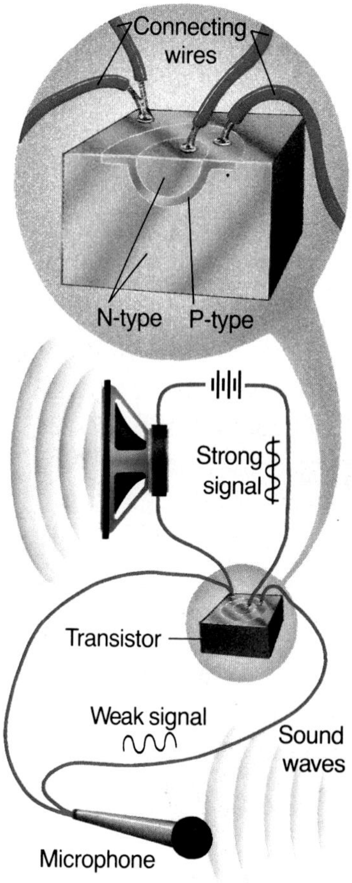

INTEGRATED CIRCUITS

When hand-held calculators first appeared on the market, they only did addition, subtraction, multiplication, and division—and they cost about $100. Each operation was performed by an entire board full of transistors, diodes, resistors, and conductors. In the late 1950s, it became possible to combine or integrate thousands of such circuits onto a single semiconductor chip, less than 5 millimeters across.

Thanks to these integrated circuits, computers that once filled a room now sit on the corner of a desk or on your lap. Even these computers are slow and simple compared with those used to model hurricanes, predict the onset of a heart attack, or describe the properties of a black hole.

FIGURE 3-14. The npn-transistor shown uses a small input current to control the flow of a much larger current.

DID YOU KNOW?

If the progress of automobile technology had been as fast as the rate of the development of semiconductor technology, today's cars would travel at over 1,000,000 miles per hour, get over half-a-million miles per gallon, and cost under $10.00!

FIGURE 3-15. The integrated circuit contains hundreds of semiconductor devices and can still pass through the eye of a needle.

Your world is becoming full of smaller and smaller electronic devices for your use. Because of the development of semiconductors and integrated circuits, you can now take your calculator, radio, or even your television to school or a friend's house . . . in your pocket.

In addition to the calculators and computers you use yourself, their small size allows computers to be part of a variety of products. Your family car may use computers to regulate the flow of gasoline. Computers can be used to regulate temperatures in office buildings and direct railroad cars in a train yard. The nature of the materials used and the design of the circuits has allowed miniature devices to produce and amplify electronic signals to bring you rich sounds, incredibly high-speed calculations, and fabulous video games.

Check Your Understanding

1. Explain how a diode can be used to convert alternating current to direct current.
2. Describe a device that could amplify a TV signal.
3. **APPLY:** Two identical LEDs are connected in series with their positive ends twisted together and their negative ends connected to the leads of an AC power supply. Describe the current flow in the diodes and how the lights would look.

3-3 Electrical Power and Energy

ELECTRICAL POWER

In previous chapters, you've learned that power is the rate at which energy is transferred. Some other common rates are speed (meters per second), and pay (dollars per week). Notice that a rate always has a time denominator. Power is the amount of energy transferred divided by the time it takes for the transfer.

Both static and current electricity can do work. Remember that work involves energy transfer. Static electricity can lift pieces of paper. Current electricity can make motors turn. Chemical energy in a battery produces electrical energy that is then converted into light and thermal energy in a glowing lamp or into the kinetic energy of a turning motor. Electrical power is best thought of as the rate at which electrical energy is converted into some other form of energy. Electrical power is measured in units of joules per second, called watts (W). When you turn on your lamp, your hair dryer, or your electric mixer, electrical energy is converted to light, heat, and kinetic energy, respectively. The rate at which each of these appliances uses energy varies. Appliances are often advertised with their power rating, which tells you the amount of electrical energy each appliance needs to operate. How can you find out how much energy an appliance uses?

OBJECTIVES

In this section, you will
- determine the amount of power used by various electrical appliances;
- calculate electrical energy used and its cost.

KEY SCIENCE TERMS

kilowatt
kilowatt-hour

FIGURE 3-16. In this section, you'll see how power is computed.

EXPLORE!

How many watts do appliances use?

Find the printed or stamped tag on several appliances in your home. Record the electrical rating information on each one. What kinds of information do these tags give you? What do the appliances with the highest power ratings have in common? Would you expect your iron to use as many watts as your hair dryer? Why or why not? Compare the power used by a table lamp,

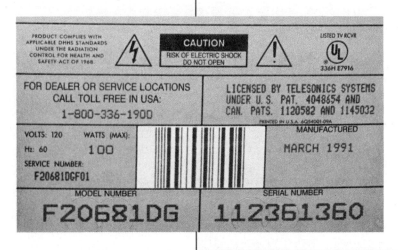

an electric can opener or toothbrush, and a hairdryer. Which appliances require the most and the least electrical power to operate? Suggest several reasons why these appliances might use different amounts of power. Why do you think it's important to be aware of the power ratings of your appliances?

You observed in the Explore that the electrical ratings for the appliances are given in watts. A watt is the electrical power needed to transfer one joule of energy in one second. The power rating for light bulbs you use in your home depends on the amount of light that you need from them: a 25-watt bulb is used in the refrigerator, a 40-watt bulb in the oven, and 100-watt bulbs in table lamps. Have you ever replaced a light bulb and found that the new bulb wasn't as bright as the original bulb? Why is that? You probably used one that had a lower power rating—that is, it was rated at fewer watts of power. Lamps and light fixtures are often labeled for the power rating of the bulb you should use with them. Light bulbs get hot when

FIGURE 3-17. Look for the manufacturers' recommendations when using electrical appliances.

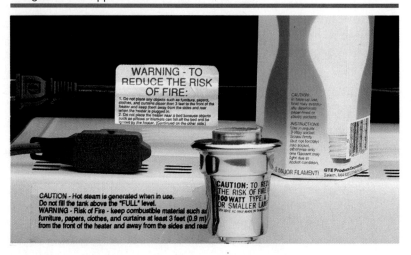

you turn them on, and some light fixtures may get dangerously hot if you use a light bulb with a power rating higher than recommended. Making sure you follow the manufacturer's recommendations for lamps and appliances is an important step in preventing fires.

Some bulbs contain two circuits that allow you to select powers of 50 watts, 100 watts, or 150 watts. The power used by devices such as hair dryers, microwave ovens, and stereo amplifiers is indicated by the number of watts at which they are rated. Since many watts of power are required to run all the appliances in the home, it is more convenient to use kilowatts (kW) rather than watts. The prefix *kilo* means 1000. Therefore, a **kilowatt** is equal to 1000 watts.

If the power rating of a device isn't shown, you can calculate it if you know the voltage, or potential difference across it, and the electrical current that flows through the device. Electrical power is the product of the potential difference and the current. That is,

$$\text{Power} = \text{current} \times \text{potential difference}$$
$$P = I \times V, \text{where}$$

power (P) is measured in watts,
current (I) is measured in amperes, and
potential difference (V) is measured
in volts.

SKILLBUILDER

MAKING AND USING GRAPHS
The power rating of a light bulb is related to the resistance of the bulb. The table gives the resistance of bulbs of various powers. Graph these data with power along the vertical axis and resistance along the horizontal axis. Connect the points with a smooth curve. Use your graph to estimate the resistance of a 30-W bulb. If you need help, refer to the **Skill Handbook** on page 682.

Light bulb size (W)	Resistance (Ω)
100	140
75	190
60	240
40	330
20	740

How do we know?

How much power does an appliance use?

Volts measure the work done when increasing the potential energy of an electrical charge. Just as lifting a book requires work done against gravity, so moving charged particles requires work done against an opposite charge. A volt is defined as the work done in moving a unit of charge. The work is measured in joules and the unit of charge is called a coulomb.

$$\text{Volt} = \frac{\text{joule}}{\text{coulomb}}$$

Current is the flow of electrical charges. One ampere of current represents a rate of flow of one coulomb of charges per second:

$$\text{Ampere} = \frac{\text{couloumb}}{\text{second}}$$

Combining these into the equation for power, we see that

$$\text{power} = \frac{\text{joule}}{\text{coulomb}} \times \frac{\text{coulomb}}{\text{second}}$$

Since the coulomb unit cancels, we are left with the power unit of joules per second—watts.

Let's see if you can use what you just learned about calculating power to find the power requirements of other electrical devices.

FIND OUT!

How much power does a toy car use?

The equation for calculating power can be used to find the power requirement of any electrical device, including a battery-powered toy car. To measure the power rating of the car, you will need an ammeter with two leads, wires, and insulating tape.

First, turn on the car and let it move across the floor or table. Is one form of energy being converted into another form? Describe these forms of energy.

Now remove the battery from the car. Use insulating tape where necessary to attach wires to the battery and the battery contacts in the car. Connect a piece of wire between one pole of the battery and the appropriate

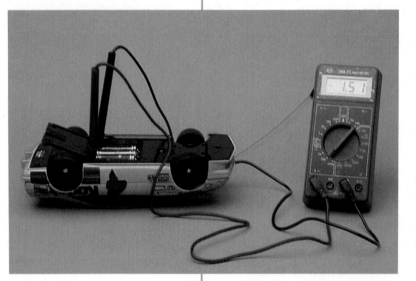

contact on the battery holder. Then, attach one wire from the ammeter to the free pole of the battery and the other wire to the appropriate contact in the battery holder. In this arrangement, the ammeter is in series with the electric motor of the car. Turn on the car and read the current on the ammeter. The voltage is shown on the battery.

Conclude and Apply

1. Use the voltage and current to calculate the power of the car in watts. If the car has more than one speed, calculate the power for different speeds.
2. Does the power usage change with the different speeds?
3. Also calculate the power when you slow the wheels gently with your finger.
4. When does the car use the most power?

USING POWER

If you operated the toy car in the Find Out for two minutes, it would change twice as much electrical energy into kinetic energy as it would in one minute. If you know the power needs of a device and the time it is used, you can find the energy used as follows:

Energy used = power × time ($E = Pt$)

Just as in the toy car, all electrical devices and appliances change electrical energy to other forms of energy. However, most household appliances use much more energy than the toy car. To measure these larger amounts, you will measure power in kilowatts instead of watts, and time in hours instead of seconds. Electrical energy, E, is measured in kilowatt-hours, kWh. A **kilowatt-hour** is the unit of electrical energy:

Energy (kWh) = power (kW) × time (h).

The energy used by any appliance may be calculated as shown in the example below.

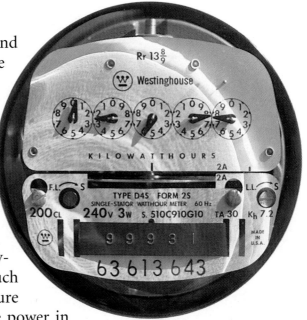

FIGURE 3-18. Meters that measure energy in your home register kilowatt-hours.

EXAMPLE PROBLEM: Calculating Energy

Problem Statement:	If a refrigerator uses 700 W and runs 24 hours a day, how much energy, in kWh, is used in one day?
Known:	$P = 700$ W $t = 24$ h
Unknown:	E
Equation to Use:	$E = Pt$
Solution:	$\dfrac{700 \text{ W}}{1000 \text{ w/kw}} = 0.700$ kW
	$E = Pt = (0.700 \text{ kW})(24 \text{ h}) = 16.8$ kWh

Electrical energy used in your home is measured by a meter, as shown in Figure 3-18. Your electric meter contains a wheel that turns when any electrical device is being used. The more power used, the faster the wheel turns.

How much electrical energy does your home use?

How much electrical energy does your home use? Make a list of appliances in your home, similar to the list in the table. List the actual power rating if you can find the tag. Otherwise, estimate from the table. Record the number of hours/day you or your family uses each device each day. Calculate the energy used (in kWh) each day and the total for one month. Then determine the cost per month of the energy used in your home. Assume electricity costs ten cents per kilowatt-hour.

Cost of Home Appliances (Assuming Electricity Costs $0.10/kWh)					
APPLIANCE	POWER (WATTS)	TIME USED (HOURS/DAY)	ENERGY (KWH/DAY)	ENERGY (KWH/MONTH)	MONTHLY COST
Hair dryer					
Microwave oven					
Radio/phonograph					
Range (oven)					
Refrigerator/freezer (15 cu ft, frostfree)					
Television					
Toothbrush, electric					
100-W light bulb					
40-W fluorescent lamp					

Conclude and Apply

1. Compare the total for one month with the energy use shown on your last electric bill. Were you close?
2. How much does your electric company charge per kWh? Make two new lists. The first should have your appliances in order of their power use, largest on top. The second should be in order of energy use, largest on top.
3. Are they the same?
4. Does this help you understand the difference?

a b

HOW DOES ENERGY REACH YOUR HOME?

Have you seen the tall steel towers like those shown in Figure 3-19 that carry electrical energy over great distances? In your home, the potential difference or voltage across an outlet is 120 V. The potential difference of the electricity delivered from the electrical generating plant to your neighborhood may range from 12,000 V to as high as 765,000 V.

Because it is dangerous to have voltages higher than 120 V or 240 V in your home, the electricity to your home passes through a transformer. You may recall from your earlier studies that a transformer is a device to increase or decrease AC voltages. The transformers near your home, such as the ones in Figure 3-20, convert the voltage of the power line to a lower voltage safe for home use.

Why are such high voltages used for transmitting electrical power? As you have learned, electrical power is the product of current and potential difference, or $P = IV$. The electric power company transmits high voltage (V) so that current (I) will be low when providing the power (P) required by all the homes in your area. Why is it preferable to transmit low current rather than high current to satisfy your home or business power requirements? You have already learned that current in a wire causes heating. Lowering the current in the transmission lines results in less heating of the wires and less loss of thermal energy to the air. Using high voltage for transmitting electrical power

FIGURE 3-20. Transformers are used to reduce voltages to consumer levels at the points of use.

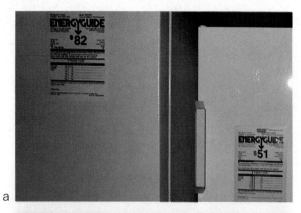

a

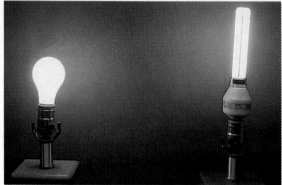

b

FIGURE 3-21. Improved manufacturing techniques and insulating materials have made some appliances (a) much more energy efficient. New designs and applications (b) also improve the energy efficiency of electrical appliances.

over long distances results in lower currents and less loss of energy as heat in the wires.

Many of you may take all the conveniences brought about by electrical energy for granted. You have now taken a close look at where this energy comes from, you've calculated how much power and energy many of your appliances require, and you have calculated some of the costs. All of these electrical devices on which you depend require power. The longer you use these devices, the more natural resources must be used up and the higher the costs. Just as automobile manufacturers are working to make cars more fuel-efficient, efforts are being made to make appliances more energy-efficient. Some changes will mean newer appliances will lose less energy to heat. Appliance motors may be more efficient. Newer refrigerators operate at a fraction of the energy used by older models. Even light bulbs have been redesigned to be more energy-efficient. There are now fluorescent bulbs that give light similar to ordinary bulbs, fit in ordinary sockets, last longer and yet, use 30 percent less electrical energy. Can you think of places in your home where these bulbs might be useful? How will you know if these products are energy-efficient? How else can you cut down on unnecessary use of energy?

Check Your Understanding

1. A lamp operates on 120 V with a current of 0.75 A. How much power does it require?
2. A 100-W light bulb is left on for 6.5 hours. How many kilowatt-hours of energy are used?
3. Assuming that the cost of a kilowatt-hour of electricity is $0.10, how much would it cost to operate a 100-W light bulb for 24 hours?
4. **APPLY:** A hair dryer has two temperature settings. It takes 12 minutes to dry your hair at the lower temperature setting of 1000 W. It takes 10 minutes to dry your hair at the higher temperature of 1500 W. Which setting would you use to save energy?

EXPANDING YOUR VIEW

CONTENTS

A CLOSER LOOK

ENERGY AND PEOPLE

In this chapter, you estimated your energy usage during a month's time and saw the differences in power requirements for different appliances. Let's look at the issue of electrical energy usage from a broader view.

A number of years ago, the futurist Buckminster Fuller estimated that an average working person, besides carrying his or her own weight, does approximately 0.0566 kilowatt hours of work each day. That's how much energy an average person *produces* in one day. How much electrical energy does the average person *use*? Do the *You Try It!* to find out.

YOU TRY IT!

Use the following information from 1975 to calculate how much electrical energy the average person used in a single day. During 1975, 589 billion kilowatt hours of electricity were sold to residences in the United States. In that same year, there were 213 million people in the United States.

1. Divide the kilowatt hours used during the year by 365 days to determine the kilowatt hours used each day.
2. Divide the answer from question 1 by the number of people in the United States to determine the number of kilowatt hours used by each person per day.
3. Use the kilowatt hours produced by an average working person to calculate how many people it would take to produce the energy used by one person in a day. Divide your answer by 0.0566 kilowatt hours/person. How many people would it take to produce the energy that one person uses?

The number of kilowatt hours used in this problem was the number sold to residences. This is only about 25 percent of the electricity used in this country, with the other 75 percent used by industry to provide us with goods and services. In other words, multiply your answer by 4 to find the number of people it would take to produce the electrical energy used by one person.

EARTH SCIENCE CONNECTION

CONDUCTORS, SEMICONDUCTORS, AND SUPERCONDUCTORS

You've learned that minerals are an important resource for gems and other materials used in industry. How are minerals and other materials found in Earth used in electrical applications?

Have you ever visited the part of California that is called Silicon Valley? If so, you know that it is not made up of sandy beaches. It is called Silicon Valley because it is a major center of electronics industries that make extensive use of semiconductors that are made of silicon chips.

Silicon is an element that is a component of ordinary sand. It is in plentiful supply throughout much of the world in deserts, on beaches, and in sand pits like the one pictured. The manufacture of semiconductors requires extremely pure silicon that contains much less than one part impurity per million parts of silicon. Refining processes must be used to extract silicon with this degree of purity from ordinary sand.

Conductors generally are made of copper or aluminum. Copper is refined from the ore found in copper mines, and aluminum is refined from an ore called bauxite. Thus, the manufacturers of electrical equipment that use conductors extensively are dependent upon countries that have large deposits of bauxite and copper ore. The United States and Canada have more than one-third of the world's copper ore deposits, but must rely upon other nations for aluminum.

A new device called a superconductor offers no resistance to the flow of electrical current. Superconductors contain exotic elements such as niobium and vanadium. They are used in exploration of atomic particles and in medical diagnosis. Superconductors are used to make the strong electromagnets used in the MRI machines discussed in Chapter 2.

Without the great variety of minerals found in Earth's crust, many of these new advances in electrical applications would not be possible. There is hope that, one day, superconductors will open a whole new field of electronic applications.

WHAT DO YOU THINK?

Can you think why countries that have large supplies of these minerals might prefer *not* to mine them all to sell to countries that manufacture conductors?

SCIENCE AND SOCIETY

ARE ELF FIELDS A HEALTH HAZARD?

Are power lines and electric blankets hazardous to your health? There are scientists on both sides of a growing debate over the biological effects of electricity and magnetism.

Alternating currents, such as those found in house wiring, produce electric and magnetic fields—electromagnetic fields. There are many sources of these fields, which are called ELF fields. ELF stands for Extremely Low Frequency. These ELF fields are found around power lines, in home wiring, electric clocks, electric blankets, televisions, and computer terminals. Twenty years ago, scientists would have said that these very weak fields could not affect biological systems. In fact, the strength of many of these fields is only about one percent of Earth's magnetic field. Fields found in cells themselves are much stronger than these ELF fields, so what harm could they possibly do?

Recently, experiments have suggested that cells may be sensitive even to the weakest ELF fields. The fields might affect the passage of materials in and out of the cells, the synthesis of certain essential compounds, and the response of cells to certain hormones. Abnormal development in chicken embryos has been observed when the eggs were incubated in the presence of ELF fields.

But the results of experiments are very complicated. There is no clear-cut conclusion that can be reached. The effect doesn't seem to be true for all fields, just for certain specific ones. Sometimes there is an effect only when the fields are turned on or off rapidly. For most health hazards, there is a certain amount of exposure or dose that causes problems. But with ELF fields, there doesn't seem to be any way to measure the amount or dose that produces an effect.

Using an electric blanket seems to have little observable effect on humans, but some studies have shown that there is an increase in brain tumors and cancers in children whose mothers slept under electric blankets while they were pregnant.

Some steps have already been taken to reduce ELF fields. Electric blankets producing smaller fields are being sold. Some computer manufacturers are making terminals that produce smaller fields. But when the dose or amount that might be hazardous is not known, how can we know that this is enough?

Part of the problem comes from the fact that electric fields can easily be blocked. Many of them cannot get through the walls of a house or even through skin. However, magnetic fields travel right through many kinds of matter without losing strength. Again, there seems to be no present way to measure which part of the ELF waves might be doing the damage.

Just because scientists do an experiment, the results are not immediately accepted by other scientists. The first experiments that seemed to show that living near power transmission lines led to higher rates of cancer and leukemia were severely criticized. The scientists who reported these findings had failed to do many of the things that are expected in solid scientific research. First, they didn't actually measure

ELF fields—they only estimated them. Secondly, the researchers did not have a control group in their experiment. That is, they already knew which homes contained people who had cancer and merely compared the location of those homes with the location of power lines.

Later studies confirmed some of these early findings. But there are still many questions to be answered. Why are certain people affected while others aren't? Is there some connection between the effect of ELF fields and other factors such as smoking or occupation? Why do children seem to be affected more than adults? Everyone agrees that more research is

WHAT DO YOU THINK?

1. Should no action be taken until results on the effect of ELF fields is clear? Or should steps be taken now to limit people's exposure to these fields?
2. Suppose a study shows that people who live near power lines have an increased rate of cancer. Does this mean that the ELF fields from the power lines cause cancer?
3. What steps could you take to reduce exposure to ELF fields?

needed before these and other questions can be answered.

TECHNOLOGY CONNECTION

SOLAR CELLS

Do you have a calculator or a watch that operates on solar energy? Have you heard about research to develop a car that operates on solar energy? Can you imagine the possibility of lighting and heating your home with solar energy?

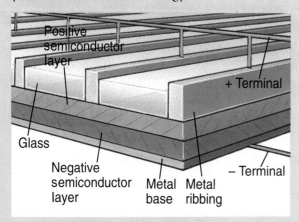

Positive semiconductor layer

Glass

Negative semiconductor layer

Metal base

Metal ribbing

+ Terminal

– Terminal

A solar cell converts solar energy into electrical energy. It can often replace a battery that converts chemical energy to electrical energy. The technical name for a solar cell like the one pictured above is a photovoltaic cell. The cell contains a silicon diode. The positive and negative layers of the diode convert solar energy and electricity.

Unfortunately, only a small amount of the solar energy is converted into electrical energy. The efficiency of a cell is the ratio of the electrical energy to the solar energy. Presently, solar cells have a less than 30 percent efficiency. Advances in the state of the art are expected to improve this efficiency in the future.

Because the sun does not always shine, solar cells are often connected to storage batteries. While the sun shines, the cells charge the batteries. The solar energy is stored as chemical energy. Thus, solar cells can, in conjunction with storage batteries, provide continuous electric energy from sunlight. This is especially true where sunshine is more abundant—in the lower latitudes and the higher elevations of Earth.

Because solar cells are expensive to manufacture and are inefficient, they are not yet looked upon as providing a significant alternative source of electrical energy. But there is every reason to believe that they may become more efficient and economical in the future.

Conventional fuels, such as coal and oil, have harmful effects on the environment and are becoming scarcer as each decade passes. Solar energy, when properly harnessed, will provide a cheap and clean supply of electrical energy in place of conventional fuels.

YOU TRY IT!

1. Do some research to find out what applications solar cells now have.
2. Describe some of the advantages of using solar cells for lighting and heating.
3. What might be some disadvantages of using solar energy rather than coal or oil?

TEENS *in* SCIENCE

COMPUTERIST ON THE MOVE

Even before he was 18 years old, Jeffery Parker was an expert on computer connections at NASA's Dryden Research Facility at Edwards Air Force Base, California. That's because he spent a summer tracing and labeling cables that run between computers at the facility.

By the time the summer was over, Jeffery had helped prepare a 50-page manual and a database, both of which explained where computer cables were placed in various buildings. The purpose of the project was to

help other NASA employees quickly find malfunctioning electrical connections. For example, if a computer quit working properly, repair persons could use the manual or database to locate important connections on the circuit.

Since the information had not been written down before, Jeffery's job was much like untangling a knot or traveling across a state without a map. First he'd start at a concentrator, another name for a multiport repeater, a device that boosts electrical signals and allows them to travel over greater distances of cable. Each concentrator could lead to as many as 48 cables and computers. So Jeffery followed and labeled each of the lines, one at a time, from the connector to its end. He traced each one over walls and through walls—anywhere the cable took him.

Next he made notes about each cable's route. With the notes he had made, he helped write the manual of connections and create the database on a Macintosh computer.

Jeffery says the database shows floor plans of various NASA buildings and displays the cable routes in color. If a NASA employee wants to know more about the electri-

cal connectors along a cable route, he or she only has to "zoom in" for more detail on the Macintosh screen.

The summer job at NASA is one of the main reasons Jeffery wants to study computers in college.

If you were to ask him how to succeed in the sciences, he'd probably tell you to develop self-discipline, work hard, and ask for lots of advice. He'd also tell you to learn from the mistakes of others and when you see an opportunity—"go for it!"

"Decide early what you're going to do," Jeffery says. "That gives you more time to get on track. It's hard sometimes to think about what you want to do, but the harder you try, the less time it takes. If you do get an opportunity for hands-on experience, then try it so you won't waste years of study to do something you don't want to do."

WHAT DO YOU THINK?

Take Jeffery's advice. Think about the kind of work you might like to do someday. What kind of hands-on experience might you be able to get now?

Reviewing Main Ideas

1. Thank goodness for parallel circuits. When one bulb burns out it's easy to find.

2. You can take your calculator to school with you in your pocket because of the development of integrated circuits and the tremendous advances in semiconductor technology.

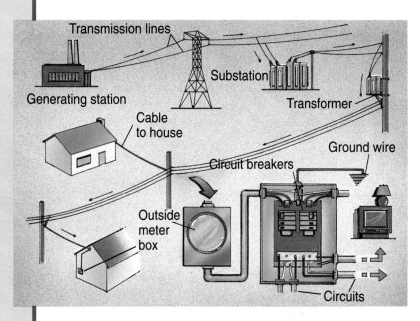

Transmission lines

Substation

Generating station

Transformer

Cable to house

Ground wire

Circuit breakers

Outside meter box

Circuits

3. Electrical energy is converted to light, heat, and kinetic energy for your use every day. Don't waste your most convenient energy resource.

Chapter Review

USING KEY SCIENCE TERMS

circuit breaker	parallel circuit
diode	semiconductor
kilowatt	series circuit
kilowatt-hour	transistor

Change the underlined words, if necessary, to make each of the following sentences correct.

1. Two lamps in a <u>parallel circuit</u> are dimmer than if there were only one lamp in the circuit.

2. Doping <u>diode</u> crystals with impurities can change their resistance and conductivity.

3. A <u>semiconductor-based device</u> in your radio amplifies an electric signal. *transistor*

4. A <u>kilowatt</u> is the unit of measure when the rate at which electrical energy is converted to a different form of energy. *kWh*

5. A <u>series circuit</u> is always used to wire the switch inside your appliances. *Parallel circuit*

6. A <u>circuit breaker</u> allows current to flow in only one direction. *series circuit*

7. A <u>kilowatt</u> is another guard against overheating a wire. *Circuit Breaker*

UNDERSTANDING IDEAS

Choose the best answer to complete each sentence.

1. Power is measured in ____.
   a. amps   c. volts
   b. watts   d. ohms

2. To find the electric power, use the equation ____.
   a. I =V/R   c. P = IV
   b. P = Et   d. E = P/t

3. For a switch to turn on a device, it must be wired ____.
   a. in series
   b. next to the power supply
   c. in parallel
   d. in two circuits

4. Electrical energy can be measured in ____.
   a. kilowatts   c. amps
   b. kilowatt-hours   d. volts

5. A diode is used to ____.
   a. change series to parallel
   b. change work to energy
   c. change power to volts
   d. change AC to DC

6. A transistor is used to ____.
   a. control current flow
   b. amplify current flow
   c. make electronic devices smaller
   d. all of the above

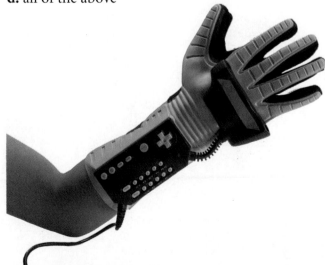

7. For a fuse to work, it must be wired ____.
   a. in series   **c.** in the wall
   b. in parallel   **d.** in a box

8. Amperes are units of ____.
   a. current   **c.** power
   b. voltage   **d.** resistance

CRITICAL THINKING

Use your understanding of the concepts developed in the chapter to answer each of the following questions.

1. Would a diode work properly if both ends were either p-type or n-type semiconductors? Explain.

2. In the figure below, if R_1, R_2, and R_3 are all lamps and R_1 burns out, what will happen to the other lamps?

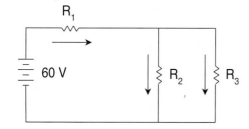

3. If a circuit breaker must constantly be reset, is it a good idea to replace it with a higher rated one? Explain.

4. Why is it important to use high voltages for power transmission?

PROBLEM SOLVING

Read the following problem and discuss your answers in a brief paragraph.

Your hair dryer is plugged into a wall outlet with a potential difference of 120 V. It draws 6 amps of current.

1. What is the power requirement of the hair dryer?

2. If you use it for 10 minutes a day, how much energy will you use in 30 days?

3. If the power company charges $.09/kWh, what will that cost?

4. How long would you have to keep a 100-W light bulb lit to use the same amount of energy?

CONNECTING IDEAS

Discuss each of the following in a brief paragraph.

1. Compare and contrast elastic, gravitational, and electrical potential energy.
2. How did the replacement of the glass tube by the diode contribute to the level of noise pollution?

3. EARTH SCIENCE CONNECTION Name three elements or minerals found in Earth and used for electrical applications. Identify the electrical application in which they're most frequently used.
4. SCIENCE AND SOCIETY What is an ELF? Explain why expo-

sure to an ELF may be unhealthful.
5. TECHNOLOGY CONNECTION Give two advantages and two disadvantages of solar energy. Is there any way to avoid the disadvantages?

DID YOU EVER WONDER . . .

How radio stations send signals through space?

Why people in warm climates wear white clothing?

Why you can see colors when you see an oil slick in the street?

You'll find the answers to these questions as you read this chapter.

Electromagnetic Waves

Waves carrying energy surround you every day, from the rainbow of colors that appears in a street puddle or a butterfly's wing, to the rays of sunshine that warm you on a summer afternoon. Some waves can be seen, the presence of others felt, but most cannot be observed directly with our senses.

Have you ever listened to music on a portable radio, cooked popcorn in a microwave oven, or had your teeth checked for cavities at a dentist's office? You've heard about radio waves, microwaves, and X rays. But what are they? These waves seem very different. Are they related to one another in some way? Are they similar to light or sound?

This chapter will help you find answers to these questions.

EXPLORE!

Do electrical appliances create disturbances?

Tune a small, battery-powered AM radio between two stations so that you hear only noise. Carry the radio around your house as you turn on and off a lamp, the television or vacuum cleaner, or a fluorescent light. Use any electrical appliances that are handy. You will probably hear clicks or pops on the radio when you turn some appliances on or off. You have learned that these appliances depend on moving electrical charges or the effects of magnetic fields. How do you think electricity or magnetism related to what you heard on the radio?

4-1 The Electro-magnetic Spectrum

WHAT'S AN ELECTROMAGNETIC WAVE?

You have learned that an electric charge exerts a force on other electric charges around it. The charge produces an electric field, a region around the charge in which the electric force acts. When you made an electromagnet, you used an electric current to produce a magnetic field. You also learned that magnetic forces can exert a force on moving electric charges. From your observations and what you learned in the previous chapters, you can see that there may be a connection between electric and magnetic fields.

You have found that any action that causes the electric field around a charge to change will also change the magnetic field. The opposite is also true. When the electric field changes the magnetic field, that magnetic field, in turn, produces another electrical field. These alternating electric and magnetic fields as shown in Figure 4-2(a) move away from the original charge in a wave-like pattern. This pattern is shown in Figure 4-2(b). Like water waves, they have crests and troughs, a wavelength, and a frequency. Unlike water waves, the waves formed by electric and magnetic fields move through space—not a medium.

The oscillating electric and magnetic wave that is produced by the charges is an **electromagnetic wave**. The opening Explore, with the portable radio, allowed you to detect electromagnetic waves coming from a variety of appliances as you changed the electrical and magnetic fields in the appliances.

FIGURE 4-1. A vibrating charge creates oscillating electric and magnetic fields.

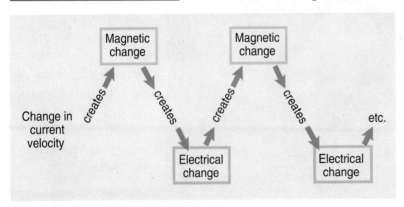

Change in current velocity → creates → Magnetic change → creates → Electrical change → creates → Magnetic change → creates → Electrical change → etc.

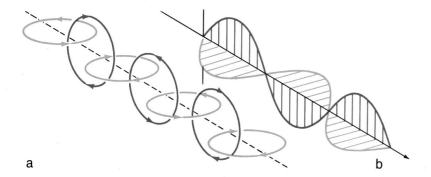

a   b

CHARACTERISTICS OF ELECTROMAGNETIC WAVES

As you recall, there are two basic kinds of waves—longitudinal and transverse. In Figure 4-3, you can see that the medium—the spring coil—carrying longitudinal waves vibrates in the same direction as the direction in which the wave is traveling. The medium—the rope in Figure 4-3(b)—carrying a transverse wave vibrates at right angles to the direction in which the wave is traveling, like shaking a rope up and down. Experiments show that electromagnetic waves have properties of transverse waves even though they do not need a medium through which to travel.

Like all waves, electromagnetic waves can be described by their frequency, their wavelength, or both. As you recall, wavelength is the measured distance from a point on one wave to the same point on the next wave. The frequency of an electromagnetic wave depends on the

FIGURE 4-3. There are two kinds of waves—longitudinal and transverse waves.

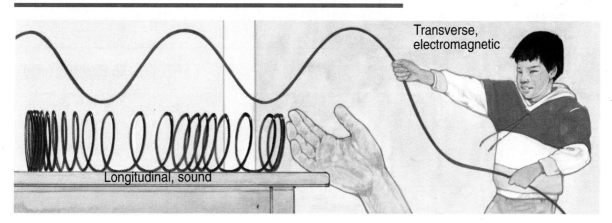

Transverse, electromagnetic

Longitudinal, sound

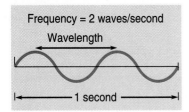

Frequency = 2 waves/second
Wavelength

1 second

FIGURE 4-4. Wavelength, frequency, and speed are three characteristics of all waves. The frequency of this wave is 2 waves per second (2 Hz).

rate of vibration of the electric charge that created it. Every time the charge goes through one vibration, or cycle, it creates one wave. As the wave is created, it moves away from the charge at the speed of light, 300,000,000 m/s.

What is the relationship among the speed, wavelength, and frequency of a wave? We can figure it out using the units in which each is measured. Speed is distance divided by time—meters/second. Wavelength is the length, in meters, of one wave. We could express this as meters/wave. Finally, frequency is in hertz, or the number of waves per second. What mathematical equation exists among these units?

$$\frac{\text{meters}}{\text{second}} = \frac{\text{meters}}{\text{wave}} \times \frac{\text{waves}}{\text{second}}$$

$$\text{speed} = \text{wavelength} \times \text{frequency}$$

You can then solve this equation for any of the terms you wish to find. What is the frequency of an electromagnetic wave which has a wavelength of 100 m?

$$\text{speed} = \text{wavelength} \times \text{frequency}$$

Dividing both sides by wavelength, we get

$$\text{frequency} = \text{speed/wavelength}$$

$$= \frac{300,000,000 \text{ m/s}}{100 \text{ m/wave}}$$

$$= 3,000,000 \frac{\text{waves}}{\text{second}} = 3,000,000 \text{ Hz}$$

Electromagnetic waves come in a wide range of wavelengths and frequencies. Each is useful in a different way. We've mentioned electricity, light, and radio. At the beginning of the chapter, we also talked about X rays and microwaves. How do the frequencies and wavelengths of these waves compare?

DID YOU KNOW?

The frequency of stations on your radio dial are marked in kilohertz (kHz) and megahertz (MHz). A station at 800 on the AM radio dial has a frequency of 800 kHz, or 800,000 Hz. On the FM dial, a station at 103 MHz has a frequency of 103 million hertz, 103,000,000 Hz.

FIND OUT!

How do frequencies of electromagnetic waves compare?

The wavelengths of various electromagnetic waves are given in the table. Use the speed of electromagnetic waves—300,000,000 m/s—and the equation above to find the frequency of each type of wave.

Wave source	Wavelength	Frequency
AM radio	500 m	
VHF TV	5.0 m	
FM radio	3.33 m	
UHF TV	1.0 m	
Radar	0.03 m	
X-rays	0.000000009 m	

300

Conclude and Apply

1. Which wave has the lowest frequency?
2. Which wave has the highest frequency?
3. What is the relationship between wavelength and frequency?

$S = \dfrac{D}{T}$ m/s

wavelength
in m/wv

Frequency hertz

wave per sec

In the Find Out, you discovered that there is an inverse relationship between the frequency and wavelength of electromagnetic waves. In other words, as long as the speed remains the same, the longer the wavelength, the lower the frequency and the shorter the wavelength of a wave, the higher its frequency as shown in Figure 4-5.

USES OF ELECTROMAGNETIC WAVES?

As we've said, the frequency of electromagnetic waves depends on the frequency of the vibrating electric charges that cause them. In the Find Out you calculated some frequencies for different types of radio waves. The entire range of electromagnetic waves, from extremely low to

FIGURE 4-5. Wave **a** has a longer wavelength and a lower frequency than wave **b**. Both waves are traveling at the same speed.

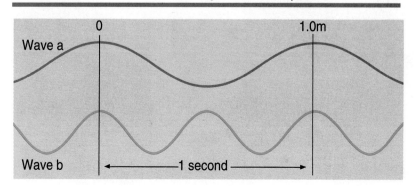

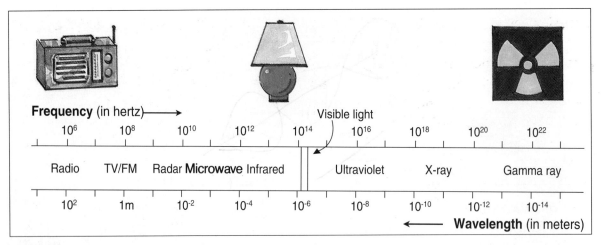

Frequency (in hertz)——→

| 10^6 | 10^8 | 10^{10} | 10^{12} | 10^{14} | 10^{16} | 10^{18} | 10^{20} | 10^{22} |

Visible light

Radio   TV/FM   Radar **Microwave** Infrared   Ultraviolet   X-ray   Gamma ray

| 10^2 | 1m | 10^{-2} | 10^{-4} | 10^{-6} | 10^{-8} | 10^{-10} | 10^{-12} | 10^{-14} |

←—— **Wavelength** (in meters)

FIGURE 4-6. All common transverse waves except mechanical waves are part of the electromagnetic spectrum.

extremely high frequencies is called the **electromagnetic spectrum**. Parts of the spectrum have been given names. The electromagnetic spectrum is shown in Figure 4-6.

How are electromagnetic waves in various parts of the spectrum used? The lowest frequency waves are called radio waves. These waves are primarily used for communications. Radio stations and TV stations use waves with these frequencies to broadcast information and entertainment to millions of people. Cordless and car telephones use radio waves to let people talk to each other.

The name microwave was given to electromagnetic waves with shorter—micro—wavelengths. Long-distance telephone calls are sent over microwaves. Television signals are sent to and from satellites using microwaves. Like radio waves, microwaves can be used for communications.

Many electromagnetic waves are used primarily to

FIGURE 4-7. Microwaves are used in communication and for cooking.

transfer) energy. Unlike the mechanical waves that you learned about previously, electromagnetic waves need no medium through which to travel. The energy is transferred from one point to another without matter carrying it. The transfer of energy by electromagnetic waves is called **radiation**.

Because the word *radiation* is often used in connection with nuclear energy, some people think all radiation is dangerous. But there are many different types of radiation, some of which are necessary for our survival. Light is certainly a familiar source of radiation, and light is an electromagnetic wave. Light has many sources including the sun, fire, and light bulbs. In all of these cases, energy is transferred to our eye by electromagnetic waves. The light from these sources reaches us through radiation.

Have you ever stood near a hot oven or under a heat lamp? Your skin gets warm even though you aren't touching anything. Infrared waves carry energy from the lamp to your body. Heat lamps, ordinary light bulbs, and hot ovens all produce infrared radiation. In fact, all objects at all temperatures above absolute zero give off some infrared radiation. The hotter the object is, the more it radiates.

What affects the amount of energy transferred by radiation? When you are warmed by a heat lamp, your skin has absorbed some or all of the energy in the infrared radiation. Does everything absorb the same amount of energy? Here's a hint. Have you noticed that people who live in hot, sunny climates often have white cars? In the next exercise you'll find out how color affects the absorption of electromagnetic radiation.

FIGURE 4-8. Infrared photography provides information, such as temperature variations, not possible with regular photography.

DID YOU KNOW?

People are warm, so they give off infrared radiation. Each person radiates about 100 joules of infrared energy each second. Recall that one joule per second is one watt. That is, a person radiates energy at the same rate as a 100 watt light bulb, 100 joules per second. Now do you understand why a room full of people warms up so quickly?

4-1 INFRARED RADIATION

In this activity, you'll measure the rate at which water in different-colored containers absorbs infrared radiation.

PROBLEM
What color absorbs infrared radiation best?

MATERIALS
3 aluminum cans of equal size: one black, one white, one shiny or wrapped in aluminum foil
water
3 thermometers
clock
heat lamp
graph paper

PROCEDURE
1. Copy the data table.
2. Fill each can halfway with water.
3. **Measure** the temperature of the water in each can.
4. Place the three cans at the same distance from the lamp and turn on the lamp.
5. **Observe** and record the temperature of the water in each can every five minutes for twenty minutes.
6. Turn off the lamp and let the cans cool. Record the temperatures every 5 minutes until the temperature stops changing.

ANALYZE
1. **Plot a graph** of temperature (vertical axis) versus time (horizontal axis).
2. In which can did the water temperature rise fastest?
3. In which can was the water temperature the highest?
4. In which did the water temperature fall fastest?
5. Did the temperature of the water in any can increase the same amount during each five-minute interval?

CONCLUDE AND APPLY
6. If you wanted the roof of your house to absorb the sun's radiation to help heat your house, would you buy black or white shingles?
7. What color shingles would you buy if you lived in a climate that was always sunny and warm?
8. **Going Further:** Builders often use insulation covered with shiny aluminum foil. How would this help to keep a house warm or cool?

DATA AND OBSERVATIONS

TIME (MINUTES)	BLACK CAN TEMP.	WHITE CAN TEMP.	SHINY CAN TEMP.
0			
5			
10			
15			
20			

You may have noticed in the Investigate activity that as the cans warmed up, their rate of warming slowed. That is, when they were cool their temperature increased rapidly. But, after they were warm, it took much longer for their temperature to increase the same amount. You can use what you know about radiation to explain this observation.

Infrared radiation is one of the common and useful parts of the electromagnetic spectrum. For instance, researchers use infrared sensitive film to determine pollution and water flow from rivers into oceans. Close to home, you've probably seen infrared lamps used at restaurants to keep food warm. There are several other forms of electromagnetic waves that are less common, but all are transverse waves that travel at the speed of light. These waves have a wide range of frequencies and wavelengths, and they transfer energy from one place to another by radiation.

Without light, you wouldn't be reading this page right now. In the next section, you'll find out why we believe that light is a form of electromagnetic energy.

SKILLBUILDER

HYPOTHESIZING
Formulate a hypothesis to explain the observations you made in the Investigate. Use your hypothesis to predict at what point the temperature of an object would become constant. It may help you to remember that all objects radiate energy. The hotter they are, the faster they radiate. If you need help refer to the **Skill Handbook** on page 689.

FIGURE 4-9. Infrared radiation shows details we ordinarily cannot see.

Check Your Understanding

1. How is an electromagnetic wave created by a vibrating electrical charge?
2. Arrange the following electromagnetic waves in order of frequency, from lowest to highest: X rays, radio waves, ultraviolet waves, infrared radiation, microwaves. Will these waves then be in the order of wavelength? Explain.
3. Keep a record of the different kinds of electromagnetic energy you use in one day. You may need to refer to Figure 4-6. Which form(s) did you use most often?
4. **APPLY:** People with swimming pools often cover them to use the sun to help heat the water. What color cover would you think would work best? White, shiny aluminum, or black?

4-2 The Wave Model of Light

OBJECTIVES

In this section, you will

- explain how diffraction through thin slits supports a wave model of light;
- describe how various observations on color and light can be explained by the wave model.

KEY SCIENCE TERMS

diffraction
diffraction grating
thin films

THE PROPERTIES OF LIGHT

You have made many observations about light during your science studies. You know that light travels in straight lines and that it can be reflected off surfaces. Light's straight-line path can be bent when light passes from air into substances like water or glass. If you try to squeeze light through a tiny slit or hole, it spreads out slightly. White light can be separated into a rainbow of colors when it goes through triangularly-shaped pieces of glass or droplets of water. How can we build a model of light that explains all these phenomena?

FIND OUT!

How does light act when it passes through a thin slit?

Use a razor blade or craft knife to cut a 5-cm long slit in the middle of an index card. With all other lights off, close one eye and hold the card in front of the other eye with one hand on each side of the card. Line the slit up with the straight filament in the lamp the teacher has turned on, as shown in the picture.

Sight the lamp through the slit in your card. Gently pull the sides of the card apart so that the slit opens slightly. What do you see?

Conclude and Apply

1. As you make the slit wider, do the bands spread out or get narrower?
2. The teacher will cover the bottom of the bulb with a red filter and the top with a blue filter. Compare the red and blue bands. Which is wider?

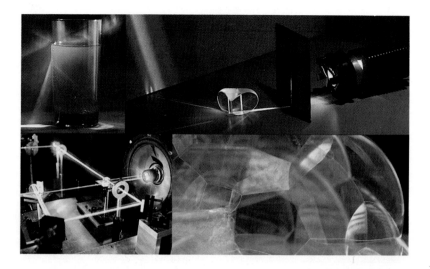

FIGURE 4-10. Each of these photographs, from the prism to the soap bubble, illustrates light's characteristic properties.

DIFFRACTION

What caused the fuzzy bands that you saw on either side of the bright filament in the Find Out? If the light traveled straight through the opening, you would see the filament. Because you saw something next to the filament, the light must have spread out in some way. It must have bent as it passed through the slit. The bending of light around a barrier is called **diffraction**. What kind of model could explain diffraction? Look at Figure 4-11.

As a straight wave approaches a barrier as shown in Figure 4-11(a), the part of the wave that touches the barrier appears to bend around it. When the straight wave approaches a small opening (b), what emerges from the other side looks very much like the circular waves produced when you tap your finger on the surface of smooth water.

a

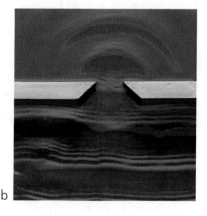

b

FIGURE 4-11. Water waves diffracted by passing the edge of a barrier (a), or through a narrow opening (b).

SKILLBUILDER

HYPOTHESIZING
When water waves pass through a thin gap the ones with a longer wavelength spread out more. Red light spreads more than blue light when passing through a thin slit. Form a hypothesis that would describe the difference between red and blue light using a wave model. If you need help, refer to the **Skill Handbook** on page 689.

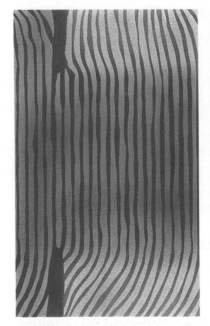 

FIGURE 4-12. Water waves spread apart after they pass through a narrow gap. The waves that passed through the narrower gap spread farther apart.

Does the wave model explain our other observations with a thin slit? Look at Figure 4-12. You see that the spreading of water waves is greater when the gap is narrowed. That agrees with what we saw. Notice also that longer-wavelength waves spread more than shorter wavelength ones. Does that agree with your observations?

INTERFERENCE

Have you seen the shimmering colors when some oil or gasoline has been spilled in water? You can see colors in the same way in soap bubbles, like those in the photo. Let's explore how light behaves when it interacts with a thin film, namely a soap bubble.

FIGURE 4-13. The thin film of a soap bubble creates a rainbow of colors.

EXPLORE!

What colors are in soap bubbles?
Assemble the equipment needed to make large soap bubbles. Dip your bubble-making device into the soap solution and create a giant bubble, allowing it to land on the cookie sheet. Watch it carefully. How many bands of red do you

see? What happens to the red bands as the time passes? Look carefully at the top of the bubble just before it breaks. How does it look?

View a bubble through a color filter so that you can see light of only one color. What do you see now?

In the Explore, you looked at light as it was reflected from a soap bubble. Then you looked at the reflection through a colored filter and you saw alternate bands of light and dark. At the top of the bubble there was no reflection; the bubble looked black. Why did this happen? Look at the reflection of a pencil in a pair of eyeglasses or a piece of window glass. You see two separate images, one reflected from the front surface of the glass, the other from the back surface. In a soap bubble, however, the two surfaces are very close together. Thin layers that produce a rainbow effect when light strikes them are called **thin films**. The wave model of light can help explain why a soap bubble separates the light into colors rather than simply reflecting it.

Figure 4-14(a) shows how waves would be reflected from both the front and back surfaces of a soap bubble. Notice that in two cases the two reflected waves have their crests and troughs at the same location. You have learned that this is called constructive interference. The reflected wave has a large amplitude. If you looked at light reflected from such a bubble you would see a strong reflection.

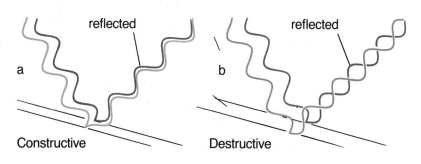

FIGURE 4-14. As light reflects from the two surfaces of a thin film, it produces constructive (a) and destructive (b) interference.

FIGURE 4-15. A soap bubble is thinner at the top than at the bottom. This creates differences in the rainbow produced.

In Figure 4-14(b), the crests of one wave line up with the troughs of the other wave. This is an example of destructive interference. The reflected wave has no amplitude. If light struck the bubble like this you would see no reflection.

The film of a soap bubble isn't all the same thickness. Gravity pulls down on the soap, making the bubble thinner on top, as shown in Figure 4-15. After a while, the film becomes so thin that it breaks. As the thickness varies, the interference alternates between constructive and destructive, as you saw in Figure 4-14.

You have seen how the wave model can explain how a wave reflected from a thin film can form areas of constructive and destructive interference. How does a soap film form colored bands? Each color has a different wavelength. As in the Explore, you saw the red bands moved down the bubble as time went on. Apparently, the red waves need a greater thickness of film to produce constructive interference. What colors formed above the red? What can you infer about the thickness of film needed for constructive interference in these colors? Which color requires the thinnest film of those observed? You can see on the electromagnetic spectrum that blue has a shorter wavelength than red. Apparently, the longer the wavelength, the thicker the film needed for constructive interference to occur.

DIFFRACTION GRATINGS

A morpho butterfly's colors aren't the result of thin films. The wing of this butterfly contains hundreds of little ridges. Each little ridge can reflect some light. How can reflections off many tiny ridges give beautiful colors? We can find out by looking at a more familiar object, a compact disc, or CD. Figure 4-16 shows what the surface of a CD looks like. It has rings of tiny pits. When it is placed in a CD player those pits are converted into music. Now we are going to see how those pits do the same thing that ridges on the morpho butterfly wing do.

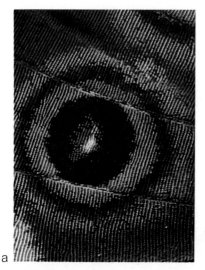

FIGURE 4-16. The surface of a morpho butterfly's wing (a), like the surface of a compact disc (b) contains thousands of microscopic pits.

EXPLORE!

Can you make rainbows in a disc?

What happens when light strikes a compact disc? You'll need either a whole or broken CD and a lamp. Sit with a lamp in front of you. Hold the compact disc, label-side down, at waist level. Tilt the disc so you see the direct reflection of the lamp. Now, slowly move your head backwards. What do you see? As you are moving your head back, which color do you see first? Which last? As you keep moving your head back, what more do you see?

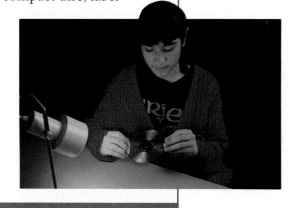

How can a wave model of light explain this spectrum? When light is reflected from a single pit it is spread out, or diffracted in the same way it would be if it were going through a slit. But in the CD there are many pits, all the same distance apart. Each one reflects light. How do these reflections produce a rainbow of colors? Let's build a model of light that will help you understand the behavior of light waves in forming rainbows.

4-2
DOUBLE-SLIT DIFFRACTION

In this investigation you will build a model that shows what happens when light is diffracted from two narrow slits close together.

PROBLEM
How does a compact disc produce a spectrum?

MATERIALS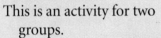
This is an activity for two groups.
For each group, one strip of shelf paper, each about 1 foot wide and 6 feet long.
Scissors

PROCEDURE
1. Draw a wave pattern along the center of one strip that matches the example by your teacher. The second group should draw a similar wave pattern, but one with a wavelength about three-quarters as long as on the first.
2. For each wave pattern, cut along the line, separating the paper into a pair of long strips. Turn one strip so the two wavy edges are up.

3. Draw two long, vertical boxes on the board, to represent two slits. Make them about 40 cm high and 10 cm wide 40 cm apart Then, using the first pair of strips, tape the end of one strip to each box with the waves pointing up.
4. Stand directly in front of the board, holding the two strips together, as shown in the figure. This represents the light waves from the two slits combining at the observer's eye. When you are the same distance from each slit, the waves' crests and troughs line up. Put a mark on the floor where you are standing.
5. Then move to the left or right, allowing the waves to slip through your fingers as you move. Stop at a point where the trough of one

wave is at the same point as the crest of the other wave. Put a mark on the floor.
6. Move farther. When the troughs and crests once again line up, mark the floor.
7. Repeat Steps 5 and 6, finding a second set of destructive and constructive interferences.
8. Repeat Steps 3 to 7 with the second pair of strips. The second set of boxes should be the same distance apart, directly below the first.

ANALYZE
1. At which points on the floor did the model show distructive interferance? Constructive interferance?
2. At the points where a trough lines up with a crest the two waves would cancel each other. Would light be seen?

CONCLUDE AND APPLY
3. Would you **predict** that both red and blue light would be bright directly in front of the two slits?
4. **Going Further:** Yellow light has a wavelength between that of blue and red. **Predict** where you would see a bright band of yellow?

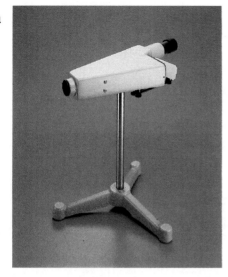

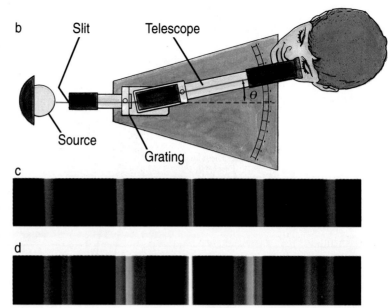

FIGURE 4-17. A spectrometer (a) is used to measure the wavelength of light emitted by a light source (b). A grating was used to produce interference patterns for red light (c) and white light (d).

A compact disc has many more than two pits, but works exactly the same way as in the Investigate. Light diffracted from each pit forms regions of constructive and destructive interference with light diffracted from other pits. Wave interference occurs naturally in some beetles and butterflies and in the feathers of a peacock. Scientists have created a device that has many rows of equally spaced grooves that also produce interference patterns. This device is called a **diffraction grating.**

Figure 4-17 shows a picture of a spectrometer. In previous chapters, you've heard about the uses of spectrometers in identifying elements in space. A spectrometer uses a diffraction grating to separate light into the different wavelengths from which it is composed. You can find out how a spectrometer works with a compact disc.

EXPLORE!

Can you see a difference in light sources?
Locate a number of different types of outdoor lights in your neighborhood. You will probably be able to find ordinary incandescent lamps, some blue-green looking lights, and others that give off a pink-colored light. You might be able to find some brightly colored neon signs.

Take your compact disc outside at night. Use it the same way you did in the last Explore. Hold the disc so you see the direct reflection. Then either move your head or rotate the disc until you see first one spectrum, then the second. Use the second spectrum in this Explore.

What spectra do the various sources of light produce? Describe what you see.

Even though the CD isn't a very accurate scientific instrument, you could use it to identify an unknown light source once you had observed the spectra formed by different sources. A chemist uses a spectrometer to identify the elements. A metallurgist looks at the light of glowing hot steel to find out the elements used to make the particular alloy. An astronomer uses the spectrum to find out which elements are in a star. Almost any source of light can be analyzed using this method.

All the properties of light we have described are well explained by a wave model. For that reason, scientists say that light is an electromagnetic wave. Light has wavelengths between infrared and ultraviolet. Therefore it is a tiny part of the electromagnetic spectrum. Of course it is very important to us because we use light to learn about our world.

Your model of light helped you to understand some of the characteristics of light. It may have helped you understand how important models are to science.

In the next chapter, you will formulate a model to help you visualize the atom and its structure.

Check Your Understanding

1. How does the behavior of light as it passes through a thin slit support the wave model of light?

2. If you see shimmering colors from oil spilled on water, where do the reflections occur that create the interference?

3. **APPLY:** You can see a rainbow-like spectrum with a phonograph record. What causes this?

EXPANDING YOUR VIEW

CONTENTS

A CLOSER LOOK

LONG-DISTANCE DETECTIVES

Using information about electromagnetic waves can turn an astrophysicist into a long-distance super sleuth. Imagine a detective collecting the equivalent of fingerprints from outer space!

Astrophysicists examine the spectrum of sunlight or of a distant star for clues to what makes up the distant body. To study a spectrum, they use a spectrometer like the one in the photo.

In 1814, Josef von Fraunhofer noticed that there were a large number of dark lines superimposed on the bright rainbow of colors of the sun's spectrum. He didn't know, however, what caused the lines. In the 1840s, Gustav Kirchoff produced the same kind of lines in the laboratory. He heated a metal block and sent the light that emerged through a spectrometer. In this way, he produced a spectrum of all the colors in white light. When he passed white light through a container filled with cool gas, however, black lines appeared on the spectrum. Different black lines appeared when light passed through a different gas. This fact seemed to imply that each gas had its own special lines. Soon it was proved that the dark lines were caused by the atoms of the gas absorbing certain wavelengths of the white light that passed through the gas. Because all other wavelengths passed through without being absorbed, the dark lines were like fingerprints, making it possible to identify the gas that had absorbed those wavelengths.

Soon physicists understood why the sun's spectrum had dark lines. They reasoned that the sun has a relatively cool atmosphere of gaseous elements. As light leaves the sun, it passes through these gases. Each element in the gases absorbs the light at its own special wavelengths. When the scientists compared the lines in the spectrum with the known lines of the various elements, they were able to determine the composition of the atmosphere of the sun. In the same way, they were able to analyze the composition of other stars.

YOU TRY IT!

Spectrometers are also important research tools in industry. Find out in what ways industry uses spectrometers.

LIFE SCIENCE CONNECTION

SUNSCREENS

As summer approaches, the lure of summer sports brings you outdoors. If you are health conscious, however, you will apply a good sunscreen to protect yourself from the sun's radiation. The greatest danger lies in the radiation you cannot see—the ultraviolet rays.

Ultraviolet waves have wavelengths about a thousand times shorter than the waves of visible light. An ultraviolet wave could have a wavelength of 0.00000028 meters—often written 280×10^{-9}.

In recent years, scientists have studied the effect of ultraviolet radiation (UV) vigorously. Sunscreens have been developed to block ultraviolet B (UVB). UVB is the name given to shorter-wavelength ultraviolet waves, the type of radiation that causes sunburn and may cause cancer in people who have a history of sunburn. Now, scientists warn that another kind of UV— UVA—penetrates the skin even more deeply than UVB. UVA, which has a longer wavelength than UVB, causes wrinkling and aging of the skin. It also increases the chances that UVB will cause skin cancer.

Whether or not your skin is harmed by UV depends on your type of skin. Darker skin has more melanin, the pigment that protects the skin against UV. The lighter your skin, the less melanin it has. Fair skin, burns quickly and painfully and then peels. If you have light brown skin, you burn little and tan easily. If you have dark brown skin, you don't burn unless exposed to the sun for a long period.

To choose the right sunscreen, you have to understand how the sunscreen works and how your skin will react to it. You should find out the shortest time needed to cause your skin to become slightly red 24 hours after exposure. This time varies according to skin type, location, and time of the year. For example, suppose you burn after 10 minutes in the sun. If you use a sunscreen with a Sun Protection Factor (SPF) 15, you could stay in the sun for 150 minutes before burning.

Sunscreen Comparison

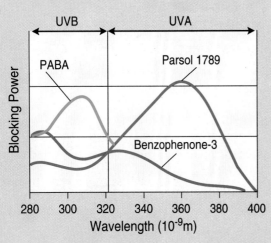

YOU TRY IT!

In order to absorb UVA rays, a sunscreen should contain a chemical called Parsol 1789. Another chemical, Benzophenone-3, absorbs UVA somewhat. PABA, an active ingredient in sunscreens, does not absorb any UVA. The graph gives a comparison of these three chemicals. Make a study of the sunscreens available at a store near you. List which contain Parsol 1789, PABA, and Benzophenone-3. Also list the SPF of the sunscreens. Which sunscreen would you buy for maximum protection?

SCIENCE A N D SOCIETY

WHO OWNS THE SPECTRUM?

As cities grow closer and closer, your chance of seeing distant stars becomes smaller. Even with better telescopes, you can see fewer stars in the sky than people did in the past. The stars are still there, but light pollution keeps us from seeing the light from the stars. It is hard to pick out the stars from the bright background of the city lights. Your grandparents may remember a time when they could see many more stars against the black background of the sky.

Observatories are usually located in remote places on mountaintops. Astronomers used to count on the black, crisp nights up there to do their sky watching. David Crawford, an

the sky. The photographs above show Tucson at night in 1959 and again in 1980. You can see that astronomers at Kitt Peak Observatory now have to compete with the bright lights of Tucson in order to see distant stars.

astronomer at Kitt Peak Observatory near Tucson, Arizona, is the founder of the International Dark Sky Association. His group has helped alert people to what is happening in

Fortunately, just as people are trying to cut down on air and water pollution, in areas of the country close to observatories, ordinances are beginning to control outdoor lighting. For example, the people of San Diego voted to change from high-pressure sodium lamps on streets and highways to low-pressure sodium lamps that interfere less with observations of the stars on Mount Palomar. Besides allowing the astronomers to see deeper into the universe, the new lights in San Diego also aid amateur astronomers in locating stars.

Another way to cut down on light pollution is to use fixtures that direct all light downward or directly at its target instead of upward. Some ordinances provide that all bright lights be turned off after midnight.

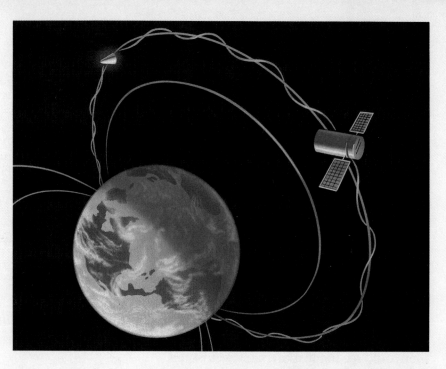

Light is not the only source of pollution spreading outward from Earth. Nuclear powered spacecraft can create pollution as well. In order to reduce costs, reactors in orbiting spacecraft are not enclosed in a protective shield. The gamma rays the reactors emit can interfere with the work of other orbiting satellites. The gamma rays make it difficult for the instruments on board a satellite to detect weak signals from distant space.

In addition, as the gamma rays pass through the surface of the reactor, they can produce charged particles. In the figure, an orbiting reactor has emitted a cloud of charged particles that spiral around Earth's magnetic field lines. As a satellite passes through this particle cloud, the particles produce X rays and new gamma rays that interfere with the operation of the satellite.

Seven or eight times a day, the satellite Solar Maximum Mission was unable to collect data on gamma rays in space because of the rays emitted by nuclear reactors in space.

CAREER CONNECTION

To prepare for a career as an astronomer, you have to study astronomy, physics, mathematics, and computer science.

WHAT DO YOU THINK?

The electromagnetic spectrum belongs to everyone, not just to one group of people. Keeping that in mind: (1) Should sports areas be regulated as to the amount and kind of light they give off at night? (2) Should nations sign a treaty to ban satellites with unshielded nuclear reactors from orbiting Earth?

Health
CONNECTION

ULTRAVIOLET AND X RAYS

Ultraviolet radiation is one of the shortest wavelength and highest frequency forms of electromagnetic wave. Sunlight and light from tanning lamps contain ultraviolet radiation. It produces vitamin D, which is needed for healthy bones and teeth. But, because of its high frequency, ultraviolet radiation can easily penetrate the skin. Prolonged and frequent exposure to ultraviolet radiation can kill healthy skin cells and produce sagging, dry skin. In the Life Science Connection, you learned that sunscreens provide some protection by absorbing some part of the ultraviolet radiation from the sun. Too much ultraviolet radiation can cause sunburn or damage cells in a way that leads to cancer. These two applications show that ultraviolet rays transmit energy.

If you have ever seriously injured your leg or arm, your doctor probably checked for broken bones using X rays. The wavelength of an X ray is so short that it is not absorbed by skin and muscle, but moves right through them. Bones are more dense and contain the heavier element calcium and so absorb X rays. Thus, when the X rays that pass through the tissue reach the photographic film, the bones leave dark shadows. In the figure below, you can see the person's ribs, shoulders, and heart as well as a pacemaker and its wires. The doctor uses the information provided by the X rays to check for breaks or other damage to the bone.

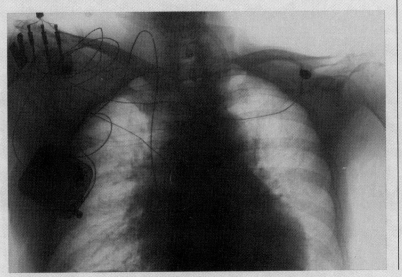

WHAT DO YOU THINK?

X rays provide valuable information to doctors. Yet, too much exposure to X rays over a long period of time can be harmful. Talk to your doctor or dentist about X rays. Ask at what point they feel an X ray is important. Ask them about other ways to gather needed information without using X rays. What do you think about the use of X rays?

HOW IT WORKS

DETECTING WEAPONS WITH X RAYS

People who travel on airplanes are routinely delayed by some kind of security check. Most travelers think it is worth the time spent if weapons such as guns and rifles as well as bombs are kept off their plane.

Guns and other weapons are often easier to detect than bombs. Weapons usually show up in an ordinary X-ray baggage check, such as the one on the left.

The kinds of bombs that have caused several airline crashes would not be detected by the usual airport X-ray machine. These bombs belong to a group of "plastic" explosives, made of a puttylike material that can be formed into any shape to fool the inspectors. The explosive is of carbon, oxygen, and mostly nitrogen. In an ordinary X ray, it would look like a dense, nonmetallic material.

Several new types of X ray and other kinds of high-tech detectors are being tested to deal with this new kind of threat to public safety.

One kind of X-ray detector sends two kinds of X rays through a piece of luggage. One is higher frequency, the other lower frequency. A computer analyzes the characteristics of the objects in the bag based on the two X rays. One X ray passes through the objects in the luggage, and the other is reflected from objects that have certain chemical makeup. Nitrogen is one of the substances that reflects low-frequency X rays. The same luggage is shown in the photograph on the right. This time the plastic explosive is indicated by the bright white image.

In another detector, a pair of X rays provides information about the mass, density, and chemical makeup of the items in the luggage. Still another uses X rays to make scan projections of luggage. The computer analyzes the contents of the bag and highlights any suspicious items in red.

YOU TRY IT!

Find out what kind of X-ray machine is used at an airport near you to examine luggage.

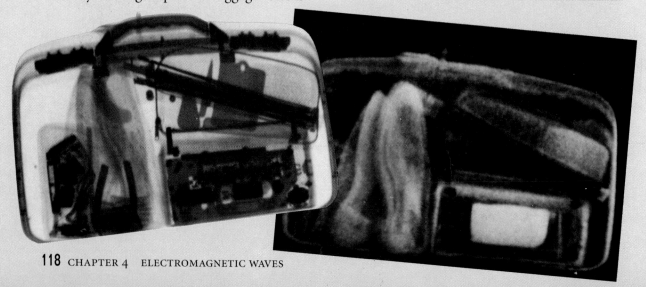

Reviewing Main Ideas

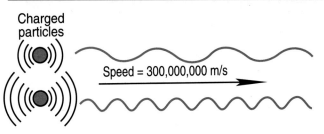

Charged particles

Speed = 300,000,000 m/s

1. Electromagnetic waves are transverse waves produced by a vibrating electric charge. One complete vibration creates one wave. The frequency times the wavelength of every electromagnetic wave equals the speed of light, about 300,000,000 meters per second.

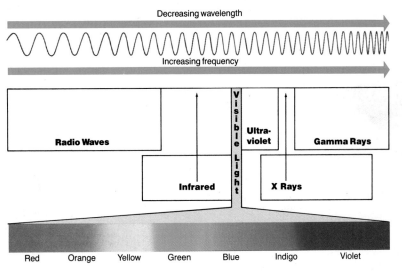

Decreasing wavelength

Increasing frequency

Radio Waves

Infrared

Visible Light

Ultra-violet

X Rays

Gamma Rays

Red   Orange   Yellow   Green   Blue   Indigo   Violet

2. Electromagnetic waves include: radio, microwave, infrared, visible light, ultraviolet, and X rays. Radio waves have the longest wavelength and lowest frequency.

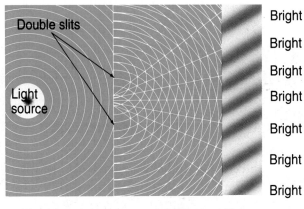

Double slits

Light source

Bright
Bright
Bright
Bright
Bright
Bright
Bright

3. Light exhibits properties of waves. The wave theory explains how a light can be diffracted and produce interference patterns.

4. Interference patterns depend on the thickness of film, the angle of viewing, the number of depressions, and other properties of objects that produce them.

Chapter Review

USING KEY SCIENCE TERMS

diffraction
diffraction grating
electromagnetic spectrum
electromagnetic wave
radiation
thin film

Using the list above, replace the underlined words with the correct key science term.

1. _The bending of light around a barrier_ is evidence that light travels in waves.

2. A _layer of oil floating on water or a soap bubble_ produces interference patterns that appear as colors of the rainbow.

3. X rays, microwaves, and visible light are examples of energy that travels in _waves with oscillating electrical and magnetic fields_.

4. Light from the sun reaches Earth by _moving through space as electromagnetic waves_.

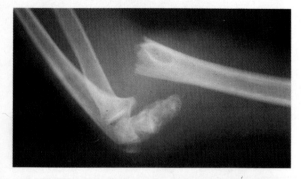

5. Radio waves, infrared waves, and X rays are part of the _range of electromagnetic waves_.

UNDERSTANDING IDEAS

Complete each sentence.

1. An electromagnetic wave is produced by a/an ____.

2. The electromagnetic wave with the next longest wavelength to visible light is ____.

3. A thin film produces colors when the light reflected from its front and back surfaces ____.

4. As the wavelength of an electromagnetic wave decreases, its ____ increases.

5. The frequency of electomagnetic radiation with a wavelength of 300 meters is ____.

6. We know that light is bent as it goes through a narrow opening because it produces ____.

7. One type of electromagnetic energy that your body gives off is ____.

8. When you know the frequency and wavelength of a type of radiation, you can calculate its speed by ____.

9. Unlike other kinds of waves, electromagnetic waves do not travel through a ____.

10. Electromagnetic waves are ____ waves rather than longitudinal waves.

11. A spectrometer relies on a ____ to separate light into different wavelengths.

CRITICAL THINKING

Use your understanding of the concepts developed in the chapter to answer each of the following questions.

1. How does a vibrating charge create an electromagnetic wave?

2. How would you use a diffraction grating to identify the source of a light?

3. Describe what would happen to the appearance of the wave after passing through the opening if the opening were much wider. What would the wave on the right side of the picture look like if there were two small openings?

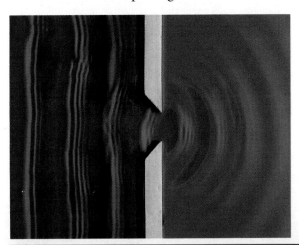

4. The color blue is seen in the left portion of a thin film and the color red in the right portion of the same film. Which portion of the film is thicker?

PROBLEM SOLVING

Read the following problem and discuss your answers in a brief paragraph.

You are going camping with a friend and expect it to get quite cold during the night. You are taking with you a foam sleeping pad that is silver on one side to put under your sleeping bag. You are also taking a "space blanket"—a very thin, shiny silver plastic blanket.

1. Which side of the sleeping pad should face up when you put it on the ground? Why?

2. Why will wrapping yourself in the plastic blanket before climbing into your sleeping bag keep you warmer than the sleeping bag alone?

3. Should you take light or dark colored clothing for your trip, or does it matter?

CONNECTING IDEAS

Discuss each of the following in a brief paragraph.

1. Discuss two ways in which electromagnetic waves differ from the electricity discussed in Chapters 1 and 3.

2. If you were able to see radio waves, do you think they would produce interference patterns? Explain your answer.

3. **LIFE SCIENCE CONNECTION** How would you decide which SPF value of sunscreen to select?

4. **SCIENCE AND SOCIETY** Describe two ways in which light pollution can be decreased.

5. **HEALTH CONNECTION** Describe one positive and one negative effect of X rays.

UNIT 1
ELECTRICITY AND MAGNETISM

CONTENTS

UNIT FOCUS

In Unit 1, you worked with electricity and magnetism. You discovered that electrical energy is used in many appliances around the home. You found out that an electric current produces a magnetic field and a changing magnetic field produces an electric current. You also learned how electromagnetic waves are created. You explored the different ways that electromagnetic waves carry information and energy for our use and enjoyment.

Try the exercises and activity that follow—they will challenge you to use and apply some of the ideas you learned in this unit.

CONNECTING IDEAS

1. Do you think that pushing the button of an electric doorbell completes a circuit or opens one? If you were designing a doorbell button, would you use an electrical conductor, an insulator, or both? Explain your answer. Describe the purpose of the coil of copper wire found inside an electric doorbell.

2. **Analyzing Data:** Suppose your electric bill rose by twenty dollars the month after your family bought an air conditioner. If the electric company charges 10 cents for each kilowatt-hour of energy, how many extra kilowatt-hours are used by the air conditioner in one month?

EXPLORING FURTHER

Draw a diagram to represent a circuit with one bulb and one electromagnet in parallel connected to a battery of three cells in series. Design a switch that will, at the same time, turn off the lamp and enable the electromagnet to produce a magnetic field.

TRY IT

In the atomic world, the size of particles and the distances between them are small indeed. Yet size and distance is relative. To an ant, a bread crumb is a full meal and a heavy load to carry back to the nest. To you, it's so small that it drops unnoticed from your sandwich to the floor. You may not know much about atoms yet, but you probably know that each has a nucleus at its center. How large do you suppose the nucleus of an atom is relative to the whole atom? If the nucleus of an atom were as large as an ant, how large would the atom be? Take out a piece of paper, draw an ant in the center of the paper, and draw a circle around the ant as large as you think the atom would be. After you've learned more about atoms, try this activity again and see how accurate you were the first time.

UNIT 2
ATOMS AND MOLECULES

CONTENTS

UNIT FOCUS

In Unit 1, you learned about electrical and magnetic properties of matter. As you study Unit 2, you'll see how the internal structure of matter determines its magnetic as well as other physical properties. You'll also learn how the structure of matter affects how substances react with one another and why they don't all react in the same ways. Chemical reactions affect your life greatly. For example, sodium and chlorine are both harmful to humans, but combine to form salt, which is needed by humans. The kinetic molecular theory helps to explain characteristics of solids, liquids, and gases and their interactions.

DID YOU EVER WONDER . . .

Why some things glow in the dark?

Where radiation comes from?

What an atom looks like?

You'll find the answers to these questions as you read this chapter.

Structure of the Atom

When you look at a globe, you know you are not looking at Earth itself. The globe is a model of Earth, a small and very useful representation of a much larger and more complicated object. While a globe is an actual physical model that you can see and touch, you can also make mental pictures of things you want to understand—mental models.

When globes were first made, no one had ever seen Earth from space. How did the globe makers know how it looked? They put together observations from astronomers, explorers, and other scientists to build their model. In the same way, scientists have built a mental model

of the tiny particles from which all matter is made—the atom.

In this chapter, you'll follow the story of how the model of the atom developed.

EXPLORE!

How can you determine the shape of an object you cannot see?

Place a paper clip, a pencil, and a brick or a small bag of sand under a piece of cardboard. Then, without looking under the cardboard, take turns rolling a marble under the cardboard. Compare the direction the marble rolled toward the object with the direction the marble rolled after it hit the object. Roll the marble from several different directions. Diagram your observations. Which object is under the cardboard?

5-1 Early Discoveries

OBJECTIVES

In this section, you will

- relate the contributions of Crookes, Thomson, Becquerel, and Rutherford to the study of the structure of the atom;
- describe radioactivity;
- list the characteristics of alpha and beta particles and gamma rays.

KEY SCIENCE TERMS

electron
radioactivity
beta particle
gamma rays
alpha particles

DISCOVERING ATOMS

The idea of atoms began more than 2400 years ago with Greek philosophers. The Greeks imagined what might happen if a material was cut repeatedly. Eventually, the piece of material would be so small it could not be cut again and still have the properties of the material. The Greeks called this basic part of matter an atom, meaning indivisible.

Acceptance of the atomic theory of matter was slow and understandably so. How can you prove the existence of something you can't see? You know from the Explore activity how difficult it is to determine the shape of something invisible. It was the mid-1800s before most scientists accepted the existence of atoms. The atomic theory offered a simple and useful explanation for the behavior of gases. Atomic theory was also useful in explaining chemical compounds and the products of chemical reactions. In all, atoms as a building block of matter accounted for observations about matter better than any earlier theory did. Yet, scientists wondered, if the atoms involved in chemistry could be further divided? The answer came from an unlikely experiment.

William Crookes was a British physicist. In the late 1800s, he was interested in the vacuum tube. A vacuum tube is a sealed glass tube with the air removed from it.

FIGURE 5-1. When a voltage is applied to the terminals of a vacuum tube, a green glow moves through the tube.

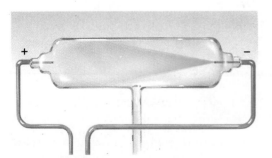

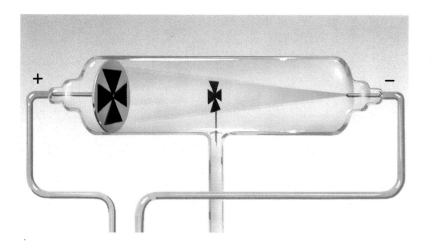

FIGURE 5-2. An object placed in the path of the beam casts a shadow.

Crookes' tube had a positive terminal at one end and a negative terminal at the other. When the terminals were connected to a high-voltage battery, a greenish glow formed at the negative terminal. The glow gradually moved toward the other end of the tube, as shown in Figure 5-1. An object in the path of the green glow cast a shadow, as in Figure 5-2. Crookes knew that shadows are cast by waves or particles traveling in straight lines. With this information, what could Crookes conclude about the green glow?

Nearly 20 years after Crookes' work, the British physicist J. J. Thomson repeated the experiment with Crookes' setup, which was now called a cathode-ray tube. Thomson observed that the waves, or beam of particles, formed in such a tube were bent when they were passed through an electric field, as in Figure 5-3. Similar observations were

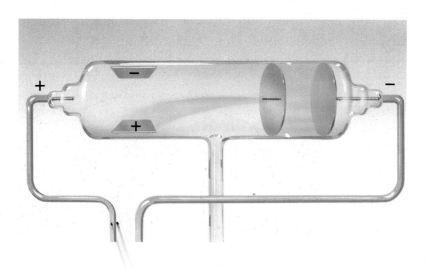

FIGURE 5-3. As they passed near electrically charged plates, the particles bent toward the positive plate.

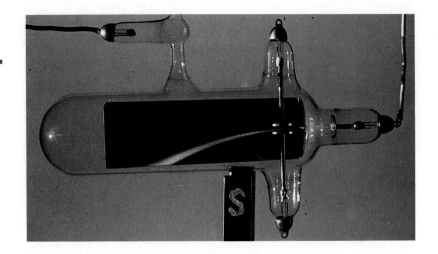

FIGURE 5-4. When a vacuum tube is placed in a magnetic field, the beam bends.

made with magnetic fields, as shown in Figure 5-4. You may recall that charged particles show such behavior in electric or magnetic fields.

In addition to showing that the beam was made up of charged particles, Thomson showed that the particles had much less mass than any atoms have. Thomson also found that the kind of material used for the tube's metal plates did not seem to affect how many charged particles were produced or how they behaved. Thomson had shown that particles even smaller than atoms existed. The particle was given the name **electron**. In 1906, Thomson received the Nobel Prize in physics for his discovery of the electron.

The electrons Crookes and Thomson observed are a form of radiation. The term *radiation* is commonly used to describe any form of energy—heat, light, or even beams of small particles—given off by an object. What caused the negative terminal in the vacuum tube to radiate these particles? Does radiation only occur when there is a voltage present? Is there any type of radiation that occurs naturally?

DID YOU KNOW?

The tube Crookes used was the ancestor of the television tube and the computer screen. Each of these modern devices relies on a vacuum tube with positive and negative metal plates. The inside of each tube is coated with materials that glow when they are struck by electrons, making the beam easy to see.

NATURAL RADIATION

Perhaps you've had a broken arm x-rayed. Maybe you've seen an X-ray photograph of a person's lungs or hand. X rays can even show cracks or breaks in steel bridges and building supports. The material to be tested is placed between the X-ray source and a sheet of film. Wherever the X rays pass through the material, the film clouds as though it has been exposed to light. Are there other forms of radiation that can affect film?

EXPLORE!

Can wrapped film be exposed?
Obtain some wrapped, undeveloped film. When you are ready to begin this activity, open one packet of undeveloped film. Describe its appearance. Your teacher will provide you with a weak source of radiation, such as a smoke detector. Place the radiation source near the unopened film for ten minutes. Unwrap the film and examine it closely. Describe the changes you observe.

The observations you made in the Explore are similar to those made nearly a hundred years ago by French physicist Henri Becquerel [BEK rell]. Becquerel accidentally left a small sample of a uranium compound on top of a photographic plate. The plate was in a drawer,

FIGURE 5-5. An X ray can travel through soft tissue to show bone structure.

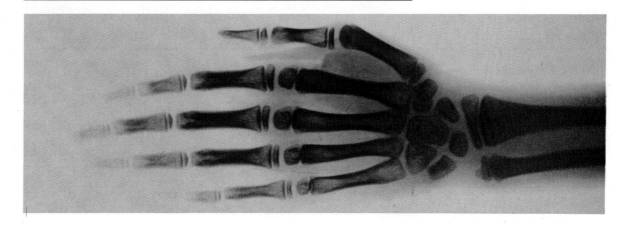

wrapped tightly in light-colored paper. Yet, when Becquerel went to use the plate, he found it fogged just like the film shown in Figure 5-6! It seemed as if the compound were giving off radiation that could go through paper. Becquerel began to study the radiation further. Radiation penetrated matter just as X rays did, and it was given off in all directions by the compound. The radiation could even be deflected by a magnetic field. Becquerel inferred that the radiation had to be—at least partly—made up of tiny, charged particles. Eventually, he concluded that the negatively charged part of the radiation was due to negatively charged particles. Becquerel further concluded that these particles were identical to those in Thomson's experiment. They were electrons. Where were the electrons coming from? The only possible source was the uranium compound, or rather the atoms of the uranium compound. Here was more evidence that the atom must have smaller parts. Furthermore, one of those parts must be a light, negatively charged, particle—an electron.

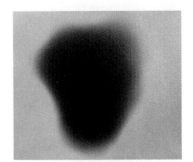

FIGURE 5-6. Becquerel was surprised to find that photographic film could look exposed if it were placed near uranium.

How do we know?

How can we detect radiation?

One method of measuring radiation uses a Geiger counter. A Geiger counter is a device that produces an electric current whenever radiation is present.

The figure illustrates the parts of a Geiger counter. The tube is filled with gas at a low pressure. A positively charged wire runs through the center of a negatively charged copper cylinder. The wire and the cylinder are connected to a voltage source. Radiation enters the tube at one end and strips the electrons from the gaseous atoms. The electrons are attracted to the positive wire. As they move to the wire, they knock more electrons off the atoms in the gas. An "electron avalanche" is produced, and a large number of electrons reach the wire. This produces a short, intense current in the wire. This current is amplified to produce a clicking sound or flashing light. The intensity of radiation present is determined by the number of clicks in each second.

Geiger counters can be made very small and portable. They are often used to test the radioactivity at job sites where workers can be exposed to radioactive materials. For example, workers in a hospital radiation lab or at a nuclear power plant could actually wear small Geiger counters to monitor their exposures.

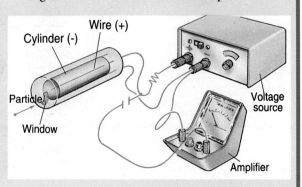

MORE ATOMIC PARTICLES

You've seen that radiation can be given off by metal plates in a vacuum tube or by elements such as uranium. Uranium is said to be an unstable element—it breaks apart on its own. Elements that break apart on their own are radioactive. The release of high-energy particles by radioactive elements is called **radioactivity.**

The study of radioactivity contributed a lot to our current ideas about an atom and its parts. Following Becquerel, Ernest Rutherford, a physicist from New Zealand, studied radioactivity. He used uranium and thorium, two radioactive elements, to make some important observations. First, he put each element in a magnetic field, as shown in Figure 5-7. Part of the radiation from the element was slightly bent in one direction. Part of the radiation was greatly bent in the opposite direction. Finally, part of the radiation Rutherford observed was unaffected by the magnetic field. This radiation did not bend in either direction.

Rutherford gave these three parts of the radiation names taken from the first three letters of the Greek alphabet: *alpha*, *beta*, and *gamma*. In addition to their

FIGURE 5-7. Alpha and beta rays are deflected by a magnetic field. Gamma rays moved through the field without being affected.

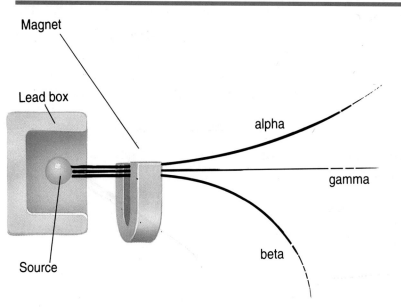

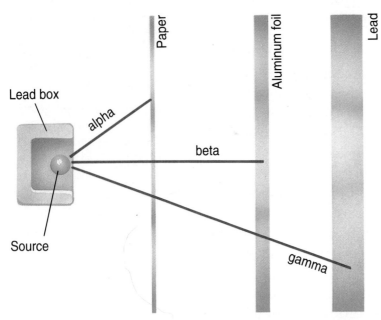

Lead box

alpha

Source

beta

gamma

Paper

Aluminum foil

Lead

FIGURE 5-8. Alpha particles can be stopped by paper, beta particles by aluminum foil, and gamma rays by lead.

SKILLBUILDER

MAKING AND USING TABLES

Make a table of the three kinds of radiation you have read about in this chapter. Make table headings for the type of radiation, response to magnetic field, charge, mass, and what material can stop the radiation. If you need help, refer to the **Skill Handbook** on page 681.

different responses to a magnetic field, the radiation differed in another way. Figure 5-8 shows that the alpha radiation Rutherford observed could be stopped by a sheet of paper. The beta radiation could go through paper and some thin metal foils. Most impressive of all was the gamma radiation which, like X rays, could penetrate even lead shielding. However, it was the beta and alpha radiation that were more important to understanding the atom.

Because beta radiation behaved like the particles in Crookes' and Thomson's experiments, Rutherford inferred that beta radiation must contain negatively charged particles. Later experiments supported this inference. Beta radiation is now known as beta particles. A high-speed electron given off by a radioactive substance is a **beta particle**.

The alpha radiation was affected by the magnetic field, but the alpha rays didn't bend as much as the beta rays had. Rutherford also observed that alpha and beta rays bent in opposite directions. These observations led Rutherford to conclude that **alpha particles** are positively charged particles given off by radioactive substances and have more mass than beta particles. The gamma radiation was not deflected by a magnetic field. And gamma radiation was more penetrating than X rays were. Could the gamma rays be electromagnetic radiation? Experiments in Rutherford's laboratory proved that **gamma rays** were electromagnetic radiation. The experiments also indicated that the wavelength of gamma radiation was shorter than the wavelength of X rays.

These observations led to other questions. One of the most puzzling was: How are the parts of an atom arranged? Where in an atom are the electrons, the beta particles, and the alpha particles?

5-1
PARTS OF AN ATOM

Think back to the Explore you did at the beginning of this chapter. Suppose you were absolutely certain the brick was under the cardboard, but the marble seemed to roll as if nothing were under the cardboard. What would you think?

PROBLEM
What's inside an atom?

MATERIALS
regular-size aluminum pie pan
4 glass marbles
12-mm steel ball
4 steel marbles
grooved ruler

PROCEDURE
1. Gently press the 4 glass marbles into the pie pan so that they make small indentations near the center of the pan.
2. Roll the 12-mm steel ball down the grooved ruler, as shown in the illustration. Try to hit the marbles.
3. **Observe** and record what happens to the steel ball. Does it ever change its path? Does the steel ball ever bounce back?
4. Place the ruler at different slopes. Record any **effect** this has on your observations.
5. Now put steel marbles into the indentations in the pie pan.
6. Repeat Steps 2, 3, and 4 rolling a glass marble (alpha particle) down the grooved ruler.

ANALYZE
1. **Compare and contrast** the results in Step 6 with the previous observations.
2. Why were the results different?
3. What **effect** did the slope of the ruler have on the way the rolling ball or marble behaved? What **hypothesis** can there be for your observation?

CONCLUDE AND APPLY
4. Which has a greater **effect** on the way the rolling ball acts after a collision, the mass of the rolling ball or the mass of the ball in the indentation?
5. **Going Further:** How would your observations change if the steel marbles and the rolling steel ball were all positively charged?

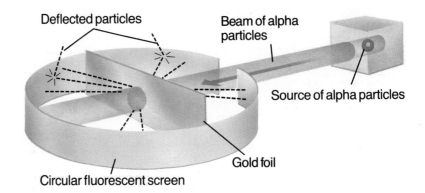

FIGURE 5-9. Rutherford aimed a beam of alpha particles at a piece of gold foil. The circular screen around the foil recorded the direction the alpha particles moved after hitting the foil.

Deflected particles

Beam of alpha particles

Source of alpha particles

Gold foil

Circular fluorescent screen

In this Investigate, you learned that the way objects interact is affected by their mass, their velocity, and whether or not they are charged. Rutherford used a similar experiment to study the way alpha particles interacted with matter.

Rutherford and his colleagues wanted to learn more about alpha particles. They designed an experiment to study the ability of alpha particles to pass through different metals. The setup is shown in Figure 5-9. Rutherford fired alpha particles at a sheet of gold foil only 1/50,000 of an inch thick. He expected the alpha particles to pass right through the foil. These particles appeared as tiny flashes of light on a coated screen. Most of these flashes appeared on the screen as if the particles passed directly through the foil. However, the boundary of the circle formed by the flashes was fuzzy. This meant that the paths of some of the alpha particles had been bent—some at small angles, some at very large angles. A few particles even bounced right back out from the foil. Rutherford, some years later, was quoted: "It was about as believable as if you had fired a 15-inch shell at a piece of tissue paper, and it came back and hit you."

Rutherford's team set out to learn more about alpha particles. Instead, they made one of history's most important observations about atoms. Look at Figure 5-10. Since most of the alpha particles passed straight through, gold atoms must be mostly empty space. Other alpha particles came out at angles. This meant that somewhere in the gold atom was a very massive charged object that would repel the positively charged alpha particles. After Rutherford's team made these observations, other scientists became very interested in just what an atom looked like and how the parts of

SKILLBUILDER

SEQUENCING
Sequence the chain of discoveries presented so far in this chapter that led to finding out about the structure of an atom. Start with the Greeks. If you need help, refer to the **Skill Handbook** on page 680.

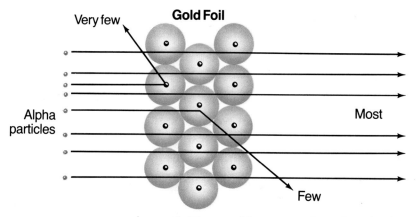

Very few

Gold Foil

Alpha
particles

Most

Few

FIGURE 5-10. Most of the alpha particles went through the foil as if it were not there. A few particles bounced back at great angles.

an atom were arranged. The problem was that they had no tools to directly observe the atom. Instead, they had to rely on mental pictures of the atom.

The development of the current idea of an atom is an example of how hard work and even luck contribute to scientific discoveries. Crookes and Thomson performed experiments to explore the possibilities of atomic structure. Meanwhile, Becquerel's accidental discovery of the radiation given off by radioactive elements offered new information about the structure of atoms. In addition, Rutherford's work with alpha, beta, and gamma particles led to more information about the atom and even more questions and problems to solve.

In the next section, you will use all the observations made during these experiments to build a model of the atom. A model is an idea, system, or structure that represents what you are trying to explain.

Check Your Understanding

1. What do you do when you want to find out what is inside a wrapped present but can't open it? How is that like what Crookes, Thomson, Becquerel, and Rutherford did to find out the composition of an atom?

2. What is the connection between the green glow in Crookes' vacuum tube and the beta particle that Rutherford discovered?

3. How would you tell a beta particle from an alpha particle?

4. **APPLY:** Draw a diagram to show what observations would be made if zeta rays were very light positively charged particles and theta rays were very heavy negatively charged particles, and they passed through a magnetic field.

5-2 A Model Atom

OBJECTIVES

In this section, you will

- trace the development of the model of the atom;
- distinguish among electrons, protons, and neutrons.

KEY SCIENCE TERMS

nucleus

proton

neutron

MODELING ATOMS

You are probably familiar with several types of models, such as the ones in Figure 5-11. A model helps you understand how an object is built or how it works. A good model of an object can explain all your observations of that object. Sometimes, rather than an object you can touch, a model is a mental picture. The following activity will give some experience in forming a mental picture.

FIND OUT!

How can you make a mental picture of an atom?
Your teacher will give you some bolts, nuts, and/or washers. Each group in the class will get different amounts of hardware. Bury your hardware in a piece of modeling clay. Form the clay into a ball so that you cannot see the hardware or determine its shape. Trade clay balls with another group.

Try to find out what is inside the clay ball. The only observations you may make are with toothpicks. To make your observations, stick toothpicks one at a time into the clay ball. Try to find out how many of which hardware pieces are hidden in the clay. Do not pull apart the clay! What did you observe?

Conclude and Apply

1. What inference can you make about the contents of the clay?
2. Evaluate the procedure for making a mental picture or a model. Why are models necessary?

As you did the activity, you probably tried to form a mental picture of what was inside the clay ball. You made a model of the clay ball and its contents.

As scientists study matter, they try to form a mental picture of what an atom might look like. Like any model, a good model of the atom must explain all the information that is known about matter and atoms. As more data are collected, a model may need to be changed. The model of the atom we use today is the result of the work of many scientists over many years.

In 1802, John Dalton, a British chemist, developed the first model of the atom. Dalton observed that the gases of the air could be compressed only so far. He concluded that air and all other matter were made up of particles too tiny to be seen. These particles were solid and indestructible, like tiny billiard balls. Dalton's model is shown in Figure 5-12(a).

Think back to Crookes and Thomson. Does Dalton's billiard ball model of the atom give any clue about the electrons Crookes and Thomson observed? The electrons had to come from atoms. To accommodate this observation, Thomson claimed the atom was a solid mass with electrons scattered throughout it, rather like the blueberries in a blueberry muffin. Thomson's atomic model is the model in Figure 5-12(b).

Does Thomson's model explain the observations Rutherford made? What about the great amounts of empty space inside the atom? Rutherford's first change to

a

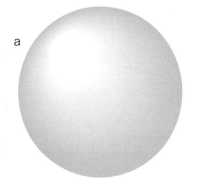

b

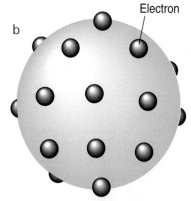

Electron

FIGURE 5-12. Dalton's solid ball model (a) and Thomson's blueberry muffin model (b) each explained some observations about atomic structure.

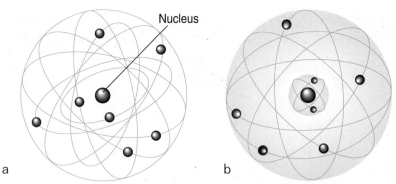

a   b

FIGURE 5-13. As more observations were made, the atomic model was refined to include electrons surrounding a nucleus (a) and electrons moving in shells (b).

the model was to give the atom a dense center. Because the positive alpha particles were sometimes scattered in large angles from this center, it must have a positive charge. The dense, positively charged center of an atom is called the **nucleus**.

Rutherford then reasoned that the positively charged alpha particles emitted by the radioactive source must have come from the nucleus of the atom. Therefore, the nucleus must contain positively charged particles. Rutherford named the positively charged particle in the nucleus of an atom a **proton**.

Remember that Thomson, Becquerel, and Rutherford all observed negatively charged particles of relatively small mass—electrons. To account for the small angle scattering, Rutherford suggested that electrons are scattered around the nucleus and that the space between the nucleus and its electrons is empty space. It took Rutherford ten years to fully understand all of his observations. He tried many different ideas and tested them before making his final inferences.

Rutherford's model of the atom, the model in Figure 5-13(a), had a major impact on the world of science. The model shown in Figure 5-13(b) was proposed by Niels Bohr in 1913. Bohr pictured the atom as having a central nucleus with electrons moving around it in well-defined paths.

In 1926, scientists changed the model of the atom again. In the new model, the electrons moved around the nucleus in a region called an electron cloud. A diagram of this model appears in Figure 5-14. Because the electron's

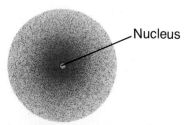

FIGURE 5-14. The electron cloud model of the atom shows regions where electrons are likely to be.

FIGURE 5-15. You can compare the spray of water from a lawn sprinkler to an electron cloud.

mass is so small, it is impossible to describe exactly where it is as it moves in the atom. The electron cloud represents the probable locations of electrons within an atom. You can compare the electron cloud to the spray of water drops from a lawn sprinkler. Each drop represents a probable location of an electron in the cloud. As you can see in Figure 5-15, most of the drops are concentrated near the center of the spray. In an atom, the most probable location of electrons is in the electron cloud, distributed about the nucleus.

The diameter of the nucleus is about $1/100,000$ the diameter of the electron cloud. Suppose you built a model of an atom with an electron cloud as wide

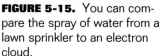

FIGURE 5-16. In an atom as wide as a football field, the nucleus would be as wide as a paper clip wire.

as a football field. The nucleus of that atom would be in the center of the field and would be about the thickness of the wire in an ordinary paper clip.

The electron cloud model of the atom answers questions about electrons and their relationship with an atom's nucleus. However, there are observations of the nucleus that have not yet been included in our model. In the early 1900s, Rutherford compared the charge and mass of several particles he had observed. He knew that of all the elements, hydrogen had the least mass. Therefore, he assigned the hydrogen nucleus a mass of one atomic mass unit. From the model, the nucleus would have one positively charged particle, a proton. There would be one electron, of very little mass, associated with this nucleus to make a hydrogen atom.

Rutherford compared this information with data he gathered about alpha particles. One alpha particle had a positive charge of two. According to the model it should have had two protons and a mass of two. Yet, when Rutherford measured the mass of an alpha particle he found it was four times as heavy as a hydrogen atom instead of twice as heavy. There were two extra units of mass! And no additional charge! What could have caused the extra mass?

How do we know?

What does an atom look like?

Many models of the atom have been presented. How do we know which one is closest to the real thing? Seeing an actual atom would answer that question once and for all. Modern techniques permit the photographing of individual atoms that are only 30 billionths of a centimeter across. The microscope works by moving a fine metal point across the object being examined. This discovery may lead to building molecules one atom at a time. The point traces the shape of the surface of the object just as your finger detects rough spots when moved across your desk. When a desired position is reached, an atom can be deposited. The picture shown here was taken using a scanning tunneling microscope. Each hill is a single xenon atom, and the atoms have been arranged to spell out "IBM."

In 1932, James Chadwick, a student of Rutherford's, answered that question. Chadwick had heard of a new type of very penetrating particle radiation obtained from beryllium that had been bombarded with alpha particles. The path of this radiation did not change when it was surrounded by an electric field. Therefore, researchers could conclude that this radiation had no charge.

Chadwick used this new radiation to bombard paraffin wax. As a result, the hydrogen atoms in the wax emitted high-speed protons. Chadwick studied the speed of the protons and proposed that the uncharged radiation was made up of particles with a mass about equal to the mass of the proton. Chadwick called the particle a neutron.

A **neutron** is a particle with no charge and with a mass about equal to that of a proton, and it is found in the nucleus of an atom. The name was chosen because the particle has no electric charge. It is neutral. This uncharged particle suited the theory nicely. It explained the extra mass of the alpha particle and did not upset the balance of charges. Thus, Chadwick's discovery of the neutron answered many questions about the structure and behavior of atoms.

With the discovery of the neutron, the model of the atom was modified to include a nucleus made up of protons and neutrons. The proton-neutron model of the nucleus is still accepted today.

Table 5-1 summarizes information about the three basic particles of atomic structure. Does it seem like a lot was learned from all these years of work? What are these findings really telling us about all matter on Earth? Researchers set to work to see how this atomic model could be used to explain the differences between one element and another. They also used the model to explain how different elements interact with one another.

a

b

FIGURE 5-17. Ernest Rutherford (a) and Niels Bohr (b) both contributed to our knowledge and understanding of atomic structure.

TABLE 5-1. Comparison of Atomic Particles

	Relative Mass	Charge	Location in the Atom
Proton	1	1+	Part of nucleus
Neutron	1	none	Part of nucleus
Electron	0.0005	1−	Moves around nucleus

ENERGY LEVELS OF ELECTRONS

Although all the electrons in an atom are contained in the electron cloud, within the cloud itself the electrons are at different distances from the nucleus. One way scientists know that electrons are different distances from the nucleus is that it takes different amounts of energy to pry the electron away from a nucleus.

■ EXPLORE! ■

Does a magnet hold everything with the same strength?

Place a horseshoe magnet in a bowl of ball bearings or tacks. When you pull the magnet from the bearings, 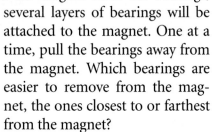 several layers of bearings will be attached to the magnet. One at a time, pull the bearings away from the magnet. Which bearings are easier to remove from the magnet, the ones closest to or farthest from the magnet?

Do you need more energy to pull the bearings farther from the magnet's poles or closest to the magnet's poles?

In the activity, you found that it takes more energy to remove the bearings that are closest to the magnet. The same is true for the electrons surrounding a nucleus. The electrons closest to the nucleus require the most energy to be separated from the nucleus. Electrons farther from the nucleus require less energy to be separated from the nucleus. Do you think the green glow in Crookes' tube was caused by electrons that had been close to or far from the nucleus of an atom?

Sulfur has 16 protons and 16 electrons. Two of these electrons are in the first energy level, eight are in the second energy level, and six are in the third energy level. The electron arrangement of sulfur is shown in Figure 5-18. Remember that, although the picture is flat, the electrons are actually spherical clouds.

You can represent the energy differences of electrons by picturing them on a flight of stairs. If the floor is the nucleus, then an electron on step 3 has more energy than an electron on step 1. The difference in heights between the steps is the difference in energy between the electrons. The atom differs from the model because the steps are not all of equal distance apart.

Because the electron cloud is spherical, the farther away the energy level is from the nucleus, the larger the energy level is and the more electrons that level can hold. Table 5-2 shows the maximum number of electrons that each of the first four energy levels can hold.

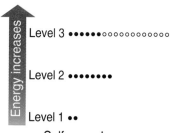

FIGURE 5-18. The diagram shows the location of electrons in the sulfur atom. More electrons can fit into the third level.

TABLE 5-2. Electrons in Energy Levels

Energy Level in Atom	Maximum Number of Electrons
1	2
2	8
3	18
4	32

ATOMS AND ELEMENTS

One of the really useful characteristics of our model of the atom is that it gives us a way to explain the wide variety of elements we can observe. Every atom of the same element has the same number of protons. It is the number of protons in an element's nucleus that distinguishes one element from another. Atoms of different elements have different numbers of protons. For example, look at Table 5-3. Every carbon atom has 6 protons. Furthermore, the model tells us that if an atom has 6 protons, it must have 6 electrons because there must be an equal number of positive and negative charges. This is because an atom is always neutral. It has no net charge. An oxygen atom has 8 protons. How many electrons does it have? What do you know about an atom that has 8 protons in its nucleus?

Because the mass of an electron is so small, the mass of a single atom is about equal to the number of particles in its nucleus. If a carbon atom has 6 protons and its mass is

COMPARE AND CONTRAST
Compare and contrast the parts of an atom. Include the following terms: *electron cloud, nucleus, electrons, protons, neutrons.* If you need help, refer to the **Skill Handbook** on page 685.

12, where will you find the remaining mass? What particle is responsible for the mass? The neutron. If an atom's mass is 12 and the number of protons is 6, then 6 neutrons provide the remaining mass. The mass of an oxygen atom is 16—its nucleus has 16 particles. How many neutrons does it have? Right, 8. In the next chapter, you'll use this idea to find out more about atoms.

FIGURE 5-19. Helium (a) copper, aluminum (b) sulfur, and nickel (c) are different because they have different numbers of protons in their nuclei.

TABLE 5-3. Number of Protons and Mass Number of Selected Elements

Element	Number of Protons	Mass Number
Hydrogen	1	1
Helium	2	4
Lithium	3	7
Beryllium	4	9
Boron	5	11
Carbon	6	12
Nitrogen	7	14
Oxygen	8	16
Fluorine	9	19
Neon	10	20
Sodium	11	23
Magnesium	12	24
Aluminium	13	27
Silicon	14	28
Phosphorus	15	31
Sulfur	16	32
Chlorine	17	35
Argon	18	40
Potassium	19	39
Calcium	20	40
Scandium	21	45
Titanium	22	48
Vanadium	23	51
Chromium	24	52

5-2
MODELS
OF ATOMIC
STRUCTURE

You have seen how models of the atom have changed. How can you make a model of an atomic structure?

PROBLEM
How can you use a model to predict similarities in atomic structure?

MATERIALS
magnetic board about
    20 cm x 27 cm
one 0.5-cm piece and 24
    2-cm pieces of rubber
    magnetic strips
circle of white paper 4 cm
    wide
marker

PROCEDURE
1. Copy the data table.
2. Use Table 5-3 to choose an element and determine the number of each kind of particle needed to make up an atom of that element.
3. Use a marker to write the number of protons and

neutrons on the paper circle. This represents the atom's nucleus.
4. Use a 0.5-cm magnetic strip to attach the model nucleus to one side of a magnetic board.
5. Use 2-cm magnetic strips to represent electrons. Arrange the model electrons around the nucleus.
6. Remove either the model nucleus or the model electrons from the magnetic board. Ask a classmate to **infer** the identity of the element.
7. Then, **observe** a classmate's board. To help you identify the element, complete the data table for each element you try.

8. Repeat Steps 2 through 6 for another element.

ANALYZE
1. In a neutral atom, **identify** which particles are always present in equal numbers.
2. **Predict** what would happen to the charge of an atom if one of the electrons were removed from the atom.

CONCLUDE AND APPLY
3. How is the model of an atom similar to an actual atom?
4. **Identify** two differences, other than size, between your model and an actual atom.
5. What happens to the atom if one proton and one electron are removed?
6. **Going Further:** Why are some models more helpful than others?

DATA AND OBSERVATIONS

ELEMENT	NUMBER OF PROTONS	NUMBER OF ELECTRONS	NUMBER OF NEUTRONS
1			
2			

FIGURE 5-20. Imagine trying to piece this puzzle together if some of the pieces were on the other side of the world.

In the Investigate, you used an atomic model to predict similarities in atomic structure and to identify an element by the number of protons in its nucleus. In the chapters to come, you will use similar models to explain the physical and chemical properties of elements, as well as the characteristics of solids, liquids, and gases.

This chapter presented the development of a model of the atom as if all the events came together in an orderly manner. You might get the impression that developing the atomic model was similar to several people working at the same time on a jigsaw puzzle. But the model of the atom did not come together that easily. Everyone was not working in the same room. Everyone did not know that he or she had a puzzle piece. The atomic puzzle pieces were in laboratories scattered throughout the world. Sometimes the results of an experiment—or accident—were not even recognized as part of the atomic puzzle. Remember Becquerel's film? At first, it did not seem at all related to Rutherford's or Thomson's work. However, newly reported results often lead researchers to re-examine their data and observations. As researchers reported their observations, the atomic model was revised and refined.

Remember, the model of the atom has been revised since the first theory was proposed by ancient Greeks. And while the model is based on previous observations, it must fit observations yet to come. It is possible that you may make observations during your career that will help further refine the atomic model.

Check Your Understanding

1. Describe the structure of the present model of an atom.
2. How did Rutherford model the atom after his famous scattering experiment was done?
3. Suppose you held a proton, a neutron, and an electron in your hand. How could you tell them apart?
4. **APPLY:** What kinds of experiments do you think were done to result in the subatomic particles or quarks?

|||||||EXPANDING YOUR VIEW||||||

CONTENTS

A **CLOSER** LOOK

YOUR NOSE KNOWS

Scientists use sophisticated equipment and complicated mathematical formulas to find out the size of particles. Those things are necessary when they are investigating atoms and tiny molecules, but we can find out some things about particle sizes with just a sniff.

For example, consider perfume or bleach bottles or hamburger wrappers. What if the particles that make up the perfume, the bleach, or the hamburger are smaller than the spaces between the particles of the glass, the plastic, or the paper that holds them? You would know what's inside the container by just sniffing. In the case of paper hamburger wrappers, that is true. Particles of chemicals in onions, meat, and even pickles can easily pass through the paper wrapper, so you can smell the hamburger before you unwrap it and take a bite.

There are experiments you can conduct to determine the relative size of particles. Place five to ten drops of vanilla extract into a balloon. Blow up the balloon and tie the end closed. You'll find that you can smell the vanilla through the inflated balloon. Because you can smell it, you know that the particles of the vanilla extract are smaller than the spaces between the particles of the balloon, so they can escape through the spaces between balloon particles.

If you put the balloon in your locker or a small room and leave it for a while, you will find that the vanilla odor continues to diffuse through the balloon walls and makes the space smell like vanilla.

The different sizes of particles are important in choosing containers for different materials. While you might enjoy the smell of a hamburger or vanilla, you wouldn't want the whole house to smell like bleach just because you want to do laundry!

WHAT DO YOU THINK?

Why do you think Mylar balloons are most often used to hold helium? Have you ever had a rubber balloon filled with helium? How did it change over a few days? What can you conclude about the particle size of helium, compared to the spaces between the particles of Mylar or rubber?

Physics Connection

QUIRK, QUORK, QUARK!

Scientists found that the atom was made up of neutrons, protons, and electrons. For some time afterward, they were happily convinced that they had discovered the smallest units of matter in the universe. As experimentation continued, however, scientists found even smaller particles within the nucleus of the atom. These particles are called quarks. Quarks have electric charges that are fractions. For example, the charge may be ⅓, -⅓, or ⅔, whereas electrons and protons always have whole-number charges.

The first quarks discovered were known as up, down, and strange. By 1990, three other types of quarks had been identified: charm, top, and bottom. All six names are used only for identification and tell nothing about the quark. Scientists lightheartedly refer to these six types as the flavors of quarks. Scientists continue to study atoms and may yet find still more quarks, or particles even smaller than quarks, as technology improves.

Murray Gell-Mann, one of the discoverers of quarks,

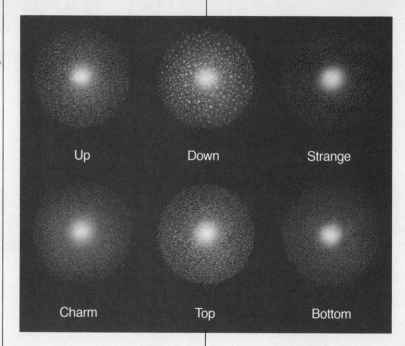

Up   Down   Strange

Charm   Top   Bottom

called them "quorks," a nonsense word by which he meant "those funny little things." Other scientists, noting their behavior, called them "quirks." Finally, Gell-Mann found a passage in James Joyce's book *Finnegan's Wake* that referred to "Three quarks for Master Mark!" He borrowed the

WHAT DO YOU THINK?

Think about an onion. Look at it from the outside. It looks solid. Peel off a layer, and you find another layer underneath. Layer after layer is revealed as one is peeled away. How does this compare with the atom model?

spelling of quark, and that is the name used now.

Quarks never appear alone in nature—they are always found in groups of two or more. When the idea of quarks was introduced in 1964, many scientists thought it an unlikely theory. Experiments much like those that led to the discovery of the nucleus proved that quarks did, indeed, exist. Today's models of quarks indicate that quarks have electrical charge, spin, and a type of strong charge called color charge. Scientists have now decided that quarks now come in six flavors, each of which can have one of three colors.

SCIENCE
A N D
SOCIETY

CAN YOU GIVE ME A FLOAT TO SCHOOL?

For centuries, people have dreamed of levitation—floating suspended in air. In ancient times, they imagined magic carpets that could whisk them anywhere they wanted to go. With the discovery of superconductivity, levitation may no longer be a fantasy.

Superconductivity is the conduction of electricity without the slightest power loss. Once electrons begin moving, they no longer have the problems associated with friction, resistance, and loss of power over long distances—they can move forever.

Scientists have known about superconductive material for a long time. The problem was that in order to have the ability to be superconductive the materials must be chilled to a few degrees above absolute zero. At this temperature, the movement of atoms slows almost to a standstill.

In 1986, however, a new era of superconducting science and technology began. Karl Alex Müller and Johann Georg Bednorz developed materials that were superconductive at much higher (although still very low) temperatures. Since then, scientists have continued to develop materials that are superconductive at higher temperatures. The goal is to develop a superconductor that will require no refrigeration at all.

One of the characteristics of superconductors allows a magnet to hover just above the material. This happens because the current moving through the supercondutor produces a magnetic field. This magnetic field repels the magnet, as shown in the photograph. It is this quality that makes levitation a real possibility in the future. Already the Japanese National Railways has built a prototype of experimental trains that levitate by carrying powerful superconducting magnets.

Scientists envision cars, toys, and furniture that can just float through the air. A physicist at a computer company says, "You could put on a pair of special shoes and make little tracks along which you as a human being could push yourself and keep going." With or without electric current, a chunk of superconductor placed above a magnet will settle calmly in midair. A chunk of magnet above a superconductor will also hang in the air.

When superconductors are developed that work at air temperature, the possibilities are limitless. However, as long as they must be cooled to extreme temperatures, the process is extremely expensive. Another problem scientists face in making levitation practical is finding out how to make objects move once they are suspended in space. Magnets, air jets, and muscle power are just three possibilities.

The test trains in Japan travel six to eight inches above their tracks at speeds of 200 to 300 miles per hour. They make almost no noise and, because the trains do not touch the tracks, there is no wear and tear on the trains or the tracks. Research continues on the trains, but the time may be soon when we can just rise up in the air and float wherever we need to go.

WHAT DO YOU THINK?

What applications can you think of for levitation? Imagine how such a capability would be used in schools, homes, and businesses. Would you want floating furniture? Why? What toys would you design making use of this technology?

*H*ealth
CONNECTION

NUCLEAR MEDICINE

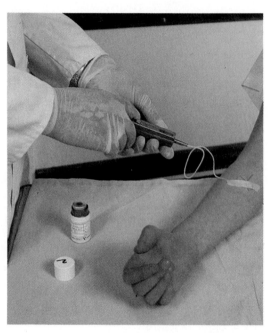

In its short history, nuclear energy has presented some terrible instances of death and destruction. On the other hand, millions of people owe their lives to the applications of nuclear energy in the diagnosis and treatment of a wide variety of diseases and disorders. Some of the simplest applications involve radioactive tracers.

Radioactive isotopes are used as tracers. In addition to its ability to emit radiation, a tracer must be nontoxic. That is, it must be a substance that can be introduced into the body without causing a dangerous reaction. The substance should be only a weak source of radiation. A stronger source could cause radiation sickness or destruction of healthy tissue. The material should have a relatively short half-life. A prolonged half-life would expose the patient to unnecessary radiation.

The isotope can be introduced into the patient's digestive, circulatory, or nervous system. Once introduced, the tracer emits radiation as it travels through the body. Physicians follow the path of the radiation to determine the location of any problems or abnormalities.

WHAT DO YOU THINK?

Do the benefits of nuclear energy to the field of medicine outweigh its negative, destructive uses? What would you think if you were in need of one of the applications of nuclear medicine?

TECHNOLOGY CONNECTION

RADON TESTING

In the past few years, many people began to worry that their homes might be hazardous to their health. Reports in the newspapers warned people that their homes might contain dangerous levels of radon.

Radon is a radioactive gas that is produced from uranium and thorium. Radon produces charged particles that are attracted to dust. When inhaled, these particles can produce a higher risk of cancer than normal. Some homes built over rocks containing uranium and thorium have been found to have high levels of radon gas.

The problem of radon gas in homes was discovered by accident. A construction worker helping to build a nuclear power plant in Pennsylvania kept setting off the radiation alarms at the plant. After it was found that he was not being exposed to radiation at work, investigators checked out his home. They found that his house was built on radioactive rocks that were filling the air in his home with radon gas.

There are also other sources of radon gas. Some modern lightning rods contain radon gas that can leak into the attics of homes.

Kits are now available to test for high radon levels. Most kits contain activated charcoal, which attracts radon particles. The kit is then sent to a laboratory for an interpretation of the results.

People who find that their homes contain high amounts of radon gas are advised to make modifications in their homes. In some cases, added ventilation solves the prob-

YOU TRY IT!

Get a radon testing kit either from your state or local health department. Check your home or school for radon gas. Usually, buildings that are well insulated collect gases more than those that are built off the ground or are not so tightly built. Compare the results of a test on a new building with those of a test on an old building.

lem. In other cases, walls, ceilings, or floors must be sealed against the gas.

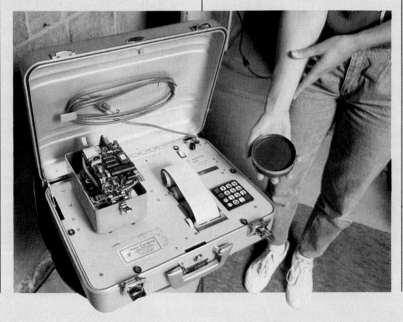

*L*iterature
C O N N E C T I O N

WISDOM IN MANY FORMS

"Our textbook said that 'atoms are the smallest particle in the universe.' And yet I knew from my tradition that 'There is nothing that is so small but that there is something smaller. There is nothing so large but that there is something larger'... When I asked my teacher, he answered 'You'd better give the answer in the book unless you want to be graded for error...Then down at the bottom of the page you can say anything you want to say...anything at all.' "

Three Strands in the Braid
by Paula Underwood

Sometimes we think of anything that cannot be proven as superstition. In some cases, however, after much study we learn that the superstition was right in the first place.

Scientists work to discover the secrets of the world. Sometimes they study atoms, sometimes rocks, sometimes human tissue. In every case, however, they are attempting to learn how things work and explain things we don't yet understand. Every scientist relies on the work of those who have gone before and builds on that information. Scientists rely on experimentation, intuition, lucky accidents, and education to develop new ideas and new products. Usually it is a combination of all those things that bring about important discoveries in science. In some cultures, however, tradition is a very important influence on what people believe about the world.

In her book, Paula Underwood tells of tribal ancestors who created Learning Stories. Each ancient story traditionally ended with the question of what may be learned from it. Listeners would be encouraged to exercise three ways of understanding the story—the way of the Mind, the Body, and the Spirit— to gain a deep and complete understanding. The three strands in the braid symbolized three ways of understanding, woven into a greater whole. Native American beliefs about the world and the universe were handed down through the telling of stories.

In some Native American cultures, there is a belief that nothing is so small that something else can't be smaller. When Paula Underwood was in school, scientists believed that the atom was the smallest unit of matter. Her own tradition, however, had taught her that although atoms were small, there were always smaller things.

WHAT DO YOU THINK?

Given what you have learned about quarks, what do you think of the Native American belief? How can you learn from many different kinds of wisdom?

Reviewing Main Ideas

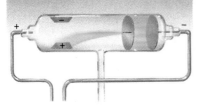

1. Using cathode-ray tubes, Thomson demonstrated the existence of a negatively charged particle he called the electron.

2. Rutherford observed the existence of alpha particles, beta particles, and gamma rays.

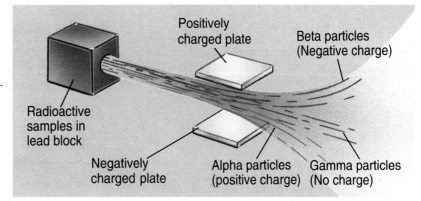

Positively charged plate

Beta particles (Negative charge)

Radioactive samples in lead block

Negatively charged plate

Alpha particles (positive charge)

Gamma particles (No charge)

3. Our model of the structure of the atom has been changed as new experiments provided more information.

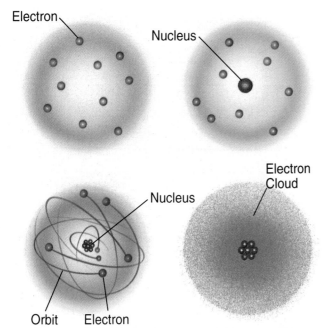

Electron

Nucleus

Nucleus

Electron Cloud

Orbit   Electron

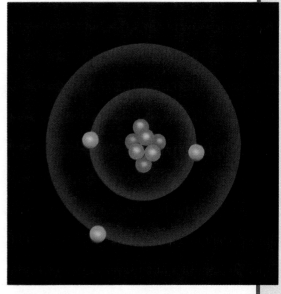

4. The atom consists of a nucleus containing protons and neutrons surrounded by electrons in energy levels within their electron cloud.

Chapter Review

USING KEY SCIENCE TERMS

alpha particle	neutron
beta particle	nucleus
electron	proton
gamma ray	radioactivity

For each set of terms below, choose the one term that does not belong and explain why it does not belong.

1. radioactivity, alpha particle, beta particle, gamma ray
2. electron, beta particle, gamma ray, negative charge
3. alpha particle, protons, neutrons, electron
4. radioactivity, proton, alpha particle, gamma ray
5. neutrons, radioactivity, protons, electron

UNDERSTANDING IDEAS

Choose the best answer to complete each sentence.

1. Because atoms have the same number of electrons and protons, atoms are _____.
   a. positively charged
   b. radioactively charged
   c. negatively charged
   d. neutral

2. The idea of an atom was first proposed by _____.
   a. John Dalton
   b. ancient Greeks
   c. Ernest Rutherford
   d. J. J. Thomson

3. In experiments, a beam of charged atomic particles will be bent by _____.
   a. an electric field
   b. wrapped photographic film
   c. a vacuum tube
   d. radioactivity

4. The particles given off by a radioactive atom come from the atom's _____.
   a. electrons   c. electron cloud
   b. nucleus   d. cathode rays

5. A 3-dimensional structure that represents an object too small to see is called _____.
   a. a model   c. a stable system
   b. an atom   d. radioactivity

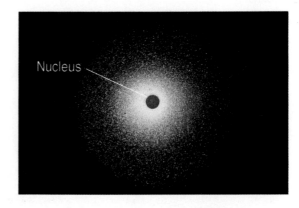

Nucleus

6. Not every atom of oxygen has the same number of _____.
   a. electrons   c. protons
   b. neutrons   d. alpha particles

7. A system that contains more energy than it can hold is said to be ____.
  a. radioactive **c.** unstable
  b. stable **d.** tracer

CRITICAL THINKING

Use your understanding of the concepts developed in the chapter to answer each of the following questions.

1. Three particles are fired into a box that is positively charged on one side and negatively charged on the other. The result is shown in the picture. Which particle is the proton? Which particle is the electron? Which particle is the neutron? Explain.

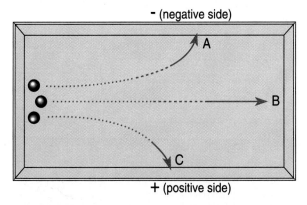

2. What evidence is there that the particles of matter are very small?

3. Radiologists at hospitals and clinics wear aprons that contain lead. Why?

4. If you wanted to repeat an experiment to test a hypothesis you didn't believe, what is most important for you to find out and do?

PROBLEM SOLVING

Read the following problem and discuss your answer in a brief paragraph.

Carbon-14 (14 particles in the nucleus) atoms are unstable. Carbon-14 is a radioactive form of carbon. Normal carbon atoms are carbon-12 (12 particles in the nucleus). It takes 5700 years for half the atoms in a sample of carbon-14 to release their extra energy and particles and become stable. In another 5700 years, half of the remaining atoms in the sample would become stable, and so on every 5700 years.

All living things have carbon atoms in them. Living organisms absorb some carbon-14 atoms from the atmosphere. When the organisms die, no new atoms are taken in. The carbon-14 atoms present begin to break down into stable atoms. How could these facts be used to determine the age of a mummy found in a newly discovered ancient Egyptian tomb?

CONNECTING IDEAS

1. What would happen to beta particles in an electric field? Explain.
2. What occurrence led Crookes to think that his green glow could be electromagnetic radiation?

3. PHYSICS CONNECTION Why do you think that quarks are always found in combination of two or more?
4. LITERATURE CONNECTION "This can't be true because science has never proven it."

Describe how you might respond to such a statement.
5. TECHNOLOGY CONNECTION What steps can be taken to reduce the level of radon in a home?

DID YOU EVER WONDER . . .

How the pioneers made soap?

Why racing bicycles are so light?

What is used to mark the white
lines on baseball diamonds and
football fields?

You'll find the answers to these questions as you read this chapter.

The Periodic Table

The repeated pattern in a beaded necklace, the movement of a clock pendulum, a playground swing, and the seasons—all have something in common. What do you think it is? Remember the last time you sat on a swing and moved back and forth, over and over, in a regularly repeating pattern?

What kind of patterns exist in the examples above? In the necklace, it is the colors of gems. In the swing, it is the height and direction of the seat. In the seasons, the pattern could be the number of daylight hours or the growth of trees and plants. Your brain always looks for such patterns—patterns in the properties of things. That is how you make sense of the world.

In this chapter, you will discover some similarities and patterns among elements. You'll also see how the elements can be placed in a pattern based on their characteristics.

EXPLORE!

Can you organize your classmates?

Identify the different characteristics of your classmates. In addition to physical appearance, don't forget things like birth month, date, or

telephone number. Be creative. Use your list to arrange your classmates in some pattern. Compare your arrangement to that of others.

6-1 Structure of the Periodic Table

OBJECTIVES

In this section, you will

- describe the arrangement of the elements in the periodic table;
- find the number of protons and electrons in an atom using the periodic table;
- explain atomic number;
- identify mass number and calculate atomic mass.

KEY SCIENCE TERMS

periodic table
atomic number
mass number
isotopes
atomic mass

FIGURE 6-1. Materials for new products are chosen because they have the most useful set of properties.

DECISIONS, DECISIONS!

You've been asked to design a new product for a very large and successful company. You'd like to know what properties the product must have to work well and sell well for the company. You find out that the material must be lightweight, strong, flexible, and resistant to heat and weather. How do you decide what to use? One way would be to obtain a list of all the thousands of available substances and start checking out their properties. Wow! What a job! Perhaps if you started with the elements in these substances, you could at least narrow the list down to a hundred or so.

You may remember from learning about elements that metals have many of the desired properties, but that still leaves a lot of work. Wouldn't it be nice if someone arranged those elements so that you could quickly find the one you want? Because it would be pretty hard to get samples of all the elements, let's try to develop a good strategy for arranging and identifying characteristics of elements by arranging something more common instead.

INVESTIGATE!

You classify things and people every day. Edible, tall, red, hard, smart, magnetic—these are all properties used to put things in groups. Let's find out how a scientist can use this tool.

PROBLEM

How can you arrange properties to **predict** and explain?

MATERIALS

squares of paper with numbers from 0 through 45

PROCEDURE

1. Place your squares faceup on the table in front of you. Imagine you had never before seen the squares organized in any meaningful way. You know that the numbers have some things in common and that they are different in other ways. You have two jobs. One is to organize the squares in a way that organizes their properties, and the other is to identify the one square that is missing.

2. Put the squares in order. Try to do this in one long row. You may have to move to the floor to do this.

3. Although you probably already know which square is missing, you aren't yet finished. How would you arrange your squares in several rows, without changing the order in which you already have them? The idea is to arrange them so that every square in a row has something in common, and every square in a column has something in common. Where would you break your original arrangement and begin a new row? Do this now.

4. Continue until you have used all the squares. Remember, you can't change the order you have them in already.

ANALYZE

1. What pattern did you use to organize your squares the first time?

2. When you completed your arrangement of rows and columns, what properties did the squares in a row have in common? In a column?

CONCLUDE AND APPLY

3. **Predict** the properties of the missing square.

4. **Observe** and **infer** which property of the numbers shows a repeating pattern.

5. **Going Further:** If you were able to arrange the elements as you did the numbers, **predict** what properties you might use to group them.

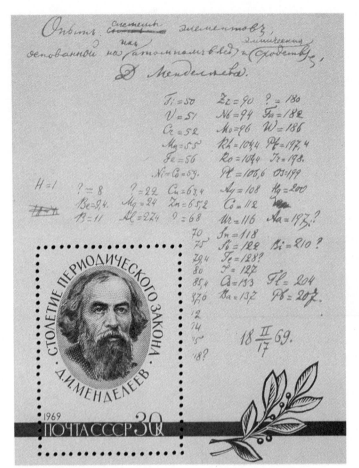

FIGURE 6-2. This is one of Mendeleev's early periodic tables.

You were able to arrange familiar numbers by using properties and repeating patterns in those properties. These properties were the beginning and ending numbers. If the numbers were elements, they would have many other properties, such as flexibility, resistance to heat, strength, and ability to combine with other elements. They could be organized in a very similar way, and you'd now be able to predict which elements would have the properties you want to make your revolutionary new product.

In the late 1800s, as more and more elements were discovered, the need arose to arrange them into a pattern that would simplify their study. Dmitri Mendeleev, a Russian chemist, searched for a meaningful way to organize the elements. He decided to put them in order of increasing masses.

When Mendeleev put the elements in order by mass, he found that other properties, such as density, malleability, and the ability to react with other elements, seemed to repeat over and over. This repeating pattern is called periodic, and he called his table the **periodic table** of the elements.

Recall that you were able to predict the properties of the missing number from your table. Mendeleev was able, in the same way, to predict properties of elements that hadn't yet been discovered.

DID YOU KNOW?

Mendeleev, the youngest of more than 12 children, was born in Siberia. Although he wasn't a very good high school student, he graduated at the top of his class from college.

ARRANGEMENT OF THE PERIODIC TABLE

Mendeleev arranged the elements by increasing mass. When he did this, some of the elements seemed to be out of order. The periodic table we use today takes care of that problem.

Recall what you learned about atoms in the last chapter. Atoms are composed of protons, neutrons, and electrons. Each element has one more proton in its nucleus than the one before it. The number of protons (positive charges) in an atom of an element is called the **atomic number** of the element. Since atoms are electrically neutral, there must be the same number of electrons (negative charges) in the atom as there are protons. The atomic number, then, tells you both the number of protons and the number of electrons. The modern periodic table shown in Appendix E is arranged in order of increasing atomic number.

Look at the information given in one box of the periodic table, shown in Figure 6-3. This box represents the element boron. The box contains the atomic number (5), the chemical symbol (B), the name, and the atomic mass (10.811) of the element. What do we mean by atomic mass?

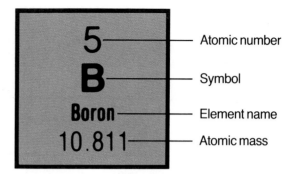

FIGURE 6-3. This is a sample representation of the element boron in the periodic table.

ATOMIC MASS

Let's say that you have a carton of eggs that contains six white eggs and six brown eggs. Someone asks you the mass of the carton of eggs. Not having a balance, you have to think fast. You decide that each egg has about the same mass and the carton is very light by comparison, so you decide to measure the *mass* of the eggs in terms of the *number* of eggs. In other words, you define the mass of an egg as one *egg mass unit (e)*. You tell the person that the mass of the carton of eggs is twelve! Twelve egg mass units—12 *e*!

Since atoms are so small, the easiest way to describe their mass is by describing the total number of protons and neutrons in the nucleus—the **mass number**. Protons and neutrons are like the brown and white eggs. They

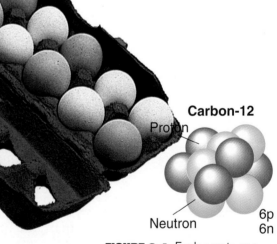

FIGURE 6-4. Each egg is one egg mass unit (e). Each particle (proton or neutron) is one atomic mass unit (u). The mass of this carbon atom is 12 u.

FIGURE 6-5. Each chocolate has a mass of 1 c. Each peanut has a mass of 2 c. What is the total mass of the candy?

have different properties, but just about the same mass. If there are 6 protons and 6 neutrons in the nucleus, you say that the mass of the atom is 12 atomic mass units (u). Why aren't the electrons included? Even if we counted all the electrons in the biggest atom, their total mass would be only a fraction of the mass of a proton.

If an atom has a mass number of 23 and contains 12 neutrons, how many protons does it have? In other words, what is its atomic number, and what element is it? Remember that the mass number, 23, is the total number of protons and neutrons in the nucleus. If 12 of them are neutrons, how many are protons? 23–12=11 protons. That is the atomic number. Find that number on the periodic table. The element is Na—sodium.

Try this. An atom has 9 protons and 10 neutrons. Look at the periodic table and figure out what element it is. Use the number of protons—the atomic number. What element has an atomic number of 9? Fluorine!

What is the mass number of this atom? That's right—19. What if you looked for the mass number on the table? Oops! There is no element with a mass number of 19. Fluorine is listed at 18.998. And 18.998 is called the atomic mass, not the mass number. Are atomic mass and mass number the same? If so, how come the atomic mass is not a whole number when you are counting protons and neutrons? Are there pieces of protons and neutrons?

ISOTOPES

Imagine that you have 100 pieces of candy-coated chocolates and peanuts. Sixty of these pieces are chocolates, each having a mass of 1 candy mass unit, and 40 of them are peanuts, each with a mass of 2 candy mass units. First, what is the total mass of the 100 pieces of candy? Let's call a candy mass unit *c*.

$$
\begin{array}{ll}
60 \times 1\ c & = 60\ c \\
\underline{40 \times 2\ c} & \underline{= 80\ c} \\
100\ \text{pieces} & =140\ c
\end{array}
$$

Now, what is the *average* mass of one piece?

$$140\ c/100\ \text{pieces}=1.4\ c/\text{piece}$$

Proton

Neutron

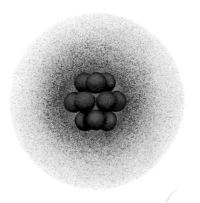
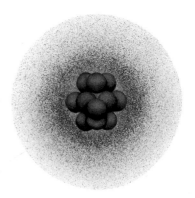

FIGURE 6-6. Two isotopes of boron.

Atoms of the same element always have the same number of protons—their atomic number. That is what identifies them as the element they are. But all atoms of the same element don't necessarily have the same number of neutrons. For example, boron is a dark, gray powder. All boron atoms have 5 protons. Four-fifths of them have 6 neutrons. What is their mass number? The other one-fifth of all boron atoms found in nature have 5 neutrons. What is their mass number? Atoms of the same element with different numbers of neutrons are called **isotopes** of that element. The two isotopes of boron discussed above are referred to as boron-11 and boron-10. The numbers indicate the mass number of that isotope.

If you have 100 boron atoms, what is their *average* mass? Well, it would be closer to 11 than to 10, because there are more boron atoms with a mass of 11 than there are with a mass of 10.

$$4/5 \times 100 \text{ atoms} = 80 \text{ atoms}$$
$$1/5 \times 100 \text{ atoms} = 20 \text{ atoms}$$
$$80 \text{ atoms} \times 11 \text{ u/atom} = 880 \text{ u}$$
$$20 \text{ atoms} \times 10 \text{ u/atom} = \underline{200 \text{ u}}$$
$$100 \text{ atoms} = 1080 \text{ u}$$
$$1080 \text{ u}/100 \text{ atoms} = 10.8 \text{ u/atom}$$

Notice the atomic mass shown for boron on the periodic table. The **atomic mass** is the average mass of the isotopes of an element found in nature. This is why atomic masses are not whole numbers.

Let's investigate more about the way isotopes and atomic mass are related.

SKILLBUILDER

SEQUENCING
What changes in the periodic table would occur in periods 1 through 4 if the elements were arranged according to increasing average atomic mass instead of atomic number? How do we know that arrangement by atomic number is correct? If you need help, refer to the **Skill Handbook** on page 680.

6-2
ISOTOPES AND ATOMIC MASS

In this Investigate, you'll use a model of isotopes to help you understand the concept of atomic mass.

PROBLEM
How do isotopes affect average atomic mass?

MATERIALS
4 red and 3 green candy-coated peanuts
2 red and 3 green candy-coated chocolates

PROCEDURE
1. Copy the data table.
2. Make a pile of four red candy-coated peanuts and two red candy-coated chocolates. The two different kinds of candy represent two isotopes of the same element.
3. Assume that a red peanut has a mass of 2 candy units, and a red chocolate has a mass of 1 candy unit.

Carbon-14

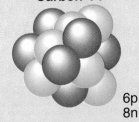

6p
8n

Calculate the average mass of the red candy as follows:

a. Multiply the number of red peanuts by the mass in candy units.

b. Multiply the number of red chocolates by the mass in candy units.

c. Add the masses and divide by the total number of candies.

4. Repeat Steps 2 and 3, but use three green peanuts and three green chocolates. Assume a green peanut has a mass of 4

units, and a green chocolate has a mass of 3 units.

5. Record your calculations.

ANALYZE
1. There were six red and six green candies. Why were their average masses not the same?
2. If a sample of element X contains 100 atoms of X-12 and 10 atoms of X-14, what is the average mass of X?

CONCLUDE AND APPLY
3. An element needed for most nuclear reactors is uranium. Its two major isotopes are U-235 and U-238. Look up the mass of uranium on the periodic table. **Infer** which isotope is the most common. Explain.
4. **Compare and contrast** mass number and atomic mass.
5. **Going Further:** Hydrogen has three isotopes. The most common one, protium, has no neutrons. Deuterium, the second isotope, has one neutron. Tritium has two neutrons. Using this information, calculate the mass number of these isotopes.

DATA AND OBSERVATIONS

	PEANUT	CHOCOLATE	AVERAGE
	(candy x candy unit)	(candy x candy unit)	(total mass) (total candies)
Red			
Green			

In the Investigate, you used a candy mass unit as a model for atomic mass. The calculations you used to find the average candy mass are similar to the calculations you used to find the atomic mass of an element. Some elements may have only identical atoms. On the other hand, several elements have as many as 6 or 7 isotopes. The atomic mass is found by calculating the average mass of a sample of atoms. Carbon has 6 isotopes, with mass numbers ranging from 10 to 15. However, almost 99 percent of carbon atoms have 6 protons and 6 neutrons—mass number 12. This is referred to as carbon-12. An atom of carbon with 8 neutrons is called carbon-14.

The days of the week, the pendulum of a clock, and multiplication tables—all occur in repeating patterns that are periodic. You've seen how we can organize elements into a table that shows repeating patterns of properties. How can we use this table to explain and predict the behavior of matter? In the next section, you'll take a closer look at the organization of the periodic table and how it is used.

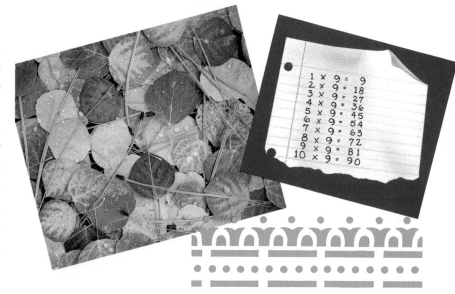

FIGURE 6-7. Patterns are all around us. Besides the items shown, what other patterns are you familiar with?

Check Your Understanding

1. How does the arrangement of the modern periodic table differ from Mendeleev's table?
2. Use the periodic table to find the name, atomic number, and atomic mass of the following elements: O, N, Ca, Ba, and Br.
3. What are three pieces of information that you can learn from an element's atomic number?

4. **APPLY:** Complete the following table.

Symbol	Atomic No.	Mass No.
N	7	
F		19
K		39
Co		59

6-2 Families of Elements

OBJECTIVES

In this section, you will

- identify a family of elements;
- recognize the alkali family;
- describe the alkaline earth family.

KEY SCIENCE TERMS

family of elements
alkali metals
alkaline earth metals

ORGANIZING THE ELEMENTS

We began this chapter by using properties to organize elements in a way that would allow us to quickly locate them and to predict other properties. These might be density, malleability, conductivity, or any other chemical or physical characteristics of the element. What else do the elements have in common?

FIND OUT!

How are elements alike and different?

Select two elements from the list provided by your teacher. For each of your chosen elements, prepare an index card. In the upper left-hand corner of the card, place a box like the one on the periodic table. This should show the atomic number, symbol, name, and atomic mass of the element. Do some research on the element and write a few sentences about its properties and uses. Attach either an object or a picture to the card that shows its properties. For example, for iron, you could attach a nail. For helium, you might have a picture of a floating balloon. Make a large periodic table using your cards and those of your classmates.

```
26
Fe
Iron
55.847
```

Conclude and Apply

1. What do you notice about the properties of elements on the left side of your table?
2. What about the right side?

Study the properties of the elements in the first column of your table. Do they seem to have some properties or characteristics in common? What are they?

On the periodic table, elements in the same column are called a **family of elements**. Look at Family 11 on the periodic table. Do you recognize the three elements? Copper, silver, and gold are the coinage metals. Although they are different colors, they have similar physical and chemical properties. They are all malleable, shiny, and resistant to change.

Recall that the noble gases—helium, neon, and argon—were called noble because, like royalty refusing to associate with common people, these elements rarely combine with other elements. Find these elements on the periodic table. What other elements would you expect to behave in the same way? On the other hand, members of Family 17, the halogens, are very reactive. They often combine with other elements.

You've seen that elements in the same family have similar properties. But why? As you recall from Chapter 5, the electrons in an atom are arranged in energy levels around the nucleus. Figure 6-9 shows atoms of several elements. The number of electrons in the outer energy level of an atom determines if and how an element will combine with other elements. These outer electrons are so important that a special system is used to represent them.

A dot diagram is simply the symbol for an element surrounded by as many dots as there are electrons in the outer energy level. How can you tell how many electrons there will be? If you skip the elements in Families 3 through 12 on your periodic table, the other columns have a very simple pattern. There will be one electron in the outer level of column 1, two in column 2, three in column 13, and so on

FIGURE 6-8. Jewelry is often made of copper, silver, and gold. These elements are members of the same family.

FIGURE 6-9. Electrons are arranged in energy levels around the nucleus.

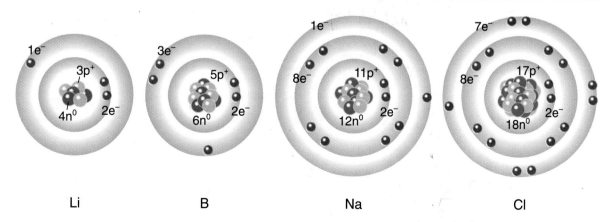

Li   B   Na   Cl

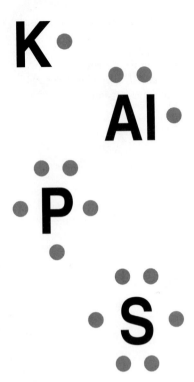

FIGURE 6-10. These are dot diagrams for potassium, aluminum, phosphorus and sulfur.

until you reach column 18, which has eight electrons in the outer level. The pattern of outer electrons is simply one through eight. How many electrons are in the last energy level of the halogens? They are in Family 17, so it's seven. Figure 6-10 shows examples of dot diagrams.

How would you write dot diagrams for the element sulfur? First, write the symbol for the element—S. Then look at its position on the periodic table. What column is it in? Family 16. How many electrons does it have in its outer energy level? Using the pattern mentioned above, we see that it has six. When the dots representing the electrons are drawn around the symbol, they are typically placed as follows: for elements with one to four electrons, the dots are drawn unpaired. They are not arranged in a circle, but rather as if there were four sides to the symbol. Study the dot diagrams in Figure 6-10 to see examples. When there are more than four electrons, the first four are placed unpaired on the four sides of the symbol, then any remaining electrons are paired. If there are six electrons, there will be two paired and two unpaired electrons.

Notice that, with the exception of helium, all of the noble gases have eight electrons in their outer energy level. Once eight is reached, the next element adds an energy level and begins again with one electron. It would seem that the presence of eight electrons makes the energy level full, or complete. You know that noble gases do not combine easily with other elements. They seem very stable—that is, they resist change.

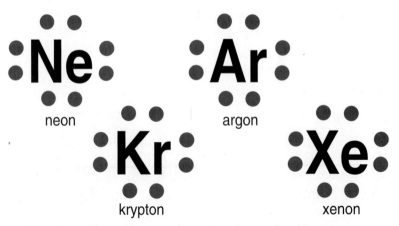

FIGURE 6-11. The noble gases have complete and stable outer energy levels.

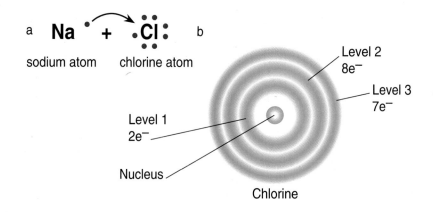

a **Na** · + · **Cl** : b

sodium atom   chlorine atom

Level 1
2e⁻

Nucleus

Chlorine

Level 2
8e⁻

Level 3
7e⁻

FIGURE 6-12. The dot diagram (a) helps us to see how sodium and chlorine combine. The cloud diagram (b) reminds us of how the electrons of chlorine surround the nucleus.

By observation, we find that when other elements combine, they tend to do so in a way that will give them eight electrons in their outer energy level. Let's look at one example. Figure 6-12(a) shows dot diagrams of an atom of sodium and an atom of chlorine. If the sodium gives its electron to chlorine, how many electrons will chlorine have in its outer level? Look at Figure 6-12(b). How many will sodium have after it loses that electron?

In Figure 6-12, one sodium atom (Na) combines with one chlorine atom (Cl). Each ends up with eight electrons in its outer energy level. They form a compound, sodium chloride (NaCl). You've just made salt!

There is an exception to this rule of having eight electrons in the outer level. Hydrogen and helium are so small that they have only one energy level. In this first energy level, there is only room for two electrons. Therefore, the noble gas helium is complete with two electrons in its outer energy level. When elements such as lithium (Li) and beryllium (Be) lose their outer electrons, their outer levels become like helium, and they are stable.

ALKALI METALS

What other elements would you expect to combine with chlorine as sodium does? Right! The other Family 1 elements. Since each element has one outer electron to lose, they all behave in the same way. What other elements, in addition to chlorine, would you expect to react with sodium?

The Column 1 elements belong to a family known as the **alkali metals**. They differ from metals you are used to

DID YOU KNOW?

Compounds of sodium are used in the manufacture of detergents and soaps. Pioneers made soap by collecting water that ran through ashes and cooking it with grease. The water contained sodium hydroxide. Alkali means to roast ashes in a pan.

FIGURE 6-13. The alkali metals are very reactive. This photo shows a small bead of sodium reacting with water.

because they are so soft they can be cut with a knife. However, they do have a metallic luster, conduct heat and electricity, and are malleable.

If you look for pure alkali metals in nature, you won't find them. When an alkali metal atom is in the presence of anything with which it will combine, it immediately reacts. To keep them in their pure state, alkali metals must be stored in kerosene or some other liquid that doesn't react with them. This keeps them from immediately reacting with air, water, or other substances in the environment.

ALKALINE EARTH METALS

The second vertical column of elements is the **alkaline earth metals**. Study this column on the periodic table your class made from index cards. In what ways do their properties seem different from those of the alkali metals?

Look at the picture in Figure 6-14. It shows a reaction between magnesium nitrate and a solution of baking soda. What do you expect will happen if strontium nitrate were added to a baking soda solution? What other nitrates should behave in the same way?

You've probably heard of magnesium. It's often used in alloys with aluminum. Your bike may be made of a magnesium aluminum alloy. Recall that an alloy is a uniform mixture of metals. These alloys may also be used in tennis rackets and backpack frames because they are strong and lightweight.

Magnesium is also used to produce the brilliant white flash in many flashbulbs and as part of spectacular Fourth-of-July displays. On a more personal level, it's found in the milk of magnesia that you or your family may use as an antacid or mild laxative.

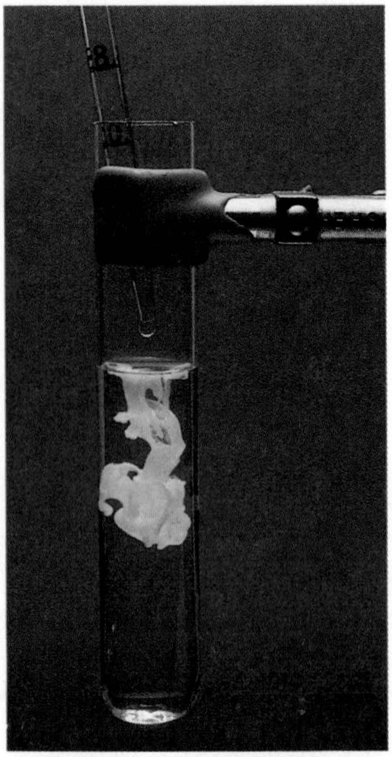

You might be surprised to find calcium in the alkaline earth family. Found in dairy products, it's an essential building block for strong bones and teeth. Calcium

FIGURE 6-14. This white solid forms when magnesium nitrate and baking soda react.

FIGURE 6-15. These racers would have to work much harder if their bikes were made of steel.

hydroxide is a white powder that you may have seen used to mark the lines of a baseball diamond or football field. Gardeners often use it to reduce the acidity of soil because it is a base and will neutralize the acid in soil. Another compound of calcium, calcium chloride, is used in winter to keep ice from forming on roads and walks.

Because members of a chemical family share the same number of outer electrons, they also share their ability to form compounds with other elements. Rather than having to test each individual element, you can simply look at the periodic table and identify the family to which an element belongs. Then you can predict how it will behave and how it might be used.

Check Your Understanding

1. List four of the elements in Family 16 of the periodic table. Draw dot diagrams for them.
2. Compare and contrast the properties of alkali metals and alkaline earth metals.
3. **APPLY:** An element is shiny, but easily cut with a knife. When dropped in water, it reacts immediately, giving off a flash of light. It is placed in a container with another element that is a gas. Nothing happens. What families would you guess these two elements are in? Explain your answer.

odic
Vhat
tion
Do
ble

EY SCIENCE TERMS

period

FIND OUT!

How can you use a table of repeating events to predict or explain?

The figure shows a familiar table of repeating properties. What is it? Of course, it's a calendar, but one with a difference. This calendar has some missing information. You can determine what is missing by examining the information surrounding the spot where the missing information goes. This periodic table is made up of families of days, Sunday through Saturday, and by horizontal periods called weeks.

Sun	Mon	Tue	Wed		Fri	Sat
				1	2	3
4	5	6	7	8	9	10
11	12	@	#	15	16	17
18	19	20	21	22	23	24
25	26	27	28	29	30	31

Conclude and Apply

1. Two of the days in Families 3 and 4 are marked with an @ and a #. What dates should go in these positions? Explain.
2. Family 5 doesn't have a name. What is the correct name for this family?
3. What dates are included in the third period of the table?
4. Assuming that the previous month had 30 days, what day would the 28th of that month have been? What period of this table would it appear in?

10	11	12	13	14	15	16	17	18	19
Ne	**Na**	**Mg**	**Al**	**Si**	**P**	**S**	**Cl**	**Ar**	**K**
Neon	Sodium	Magnesium	Aluminum	Silicon	Phosphorus	Sulfur	Chlorine	Argon	Potassium
20	21	22	23	24	25	26	27	28	29
Ca	**Sc**	**Ti**	**V**	**Cr**	**Mn**	**Fe**	**Co**	**Ni**	**Cu**
Calcium	Scandium	Titanium	Vanadium	Chromium	Manganese	Iron	Cobalt	Nickel	Copper

FIGURE 6-16. The second row and third row of Investigate 6-1 are each a period.

The calendar is just one example of a table of periodic events. Recall that in the first Investigate, the properties of the numbers changed gradually as you moved across a row. Each number increased by one—from 0 to 9. But at this point, both the first and last number changed. You began a new row as the pattern repeated, increasing again from 0 to 9. One repeat of this pattern is called a **period**.

On the periodic table of elements, each row begins as the pattern of physical and chemical properties of elements begins to repeat itself. When arranged in this manner, the 100+ known elements form 7 horizontal rows. These rows are called periods because of the periodic repetition of properties as you move from left to right. Breaking the sequence of elements into periods created 18 columns called families. This is similar to the calendar in the Find Out activity.

METALS AND NONMETALS

On the periodic table, locate the stair-step line toward the right side. Notice that it divides the table, though not in half. The elements to the left of this line are metals, except hydrogen. Notice that the box containing hydrogen is slightly above the rest of the table. Although hydrogen has one electron in its outer energy level, you might also say that it has one less than it needs to become nonreactive like helium. In that case, it would be placed at the top of the halogen family. As you know, hydrogen is a gas and has properties of a nonmetal. It is placed in Family 1 because the formulas for its compounds are similar to those formed by Family 1 elements.

You've learned that most metals are solid at room temperature, shiny, and good conductors of heat and electricity. In your index card periodic table, locate examples of metals you are familiar with, such as iron, zinc, copper, and silver.

SKILLBUILDER

CLASSIFYING
Use the periodic table in Appendix E to name and classify the following elements into families: If you need help, refer to the **Skill Handbook** on page 680.
K Cu Cr C Sn Li
As F Na Pb Ag I
1. How many families of elements are represented here?
2. How many periods of elements are represented here?
3. What is the atomic number of carbon?

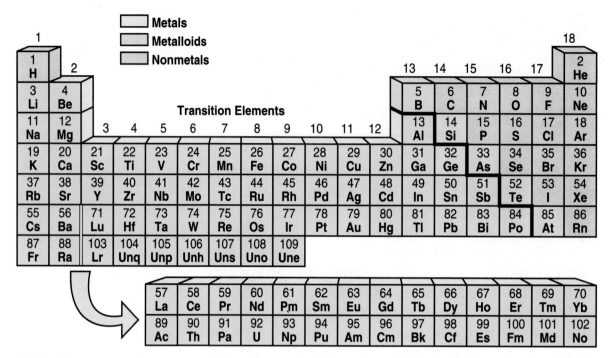

FIGURE 6-17. Every element to the left of the line is a metal, except hydrogen and three metalloids.

Elements in Families 3 through 12 are called transition elements. They include many of the metals found in objects you use every day.

Now examine the elements to the right of the stair-step line. You should recognize these as the nonmetals. Many of them are gases. The solids, such as carbon and sulfur, are easily crushed and do not shine.

You know that the properties of elements change gradually as they move from left to right. Therefore, there is no quick change from metal to nonmetal. Instead, on either side of the stair-step line is a special group of elements called metalloids. You learned earlier that these elements have some properties of both metals and nonmetals. They are dull rather than lustrous. They are not malleable or ductile, but they conduct a current. Silicon and germanium are examples of metalloids. Because metalloids do not conduct as well as a metal, they are called semiconductors. As you already know, these elements are used to make transistors, integrated circuits, and other critical parts of electronic devices, such as portable radios, computers, and video games.

Where are the elements in the table that are most likely to react? Well first, let's separate the metals and non-

FIGURE 6-18. Shown here are samples of the transition elements. From left to right in the first row are scandium, titanium, vanadium, chromium, and manganese. From left to right in the back row are cobalt, nickel, copper, and zinc.

metals. You learned that the metals in Family 1, or alkali metals, are so reactive that they are never found uncombined in nature. Of the alkali metals, those nearest the bottom are the most active. The most active metals are in the lower left corner of the periodic table. Their outer electrons are so far away from the nucleus that the attraction between the electrons and the protons is much weaker. Therefore, these elements easily lose electrons.

FIGURE 6-19. Your knowledge of the periodic table can help you understand why chlorine spills are dangerous.

The opposite is true of the nonmetals. If you don't count the noble gases, Family 18, the most active nonmetals are found in the upper right corner. Recall that nonmetals gain electrons from other elements, rather than losing them. Since the nucleus is positive and will attract electrons, the closer the outer energy level is to the nucleus, the easier it is for the atom to attract electrons. In the case of fluorine, the outer energy level is closer to the nucleus than any of the larger atoms in Family 17.

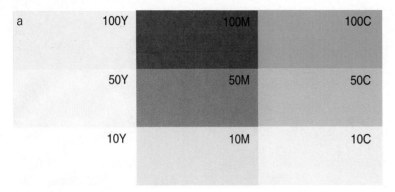

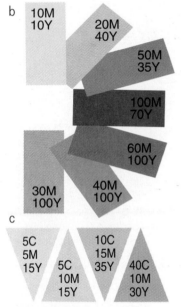

FIGURE 6-20. By following the color pattern in chart (a), paint or ink manufacturers can create the colors in chart (b) and (c).

Therefore, fluorine is the most active nonmetal.

You've taken a short trip through the periodic table. If you had the task of designing the new product mentioned at the beginning of the chapter, you can see how it would be simplified by using the table.

But you may have noticed that there's one section we haven't discussed. What are those two rows doing down at the bottom of the table? The atomic numbers would indicate they should be placed between Families 2 and 3 in periods 6 and 7. Why aren't they there? Simple—the table wouldn't fit on the page! The table is made more compact and useful by placing them at the bottom.

As you continue your education, you'll find that organizing information according to systematic patterns can help you study, learn, and recall important facts more easily. Lists and tables are one way to do this. You're sure to discover other methods of organization that will also work well for you. Even now, you can probably recall the names of families of elements that appear in columns one, two, and eighteen of the periodic table. Working with an organized system can make studying fun. You may want to experiment with a system something like this in some of your other classes.

Check Your Understanding

1. What happens to the atomic number as you follow a period across the periodic table? Why is it called a period?
2. Locate the positions on the periodic table for metals, nonmetals, and metalloids. Sequence these three categories from the one containing the largest number of elements to the smallest.
3. Give the period and family in which each of the following elements are found: nitrogen, sodium, iodine, and mercury. Tell whether the element is a metal, nonmetal, or transition element.
4. **APPLY:** Which element is more reactive?
   a. potassium or magnesium
   b. phosphorus or chlorine
   Explain your answer.

CONTENTS

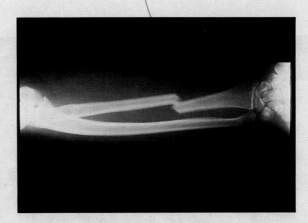

A CLOSER LOOK

MEDICAL USES OF RADIATION

Although people are concerned about the possible health risks due to radiation, doctors sometimes choose to expose their patients to radiation. The earliest and best-known medical use of radiation involves X rays. X rays travel easily through most body tissue but are stopped by bone. X rays help locate breaks in the bones.

Radioactive isotopes release radiation that can be measured. The measurements can then be interpreted by a computer and a picture of soft tissue such as the brain, kidneys, and lungs is produced. In this way doctors can determine the extent of a tumor or other abnormality.

Radioactive isotopes can also be used to determine—very precisely— how much of a virus, hormone, or drug is in a patient's body. The technique, radioimmunoassay (RIA), was pioneered in the 1950s by Rosalyn Yalow and Soloman Berson. Yalow was awarded a Nobel Prize for her work. In an RIA test, the patient is given a precise amount of a radioactive compound. Compounds used in the test are chosen for their ability to take the place of the virus, hormone, or drug normally present in the body's fluids. Then a precise measurement of the radioactivity given off by the patient's blood or urine is made. By comparing the measurements, physicians can determine the amount of the substance under study present in a patient's body. For example, it was widely believed that diabetes was a condition that resulted from a total lack of insulin in the patient's blood. RIA showed that diabetes can occur even if insulin is present.

RIA has been used successfully to treat diabetes, reduce the risk of transmitting hepatitis in transfused blood, and in identifying infectious diseases such as tuberculosis.

WHAT DO YOU THINK?

Survey the members of your family to learn if any of them have had any radiation treatment. How does that make you feel about the dangers of radiation?

LIFE SCIENCE CONNECTION

THE CHERNOBYL DISASTER

History's worst accident at a nuclear power plant occurred on April 26, 1986, in Chernobyl in the Soviet Union. This reactor used graphite to regulate the nuclear reaction, and water to carry the thermal energy to the turbine, which then produced electrical energy. On that day, the water flow past the core (where the nuclear reaction occurs) was stopped. Part of the reactor got so hot that the graphite caught fire and caused an explosion that ripped apart the reactor and released large amounts of radioactive material into the atmosphere. At least 31 people died from radiation sickness or burns. Many more may die in the coming years as a result of this accident.

People who lived in the Soviet Union were not the only ones affected by the Chernobyl disaster. Some radioactive material was carried by wind into northern and central Europe. Health experts in Europe were particularly concerned about strontium-90, an isotope of the element strontium that has a half-life of 28 years.

If you look at the periodic table, you will notice that strontium is just beneath calcium. Elements that belong to the same group in the periodic table have many similar characteristics. Strontium, therefore, can take the place of calcium in many chemical reactions.

Our bones are made up almost entirely of calcium. If strontium-90 enters the human body, it replaces some of that calcium and exposes the bones to radiation. Constant exposure to this type of radiation can seriously damage bone marrow, causing diseases such as leukemia.

Strontium-90 enters our bodies the same way that calcium enters our bodies. When grass grows, it absorbs calcium from the soil. Cows eat the grass and produce milk. When we drink milk or eat milk products, such as butter and cheese, our bodies absorb the calcium.

That's why, in the aftermath of the Chernobyl explosion, European health officials carefully monitored the level of strontium-90 in milk. Some milk had to be thrown away because it contained too much of the radioactive material.

WHAT DO YOU THINK?

Many people were evacuated from the vicinity of the Chernobyl nuclear power plant when it caught fire in 1986. From what you've learned about strontium-90, do you think they have been allowed to return?

SCIENCE AND SOCIETY

SYNTHETIC ELEMENTS

You could take apart the Earth, piece by piece, but you would never find even the slightest trace of an element called promethium. That's because promethium is a synthetic element, one that is produced only in laboratories. Like all other synthetic elements, promethium is radioactive. It has been used as a miniature electric power source for pacemakers and artificial hearts like the one shown.

Promethium belongs to a part of the periodic table known as the lanthanide series, which is a group of elements with atomic numbers from 57 through 71. These elements all have similar electron configurations, so they share similar chemical properties. The same is true of elements belonging to the actinide series, which includes atomic numbers from 89 through 103. Most synthetic elements are found in the actinide series, and most are known as transuranium elements. Transuranium literally means "beyond uranium." A trans-

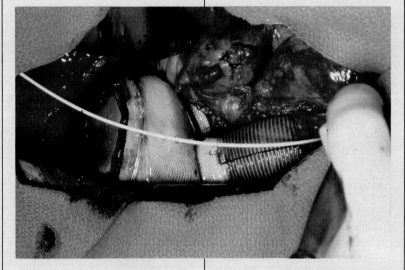

uranium element has an atomic number greater than 92, which is the atomic number of uranium.

Edwin McMilan and Philip Abelson were among the first physicists to create a transuranium element by bombarding uranium with slow neutrons. The element was named neptunium because uranium was named after the planet Uranus, and Neptune is the next planet in the solar system. Another transuranium element, discovered later that year, was named after the planet Pluto. This element was called plutonium.

Plutonium is perhaps the best known of all the synthetic elements. It has been used in nuclear warheads. Small amounts of plutonium provided electric power for the Apollo spacecraft that went to the moon.

Nearly 40 metric tons of plutonium are produced each year. Most of it is in the form of nuclear waste. Finding ways to dispose of plutonium is one of the most challenging problems facing society today. Plutonium is one of the most toxic substances on Earth—a lump the size of an orange could poison an entire city. To make matters worse, plutonium remains radioactive for more than 24,000 years.

How, then, do you dispose of plutonium? There have been many suggestions made over the years. One possibility would be to load it up on rockets and launch it into space. But what if the rocket explodes or crashes shortly after lift-off? Another idea is to bury containers filled with nuclear waste beneath the polar ice caps. But what if the radioactive heat melts the polar ice caps and causes worldwide flooding?

Many experts believe that the safest way to dispose of plutonium would be to bury it deep underground. The United States government recently selected a place to bury highly radioactive nuclear waste beneath the Yucca Mountains in Nevada shown in the photo.

Before the plutonium is buried, it has to be sealed in specially constructed stainless steel canisters. These canisters have already been tested in laboratories, where they have been dropped from a height of 600 meters, crashed into a concrete wall at 128 kilometers per hour, and submerged in burning fuel. Despite all of this punishment, none of the containers ever sprang a leak. Even so, no one can be certain what would have happened if the containers had been filled with plutonium when they were tested.

The canisters are placed in tunnels dug more than 300 meters beneath the Yucca Mountains. Most of the mountain is composed of volcanic rock, which will carry heat away from the canisters as they cool down.

After 60 years, the canisters will be inspected. If there are no leaks, the tunnels will be permanently sealed. In all, the dump site will contain more than 187 kilometers of tunnels, enough to hold nearly 70,000 metric tons of radioactive waste.

Some people who live in Nevada are worried about the dump site. What would happen if there were ever a volcanic eruption beneath the Yucca Mountains? Or an earthquake? What if the canisters ever came in contact with underground water? Can these canisters resist corrosion over a period of 24,000 years? Only time will tell.

WHAT DO YOU THINK?

Energy creates pollution. When you burn fossil fuels—such as natural gas, coal, and oil—you release toxic chemicals into the air. Nuclear power, by comparison, is a very clean source of energy. But nuclear waste, such as plutonium, is a potential threat to the environment. Some people feel that no more nuclear power plants should be constructed until scientists develop a foolproof way to store nuclear wastes. How do you feel about the use of nuclear power?

TECHNOLOGY CONNECTION

SEARCHING FOR THE IDEAL SUPERCONDUCTOR

Every time you turn on the lights in your home, you can thank the local electric company for sending energy through power lines from an electric generation plant.

You might think of the wires as highways for electrons. And like highways, not all wire is equally effective in allowing traffic—electricity—to pass through.

In the case of power lines, some electrical energy is lost between the generation plant and your home. Because it is expensive to operate generation plants, any lost electrical energy is quite costly.

But what would happen if a truck on a highway, or the electricity from a power plant, used almost no energy while traveling? The bills would drop and there would be little waste of energy.

In the early 1900s, a scientist (H. Kamerlingh Onnes) discovered that super-cold mercury could conduct electricity with virtually no waste. Electrons flowed through the mercury without effort. Gradually, scientists

learned that other super-cooled metals could also conduct electricity without waste. Scientists call this superconductivity.

The discovery of superconductivity was terribly exciting news, but there was a major problem: it was extremely expensive to cool the wire. In order for mercury to become superconductive, scientists had to cool it to about -450°F!

Today, scientists continue to search for new superconductive materials, especially ones that become superconductive at room temperature. When they find the material they are looking for, they will be able to develop wires that conduct electricity over great distances without waste.

The transfer of electricity to your home is not the only use for superconductive materials. Scientists, for example, hope some day to develop more efficient motors and faster computers.

Researchers continue to develop materials that super-

conduct at warmer temperatures, but even those new materials must be cooled to far below 0°F.

While they continue to look for the ideal material, scientists use some superconducting materials for special purposes—some medical instruments, for example. For most purposes, however, such as for use as electric power lines, the cost of cooling continues to prohibit superconducting materials from being used.

WHAT DO YOU THINK?

Scientists hope one day to develop materials that would be superconductive at room temperature. What impact do you think this might have on the environment?

*H*istory
C O N N E C T I O N

ALCHEMY: QUEST FOR GOLD AND HEALTH

Alchemy was the medieval form of chemistry. Back then, there was no such thing as a periodic table of elements. In the middle ages, scholars thought that all matter was a mixture of four basic elements: earth, air, fire, and water. Alchemists believed that by changing the proportions of this mixture—by adding more fire and water, for instance—it would be possible to transform one substance into another. Much of their time was devoted to trying to change various elements, such as lead, into gold. Alchemists also hoped to find a universal cure for illness.

Today, most people remember Sir Isaac Newton as a great physicist and mathematician. He was, after all, the man who formulated the Three Laws of Motion and began the development of calculus. What many people don't realize, however, is that Sir Isaac Newton was also an alchemist who spent much of his life working in a secret laboratory.

Alchemists were in great demand among kings and nobility, who were always eager to add more gold to their personal treasuries. In seventeenth-century Prague, the Holy Roman Emperor Rudolf II surrounded himself with prominent alchemists from all over Europe. Some of these alchemists were imprisoned or executed when they could not provide the emperor with the gold they had promised.

Alchemy eventually disappeared in the late eighteenth century, upon the emergence of modern chemistry. Of course, no one was ever able to turn lead into gold. But that does not mean that alchemy was a complete failure. Many of the techniques used by laboratories today for mixing and preparing chemicals were first developed by alchemists many centuries ago.

YOU TRY IT!

When alchemists wrote about their experiments, they used a complex system of symbols. It was a type of code to prevent other people from learning their secrets. A drawing of the sun, for instance, symbolized gold, since gold has a bright yellow color. The moon, on the other hand, symbolized silver.

Take a look at the periodic table. What symbols would you draw to represent some of the different elements? What symbol would you create for uranium? Or helium?

Reviewing Main Ideas

1. Your life is full of events that repeat and thus are periodic. Chemical and physical properties of elements repeat periodically and can be represented by the periodic table.

Sun	Mon	Tue	Wed	Thur	Fri	Sat
	1	2	Birthday 3	4	5	6
7	New moon 8	9	10	11	12	13
14	Taxes due 15	16	Photo club 17	18	19	20
21	22	23	School starts 24	25	26	27
28	29	30	31			

2. A period is made up of a series of elements with increasing atomic numbers. A new period starts when similar properties repeat.

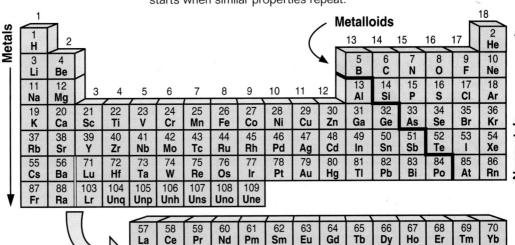

3. Elements with like properties are placed in columns called families.

4. An approximate diagonal from the top left corner of the periodic table to the lower right corner roughly separates the metal elements from the nonmetals. The elements that occur close to the diagonal have properties in between and are called metalloids.

| 37 Rb 85.468 | 38 Sr 87.62 | 39 Y 88.906 | 40 Zr 91.224 | 41 Nb 92.906 | 42 Mo 95.94 | 43 Tc 97.91 | 44 Ru 101.07 | 45 Rh 102.91 | 46 Pd 106.42 | 47 Ag 107.87 | 48 Cd 112.41 | 49 In 114.82 | 50 Sn 118.71 | 51 Sb 121.75 | 52 Te 127.60 | 53 I 126.90 | 54 Xe 131.29 |

Chapter Review

USING KEY SCIENCE TERMS

alkali metals   isotopes
alkaline earth metals   mass number
atomic mass   period
atomic number   periodic table
family of elements

The sentences below include terms that have been used incorrectly. Change the incorrect terms so that the sentence reads correctly. Underline your change.

1. The atomic mass of an element represents the total mass of all its isotopes.

2. Family 1 on the periodic table is called the alkaline earth metals.

3. A horizontal row in the periodic table is called a family.

4. The halogens are a very reactive period in the periodic table.

5. The atomic number of an element is the number of neutrons in its nucleus.

6. Magnesium and calcium are alkali metals.

7. Atoms of the same element that have differing numbers of electrons are called isotopes.

UNDERSTANDING IDEAS

Use the periodic table in Appendix E to choose the best answer to complete each sentence.

1. Of the following, the element that is not an alkaline earth metal is ____.
   a. magnesium   c. calcium
   b. potassium   d. barium

2. An example of a noble gas is ____.
   a. nitrogen   c. neon
   b. oxygen   d. hydrogen

3. An element has an atomic number of 11. The atomic number of the next heaviest element with similar properties would be ____.
   a. 19   c. 16
   b. 14   d. 21

4. The atomic numbers of the elements in period four are ____.
   a. 22–104   c. 3–10
   b. 19–36   d. 55–85

5. Of the following, the element that is not a metal is ____.
   a. chromium   c. titanium
   b. lithium   d. phosphorus

6. The mass number of an atom is ____.
   a. the total mass of the electrons
   b. the sum of the masses of the electrons and protons
   c. the total mass of the protons
   d. the sum of the masses of the protons and neutrons

7. The element with an atomic number of 14 is ____.
   a. sulfur   c. gold
   b. iodine   d. silicon

8. An element has an atomic number of 7 and a mass number of 14. It has ____ neutrons in its nucleus.
   a. 7   c. 21
   b. 28   d. 24

9. Oxygen has an atomic mass of 15.9994 and isotopes with masses of 15, 16, and 17. The most common isotope is ____.
   a. 15   b. 16   c. 8   d. 15.9994

10. The halogens have _____ electrons in
    their outer energy level.
    a. 7   **c.** 6
    b. 8   **d.** 2

CRITICAL THINKING

Use your understanding of the concepts
developed in the chapter to answer each of
the following questions.

1. A silver sample contains 52 atoms, each
   having 60 neutrons, and 48 atoms, each
   having 62 neutrons. What is the sample's
   average atomic mass?

2. U and Pu are named for objects in nature.
   What are these objects, and what other
   element is named after a similar object?

3. According to the periodic table, what is
   the most active metal? The most active
   nonmetal? What would you expect if
   these two elements were brought
   together?

4. A certain element has isotopes with masses of 20, 21, and 22. If 50 percent of its
   atoms have a mass of 20 and the rest of
   the atoms are equally divided between the
   other isotopes, what is its atomic mass?

5. What is the family number of the
   elements in the diagram?

PROBLEM SOLVING

Read the following problem and discuss your
answers in a brief paragraph.

You are a public official in a town that has
been isolated by a natural disaster. A major
factory in your town uses cadmium in a process that is vital to the town's survival. All
sources of cadmium have been cut off.

1. Suggest two elements that might replace
   cadmium in the factory's process. Explain
   your suggestions.

2. The town workers must handle this ele-
   ment in the manufacturing process.
   Explain which of your two choices from
   Question 1 you would recommend.

CONNECTING IDEAS

Discuss each of the following in a brief paragraph.

1. When an atom of element
X emits an alpha particle,
one of the products is
Pb-214. What are the atomic
number and mass number
of element X? What element
is it?

2. Atoms in a family of elements increase in size.
Explain why this is so.

3. LIFE SCIENCE CONNECTION
What radioactive element
could easily replace the calcium in human bones?

4. SCIENCE AND SOCIETY List
four benefits and four risks
associated with synthetic

elements. Do you think the
benefits outweigh the risks?
Explain.

5. TECHNOLOGY CONNECTION
Describe how superconduc-
tors could decrease our
country's energy needs.

DID YOU EVER WONDER . . .

Why fire fighters put water on a fire?

Why water is called H_2O?

How a detergent gets your clothes clean?

You'll find the answers to these questions as you read this chapter.

Combining Atoms

id you ever dream of being a fire fighter? Fire fighters live exciting and dangerous lives. Every year they save many lives and protect valuable properties.

Today's fire fighters do more than just pour water on fires. If a tanker truck full of chemicals has an accident, the fire department may deal with it, spraying a special foam over the truck. If there is a gas leak, fire fighters may be first on the scene, deciding what precautions need to be taken until the leak is stopped. Perhaps they should be renamed "chemical reaction technicians."

Fire is a very rapid chemical reaction that releases heat and produces new compounds. Putting out a fire also involves chemical reactions. In this chapter, you'll learn more about the special language scientists use to describe such reactions.

EXPLORE!

What is in a fire extinguisher?

Put 20 grams of baking soda in a small test tube. Pour 50 mL of vinegar in a 500-mL flask. Carefully lower the test tube into the flask, making sure the baking soda does not contact the vinegar. Put a one-hole stopper containing a piece of tubing into the mouth of the flask. While pointing the tubing into the sink, tilt the flask so that the vinegar wets the baking soda. Watch what happens. **CAUTION:** *If the contents react too fast, the stopper can blow out.*

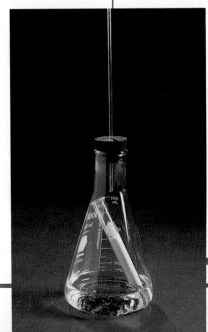

7-1 Kinds of Chemical Bonds

OBJECTIVES

In this section, you will

- describe ionic and covalent bonds;
- identify particles produced by ionic and covalent bonding;
- distinguish between a nonpolar covalent and a polar covalent bond.

KEY SCIENCE TERMS

ion
ionic bond
molecule
covalent bond
polar molecule
nonpolar molecule

FIGURE 7-1. Is there a fire extinguisher like this in your school?

STOPPING A REACTION

Although you may not have been aware of all of them, three different products were formed when you mixed ordinary vinegar, also called acetic acid, with baking soda, also called sodium hydrogen carbonate, in the Explore. These products were water, carbon dioxide, and sodium acetate, a salt. Each of these products can put out a fire. The salt cuts off the oxygen supply and suffocates the fire. Water lowers the temperature of the burning materials below their ignition point and reduces the oxygen supply to the fire. Carbon dioxide is more dense than air, so it forms a blanket over the flames and cuts off the supply of oxygen to the fuel. Some of the fire extinguishers around your school and neighborhood work just like the one you made.

But how and why do the atoms in these chemicals bond together in the first place? Is there some special atomic glue that keeps them together? And why do some elements form compounds much more easily than others do?

ATOMIC GLUE

Recall from Chapter 6 that having a complete outer energy level makes an atom very stable. Look at the example of sodium and chlorine in Figure 7-2(a). If a sodium atom loses the single electron it has in its outer level, the remaining outer level is full. Chlorine, on the other hand, needs the electron lost by sodium to fill its outer level. When sodium gives its electron to chlorine, both will have filled outer levels.

Figure 7-2(b) shows what happens when a small amount of the metal sodium is placed in a flask of chlorine gas. What is the white smoke? Where did it come from? Let's see if we can figure it out. Recall from Chapter 5 that atoms are neutral—that is, they have equal num-

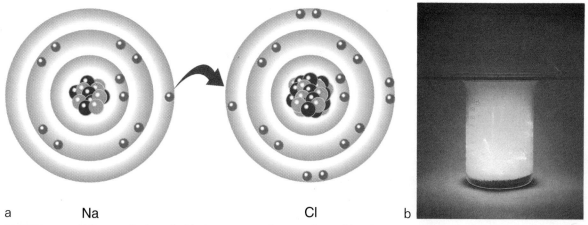

a   Na   Cl   b

FIGURE 7-2. When sodium and chlorine react to form sodium chloride, sodium gives up an electron and chlorine gains one (a). This reaction is quite violent (b).

bers of positive and negative charges. Sodium has 11 protons (11+) and 11 electrons (11-). When it loses one of those electrons, what happens to the overall charge? It now has only 10 electrons (10-) and thus has an overall charge of 1+. (11+) + (10-) = 1+. This charged atom is called an **ion**. In this case the ion is positively charged because it has one fewer electron than proton. It is written Na^+.

In the meantime, what has happened to the chlorine atom with its 7 outer-level electrons? When chlorine gains 1 electron from sodium, it has 8 electrons in its outermost energy level. Sodium and chlorine now both have full outer energy levels. But chlorine has 17 protons with a charge of 17+ and 18 electrons with a charge of 18-. Is the ion formed by chlorine negative or positive? To find out, add (17+) + (18-) = 1-. Chlorine is a negative ion because it contains one more electron than proton. Scientists call it a chloride ion and write it as Cl^-.

Notice that when we write the shorthand for the ions Na^+ and Cl^-, the sign is slightly above the symbol. This is called a superscript, super- meaning above. You'll see superscripts, such as Al^{3+} and O^{2-} throughout the chapter. They describe the charge on the ion. When the superscript is simply + or -, it is understood to mean 1+ or 1-.

The charges of the two ions are opposite. Therefore, they attract each other to make up the compound NaCl. NaCl is the white smoke you see as the reaction takes place. Because

FIGURE 7-3. Getting your daily dose of ions is important. Many systems in the human body need ions to work correctly.

the positive charge of the sodium ion is equal, but opposite in sign, to the negative charge of the chloride ion, the compound NaCl, sodium chloride, is neutral.

IONIC BONDING

There are many compounds that form in a similar way to sodium chloride. When atoms gain or lose electrons, they become ions. Because these ions are positively and negatively charged, they attract one another. This attraction of positive ions for negative ions is called an **ionic bond**. Compounds that are made up of ions are ionic compounds. Is NaCl an ionic compound? Yes, it is, because it is made up of ions, and the bonds that hold it together are ionic bonds—not atomic glue!

EXPLORE!

Can you see an ionic reaction?
Examine a camera flashbulb. List the properties of the substance(s) inside the bulb. Without looking directly at the bulb, set it off. After it has cooled, examine it again. How have the properties changed? What other invisible substance do you think was in the bulb before you set it off? Have you seen other similar reactions?

The fine wire you saw in the flashbulb before setting it off was the element magnesium. You know that a chemical reaction must have taken place because energy was given off in the form of light, and a new substance formed. The magnesium reacted with oxygen gas, which was also present in the flashbulb. Figure 7-4 shows the formation of magnesium oxide, MgO, that you just saw in the Explore. Magnesium is in Family 2 of the periodic table. How many electrons are in its

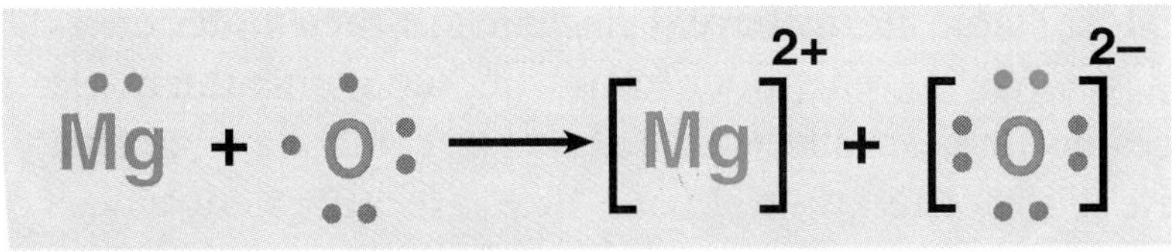

FIGURE 7-4. In this ionic reaction, magnesium loses two electrons to oxygen to form magnesium oxide.

outermost energy level? Find oxygen. From its family, how many outer electrons does it have? If you said 6, you are correct.

When magnesium reacts with oxygen, a magnesium atom loses 2 electrons and becomes a positively charged ion, Mg^{2+}. We write the superscript $^{2+}$ on the symbol for magnesium to remind us of the ion's charge. At the same time, the oxygen atom gains the 2 electrons and becomes a negatively charged oxide ion, O^{2-}. The compound as a whole is neutral. Why? Because the sum of the charges of the ions is zero. Predict what ions would form when magnesium reacts with chlorine. Remember that the final sum of the charges must be zero.

You know that magnesium loses 2 electrons, but chlorine needs only 1 electron to be complete. In order for the elements to combine, both must be able to get complete outer energy levels. In this case, there must be 2 chlorine atoms for every 1 magnesium atom. Magnesium gives 1 electron to each chlorine atom. You now have 1 Mg^{2+} ion and 2 Cl^- ions. These ions attract one another and the compound magnesium chloride, $MgCl_2$, is formed.

The small 2 after Cl is called a subscript. Sub- means below. The subscript indicates the number of atoms of the element in the compound. When there is no subscript, as in Mg, the number of atoms is understood to be 1. The compound is neutral because $(1 \times Mg^{2+}) + (2 \times Cl^-) = 0$.

FIGURE 7-5. Why do 2 chlorine ions combine with 1 magnesium ion?

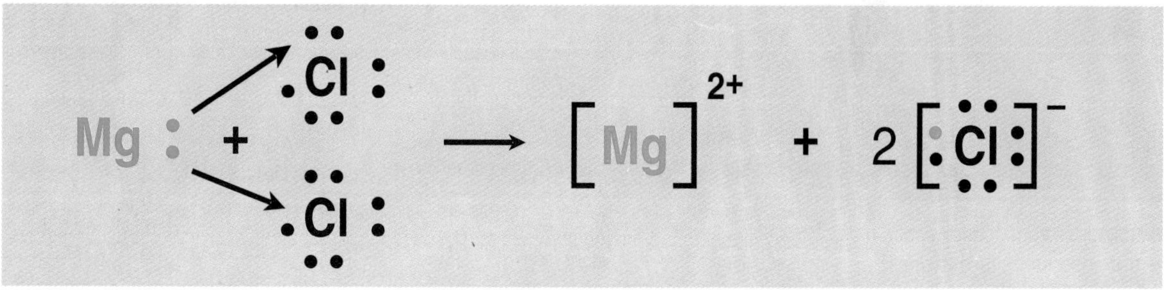

Most stable atoms have 8 electrons in their outer energy level. As you remember from Chapter 6, only the noble gases occur naturally with 8. They not only have a complete outer energy level, but they are also neutral. As you've seen, some atoms without 8 electrons may get a complete outer energy level by gaining or losing electrons, but they do so at the expense of becoming charged. The more electrons an atom gains or loses, the higher its charge. As charges increase, the ionic bond becomes less stable. But there is a path to stability other than forming charged ions.

FIGURE 7-6. Hydrogen, water, and chlorine are held together by covalent bonds.

MOLECULES AND COVALENT BONDS

Some atoms become more chemically stable by sharing electrons, rather than by losing or gaining electrons. The neutral particles formed as a result of atoms sharing electrons are called **molecules**. The bond that forms between atoms when they share electrons is called a **covalent bond**. Notice that covalent molecules aren't charged. Because no electrons have been gained or lost, only shared, both the atoms and molecule remain neutral.

You can get a better understanding of how atoms gain, lose, or share electrons by working with models of electron energy levels in the following Investigate.

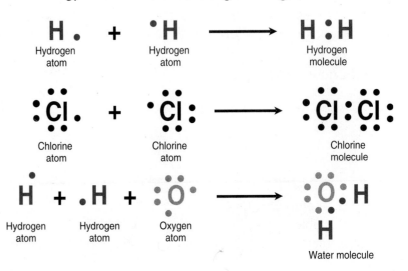

FIGURE 7-7. Atoms of covalent compounds stay together because they share electrons.

7-1 MODELS OF COMBINING ATOMS

You know that atoms combine in order to fill their outer energy levels. Let's use models to see how this can happen.

PROBLEM
How can a model show the way atoms gain, lose, or share electrons?

MATERIALS
modified egg cartons
marbles

PROCEDURE
1. Obtain a modified egg carton and marbles from your teacher. The carton will represent the first and second energy levels of an atom, and the marbles will represent electrons.
2. Put one marble in each depression of the carton, starting with the pair of receptacles representing the first energy level.
3. Place the remaining marbles in depressions representing the second energy level. What is the element? In which column of the periodic table would your element appear?

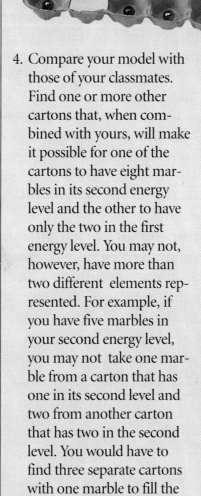

4. Compare your model with those of your classmates. Find one or more other cartons that, when combined with yours, will make it possible for one of the cartons to have eight marbles in its second energy level and the other to have only the two in the first energy level. You may not, however, have more than two different elements represented. For example, if you have five marbles in your second energy level, you may not take one marble from a carton that has one in its second level and two from another carton that has two in the second level. You would have to find three separate cartons with one marble to fill the three spaces in your carton.
5. Make a list of combinations that you made with your classmates' models.
6. **Observe** your classmates' models again. Are there any combinations that could make it possible for both cartons to have eight marbles in the second energy level? What are they?

ANALYZE
1. Would you **infer** that your model is a metal or a nonmetal? How did you know?

CONCLUDE AND APPLY
2. Which of the combinations that you made in Steps 5 and 6 were ionic bonds and which were covalent? How do you know?
3. **Predict** what combinations of B and F will give you complete energy levels.
4. **Going Further:** How would you have to change you model to show how sodium (Na) combines?

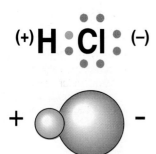

FIGURE 7-8. HCl is a polar molecule. The pair of electrons is attracted more by the chlorine than the hydrogen.

In the Investigate, you modeled the role electrons play in forming compounds. Even though you only used the elements in one row of the periodic table, you can see from the models that many different combinations could be made. Metals and nonmetals can gain and lose electrons to complete their outer energy level. Elements with four electrons tend to share those four with other atoms so that each of them possesses a full outer energy level as long as they stay together.

POLAR AND NONPOLAR MOLECULES

Do atoms share electrons equally? You know that an atom like chlorine has more protons than an atom like hydrogen. The chlorine nucleus has 17 positively charged protons, and hydrogen has only 1. For this reason, a chlorine atom will have a greater attraction for electrons than hydrogen.

The diagram and model of hydrogen chloride in Figure 7-8 show how this difference in attraction can affect the overall charge, and sometimes the shape, of the molecule. The chlorine atom has a stronger attraction for the shared pair of electrons than does the hydrogen atom. As a result, the electrons will spend more time near the chlorine atom than near the hydrogen atom. This makes the chlorine end a little more negative and the hydrogen end a little more positive than if the electrons were shared equally. We call this type of bond a polar bond. Polar means having two opposite ends or poles. Polar bonds

FIGURE 7-9. The way in which oxygen and hydrogen bond produces water, a polar molecule.

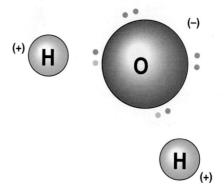

may result in polar molecules. A **polar molecule** is one that has a slightly positive end and a slightly negative end. Molecules that do not have unbalanced charges like this are called **nonpolar molecules**.

Water is another example of a compound with polar molecules, as shown in Figure 7-9. A water molecule contains two polar covalent bonds, one between each hydrogen atom and the oxygen atom. The oxygen atom has a stronger attraction for electrons than the hydrogen atoms do. As a result, the oxygen end of the water molecule is slightly negative, and the hydrogen end of the molecule is slightly positive. One interesting consequence of this is shown in Figure 7-10.

You've read about two ways in which chemical bonding takes place, producing two kinds of compounds—ionic and covalent. In ionic bonding, elements gain and lose electrons to complete their outer energy levels. The positive and negative ions then attract. In covalent bonding, atoms share electrons and form molecules. In the next section, you will find out more about the scientific shorthand used to describe compounds.

SKILLBUILDER

COMPARE AND CONTRAST
Compare and contrast ionic, polar covalent and nonpolar covalent bonds. If you need help, refer to the **Skill Handbook** on page 685.

FIGURE 7-10. If you comb your hair and hold the charged comb near a thin stream of water, the water will bend toward the comb.

Check Your Understanding

1. What is the smallest unit in each of the following bonds: (a) ionic ; (b) polar covalent ; (c) nonpolar covalent?
2. Sodium reacts in air to form a white compound. Write a formula for this compound.
3. **APPLY:** Most laundry detergents work because one end of their molecule is soluble in dirt and the other in water. What is the most probable type of molecule in these detergents?

7-2 Chemical Shorthand

OBJECTIVES

In this section, you will

- explain how to determine oxidation numbers;
- give formulas for compounds from their names;
- name compounds from their formulas.

KEY SCIENCE TERMS

oxidation number
binary compound
polyatomic ion

THE WORLD OF ALPHABET SOUP

If you take a close look at many of the containers around your home and school, you'll find enough combinations of letters and numbers to fill a can of alphabet soup. Let's explore several possibilities.

EXPLORE!

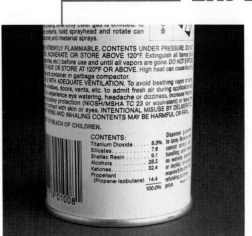

CONTENTS:
Titanium Dioxide 8.3%
Silicates 7.6
Shellac Resin 9.1
Alcohols 28.2
Ketones 32.4
Propellant
(Propane-Isobutane) 14.4
100.0%

What's it made of?

Study the chemical content on a bag of lawn fertilizer, dog or cat food, a can of paint, and a box of laundry detergent or bleach. List the ingredients by name and include any symbols or numbers used to describe the ingredient. Do these products have any elements in common?

How could the lists of chemicals you saw on the packages have been written in a shorter form so that everyone would still understand them? Lets see how we can combine symbols to describe how elements form compounds.

The two people in Figure 7-11 seem to have little in common. Yet, in a sense, the medieval alchemist is the ancestor of the modern chemist. Both are shown at work investigating matter. Notice how each would write symbols for the elements silver and sulfur. If the alchemist knew the composition of tarnish, how might he write its formula? The modern chemist does know its composition. She would write it Ag_2S. Being able to use this kind of shorthand can enable you to write a great deal of information in just a short time.

A chemical formula is a kind of code used by scientists around the world. When you write Ag_2S, chemists in Spain, Germany, or Japan would know exactly what you mean. Chemical formulas allow scientists to communicate and share research. In our world, which is changing so rapidly, this is most important. Where do formulas come from, and what do they mean?

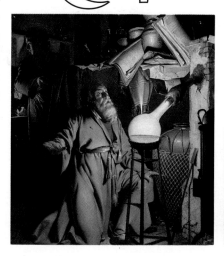

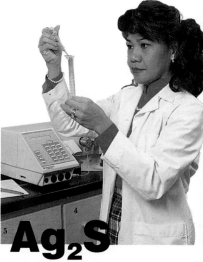

FIGURE 7-11. An ancient alchemist and today's chemist may have more in common than you think.

In a previous chapter, you learned to write word equations for chemical reactions. Recall the fire extinguisher you made at the beginning of this chapter. A scientist would write the reaction like this:

acetic acid + sodium hydrogen carbonate → sodium acetate + water + carbon dioxide

$$HC_2H_3O_2 + NaHCO_3 \rightarrow NaC_2H_3O_2 + H_2O + CO_2.$$

Notice that the words you've used before to name compounds have been replaced by a kind of chemical shorthand called a formula. The formula of a compound tells a chemist how much of each element is present. For example, in the formula, H_2O, the subscript 2 shows 2 atoms of the element hydrogen. Since there is no subscript on the O, 1 atom is understood. How are these numbers determined?

OXIDATION NUMBER

Recall that you can tell how many electrons an element has in its outermost energy level from its family number on the periodic table. If the element is a metal, it tends to lose electrons, leaving the new outer level complete. If the element is a nonmetal, it's likely to gain electrons, completing the outer level.

Sometimes, as you've learned, an atom shares electrons to become stable. The number of electrons that an atom

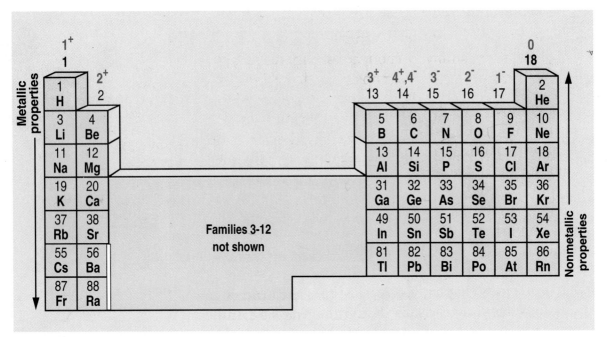

FIGURE 7-12. The oxidation number shown in red is the same for each element in a family.

gains, loses, or shares when bonding with another atom is called its **oxidation number**. An oxidation number can be positive or negative. For example, when sodium forms an ion, it loses an electron and has a charge of 1+. So the oxidation number of sodium is 1+. When chlorine forms an ion, it gains an electron and has a charge of 1-, so its oxidation number is 1-. Notice that when one sodium combines with one chlorine, the net charge is zero.

You may have noticed the red numbers printed on the periodic table shown in Figure 7-12. These are the oxidation numbers for many elements that form binary compounds. The prefix bi- means two. Thus, a **binary compound** is one that is composed of two elements. Sodium chloride is a binary compound consisting of two elements, sodium and chlorine. The transition elements have been omitted since their oxidation numbers may change from compound to compound.

You'll recall that the alkali metals in Family 1 are extremely reactive. Like sodium, each metal in this group loses its 1 outer electron in bonding. So you can say that each of these elements has an oxidation number of 1+.

Like chlorine, each of the other nonmetals in Group 17 gains 1 electron in bonding, so each of these elements has an oxidation number of 1-. One easy way to remember an element's oxidation number is that it is the same as the electrical charge on the element's ion.

Some elements, strangely enough, have more than one oxidation number. Copper, as shown in Figure 7-13, can be both Cu^+ and Cu^{2+}. When an element can have more than one oxidation number, a Roman numeral is used in the name of the compound to indicate the oxidation number. Thus the oxidation number of copper in copper(II) oxide is 2+. Iron is another element with two oxidation numbers. It may be Fe^{2+} or Fe^{3+}. You can tell that the oxidation number of iron in iron(III) oxide will be 3+.

copper(I)	Cu^+
copper(II)	Cu^{2+}
iron(II)	Fe^{2+}
iron(III)	Fe^{3+}
chromium(II)	Cr^{2+}
chromium(III)	Cr^{3+}
lead(II)	Pb^{2+}
lead(IV)	Pb^{4+}

FIGURE 7-13. Some elements can have more than one oxidation number.

FORMULAS FOR BINARY COMPOUNDS

Once you know how to find the oxidation numbers of elements in binary compounds, you can write the formulas by using these rules.

1. Write the symbol of the element with the positive oxidation number. Hydrogen and all metals have positive oxidation numbers: Ca.
2. Then write the symbol of the element with the negative oxidation number: F.
3. Look up the oxidation numbers on the periodic table and write them above the symbols: $Ca^{2+} F^-$.
4. In the completed formula, there must be an equal number of positive and negative charges. The charge is calculated by multiplying the number of atoms of the element by its oxidation number. When $Ca^{2+}F^-$ combine, we see that one Ca atom will combine with two F atoms. We know this because one atom of Ca times a charge of 2+ equals 2+. Two atoms of F times a charge of 1- equals 2-. The sum of 2+ and 2- is zero, and the compound is neutral.
5. The last step is to put subscripts in so that the sum of the charges in the formula is zero. In this example, the formula becomes CaF_2.

FIGURE 7-14. No matter how many atoms combine, the overall charge of the molecule is zero.

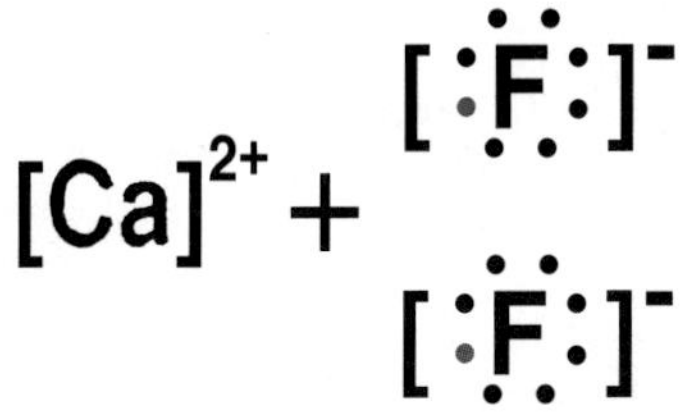

$$[Ca]^{2+} + \begin{matrix} [:\ddot{F}:]^- \\ \\ [:\ddot{F}:]^- \end{matrix}$$

WHAT WOULD YOU CALL $AlCl_3$?

Now that you've learned to write the formulas from the name, how can you tell the name from the formulas? You can name a binary compound from its formula by

TABLE 7-1. Elements in Binary Compounds

Element	*-ide* Naming
Chlorine	Chloride
Fluorine	Fluoride
Nitrogen	Nitride
Oxygen	Oxide
Phosphorus	Phosphide
Sulfur	Sulfide

using these rules.

1. Write the name of the first element.
2. Write the root of the name of the second element.
3. Add the suffix -ide to the root.

Table 7-1 lists several elements and their -ide counterparts. The example, $AlCl_3$ is named aluminum chloride.

Now, we have another problem—compounds of elements with two oxidation numbers. To name the compounds of elements having two oxidation numbers, you must first figure out the oxidation numbers of each of the elements.

For example, suppose you wanted to name CrO. First you would look up the oxidation number of the negative element. The oxidation number of oxygen is 2-. Next, figure out the oxidation number of the positive element. That number added to 2- will give a total charge of zero. $(2+) + (2-) = 0$. Finally, if necessary, write the name of the compound using a Roman numeral for the positive oxidation number. In this case the positive oxidation number is II and the compound is chromium (II) oxide.

COMPOUNDS WITH POLYATOMIC IONS

Have you ever used baking soda in cooking, as a medicine, or to brush your teeth? You'll remember that baking soda was one of the ingredients in our homemade fire extinguisher. Some compounds, including baking soda, are composed of **polyatomic ions**. The prefix poly-means many, so polyatomic means having many atoms. A polyatomic ion is a group of positively or negatively charged covalently-bonded atoms. In the case of baking soda, Na^+ is the positive ion, and HCO_3^- is the negative, polyatomic ion.

FIGURE 7-15. Iron can combine with the polyatomic sulfate ion forming $FeSO_4$ or $Fe_2(SO_4)_3$

Table 7-2 lists several polyatomic ions. To name a compound that contains one or more of these ions, use the same rules used for a binary compound. For example K_2SO_4 is potassium sulfate. What is the name of $Sr(OH)_2$ and NH_4Cl?

TABLE 7-2. Polyatomic Ions

Charge	Name	Formula
1+	Ammonium	NH_4^+
1-	Acetate	$CH_3CO_2^-$
1-	Chlorate	ClO_3^-
1-	Hydroxide	OH^-
1-	Nitrate	NO_3^-
2-	Carbonate	CO_3^{2-}
2-	Sulfate	SO_4^{2-}
3-	Phosphate	PO_4^{3-}

SKILLBUILDER

USING TABLES
Name the following compounds: Li_2S, MgF_2, FeO, $CuCl$. Strategy Hint: For names of elements with more than one oxidation number, remember to include the Roman numeral. For more names of non-metals in binary compounds, use Table 7-2.
If you need help, refer to the **Skill Handbook** on page 681.

To write formulas for compounds containing polyatomic ions, follow the rules for writing formulas for binary compounds, with one addition. Use parentheses around the group representing the polyatomic ion when more than one of that ion is needed, such as $Mg(OH)_2$. Without the parentheses, it appears as though there are two hydrogen atoms, rather than two hydroxide ions.

EXAMPLE PROBLEM: Writing Formulas with Polyatomic Ions

Problem Statement: What is the formula for calcium nitrate?

Problem-Solving Steps: 1. Write symbols and oxidation numbers for calcium and the nitrate ion.

2+ 1−
Ca NO_3

2. Write in subscripts so that the sum of the oxidation numbers is zero. Enclose the NO_3 in parentheses.

2+ 1−
Ca $(NO_3)_2$

Solution: Final Formula:
Ca $(NO_3)_2$

NAMING BINARY COMPOUNDS

Although there are thousands of possible compounds making up the substances in your world, they can all be named using the simple rules that you have just learned to

How do we know?

Common and Systematic Names

What is the formula for dihydrogen monoxide? H_2O! But, you say, that's water. Everyone knows that. It may sound difficult, but a systematic name gives a lot of useful information. When you're thirsty, you wouldn't ask for a glass of ice cold dihydrogen monoxide! You would go by the common name and ask for a glass of water. However, if you need to plan a scientific experiment involving water, you'll be glad that the systematic name for water tells you its exact composition.

SKILLBUILDER

USING TABLES
Using Table 7-2, write the formulas for the following compounds: sodium sulfate, magnesium chlorate. If you need help, refer to the **Skill Handbook** on page 681.

use with binary compounds and those containing polyatomic ions. The fact that all scientists use these same rules makes it possible for them to communicate their work from country to country. In the next section, you will see how this chemical shorthand is used in describing chemical reactions.

Early in the history of the science of chemistry, the discoverer of a new compound would name it. Often the discoverer would choose a name that described some chemical or physical property of the new compound. A common name for potassium carbonate, K_2CO_3, is potash. The name came from the fact that the compound could be produced by boiling wood ash in iron pots. Laughing gas was named for the effect it has on humans when it is inhaled. Sodium hydrogen carbonate, written $NaHCO_3$, is commonly called baking soda. It's one of the compounds that helps baked goods rise. Sulfuric acid was once called oil of vitriol. Lye and plaster of paris are other common names of compounds. While these names may be very descriptive, they tell us nothing about the chemical composition of the compound.

As the number of known compounds grew, it became necessary to establish a systematic system of names, part of which you have learned. There are 217 different known compounds that have the simple formula C_6H_6. Each of them has a unique name based on a system accepted by chemists worldwide. Since hundreds of thousands of new compounds are made each year, it's clear that a systematic naming system is necessary. The next time you want to impress your family or friends, just ask for a glass of ice cold dihydrogen monoxide!

Check Your Understanding

1. Name the following: NaI, FeI_3, NH_4Br.
2. Write formulas for compounds composed of (a) lithium and sulfur, (b) calcium and the acetate ion, and (c) barium and oxygen.
3. Assign an oxidation number to each element in the following: Al_2O_3 ; $ZnCl_2$; $FeBr_2$
4. **APPLY:** The label on a package of plant food lists potassium nitrate as one ingredient. What is the formula for potassium nitrate?

7-3 Balancing Chemical Equations

CHECKING FOR BALANCE

If you were to write an equation for making applesauce, you might say that you take 10 apples + 1 pound of sugar = 3 cups of applesauce. The apples and sugar are reactants. When heated together, they make applesauce, the product. The numbers in front of each substance are called coefficients. They describe how many units of that substance are involved in the recipe. Let's learn more about this type of equation in the following activity.

OBJECTIVES

In this section, you will
- explain what is meant by a balanced chemical equation;
- demonstrate how to write a balanced chemical equation.

KEY SCIENCE TERMS

balanced chemical equation

EXPLORE!

Must the sum of the reactant and product coefficients be equal?

Obtain a marked card from your teacher. With others in your class, assemble all the cards to represent a basketball team. When you write this as an equation, you have something like this: 2 guards + 2 forwards + 1 center = 1 team.

Why aren't the sums of the coefficients on each side of the equation equal? What other examples like this can you think of?

FIGURE 7-16. The action of silver polish is not a chemical reaction. It is an abrasive that wears away the thin coating of tarnish.

Let's see how the coefficients for the reactants and products in a chemical reaction compare to the Explore. Have you ever seen silver polish in the hardware store or supermarket? It's used to remove tarnish from silver. Tarnish can make silver appear almost black. Where does tarnish come from? It forms when sulfur-containing compounds in air or food react with silver to form silver sulfide, the black tarnish.

Let's write the chemical equation for tarnishing:

$$Ag + H_2S \rightarrow Ag_2S + H_2 .$$

Look at the equation closely. Remember that matter is never created or destroyed in an ordinary chemical reaction. Notice that one silver atom appears in the reactants, $Ag + H_2S$. However, two silver atoms appear in the product, $Ag_2S + H_2$. As you know, one silver atom can't just become two. The equation must be balanced so that it shows a true picture of what takes place in the reaction. A **balanced chemical equation** has the same number of atoms of each element on both sides of the equation. In the Explore, even though there were 2 guards, 2 forwards, and 1 center on one side and 1 "team" on the other, no players had been lost. The player "equation" was balanced. To find out if this equation is balanced, make a chart like that shown in Table 7-3.

TABLE 7-3. Atoms in an Unbalanced Equation

Kind of Atom	Number of Atoms $Ag + H_2S = Ag_2S + H_2$	
Ag	1	2
H	2	2
S	1	1

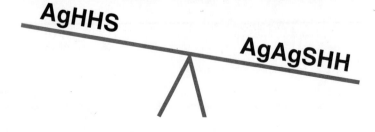

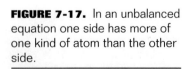

FIGURE 7-17. In an unbalanced equation one side has more of one kind of atom than the other side.

The number of hydrogen and sulfur atoms are balanced. However, there are two silver atoms on the right side of the equation, and only one on the left side. We cannot change the subscripts of a correct formula in order to balance an equation. Instead, we place whole number coefficients to the left of the formulas of the reactants and products so that there are equal numbers of silver atoms on both sides of the equation. If the coefficient is one, no coefficient is written. How do we choose which coefficients to use to balance this or any other equation?

CHOOSING COEFFICIENTS

The decision for choosing coefficients is a trial-and-error process. With practice, the process becomes simple to perform.

In the chemical equation for tarnishing, you found that both the sulfur atoms and the hydrogen atoms were already balanced. So look at the formulas containing silver atoms: Ag and Ag_2S. There are two atoms of silver on the right side and only one on the left side. If you put a coefficient of 2 before Ag, the equation is balanced, as shown in Table 7-4.

TABLE 7-4. Atoms in a Balanced Equation

Kind of Atom	Number of Atoms $2Ag + H_2S = Ag_2S + H_2$	
Ag	2	2
H	2	2
S	1	1

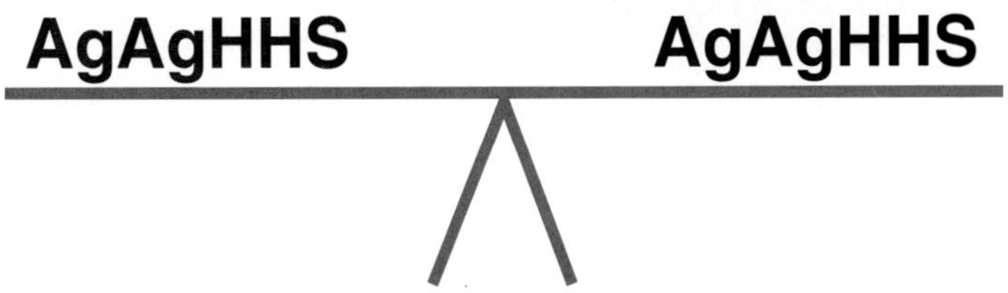

AgAgHHS   **AgAgHHS**

FIGURE 7-18. In a balanced equation, there is the same number of atoms on both sides.

WRITING BALANCED EQUATIONS

FIGURE 7-19. Notice the reaction between silver nitrate and sodium chloride solutions.

Figure 7-19 shows that when a silver nitrate solution is mixed with a sodium chloride solution, a white, insoluble solid is formed. This silver chloride solid falls to the bottom of the container. The sodium nitrate formed remains in solution. Write a balanced equation for this reaction.

1. Describe the reaction in words:
   Silver nitrate plus sodium chloride produces silver chloride plus sodium nitrate.

2. Write a chemical equation for the reaction using formulas and symbols for each term. Review Section 7-2 on how to write formulas for compounds. The formulas for elements are generally just their symbols.

$$AgNO_3 + NaCl \rightarrow AgCl + NaNO_3$$

3. Check the equation for balance. Set up a chart similar to Table 7-5 to help you. Notice that there are already equal numbers of each element on both sides of the equation. This equation is balanced.

4. Determine coefficients. This equation is balanced, so only the understood coefficients of one are needed.

   In the next section, you will take a closer look at a number of familiar and unfamiliar types of chemical equations and how they are classified.

TABLE 7-5. Atoms in a Balanced Equation

Kind of Atom	Number of Atoms			
	$AgNO_3$ + NaCl	$\rightarrow$	AgCl +	$NaNO_3$
Ag	1		1	
N	1			1
O	3			3
Na		1	1	
Cl		1	1	

Check Your Understanding

1. Write balanced chemical equations for the following reactions: (a) copper plus sulfur produces copper (I) sulfide, (b) sodium plus water produces sodium hydroxide plus hydrogen gas.

2. Rust, iron (III) oxide, can be formed when iron is exposed to oxygen in the air. Write a balanced equation for this reaction.

3. **APPLY:** When charcoal burns, it appears that the ashes have less mass and take up less space than the charcoal did. How can this be explained in terms of a balanced equation?

7-4 Chemical Reactions

CLASSIFYING CHEMICAL REACTIONS

Scientists have developed a system of classification for chemical reactions. It is based on the way that atoms rearrange themselves in the reaction. Most reactions can be placed in one of four groups: synthesis, decomposition, single displacement, or double displacement reactions. You've worked with three of these in word equations. Now you'll be able to write balanced chemical equations for these reactions.

In the following activity, you'll discover how chemical reactions enable a space shuttle to be launched.

OBJECTIVES
In this section, you will:
- describe four types of chemical reactions, using their general formulas;
- classify various chemical reactions by type.

FIND OUT!

How does a chemical reaction enable a space shuttle to be launched?

A space shuttle is powered by a chemical reaction between pure liquid hydrogen and pure liquid oxygen. Liquid hydrogen actually serves as the fuel. The fuel tank contains 1,464,000 liters of H_2. The oxidizer tank contains 544,734 liters of O_2. The reaction between H_2 and O_2 is a synthesis reaction. You'll recall that in a synthesis reaction two or more reactants produce a single product.

Conclude and Apply
What do you predict the product of H_2 and O_2 will be? Write a balanced equation for the reaction.

SYNTHESIS REACTIONS

The easiest reaction to recognize is a synthesis reaction. In a synthesis reaction, two or more substances combine,

DID YOU KNOW?

Of prime importance to firefighters is this reaction:

$C + O_2 = CO_2 + heat$.

Most combustible materials are made of carbon-based compounds. When something burns, this is the key reaction.

forming another substance. Typically, synthesis reactions give off energy in the form of heat and light. The general formula for a synthesis reaction is: A + B → AB. The reaction in the Find Out was a synthesis reaction in which hydrogen burns in oxygen forming water.

DECOMPOSITION REACTIONS

The opposite of a synthesis reaction is a decomposition reaction. In a decomposition reaction, one substance breaks down, or decomposes, into two or more simpler substances. The general formula for this type of reaction is: AB → A + B.

Most decomposition reactions require the addition of energy in the form of heat, light, or electricity. For instance, the decomposition of water produces hydrogen and oxygen.

$$\text{electrical energy}$$
$$2H_2O \rightarrow 2H_2 + O_2.$$

DISPLACEMENT REACTIONS

A single displacement reaction occurs when one element replaces another in a compound. There are two general formulas for this type of reaction. In the first case, A replaces B as follows:

$$A + BC \rightarrow AC + B.$$

In the second case D replaces C as follows:

$$D + BC \rightarrow BD + C.$$

There may not appear to be much difference between these two reactions. However, if you look closely you will see in the first case the positive ion is replaced and in the second case it is the negative ion that is replaced as shown in Figure 7-20.

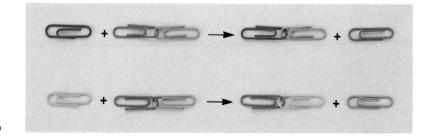

FIGURE 7-20. There are two types of single displacement reactions.

7-2 DOUBLE DISPLACEMENT REACTIONS

One other type of equation is called double displacement. Let's investigate one way you can tell when this type of reaction occurs.

PROBLEM

How does a water softener work?

MATERIALS

5 test tubes and rack
small beaker
saturated solutions of
    calcium sulfate, $CaSO_4$
magnesium sulfate, $MgSO_4$
distilled water
soap solution–1%
sodium carbonate, Na_2CO_3
graduated cylinder–25 mL
filter paper
funnel   stoppers
dropper   stirring rod

PROCEDURE

1. The $CaSO_4$ and $MgSO_4$ solutions represent hard water. Place 10 mL of distilled water and 10 mL of each of the hard water solutions in separate test tubes.

2. Place 2 mL (about 40 drops) of soap solution in each tube. Stopper each

tube and shake. **Observe** the amount of suds formed.

3. Place 15 mL of one of the hard water samples in a small beaker. Add 5 mL of sodium carbonate solution. Stir thoroughly. Record your observations.

4. Filter the solution, collecting the clear liquid in a test tube. Add 2 mL of soap solution and shake. Compare the suds formed with the same solution before the reaction.

5. Repeat Steps 3 and 4 with the other hard water solution.

ANALYZE

1. What evidence of a chemical reaction did you **observe** in Step 3?

2. **Compare** the suds formed

in the hard water solutions before the reaction with sodium carbonate with the suds formed after the reaction.

CONCLUDE AND APPLY

3. Write a word equation for the reaction in Step 3. Based on your knowledge of single displacement reactions, what would you **infer** the products to be in this double displacement reaction? Can you write a balanced equation for what you see?

4. How would you account for the fact that more suds formed after the reaction in Step 4?

5. **Going Further:** In terms of cleanliness and cost, what are the advantages of having a water softener?

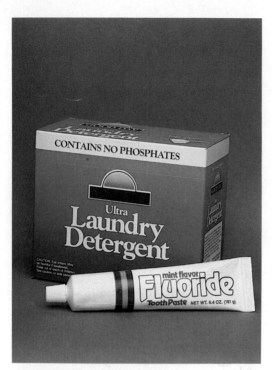

FIGURE 7-21. Some or all of the active ingredients listed in these products take part in chemical reactions and make the products work.

DOUBLE DISPLACEMENT REACTIONS

A precipitate is a common product when solutions of two compounds react as they did in the Investigate. This type of reaction is called double displacement reaction. In a double displacement reaction, the positive ion of one compound replaces the positive ion of the other compound, forming two new compounds. The general formula for this type of reaction is:

$$AB + CD \rightarrow AD + CB.$$

The two reactions in Investigate are both double displacement .

calcium sulfate + sodium carbonate = calcium carbonate + sodium sulfate.

$$CaSO_4 + Na_2CO_3 \rightarrow CaCO_3 + Na_2SO_4$$

The reaction with magnesium is identical except that Mg is used instead of Ca.

Life could not exist without chemical reactions. You get up in the morning, wash your face, and brush your teeth. Toothpaste and soap are both made with chemicals. Some reactions that occur when you wash and brush your teeth are chemical. Eating involves more chemical reactions occurring within your body.

Chemistry is all around you. Understanding how chemical reactions occur can help you understand your world.

Check Your Understanding

1. Which type of reaction is each general formula?
   (a) $XY \rightarrow X + Y$
   (b) $XY + Z \rightarrow XZ + Y$
   (c) $X + Z \rightarrow XZ$
   (d) $WZ + XY \rightarrow WY + XZ$

2. Classify the following reactions by type:
   (a) $2KClO_3 \rightarrow 2KCl + 3O_2$
   (b) $CaBr_2 + Na_2CO_3 \rightarrow CaCO_3 + 2NaBr$

3. **APPLY:** The copper bottoms of some cooking pans turn black after being used. The copper reacts with oxygen forming black copper(II) oxide. Write a balanced chemical equation for this reaction.

EXPANDING YOUR VIEW

A CLOSER LOOK

SILVER STREAKS AND SPEEDING ELECTRONS

Silver is a beautiful, shiny metal that is easily shaped. Its unique traits are determined by the action of its electrons.

The atoms in every element contain a specific number of negatively charged electrons around the nucleus of the atom. Silver has 47 electrons. The electrons nearest the nucleus (in the inner energy levels) are relatively stable and closely bound to the nucleus. Those in the outer energy levels, however, are so far from the nucleus that they are loosely held. They easily move completely away from their own atom to bond with other atoms.

The electrons in the outer energy levels of silver and many other metals actually move freely among all the millions of atoms that make up a piece of silver. In fact, they form a kind of electron gas that makes silver shiny and lustrous, as well as a good conductor of heat and electricity.

The ability of these roving electrons to combine with other elements, however, allows silver to become easily tarnished. Silver atoms bond readily with sulfur in the air to create silver sulfide. The silver sulfide sits on top of the silver, dulling its shine and creating a black residue. Silver polishes remove the silver sulfide and make the metal shiny again. But every time you polish silver, you take a little of the silver away.

YOU TRY IT!

Can you to take the tarnish off silver without losing the silver? Line a glass bowl with aluminum foil. Place a tarnished silver spoon or fork into the bowl. Dissolve several tablespoons of baking soda in enough boiling water to cover the silver. Pour the water over the silver. With a wooden or plastic spoon, press the ends of the aluminum foil loosely over the silver. It only has to touch the top of the silver in a few places.

After fifteen minutes, pour out the water and rinse off the silver. How do the silver and aluminum foil look? Write down "in the presence of baking soda" and the equation for the single displacement reaction that you think might have occurred here. What is the black substance on the aluminum?

LIFE SCIENCE CONNECTION

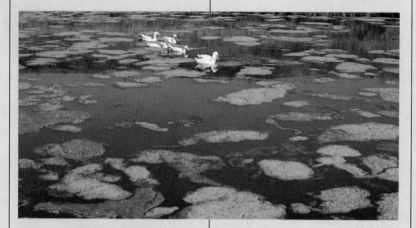

POND SCUM BE GONE!

If your pond is green and scummy, just throw in a few bales of rotting straw. Scientists in England have discovered that rotting straw produces a chemical that initiates a reaction that destroys pond scum.

Algae—microscopic protists—flourish in water that is high in phosphates. Phosphates are compounds that contain the phosphate ion. Phosphates run into water from many sources. They are found in detergents. They come from fertilizers that are spread on crops in the country and on lawns and golf courses in the city. Phosphates are present in the manure that farm animals deposit on the ground and in sewage that has been treated by city treatment plants. The phosphorus from the phosphate ion acts as fertilizer for the algae and encourages it to grow with incredible speed. Soon the entire surface of the water is covered with green.

The result of this speedy growth is that the algae use up all the oxygen that is in the water and that is necessary for other life. Fish of all sizes must have oxygen to survive. In ponds and lakes where algae are rampant, the other life-forms die out.

Scientists decided to follow up on a lead from a farmer who accidentally dropped rotten bales of straw into his lake and was amazed to see the algae disappear. They found that rotting straw produces a chemical that stops algae growth. They don't yet know the exact identity of the chemical, and are still studying it. They have, however, found that fish and plants do not seem to be affected by it. Different kinds of straw work differently. Barley straw works best. Wheat straw works, but more slowly.

Researchers recommend throwing hay into the pond twice a year, once in the fall, and again in the spring before algae start growing.

WHAT DO YOU THINK?

Find a lake or pond in your area. Look for algae growing on the water. Then look around you. Are there farms or manicured lawns nearby? What could be leading to phosphorus runoff that encourages the growth of algae?

SCIENCE AND SOCIETY

CHEMICAL DETECTIVES

It's an unfortunate fact, but where there are people, some sort of criminal activity usually exists. In recent times, science, particularly in the field of chemistry, has provided law enforcement agencies with a powerful tool. This tool, known as forensic chemistry, not only helps police to understand more about the crime itself, but often leads to identification of the criminal.

Who does the blood found at the scene of the crime belong to? Was the fire an accident or was it deliberately set? Is the piece of art or the letter from Abraham Lincoln real or a forgery? The forensic chemist can answer these questions.

Law enforcement agencies are becoming more and more systematic and careful about collecting and preserving evidence at the scene of a crime. Even the oil from the fingers of the detective may prevent evidence from giving clear-cut information. Police now often call in evidence technicians to collect the evidence rather than do it themselves.

Forensic chemists work with the tiniest bits of hair, skin, and fibers from clothing or rugs, blood, or other materials that the untrained eye might overlook. Evidence is sent to one of several hundred crime labs around the United States and Canada. These labs are fully equipped with the latest computerized testing equipment and staffed with highly trained personnel who examine evidence from crime scenes.

Other laboratories work solely on evidence in cases concerning violations of federal or state laws. These may involve identifying pollutants, testing imported materials or

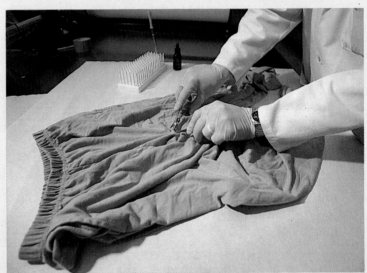

WHAT DO YOU THINK?

Imagine that you are a forensic chemist. You have tested some fibers found at the scene of a murder and fibers from the jacket of the person arrested. The fibers match. What kind of evidence is this? What would you say when you testified in court?

products sold to the public, or verifying that a particular substance is an illegal drug.

In crime labs, body fluids and internal organs are commonly analyzed for poisons, drugs, and alcohol. Even knowing what the victim ate at his or her last meal can provide information as to where he or she might have been before the crime. Blood, saliva, and hair can be classified as to type. Blood, for example, can be classified as A, B, O, RH negative, or RH positive. While once it was only possible to identify a couple of different blood types, it is now possible to compare 30 or more characteristics of a tissue sample.

Evidence can be divided into several categories. For example, the paint from a car can be identified as to the car manufacturer who uses it and possibly the years in which it was used. This type of qualitative testing identifies that the evidence comes from a certain class of substances. It cannot, however, show that the sample came from a specific car. The sample could come from any car from that manufacturer produced during those years.

What if the car has been repainted on several occasions? If the sequence of paint colors in the sample matches that of the suspect car, there is a much greater probability that they match. This is more of an individual type of evidence. The composition of the water in the lungs of a drowning victim could, if not identify where the victim drowned, at least rule out bodies of water that did not possess the same composition.

Forensic chemists can restore charred documents and analyze debris from a fire scene.

CAREER CONNECTION

A career in forensic chemistry, the study of evidence connected with criminal activity, requires a degree in chemistry with further training in the chemistry of identifying substances—analytical chemistry. Forensic chemists need to be good problem solvers and they need to be able to explain complex procedures in simple terms.

Residues of flammable substances are still present after a fire. These may be indications of arson.

Forensic chemistry is an extremely valuable tool in solving various crimes. While the present techniques are excellent, new equipment is constantly being developed. It's possible to identify a substance if it is present in amounts of only a few parts per million. That's like finding one specific person in a city with a population of a million people.

When forensic chemists testify in court, they are considered expert witnesses. That means that they can testify to what their tests have shown and under what circumstances one could expect to observe the same findings. They may not, however, testify as to the guilt or innocence of the person on trial.

*H*istory

C O N N E C T I O N

DYNAMITE AND THE NOBEL PRIZE

You probably know that nitroglycerine is highly explosive. You may have heard of bombs made of nitro that destroyed whole city blocks. But do you know that people with a heart condition can just pop a tiny tablet of nitroglycerine in their mouth and go on their way?

An explosion occurs when a substance combines with oxygen at an extremely fast rate, giving off large amounts of heat and energy. Nitroglycerine is a dangerous explosive liquid with the formula $C_3H_5O_9N_3$. Because nitro already contains enough oxygen of its own, it doesn't need to be combined with more oxygen to react. All it needs is a little shake.

Alfred Nobel (1833-1896) knew that nitroglycerine was very unstable. His family produced the compound for use in the mining industry. Even though they took great care in the production of nitroglycerine, the Nobel family factory exploded, killing Alfred's brother.

Nobel set out to find a way to make nitroglycerine safer to use. Experimenting on a barge in the middle of a lake, he almost accidentally made the discovery that ended his search. A container of nitroglycerine had leaked. Fortunately, it had been packed in dirt to absorb the shocks involved in moving it. Nobel found that when the nitroglycerine was mixed with this dirt, it could only be set off with a blasting cap. Nobel named his invention dynamite. It was eagerly received by the mining industry because of its relative safety in handling.

It was many years after Nobel's death that doctors found that nitroglycerine was especially helpful in treating a heart condition called *angina pectoris.* This is a condition which produces the sensation of suffocation and pain in the chest and is often caused by an anemia of the heart muscle. Tiny amounts of nitroglycerine act directly on the walls of the blood vessels and enlarge them so that blood supply is quickly increased. As the blood flows more freely, the heart doesn't have to work as hard, and blood pressure is reduced.

Nobel probably would have been very happy to know that the substance that had killed his brother had saved so many lives. Nobel left his entire estate to a fund that provides annual prizes in five fields. He chose the fields of chemistry, physics, physiology and medicine, literature, and peace. Receiving a Nobel Prize is considered the highest honor a person can receive for work in these fields.

*E*conomics

C O N N E C T I O N

USING IT UP

As our knowledge of chemistry and chemical reactions has improved, we have found many ways of using these reactions to produce the products we all use. As the technology of such production improves and spreads throughout the world's countries, there is increased competition for raw materials. In many countries, these raw materials are found as minerals in Earth. But the supply of these minerals is limited.

The graph shows three different possible outcomes for how soon the raw materials from which metals are produced might be used up in the United States. Line A shows what will happen if, in the future, we continue to use raw materials at the present rate. What would produce the lines shown in B and C?

YOU TRY IT!

Your teacher will divide the class into small groups and will assign each group a certain course of action. Discuss this action with your group and answer the following questions.

1. Which of the lines on the graph would indicate the results of the action you take?

2. What are the advantages and disadvantages of this action in terms of the country's economy? In terms of the environment?

3. How would this action affect your own personal lifestyle?

After discussing your action, share your results with the class. Since most of these actions would probably require government action, what groups might oppose the passage of each of the laws?

Working with your team, think of several other actions that will move our use of metal-containing resources toward line C on the graph.

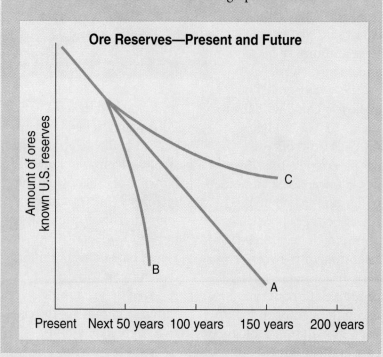

Ore Reserves—Present and Future

Amount of ores known U.S. reserves

C

B

A

Present   Next 50 years   100 years   150 years   200 years

Reviewing Main Ideas

1. A knowledge of chemical reactions can be both helpful and life-saving.

$$6HCl + 2Fe \longrightarrow 2FeCl_3 + 3H_2$$

3. The total number of atoms of each element in the reactants equals the total number of atoms in the products. All chemical reactions must be balanced.

Na +
K +
Fe^{2+}
O_2
H_2O
CO_2

Na +
K +
Fe^{2+}
O_2
H_2O
CO_2

a

b

c

d

4. Four major types of reactions are synthesis (a), decomposition (b), single displacement (c), and double displacement (d). All can be expressed as balanced chemical equations.

2. Ions and covalent molecules are found in all living things.

Chapter Review

USING KEY SCIENCE TERMS

balanced chemical equation
binary compound
covalent bond
ion
ionic bond
molecule
nonpolar molecule
oxidation number
polar molecule
polyatomic ion

Use one of the above terms to complete each sentence.

1. $AgNO_3 + NaCl \longrightarrow AgCl + NaNO_3$ is a(n) ____.
2. HCO_3^- is an example of a(n) ____.
3. NaCl is an example of a(n) ____.
4. A(n) ____ shows how many electrons an atom has gained, lost or shared when bonding with other atoms.
5. A molecule whose ends have neither a positive nor a negative charge is an example of a(n) ____.
6. A compound that is composed of two elements is a(n) ____.
7. When an atom gains electrons, it becomes a(n) ____.
8. Opposites attract could describe what happens in a(n) ____.

UNDERSTANDING IDEAS

Choose the best answer to complete each sentence.

1. In a formula, a number written after and below a symbol tells ____.
   a. the coefficient
   b. the number of atoms of that element that are in the compound
   c. the number of atoms in the compound
   d. the number of atoms needed to balance the equation
2. A bond that forms between atoms when they share electrons is called ____.
   a. an ionic bond
   b. an atomic bond
   c. a covalent bond
   d. a government bond
3. In a polar molecule ____.
   a. electrons are evenly shared
   b. electrons are gained and lost
   c. magnetic poles form
   d. electrons are unevenly shared
4. In iron(III) oxide, the Roman numeral equals ____.
   a. the number of electrons in the outer energy level
   b. the number of protons in the atom
   c. the oxidation number
   d. the binary number
5. The formula for iron (III) chlorate is ____.
   a. $FeClO_3$
   b. $FeCl$
   c. $Fe(ClO_3)_3$
   d. $FeCl_3$

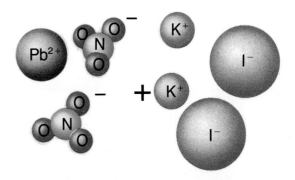

6. The oxidation number of Fe in Fe_2S_3 is ____.
  a. 1+   **c.** 3+
  b. 2+   **d.** 4+

7. $Mg + O_2 \longrightarrow MgO$.
  The coefficients which would balance this equation are ____.
  a. 2,1,2   **c.** 1,1,2
  b. 2,2,1   **d.** 2,1,1

8. $H_2 + S \longrightarrow H_2S$ is an example of a ____.
  a. synthesis reaction
  b. decomposition reaction
  c. single displacement reaction
  d. double displacement reaction

2. Balance the following equation:
  $Fe_3O_4 + H_2 \longrightarrow Fe + H_2O$

3. The diagram shows the reactants in a chemical reaction. Write a balanced equation for this reaction.

CRITICAL THINKING

Use your understanding of the concepts developed in the chapter to answer each of the following questions.

1. Element X has oxidation numbers of 3+ and 5+. Element Z has oxidation numbers of 2- and 3-. Write formulas for the four different compounds of X and Z.

PROBLEM SOLVING

Read the following problem and discuss your answers in a brief paragraph.

You are living on the shore of a body of water and you get 250 days of sunshine a year. The problems of storing and transporting hydrogen have been solved. Suggest how you would use the electricity from solar cells to produce a clean, nonpolluting fuel.

What use(s) could you make of any other products of this reaction?

CONNECTING IDEAS

Discuss each of the following in a brief paragraph.

1. In nature, tin is found in ore as tin(IV) oxide. When the tin(IV) oxide is heated with carbon, the products are tin and carbon dioxide. Write a balanced equation for this reaction.

2. The unbalanced reaction involved in photosynthesis is $CO_2 + H_2O \longrightarrow C_6H_{12}O_6$ (sugar) $+ O_2$. This takes place in the presence of light energy and chlorophyll. What set of coefficients will balance this equation?

3. SCIENCE AND SOCIETY What's the difference between class

and individual evidences?

4. EARTH SCIENCE CONNECTION Why do phosphates cause ponds to be overrun with plant growth?

5. A CLOSER LOOK Why does silver bond so readily with other elements?

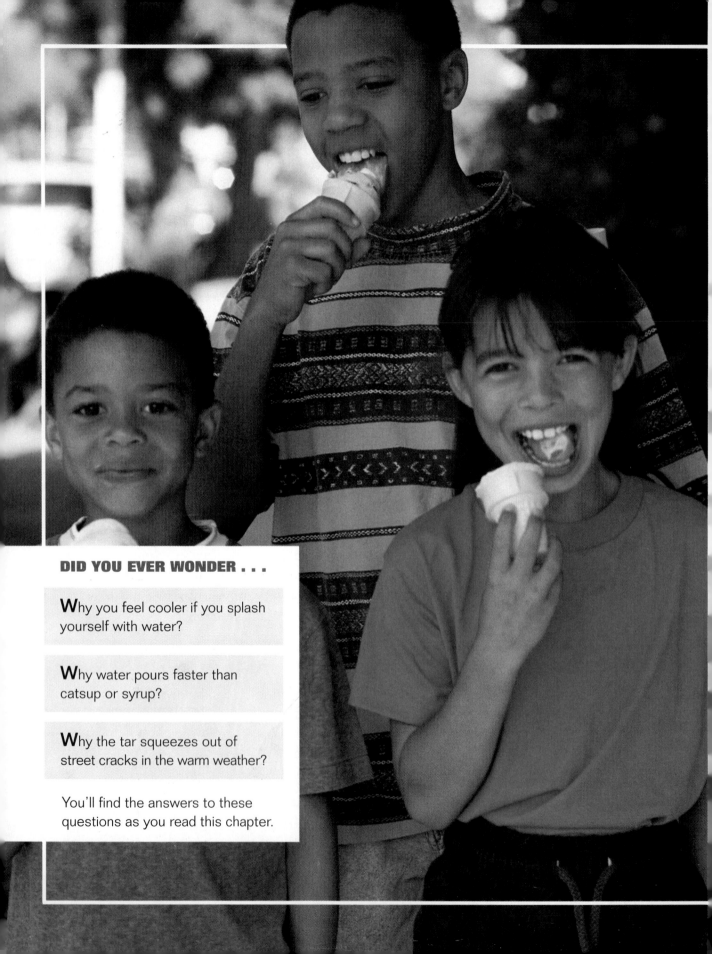

DID YOU EVER WONDER . . .

Why you feel cooler if you splash yourself with water?

Why water pours faster than catsup or syrup?

Why the tar squeezes out of street cracks in the warm weather?

You'll find the answers to these questions as you read this chapter.

Molecules in Motion

I t's a warm, clear, sunny day, and you and your friends are on the way home from the beach. You had arrived early enough in the day to get a choice spot on the beach, put on a sunscreen, and then you waded kneedeep into the water to test the temperature. Perfect!

After lying in the sun for 20 minutes, you were so warm that you began to sweat. You decided it would be a good time for a swim. You dove into the surf and came up shivering. How could the water become so cold when it was perfect when you arrived?

Now, walking home, you are starting to get hot again. You and your friends decide

to buy ice cream cones. But you must finish the cones fast before they melt all over your hands.

What causes all these changes? You'll find out in this chapter with the help of an interesting idea called the kinetic-molecular theory.

EXPLORE!

How does heat move?

Place 75 mL of ice water into one beaker, 75 mL of tap water into a second beaker, and 75 mL of hot water into a third.

Record the temperature in each beaker, then drop a piece of brightly colored hard candy in each beaker. Record your observations over the next few minutes. How do you account for what you observe?

8-1 Solids and Liquids

FIGURE 8-1. In Joule's device (a), potential energy turned into kinetic energy and the temperature of the water increased. The same energy change occurs at a waterfall (b).

THE KINETIC-MOLECULAR THEORY

In the mid-1800s, the British physicist James Prescott Joule found a way to measure the increase in temperature produced by a measured amount of work. Joule attached a weight on a cable and the cable to a paddle wheel, as shown in Figure 8-1(a).

With the paddle wheel in a container of water, he allowed the weight to fall. When the weight fell, its potential energy turned to kinetic energy. The wheel turned, churning the water and raising its temperature.

Joule measured these temperature changes in many trials. He found that the ratio of the increase in temperature to the distance the weight fell was always the same. In other words, the increase in thermal energy produced by a given amount of mechanical work was always the same. The experiment shows that work can be changed into thermal energy. But how was energy transferred from the falling weight to the water in the container?

Joule used the idea that all matter is made up of vibrating atoms and molecules to explain what happened. The movement of the paddle wheel in the water caused the water molecules to move faster. Of course, the paddle wheel caused currents of water to move. These could be seen. But Joule said that the paddle wheel also increased the invisible random motion of the water molecules. A faster-moving molecule has more kinetic energy. The more kinetic energy each molecule had, the hotter the water became. The explanation of thermal energy as the random move-

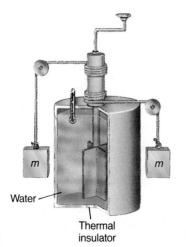

Water

Thermal insulator

a

b

ment of atoms or molecules is part of what is called the **kinetic-molecular theory**.

In this section, you'll take another look at some familiar properties of matter. You'll see how the kinetic-molecular theory helps us explain those properties and predict the behavior of matter.

WHAT MAKES A SOLID SOLID?

In your day at the beach, you might buy a soft drink to cool off. The paper cup, the ice, and the coins you get as change are each examples of solid materials. A solid material has a definite shape and fills a definite amount of space. What is it that keeps solid things together? Solids are made of particles—ions, atoms, or molecules. Because solids are rigid, there must be forces of attraction that hold the particles in a fixed arrangement giving solids their definite shape. Because solids cannot be compressed easily, the particles must be close together and there must be forces that keep the particles from being pushed even closer together.

The kinetic theory says that the ions, atoms, or molecules in matter are in motion. A model of a solid is shown in Figure 8-2. In this model, the particles are represented by small balls and the forces between them as springs. Try to pull the particles apart and the force of the springs keeps them together. Try to push the particles closer together, and the springs will oppose that push. But the particles can vibrate back and forth in all directions around their fixed, or home, positions. The greater the vibration, the greater the temperature. Of course, metal springs don't exist between real particles of a solid, but the forces between the particles act like the springs. Inside even the most solid-looking solid, the particles are always moving. The strength of a solid's forces between particles keeps the solid in its general shape.

What happens to a solid when its temperature rises? We will investigate this question using a common soda straw.

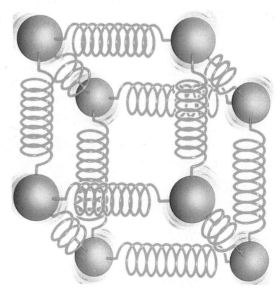

FIGURE 8-2. In a solid, particles are held in a definite shape by forces acting between them.

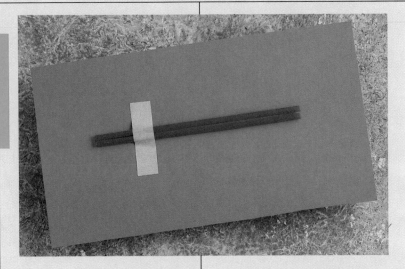

8-1 THERMAL EXPANSION OF A STRAW

An increase in temperature of a solid indicates an increase in the kinetic energy of the particles in the solid. What are some effects of this increased motion?

PURPOSE
What happens to a solid as its temperature rises?

MATERIALS
3 drinking straws
cardboard sheet
2 drinking cups
sticky tape
very hot water
scissors
1 pencil
thermal mitt

PROCEDURE
1. Tape two of the straws tightly together, side by side, as shown. Then tape these straws to the cardboard.
2. Mark the positions of the bottoms of the straws.
3. Use the third straw as a funnel to help you pour water into one of the side-by-side straws. It will help if you slice the top end of the third straw diagonally. Slightly fold its bottom end and slide it into one of the two taped straws.
4. Put on the thermal mitt. With one cup, slowly pour the hottest water that is available into the funnel straw. Catch the water in the other cup as it runs out the bottom end of the straw. Make sure that only the one straw comes in contact with the hot water.
5. **Observe** and record any change in the position of the end of this straw.

ANALYZE
1. Describe the direction in which the two-straw combination curved when heated.
2. Make a drawing that shows the two straws in the bent position. Which straw is longer—the one on the outside of the bend or the one on the inside of the bend?

CONCLUDE AND APPLY
3. Did the heated straw get larger or smaller? Use the kinetic-molecular theory to **hypothesize** why this happened.
4. **Predict** how you could make the straws bend back.
5. **Going Further:** You have a metal storm door that opens and closes very easily in the winter, but sticks in the summer. Explain why this happens.

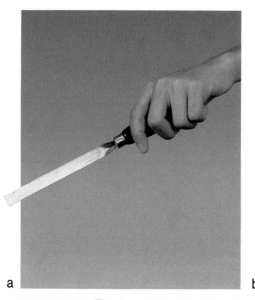
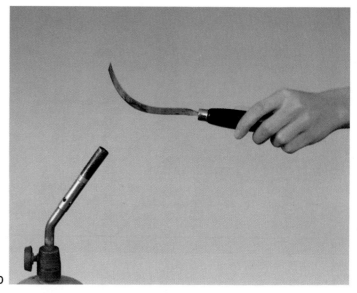

FIGURE 8-3. This bimetallic strip (a) is steel on one side and brass on the other. Each metal expands at a different rate (b).

Of course, you normally would have no reason to consider how drinking straws change when heated. But you probably have observed the effect of temperature on other solids in your home. Have you ever removed a metal cap from a jar by running the cap under hot water? Or separated two nested glasses by putting cold water into the inner glass and standing the outer one in hot water?

When the temperature increases, a solid tends to expand. The expansion you observed was small, but it is important to the design of structures such as highways, railroads, and bridges. When a highway is built, the concrete is poured in sections that are separated by small spaces. On a hot day, the concrete expands to fill the spaces. Without these spaces, concrete might crack or buckle. Figure 8-4 shows the expansion joints that are part of a bridge. Each section of the bridge expands or contracts as the temperature changes.

The expansion that occurs as a solid is heated is called **thermal expansion**. How can we use kinetic theory to

FIGURE 8-4. The spaces between bridge sections allow for thermal expansion.

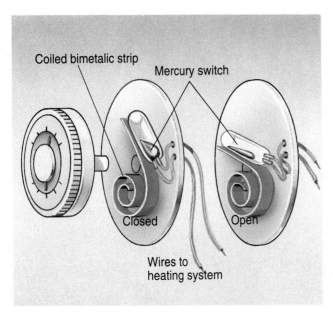

FIGURE 8-5. In this thermostat, there is a bimetallic strip that expands as the room gets warmer.

SKILLBUILDER

INTERPRETING SCIENTIFIC ILLUSTRATIONS

The thermostat that controls a furnace works a little like the side-by-side straws. In Figure 8-5, what happens as the loop in the thermostat expands? What happens when it contracts? How does this control the furnace? If you need help, refer to the **Skill Handbook** on page 691.

explain thermal expansion? As the temperature of a solid increases, its atoms or molecules vibrate with greater speed and amplitude. The atoms move a little farther from their home position. In terms of the ball-and-spring model, the balls vibrate faster and with greater amplitude. The average length of the springs increases. When you heat the metal jar lid, the average distance between the metal's atoms increases, and so the lid expands. How does the kinetic molecular theory explain the characteristics of liquids?

THE NATURE OF LIQUIDS

Have you ever put an ice cube in a glass, left for a while, and come back some time later? The solid, with its fixed shape, has become a liquid, whose shape depends on the shape of the glass. Early in your science studies, you learned that a liquid has a definite volume and tends to be hard to compress. A liquid expands as its temperature rises. Kinetic theory explains this expansion in the same way that it explains the expansion of a solid. The thermal expansion of some liquids like mercury and alcohol is regular and constant over a wide range of temperatures. This allows the liquids to be used in a thermometer to measure temperature.

Unlike a solid, a liquid does not have a definite shape. It takes on the shape of its container. How does kinetic theory explain this and other properties of a liquid? Let's investigate a few more properties of liquids before answering that question.

FIGURE 8-6. Why are alcohol and mercury suitable for thermometers?

8-2 PROPERTIES OF LIQUIDS

What conditions must be true for us to call a substance a liquid? In this Investigate, you'll have an opportunity to decide.

PROBLEM
How can properties of a material be used to classify it?

MATERIALS
dropper
goggles
food coloring
apron
wooden stick
paper cup
50-mL graduated cylinder
4% solution of powdered borax, in water
4% solution of polyvinyl alcohol (PVA)

PROCEDURE
1. Copy the data table and record all observations.
2. Using a graduated cylinder, measure 30 mL of PVA solution into a paper cup. Add 2 drops of food coloring.
3. Using a dropper, add about 3 mL of borax solution to the PVA in the cup and begin to stir vigorously with the stick.
4. After stirring for two minutes, what is the consistency of the material?
5. Transfer the material to your hand. **CAUTION:** *Do not taste or eat the material and be sure to wash your hands after the activity.* How easily does the material flow?
6. Form the material into a ball and then place it in the cup. Does it take the shape of the container?
7. **Compare** the volume of the new material with the volume of the original material before stirring.

ANALYZE
1. Would you **infer** that the new material is more like a solid, a liquid, or a gas?
2. Considering the slow flow of the new material, rate the strength of the attraction among its particles.

CONCLUDE AND APPLY
3. **Compare and contrast** the properties of your new material with those of a wood block and water.
4. **Going Further:** At what point might it become very difficult to decide whether a substance is a liquid or solid? What does this tell you about the definitions of these states?

DATA AND OBSERVATIONS

PROPERTY	OBSERVATION	INTERPRETATION
Ability to flow		
Shape changes		
Volume changes		

In the Investigate, you observed evidence that there is a difference in the forces holding particles together. Attractive forces must exist between a liquid's molecules, or else the liquid would not stay together at all. As in solids, the molecules resist being squeezed together. Unlike solids, however, the attractive forces between the liquid's molecules are too weak to maintain a particular shape. The molecules are able to slip and slide over each other and assume any possible arrangement.

Is this force between molecules the same for all liquids? Or, like solids, are some liquids held together more tightly than others? Can the molecules of one liquid move more freely than those of others? Let's find out.

FIND OUT!

How do the molecular forces within liquids compare?

You can't directly observe the forces between a liquid's molecules. You can, however, observe how easily a liquid changes shape and use these observations to infer how strongly a liquid's molecules are held together. You will need three clear glasses and three large plates or pie pans. Put about 25 mL of water in one glass. Try to coat the inside of the glass with water by twisting and turning the glass as in the picture. Record your observations. Then hold the glass about 10 cm above the pie plate. Slowly turn the glass upside down and notice how quickly or slowly the water pours out of the glass. What happens as the water reaches the pie plate? Repeat the activity for two or three other liquids, such as syrup, molasses, motor oil, salad oil, or liquid soap.

Conclude and Apply
1. Make a list of the liquids you tested, sequencing the liquids from fastest to slowest pouring.
2. Explain this difference in pouring speed in terms of the attraction between molecules in the different substances.

As you discovered in the Find Out, one liquid may change shape less readily than another. A liquid's resistance to changing shape is called its **viscosity**. A liquid with high viscosity, such as syrup, pours more slowly than a liquid with low viscosity, such as water. Viscosity depends on the attractive forces between a liquid's molecules. The stronger the force, the more viscous the liquid. You already know from the kinetic theory that the temperature of the liquid affects the strength of this force. This is not because the force itself changes, but because molecules with less kinetic energy are closer together. A cold liquid tends to be more viscous than a hot liquid. On a cold morning, the lubricating oil in an automobile engine may be so viscous that it does not flow freely enough to form a protective coating when the engine is first cranked. Many motor oils are now manufactured to lessen the effect of temperature on viscosity.

FIGURE 8-7. Which liquid is more viscous?

FREEZING AND MELTING

If you heat almost any solid, it will change into a liquid. The change from a solid to a liquid is called melting. You have to add energy to a solid to melt it. If you drop an ice cube into water, the energy that melts the ice comes from the water. The water temperature drops as a result.

Once again, we need to go below the surface and use kinetic theory to understand how a solid turns to a liquid.

FIGURE 8-8. As a solid melts, the particles move more freely and lose their regular shape.

When a solid is heated, each of its molecules receives additional energy. The molecules vibrate faster and farther away from their home positions. Eventually, the molecules have so much energy that they break free of the bonds that hold them in a regular arrangement. The solid becomes liquid.

In the reverse process to melting, a liquid is cooled. As the liquid's temperature drops, its molecules become increasingly sluggish. When the temperature is low enough, the molecules cluster together, and the liquid becomes a solid. The process in which a liquid changes into a solid is called freezing or solidification. Does the volume of a material change during this process?

EXPLORE!

How does freezing or solidification affect volume?

Pour water into a tray or square cake pan until the tray is two-thirds full. Mark the level of the water on one side of the tray. Then place the tray in the freezer. After the water has frozen, observe the level of the ice. Does the ice take up more space or less space than the water did?

Repeat the experiment, using some paraffin. Gently heat the wax in a pan until the wax melts. If you use a gas burner, be careful not to spill the wax while heating it because the wax can catch fire. Make a mark about halfway up one side of a small, clear container. Fill the container with the melted wax up to the mark. Let the wax cool at room temperature until it is solid. Check the level of the solid wax in the container. Did the wax expand or shrink when it turned into a solid?

Knowing how a drop in temperature affects the interaction of molecules, you might have accurately predicted the behavior of the wax. Generally, the solid phase of a substance occupies a smaller volume than the liquid phase

FIGURE 8-9. As water freezes, it expands. Ice is less dense than water.

does. Molecules will, on the whole, move more slowly and stay closer together as the substance freezes or solidifies. However, water's behavior may have surprised you. Water turns out to be the chief exception to this behavior.

Water expands when it freezes. This unique characteristic of water is important to life on Earth. A ten-gram mass of ice has a larger volume than a ten-gram mass of water. Therefore, the density of ice is less than the density of water and ice floats on water as Figure 8-9 illustrates. As a result, a river, lake, or pond freezes from the surface down. This allows most plants and animals in the water to live through the winter beneath the ice.

EVAPORATION AND CONDENSATION

Solids change to liquids when their temperature reaches their melting point. Above this point, more molecules leave a solid than join it, and the solid shrinks. At its melting point, the solid and liquid phases or states of a substance are in thermal equilibrium. The solid is melting at the same rate as the liquid is freezing.

You have seen that, at the melting point, a substance is in equilibrium between the solid and liquid state. What happens when the liquid is heated?

In your trip to the beach, you were very wet when you first left the water. After a few moments in the sunlight, your skin was dry. Where did the water go?

FIGURE 8-10. Which shape allows for more evaporation?

EXPLORE!

Do you need sunlight to make a liquid change state?

Using a dropper, place 5 drops of rubbing alcohol on the back of one hand. Wait two minutes. What did you feel? What change of state did you observe? Has energy entered or left your hand? Where did the energy for this process come from?

The alcohol molecules on your skin are in motion. As the energy moves from your skin to the alcohol, the alcohol molecules move faster. The fastest ones soon gain enough energy to break free into the open air as an invisible gas. This process of a liquid changing to a gas or vapor is called **evaporation**. How did your hand feel as the alcohol evaporated? It cooled off. As the water evaporates from your skin when you come out of the water at the beach, you also feel cold. Why?

According to kinetic theory, the molecules with the highest kinetic energy in a liquid are the ones that escape into the air as a gas. This lowers the average kinetic energy of the molecules that stay behind. In addition, thermal energy is transferred from your skin to the water, increasing the temperature of the water molecules, allowing some molecules to escape. This decreases the temperature of molecules in your skin. You experience this as a cool feeling. If you measure the temperature of a container of water after evaporation has been going on for some time,

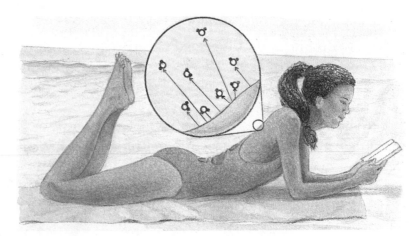

FIGURE 8-11. As water evaporates, thermal energy from your skin is transferred to the water, making you feel cooler.

it will indicate a lower temperature than before evaporation began. Evaporation is a cooling process.

BOILING

Evaporation takes place faster from your warm skin than it does from a container at room temperature. If you warm the water in the container on the stove, it will evaporate even faster. If you heat the water further, bubbles will begin to form on the bottom of the pan and rise to the surface. Soon, the entire liquid will be filled with rapidly forming and rising bubbles. The water is **boiling.** If the boiling continued, the pan would soon be empty. All of the water would have turned into water vapor.

Any pure liquid will boil when it reaches a temperature called its boiling point. When energy is added to a liquid at the temperature of its boiling point, the energy separates some molecules from other molecules in the liquid. These move so far away from the others that the forces between them can no longer hold them together. At this point, the liquid becomes a gas or vapor. The boiling point is a unique temperature for each liquid. Some substances do not need to boil to change to a gas.

FIGURE 8-12. When water boils, bubbles of gas particles form below the surface, rise to the top, and escape (a). When a liquid evaporates, individual gas particles escape from the surface (b).

a

b

FIGURE 8-13. As solid CO_2 sublimes, water vapor in the air condenses on the cold CO_2 gas molecules.

SUBLIMATION

Solids can undergo a process similar to evaporation. Have you ever left a tray of ice cubes in the freezer for several months? You find that the once-full tray now has only small cubes of ice in it. The temperature was below freezing, so the water in the cubes couldn't have changed to a liquid and evaporated in the normal sense. Instead, they changed directly from solid to gas. In the process, called **sublimation**, a solid changes into a gas without first becoming a liquid. Sublimation can occur when wet clothes are hung out to dry and the temperature is below freezing. The water on the clothes soon freezes. After several hours, however, the clothes are dry, even though the ice never thawed. The ice vanished into the air as vapor.

Dry ice is actually solid carbon dioxide. A block of it left at room temperature will gradually disappear, without passing through a liquid state. Moth balls are another example of a substance that undergoes sublimation. When a block of moth repellant is hung in the closet, it gradually gets smaller. You smell the vapor in the air, but there is no liquid state.

CONDENSATION

If you've had a cold glass of water on a hot day, you've probably noticed that water collects on the outside of the glass. Where did this water come from? Did water inside the glass somehow pass through it? You could find out by adding food coloring to the water inside and then seeing whether the water on the outside is colored. Or you could place an empty glass in a bowl of water and see if water can move through the glass from the outside in.

Either activity would show you that the water did not move through the glass. It must have come, then, from the surrounding air. If you compare the amount of water that collects on a glass of water on a hot, dry day and the amount that collects on a hot, humid day, you will find much more water on the glass on the humid day. Molecules of water vapor in the air must have changed into liquid. When a gas becomes a liquid, **condensation** is said to take place.

FIGURE 8-14. Water vapor from the air condenses on the cool sides of a glass.

Condensation is evaporation in reverse. As the temperature of a gas decreases, the kinetic energy of its molecules decreases. They slow down, and, the force of attraction between them holds them closer together. The gas has changed into a liquid. This happens when warm water vapor in the air comes in contact with the cold glass of water. It's also what happens as warm air rises in the atmosphere to cooler levels. The water vapor condenses into the cluster of tiny water droplets that you know as a cloud.

The kinetic theory can explain the properties of solids and liquids in terms of moving particles and the forces between them. In solids, strong bonds between particles restrict their movement to vibrations about fixed points, so solids are rigid and have definite volumes.

As you heat a solid, its particles vibrate increasingly faster. Solids melt when the strength of the vibrations is greater than that of the forces holding the particles together. Thus a solid becomes a liquid, whose bonds still are strong enough to give it a definite volume but are too weak to give it a particular shape. If you bring the liquid to a boil, the particles gain enough kinetic energy to break their bonds and escape as a gas. In the next section, you'll explore the properties and characteristics of gases more fully.

Check Your Understanding

1. Compare and contrast the way the particles in a solid and liquid are organized.
2. Suppose you have filled a gasoline can to the brim on a cool morning. You come back to it in the hot afternoon to find that some gasoline leaked from the can. What can you conclude?
3. Explain melting in terms of the kinetic theory.
4. Label each of these examples as evaporation, condensation, or sublimation.
   a. A piece of meat taken from the freezer has freezer burn. It is dry and looks gray. What happened?
   b. When you are boiling a pot of water on the stove, you find that the metal surface above the burners is wet.
   c. Your skin feels dry and flaky after a day in the sun.
5. **APPLY:** Experiments have shown that it takes more than five times as much energy to change 1 g of water at 100° C to water vapor at 100°C, as it does to heat that gram of water from 0°C to 100°C. In terms of energy transfer, why do you get a more severe burn from steam than you do from boiling water?

8-2 Kinetic Theory of Gases

OBJECTIVES

In this section, you will

- describe pressure in terms of kinetic theory;
- explain the meaning of temperature in gases;
- discuss what absolute zero means.

KEY SCIENCE TERMS

absolute zero

PRESSURE

Of the three phases of matter, the gas phase has the most interesting behavior of all. Consider how air behaves when you blow up a party balloon. You take a deep breath, put the balloon to your lips, and try to force air into the balloon. The balloon pushes the air back, and you feel it pushing against your cheeks. Finally, the rubber begins to stretch. The more air you can keep inside the balloon after each breath, the more readily the balloon expands. How can something like air, made up of tiny moving particles with relatively large spaces between them, exert pressure?

FIND OUT!

How do collisions produce pressure?
Get some classmates to stand about two meters from a large cardboard carton. Place the carton so that one side faces your friends. Have your friends throw tennis balls at the carton. What happens? Have your friends throw ten balls in one second, then only five in one second. Record the results. Then have your friends throw the balls very fast, one at a time. Then throw them very slowly. Record these results as well.

You've seen that the force exerted on the carton depended on the speed and number of balls thrown at it. In the same way, the force that molecules in the air exert is proportional to their speed and number. Although the motion of the box may have been uneven, moving only when a ball hit it, imagine billions of balls hitting the box—billions of moving molecules in the air striking every surface with which they come in contact. You can feel this force when you inflate the balloon.

Why is inflating a balloon so difficult? The rubber of the balloon must exert a force inward on the air trapped inside. You feel the result of that force as you blow. The air you blow into the balloon must exert a force outward on the balloon greater than the force the balloon exerts inward.

PRESSURE CHANGES WITH VOLUME

What happens when you squeeze an inflated balloon? In the chapter on gases, you studied Boyle's Law, which describes the relationship between the pressure and volume of a gas. For a fixed amount of gas at a constant temperature, pressure and volume are inversely proportional. That is, as volume goes up, pressure goes down. Figure 8-15 shows how kinetic theory explains this relationship. If the volume of a gas increases, then the area of the container also increases. Fewer particles strike a given area, and thus the overall pressure drops.

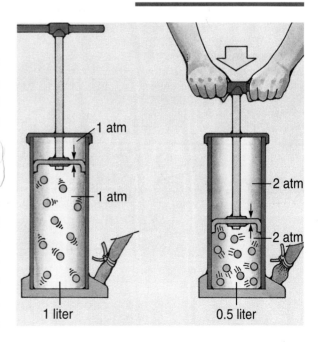

FIGURE 8-15. As the volume of a gas decreases, its pressure increases.

You saw this in Find Out when fewer balls were thrown at the carton. Similarly, if the volume is decreased, the surface area is decreased. The collisions per unit area increase, so the pressure rises.

PRESSURE CHANGES WITH TEMPERATURE

How else can you change the pressure of a gas? Figure 8-16 shows a sample of gas in a container with a fixed volume. If you heat the gas, its pressure increases. If you cool the gas, its pressure decreases. For a fixed amount of gas at a constant volume, the pressure is directly related to its temperature. The area of the container's surface did not change, but the gas pressure did. In terms of kinetic theory, the speed of the gas particles must have increased as the temperature rose. This is similar to what happened in the Find Out when the balls were thrown with greater speed. Each ball exerted more force on the carton.

If a gas in a sealed container is heated it can generate enormous pressure. This explains why you should never throw a container of pressurized gas, such as an aerosol can, into a fire. The temperature of the gas inside the can will rise, and then the pressure may rise to a point where the container can no longer withstand the pressure. At that point, the container will explode.

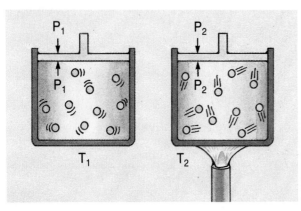

FIGURE 8-16. For a fixed amount of gas, as temperature increases, pressure increases.

VOLUME CHANGES WITH TEMPERATURE

So far, you've seen that a change in either the volume or the temperature of a gas changes its pressure. How does a change in temperature affect the volume of a gas? You learned earlier that Charles' law describes this relationship. At constant pressure, volume and temperature are directly proportional. That is, as one increases the other increases. How does kinetic theory explain this? If thermal energy is added, the kinetic energy of the molecules is increased. If the volume stays the same, the number of collisions between the particles and the container would increase and the pressure would be greater. But to apply Charles' law, the pressure must remain constant. Therefore, the surface which the molecules strike must get larger so that the number of collisions per unit of area (pressure) remains the same.

Can the volume of a gas ever be zero? No, of course not. Molecules are matter and matter takes up space. The volume would eventually reach a level below which it wouldn't go no matter how cold the gas got. At that point, the molecules in the gas would be so close together that no matter how weak the forces of attraction between them were, the gas would condense or even solidify. But suppose this gas were an "ideal" gas and could be cooled to a volume of zero. What would the kinetic energy of the molecules be at that point?

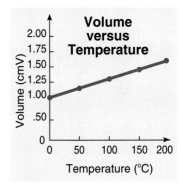

FIGURE 8-17. Volume and temperature are directly related.

ABSOLUTE ZERO

As far as we know, there is no upper limit to how hot matter can get, but there is a limit to coldness. The temperature of a gas measures the average kinetic energy of the molecules. Suppose that a substance could be cooled to −273°C. At that temperature, known as **absolute zero**, the kinetic energy of molecules would have decreased to zero. And if the molecules had no more energy to remove, there could be no further cooling. Absolute zero is a coldness limit. It is now known that, even at this temperature, molecules would still have a tiny amount of energy that could never be taken away. Therefore, absolute zero represents the lowest possible energy that matter can have.

While the Celsius temperature scale is constructed with the freezing and boiling points of water as its reference points, you can see that 0°C doesn't mean much in terms of other substances. A new scale, the Kelvin scale, begins at absolute zero. The kelvin is the SI unit of temperature. Because one kelvin is equal in size to one Celsius degree, this means that the freezing point of water on the kelvin scale is 273 kelvins or 273 K and the boiling point is 373 K. This is very useful when solving problems such as the relationship in Charles' law. You know that as temperature increases, volume increases proportionately. So if you double the temperature, you would double the vol-

SKILLBUILDER

MAKING AND USING GRAPHS
Make a graph like the one in Figure 8-17, but begin your horizontal axis at −300°C. and your vertical axis at 0 cm^3. Graph the following points:
   V=100 cm^3 when T=0°C.
   V=118 cm^3 when T=50°C.
   V=137 cm^3 when T=100°C.
Connect the points to form a line. Extend the line until it crosses the horizontal axis. What is that temperature? If you need help, refer to the **Skill Handbook** on page 682.

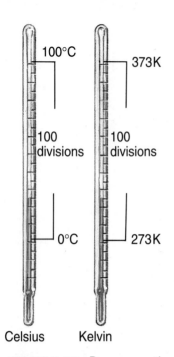

100°C
373K

100
divisions

100
divisions

0°C

273K

Celsius   Kelvin

FIGURE 8-18. Degrees on the Celsius and Kelvin temperature scales are the same size.

ume. How can you double a temperature of 0°C? Using the Kelvin scale eliminates this problem.

In this section, we've discussed the behavior of gases in kinetic-molecular terms. But scientists established the laws that describe this behavior before they were even sure that atoms and molecules exist. In fact, the laws relating the temperature, pressure, and volume of gases provided strong evidence for the existence of these particles.

We now picture a gas as a group of widely separated atoms or molecules in constant, random motion. These particles are always colliding with each other and, when contained, with the walls of their container. These collisions produce pressure. More collisions result in more pressure. Boyle's law tells us that this is exactly what occurs. If volume decreases, pressure increases.

The next time you spend a day at the beach, think of all the ways in which the kinetic theory operates around you. Substances may look like solids, liquids, and gases, but now you know that they are all made up of moving particles.

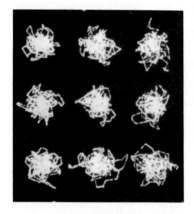
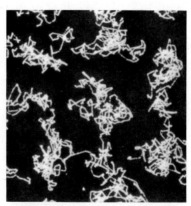
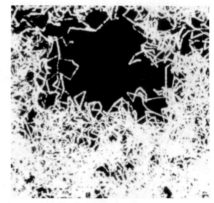

FIGURE 8-19. The motion of particles in solids, liquids, and gases is illustrated by this computer-generated model.

Check Your Understanding

1. Explain how air exerts pressure on the top of your desk.
2. Define the temperature of a gas in terms of kinetic theory.
3. Explain why no gas can be cooled to a temperature of absolute zero (0°K).
4. **APPLY:** When you are eating hot soup, why does blowing on a spoonful make it cool off faster?

CONTENTS

A CLOSER LOOK

CRYSTAL CLEAR

What do salt, diamonds, and snowflakes all have in common? They are all crystals.

Crystals are everywhere—even in your pencil. A pencil's lead is really clay mixed with graphite—a crystal form of carbon. Draw a line on a piece of paper with your pencil. Then look at that line under a magnifying glass. What do you see?

Today, solids whose atoms are arranged in a pattern repeated over and over again are called crystals. But, in ancient times, the word *crystal* referred to only transparent solids.

Crystal comes from the Greek word *krystallos,* which means frozen water. The ancient Greeks thought crystals were made from water that was frozen under intense cold. This belief lasted into medieval times. Even today, we refer to water that is very clear as being crystal clear.

The first recorded scientific observation of crystals was in 1597. That was when Andreas Libavius saw that crystals of different substances had their own distinct shapes. He discovered that the salts dissolved in mineral waters could be identified by looking at the shapes of crystals that were left after the water dried.

Crystals can form in solutions, from molten solids, or from vapors. Perfect crystals form only under ideal conditions. They need steady temperatures, steady pressure, and a steady supply of atoms. This is because even the smallest crystals consist of millions of subatomic connections. It's calculated that the growth of one cubic inch of crystal requires 1.0×10^{24} atoms to line up in an orderly fashion. (1.0×10^{24} is a 1 with 24 zeros after it—imagine what a large number that is.) Imagine trying to line up that many dominoes without knocking any over!

YOU TRY IT!

Try your own version of Libavius's experiment. Dissolve some salt in a jar of water. In another jar of water, dissolve some sugar. Leave the jars uncovered, and let the water evaporate. Use a magnifying glass to look at the residue. Describe what you see.

LIFE SCIENCE CONNECTION

SOUNDS FISHY TO ME

Imagine fish living in the frigid Arctic waters near the North Pole. How do they survive without being frozen solid?

Fish are cold-blooded animals. That is, unlike us, they are not able to increase their body temperature by breaking down foods to produce thermal energy. The reason many fish can survive in freezing waters is because they have what scientists call a natural antifreeze.

Antifreeze in a car's radiator does not warm up the car. Instead, it keeps cars running in frigid weather by lowering the freezing temperature of water.

Water freezes at 0°C. If water turned to ice inside a car, it would expand and crack the radiator. If a fish's blood froze inside its body, the sharp ice crystals would break cell membranes and do all sorts of damage. A fish's natural antifreeze works by lowering the freezing point of its blood and other body fluids.

Some fish, like the Alaskan blackfish pictured, live near the bottom of freshwater lakes that are almost completely frozen.

The super-cooled lake bottom waters remain unfrozen—even at temperatures below 0°C—because flowing water currents prevent ice crystals from forming. Most fish avoid the higher waters where ice is forming to avoid ice crystals from forming in their bodies. But fish with natural antifreeze can swim almost anywhere.

An active ingredient in car antifreeze is a substance called glycerol. Scientists have discovered that an active ingredient in fish's natural antifreeze is a substance called glyco-protein. It's also been found that fish that live closer to the frozen surface, where ice crystals form, have more glyco-protein than fish that stay near the bottom, where ice crystals don't form.

WHAT DO YOU THINK?

The Alaskan blackfish is one type of fish that lives in frigid waters. Read about other fish that live in frigid waters and share that information with your classmates.

SCIENCE AND SOCIETY

KEEPING YOUR COOL

No matter how hot and sweaty you are, walking inside a cool, air-conditioned building on a hot day can refresh you immediately. Just think, would you enjoy going to the movies in the summer if the theater wasn't air-conditioned?

Air-conditioning technology began in the 1920s. But home air conditioning was too expensive for most people until the 1960s. The common use of air conditioning helped turn Southern cities like Houston, Texas, and Atlanta, Georgia, into major business centers.

Houston's average summer temperature is around 82° F. Atlanta's is a humid 78° F. Many people used to think it was too hot to live and work in these areas. Air conditioning changed that. As a result, the population of these and other southern states has grown tremendously in the last 30 years. These states, which are characterized by a warm, sunny climate and rapid population growth, are sometimes referred to as *The Sunbelt.*

What do you think people in sunbelt states drive? Most likely, they drive air-conditioned cars. Actually, people in other states must be driving air-conditioned cars, too, because about 95 percent of all cars built in the United States now have air conditioning.

In the summer, millions of people drive from their air-conditioned homes in air-conditioned cars to go to work in air-conditioned office buildings.

Modern office buildings, such as the one pictured, are designed to maximize air-conditioning efficiency. They are well insulated to keep cooled air (and heated air in the winter) inside. Windows are often sealed, so cooled air won't escape. In some buildings, electronic sensors monitor the temperature of individual rooms. As soon as the temperature rises beyond a certain level, the air conditioner kicks in. As soon as it's cool enough, computers automatically shut the air conditioning off. With modern air-conditioning technology, people can work in comfort. They can concentrate on their work without having to get up to open or close windows, worry about fans, or listen to people complain about how hot it is.

But not all the effects of air conditioning have been beneficial to society. For example, in some of these tightly sealed office buildings, not enough fresh air gets in. The same

air is recirculated over and over again. Cigarette smoke, food odors, germs, and chemical fumes from office machines can circulate through air vents. Under these conditions, some workers get frequent colds. In places where this happens a lot, the office is said to have *sick building syndrome.*

Using air conditioning also means using more energy—especially on extremely hot days. Most often, this electrical energy is produced at coal, oil, or nuclear power plants. Coal- and oil-generated electric plants create air pollution. Radioactive waste from nuclear power plants is another problem.

Also, many air conditioners use a coolant that uses a compound containing chlorine and fluorine atoms. When they are released into the air as chlorofluorocarbon gas molecules, commonly called CFCs, they damage the atmosphere's ozone layer. This is a layer in Earth's atmosphere where the concentrations of ozone are high. Ozone is a compound whose molecules are composed of three oxygen atoms bonded together. This layer filters and protects us from the sun's rays.

CFC molecules are harmful because, over a long period of time, their chlorine and fluorine atoms separate. The free particles of chlorine then react with the ozone molecules and produce other substances.

Because of the growing use of air conditioning, scientists and others are working to find solutions to some of the problems associated with it. They are, for example, working to replace CFCs with HFCs, or hydrofluorocarbons. HFCs don't have ozone-damaging chlorine atoms. More research, however, needs to be done to find out if HFCs will cause other problems. People are also working to make air conditioners more fuel efficient. If such problems could not be solved, would you be willing to give up air conditioning?

WHAT DO YOU THINK?

The United States has more air conditioners than any other country in the world. Developing countries like India and China are just starting to be able to afford more air conditioning. What might happen to the environment if every country used as many air conditioners as the United States does?

*L*iterature
CONNECTION

ANCIENT WISDOM

The ancient Greek philosopher Lucretius observed the world around him. In the third century B.C.E., he recorded his observations and his theories about the natural world. Read the following translation from "Movements and Shapes of Atoms," by Lucretius. Compare his ideas with what modern science has proven.

Things that seem to us hard and stiff must be composed of deeply indented and hooked atoms and held firm by their intertangling branches. In the front rank of this class stand diamonds, with their steadfast indifference to blows. Next come stout flint and stubborn steel and bronze that stands firm with shrieking protest when the bolt is shot. Liquids, on the other hand, must owe their fluid consistency to component atoms that are smooth and round. For poppy-seed can be poured as easily as if it were water; the globules do not hold one another back, and when they are jolted they tend to roll downhill as water does.

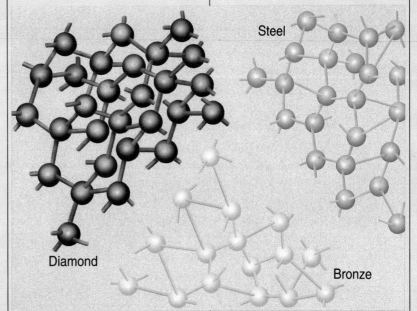

Steel

Diamond

Bronze

A third class is constituted by things that you may see dissipated instantaneously, such as smoke, clouds, and flames. If their atoms are not all smooth and round, yet they cannot be jagged and intertangled. They must be such as to prick the body and even to penetrate rocks but not to stick together; so you can readily grasp that substances hurtful to the senses but not solid are sharp-pointed but without projections.

WHAT DO YOU THINK?

How accurate were Lucretius's theories in terms of whether the shapes of atoms caused their properties? Look at the illustration of the molecular structure of diamonds, bronze, and steel. Would Lucretius say that their atomic connections hooked and intertangled? What about common liquid atoms?

TECHNOLOGY CONNECTION

SWEET EVAPORATION

What tastes sweet, sprinkles easily, and comes from beets or sugar cane? Chances are you know the answer—sugar. But do you know how sugar is made?

People have known about the sweetness of maple tree sap and sugar cane juice for thousands of years. They realized that if they removed some of the water from the sap or juices, the resulting product would be sweeter than the original sap or juice.

In the eighteenth and nineteenth centuries, the process of getting concentrated sweetness from sugar cane was a slow and costly process. Sugar refining was accomplished by pouring and ladling boiling sugar cane juice from one open steaming kettle to another. In the last and smallest kettle, the juice was heated to crystallization.

There was no way to control the temperature of these open boiling kettles. Because sugar has a low boiling point and readily caramelizes, the sugar from this process was dark, crude, and occasionally looked like molasses.

By 1840, engineers had applied some of the principles you've studied to sugar refining. They knew that a liquid can be made to boil at a lower temperature if the pressure is reduced. This means that if sugar cane were boiled in a partial vacuum, the boiling temperature could be kept lower than the caramelization temperature. Vacuum pans and evaporating coils were used to boil sugar cane juice at a relatively low temperature. Water in the sugar cane juice boiled, evapo-

rated, and was removed from the system. Norbert Rillieux, however, took the process one step further.

Rillieux, an African-American engineer, designed a process that started with the same simple vacuum pans and coils others had used. But he added a second evaporation chamber kept at a lower pressure than the first.

The vapor from the first condensing chamber was used to heat the juice in the second chamber. The temperature could be controlled and kept below the caramelization temperature. Best of all—no additional heat source was needed! Rillieux patented his process—which produced a better sugar than any earlier process and used only half the fuel—in 1843 and again in 1846. White crystal sugar moved from a luxury for special occasions to a commodity for everyday use.

His improved process for sugar cane and sugar beets was patented in 1881. Today, this same process is the foundation for processing products as varied as condensed milk, soap, gelatin, and glue. For those with a sweet tooth, Rillieux will always be remembered for his contribution to the sugar industry.

YOU TRY IT!

List the steps, in order, that occur in the Rillieux process. Include three evaporation stages. Indicate which stages have higher and which have lower temperatures. Which have higher and lower pressures?

Chapter 8

Reviewing Main Ideas

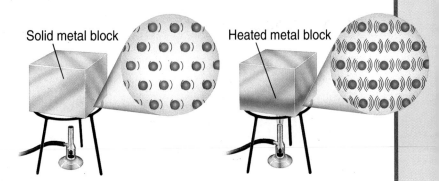

2. Temperature of a gas is a measure of the particles' average kinetic energy. The greater the temperature, the faster the particles move and the harder they collide.

1. Kinetic molecular theory states that the tiny particles (atoms, ions or molecules) that compose all forms of matter are constantly moving and colliding.

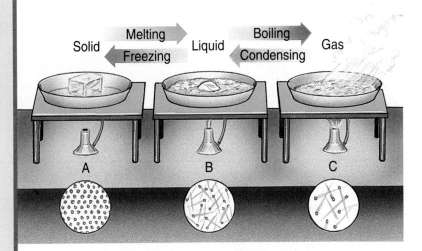

3. Kinetic theory explains the behavior of matter, including expansion, viscosity, and phase changes.

4. As temperature changes, matter changes form. Solid—strong bonds between particles restrict their movement to vibrations about fixed points. Liquid—weaker bonds allow particles to move faster past each other. Gas—particles gain enough kinetic energy to break their bonds and move freely.

Chapter Review

USING KEY SCIENCE TERMS

absolute zero
boiling
condensation
evaporation

kinetic-molecular
theory
sublimation
thermal expansion
viscosity

Using the list above, replace the underlined words with the correct key science term.

1. If you leave moth balls in the open air, they will undergo <u>a direct change from solid to vapor</u>.

2. The coldest temperature that is possible is <u>zero on the Kelvin temperature scale</u>.

3. <u>The escape of molecules from the surface of a liquid</u> occurs when the molecules gain enough energy to overcome the forces that hold them as part of the liquid.

4. When laying a sidewalk, a builder must allow for <u>an increase in volume caused by an increase in temperature</u>.

5. <u>The idea that thermal energy is the motion of atoms or molecules</u> explains why gases take up more space than the liquids they came from.

6. Dew results from <u>the conversion of water vapor in the air to liquid water</u>.

UNDERSTANDING IDEAS

Choose the best answer to complete each sentence.

1. The process by which a solid changes to a liquid is ____.
   a. condensation
   b. freezing
   c. sublimation
   d. melting

2. If an inflated balloon is put in the freezer, the volume and pressure of the air in the balloon ____.
   a. both increase
   b. both decrease
   c. stay the same
   d. vary inversely

3. When vapor condenses, ____.
   a. the molecules move slower
   b. the molecules get closer together
   c. the molecules get smaller
   d. both a and b

4. Temperature of a gas is a measure of ____.
   a. the total heat contained in molecules
   b. the average mass of molecules
   c. the average kinetic energy of molecules
   d. the average potential energy of molecules

5. For gas at a constant temperature, as the volume ____.
   a. increases, the pressure decreases
   b. decreases, the gas particles expand
   c. increases, the pressure increases
   d. increases, the gas becomes a liquid

6. Particles separate completely from one another in a(n) ____.
   a. solid
   b. liquid
   c. gas
   d. crystal

7. The temperature at which molecular motion would stop is _____.
   a. 0° C   **c.** 0 K
   b. 0° F   **d.** 0° A

CRITICAL THINKING

Use your understanding of the concepts developed in the chapter to answer each of the following questions.

1. A group of students heated ice until it melted and turned to water vapor. They measured the temperature each minute and made the following graph. Explain what is happening to the molecules in each section of the graph.

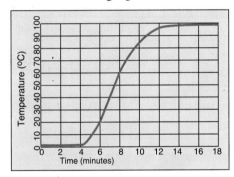

2. How would you use temperature to remove a tight gold ring from a finger?

3. What happens on the molecular level that causes a bottle of soft drink placed in the freezer to break?

4. A metal pot full of water overflows when heated. What does this tell you about the the relative expansion of solids and liquids?

5. What happens to an inflated balloon if you take it outside on a cold day?

PROBLEM SOLVING

Read the following problem and discuss your answers in a brief paragraph.

You've been asked to prepare the tires on a car for a vacation trip. The car has just been dropped off to you after being driven for several miles.

1. You want to know if the tires have been inflated to the manufacturer's recommendations. Would you check the pressure now or would you wait? Explain.

2. The owner of the car is taking a trip into an area that is experiencing very cold temperatures. Would you recommend that more or less air than normal be put into the tires? Explain.

CONNECTING IDEAS

Discuss each of the following in a brief paragraph.

1. Why is there generally more snowfall near a body of water than 10 or 15 kilometers away?

2. Use the kinetic theory to explain the cracks that appear in rock during the process of weathering.

3. **LIFE SCIENCE CONNECTION** Describe how some fish keep from freezing in arctic environments.

4. **SCIENCE AND SOCIETY** List some advantages and some disadvantages of air conditioners.

5. **TECHNOLOGY CONNECTION** What relationship between temperature and pressure was used to improve sugar refining?

LOOKING BACK ▨▨▨▨▨▨▨▨

UNIT 2 ATOMS AND MOLECULES

CONTENTS

UNIT FOCUS

In this unit, you investigated the development of atomic models from concise drawings as attempts to show the true nature of an atom. You have learned that the number of electrons located in the outer energy shell of an atom determines how it reacts in the presence of other atoms. The periodic table of elements is based on atomic mass and structure and helps you predict how one element will react with another.

Try the exercises and activity that follow—they will challenge you to apply some of the ideas you learned in this unit.

CONNECTING IDEAS

1. Elastic collisions do not lose kinetic energy when they collide. What do you think would happen if the collisions between particles of matter were not perfectly elastic? Explain your answer.

2. Using the periodic table, select three elements—a solid, a liquid, and a gas—in the natural state. Prepare a chart showing how the kinetic molecular theory explains their states. Give at least one use of each element that depends on its state.

EXPLORING FURTHER

Some air fresheners are heated. Some are plugged into an electrical outlet. Using the concept of thermal expansion, explain why this is so. Design an experiment to time how long it takes to smell the air freshener at a certain place in the room for three different temperatures. How might the usefulness of air fresheners be affected if they were made from elements having very large masses?

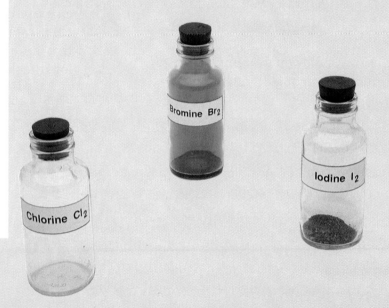

UNIT 3 OUR FLUID ENVIRONMENT

CONTENTS

UNIT FOCUS

In Unit 2, you learned how the structure of atoms affects how they combine to form molecules and how the movement of these molecules produces properties of solids, liquids, and gases. In this unit, you will learn how the movement of molecules is related to the overall movement of air and water in Earth's atmosphere and oceans and the movement of blood in your body. You will also learn how your body digests important chemicals and then carries them to where they are needed.

TRY IT

Molecules are constantly moving everywhere on Earth—inside buildings, in the sky and oceans, and even inside your body. Unless you have special equipment, you cannot see the movements of individual molecules. You can, however, observe the direction that groups of them move. Make a loop in one end of a paper clip. Use the other end of the clip as a handle, and dip the loop into liquid soap. Lift up the loop, and gently blow on the film inside the loop. A bubble will float into the air. On a piece of paper, draw the motion of your bubble throughout the room. In what direction were molecules moving around the bubble? How do you know? How might this relate to the mass of the elements contained in the molecules of air surrounding the bubble? Repeat several times, in several places in the room. After you've learned more about the motions of molecules, try this activity again and see if the movements are easier to explain and whether you can relate them to the kinetic molecular theory.

DID YOU EVER WONDER . . .

What fog is?

What causes clouds?

Why weather changes?

You'll find the answers to these
questions as you read this chapter.

Weather

You look out the window at the beautiful, sunny day, daydreaming about your after-school plans. By three o'clock, the wind has blown huge storm clouds overhead, and the rain is coming down in sheets. Your plans for going to the park or playing basketball with your friends have to be canceled. In some parts of the country, the weather seems to change continually. If you live in such an area, your first thought in the morning might be, "What's the weather going to be like today?" You'd want to know whether you need to take an umbrella to school or whether you might need sweatpants for track practice afterward. Sometimes you might think you know what the weather will be like, but it changes! Sometimes the weather suddenly turns so violent that it's dangerous to be outside.

In this chapter, you'll discover how the exchange of water from Earth's surface to the atmosphere and back again provides the key to understanding different kinds of weather.

EXPLORE!

What kind of data can you find on a weather map?
Look at the weather map in a newspaper for two consecutive days. Write down the changes you observe in symbols and other graphics between the map from the first day and the map from the second day.

9-1 What Is Weather?

OBJECTIVES

In this section, you will

- explain the role of water vapor in the atmosphere and how it affects weather;
- relate relative humidity to weather;
- explain how clouds form.

KEY SCIENCE TERMS

relative humidity
saturated
dew point

FACTORS OF WEATHER

"I don't think we should play basketball this afternoon. It looks like it might storm."

"Better close the windows, Latanya. The wind is starting to blow the curtains into the plants."

You have probably had a conversation like this. You talk about weather all the time because it affects you every day. Can you explain what weather is? Try this next activity and find out.

EXPLORE!

What things make up the weather?
Look out the window and write down everything you can about today's weather. Observe the sky closely. Are there clouds? If so, what do they look like? Are they moving? Observe objects near the ground. Are the leaves on the trees blowing? Is the ground wet? Some of the things you should be describing are the presence and strength of the wind, the temperature, the amount and type of cloud cover, and whether it is raining or snowing. Are these things you think of when you think of weather?

As you discovered in the Explore activity, several factors determine what kind of weather you see outside the window each day. Some of these factors are plainly visible, such as cloud cover and whether or not the wind is blowing the leaves on trees. Other factors can be felt, such as the temperature or the amount of moisture in the air.

In addition to the thermal energy from the sun and the resultant movement of air, weather is greatly affected by one of Earth's most abundant substances: water.

WATER AND WEATHER

How much do you know about the water cycle? Figure 9-2 will remind you that water on Earth's surface does not stay in one place for long. Some water sinks into the ground. Other water runs off the surface into rivers and then into lakes and oceans. A great deal of water evaporates into the atmosphere.

FIGURE 9-1. Weather can influence what you do and wear.

The sun provides the energy to evaporate water from the oceans and other bodies of water. Then, as the water vapor cools in the upper atmosphere, it condenses and forms clouds. The water eventually falls back to Earth as rain, snow, or some other form of precipitation. This water cycle forms the basis of Earth's weather.

Water vapor is a large component of the water cycle. The amount of water vapor in the air is called humidity. You've probably heard this term used before. People sometimes comment about how humid it is on hot summer days.

FIGURE 9-2. The water cycle is a key factor in Earth's weather.

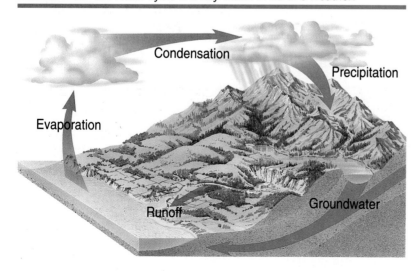

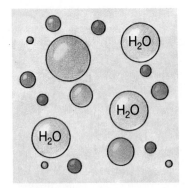

FIGURE 9-3. The spaces between molecules that make up air may contain water molecules.

No doubt you've also heard a weather forecaster mention relative humidity. **Relative humidity** is a measure of the amount of water vapor in the air at a particular temperature, compared with the total amount of water vapor the air can hold at that temperature.

Think of the air as a sponge. A sponge has holes that allow it to hold water. The holes can be completely full of water or partially full of water. As you can see in Figure 9-3, the air doesn't exactly have holes, but there are spaces between the molecules that make up the air. The water molecules in water vapor fill in those spaces. All the spaces may be filled with water or only some of them.

Relative humidity is a percentage that tells how much of the available space in air has been filled by water vapor. For example, if the relative humidity is 50 percent, the air is holding only 50 percent of the water vapor it is capable of holding at its current temperature. Weather forecasters have developed a simple instrument for measuring relative humidity. It is called a psychrometer (si KRAH muh tur).

TABLE 9-1. Determining Percent Relative Humidity

Dry Bulb Temperature	Dry Bulb Temperature Minus Wet Bulb Temperature, °C									
	1	2	3	4	5	6	7	8	9	10
10°C	88	77	66	55	44	34	24	15	6	
11°C	89	78	67	56	46	36	27	18	9	
12°C	89	78	68	58	48	39	29	21	12	
13°C	89	79	69	59	50	41	32	22	15	7
14°C	90	79	70	60	51	42	34	26	18	10
15°C	90	80	71	61	53	44	36	27	20	13
16°C	90	81	71	63	54	46	38	30	23	15
17°C	90	81	72	64	55	47	40	32	25	18
18°C	91	82	73	65	57	49	41	34	27	20
19°C	91	82	74	65	58	50	43	36	29	22
20°C	91	83	74	67	59	53	46	39	32	26
21°C	91	83	75	67	60	53	46	39	32	26
22°C	92	83	76	68	61	54	47	40	34	28
23°C	92	84	76	69	62	55	48	42	36	30
24°C	92	84	77	69	62	56	49	43	37	31
25°C	92	84	77	70	63	57	50	44	39	33
26°C	92	85	78	71	64	58	51	46	40	34
27°C	92	85	78	71	65	58	52	47	41	36
28°C	93	85	78	72	65	59	53	48	42	37
29°C	93	86	79	72	66	60	54	49	43	38
30°C	93	86	79	73	67	61	55	50	44	39

In the following activity, you will make a psychrometer to **measure** the relative humidity in three different areas around your school.

PROBLEM

How do you determine relative humidity?

MATERIALS

2 identical Celsius ther-
    mometers
piece of gauze, 2 cm^2
string
tape
cardboard
beaker of water

PROCEDURE

1. Attach the gauze to the bulb of one thermometer with string as shown in the picture.
2. Thoroughly wet the gauze on the thermometer by dipping it into the beaker of water. This is called a wet bulb thermometer.
3. Tape both thermometers side by side on the cardboard with the bulbs hanging over the edge of one end. You have created a psychrometer.

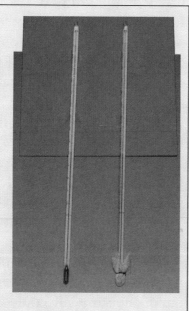

4. Create air motion across both thermometer bulbs by gently fanning them with a sheet of paper.
5. Wait until the alcohol in the thermometers stops moving and record the temperatures.
6. Subtract the wet bulb temperature from the dry bulb temperature.
7. Determine relative humidity **using the table** on the opposite page. Find the temperature difference you computed in Step 6 by reading across the top of the table. Keep one finger on this number. Find the dry bulb temperature in the first column of the table. Look across this row until you find the column you marked with your fin-

ger. Record the number where the row and column intersect. This is the percent relative humidity.

8. Repeat Steps 4–7 at a different location inside your school. Be sure to resoak the wet bulb thermometer at your new test site. Wait at least 5 minutes between trials in order to let the thermometers adjust to the new location.
9. Repeat Step 8 at a test site outside your school.

ANALYZE

1. How did the wet bulb temperature **compare** with the dry bulb temperature at each site?
2. Which area in your school had the highest relative humidity? Which area had the lowest?

CONCLUDE AND APPLY

3. What would the relative humidity be if the wet bulb and dry bulb thermometers recorded the same temperature?
4. **Going Further**: Use the table to determine whether two spots having the same relative humidity must also have the same temperature. Is there the same amount of water vapor in the air at both spots? Explain your answer.

SKILLBUILDER

DETERMINING CAUSE AND EFFECT

Suppose the relative humidity of the air in a room is 50 percent. If the thermostat is turned up, will the relative humidity change? Explain your answer. If you need help, refer to the **Skill Handbook** on page 685.

The amount of water vapor that air can hold depends on the temperature of the air. Warmer air can hold more water molecules than cooler air. You may have begun to realize this as you were doing the Investigate activity. Why do you think this is true? Recall from Chapter 8 that matter expands when it is heated. In cold air, the molecules are close together and are moving very slowly. They have little kinetic energy. This slow movement makes it easier for water vapor molecules to join together or condense. In warm air, the kinetic energy of the molecules is much greater, and the molecules move more quickly. Water vapor molecules can't join together or condense as easily. Therefore, warmer air can hold more water vapor than cooler air.

For example, a cubic meter of air can hold a maximum of 22 grams of water vapor at 25°C. On the other hand, the same air cooled to 15°C can hold only about 13 grams of water vapor. An interesting thing happens when air is cooled to the point where it cannot hold any more water. The next Find Out activity will help you see more clearly how water vapor in the air responds to changes in temperature.

FIGURE 9-4. This chart shows that the amount of water vapor that air can hold increases when the temperature of the air increases.

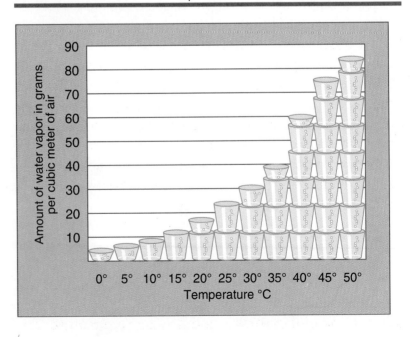

What happens to air that is cooled to the point where it cannot hold any more water?

Partially fill a shiny metal container, such as a cup or can, with water at room temperature. While slowly stirring the water with a thermometer, carefully add small amounts of ice. Watch the outside surface of the container. Note the exact temperature at which a thin film of moisture first begins to form there.

Repeat the procedure two more times, making sure that you start with water at room temperature and with the outside of the container dry. Find the average of the three temperature readings.

Conclude and Apply

1. Where did the water on the outside of the container come from?
2. What happened to the air surrounding the container as you added ice to the water?
3. Why did the water on the outside of the container appear?

When the relative humidity of air reaches 100 percent, the air is holding all the moisture it possibly can at that temperature. When this happens, the air is **saturated**. As you saw in the Find Out activity, when the temperature of the air around the container was cooled to the point of saturation, water vapor in the air condensed on the container's outside surface. Dew that forms on grass and other cool surfaces in the early morning forms in the same way. When air near the ground is cooled to the point where the air is saturated with water, water vapor condenses and forms droplets on the grass. The temperature at which air is saturated and condensation takes place is called the **dew point**.

CLOUDS AND PRECIPITATION

When you think of a cloud, what kind of cloud do you imagine? Some people think of fluffy, white clouds, while others think of dark storm clouds. There are many differ-

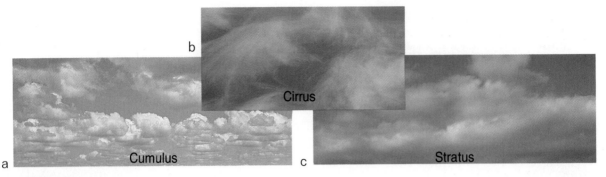

b

Cirrus

a

Cumulus

c

Stratus

FIGURE 9-5. Cumulus clouds (a) are dense, billowing clouds that may build up to great heights. Cirrus clouds (b) are high, thin, white clouds that are seen during fair weather but may signal an approaching storm. Stratus clouds (c) are low-lying gray clouds associated with light precipitation.

ent types of clouds. They vary in shape and in the altitude at which they form.

Some clouds are towering, reaching high into the atmosphere, while others lie low and flat. Some dense clouds bring rain and snow, while other, thin clouds appear on mostly sunny days. Figure 9-5 pictures three major cloud types. What kind, if any, do you see outside today?

Would you like to walk through a cloud? Then walk outside on a foggy day. Fog is simply a stratus cloud that has formed at Earth's surface. How do fog and other clouds form? Do this Explore activity to see.

EXPLORE!

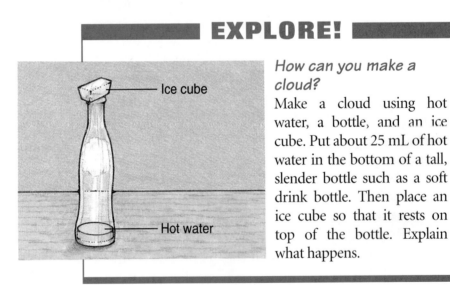

Ice cube

Hot water

How can you make a cloud?

Make a cloud using hot water, a bottle, and an ice cube. Put about 25 mL of hot water in the bottom of a tall, slender bottle such as a soft drink bottle. Then place an ice cube so that it rests on top of the bottle. Explain what happens.

A similar process happens in the atmosphere. Clouds form as humid air is cooled to its dew point. The water vapor in the air condenses. The condensing water vapor forms tiny drops of water around dust particles in the atmosphere. These tiny drops of water in the atmosphere are called cloud droplets.

Cloud droplets are so small that the slightest air movement keeps them from falling to the ground. When millions of these drops cluster together, a cloud forms.

In the last Explore activity, you made a cloud. Do you think you could also make rain? Actually, you did make rain. Did you notice that where the fog came in contact with the inside of the bottle, water droplets joined together and slid down the sides of the bottle? These large droplets were rain.

Cloud droplets in a cloud swirl around and bump into one another. When they collide, they merge into bigger droplets. When these water droplets reach a diameter of 0.2 milllimeters, they are too heavy to remain suspended in the atmosphere. As a result, the drops fall out of the clouds as precipitation. Precipitation refers to water that falls to Earth in the form of rain, snow, sleet, or hail.

FIGURE 9-6. Fog is a common occurrence in San Francisco. Why do you think this is true?

FIGURE 9-7. A raindrop is much larger than a cloud droplet.

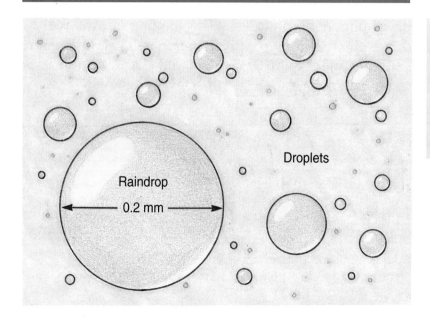

Raindrop

0.2 mm

Droplets

DID YOU KNOW?

Arica, Chile, is the driest place on Earth. During one 14-year period, no rain fell at all. During a 59-year period, the average annual rainfall was 0.76 mm.

FIGURE 9-8. From this cross-sectional view, you can see the layers of ice in a hailstone. These layers are added as a hailstone rises and falls within a storm cloud.

The form of precipitation depends on the temperature of the air the droplets fall through and how close the clouds are to the ground. Air temperature determines whether the water droplets form rain, snow, sleet, or hail—the four main types of precipitation. Droplets that fall in temperatures above freezing fall as rain. Snow forms when the temperature is below freezing and water vapor changes directly into snow. Snowflakes that pass through a layer of warm air, melt, and then refreeze near the ground form sleet.

Hail forms in air that is very active, such as in a thunderstorm where cumulus clouds are present. Hail forms when drops of water freeze in layers around a small nucleus of ice, as you can see in Figure 9-8. Hailstones grow larger as they're tossed up and down by the rising and falling air currents in a storm.

In this section, you've seen how temperature and humidity affect precipitation. You have learned that the amount of water vapor that air can hold depends on the temperature of the air. Saturated air has 100 percent relative humidity. Clouds form as water vapor is cooled to its dew point and condenses. The temperature of the air determines what type of precipitation will fall. In the next section, you'll explore how wind and air-pressure masses can cause changes in the weather.

Check Your Understanding

1. How does air temperature affect the type of precipitation that falls?
2. What is the relative humidity when dew forms? Explain.
3. Explain why cold air can hold less moisture than warm air.
4. Use the terms *evaporation* and *condensation* to explain how clouds form.
5. **APPLY:** Two rooms of the same size have the same humidity. It is colder in room A than room B. Which room has the higher relative humidity?

9-2 Changes in Weather

AIR MASSES

Have you ever noticed that the weather you're having today may be gone tomorrow? It could move to another town or even to another state. That's because the air is moving. The changes in weather are caused by the development and movement of large air masses.

An **air mass** is a large body of air whose properties are determined by the part of Earth's surface over which it develops. For example, an air mass that develops over land is dry compared with one that develops over water. And an air mass that develops near the equator is warmer than one that develops at a higher latitude. What characteristics might you expect of an air mass that forms over northern Canada?

Air masses move and swirl over the surface of Earth. Because they move in different directions and at different speeds, they often bump into each other. What happens then? The next activity will show you.

FIGURE 9-9. Different types of air masses form over different areas.

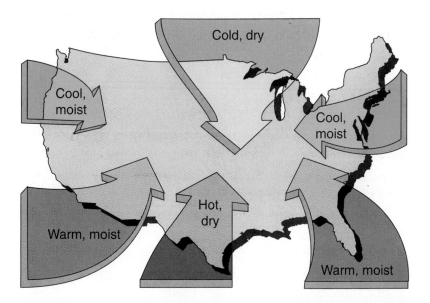

What happens when two air masses meet?
Get an aquarium with a glass lid, a cold bag of sand or marbles, and a pan of very hot water. Place the pan of water inside the aquarium next to the cold bag. Cover the aquarium with the glass lid. Observe and record what happens.

Conclude and Apply
Why is there no cloud above the pan of hot water?

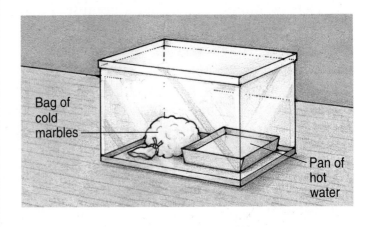

Bag of cold marbles

Pan of hot water

Rain, thunderstorms, snow, tornadoes—all of these weather-related events can result when air masses meet. When an air mass moves and collides with another air mass, a boundary forms between the two air masses. This boundary is called a **front.** You created a model of a front in the Find Out activity. Although you couldn't see it, the front formed where the cool air and warm air met. There are four types of fronts.

Warm Front

Have you ever been in a snowstorm or seen a blizzard on the news? You didn't know it then, but it was probably snowing because a warm air mass had met a cold air mass. The type of boundary that forms when this happens is called a warm front.

Precipitation can form at a warm front. Why? The answer has to do with temperature. Remember that warm air is less dense than cold air. As the warm air mass meets the cold air mass, the leading edge of the warm air mass is forced up over the edge of the cold air mass. Look at Figure 9-10. Is the slope of a warm front gentle or steep? As the warm air mass is forced upward by the cold air mass, its temperature drops and the water vapor in the air condenses to form clouds. These first clouds form at high altitudes. Cirrus clouds are your first sign that a warm front is approaching. As the front continues to move, the clouds form at lower and lower altitudes. A warm front may lead to the formation of stratus clouds that often bring rain and snow.

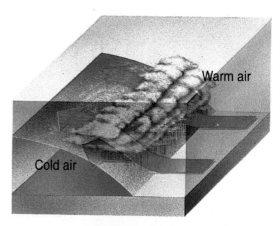

FIGURE 9-10. At a warm front, a warm air mass bumps into a cold air mass.

Cold Front

A cold front forms when a cold air mass moves into a warm air mass. Figure 9-11 shows how the cold air hugs the ground as it moves forward. It works almost like a plow, forcing the warm air mass to rise rapidly along the steep front. The air cools quickly, causing rapid condensation. Tall, cumulus clouds form along the front, often producing rain and thunderstorms.

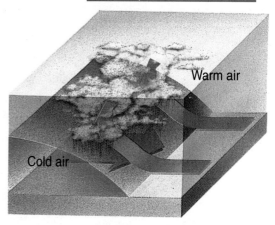

FIGURE 9-11. At a cold front, a cold air mass bumps into a warm air mass.

Stationary Front

Have you ever been annoyed that the skies have been gray and rain has been falling for days? That is what happens when a stationary front forms. In a stationary front, the air masses have stopped moving. Therefore, the front is no longer moving. This type of front may remain in the same place for several days, bringing light winds and a steady rain.

Occluded Front

The fourth type of front is called an occluded front. This type of front forms when two cold air masses merge, forcing a warm air mass between them to rise completely off the ground. Figure 9-12 shows an occluded front. The weather at an occluded front is often difficult to predict. Instead of two air masses meeting, as in a cold, warm, or stationary front, occluded fronts involve three air masses. The temperature differences between these air

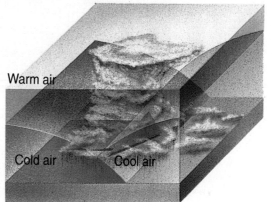

FIGURE 9-12. Occluded fronts occur when two cold air masses meet and warm air is trapped between them.

SKILLBUILDER

MAKING A TABLE
Make a table that shows the four types of fronts and the weather associated with each. If you need help, refer to the **Skill Handbook** on page 681.

masses help determine what weather conditions will be like at an occluded front. Strong winds and heavy precipitation may occur at such a front.

Think about what happens at each of the four fronts. Did you notice that all fronts have precipitation associated with them? That's because all along each of these fronts, warm air is being cooled. You learned earlier that when air is cooled, its ability to hold water is reduced. When the air cools, it becomes saturated. Water vapor in the atmosphere condenses and forms clouds, and precipitation may fall.

PRESSURE SYSTEMS

Differences in pressure have a great effect on the weather. High pressure usually means clear weather, and low pressure means cloudy weather.

As you already learned, air molecules have mass, and as they collide, they exert pressure on one another. When air molecules are densely packed, high pressure occurs. Let's explore how such an air mass moves.

EXPLORE!

How do pressure systems move?
Place an empty, capped thermos bottle in the freezer for several hours. Then remove the thermos from the freezer and take off the cap. Hold the thermos upside down above your head. Do you feel the cool air pouring out of the thermos and onto your head? Describe what is taking place.

How did cooling the air in the thermos affect the density and pressure of the air? As you know, dense air sinks. You felt this for yourself in the Explore activity. The cold air in the thermos was more dense than the air in the room, so it flowed out and down onto your head. This also happens in high pressure systems. As cool, dense air sinks toward Earth's surface, it starts to become warmer. As the air becomes warmer, it can hold more water vapor. Because it now contains a lower percentage of water vapor than it can hold, its relative humidity decreases. Droplets of water in clouds evaporate. That is why high pressure usually means fair weather. Moisture in the air is evaporated, so few clouds form.

The reverse is true with low pressure systems. Because its density is low, warm air of a low pressure system is forced upward by surrounding, denser air. As it gains altitude, the air cools. As the air cools, its relative humidity increases. The air eventually reaches its dew point. Condensation takes place, and clouds form. You can see how low pressure often leads to rain in the forecast.

Because high and low pressure systems are constantly moving and shifting, the National Weather Service uses information gathered at many different locations. Each location communicates its data, and the Weather Service combines them to make weather maps used to forecast the weather. These maps show information collected in specific locations as shown in Figure 9-13. This information shown in symbols is called a station model. A complete key to the symbols is shown in Appendix K.

Symbols are used because if words were written on such maps, they would be too cluttered to read.

In the next activity, you can use these symbols and see if your understanding of fronts and pressure systems can help you predict the weather.

FIGURE 9-13. A station model shows the weather conditions at one specific location.

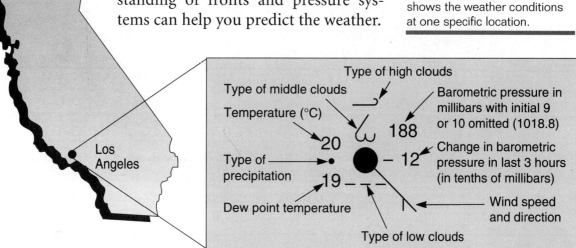

INVESTIGATE!

9-2 READING A WEATHER MAP

In this activity, you'll read and interpret the symbols on a weather map so that you can **predict** the weather.

PROBLEM

How can you use symbols on a weather map to forecast the weather?

MATERIALS

hand lens (optional, if needed)
Appendix K

PROCEDURE

Use the information that is provided in the questions and Appendix K to read a weather map.

ANALYZE

1. Find the station models on the map for Tucson, Arizona, and Albuquerque, New Mexico. Find the dew point, cloud coverage, pressure, and temperature at each location.

2. Determine the type of front located near Key West, Florida.

3. The triangles or half circles on the weather front symbol are on the side of the line that indicates the direction the front is moving. Determine the direction that the cold front located over Colorado and Kansas is moving.

CONCLUDE AND APPLY

4. The prevailing westerlies are the winds responsible for the movement of weather across the United States and Canada. Based on this fact, would you **predict** that Charleston, South Carolina, will continue to have clear skies over the next several days? Explain your answer.

5. The line on the station model that indicates wind speed shows from which direction the wind is blowing, and the wind is named according to the direction from which the wind blows. What is the name of the wind at Jackson, Mississippi?

6. **Going Further:** Locate the pressure system over Winslow, Arizona. **Determine the effect** this system would have on the weather of Wichita, Kansas, if it moved there.

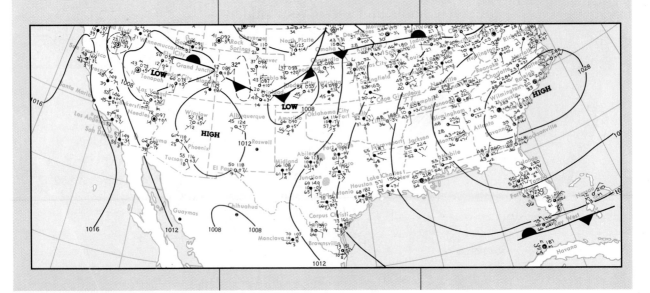

From the Investigate, you have begun to see how you can use your knowledge of fronts and pressure systems to predict weather. Look at Figure 9-14. What would happen if the air mass over the location shown in Figure 9-14 (a) moved into the area shown in (b)?

When you witness a change in the weather from one day to the next, it is due to the movement of air masses. The movement and collision of air masses cause weather conditions to change. The boundary formed between these moving air masses is a front. A warm front develops when a warm air mass meets a cold air mass. A cold front forms when a cold air mass invades a warm air mass. Low pressure usually forms along fronts where warm and cold air meet. These low pressure systems cause most of the weather changes in the United States.

A stationary front results when a warm or cold front stops moving. An occluded front results when two cold air masses meet and trap warm air between them. Along each of these fronts, the warm air is being cooled. When the air becomes saturated, precipitation falls.

You'll learn more about the severe weather associated with low pressure systems in the next section.

FIGURE 9-14. What kinds of pressure systems and air masses are determining the weather in each of these locations?

a

b

Check Your Understanding

1. Compare and contrast warm fronts and cold fronts.
2. Suppose a weather report states that a high pressure system will cover your area tomorrow. Why can you expect the skies to become clear?
3. **APPLY:** Air that stays over the Gulf of Mexico for a period of time forms an air mass. Describe the humidity and temperature of that air mass in general terms.

9-3 Severe Weather

OBJECTIVES

In this section, you will
- describe what causes thunderstorms;
- relate how tornadoes evolve from thunderstorms;
- compare and contrast tornadoes and hurricanes.

KEY SCIENCE TERMS

tornado

hurricane

SEVERE WEATHER

Even though weather affects you every day, you can usually still go about your business regardless of the weather. If it's raining, you can still go to school, and if it snows a little, you can still get to the store. But some weather conditions prevent you from going about your normal routine. Severe weather conditions can pose danger to life on Earth.

THUNDERSTORMS

What's the most impressive thing you've ever seen happen during a thunderstorm? Maybe it rained so hard that you couldn't see across the street. Perhaps you saw lightning strike a tree or felt thunder shake your house. Or maybe you saw hail pounding the ground and bouncing in the grass. What powerful forces cause such extreme weather conditions?

Thunderstorms are formed by the rapid upward movement of warm, moist air. They can occur within warm, moist air masses but often occur at cold fronts. As the warm, moist air is forced upward, it cools, and its water vapor condenses, forming cumulus clouds that can reach heights of 10 kilometers. Water droplets that form in the

FIGURE 9-15. When you see dark clouds like these, you know a thunderstorm is probably forming.

clouds begin falling the long distance toward Earth's surface. As the droplets fall through the clouds, they collide with other droplets and become larger. These falling droplets create a downward motion of air that spreads out at Earth's surface and causes some of the strong winds associated with thunderstorms.

Lightning is also associated with thunderstorms. As storm clouds form, air currents carry some water vapor to the cool, upper parts of clouds, where it forms ice crystals. Other water vapor condenses near the bottom of the clouds in the form of water droplets. Recall from Chapter 5 that atoms in matter contain protons and electrons. Protons have a positive charge, while electrons have a negative charge. The top of the storm clouds become positively charged. The water droplets in the bottom of storm clouds become negatively charged, while containing small areas with a positive charge. Figure 9-16 illustrates how the top of the cloud develops a positive charge and the bottom a negative charge. Lightning, which is nothing more than electricity, occurs when current flows between regions of opposite electrical charge. Bolts of lightning can leap from cloud to cloud, from a cloud to Earth's surface, or from Earth's surface to a cloud.

If you've seen lightning, you've probably heard thunder, too. Thunder results from the rapid heating of the air around a lightning bolt. It's hard to believe, but lightning can reach temperatures of about 28,000°C. That's more than five times the temperature of the sun's surface! This extreme heat causes the air close by to expand rapidly, forming a sound wave that you hear as thunder.

Thunderstorms can cause a great deal of damage. The heavy rains sometimes cause flooding and mudslides. Lightning can strike trees and other objects, setting them on fire, and can electrocute people and animals. Strong winds from thunderstorms can also cause damage. If a thunderstorm has winds traveling faster than 80 kilometers per hour and hail more than 2 centimeters in diameter, weather forecasters classify it as a severe thunderstorm.

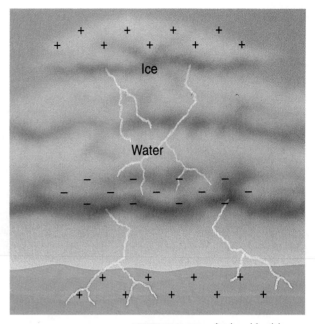

FIGURE 9-16. A cloud builds up a static electrical charge as ice and water move to different areas within the cloud.

FIGURE 9-17. Lightning can cause a great deal of damage.

Hail this size can dent cars and the siding on houses. It can also flatten and destroy a crop in a matter of minutes.

TORNADOES

As scary as thunderstorms can be, they're gentle compared with the fury of a tornado. You've probably seen films of tornadoes in action. What does a tornado look like? Make a model of a tornado and observe some of its characteristics.

FIND OUT!

How does air in a tornado move?
Obtain two 2-liter plastic bottles. Fill one about three-quarters full of water and add one drop of dishwashing soap. Tape the mouth of the empty bottle to the mouth of the bottle with water in it. Make sure the tape secures the bottles together so that they won't leak. Now, flip the bottles so that the one with the water is on top. Move the top bottle in a circular motion.

Conclude and Apply
1. What do you see forming in the bottle?
2. How is this model of a tornado similar to a real tornado?

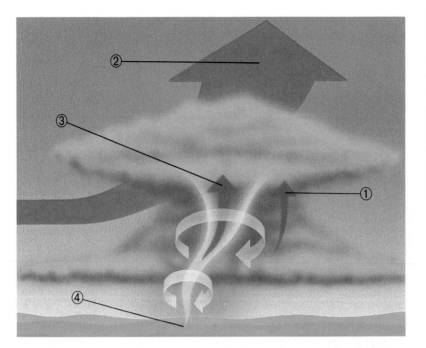

FIGURE 9-18. A tornado begins to form when warm air rises through a storm (1). The warm air collides with cool air flowing above, causing the warm air to begin twisting (2). As rotation of the rising air increases, a low pressure area is created in the center of the funnel; more warm air is drawn up (3). The funnel may sometimes extend to the ground (4).

Just as the model tornado you created in the plastic bottles swirled around, so do real tornadoes. A **tornado** is a violent, funnel-shaped storm whose whirling winds move in a narrow path over land.

Tornadoes form from severe thunderstorms. As with regular thunderstorms, tornado-producing thunderstorms involve the rapid upward movement of warm, moist air. Scientists aren't exactly sure what causes this upward-moving air to rotate. They think the upward-moving air is twisted when it comes in contact with the cooler winds moving in a different direction at the top of the cloud. As the speed of the rotating air mass increases, even more warm air is drawn into the low pressure at the center. A funnel-shaped cloud then extends from the bottom of the storm cloud, sometimes touching the ground. The funnel cloud picks up dirt and debris from the ground, which give the funnel its dark gray or black color.

When a tornado touches the ground, buildings and trees are destroyed by winds that can reach up to 500 kilometers per hour. The pressure in the center of a tornado is so low that when it passes over a building, the building can actually explode. This happens when the pressure inside the building is greater than the pressure outside in the tornado. The updraft in a tornado is so

SKILLBUILDER

INTERPRETING SCIENTIFIC ILLUSTRATIONS
Use Figure 9-18 to answer these questions. If you need help, refer to the **Skill Handbook** on page 691.

1. What causes rising warm air to begin swirling?
2. What kind of pressure area exists within the tornado?

FIGURE 9-19. A tornado is a destructive but narrowly based storm.

strong it can lift animals, people, cars, and even houses into the air. Although tornadoes average only 200 meters in diameter and usually last less than 10 minutes, they are one of the most destructive types of storms. There is, however, a more powerful and threatening storm—the hurricane.

HURRICANES

The largest storm that occurs on Earth is the hurricane. A **hurricane** is a very large, swirling, low pressure system that forms over tropical oceans. For a storm to be called a hurricane, it must have winds that blow at least 120 kilometers per hour. Hurricanes may be many kilometers in diameter. Because they form over large bodies of water and have a steady supply of energy, they may go on for many days, until they reach land.

Hurricanes form over warm, tropical oceans where two opposing winds meet and begin to swirl. For example, in the Atlantic Ocean north of the equator, the southeast trade winds and the northeast trade winds sometimes meet and spin around each other. A low pressure area forms in the middle of the swirl and begins rotating. Figure 9-21 shows how warm, moist air is forced up into the middle of the low pressure area. You already know what happens when warm, moist air rises. It cools, and moisture starts to condense.

Just as in a tornado, the dropping air pressure inside the low pressure area pulls air toward the center, causing even greater winds and lower air pressure. As long as a hurricane is over warm water, the warm, moist air continues to provide energy for the storm. Hurricanes weaken when they strike land because they no longer receive energy from the warm water.

However, a hurricane that strikes land can be a very destructive force. The winds, which can blow up to 300 kilometers per hour, can uproot trees and demolish buildings. With these powerful winds come heavy rains that can cause flooding.

FIGURE 9-20. From a weather satellite, it's easy to see the swirling winds of a hurricane.

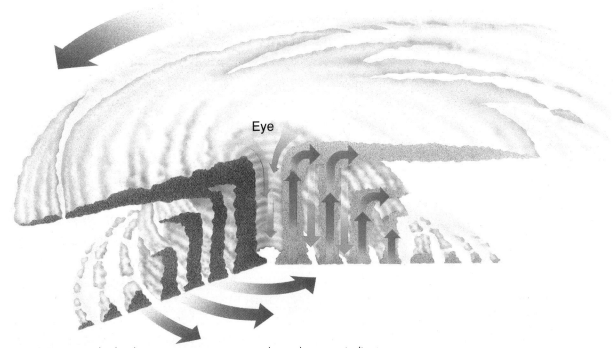

Eye

FIGURE 9-21. In this hurricane cross-section, the red arrows indicate rising warm, moist air forming cumulus clouds in bands around the eye. The blue arrows indicate cool, dry air sinking in the eye and between the cloud bands. The purple arrows indicate the circular motion of the spiral cloud bands.

What is the difference between a storm watch and a storm warning?

Because storms like hurricanes, tornadoes, blizzards, and thunderstorms can be very dangerous, meteorologists at the National Weather Service issue advisories when severe weather has been observed or when the conditions are such that severe weather could occur. When a watch is issued, conditions are right for a storm to occur. Watches are issued for severe thunderstorms, tornadoes, floods, blizzards, and hurricanes. During a watch, stay tuned to a radio or television station that is reporting weather updates. When a warning is issued, severe weather exists, and you should take immediate action because the weather has already been observed in your area. In the case of a tornado, a warning is issued when one has been sighted in the vicinity. Take shelter during a severe thunderstorm warning. During a tornado warning, go to the basement or a room in the middle of the house away from windows.

The most dangerous part of a hurricane is the storm surge. A storm surge is a bulge of sea water pushed onshore by the hurricane. The sea level in a particular area may quickly rise as much as 5 meters, bringing the pounding waves far onto the land. For some coastal areas, such a rise in sea level can be devastating. For example, the country of Bangladesh is only a meter or so above sea level in many areas. When a huge hurricane hit Bangladesh in 1991, the storm surge swept over the country, killing thousands and leaving millions homeless.

FIGURE 9-22. Hurricane Hugo caused a great deal of damage when it struck South Carolina in 1989.

Such severe weather might seem like a lot to get from sunlight, wind, differences in air pressure, and water vapor in the air. But both fair and frightful weather result from the water cycle that carries water from the sea, through the atmosphere, to your street, and back again.

Check Your Understanding

1. Describe how thunderstorms occur.
2. Explain how tornadoes evolve from thunderstorms.
3. How does a tornado differ from a hurricane? What are the similarities between the storms?
4. **APPLY:** Tornadoes sometimes form when hurricanes come onto land. Discuss how the tornadoes might form.

EXPANDING YOUR VIEW

CONTENTS

A CLOSER LOOK

FORECASTING THE WEATHER

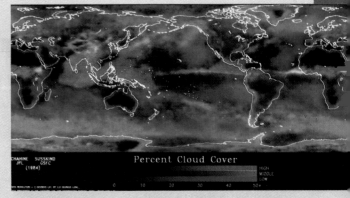

You can tell what current weather conditions are by simply making observations. However, the weather is continually changing, so you can't always rely on your own observations to predict what the weather will be like later. Instead, you rely on the people who make the weather forecasts on TV, radio, and in the newspaper—the meteorologists.

You've learned that thermometers measure temperature and that psychrometers measure relative humidity. In the *How it Works* section you'll learn how barometers measure atmospheric pressure. In addition to these instruments, meteorologists use satellites, radar, and computers to help them forecast the weather.

Some satellites gather information on global weather patterns by recording information on the temperature and moisture of the air at different heights. Stationary satellites remain at the same spot above the equator and record air currents and cloud formation. Information from these satellites is entered into computers and the data are shared with weather stations around the world. Radar, or radio wave pictures, is used by meterologists to detect raindrops and ice particles up to 400 kilometers away, revealing what type of weather is approaching.

Once these data are gathered, meteorologists can make predictions, or forecasts, about the weather. To make short-range forecasts, meteorologists use a combination of computer analysis of data and human interpretation. Long-range forecasts are made by computers that compare current weather information with information from previous years.

YOU TRY IT!

Make your own observations of the weather in your city. Observe such things as temperature, barometric pressure, clouds, rainfall, and wind direction and speed. Record your observations at the same time each day, over a period of several days or a week. Based on your data, forecast the weather for the next three days. Check your results against actual weather forecasts.

Physics Connection

THE SOUND OF THUNDER

In this chapter, you learned that thunder is caused by the rapid heating of the air around a bolt of lightning. A flash of lightning is always seen before we hear the thunder, although it may seem at times that the two happen at the same time. This is because light waves travel faster than sound waves—about 299,800 kilometers (185,876 miles) per second. Sound waves are produced by vibrations and travel at the speed of about 330 meters (1100 feet) per second or about 1200 kilometers (750 miles) per hour. Because of the difference between the speed of light and the speed of sound, you can estimate how far away a thunderstorm is by the time that elapses between a flash of lightning and the clap of thunder that follows it.

YOU TRY IT!

Count the number of seconds between a flash of lightning and the clap of thunder that follows it. If you don't have an accurate stopwatch, count seconds by saying slowly, "a thousand and one, a thousand and two," etc. This will give you the approximate number of seconds. Use the chart to calculate how far away the lightning was.

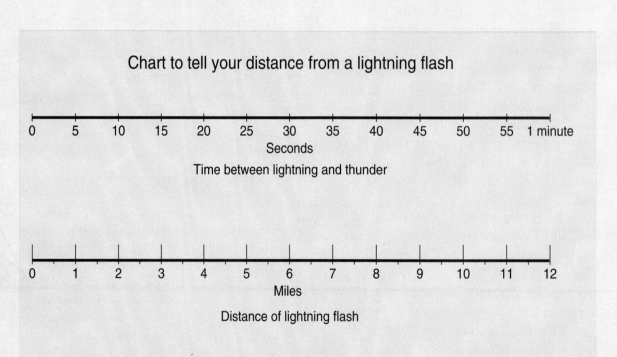

Chart to tell your distance from a lightning flash

0 5 10 15 20 25 30 35 40 45 50 55 1 minute

Seconds

Time between lightning and thunder

0 1 2 3 4 5 6 7 8 9 10 11 12

Miles

Distance of lightning flash

SCIENCE AND SOCIETY

IS CLOUD SEEDING A GOOD IDEA?

As you know, weather is extremely changeable and often difficult to predict. Human activities can cause weather changes. The use of fossil fuels, such as coal and oil, have released so much carbon dioxide into the atmosphere, trapping the sun's heat, that a period of global warming is predicted. Cutting down tropical rain forests may also contribute to the problem. People did not try to purposely alter the weather through these activities, but cloud seeding is an example of how people intentionally try to change the weather.

With cloud seeding, fog can be dispersed at airports, dangerous lightning can be reduced inside thunderclouds, large hail can be reduced in size so that it is less damaging to crops. The corn crops shown in the photo were completely ruined by hail. Also with cloud seeding, snow can be increased in mountain resorts, wind speed can be reduced near the eyes of hurricanes, and rainfall can be increased 10 to 30 percent.

The process of seeding clouds was pioneered in 1946. Dry ice, or frozen carbon dioxide, was first used to cause the moisture in supercooled clouds (temperatures below −5°C) to adhere to the dry ice crystals. The crystals get heavier and soon begin to fall as snow or rain. Silver iodide is now the most common chemical used for cloud seeding. Silver iodide's crystalline structure is like that of dry ice and causes silver iodide to act like dry ice. Ice crystals form, grow, absorb the moisture in the clouds, and eventually drop out of the clouds as rain.

Cloud-seeding aircraft feed smoke trails of silver iodide into the updrafts of clouds. In other cases, rockets filled with silver iodide are shot from the ground into clouds, where water droplets are collecting, to prevent the formation of large hailstones.

While the results seem positive, there are problems. Some cloud-seeding projects have led to court battles.

Some communities accuse the seeders of "cloud rustling" because they take the water out of clouds that normally drop moisture on their towns. The courts must decide whether a cloud and its precipitation is owned by the community beneath it or whether nature should be allowed to take its course.

WHAT DO YOU THINK?

You love to ski, but the ski resort nearest your home hasn't had enough snow this year to open. Should they seed the clouds?

Your parents own an amusement park in a farming area. Your family's income depends on the tourists who come to the park in the summer. Local farmers keep seeding the clouds to make it rain. How would you vote at a city council meeting if it were up to the council to decide whether or not cloud seeding should be continued?

HOW IT WORKS

BAROMETERS

Barometers are instruments used to determine atmospheric pressure. How do barometers work?

One common type of barometer, pictured on the right here, is an aneroid barometer. It works on the principle that a sealed metal chamber contracts and expands with changes in the atmospheric pressure. For example, if high pressure moves in, pressure outside the chamber is greater than pressure inside the chamber, and the chamber contracts. If low pressure moves in, pressure outside the chamber is less than pressure inside the chamber, and the chamber expands.

A small chain extends between the chamber to a pointer on a dial that is read on the face of the barometer.

YOU TRY IT!

Take barometric pressure readings regularly each morning and evening for a week. Be sure it is about the same time each day. Draw a graph to show the pressure readings. Based on what you know about high- and low-pressure systems, what can you predict using only the pressure data?

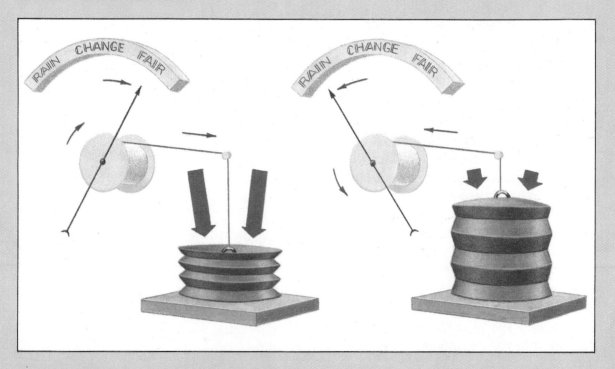

Literature
CONNECTION

THE HURRICANE

You've probably seen pictures of hurricanes in newspapers or on television. These powerful storms, with winds near their center blowing at least 120 kilometers per hour, form over oceans in tropical areas. The violent winds, and huge waves that result, may cause massive damage and destruction.

Vivid images of hurricanes can be evoked in ways other than through pictures, however. A poet uses words to paint pictures, and his or her writing forces us to dip into our imagination.

Read the poem "The Hurricane," by Puerto Rican poet Pales Matos (Ferris, Helen, ed,.

Favorite Poems Old and New). Notice the images the poet uses to convey his perception of a hurricane.

YOU TRY IT!

Do you think of an "agile dancer" when you think of a hurricane or does a more powerful image come to mind? Rewrite portions of "The Hurricane" to change the mood of the poem. Think of other words to describe the strength of the wind and the panorama of the sea.

TEENS *in* SCIENCE

WEATHER WATCH

Christopher Maiorino's science teacher invited him to see the Lakeland High School's weather station three and a half years ago. "I thought, 'Why not?'" said Chris. "I never left. I'd like to do this as a career."

Chris and his teacher arrive at the weather station every day at 6:30 A.M. Together they call weather stations from Salt Lake City to Connecticut, which are equipped with satellite weather maps as shown in the photo, for the daily weather data. The station has a fully equipped weather laboratory with a computer and modem, barometer, weather radio, and other equipment for measuring temperature, air pressure, wind, and humidity. More members of the Weather Club come in later to discuss the predictions. Then Chris broadcasts the weather forecast in the morning and in the afternoon over the local radio station.

Chris's teacher took over the Lakeland High School Weather Club in 1976, and since that time has installed a lot of new equipment, including a satellite dish. "Weather prediction gets exciting when there's a potential for a good storm."

Reviewing Main Ideas

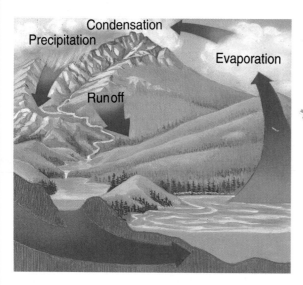

1. Water that evaporates into the atmosphere condenses to form clouds and then falls back to Earth in some form of precipitation.

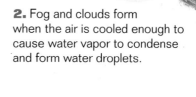

2. Fog and clouds form when the air is cooled enough to cause water vapor to condense and form water droplets.

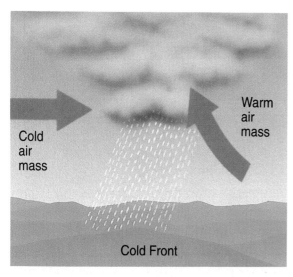

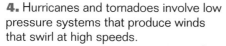

3. The weather at a front depends on the types of air masses that meet.

4. Hurricanes and tornadoes involve low pressure systems that produce winds that swirl at high speeds.

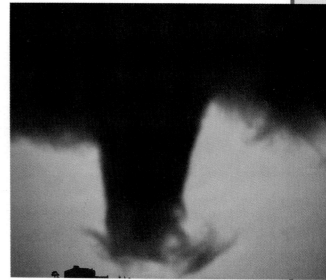

Chapter Review

USING KEY SCIENCE TERMS

air mass	relative humidity
dew point	saturated
front	tornado
hurricane	

For each set of terms below, explain the relationship that exists.

1. air mass, front
2. dew point, saturated
3. relative humidity, dew point
4. hurricane, tornado

UNDERSTANDING IDEAS

Choose the best answer to complete each sentence.

1. Water evaporates more rapidly on days when the air is ____.
   a. hot and dry   **c.** cool and dry
   b. hot and humid   **d.** cool and humid

2. A cloud that forms at Earth's surface is called ____.
   a. dew   **c.** cumulus
   b. frost   **d.** fog

3. Hurricanes weaken when they move over ____.
   a. warmer water
   b. land
   c. deep water
   d. water near the equator

4. Relative humidity drops when ____.
   a. warm air cools
   b. warm air is heated
   c. the dew point is reached
   d. evaporation increases

5. An air mass that forms over Canada is ____.
   a. cool and moist   **c.** warm and moist
   b. cool and dry   **d.** warm and dry

6. Air that is saturated has a relative humidity of ____ percent.
   a. 0
   b. 50
   c. 100
   d. an unknown

7. Relative humidity is measured with a(n) ____.
   a. thermometer   **c.** altimeter
   b. barometer   **d.** psychrometer

8. A large body of air with the same temperature and humidity is called a(n) ____.
   a. front   **c.** air mass
   b. air pocket   **d.** cloud

9. The first signs of an approaching warm front might be ____.
   a. cumulus clouds   **c.** rain
   b. cirrus clouds   **d.** stratus clouds

CRITICAL THINKING

Use your understanding of the concepts developed in the chapter to answer each of the following questions.

1. Why would an air mass formed off the coast of Oregon have different qualities after it moved across the western United States and crossed the Rockies?

2. Fred walks out of an air-conditioned building. His eyeglasses immediately fog up. Why?

3. You go into the basement of your school building. In the ceiling, you see two identical copper pipes. You know one carries cold water, the other hot water. The left pipe is moist on the outside. Without touching the pipes, how can you tell which pipe has the hot water?

4. The relative humidity of the air outside has remained 50 percent all day, despite an increase in temperature. Explain why this can happen.

5. How could you lower the relative humidity in your classroom?

6. Describe the weather conditions shown on the station model in the diagram.

The initial 10 is omitted from the barometer reading.

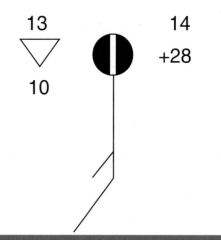

PROBLEM SOLVING

Read the following problem and discuss your answers in a brief paragraph.

Jason and Kim were helping their father by fixing spaghetti for supper. They filled a pot two-thirds full of water and put it on the stove to heat. Then they went to watch television. When Jason went to check the pot a while later, it was only half full of water. On the wall above the stove were droplets of water. What had happened? What happened to the relative humidity of the room as the water boiled?

CONNECTING IDEAS

Discuss each of the following in a brief paragraph.

1. Explain how convection is related to the formation of weather systems.

2. How is the water cycle related to the weather?

3. How are temperature and pressure related in air masses?

4. **A CLOSER LOOK** What are some of the weather factors that forecasters must collect data on in order to predict the weather?

5. **SCIENCE AND SOCIETY** Explain how the process of cloud seeding works.

DID YOU EVER WONDER . . .

How the oceans were formed and where all that water came from?

Why the water level at the seashore rises and falls each day?

How the creatures that scurry on the beach can live with waves continually crashing around them?

You'll find the answers to these questions as you read this chapter.

Ocean Water and Life

Surf's up! That's what you and your friend have been waiting all morning to hear. You grab your surfboards and start paddling out to the breaking waves.

You bravely stand on your board—feet apart, knees bent, arms out for balance—and, for the next few seconds, ride a wall of water nearly 20 feet tall.

But look—your friend has been snagged by the top of the wave! She loses her balance and tumbles into the water. After the wave passes, however, she surfaces and catches her breath. So do you.

Surfing is a lot of fun, but it can also be dangerous. If you've ever been knocked over by a wave, you know how much energy water in motion can have.

In this chapter, you'll learn how ocean water moves. You'll also discover what effects this movement has on life on Earth.

EXPLORE!

Can you make a human wave?
Have you seen excited fans leap from their seats, raise their arms, then flop back down again, forming a gigantic human wave? You try it. Have a group of classmates put their chairs in a row and one by one stand up, then sit down again. How can people create the illusion of movement without changing seats?

10-1 Waves and Tides

OBJECTIVES

In this section, you will

- explain the relationship between wind and waves;
- differentiate between the movement of water particles in a wave and the movement of wave energy;
- explain the cause of tides;
- discuss ways in which organisms are adapted to life in intertidal zones.

KEY SCIENCE TERMS

intertidal zone

WAVES

It's a great day for the beach. You've covered yourself with sunscreen and spread out your blanket. With your radio to your left and a can of soda to your right, you sit and watch the waves roll in.

Water waves are movements in which the water alternately rises and falls. Water waves have a lot in common with light waves and sound waves. You may remember that all waves have a crest and a trough and that waves can be measured in terms of height and length. These wave characteristics are shown in Figure 10-1. But what causes water waves to form, and why are some waves very tall, while others are barely ripples?

How Waves Form

In the ocean, waves are usually caused by the wind. The same stiff breeze that uproots your beach umbrella causes waves to form. As wind blows across a body of water, friction causes the water to move along with it. If the wind speed is great enough, the water will begin to pile up on itself and form a wave.

Wind-generated waves stop forming when the wind stops blowing. But once waves have been set in motion, they will continue to travel over long distances. The waves you see at the beach may have originated many thousands of kilometers away. In the following Investigate activity, you will learn how wind affects wave height.

FIGURE 10-1. Each water wave has the characteristics shown in the illustration.

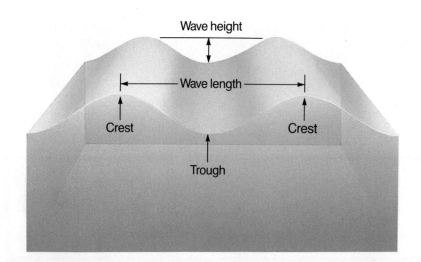

Wave height

Wave length

Crest

Crest

Trough

10-1 WIND AND WAVE HEIGHT

You've learned that the height of a wave is the vertical distance from trough to crest. In this activity, you'll study how wind affects wave height.

PROBLEM
How do wind speed and duration affect the height of waves?

MATERIALS
white paper
electric fan (3-speed)
light source
clock or watch
clear plastic storage container
ring stand   water
metric ruler   pencil

PROCEDURE
1. Copy the data table.
2. Set up the light source, ring stand, and piece of paper under the plastic container as shown.

3. Shine the light source directly on the plastic container.
4. Pour water into the container so it is almost full.
5. Place the fan at one end of the container as shown. Turn the fan on low. **CAUTION:** *Do not allow any part of the light, the fan, or their cords to come in contact with the water.*
6. **Observe** the shadows of the waves on the paper through the container. After 3 minutes, **measure** the height of the waves. Record your observations.

7. After 2 more minutes, measure the waves again and record your observations.
8. Repeat Steps 6 and 7 with the fan on medium speed and then high. Record your findings.
9. Turn off the fan and observe what happens.

ANALYZE
1. **Determine the cause** of the shadows that appeared on the white paper.
2. How does an increase in fan speed affect the pattern of these shadows?
3. What was the effect on the shadows when you turned off the fan?
4. **Identify the two variables** in this activity.

CONCLUDE AND APPLY
5. **Determine** if wave height is affected by the length of time that the wind blows by interpreting the data in your table. Explain.
6. **Determine the effect** of wind speed on the height of the waves. Explain.
7. **Going Further:** Where does the energy that generates waves come from?

DATA AND OBSERVATIONS

FAN SPEED	TIME	WAVE HEIGHT	OBSERVATIONS
Low	3 min.		
	5 min.		
Medium	3 min.		
	5 min.		
High	3 min.		
	5 min.		

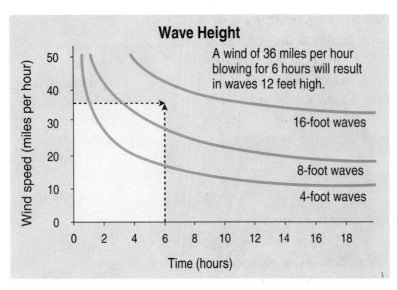

Wave Height

A wind of 36 miles per hour blowing for 6 hours will result in waves 12 feet high.

16-foot waves

8-foot waves

4-foot waves

Wind speed (miles per hour)

Time (hours)

FIGURE 10-2. The size of a wave depends partly on wind speed and how long the wind has been blowing.

As you learned in the Investigate activity, the height of wind-generated waves depends on the speed of the wind as well as the length of time the wind blows. Study the graph in Figure 10-2. How long would it take for a 40-mph wind to generate a 16-foot wave?

A third factor that affects wave height is the distance over which the wind blows. The greater the distance, the higher the wave. This is why waves on the oceans can reach greater heights than waves on smaller bodies of water.

How Waves Move

When you watch a wave, it looks like the water is moving forward with the wave. The water is moving, but not in the way you may think.

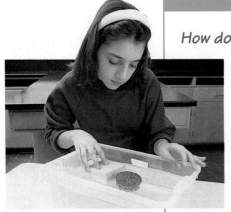

FIND OUT!

How do waves move?

Fill a clear plastic storage container or a glass baking dish with water. Place a cork in the middle of the container. Use tape to mark the approximate location of the cork on each side of the container. At one end of the container, gently lower and raise a small wooden block in and out of the water to create waves. Observe the effect on the cork.

Conclude and Apply

How and where does the cork move? Explain.

If water moved forward with a wave, all the water would eventually drain from the oceans and lakes and pile up on shore. Water waves actually consist of two motions: the forward progress of the energy of the wave and the circular motion of the water particles this energy displaces as it passes by. These two motions are shown in Figure 10-3. The activity you did with the cork demonstrates that as the crest of a wave passes, water particles are lifted and moved briefly forward before they sink back down to their original position. The cork, along with the water, was only temporarily displaced as the energy of the wave passed by.

How Waves Break

Have you ever heard the sound of waves tumbling on the beach? You cannot hear waves as they move over the ocean. Only when they break do they make sound. What do you think causes a wave to break? Figure 10-4 illustrates the cause.

As a wave approaches a sloping shore, it changes shape. As it reaches shallow water, the water at the bottom of the wave is slowed down by friction with the ocean floor. Wave height increases and wavelength decreases, until finally the wave becomes so tall it collapses, or breaks.

Therefore, the height of the waves and the depth of the water determine where waves will break, with high waves usually breaking farther from shore than low waves. Is the breaker shown in Figure 10-4 very close to shore?

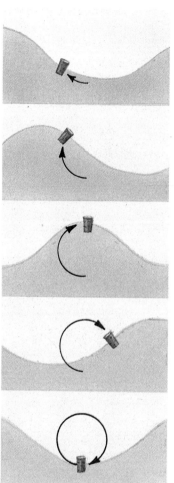

FIGURE 10-3. A floating cork shows that a waveform travels but the water itself does not.

FIGURE 10-4. A wave breaks when it becomes too tall for the depth of the water in which it is moving.

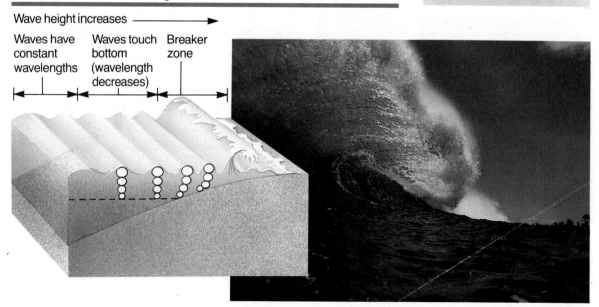

Wave height increases ⟶

| Waves have constant wavelengths | Waves touch bottom (wavelength decreases) | Breaker zone |

DID YOU KNOW?

Commercial fisheries rely on tide charts to tell them what time of day is best for fishing. Fish feed most heavily about one hour before and one hour after high or low tide. The tide chart tells the fisheries exactly what time high or low tide will occur.

TIDES

Have you ever spent an entire afternoon at the seashore? Then you have probably seen the tides. Tides are long, slow waves that result in an alternate rise and fall of the surface level of the ocean. As a tide comes in along a stretch of seashore, the water level rises, and waves break farther and farther inland. At high tide, the surface level of the ocean along a particular stretch of seashore is at its highest point, and the water line reaches its farthest point inland.

Once high tide has been reached, the water level slowly starts to drop again. A tide is then said to be going out. Gradually, the water line recedes, and parts of the beach that were previously underwater become exposed again. When the surface level of the ocean is at its lowest point along a stretch of beach, low tide occurs. Then the cycle starts all over again. Figure 10-5 shows high tide and low tide at the same location.

Tides are mainly an ocean phenomenon; people who live inland rarely observe tides. Even the largest lakes don't contain the volume of water necessary to be affected by the same forces that cause water levels along coastal areas to rise and fall. What are the forces that cause tides?

FIGURE 10-5. The difference between high tide (a) and low tide (b) is easily seen at Mont Saint Michel off the northwestern coast of France.

a

b

The Gravitational Pull of the Moon

Tides are caused by the gravitational attraction among the sun, the moon, and Earth. The gravitational force of the moon pulls on Earth. This force affects all parts of Earth including the solid part. But it is the oceans that are most affected by this force. On the side of Earth closest to the moon, the moon's gravity pulls the water with greater force than it does matter farther away. This causes water to form into a bulge facing the moon. This variation in pulling results in a stretching of Earth. Although the solid portion of Earth is stretched only slightly, the world's oceans are changed quite dramatically to produce two opposing tidal bulges. You can see this in Figure 10-6.

Recall that the moon revolves around Earth about every 29 days. Because the position of the moon changes very little in a day, it is the bulges that stay in place while Earth rotates beneath them. As Earth rotates, different locations on Earth's surface experience the high and low tidal water levels. Because there are two high tide bulges, a single location on Earth's surface experiences each of them in one 24-hour period—the time it takes Earth to rotate once on its axis. There are some coastal areas that experience two high tides and two low tides each day.

Examine the tide chart for Boston Harbor in Table 10-1. You will notice that a high tide occurs about every 12¹/₂ hours. A low tide occurs a little more than 6 hours after every high tide.

If the water level of the oceans is highest when the moon pulls on it, then you might think that a high tide should occur at a location when the moon is directly over that location. But high tides occur some four to six hours later than that. Actually, when the moon is overhead, there are low tides. How can this be explained?

When the moon's gravity pulls the oceans, it takes time for the water to move and form tidal bulges. This is because of the inertia of the water, friction, and the distance the water must travel—often hundreds of kilometers—to form the bulge. Thus, there is a delay in the time it takes to form high and low tides. This delay is about half the time between one high tide and the next.

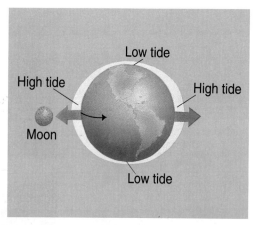

FIGURE 10-6. Locations facing the moon and on the opposite side of Earth experience tidal bulges. This is an idealized diagram of tidal bulges. The actual positions of tidal bulges vary due to the inertia of water, friction, and other variables.

TABLE 10-1. Tide Chart For Boston

Date	Morning		Afternoon	
SUNDAY **6**	High height Low height Sunrise	9:28 10.8 3:12 -0.3 5:44	High height Low height Sunrise	9:52 10.8 3:38 -0.5 5:21
MONDAY **7** NEW MOON	High height Low height Sunrise	10:15 11.1 4:00 -0.4 5:45	High height Low height Sunrise	10:42 10.7 4:28 -0.8 5:19
TUESDAY **8**	High height Low height Sunrise	10:59 11.2 4:45 -0.3 5:47	High height Low height Sunrise	11:29 10.5 5:15 -0.9 5:18
WEDNESDAY **9**	High height Low height Sunrise	11:41 11.2 5:29 -0.1 5:48	High height Low height Sunrise	— — 6:00 -0.8 5:16
THURSDAY **10**	High height Low height Sunrise	12:14 10.2 6:11 0.3 5:49	High height Low height Sunrise	12:24 11.0 6:45 -0.5 5:14
FRIDAY **11**	High height Low height Sunrise	12:57 9.8 6:56 0.7 5:50	High height Low height Sunrise	1:06 10.6 7.29 0.0 5:13
SATURDAY **12**	High height Low height Sunrise	1:43 9.3 7:41 1.2 5:51	High height Low height Sunrise	1:52 10.2 8:15 0.5 5:11

Eastern Standard Time –
Add 1 Hour For Daylight Savings Time

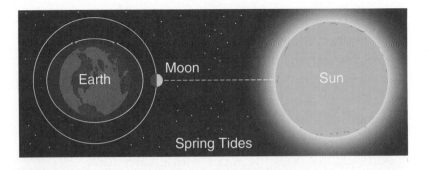

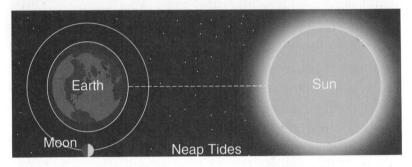

FIGURE 10-7. When the sun, the moon, and Earth are aligned, spring tides occur. When the sun, the moon, and Earth form a right angle, neap tides ocur.

The sun also affects tides by strengthening or weakening the moon's effects. When the moon, Earth, and the sun are aligned, high tides are higher and low tides are lower than normal. These are called spring tides. When the moon, Earth, and the sun form a right angle, high tides are lower and low tides are higher than normal. These are called neap tides. Spring tides and neap tides are shown in Figure 10-7.

If you were in a boat in the middle of the ocean, you would not notice a change in the water level produced by the tides. The rising and falling water level is mainly evident where the land meets the sea. This area is called the intertidal zone and it is home to an astonishing variety of organisms.

LIFE IN THE INTERTIDAL ZONE

You may think that not many organisms could live in an area that is pounded by waves, raked over by rocks and sand, and exposed to wind and light day after day. If

FIGURE 10-8. A hermit crab protects its soft body by occupying a discarded shell.

you examine the sand at low tide closely, however, you will see many tiny holes. These holes mark the hiding places of animals.

A wide variety of plants and animals thrive in the **intertidal zone**, the area of a coastline between high and low tide. The intertidal zone is one of Earth's ecosystems. Recall that in an ecosystem, a community of different organisms interact with one another and with their environment. For the organisms that live in the intertidal zone, however, it's a dangerous way of life. They are threatened daily with the possibility of being dried up, eaten by birds and other animals, or washed out to sea. But the intertidal organisms have adapted to these conditions in some surprising ways.

Microscopic organisms live in water between the grains of sand in a sandy intertidal zone. Burrowing animals like clams, crabs, and lugworms also live in muddy or sandy shores. During low tide, animals living in this zone burrow down into the wet sand or mud, crawl or swim into the water, or pull their bodies into moist shells and wait inside until they are covered with water again.

Along rocky shores, oysters, mussels, and barnacles, like those in Figure 10-9, grip the rocks so tightly that even storm waves can't pry them loose. These animals rely on the tides to bring them their food. Their hard shells protect them from the pounding surf and abrasive sand, as well as from hungry predators.

In this section, you learned that ocean waves and tides are movements of seawater. But what is the ocean made of? What was the origin of ocean water? Why is water important for life in and around the oceans? You will learn the answers to these questions in the next section.

FIGURE 10-9. Barnacles and sea stars attach themselves to rocks and other stationary objects to keep from being swept away by the change of tides.

Check Your Understanding

1. How does wind relate to water waves?
2. What effect does the moon have on Earth's oceans?
3. Describe the living conditions in the intertidal zone and name two characteristics that enable animals to survive there.
4. **APPLY:** When a wave passes, why do harbor markers bob up and down in the water?

10-2 The Origin and Composition of Oceans

OBJECTIVES

In this section, you will

- describe the origin of ocean water;
- discuss the origin of ocean salts, and explain why the salinity of the ocean does not change;
- describe the benefits that organisms get from seawater.

KEY SCIENCE TERMS

salinity

manganese nodule

THE ORIGIN OF OCEAN WATER

Ocean water covers nearly three-quarters of Earth's surface. Where do you think all this water came from? Scientists can only hypothesize about the origin of ocean water. They think that in Earth's younger years, it was much more volcanically active than it is today, and that the water in our oceans came from volcanoes.

Not only do volcanoes spew lava and ash, but they also give off water vapor, as you can see in Figure 10-10. About 4 billion years ago, water vapor from volcanoes began to accumulate in Earth's atmosphere. The vapor eventually cooled enough to condense. Precipitation began to fall, and oceans formed over millions of years as this water filled low areas. But why is ocean water so salty?

THE ORIGIN OF OCEAN SALTS

If you've ever accidentally swallowed a mouthful of ocean water, you could tell immediately that it was different from the water you drink at home. Ocean water contains many dissolved materials, including sodium, chlorine, silicon, and calcium. Where do these materials come from?

One source is the water that soaks into the ground and collects between particles of rock and soil. This groundwater very

FIGURE 10-10. Volcanoes may have been the source of ocean water.

slowly dissolves elements such as calcium from rocks and minerals that are in the ground. The elements are then carried by rivers to the ocean. Another source of dissolved elements is volcanoes that erupt and release gases into the atmosphere. These gases are eventually deposited in the ocean.

Two elements in ocean water combine to form the most abundant dissolved compound in the ocean. Sodium is dissolved in river water that flows into the ocean. Chlorine gas is added from the atmosphere. When sodium and chlorine combine in ocean water, they form sodium chloride, a salt. In solid form, sodium chloride is known as halite, the common table salt that we all know. As you can see in Figure 10–11, chlorine and sodium make up more than 80 percent of the elements that form salts in the oceans. It is sodium chloride and a few similar compounds, that make ocean water salty.

SALINITY

Salinity is a measure of the amount of solids—primarily salts—dissolved in ocean water. On average, every 1000 grams of ocean water contains about 35 grams of dissolved salts. Do the following experiment to compare the characteristics of different saltwater solutions.

FIGURE 10-11. The composition of seawater includes salt compounds.

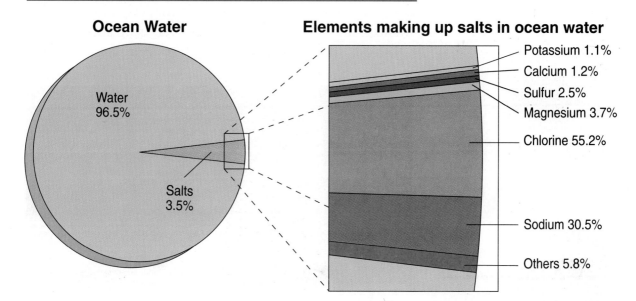

Ocean Water

Water 96.5%

Salts 3.5%

Elements making up salts in ocean water

Potassium 1.1%
Calcium 1.2%
Sulfur 2.5%
Magnesium 3.7%
Chlorine 55.2%
Sodium 30.5%
Others 5.8%

How does salt affect the density of water?
Place a small weight in a test tube. Push a small wad of clay into the tube to hold the weight in place. Cork the tube and place it in a jar of warm tap water. Note the water level on the floating test tube and mark it with a grease pencil. Next, add 1 tablespoon of salt to the water in the jar and note the new water level of the tube. Is it higher or lower? Add another tablespoon of salt to the water. What has happened to the water level now?

Conclude and Apply
Is seawater more or less dense than fresh water?

As this experiment showed, the saltier the water, the higher the test tube floated. This is because the presence of salt in water causes the water to become denser, and objects float more easily in dense water.

Generally speaking, the salinity of ocean water does not change. Although substances are added constantly by rivers, volcanoes, and the atmosphere, they are being removed at the same rate by plants and animals, or they are forming solids on the ocean bottom.

Some marine animals use calcium to form bones, while others use silicon and calcium to form shells. Because there are so many sea plants and animals, calcium and silicon are constantly removed from seawater.

DID YOU KNOW?

The Dead Sea is a salt lake between Israel and Jordan. The salinity of this body of water is nearly eight times that of the ocean. People float easily in the Dead Sea because the abundance of salt makes the water very dense. This peculiar characteristic makes it a popular vacation spot for people from all over the world.

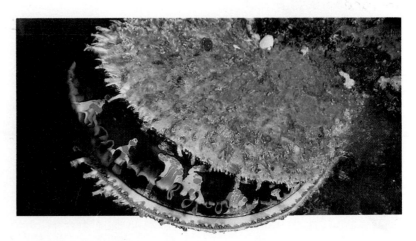

FIGURE 10-12. The shell of this oyster is made of calcium and other elements found in ocean water.

The ocean is like a giant solution. Substances in the ocean behave in ways similar to how they might behave chemically in a laboratory beaker. The following Find Out activity will show you another way solids can be removed from seawater.

FIND OUT!

What happens to saltwater when it is cooled?

Use the saltwater solution from the previous Find Out activity for this activity. Put the jar in a refrigerator overnight. The next day, check the solution. What do you see at the bottom of the jar?

Conclude and Apply

Where did the substance at the bottom of the jar come from?

As you just observed, solids in solution, such as the sodium chloride in the Find Out activity, can precipitate out of a solution as it is cooled. In a similar manner, solids dissolved in seawater can precipitate out of the solution and fall to the ocean floor. One solid that forms this way is a manganese nodule. A **manganese nodule** is a rounded rock the size of a golf or tennis ball that forms when minerals collect around a small object such as a shark's tooth. Manganese nodules consist mostly of oxides of iron and manganese. Some also contain cobalt, titanium, zirconium, and vanadium.

How do these dissolved substances affect life? Most land animals and plants need fresh water to survive—their systems cannot tolerate the level of salt in seawater. Yet fresh water is becoming less plentiful as the world develops. Fresh water supplies are being used in homes and businesses faster than they can be replaced by rain. In addition, humans have polluted or contaminated some supplies of fresh water. Ocean water can be used only if the salts and other dissolved substances are removed. The next activity shows you one method of removing salt from salt water.

SKILLBUILDER

IDENTIFYING CAUSE AND EFFECT

Discuss what would happen to the composition of seawater if all organisms having bones or shells suddenly died. If you need help, refer to the **Skill Handbook** on page 685.

DID YOU KNOW?

There is a little bit of ocean in each of us. The adult human body contains about 18 L of salt water. The chemical composition of this fluid is similar to seawater.

10-2 FRESH WATER FROM SALT WATER

In this activity, you'll learn one way of removing salt from salt water.

PROBLEM

How can you make drinking water from ocean water?

MATERIALS

pan balance
table salt
water
2 500-mL beakers
1000-mL flask
1-hole rubber stopper
rubber tubing
hot plate
cardboard
ice
shallow pan
polyethylene plastic tubing
glycerine
towel
scissors
washers

PROCEDURE

1. Be sure the glassware is clean before beginning this experiment. Measure and dissolve 18 g of table salt into a beaker containing 500 mL of water. Carefully taste the solution.

2. Pour the solution into the flask.

3. Rub a small amount of glycerine on both ends of the plastic tubing. Hold the tubing with a towel, and gently slide it into the stopper and rubber tubing as shown in the photo.

4. Insert the tube-stopper assembly into the flask. Make sure the plastic tubing is above the surface of the solution.

5. Cut a small hole in the cardboard. Insert the free end of the rubber tubing through the hole. Be sure to keep the tubing away from the hot plate.

6. Place the flask on a hot plate, but do not turn on the hot plate yet.

7. Set the beaker in a shallow pan filled with ice.

8. Place the cardboard over a clean beaker. Add several washers to the cardboard

to hold it in place.

9. Turn on the hot plate. Bring the solution to a boil. **Observe** the flask and the beaker.

10. Continue boiling until the solution is almost boiled away.

11. Turn off the hot plate, remove the flask, and let cool.

ANALYZE

1. What happened to the water in the flask as you boiled the solution?

2. What happened inside the beaker? Explain.

3. Taste the water in the beaker. Is it salty?

4. What remains in the flask?

5. Is the combined water in the flask and in the beaker the same volume you placed in the flask at the beginning? Explain.

6. What is on the sides of the flask?

CONCLUDE AND APPLY

7. Explain how evaporation can be used to obtain fresh water from salt water.

8. **Going Further: Infer** how this process could be used to extract minerals from seawater.

You just discovered a method for removing salt from seawater to produce fresh water. Desalination plants use a similar method for producing fresh water. Ocean water is heated until water vapor forms. The vapor is collected and cooled. The condensed product is fresh water.

FIGURE 10-13. Desalination plants often provide fresh water to people living in desert areas.

OCEAN WATER SUPPORTS LIFE

Although land organisms require fresh water, you've already seen how marine organisms need the calcium and silicon dissolved in ocean water to carry on certain life processes. Oxygen and carbon dioxide, also necessary for life, are dissolved in ocean water too. Animals use oxygen to breathe. Protists, such as the green algae shown in Figure 10-14, need carbon dioxide to photosynthesize. The actual water in seawater is also very important because it transports food to organisms and carries away wastes. It also provides the buoyancy that allows marine organisms to move more easily, and, of course, it provides the moisture the organisms need to survive.

In the next section, you will learn about how changes in the salinity and temperature of ocean water affect the way it moves. The next section examines ocean currents.

FIGURE 10-14. Green algae use carbon dioxide during the process of photosynthesis.

Check Your Understanding

1. What role do scientists think volcanoes played in the formation of the oceans?
2. What makes ocean water salty, and where do these substances come from? Why doesn't the salinity of the ocean change?
3. Discuss how organisms benefit from ocean water and its dissolved substances.
4. **APPLY:** What might happen to sea animals if all the green algae in the ocean died? Explain.

10-3 Ocean Currents

OBJECTIVES

In this section, you will

- contrast surface currents and density currents;
- discuss ways that ocean currents affect organisms;
- describe the movement of water in an upwelling.

KEY SCIENCE TERMS

surface current
plankton
nekton
density current
upwelling

WHAT ARE CURRENTS?

When you stir chocolate syrup into a glass of milk, you make currents. These currents are the dark swirls of chocolate made by stirring with your spoon.

Oceans have currents too. You know that water particles in ocean waves do not travel forward. Rather, they move in a circle as the energy of the wave temporarily displaces them. In currents, however, water particles flow in one direction like giant rivers in the ocean.

SURFACE CURRENTS

In the late 1760s, the American colonists complained that it took their mail ships two weeks longer to travel from England to America than it took whaling ships to make the same trip. Deputy Postmaster General Benjamin Franklin decided to investigate. Franklin learned that the whalers knew of a place in the ocean where the water moved in a northeasterly direction. When they wanted to travel southwest from Europe to America, the whalers sailed outside this area. The following Find Out activity will show you why.

FIND OUT!

Do currents affect a ship's speed?
Fill a shallow pan with water. Have a partner stand beside you and, with a spoon, create a current that moves to the far end of the pan. Place a cork in the water to represent a ship. Blow on the cork so that it moves in the same direction as the current. Observe what happens. Now blow the cork in the same direction as before, but this time have your partner stand at the far end of the pan and create a current that moves the water toward you.

Conclude and Apply
Is it harder to move with or against a current?

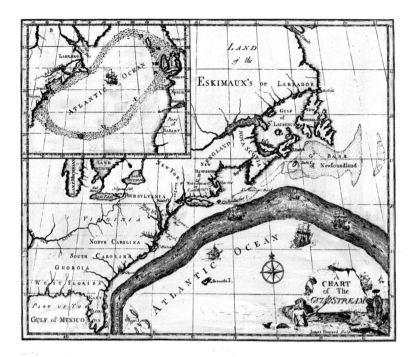

If you answered that it's harder to move against a current than with a current, you could make a good sailor. Franklin found that on the way to England, the mail ships traveled with the current. However, when the ships traveled in the opposite direction, they sailed against the current and lost speed. This made their return trip longer.

Franklin was told that the current was only about 100 kilometers wide. With a good map, the mail ship captains could avoid the current on their way back to America. Franklin drew the first map of the current in 1770. He called the current the Gulf Stream because it seemed to flow out of the Gulf of Mexico. Franklin's map is shown in Figure 10-15.

The Gulf Stream is one of several surface currents in Earth's oceans. A **surface current** is movement of water that affects only the upper few hundred meters of seawater. Most surface currents are caused by wind. Friction between wind and water surface causes the water to move.

You've seen in your earlier science classes that surface winds are influenced by Earth's rotation. Earth's rotation affects ocean currents too. The direction of Earth's rotation causes most currents north of the equator to move in a clockwise direction, as the Gulf Stream does.

DID YOU KNOW?

The Gulf Stream, called "a river in the ocean," is bigger than any river on land. It is approximately 800 m deep and 100 km wide. It flows at an average speed of 6.5 kph and transports 1000 times as much water as the Mississippi River in the same period of time.

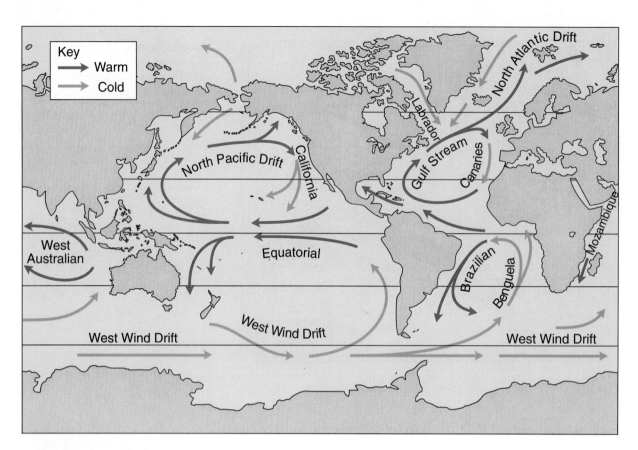

FIGURE 10-16. Surface currents flow in the Northern Hemisphere and Southern Hemisphere.

In Figure 10-16, which way do currents south of the equator move? Most currents south of the equator move in a counterclockwise direction.

Another factor that affects the movement of currents is the continents that deflect them. For example, in the Pacific Ocean, currents moving west are deflected northward by Asia and southward by Australia. These currents then move eastward until they meet North and South America, which deflect them toward the equator.

Figure 10-16 shows that many surface currents on the western coasts of continents are cold, whereas currents on the eastern coasts of continents are warm. The reason is that currents on the western coasts generally originate far from the equator, in the cooler latitudes. Currents on the eastern coasts originate near the equator and, therefore, are warmer.

Surface Currents and Climates

If you live near a seacoast, how do you think the warm or cold currents off your coastline affect your climate? Do you know that currents can have an effect on you even if you don't live along the coast?

Iceland is located near the Arctic Circle, so you would expect it to have a very frigid climate. But the Gulf Stream flows past Iceland, carrying with it warm water from the Gulf of Mexico. The current's warm water heats the surrounding air, causing the entire country to have a surprisingly mild climate.

Surface Currents and Marine Organisms

Surface currents also greatly affect marine life. Most photosynthetic protists such as algae live in the upper 140 meters of the ocean because this is about how far sunlight will penetrate ocean water. Most animals live where there are algae because of the food and oxygen the algae provide. Therefore, most marine organisms live where there are surface currents.

One way of classifying marine organisms is by how they move. Drifting protists and animals are called **plankton** (PLANGK tuhn). Most plankton are micro-

SKILLBUILDER

INTERPRETING SCIENTIFIC ILLUSTRATIONS
The latitudes of San Diego, California, and Charleston, South Carolina, are exactly the same. However, the average yearly water temperature in the ocean off Charleston is much higher than the water temperature off San Diego. Use Figure 10–16 to help explain why. If you need help, refer to the **Skill Handbook** on page 691.

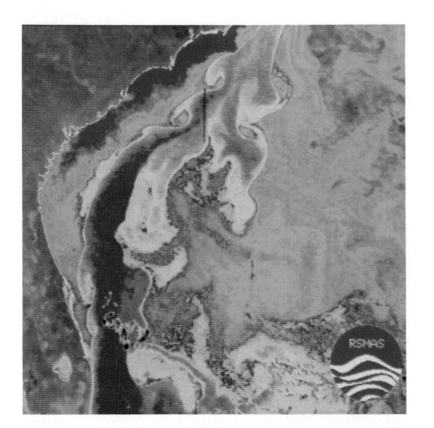

FIGURE 10-17. Ocean temperature data collected by satellite were used to make this surface temperature image of the Atlantic Ocean off the coast of Florida. The warm Gulf Stream waters appear red and orange; the cooler water appears blue and green.

scopic and depend largely on dissolved substances in the seawater for their survival. The currents carry nutrients to these organisms and carry the wastes away. Surface currents also transport plankton.

Nekton (NEK tuhn) include all swimming forms of fish and other animals, from tiny herring to huge whales. Nekton can move from one depth to another. Some nekton come to the ocean surface only at night to feed on plankton. They spend the rest of their time in water that is too deep to be affected by surface currents. But at these depths, density currents are present.

DENSITY CURRENTS

Water below a few hundred meters is too deep to be affected by winds, and yet it also has currents. These currents are called density currents. A **density current** is movement of water that occurs when dense seawater moves toward an area of less dense seawater. What do you think would cause differences in the density of seawater?

EXPLORE!

Can temperature affect water density?

Fill a large glass jar with warm water. Gently add a drop of food coloring in the center. Now carefully float an ice cube on top of the food coloring. Observe for one minute. What happens to the food coloring? Add two drops of food coloring directly on the ice cube to help you see what is happening.

In the Explore activity, you saw that temperature affects the movement of water. The molecules in cold water are less active and are closer together than molecules in warm water, making the cold water more dense. Dense water sinks, forming a vertical current.

In the ocean, cold air near the North and South poles cools the water, causing it to become more dense than water in nonpolar areas. Can you think of something else besides temperature that might affect the density of seawater?

How are density and salinity related?
Fill a large jar three-quarters full with water at room temperature. Mix several teaspoons of table salt into a small glass of water of the same temperature as the water in the jar. Add a few drops of food coloring to the salt water and pour the solution very slowly and gently into the jar of water. Describe what happens.

As you can see from this activity, salinity affects the density of water. The colored salt solution sank to the bottom of the jar because it was more dense than the fresh water around it. What do you think causes salinity differences in the ocean?

Think about the water at the poles. The temperature at the poles is so cold that it freezes some of the water. But only the water freezes, not the salts in the seawater. Therefore, the concentration of salts in the seawater that remain unfrozen increases. Once the salinity increases, the seawater becomes quite dense and sinks. But the dense water doesn't stay near the poles. It sinks and travels along the ocean floor toward the equator. As it moves, it displaces warm, less dense water. This warm water is forced to flow toward the poles. These two events form a continuous cycle that circulates ocean water. This cycle is shown in Figure 10-18.

FIGURE 10-18. Density currents flow to and from the poles and the equator.

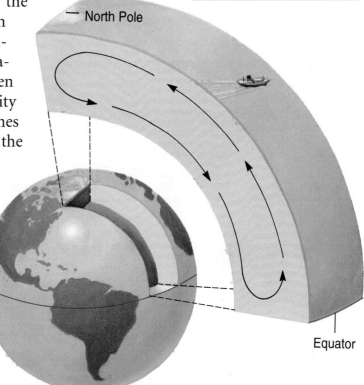

North Pole

Equator

UPWELLINGS

In some regions of the world, the density current cycle is interrupted. This happens where strong, wind-driven surface currents carry warm surface water away from an area. In such an area, cold water from deep below rises to replace water at the surface. This upward movement of cold water is called an **upwelling**.

Where there are upwellings, there are usually a lot of fish. Can you guess why? When organisms die, they sink into deep water, making this water extremely rich in nutrients. As a result, upwellings bring high concentrations of nutrients to the surface. Where there are high concentrations of nutrients, there is a surplus of food for fish. Because of these nutrients, upwellings are usually good fishing areas. Upwellings along the coast of Oregon, Washington, and Peru are among the most well known. Can you guess how many of the people living in these areas might make their living by fishing?

Whether your family makes its living from the ocean, or you occasionally visit the coast, or you have never even seen the ocean, the composition and movement of the ocean has a tremendous effect on your daily life. What would life on Earth be like without oceans?

FIGURE 10-19. Upwellings are caused by strong winds blowing surface currents away from shore.

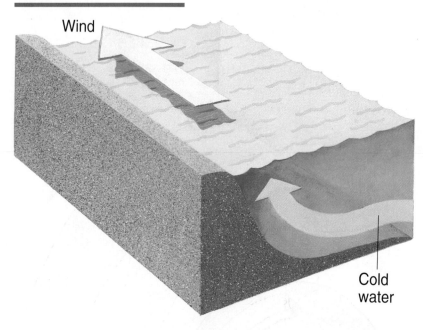

Wind

Cold water

Check Your Understanding

1. What is the difference between surface currents and density currents?
2. How do ocean currents affect organisms?
3. What causes an upwelling? Why might commercial fisheries be on the lookout for upwellings?
4. **APPLY:** How are density currents similar to convection currents?

EXPANDING YOUR VIEW

CONTENTS

A CLOSER LOOK

A LONG DRINK OF WATER

In this chapter, you investigated one way to solve a problem plaguing desert and some landlocked countries: finding a reliable supply of fresh drinking water. Your method was to take the salt out of seawater. An intriguing alternative—melting the fresh water captured in icebergs—has been explored for many years.

Icebergs are pieces of floating glacial ice broken from the front of a glacier or ice sheet. Icebergs can be more than 80 kilometers in length and their water is very pure. Though they often contain traces of rock fragments, they have little trapped organic matter because relatively few organisms live in the regions where icebergs are common. If icebergs could be transported to areas in need of fresh water, they would be stationary sources of water, more dependable than rainfall.

Although icebergs have been towed 3900 kilometers from southern Chile to Peru, melting prevents iceberg-towing from becoming a standard practice. The conventional method for towing icebergs would be to attach several lines to the iceberg and haul it with several tugboats at the slow speed of one nautical mile per hour. Melting is a big problem. As one discouraging glaciologist, a scientist who studies glaciers, warns, "Once you get into warm waters near the equator, you'll have nothing but a rope at the end of your tow."

The top of an iceberg is relatively immune to melting, because its icy-white surface deflects 90 percent of the sun's rays and thus absorbs little heat. The vulnerable part is the 85 to 90 percent of the iceberg that is underwater. Warmer water and friction from towing would cause most of the melting loss.

Encasing the underwater part of the iceberg in plastic to insulate against melting has been proposed, but it would be an enormous project that would cost millions of dollars or more.

WHAT DO YOU THINK?

Even if the transportation problem can be settled, questions about the use of icebergs for fresh water remain. What effect do you think anchoring a huge block of ice off an arid coast might have on the environment? How could weather in the region be affected?

LIFE SCIENCE
CONNECTION

THE OCEAN'S SKIN

You've read in this chapter that most marine life exists in the "sunlight zone," the upper 180 meters of the ocean, where protists can photosynthesize and provide food for marine animals. A narrower, paper-thin habitat exists on the surface of the ocean that separates the water from the atmosphere. This microlayer or, "skin," is a rich ecological niche where thousands of insects, fish, crustacean larvae, protists, and monerans—most invisible to the naked eye—cluster near the water's surface.

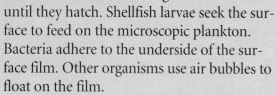

Because of its special ability to nurture life, the surface serves as a nursery for many fish species. Billions of fish eggs float to the surface where they attach themselves with fat globules to the film until they hatch. Shellfish larvae seek the surface to feed on the microscopic plankton. Bacteria adhere to the underside of the surface film. Other organisms use air bubbles to float on the film.

This surface area is like a large dining room for multitudes of species. Tiny life-forms inhabiting the water's surface, invisible to the naked eye, are the base of an extensive food web. Small fish feed on these plankton, only

You can see for yourself that water that appears clear and empty can be full of life. Take a trip to an ocean, pond, lake, or stream and collect some water in a glass jar. If possible, get some samples from different water sources.

Look at your samples through magnifying glasses and microscopes, slowly increasing the magnification as you view the samples.

Take a drop of water from one of your samples with an eyedropper. Make a slide and look through a high-powered microscope. How many more organisms can you find?

Draw pictures of what you see. Try to identify the organisms from a field guide.

to constitute a meal for larger and larger fish that swim upward to feed at the top. Seabirds feast by skimming food from the water's surface.

SCIENCE AND SOCIETY

AQUACULTURE

One of the most difficult problems facing the world of tomorrow is how to feed our growing population when food-producing areas on land remain the same size or get smaller. Where will we turn for new food sources?

A good place to find them is under water. Aquaculture is the controlled raising, or farming, of shellfish, fish, and plants that live in water. Aquaculture is done in both fresh water and seawater, and is done in both natural bodies of water and enclosures built on land. By controlling the environment—providing proper nutrients, providing protection from predators, and controlling breeding— farm-raised plants and animals often grow faster and larger than those in the wild.

In Japan's Inland Sea, oysters and other bivalves, such as clams and mussels, are cultivated on ropes hanging into the water from rafts. The Hanging Gardens of the Inland Sea are really very large undersea fields for growing bivalves. Many hundreds of bivalves are hung into the sea from floating rafts that give the animals a place on which to grow and mature. The bivalves get their food in the form of algae and are ready to harvest in a few months to a couple of years, depending on the animal. The process of cultivating oysters in this way is one of the oldest and most successful forms of aquaculture. This form of aquaculture is also practiced in parts of the United States.

Besides shellfish, many types of fish are also raised as aquaculture crops. Fish farms in the United States raise mostly salmon, catfish and trout. Many other countries—including China, India, Chile, and Norway— also have fish farms.

Some of these countries— the Asian ones in particular —raise large amounts of plants, as well as shellfish and fish, through aquaculture. Seaweeds are raised most often. They are used as food or as other products, such as thickeners for foods and drugs.

Aquaculture is not a recent invention. It has been practiced in China for more than 3000 years. But the industry has grown rapidly since about 1970. Its importance in providing food will continue to grow in the future.

WHAT DO YOU THINK?

Shellfish, fish, and plants raised through aquaculture are often raised in a controlled environment. For example, their eating and breeding habits may be controlled. What effects do you think this may have on these plants and animals?

*L*iterature
C O N N E C T I O N

TWO VIEWS OF THE OCEAN

Writers have written about water and the seas for thousands of years. The images they have presented have brought clear pictures, even to those who have never seen the ocean. Read the following excerpt from "The Rime of the Ancient Mariner" by Samuel Taylor Coleridge.

Day after day, day after day,
We stuck, nor breath nor motion;
As idle as a painted ship
Upon a painted ocean.

Water, water, everywhere,
And all the boards did shrink;
Water, water, everywhere,
Nor any drop to drink.

WHAT DO YOU THINK?

Using information from Carson's book, write a poem in the style of Samuel Taylor Coleridge.

Rachel Carson (1907-1964) presented another view of the ocean. As a marine biologist who spent most of her life working for the United States Fish and Wildlife Service, the author was especially interested in the sea.

In her writing, Carson emphasized how all living things are interrelated. You can see an example of this by reading the chapter "A Changing Year" from Carson's book *The Sea Around Us*. The book tells about the history, geography, biology, and chemistry of the sea. "A Changing Year" describes life in the sea as the seasons change. It tells us that nothing is ever wasted in the sea. Instead, it is used and then passed on from one creature to another. The minerals in the sea water are vital to the life of even the smallest of marine protists. Everything in the ocean is necessary for the survival of something else in the ocean.

History
CONNECTION

DID COLUMBUS SAIL WEST?

If you were an explorer in the days before steamships, would you take advantage of the strong currents in the ocean? Columbus did. Look at the world map shown below. America is west of Europe. But Columbus did not sail due west from Europe. His ships could only sail with the wind, and the winds off the coast of Spain did not blow in the direction of America. Therefore, he had to take a southerly route to the Canary Islands before he turned west toward what he thought was Asia.

Had Columbus sailed 20 degrees farther south in latitude, he would have met both the equatorial current moving east and areas where winds seldom blow, making the crossing impossible. The southward-moving Canaries current took him to the area of the westward-moving North Equatorial trade winds and current. The expedition sighted land—possibly what we now call San Salvador—on the 36th day of the journey. Columbus wrote in his journal, "my people were very much excited because they thought that in these seas no winds ever blew to carry them back to Spain." Indeed, returning the way they came would have been impossible because the current flowed westward, and he took advantage of a north-blowing wind to sail northeast and then due east to the Azores and Portugal.

> **YOU TRY IT!**
>
> Using a map of worldwide currents, plan a trip—short or long—that you could undertake in a vehicle that must drift or sail.

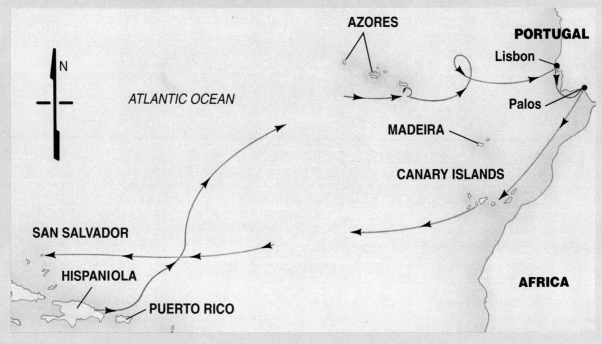

TEENS *in* SCIENCE

DESIREE SICULIANO

At the age of 12, Desiree Siculiano started as a volunteer guide in the New York City Aquarium. She worked at the touching tank, a large tank holding various aquatic animals, such as turtles and snakes, that visitors are encouraged to touch. She was the youngest volunteer at the Aquarium when she started. How did she have the self-confidence to volunteer at such a young age? "My science teacher said it would be a good program for me for the summer. If he thought I could do it, so did I." Desiree convinced her brother to volunteer with her, and they worked as a team for four years.

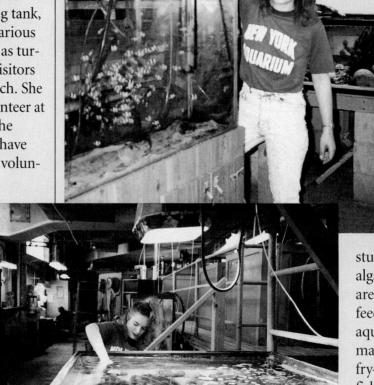

Desiree is in the *College Now* program at John Dewey High School in Brooklyn. She takes college-level courses after the regular school day and plans to study marine biology in college. To help her reach this goal, she works in the culture room at the aquarium where she studies brown algae, which are used to feed small aquatic animals, and fry—baby fish—at the aquarium. Miscroscopic animals also eat algae. "This type of organism (algae) is at the very bottom of the food chain," says Desiree, whose task is purifying the water in which the algae grow.

Reviewing Main Ideas

1. In a water wave, water particles are temporarily displaced while the energy of the wave passes. The water itself does not move forward with the wave.

2. Water waves are usually caused by wind, but tides are kinds of waves caused by the gravitational attraction among the moon, the sun, and Earth.

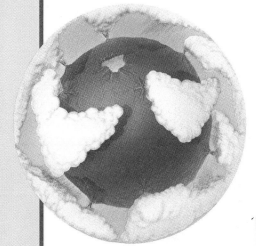

3. Scientists think that oceans were formed when water vapor from volcanoes condensed and fell to Earth as precipitation. Ocean water contains dissolved solids such as salt and dissolved gases such as oxygen and carbon dioxide.

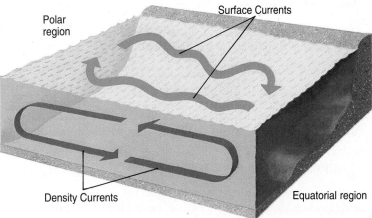

Surface Currents

Polar region

Density Currents

Equatorial region

4. Ocean currents are like rivers of water in the sea. Marine protists and animals depend on currents to bring them food, carry away waste, and provide them with transportation.

Chapter Review

USING KEY SCIENCE TERMS

density current
intertidal zone
manganese nodule
nekton
plankton
salinity
surface current
upwelling

Using the list above, replace the underlined words with the correct key science term.

1. <u>Swimming fish and sea animals</u> may be found in surface and density currents.

2. The <u>measure of saltiness</u> of ocean water can vary.

3. A/An <u>ocean river moving from more dense to less dense seawater</u> results from temperature and salinity differences.

4. Many <u>drifting protists and animals</u> near the ocean surface are microscopic.

5. The <u>zone of land covered and uncovered by tides</u> is home to such sea creatures as hermit crabs.

6. A <u>riverlike water movement caused by wind</u> can affect the speed of sailing ships.

7. An <u>ocean water movement of cold, deep water to the surface</u> usually occurs along coastlines.

8. A <u>rounded rocky object formed by minerals collecting around an object</u> may be found on the ocean floor.

UNDERSTANDING IDEAS

Complete each sentence.

1. Wave height depends on the distance over which the wind blows, the speed of the wind, and the _____ the wind blows.

2. Scientists think that Earth's ocean water first came from _____.

3. The most abundant dissolved salt in the ocean is _____.

4. Temperature and salinity affect _____ of ocean water.

5. Upwellings bring water that has a high concentration of _____ to the ocean's surface.

6. Unlike ocean waves, the water particles in a current move _____.

7. Surface currents on the western coasts of continents tend to be _____.

CRITICAL THINKING

Use your understanding of the concepts developed in the chapter to answer each of the following questions.

1. In which direction would you expect a surface current off the southern coast of Africa to flow?

2. *Thermo* refers to temperature and *haline* to salinity. Why do you think density currents are sometimes called thermohaline currents?

3. There has been virtually no wind where you are for a day. Would you expect to see waves on a small lake? The ocean? Explain.

4. Look at the map below. How are commercial fishing grounds related to the location of surface currents, as shown in Figure 10-16?

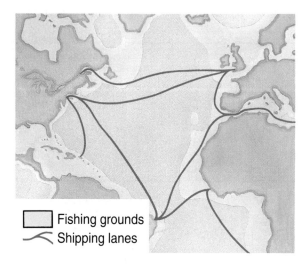

☐ Fishing grounds
⌒ Shipping lanes

5. How are the shipping lanes shown on the map related to the location of surface currents?

6. Why do you think 80 percent of the kinds of seaweed found off the east coast of North America are also found off the west coast of Great Britain?

PROBLEM SOLVING

Read the following problem and discuss your answers in a brief paragraph.

Suppose your local park district is running a contest to design a water amusement park for the city. After reading this chapter, you decide to enter the contest. Using what you know about the movement of water in currents and waves, describe in words and pictures three different water rides you would design.

1. Compare the motion of water in your rides to the movement of ocean water.

2. Identify the source of energy for each ride.

3. Discuss how objects or people move in the ride.

4. Make diagrams of your rides.

CONNECTING IDEAS

Discuss each of the following in a brief paragraph.

1. What do ocean waves and sound waves have in common? How are they different?

2. If the moon is full, what kind of tide would you expect? Why?

3. Look at the graph in Figure 10-2. How much longer would it take a 20-mph wind to result in a 4-foot wave than it would a 30-mph wind?

4. A CLOSER LOOK Why is the fresh water trapped in icebergs largely free from organic matter?

5. HISTORY CONNECTION What kind of movement of ocean water did Columbus use to sail to America? How did he use this movement?

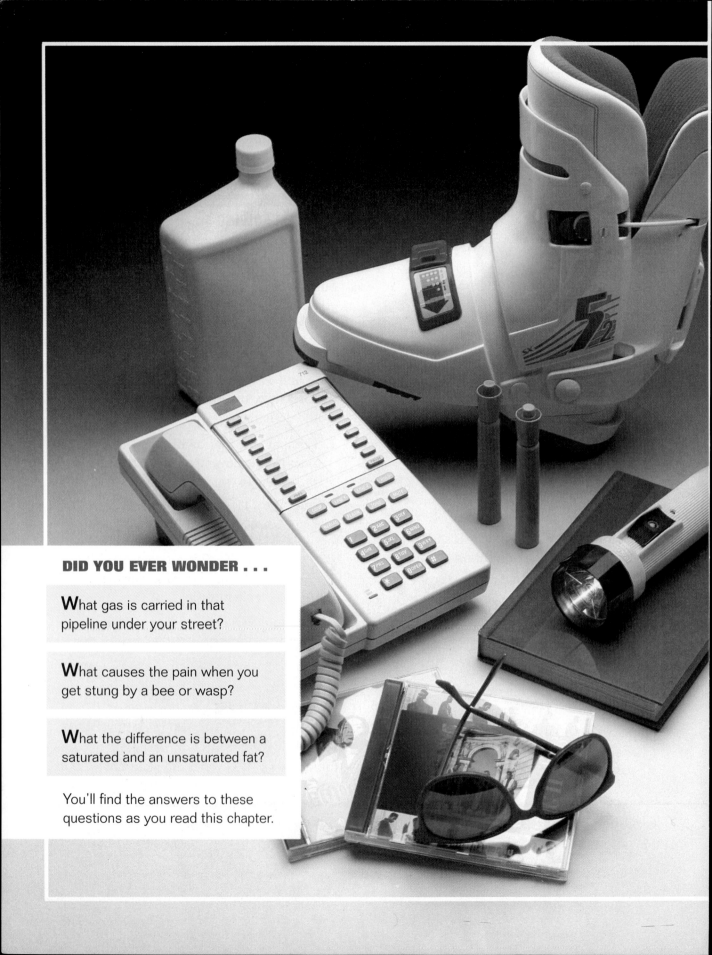

DID YOU EVER WONDER . . .

What gas is carried in that pipeline under your street?

What causes the pain when you get stung by a bee or wasp?

What the difference is between a saturated and an unsaturated fat?

You'll find the answers to these questions as you read this chapter.

Organic Chemistry

Every day you wake up, get dressed, eat something, and head out the door to face the world. You may ride the bus to school while talking to your friends. Your pack of notebook paper is covered in plastic wrap. The body of your ballpoint pen is made of hard plastic. Your sweater may be knitted with acrylic yarn and your backpack constructed of nylon.

If it is not a school day, you may turn on the radio or tape player and listen to music, or slip on your athletic shoes to play basketball.

You may never give it a second thought, but most things you experience today involve carbon in some way. The clothes you wear, the food you eat, the fuel in the bus, the cassette tape you use to play music, even the basketball you play with are made of carbon compounds. Why does carbon make so many different compounds? How can carbon be used to make fuels and foods? This chapter will help you answer these questions.

EXPLORE!

How can you test for carbon?

Take a small piece of marshmallow, tomato, bread, apple, butter, and sugar. Heat each one separately in an open crucible, over a flame, until it changes. What did each substance look like after heating?

11-1 Simple Organic Compounds

ORGANIC COMPOUNDS

Would you eat a piece of charcoal? If you have ever eaten a marshmallow, you might be surprised to learn that both marshmallows and charcoal are composed mainly of the element carbon. A substance that contains carbon is called an **organic compound**. In 1828, a German scientist named Friedrich Wohler accidentally formed the organic compound urea from inorganic materials. This made other scientists realize that living organisms weren't always necessary to form organic compounds.

Today, the term *organic* is used to describe nearly all carbon-containing substances, whether or not they are found in living organisms. You have already seen how you can turn simple substances, such as bread and butter, into carbon. How can you make other forms of carbon, such as charcoal?

FIGURE 11-1. When concentrated sulfuric acid is poured over sugar, carbon is produced. Sulfuric acid pulls the water out of sucrose, a compound with the formula $C_{12}H_{22}O_{11}$. The reaction yields carbon and water.

How do you make charcoal 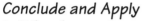 *from wood?*

Fill a clean, empty $1/4$-pint varnish or paint can with sawdust from either a white pine or an oak. Punch a small round hole (about $1/4$" in diameter) through the center of the lid with a nail. Press the lid firmly in place and place the can on a hot plate. Begin heating until white smoke comes out of the hole. Carefully light the smoke with a match until a yellow flame appears. Continue heating until the flame disappears from the hole. Turn off the hot plate and allow the can to cool overnight. Open the can the following day.

Hot plate

Conclude and Apply

1. What do you observe?
2. What happened to the sawdust?

Most of the millions of different organic compounds that exist can be synthesized from carbon-containing raw materials such as wood, oil, natural gas, and coal. When you made charcoal in the last activity, you started with a carbon-containing material. The manufacturing of organic compounds is one of the world's largest industries. Petrochemical plants, such as the one shown in Figure 11-2, make organic compounds from petroleum or natural gas.

FIGURE 11-2. Many useful organic compounds are made in petrochemical plants like this one.

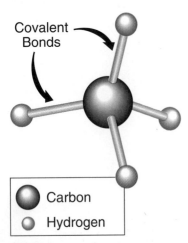

Covalent
Bonds

Carbon
Hydrogen

FIGURE 11-3. A carbon atom can form four stable covalent bonds with other atoms.

Why does carbon form so many different compounds? The reason is that carbon has an atomic structure that allows it to combine with a tremendous number of different elements. A carbon atom has four electrons in its outer energy level. This electron arrangement means that the carbon atom can form four covalent bonds, as shown in Figure 11-3, with either another carbon atom or with atoms of other elements such as hydrogen, oxygen, nitrogen, and chlorine.

As you may recall from Chapter 7, a covalent bond forms when two atoms share a pair of electrons. Besides forming single bonds, carbon can form double or triple covalent bonds with other atoms. Single covalent bonds contain one pair of shared electrons. Double bonds contain two pairs of shared electrons, and triple bonds contain three shared electron pairs.

Carbon atoms form an enormous number of compounds with hydrogen alone. This type of compound is called a **hydrocarbon**. Hydrocarbons form the basis for the structure and chemistry of a number of other organic compounds.

HYDROCARBONS

Does the furnace, stove, or water heater in your home burn natural gas? This is the fuel brought to homes through the pipeline underneath the street. If your home uses natural gas, you've been keeping warm and cooking food by burning methane. Why do you suppose it's called natural gas?

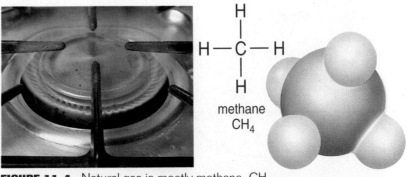

methane
CH_4

FIGURE 11-4. Natural gas is mostly methane, CH_4.

Methane is the first and simplest member of the hydrocarbon family. Its chemical formula is written CH_4, but we can also represent methane by a structural formula that shows how its atoms are arranged. Figure 11-4 shows the structural formula for methane. Each line between atoms represents a single covalent bond. In methane, the carbon atom has four single covalent bonds to hydrogen atoms.

Other hydrocarbon molecules in this family are made by joining additional carbon and hydrogen atoms to methane in a straight line, or chain. Each carbon atom appears to be a link in the chain within the molecule. Every time another carbon atom is added, a new molecule is formed with its own set of properties.

If you were to add another carbon atom and two hydrogen atoms (CH_2) to methane, you would form ethane, the next member of the methane family. Ethane has the chemical formula C_2H_6 and the structural formula shown in Figure 11-5. Ethane burns easily and is found in small amounts in natural gas.

Hot-air balloons and outdoor grills burn the bottled gas propane. Propane is the third member of the methane family and has the chemical formula C_3H_8. This compound is formed when another $-CH_2$ group is added to ethane. Its structural formula is shown in Figure 11-6.

Methane, ethane, propane, and their cousins make up a family of molecules known as saturated hydrocarbons.

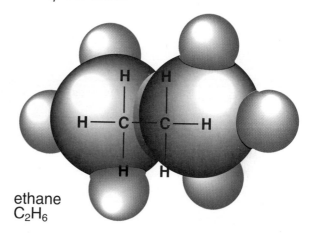

ethane
C_2H_6

FIGURE 11-5. Ethane is formed by adding a $-CH_2$ group to methane.

FIGURE 11-6. Bottled gas is mostly propane, C_3H_8.

propane C_3H_8

A hydrocarbon that is saturated contains only single covalent bonds. In this group, the carbon atoms are joined by single covalent bonds. What would be the chemical and structural formulas for the next members of the methane family? Table 11-1 shows formulas for the first ten saturated hydrocarbons.

The shorter hydrocarbons are lighter molecules. In general, these compounds have low boiling points, and so they evaporate and burn more easily. This makes them

TABLE 11-1. Names and Formulas for the First Ten Hydrocarbons

NAME	CHEMICAL FORMULA	STRUCTURAL FORMULA
Methane	CH_4	
Ethane	C_2H_6	
Propane	C_3H_8	
Butane	C_4H_{10}	
Pentane	C_5H_{12}	
Hexane	C_6H_{14}	
Heptane	C_7H_{16}	
Octane	C_8H_{18}	
Nonane	C_9H_{20}	
Decane	$C_{10}H_{22}$	

SKILLBUILDER

MAKING AND USING GRAPHS
Make a graph of the information in Table 11-1. For each compound, plot the number of carbon atoms on one axis and the number of hydrogen atoms on the other axis. Use this graph to predict the formula for the saturated hydrocarbon that has 11 carbon atoms. If you need help, refer to the **Skill Handbook** on page 682.

useful as fuel gases. Longer hydrocarbons are heavy molecules that form solids or liquids at room temperature. They can be used as oils, as waxes, or even in the black asphalt in the road you drive on.

Have you ever opened your refrigerator and wondered why some foods seem to spoil quickly? How can you find out how this process works?

FIND OUT!

What causes fruits and vegetables to ripen?
Place a rotten apple in a clear plastic box along with a fresh unripe apple. Seal the lid of the box with aluminum foil and a rubber band. Set another unripe apple on top of the box. Observe the changes in each apple over the course of a week. Repeat this experiment with two green tomatoes instead of apples.

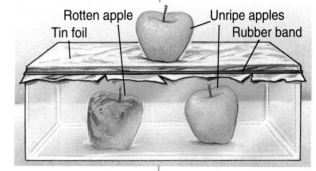

Rotten apple   Unripe apples
Tin foil   Rubber band

Conclude and Apply
1. Which apple ripens faster? Why?
2. Does the same thing occur when you use tomatoes instead of apples?

In some of the hydrocarbons, the carbon atoms form double or triple covalent bonds with another carbon atom. These new molecules have different properties than the molecules that have a single carbon-carbon bond.

The hydrocarbon ethene, C_2H_4, has a double bond between the carbon atoms. This gas, commonly called ethylene, helps ripen fruits and vegetables at the warehouse before they are sold. Foods that are allowed to spoil in your refrigerator produce large quantities of this gas, which then causes other foods to spoil as well. You saw this happen in the Find Out activity.

Hydrocarbons that contain double or triple bonds between carbon atoms are called unsaturated hydrocarbons. Remember that saturated hydrocarbons contain only single bonds. As you will see in a later section, fats and oils can also be classified as saturated or unsaturated.

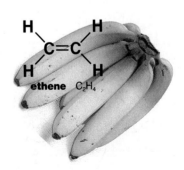

FIGURE 11-7. This is the structural formula for ethene, showing the double bond.

FIGURE 11-8. Carbon atoms can bond together in straight or branched chains (a) or closed rings (b).

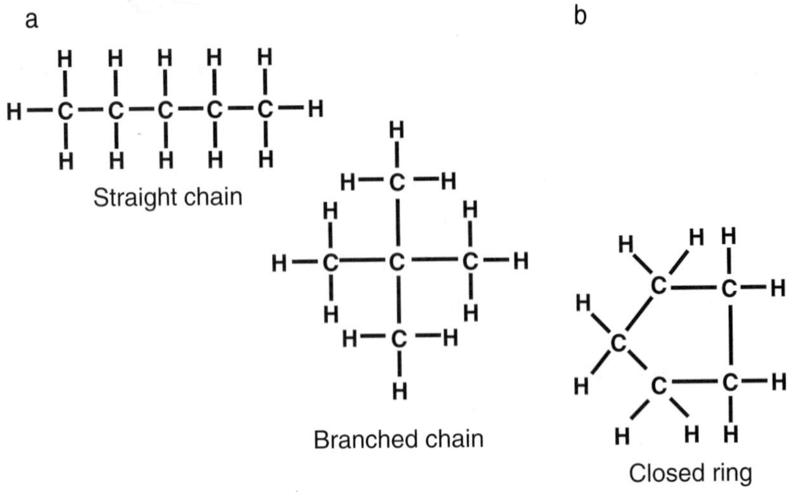

Straight chain

Branched chain

Closed ring

ISOMERS

Imagine that you could move the desks around in your classroom. You might place them all in two long rows or in six short rows. How many combinations can you think of?

Just as you could move your desks into different arrangements, the atoms in a hydrocarbon can form several different molecular structures, all having identical chemical formulas. Each carbon atom will still have four covalent bonds, but the overall shape of the molecule may vary.

Perhaps you have heard of butane, C_4H_{10}, a gas sometimes burned in camping stoves and lighters. In its molecular structure, shown in Figure 11-9, you can see the carbon atoms form a continuous straight chain. Another hydrocarbon, however, has the same chemical formula as butane, but its carbon chain is branched. This compound is called isobutane. Its structure is also shown in Figure 11-9. Butane and isobutane are called isomers. **Isomers** are compounds that have identical chemical formulas but different molecular structures, or shapes. Can you make isomers from any other hydrocarbons?

FIGURE 11-9. Butane and isobutane have the same chemical formula, C_4H_{10}, but they each have different structural formulas.

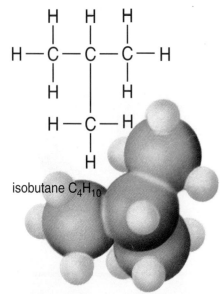

isobutane C_4H_{10}

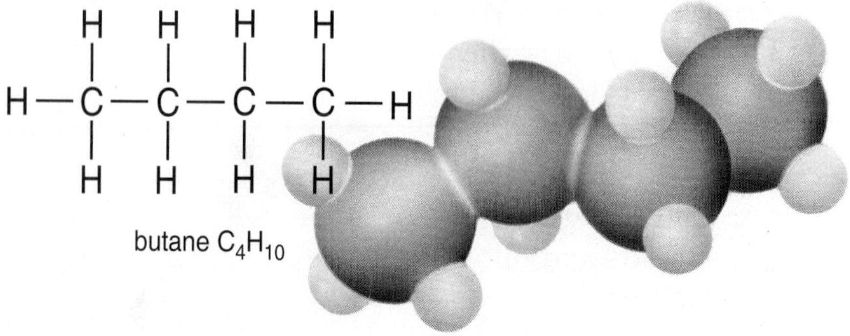

butane C_4H_{10}

EXPLORE!

Do pentane and hexane have isomers?
Using gum drops for carbon atoms, raisins for hydrogen atoms, and toothpicks for covalent bonds, try to make a model of pentane, C_5H_{12}. Remember that each carbon atom must have four bonds, while each hydrogen atom can have only one bond. How many different models of pentane can you build?

Try to make a model of hexane, C_6H_{14}. Follow the same rules as for pentane. How many different models can you build now?

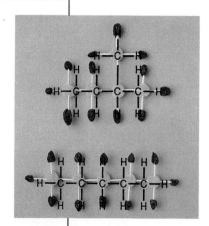

Were you surprised at how many different models you could make with only five or six carbon atoms? The properties of isomers may not be identical, even though the chemical formulas are the same. The shape of the molecule seems to determine some of the properties. Table 11-2 shows the differing properties of butane and isobutane.

Even the complicated-looking isomers, such as those you made for pentane and hexane, are still members of the methane family. They are all formed by adding more carbon and hydrogen atoms to methane, as if they were links in a chain. If there is a double or triple covalent bond in the compound instead of a single bond, the hydrocarbon is an entirely new compound with its own unique properties.

Most hydrocarbons form isomers. Because the larger molecules have more carbon atoms they form more isomers. Octane, C_8H_{18}, the hydrocarbon used in gasoline,

TABLE 11-2. Properties of Butane Isomers

	Butane	Isobutane
Description	Colorless gas	Colorless gas
Density	0.6 kg/L	0.6 kg/L
Melting Point	−138°C	−160°C
Boiling Point	−0.5°C	−12°C

How are octane numbers assigned?

When fuel burns in an engine, small amounts of it will occasionally explode rather than burning evenly. These tiny explosions can be heard and are referred to as knocking. You might also notice that the car does not run as smoothly when knocking occurs. Fuels are rated on their ability to burn evenly, rather than explode. The rating is called the octane number.

Two compounds are used as standards in creating the scale for octane numbers. Iso-octane, which resists knocking very well, is assigned an octane number of 100. Heptane, which knocks very badly, has an octane number of 0. The amount of knocking in a fuel is compared with a known mixture of these two compounds. For example, a sample of gasoline which knocks the same amount as a mixture of 90 percent isooctane and 10 percent heptane would have an octane number of 90. If a fuel knocks less than pure isooctane, it can have an octane number greater than 100.

has 18 possible isomers. These isomers can have a straight chain or branched chain.

You may have heard of octane rating applied to gasoline. Octane rating does not measure the amount of octane in the fuel, but rather the tendency of fuel to knock. Knocking occurs when a fuel does not burn evenly.

Hydrocarbons directly affect you. The major source of energy in the world comes from chemicals made from organic compounds found in petroleum or natural gas. Over 90 percent of the energy used in homes, schools, industry, and transportation comes from methane and the other hydrocarbons. Products ranging from fertilizer to skateboards are manufactured from hydrocarbons. Can hydrocarbons be used to make more complicated molecules? In the next section, you will learn how three special types of organic compounds are synthesized from hydrocarbons.

Check Your Understanding

1. Why can carbon form so many different organic compounds?
2. How is an unsaturated hydrocarbon different from a saturated hydrocarbon?
3. How many isomers can you make from heptane, C_7H_{16}?
4. **APPLY:** Cyclopropane is a saturated hydrocarbon containing three carbon atoms. In this compound, each carbon atom is bonded to two other carbon atoms. Draw its structural formula. Are cyclopropane and propane isomers? Explain.

11-2 Other Organic Compounds

SUBSTITUTED HYDROCARBONS

Usually a cheeseburger is a hamburger covered with American cheese and served on a bun. However, you can make a cheeseburger with Swiss cheese and serve it on slices of rye bread. If you ate this cheeseburger, you would notice how the substitutions affected the taste.

Chemists make similar changes to organic compounds. These changes produce compounds called substituted hydrocarbons. A substituted hydrocarbon has had one or more of its hydrogen atoms replaced by atoms or groups of atoms of other elements.

OBJECTIVES

In this section, you will

- classify substituted hydrocarbons as belonging to the alcohol, carboxylic acid, or amine family;
- describe the structure of an alcohol, a carboxylic acid, and an amine;
- draw the structural formula for the simplest alcohol, carboxylic acid, and amine.

KEY SCIENCE TERMS

alcohol
carboxylic acid
amines

EXPLORE!

Can you make new models from your hexane structures?

Make a gumdrop/raisin/toothpick model for hexane. Remove a hydrogen raisin and replace it with a mini marshmallow. Then exchange the marshmallow with a raisin already on your model. Replace another raisin with a gummy candy. Make as many different models as you can.

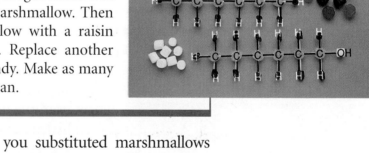

In the Explore activity, you substituted marshmallows and gummy candy for the raisin/hydrogen in the gumdrop/hexane model. Substituting even one new chemical group on a hydrocarbon forms an entirely new class of compounds with chemical properties different from those of the original compound. Sometimes two or more chemical groups can replace hydrogen atoms. You can imagine how complicated these new molecules can become. This is why millions of organic compounds exist in our world.

Perhaps you have encountered some substituted hydrocarbons, but didn't know what they were. Have you

TABLE 11-3. Names, Formulas, and Uses for Some Common Alcohols

Uses	METHANOL $H-\overset{\displaystyle H}{\underset{\displaystyle H}{C}}-OH$	ETHANOL $H-\overset{\displaystyle H}{\underset{\displaystyle H}{C}}-\overset{\displaystyle H}{\underset{\displaystyle H}{C}}-OH$	ISOPROPYL ALCOHOL $H-\overset{\displaystyle H}{\underset{\displaystyle H}{C}}-\overset{\displaystyle OH}{\underset{\displaystyle H}{C}}-\overset{\displaystyle H}{\underset{\displaystyle H}{C}}-H$
Fuel	√	√	
Cleaner	√	√	√
Disinfectant		√	√
Manufacturing chemicals	√		√

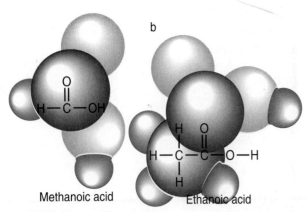

ethanol C_2H_5OH

FIGURE 11-10. Ethanol is one of many alcohols.

Methanoic acid

Ethanoic acid

FIGURE 11-11. Two simple carboxylic acids are methanoic acid (a), formed from methane, and ethanoic acid (b), formed from ethane.

ever ridden in a car fueled by ethanol? Ethanol, shown in Figure 11-10, is an example of an alcohol. **Alcohol** is the name of a family of compounds formed when a hydroxyl (-OH) group replaces one or more hydrogen atoms in a hydrocarbon. Ethanol is produced naturally by sugar fermenting in corn, grains, and fruits. Alcoholic beverages contain ethanol. You will learn more about mixing ethanol with gasoline to fuel cars in the Expanding Your View section of this chapter. Table 11-3 lists some common alcohols and their uses.

You may have eaten foods containing another substituted hydrocarbon. If you have ever tasted salad dressing made with too much vinegar, you probably made a face because of the sour taste. Vinegar contains acetic acid, which causes that sour taste. Acetic acid is the common name of ethanoic acid, an example of another class of substituted hydrocarbons called carboxylic acids.

A **carboxylic acid** is formed when a -CH$_3$ group is displaced by a carboxyl (-COOH) group. Notice that in both carboxyl groups in Figure 11-11, the carbon has a double bond to the oxygen atom, a single bond to the hydroxyl (-OH) group, and a single bond to what remains of the original hydrocarbon molecule.

The simplest carboxylic acid is methanoic acid, more commonly called formic acid. This acid is made by ants and other insects and causes the pain when you are stung

330 CHAPTER 11 ORGANIC CHEMISTRY

by a bee or wasp. If you have ever accidentally eaten an ant at a picnic, you know that carboxylic acids have a sour taste. They have a sharp, often unpleasant aroma. Figure 11-11 shows the structures of methanoic and ethanoic acids.

In another group of substituted hydrocarbons you may have encountered, nitrogen forms covalent bonds with the carbon and hydrogen in the molecule. Have you ever been given novocaine at a dentist's office? Do you take vitamins that include niacin? Does your soft drink contain caffeine? These are all hydrocarbons substituted with nitrogen.

You can picture the way that nitrogen combines with hydrocarbons by beginning with ammonia. Ammonia is a sharp-smelling household cleaner with the chemical formula NH_3. If a hydrogen is removed from ammonia, the resulting $-NH_2$ group is called an amine group. When the amine group replaces the hydrogen in a hydrocarbon, organic compounds called **amines** are formed. Methylamine, CH_3NH_2, shown in Figure 11-12, is the simplest amine.

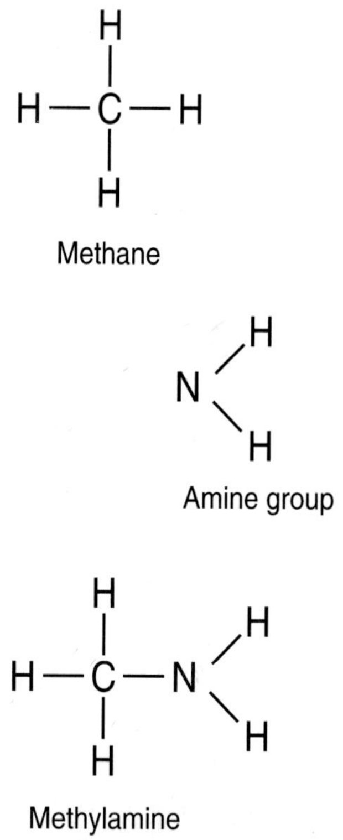

As well as being in novocaine, niacin, and caffeine, amines occur in many other biological compounds. A special type of amine-substituted hydrocarbon forms when both the $-NH_2$ group and the $-COOH$ group replace hydrogens on the same molecule. This type of compound is called an amino acid, which is a building block for the formation of proteins. You will learn more about amino acids in the next section.

You may have eaten an amino acid lately if you like gelatin desserts. The material that makes gelatin gel is called glycine. This compound is made of ethane (C_2H_6) with an amino group substituted for one hydrogen and a carboxylic acid group replacing another hydrogen, as shown in Figure 11-13. Glycine is a natural substance made by boiling animal tissue, especially hooves. Glycine strengthens fingernails in people.

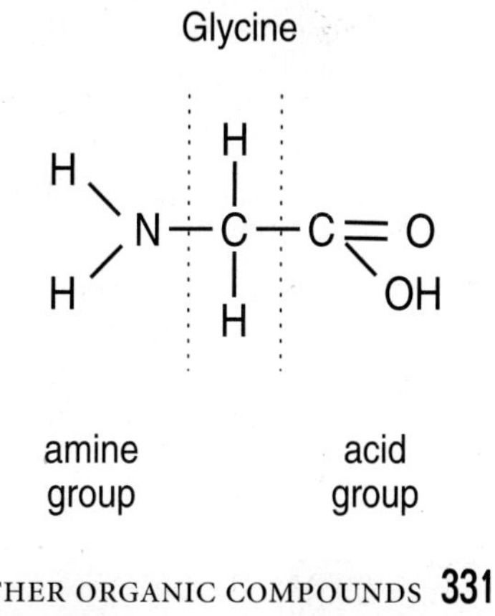

Many organic compounds are composed of different combinations of carbon, hydrogen, oxygen, and nitrogen atoms. These compounds occur naturally in your body and can also be found in the foods you eat. You have already learned about alcohols, carboxylic acids, and amines. Can one of these types of hydrocarbons be converted into another?

Methane

Amine group

Methylamine

FIGURE 11-12. Methylamine, CH_3NH_2, is formed when an amine group replaces a hydrogen in methane.

FIGURE 11-13. The structural formula of glycine shows that it is an amino acid.

Glycine

amine group   acid group

I N V E S T I G A T E !

Natural materials, such as air or bacteria, can cause changes in alcohols. A bottle of wine containing ethanol can sometimes be spoiled by such a natural chemical process. This chemical conversion can be demonstrated in this activity.

PROBLEM
What new compound can be formed from an alcohol?

MATERIALS
test tube and stopper
1 mL potassium permanganate solution
1 mL sodium hydroxide solution
3 drops of ethanol
goggles
apron
pH test paper

PROCEDURE
1. **Measure** and pour 1 mL of potassium permanganate solution and 1 mL of sodium hydroxide solution into a test tube. **CAUTION**: *Handle both of these chemicals with care; immediately flush any spill with water and call your teacher.*
2. Test the sample with pH paper. Record the result.
3. Add three drops of ethanol to the test tube.
4. Stopper the test tube and gently shake it for one minute.
5. **Observe** what happens in the test tube. Record any changes you notice for the next five minutes.
6. Test the sample with pH paper again. Record your observation.
7. Dispose of solutions as directed by the teacher.

ANALYZE
1. What is the chemical formula for ethanol?
2. What part of a molecule identifies a compound as an alcohol?
3. What part of a molecule identifies a compound as a carboxylic acid?

CONCLUDE AND APPLY
4. What would lead you to **infer** that a chemical change took place in the test tube?
5. In the presence of potassium permanganate, an alcohol may undergo a chemical change into an acid. If the alcohol used is ethanol, what would you **predict** to be the chemical formula of the acid produced?
6. **Going Further:** The acid from ethanol is found in a common household product. What is the acid's name? In what common household product is the acid found? What happens to a bottle of wine that undergoes this change?

FIGURE 11-14. Substituted hydrocarbons are commonly found in pesticides, such as those spread by crop dusters.

As you saw in the Investigate activity, some substituted hydrocarbons can be changed into other substituted hydrocarbons. You used potassium permanganate and sodium hydroxide to change ethanol to vinegar (acetic acid). There are many other types of substituted hydrocarbons. They are found in such varied products as refrigerants, fire extinguishers, pesticides, anesthetics, and moth repellants. Freon™ and DDT are two commonly known substituted hydrocarbons.

In the following section of this chapter, you will find out more about the complicated hydrocarbons that make up your body and why you need to eat foods to rebuild yourself.

Check Your Understanding

1. What major chemical group is characteristic of an alcohol? A carboxylic acid? An amine?
2. Can a substituted hydrocarbon have more than one chemical group replacing its hydrogen atoms at one time? Give an example.
3. Methylamine is a compound in which one hydrogen in ammonia has been replaced with a -CH$_3$ group, another hydrogen has been replaced with a -CH$_2$CH$_3$ group, and a third hydrogen remains. Draw its structural formula.
4. **APPLY:** Rubbing alcohol is isopropyl alcohol. How does its structure differ from propyl alcohol?

11-3 Biological Compounds

OBJECTIVES

In this section, you will

- describe polymers and examine their importance as biological compounds;
- compare and contrast proteins, carbohydrates, and lipids.

KEY SCIENCE TERMS

polymers
proteins
carbohydrates
lipids

POLYMERS

What do milk, muscles, blood, cassette tapes, and athletic shoes have in common? Not only are these things made up of organic compounds, but the compounds are made of tremendously large molecules. How can this be demonstrated?

EXPLORE!

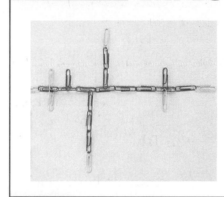

Can you build a complex molecule? Loop together different colored strips of paper into a chain, or string colored paper clips together. Who can make the longest, most complicated chain?

When you made the paper loops or strung together a chain of paper clips, you showed one way that large molecules can be formed from tens of thousands of different molecules. These types of compounds are called polymers. **Polymers** are huge molecules made of many smaller organic molecules that are linked together to form new bonds. The smaller molecules, called monomers, are usually similar in size and structure. You can imagine a monomer as a single loop of paper or one paper clip in your chain. Mono- means one, and poly- means many.

The polymer polyethylene is used to make clear plastic bags like the ones in which you may carry your lunch. It is also used to make milk and soft drink bottles.

FIGURE 11-15. The polymer polyethylene is commonly used in some plastic products.

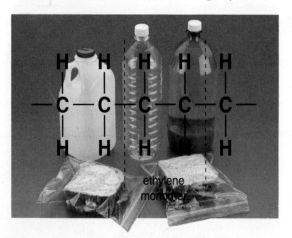

ethylene monomer

The polyethylene polymer is synthesized by linking together the small, six-atom ethylene molecules, C_2H_4. The resulting polyethylene molecule, part of which is shown in Figure 11-15, could have as many as 25,000 ethylene molecules linked in one continuous chain.

Besides being used in plastics, where they can be formed into almost any shape, polymers are found in the compounds that compose living things. These substances are called biological compounds. There are three major groups of biological compounds: proteins, carbohydrates, and lipids. Let's take a closer look at each of these groups.

PROTEINS

Milk contains a protein, a particular kind of hydrocarbon polymer that is a necessary part of all living cells. **Proteins** are polymers formed by linking together various amino acids. Figure 11-16 shows how amino acids combine to give a protein segment. Actual proteins contain 100 or more amino acids. Even though there are millions of proteins, there are only about 200 amino acids. Of these acids, 20 of them, shown in Table 11-4, are of biological significance.

You'll find proteins in your muscles, hair, bones, fingernails, and even in organs. Eight of the amino acids found in proteins are absolutely essential for your body to function properly, but your body cannot make them. You need to eat protein-rich foods every day for your body to get adequate protein so it can grow and renew itself. How can you tell whether a certain food contains proteins or not?

TABLE 11-4. Amino Acids

Amino Acid	Abbreviations
Alanine	Ala
Arginine	Arg
Asparagine	Asn
Aspartic acid	Asp
Cysteine	Cys
Glutamine	Gln
Glutamic acid	Glu
Glycine	Gly
Histidine	His
Isoleucine	Ile
Leucine	Leu
Lysine	Lys
Methionine	Met
Phenylalanine	Phe
Proline	Pro
Serine	Ser
Threonine	Thr
Tryptophan	Try
Tyrosine	Tyr
Valine	Val

FIGURE 11-16. Two amino acids (a) combine by means of a peptide bond and form a protein segment (b). Notice that a water molecule is produced as the amino acids combine.

11-3 BIOLOGICAL COMPOUNDS **335**

EXPLORE!

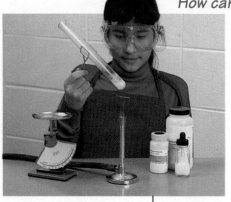

How can you test for protein in food?

Add 5 g of sodium hydrogen sulfate and 5 g of potassium nitrate to a large test tube. Add one drop of milk to the test tube and heat the contents gently over a burner. Describe what happens inside the test tube. Yellow indicates the presence of protein in your milk sample.

Repeat this test with samples of egg white, meat, and chocolate. Do all of these foods contain protein?

Sodium hydrogen sulfate reacts with potassium nitrate to form nitric acid. When proteins react with nitric acid, a yellow color is produced. This yellow color confirms the presence of protein in a food sample. Meats and dairy products, such as those you tested in the last exercise, are good sources of protein. Beans, nuts, and fish, along with other items shown in Figure 11-17, are also foods with high protein content. At least 20 percent of your daily diet should consist of proteins in order to give your body the necessary nutrients it needs to grow, and to repair damaged tissues.

Many important proteins are found in your body. One protein in your blood that carries oxygen is called hemoglobin. Other proteins are the hormones and enzymes that control chemical reactions in your body. Insulin is an example of a hormone that regulates your blood sugar level. Proteins account for 15 percent of your total weight. This amounts to about half of the weight of all the materials other than water in your body!

FIGURE 11-17. The foods pictured here are high-protein sources.

CARBOHYDRATES

What do you think of when you hear the word *carbohydrate*? A sweet fruit or a sugary treat? Have you ever heard of carbohydrate loading by athletes? Runners

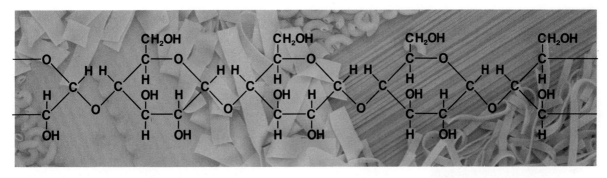

FIGURE 11-18. Starch is the major component of pasta.

often get ready for a long-distance race by eating, or loading, the carbohydrates found in starchy foods like pasta, bread, and vegetables. Sugars and starches are known as **carbohydrates**; this class of food provides energy for your body. It is recommended that 50 percent of your diet be made up of carbohydrates.

Glucose ($C_6H_{12}O_6$) and sucrose ($C_{12}H_{22}O_{11}$) are common sugars. Glucose is found in many sweet foods such as grapes and honey. In your body, glucose is directly absorbed into the bloodstream without needing to be digested, and provides energy to all of your cells. Another sugar found in foods is sucrose, the white table sugar produced from sugarcane. Sucrose breaks down into glucose and other simple sugars during digestion.

Larger molecule carbohydrates are polymers called starches. They occur naturally in plants, chiefly in corn, wheat, rice, and potatoes. Pasta is made from wheat, so it also contains carbohydrates. In Figure 11-18, a part of a starch molecule is shown. During digestion, the body converts starch into glucose to provide energy.

Carbohydrates are organic compounds in which there are twice as many hydrogen atoms as oxygen atoms. Count the hydrogen and oxygen atoms in the formulas for yourself to prove that this is true. The simple sugars are straight-chain polymers, but the larger molecule sugars and starches can be branched.

LIPIDS

The third major type of biological compound is called a lipid. **Lipids** are organic compounds that feel greasy, and will not dissolve in water. Fats, oil, waxes, and related

DID YOU KNOW?

Rubber is a polymer that we sometimes eat. Bubble gum is stretchy because it contains a little synthetic rubber, other synthetic polymers, flavoring, and vegetable oil for softening.

compounds make up this group. Some vitamins are lipids. Lipids include the fats that french fries are cooked in, the oil part of salad dressings, and the butter or margarine you spread on bread for your lunch. Can you tell the difference between a fat and an oil?

EXPLORE!

How can you tell a fat from an oil?
Obtain small samples of butter, soybean oil, paraffin, margarine, olive oil, and solid shortening. Observe them at room temperature. Which ones would you say have similar properties? Why?

Although lipids contain the same elements—carbon, hydrogen, and oxygen—that carbohydrates do, they are put together in different proportions. As you saw in the Explore activity, different lipids can have different properties, depending upon whether they are in solid or liquid forms. Lipids are a source of energy for the body just as carbohydrates are, but the energy in lipids is much more concentrated. They provide twice as much energy per gram as carbohydrates.

Have you heard that eating too much saturated fat can be unhealthy? What are saturated and unsaturated fats?

FIGURE 11-19. Fats and oils provide large numbers of calories in your diet.

Fats and oils can be classified as saturated or unsaturated, according to the types of bonds in their carbon chains. Saturated fats contain only single bonds between carbon atoms and are usually solid at room temperature. Unsaturated fats contain at least one double or triple bond and are liquid at room temperature. Fortunately, these two types of fats do not naturally occur together. Saturated fats are found mostly in foods from animal sources, such as butterfat in ice cream and white fat around the edges of meat. Oils from plants and other vegetables are mostly unsaturated. Examples of each type of fat are shown in Figure 11-19.

A properly balanced diet includes some fats, just as it includes some proteins and carbohydrates. It is recommended that less than 30 percent of your diet be made up of fats. Let's test for the presence of fats and starches in various foods.

I N V E S T I G A T E !

11-2
FATS AND STARCHES

Simple tests can be performed to discover if lipids and carbohydrates are present in foods.

PROBLEM
Which foods contain starch and fats?

MATERIALS

liquid cooking oil
iodine solution in dropper bottle
bread, cheese, cooked egg white samples, raw potato slice, cooked bacon, potato chip
scissors
large brown paper bag

PROCEDURE
1. Copy the data table.

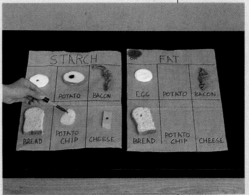

2. Open a brown bag and cut it in half. Mark one part *Fat* and the other part *Starch*. Mark off each part into six sections. Label each section with the food name. All foods are to be named on both papers, and checked for both fat and starch. **CAUTION:** *Put on an apron and goggles to protect clothing and eyes.*

3. Place a drop of oil in a corner of the paper marked *Fat*. Hold the paper up to a light and **observe** the spot. Foods with fat leave a grease spot like this on brown paper.

4. **Predict** which test foods contain fat.

5. Rub each food on its labeled section. Let the spots dry.

6. Hold the paper up to a light source. Record your observation.

7. **Predict** which foods contain starch. Foods that contain starch turn dark blue when iodine solution is dropped on them. **CAUTION:** *Iodine is poisonous and will stain clothing and skin.*

8. Place foods on the labeled sections of the *Starch* paper. Place a drop of iodine solution on each food on the paper. **Observe** and record any color changes.

ANALYZE
1. What evidence did you have that fat or starch was present in the food?

CONCLUDE AND APPLY
2. Which of the foods would you **infer** contained fat?
3. **Going Further:** What might you do to test whether the fat present was saturated or unsaturated?

DATA AND OBSERVATIONS

TEST FOOD	FAT		STARCH	
	Predict yes/no	Test yes/no	Predict yes/no	Test yes/no
Bread				
Cheese				
Egg white				
Raw potato				
Bacon				
Potato chip				

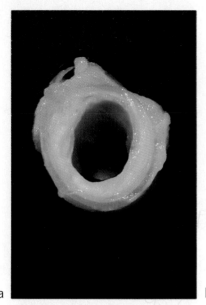

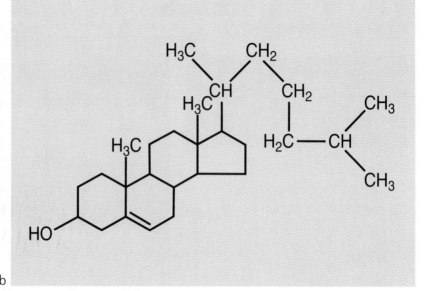

FIGURE 11-20. This figure shows a photo micrograph of a build-up of cholesterol in an artery (a), and the structural formula for cholesterol (b).

Besides saturated fats, animal foods contain another lipid called cholesterol. Do you know that even if you never eat foods containing cholesterol, your body will still make its own supply? Cholesterol is needed by your body to build cell membranes and is also found in bile, a fluid made by the liver and needed for digestion.

We have discussed three important classes of biological hydrocarbon compounds: proteins, carbohydrates, and lipids. Many of these compounds are very long and complicated polymers. Carbohydrates and lipids are in foods that provide energy for the body. Proteins are present in every living substance and are needed in food for growth and to renew the body. Each of these compounds exists because of carbon's unique ability to form covalent bonds with other atoms.

Check Your Understanding

1. How are polymers formed?
2. Name some examples of biological compounds. Where are they found?
3. What do proteins, carbohydrates, and lipids in the foods you eat provide for your body?

4. **APPLY:** Unlike animals, plants cannot digest the foods necessary to form biological compounds. Explain how plants make the biological compounds they need.

EXPANDING YOUR VIEW

CONTENTS

A CLOSER LOOK

THE DISCOVERY OF DNA STRUCTURE

Almost everyone has heard of DNA today, but in the 1950s, DNA structure was a mystery. In fact, one of the major scientific events of the 20th century was the discovery of the structure of DNA. James D. Watson, Francis Crick, and Maurice Wilkins received the Nobel Prize for this discovery in 1962.

Dr. Watson's book, *The Double Helix*, tells of the long discovery process. The research leading to the discovery involved cut-throat competition, secrets, intrigue, and many surprising turns.

There are tales of secret meetings, scornful colleagues, and false turns. There are garden parties complete with champagne and smoked salmon, trips to Paris, and long nights of staring blankly at drawings of atoms. The discovery itself was surprisingly sudden. Finally there is the dramatic rush of Watson's team to beat competing scientists to the same discovery. The original model that Crick and Watson built in 1953 is shown above.

Watson and Crick met in England in 1951. At the time, a great deal was known about DNA. Scientists knew that it was a large molecule composed of sugar and phosphate groups linked in long chains plus nitrogen-containing compounds called bases. They did not know, however, how all these components fit together.

Crick taught Watson the basics of a technique called X-ray crystallography, a key technique leading to the discovery. In X-ray crystallography, X rays are sent through a substance to find out how atoms are arranged.

Yet, many questions remain. Dr. Watson is still working in the field to expand our knowledge of the three billion chemical building blocks of human genetic material.

WHAT DO YOU THINK?

Consider your own experience in solving problems. Do you always work straight through from beginning to end? Did you ever wake up in the middle of the night knowing just how to solve a problem? Can you draw any conclusions about how the mind works from these experiences?

LIFE SCIENCE
CONNECTION

POISONOUS PROTEINS

The next time you visit the zoo to learn about the exotic animals, you just might want to bring along a chemistry book! Why?

In this chapter, you learned that living organisms are made of the biological compounds—proteins, carbohydrates, and lipids. As you know, these compounds are important for the metabolic processes of cells. Cell structures are made primarily of proteins, and carbohydrates and lipids are important for the functioning of cells.

It's clear that if the cells of organisms did not manufacture proteins from amino acids, organisms couldn't stay alive. But would you believe that there are many animals and plants that produce proteins that can mean immediate death for other organisms? Such proteins are organic poisons that are known as biotoxins, and they are produced and used by animals, plants, fungi, and bacteria for defense against predators and for obtaining food.

The reptile house at the zoo is a great place to learn about animals that produce biotoxins. Many species of snakes, including North American snakes, produce a substance called venom. Some types, similar to the snake shown in the photo at the left, are more poisonous to humans than others.

Scientists know more about the chemical makeup of snake venom than any other animal biotoxin.

Proteins in snake venom are of a special group called enzymes. Enzymes are large and complex protein molecules that work by breaking down other organic molecules. The most common protein in snake venom is an enzyme called cholinesterase, which disrupts the functioning of the nervous system.

The most poisonous land snake in the world is the tiger snake from Australia, shown in the photo at the right. Tiger snake venom is extremely poisonous. A fatal dose of tiger snake venom for a 154 pound human is only 0.609 milligrams.

WHAT DO YOU THINK?

Besides snakes, many other species of animals, including insects, frogs, toads, and fish produce biotoxins that are poisonous to humans. More is known about snake venom for two reasons. First, scientists are able to obtain more venom from snakes than biotoxins from other animals. More importantly, the enzymes in snake venom are important for the development of drugs to treat illness. How do you suppose studying the proteins found in snake venom can help scientists develop new types of drugs?

SCIENCE AND SOCIETY

PILE IT ON!

Do you have a compost pile in your backyard? Compost is one of the best fertilizers available to gardeners and is free for the making. In fact, compost has been produced for eons without any help from people. Before farmers and homeowners began moving things around, leaves and weeds fell on the ground, rotted there, and provided a constant source of food for growing plants. Without knowing it,

Composting is the process of breaking down waste material and changing it into useful products. The main ingredients in compost are carbon and nitrogen. All plant materials contain both of these elements.

Some are higher in carbon, such as twigs, sawdust, dried leaves, and hay. Others are higher in nitrogen, such as green grass clippings, kitchen vegetable waste, and animal by-products. The ratio of carbon to nitrogen determines how quickly the waste will be

landowners created an ideal environment for encouraging growth. When we rake leaves, plant grass, and pull weeds and throw them away, we break that natural cycle.

turned into useful fer-
tilizer. Most materials
have more carbon than
nitrogen, so adding
nitrogen makes the
process go faster. A pile
of sawdust, which is
mostly carbon, can take
years to break down,
but if you mix the saw-
dust with green grass
and animal manure, it
will turn into rich
compost in a matter of
months.

The process of com-
posting is done in two
ways. Anaerobic com-
posting (without air) is done in closed bins.
By keeping the air out, you are able to prevent
the loss of valuable nitrogen. Nitrogen is necessary for all plant growth and is the main
ingredient in most fertilizers. With this kind
of composting, methane gas is produced and
can then be used as a fuel for heating or lighting. Many small farms use this free source of
fuel gained from anaerobic composting.

Most composting, however, is done aerobi-
cally (with air). The materials are piled in bins
or simply in piles and turned occasionally to
let the air circulate through and speed up the
decomposition process. The heat produced
from the chemical reaction kills harmful bacteria and weed seeds and is then changed into
carbon dioxide, which passes into the air.

In either method of composting, the result
is nitrogen-rich soil that will feed your plants
and encourage them to grow. Addition of
many different kinds of materials to your
compost heap will also add beneficial
minerals, such as calcium, phosphates, and
potash.

Composting is also one of the easiest and

most beneficial ways everyone can protect the
environment. Many communities now have
laws that prohibit yard waste from being put
in landfills. It takes up space and is wasteful!
Instead of throwing all these valuable
resources away, you can easily return them to
nature to help the trees, grass, flowers, and
vegetables grow healthier and faster.

YOU TRY IT!

Build a compost pile in the corner of your
yard and watch a bunch of trash turn into
rich soil. Layer kitchen scraps (vegetable
only) with grass clippings, leaves, and whatever other waste you find in the yard. Keep
the pile damp but not wet and turn it every
few days to keep the materials well mixed.
Notice that the middle of the pile gets hot as
the carbon is changed into carbon dioxide.
In a few weeks, you will have a free supply of
the best fertilizer available.

TECHNOLOGY CONNECTION

ORGANIC MOTOR FUELS

Did you know that about 90 percent of the total United States energy needs are met by fossil fuels, such as oil and natural gas?

Oil, of course, is used for a variety of purposes, from plastics production to the food manufacturing industry. One of the most important uses of oil is as a fuel to power the engines of automobiles and other forms of transportation.

As you know, fossil fuels are considered to be non-renewable energy sources. In other words, once they have been used up, they're gone forever. Right now, we are using up fossil fuels much faster than can be replaced by Earth. What fuels will power the engines of the transportation vehicles of the future?

Since the energy crisis of the 1970s, scientists have been working on the development of new sources of energy, especially ones that can be used to power engines.

Did you ever see a sign like the one pictured here? Gasohol is a combination of the alcohol ethanol and gasoline. The gasohol used currently contains about 90 percent gasoline and 10 percent ethanol. As you recall, ethanol is the substituted hydrocarbon found in all alcoholic beverages.

Gasohol has many advantages over gasoline. Ethanol is produced commercially by the fermentation of potatoes, sugar cane, and grains, such as corn and wheat. Because it is produced from plant materials, ethanol is considered to be a renewable energy source.

Another advantage of using gasohol is that most car engines do not have to be modified to burn the gasohol manufactured today. In fact, car engines can be made to burn pure ethanol, and engineers are working hard to design engines that can use ethanol efficiently.

WHAT DO YOU THINK?

Clearly, we need to develop new sources of fuel for our transportation vehicles. Gasohol shows some promise as an alternative fuel, but there are some disadvantages to gasohol as well. Commercial production of ethanol results in numerous environmental problems. Among these are disruption of the ecosystem, fertilizer runoff, and erosion. Do you think gasohol is an answer to our fossil fuel problems? Explain your answers.

TEENS *in* SCIENCE

CLEANING UP EARTH

Teenagers may be more environmentally sensitive than their parents were at the same age. They know that the world they are inheriting needs cleaning up, and they want it to be in good shape when they hand it over to their own children. Individuals and groups such as bands, scouts, and science clubs routinely gather up recyclable material such as newspapers and aluminum cans and raise money by taking them to recycling centers. Many others are going even farther to clean up the environment.

Teenagers from Quincy High School in Illinois monitor the Mississippi River for pollutants. They use tests that show levels of dissolved oxygen. If there is a low level of oxygen, life in the river suffers. The students are working directly with The Illinois Rivers Project to make sure that the river is clean and that those who use the water do so responsibly.

Eighteen-year-old Roland Ng of Tracy, California, headed up a recycling project

YOU TRY IT!

Locate the recycling centers in your area. Do they take aluminum, glass, plastic, and paper? Do they pay for these materials? Start recycling materials from your own home and see how much less waste there is to go to the landfill.

CAREER CONNECTION

Environmental scientists have many options. They monitor bodies of water, air, and industry for possible pollutants. They research ways to control or eliminate pollutants. They work for government agencies, industry, or have their own consulting or research businesses.

that collected throw-aways—cans, bottles, and paper all over town. Roland coaches a team of seven year olds at the Boys and Girls Club in Tracy, and uses the money earned from recycling to buy basketballs and other sports equipment for the children.

Reviewing Main Ideas

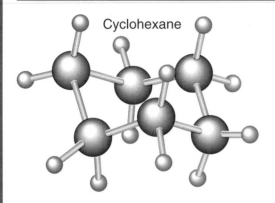

Cyclohexane

1. Carbon's unique ability to form four covalent bonds with other atoms enables it to make a huge number of compounds.

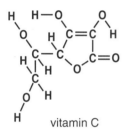

vitamin C

2. Hydrocarbons can be composed of hydrogen and carbon alone, or other chemical groups may be substituted for hydrogen on the molecule to form new compounds, as with Vitamin C.

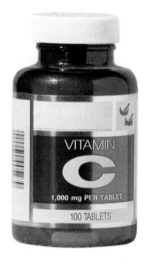

3. Biological compounds are complex hydrocarbons that make up living things. Your body needs the proteins, carbohydrates, and lipids that are found in food to provide energy and to repair or replace cells.

Chapter Review

USING KEY SCIENCE TERMS

alcohol · isomers
amines · lipids
carbohydrates · organic compound
carboxylic acid · polymers
hydrocarbon · proteins

For each set of terms below, choose the one term that does not belong and explain why it does not belong.

1. proteins, lipids, isomers
2. hydrocarbon, alcohol, amines
3. organic compound, isomers, alcohol
4. carbohydrates, proteins, carboxylic acid
5. polymers, alcohol, amines

UNDERSTANDING IDEAS

Choose the best answer to complete each sentence.

1. Two compounds with the same chemical formula but different molecular structures are called ____.
   a. isomers   c. saturated
   b. fuel gases   d. polymers

2. An organic compound not found naturally in food is ____.
   a. alcohol   c. lipids
   b. proteins   d. polystyrene

3. The component monomers in the protein polymers are ____.
   a. oils   c. starches
   b. amino acids   d. amine groups

4. Alcohols and organic acids are both ____.
   a. aromatic hydrocarbons
   b. saturated hydrocarbons
   c. substituted hydrocarbons
   d. unsaturated hydrocarbons

5. If a carbohydrate has 16 oxygen atoms, it has ____ hydrogen atoms.
   a. 4   c. 16
   b. 8   d. 32

6. Cholesterol is a type of ____.
   a. sugar   c. protein
   b. starch   d. lipid

7. Shorter hydrocarbons have ____ than longer hydrocarbons.
   a. more alcohol molecules
   b. more lipids
   c. lower boiling points
   d. more methane molecules

8. Lipids contain the same atoms as do ____.
   a. hydrocarbons   c. proteins
   b. carbohydrates d. hemoglobin

CRITICAL THINKING

Use your understanding of the concepts developed in the chapter to answer each of the following questions.

1. Using the information in Table 11-1 on page 324 as a guide, draw the structural formula for decane.

2. Compare and contrast saturated and unsaturated fats.

3. Octane number is used as a measure of a gasoline's ability to burn evenly. The higher the octane number for a gasoline, the less likely it is to cause an engine to knock or ping when driving. Look at the diagram. It shows three types of gasolines, and their octane numbers. What do you think is the relationship between even burning and molecular structure?

1) Heptane — Octane Number 0

2) 2-methylheptane — 23

3) Isooctane — 100

4. Why do butane and isobutane have different properties?

5. How does an amino acid differ from a carboxylic acid?

6. For each of the following, tell whether the compound given is an alcohol, amine, or carboxylic acid:
   a. C_3H_7OH
   b. CH_3CH_2COOH
   c. $CH_3CH_2NH_2$
   d. CH_3OH
   e. $C_8H_{17}COOH$

7. Describe the substitution process in which butane changes to butyl alcohol.

PROBLEM SOLVING

Read the following problem and discuss your answer in a brief paragraph.

Maria goes to the store for bananas to bake her father a cake for his birthday tomorrow. The only bananas she can find are too green to mash. What can she do to get them to ripen faster between now and tomorrow?

CONNECTING IDEAS

Discuss each of the following in a brief paragraph.

1. What foods should be included in a properly balanced diet?

2. One gram of a lipid yields about 9 calories in energy, while one gram of a carbohydrate only yields 4 calories. If lipids produce more energy than carbohydrates, why shouldn't they make up the larger part of a healthful diet?

3. **LIFE SCIENCE CONNECTION** What are biotoxins, and what organic molecules are many of them composed of?

4. **TECHNOLOGY CONNECTION** How is ethanol produced, and what benefits might it have for the transportation industry?

5. **SCIENCE AND SOCIETY** Describe some of the benefits of composting.

DID YOU EVER WONDER . . .

How long someone could live without food?

Why your stomach makes noises when you're hungry?

How large the area of your small intestine is?

You'll find the answers to these questions as you read this chapter.

Fueling the Body

Welcome to Blanca Hidalgo's garden. Those red-ripe tomatoes soon will find their way into a spicy salsa. The carrots and zucchini will become part of a fresh vegetable salad. And those onions and peppers will add zip to tonight's tacos.

The Hidalgos aren't the only ones to benefit from Blanca's well-tended garden. Pesky crows swoop down during the day to sample the ripening corn. A rabbit sneaks in later to nibble at the lettuce. And those tomato plants have dinner guests, too. Bees draw nectar from the tomato blossoms. Tiny aphids suck juices from the tomato stems. Later, ants milk the aphids for nourishment.

All living things—from the largest animal to the tiniest cell—require nourishment. In this chapter you will learn about the fuel your body needs and how your body processes that fuel to keep you healthy.

EXPLORE!

How is your diet different from that of your classmates?
Not everyone eats the same kinds of food. Make a list of the foods you eat most often at home. Be honest about your snacking habits, too! Compare your list with your classmates'. What foods are common to both lists? What foods are different?

12-1 Nutrients: The Spice of Life

OBJECTIVES

In this section, you will
- identify different types of nutrients and describe the importance of each;
- evaluate your own diet and plan a healthy one.

KEY SCIENCE TERMS

nutrients
minerals
vitamins

NUTRIENTS AND YOUR DIET

You've probably heard the expression "you are what you eat." No, it doesn't mean that you'll turn into a pizza if that's your favorite food. But suppose you *did* eat nothing but pizza. What would happen to your body? What if you never drank any milk? Suppose you stopped eating citrus fruits or drinking citrus juice. Do you know what happens to a body when it doesn't get the food it needs?

Do you often wonder what's for dinner long before dinnertime? People spend a lot of time thinking about food. Your body not only requires the nourishment that food gives, it requires the *right kind* of nourishment—a healthful variety of different foods. Exactly what does food do for you?

FIND OUT!

Does your diet include a healthful variety of foods?

Make a chart. Across the top of the chart write the days of the week. Along the left side of the chart write *Breakfast, Lunch, Dinner,* and *Snacks.* Fill out the chart for an entire week, listing every food you eat at every meal and the foods you eat between meals.

Analyze your chart. Do you know which foods came from animal sources? Which foods came from plants? How many were fruits, and how many were vegetables? Which food choices came from grain sources, such as bread or pasta? Which foods do you think had a great deal of fat? How much water did you take in?

Conclude and Apply

Based on your analysis, explain why you think you are or are not eating a healthful variety of foods.

In the activity, you discovered whether or not you are eating a healthful variety of foods. Some foods, however, are more healthful than others. How can you tell?

Take a look at a box of breakfast cereal. Besides the colorful images and the free offers, you'll also notice a label on the side panel listing nutritional information, like the one in Figure 12-1. You may think you're just eating toasted corn with raisins, but you're actually taking in nutrients. **Nutrients** are substances in food that provide energy and materials for the development, growth, and repair of cells. Nutrients are the fuel your body needs to function efficiently.

Suppose your body doesn't get the proper mix of nutrients. Take a look at the two skeletons in Figure 12-2. The skeleton on the left is normal. The skeleton on the right, however, shows evidence of a disease called rickets (RIK its). Rickets is caused by the lack of an important nutrient, vitamin D. How did the lack of vitamin D affect the development of this person?

SIX IMPORTANT NUTRIENTS

You learned about the chemistry of organic compounds, including proteins and carbohydrates in Chapter 11. These are just two of the six nutrients your body needs to function

FIGURE 12-1. Nutritional labels can help you to make healthful food choices at the supermarket.

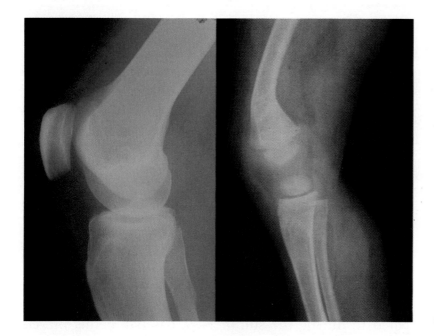

FIGURE 12-2. Improper nutrition can lead to disease. The skeleton on the left is healthy. The one on the right shows signs of rickets, a disease caused by a lack of vitamin D.

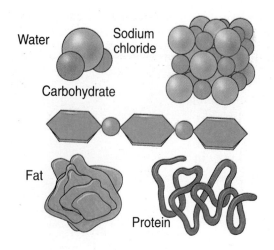

Water

Sodium
chloride

Carbohydrate

Fat

Protein

FIGURE 12-3. Compare these molecules of water, mineral (sodium chloride, or table salt), fat, carbohydrate, and protein.

properly. The other nutrients are fats, vitamins, minerals, and water. Fats and vitamins are also organic compounds because they contain carbon atoms. Water and minerals are inorganic compounds. They contain no carbon atoms.

Besides the presence of carbon atoms, how else do organic compounds differ from inorganic compounds? Look at the molecules of water, mineral, carbohydrate, protein, and fat in Figure 12-3. What do you notice about the size and complexity of these different molecules?

Organic molecules are larger and more complex than inorganic molecules. Carbohydrates, fats, and proteins in foods are usually in a form that must be broken down into simpler molecules before they can be absorbed and used by your body. In contrast, small molecules, such as water, vitamins, and minerals, are absorbed quickly.

EXPLORE!

How nutritious is one breakfast cereal?

Look again at the list of nutrients on the cereal box label in Figure 12-1. Which of the six nutrients does the cereal contain? How much of each nutrient is present in the cereal? Nutrients are measured in grams and milligrams. What vitamins are present? In what amounts? To get a better idea of just how much of each nutrient is present, measure out a gram of salt or sugar for comparison. What minerals are present? Which of the nutrients will be absorbed most quickly by your body? Why?

Water

How much water was in the cereal you just read about? Water probably wasn't listed. Yet water is a critical nutrient for life. Think back to an athletic event you participated in during the summer—a baseball game, bicycle race, or skateboarding. You probably noticed that the harder you worked, the more you perspired. After a while, you felt thirsty and needed a long drink before your thirst was satisfied. Your body can function for weeks, maybe even months, on limited amounts of food. But without water, your body would remain alive only for a few days.

FIGURE 12-4. During hard physical exercise, it's important to replenish the body's supply of water.

Why is water so important? Well, most of your body is water. The blood that carries oxygen and other nutrients throughout your body is mostly water. In fact, all of the cells of your body are mostly water. All chemical reactions and other cellular functions take place in the cell's cytoplasm, a gel-like substance that is primarily water.

EXPLORE!

How much of you is water?

Believe it or not, by weight, your body is nearly two-thirds water. Generally, when a person diets, the first pounds lost are actually pounds of water. To figure out how much of you is water, multiply your weight by 66 percent. What figure do you get?

You lose water every day of your life. You will lose more than two liters of water today from perspiration, through exhaled breath, and through urination. Even as you read these words, your body is losing water. You may not be perspiring noticeably, but water is evaporating from your skin. When something evaporates, it turns into a vapor that is released into the air.

DID YOU KNOW?

Why does corn pop? All dry seeds, including corn kernels, contain some water to keep them alive until it's time to sprout in the spring. When corn kernels are heated, this water turns to steam, and the kernels explode.

How do you know when your body needs water? Why do you feel thirsty? It's due to a process called homeostasis (hoh mee oh STAY sis). Homeostasis results in the body maintaining a balanced internal condition. When your body's water level dips too low—perhaps from exercise, excess perspiration, or urination—messages are sent to your brain. Your brain processes these messages, and you feel thirsty. As you replenish your body's water supply by drinking water or juices, your body sends more messages to your brain to hold back or slow down the feeling of thirst. As a result, you no longer feel thirsty.

Minerals

Like water, minerals are also important nutrients for your body. The next time you sprinkle salt on your broccoli (You *do* eat broccoli, don't you?), think of this. You're actually sprinkling part of the planet on your vegetable! Salt is a mineral, and minerals come from Earth. **Minerals** are inorganic compounds that regulate many of the chemical reactions that take place in your body. But why is your body composed of molecules from Earth?

Scientists think that all life on Earth began in the sea. The sea is rich in minerals, so it makes sense that organisms that began life in this "mineral soup" are mineral-rich themselves. In fact, the water in your body contains dissolved minerals that make it chemically similar to the water in the ocean. What evidence can you think of that shows that your body is chemically similar to ocean water?

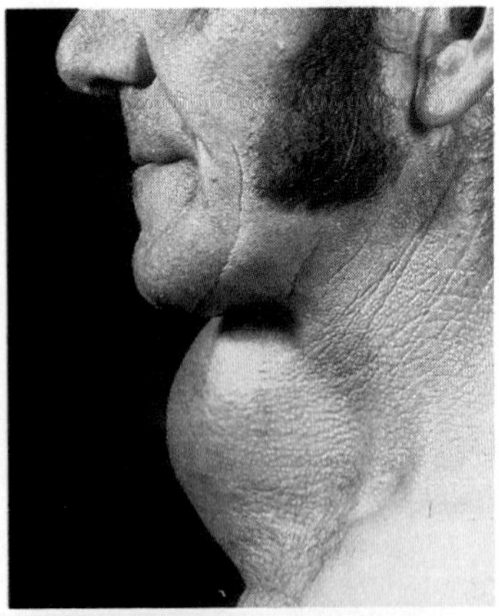

FIGURE 12-5. An iodine deficiency can cause a goiter, an enlargement of the thyroid gland.

Of all the elements listed in the periodic table, your body requires about 14 to regulate its chemical reactions. These include calcium, phosphorous, sodium, potassium, magnesium, and iron. They are required by your body in small amounts. Even so, your body must have them. A deficiency in any one mineral, however small, can result in disease, as shown in Figure 12-5.

Examine Table 12-1. It lists some of the most important minerals your body needs, how they function in your body, and which foods contain them. What would happen to your body if you didn't get enough calcium? Iron? Potassium? Look back at the chart of foods you've been eating during the past week. Are you eating foods that provide your body with the minerals it needs? If not, what foods do you think you should add to your diet?

TABLE 12-1. Common minerals, their uses and sources.

Mineral	Main Functions in the Body	Best Food Sources
Calcium	Structure of bones and teeth; work of nerves and muscles; blood clotting.	Milk, other dairy products, green vegetables.
Phosphorous	Energy storage in cells; key element in chemical reactions in cells.	Meat, dairy products, beans, peas, and grains.
Sodium	Water balance; work of nerves and muscles.	All foods; table salt; sea salt.
Potassium	Water balance; work of nerves and muscles;chemical reactions in cells.	Bananas, apricots, avocados, potatoes, other fruits and vegetables.
Iron	To make red blood cells carry oxygen.	Liver, meat, eggs, and fortified cereals.
Iodine	Needed by the thyroid gland.	Seafood; iodized table salt; sea salt.
Magnesium	Digestion of proteins and carbohydrates.	Beans, peas, nuts and cereals; leafy green vegetables.

Carbohydrates

The next time you come home from school feeling tired and listless, do what the nutrition pros do when they need an energy boost. Eat a potato!

A potato? That's right, or maybe you'd prefer a dish of three-bean salad or a plate of spaghetti. All of these foods, as well as those pictured in Figure 12-6, contain carbohydrates. Carbohydrates are organic compounds and the main source of energy for all living organisms.

FIGURE 12-6. These foods contain complex carbohydrates, an important source of energy for your body.

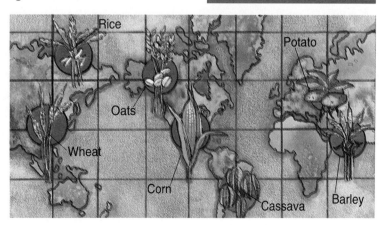
Rice Potato Oats Wheat Corn Cassava Barley

Which foods contain carbohydrates?
Look at the nutrition labels on the packages of ten foods that you eat often, such as frozen pizza, pasta, orange juice, bread, and so on. Which foods contain carbohydrates? How many total grams of carbohydrates does a serving contain? Can you tell what types of carbohydrates are present in each food? How much sugar does each contain?

Carbohydrates come in three forms: sugars, starches, and cellulose. Sugar is a simple carbohydrate. Energy that you use for all your body's activities is released from simple carbohydrates when they are broken down in your cells. Sugar comes in many forms, including glucose, dextrose, fructose, corn syrup, and molasses.

Starches, found in foods such as pasta, potatoes, and cassava root are complex carbohydrates. So is cellulose, the tough fiber that makes up the cell walls in plants. Complex carbohydrates can't be used right away by your body. They are made up of large molecules that have to be broken down into smaller forms called simple carbohydrates.

Complex carbohydrates, especially grains, are the most important foods in diets all over the world because they are more plentiful and less expensive than fats and proteins. For example, millet, oats, and soybeans are three complex carbohydrate dietary staples. Many cultures are closely associated with a particular grain or carbohydrate source. Rice is a grain usually associated with Asian cultures and corn with Latino cultures. What other grains can you think of?

DID YOU KNOW?

Blood supplies nutrients, including sodium, protein, and iron. In some cultures, blood is used as food, a regular part of the diet. The Slavic people make a soup from duck's blood. The British make blood sausage. And the Masai people of Africa milk blood from the cattle they herd to supplement their diet during the dry season.

Fats

Fats are large organic molecules. Like carbohydrates, fats are broken down to release energy to fuel your body. In fact, fats release more energy per molecule than carbohydrates do. Usually, however, you get your energy from carbohydrates because they make up the largest part of your diet. Only in an emergency, when your supply of carbohydrates is low, does your body turn to its fat reserves for energy.

The next time you're in the kitchen at home, open the refrigerator and see just how "fat" it is. Chances are you'll see some butter or margarine. Maybe there's some cheese in there, too. All of these foods contain fats. Now look in the pantry or the kitchen cabinets. Do you see any oils, such as corn oil or olive oil? These are fats also. So is solid vegetable shortening. In addition, fats are present in many of the foods you eat, such as meat, nuts, ice cream, cookies, pastries, and other foods like those shown in Figure 12-7.

Just how much fat do you need to eat to maintain the right amount of body fat? Not long ago, most nutritionists thought that no more than 30 percent of your diet should come from fats. Today, some think that figure should be 20 percent or even lower. The fact is, your body does need *some* fat, but most people eat too much of it. Not only does excess fat contribute to becoming overweight, but saturated fats—such as those found in meat, dairy products, and some tropical oils—can cause serious heart and artery disease. The result may be a narrowing of the arteries, preventing an adequate blood supply from reaching the heart muscle. Unsaturated fats, such as those found in vegetable oils, are much healthier.

SKILLBUILDER

MAKING AND USING TABLES
As you learn about the six nutrients needed by your body, organize this information into a table that lists each nutrient, its sources, and its nutritional value. If you need help, refer to the **Skill Handbook** on page 681.

FIGURE 12-7. Nutritionists recommend that no more than 20 percent of your calories come from high-fat foods like these.

What percentage of the Calories you consume comes from fat?

You can use a simple mathematical formula to calculate your fat intake from certain foods. You can find the information that you need to know on nutrition labels.

1. total number of Calories per serving
2. total grams of fat per serving

Suppose that you're eating one serving of breakfast cereal. One serving has 65 Calories and 1 gram of fat. To find out what percentage of your breakfast Calories comes from fat, multiply the grams of fat by 9. There are 9 calories in each gram of fat. Then divide the result by the total Calories:

$$1 \times 9 = 9$$
$$9 \div 65 = .1384, \text{ or } 14 \text{ percent}$$

Is your breakfast a healthful one? What makes you think so?

Conclude and Apply

1. Suppose you ate cheesecake that has 300 Calories and 25 grams of fat. What percentage of the Calories comes from fat?
2. Is this a healthful food choice? Why?

Protein

How do you feel about insects? If you're like most people, the fewer insects you see, the better. In some cultures, however, insects play an important role in diet. You'd probably be surprised to learn that in parts of Africa, for example, termites are considered quite a delicacy. African termites are much larger than those found in the United States, and they are enjoyed both fresh and fried.

Why termites? Well, termites are an important source of protein. Termites are just about 50 percent protein. Protein is an organic compound containing nitrogen that is used throughout the body for growth and to replace and repair cells. Proteins are the building blocks of body tissue.

Proteins are composed of long chains of molecules called amino (uh MEE noh) acids. Your body requires twenty different kinds of amino acids. Sixteen of these

DID YOU KNOW?

Some of the largest and most powerful animals on Earth, including the elephant, hippopotamus, rhinoceros, and American buffalo, are all vegetarians!

amino acids, called nonessential amino acids, can be made in the cells in your body. The other eight, called essential amino acids, have to be supplied by the food you eat.

 Don't worry, though. You don't have to start eating termites. The protein in meat, eggs, and dairy products contains the eight essential amino acids your body cannot produce. That's why the protein in these foods is called complete protein. The protein in plants is incomplete—that is, it contains some, but not all, of the eight essential amino acids. By combining different types of plant proteins, however, you can get all eight essential amino acids in your diet. Beans, rice, and grains are all excellent sources of protein. Figure 12-8 shows a completely vegetarian meal that includes all of the essential amino acids.

FIGURE 12-8. This delicious, protein-rich dinner includes only grains, fruits, and vegetables.

Vitamins

 Suppose your body is getting all the proteins, carbohydrates, and fats it needs. You're drinking plenty of water and taking in all the important minerals. You're bound to be a picture of good health, right?

 Maybe not. If you're not getting the right vitamins, you might actually be suffering from malnutrition! **Vitamins** are organic nutrients necessary to your continued good health. Most vitamins are required in extremely small amounts. However, a deficiency in any one vitamin can

How do we know?

What is the importance of vitamin C?

Scurvy is a disease caused by a lack of vitamin C. It was once common among sailors who spent many months at sea eating mostly salted beef and dry biscuits. The sailors' diet rarely included fresh fruits and vegetables. The result of this nutritional imbalance was a disease that caused mouth sores, painful joints, anemia, and often death. In 1499, Portuguese navigator Vasco da Gama lost many of his crew to scurvy on a voyage from India to the East African coast.

In 1753, a Scottish physician named James Lind demonstrated that eating oranges and lemons could prevent and cure this terrible disease. By 1795, the British Navy was issuing daily rations of citrus juice and fruits—oranges, lemons, and limes—to its sailors. The necessity of a healthful diet had been clearly demonstrated, even though the key factor, vitamin C, would not be identified for about another 100 years.

TABLE 12-2. Common Vitamins, Their Sources and Uses

Vitamin	Main Functions in the Body	Best Food Sources
vitamin A	needed by the eyes, lining of the lungs and digestive system, bones and teeth	liver, milk, eggs, fruits and vegetables
vitamin B1	needed for burning of carbohydrates	whole grains, cereals, nuts, beans, peas
vitamin B2	needed by cells for energy release and repair	milk, cheese, eggs, liver, chicken
vitamin B6	needed by nerves and red blood cells	liver, meat, milk, eggs, whole grains
vitamin B12	needed by bone marrow to make red blood cells and by nervous system	eggs, meats, milk and dairy products
other B vitamins	needed by cells for burning of fuel and oxygen needed by cells for energy production needed by circulatory system and skin needed by bone marrow to make red blood cells	whole grains, cereals, liver, chicken eggs, meats, nuts, fresh vegetables, fish
vitamin C	needed by bones, teeth and other tissues for repair	citrus fruits, tomatoes, cabbage, strawberries
vitamin D	needed for bone growth; Note: some is produced in the skin by sunlight.	milk and dairy products, eggs, oily fish
vitamin E	needed for cell membranes	vegetable oils
vitamin K	needed for blood clotting; Note: some is produced in the intestine by bacteria.	leafy vegetables

sometimes cause serious health problems. Study Table 12-2. Notice how each vitamin contributes to the functioning of your body. What might happen to your body if you weren't getting enough B12? If you were deficient in vitamin A?

EXPLORE!

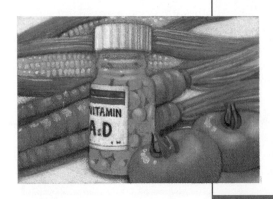

How can you be sure you're getting enough of the right kinds of vitamins?
Generally speaking, if you're eating a balanced diet, you're almost certainly getting the right vitamins. However, you may be taking a daily vitamin supplement. Look at the label on a vitamin bottle. What vitamins does it contain? How much of each vitamin is in each pill? Do the vitamin pills contain any minerals as well? Which ones?

12-1
VITAMIN C

This activity will allow you to test various orange juices and determine which has the highest vitamin C content.

PROBLEM

Which orange juice contains the most vitamin C?

MATERIALS

10 test tubes
test-tube rack
masking tape
safety goggles
apron
graduated cylinder
indophenol solution
4 dropper bottles containing (A) vitamin C solution, (B) frozen orange concentrate mixed according to directions, (C) bottled orange juice, and (D) fresh-squeezed orange juice

PROCEDURE

1. Copy the data table. Put on safety goggles and an apron.

DATA AND OBSERVATIONS

DROPS OF JUICE TO CHANGE INDICATOR			
TRIAL	FROZEN (B)	BOTTLED (C)	FRESH (D)
1			
2			
3			
Ave.			

2. Label four test tubes 1 through 4.
3. **Measure** 15 mL indophenol solution into each of the four test tubes. **CAUTION:** *Indophenol is poisonous, and can stain skin and clothing. Notify your teacher if any is spilled.* Indophenol is an indicator that changes from blue to colorless when enough vitamin C is present.
4. Add 20 drops of vitamin C solution from dropper bottle A to test tube 1. Swirl the mixture carefully. The solution will turn clear. This is your color control.
5. Add orange juice B, one drop at a time, to test tube 2. Keep an accurate count. Compare with your control after each drop. Add one drop at a time until the indicator changes from blue to colorless. Record the number of drops of juice B it took to make the indicator colorless.
6. Repeat Step 5 for juice C, then for juice D.
7. Test each juice, B, C, and D, two more times.
8. Average the data for the three trials.

ANALYZE

1. **Compare and contrast** the amount of vitamin C in the orange juices tested. Which orange juice contained the most vitamin C? Which contained the least? How do you know?
2. Why did you test each juice three times and average the results?

CONCLUDE AND APPLY

3. If the amount of vitamin C varied in the orange juices, suggest a reason why.
4. **Going Further: Hypothesize** what would happen to the vitamin C content of orange juice that was not refrigerated for several days. How would you test your hypothesis?

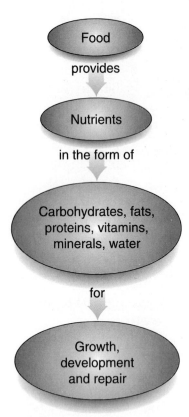

```
      Food
        │
     provides
        ↓
    Nutrients
        │
   in the form of
        ↓
Carbohydrates, fats,
proteins, vitamins,
 minerals, water
        │
       for
        ↓
     Growth,
   development
   and repair
```

FIGURE 12-9. Food from a variety of sources provide your body with six types of nutrients.

In the Investigate, you tested the vitamin C content in various kinds of orange juice. There are similar tests that can be done to test for the presence of other vitamins, minerals, and nutrients in foods. For example, in the next section, you will be testing for sugars in foods using another chemical indicator. Tests such as these help provide accurate nutritional information that can then be listed on food labels.

The nutrient content of many foods can change greatly from the time they are harvested until they are consumed. Tests show that certain methods of storage and preparation can cause a significant decrease in the amount of useful nutrients in a food. Oxygen from the air and excessive cooking are two culprits that break nutrients down into less useful substances or remove them from the foods. Steaming vegetables, rather than boiling, is one good way to preserve the essential nutrients contained in them.

As you can see in Figure 12-9, all of the nutrients that we have discussed in this section, including carbohydrates, proteins, fats, minerals, and vitamins, are essential to your good health. To be sure you're getting the right kinds of nutrients in the right amounts, eat a sensible, well-balanced diet. The more scientists study the relationship between diet and health, the more convinced they are that what we eat has a direct effect on how we feel and how our bodies respond to the stresses of daily life. In this sense, you really are what you eat! In the next section, you'll learn how the human digestive system breaks down the foods that you have eaten so your body can use the nutrients to maintain itself.

Check Your Understanding

1. It has been said that we "cannot live by bread alone." Explain why this statement is true from a nutritional point of view.

2. Describe the six different types of nutrients and explain how your body uses each type.

3. Describe a situation in which your body might begin burning its own fat for energy.

4. **APPLY:** Using what you've learned about nutrients, plan a healthy meal for you and your classmates. Explain which nutrients are present in your meal and why you think it is healthy.

12-2 Digestion: A Disassembly Line

GETTING THOSE NUTRIENTS

Remember all the nutritious foods growing in Blanca Hidalgo's garden? All those fruits and vegetables were packed with all the nutrients your body needs to grow strong and healthy. But how does your body "get to" those nutrients so it can use them for energy, tissue growth and repair, and other important body functions? The answer is a remarkable process called digestion.

THE DISASSEMBLY LINE

You've heard of assembly lines in factories where products are put together quickly and efficiently? Your digestive system, shown in Figure 12-10, works in reverse. Digestion is a disassembly line where foods you eat are taken apart. **Digestion** is the process that breaks down carbohydrates, fats, and proteins into smaller and simpler molecules that can be absorbed and used by the cells in your body. Later, your cells use these molecules as building blocks for growth and repair and as fuel from which energy is released. Any molecules that are not absorbed by your cells eventually pass out of your body as solid wastes.

Chemical digestion works on individual molecules, breaking down large molecules into smaller molecules using chemicals produced by your body. Chemical digestion is one process of metabolism, which includes all of the chemical changes that take place in your body— including the breakdown of fuel molecules for energy.

THE MOUTH

You've just returned home from gymnastics practice, and you're ready for a snack. You pop two slices of pepperoni pizza in the microwave, and in a few minutes

OBJECTIVES

In this section, you will
- describe the purpose of the mechanical breakdown of food in your digestive system;
- explain the role of enzymes in chemical digestion;
- describe what happens to food as it passes through each organ of the digestive system.

KEY SCIENCE TERMS

digestion   peristalsis
enzyme   villi

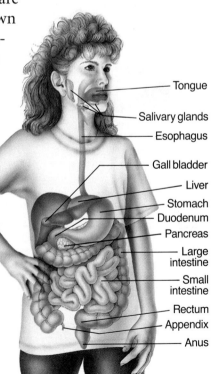

Tongue
Salivary glands
Esophagus
Gall bladder
Liver
Stomach
Duodenum
Pancreas
Large intestine
Small intestine
Rectum
Appendix
Anus

FIGURE 12-10. The Human Digestive System

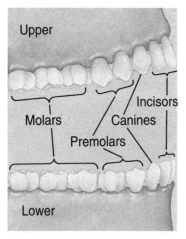

FIGURE 12-12. Your teeth are shaped differently for eating and breaking down foods.

you're biting into a delicious treat. Let's follow that pizza as it moves through your digestive system, beginning in your mouth.

Digestion begins as teeth start to work on food. Teeth are adapted to the kinds of food an animal eats. Look at the illustration of human teeth in Figure 12-12. You'll use your incisors to take that first bite of pizza. Then you'll use your molars at the back of your mouth to grind the pizza into smaller bits. This is mechanical digestion. But that's not all that's going on in your mouth.

EXPLORE!

Where does digestion begin?
Chew a saltine cracker, but don't swallow it. It won't be too easy, but hold it in your mouth for about five minutes. Now, how does the cracker taste? Why has the taste of the cracker changed?

The cracker you chewed was made from wheat flour or some other grain and contains complex carbohydrates. Remember, carbohydrates are broken down into smaller sugar molecules before they can be used as fuel for your body. What's going on in your mouth? Let's investigate.

12-2 CHEMICAL DIGESTION

This investigation will demonstrate the conversion of starch to sugar that takes place in your mouth.

PROBLEM:
Does chemical digestion begin in the mouth?

MATERIALS
4 test tubes
test-tube rack
100-mL graduated cylinder
250-mL beaker
tap water
non-instant oatmeal
sugar
tablespoon
medicine dropper
iodine solution
Benedict's solution
hot plate
safety glasses
test-tube clamp

PROCEDURE
1. **CAUTION:** *Put on your safety glasses.* Copy the data table.

2. Label four test tubes 1 through 4.
3. Fill a beaker with 100 mL of water. Soak a handful of oatmeal in the water. Allow to stand for 10 minutes, stirring once or twice. Pour off the milky-white liquid. Use this as your starch solution.
4. Measure 10 mL starch solution into test tubes 1, 3, and 4.
5. Completely dissolve 1 teaspoon of sugar in 25 mL of water. Measure 10 mL sugar solution into test tube 2.
6. Wash the starch solution out of the beaker, fill it half full with hot tap water, and place it on a hot plate.
7. Add 4 drops of iodine solution to test tube 1. Iodine will turn blue-black in the presence of starch. **Observe** the test tube and record your observations by indicating a positive (starch present) or a negative (no starch present) result.
8. Add 4 drops of Benedict's solution to test tube 2 and

heat in the hot water in the beaker. Benedict's solution is an indicator. If sugar is present, it turns muddy green to yellow to rust to red. Record your observations in the data table.
9. Add several drops of saliva to test tubes 3 and 4, and swirl carefully. Wait 5 minutes.
10. Add 4 drops of iodine solution to test tube 3. Record your observations.
11. Add 4 drops of Benedict's solution to test tube 4. Wait for the water bath to boil. Using a test-tube clamp, place test tube 4 in the water bath and leave it there for 5 minutes. Record your observations.

ANALYZE
1. How did you test for the presence of starch?
2. How did you test for sugar?

CONCLUDE AND APPLY
3. What can you **conclude** from your data table? What process begins as you chew food?
4. **Going Further: Infer** why chewing your food is an important part of the digestive process?

DATA AND OBSERVATIONS

TEST TUBE	STARCH	SUGAR
1. Starch-iodine		
2. Sugar-Benedict's		
3. Starch-saliva-iodine		
4. Starch-saliva-Bndt's		

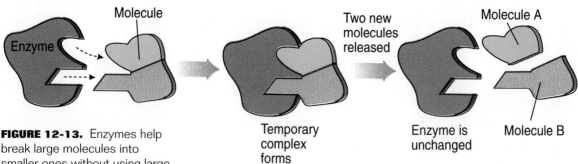

FIGURE 12-13. Enzymes help break large molecules into smaller ones without using large amounts of energy.

Molecule

Enzyme

Two new molecules released

Molecule A

Temporary complex forms

Enzyme is unchanged

Molecule B

The Investigate showed that digestion begins in your mouth. Saliva contains an enzyme that begins the process by which starch is broken down into sugar. An **enzyme** is a protein molecule that controls the rate of different processes in your body. Enzymes are a vital part of chemical digestion. They work on nutrient molecules like keys in a lock. Each enzyme fits just one type of molecule, breaking the nutrient into smaller molecules, as in Figure 12-13.

You have over 700 different enzymes in your body, each with a unique function. When an enzyme in your saliva mixes with the starchy wheat crust of the pizza you're eating, chemical digestion begins and starch is broken down to sugar.

From Your Mouth to Your Stomach

You've just swallowed your first mouthful of pizza. How does food get from your mouth to your stomach? Is gravity responsible? Let's find out.

FIND OUT!

Does gravity move food to your stomach?
Get a glass of water with a flexible straw. Lie down on an exercise slant board with your head at the lower end. Lift up your head and take a *small* mouthful of water through the straw. Don't swallow it yet! Rest your head back on the slant board and *carefully* swallow the water in your mouth.

Conclude and Apply
What role does gravity play in digestion?

Even though your head was tilted downward, you were still able to swallow the water. If gravity played a role in swallowing, the water would have stayed in your mouth. In addition, astronauts swallow with no trouble in the zero-gravity of outer space.

Here's what does happen when you swallow. Your esophagus is lined with muscles that move food and liquid from your mouth to your stomach—even if you're standing on your head! When these muscles contract, the pizza you swallow is forced down your esophagus.

Figure 12-14 illustrates the process of **peristalsis** (pe ruh STAHL suhs). During peristalsis, the smooth muscles of the esophagus contract in waves, carrying bites of pizza or any food to your stomach. This same muscle action moves food through your entire digestive system.

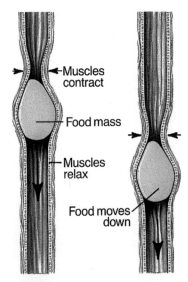

FIGURE 12-14. Peristalsis, muscle contractions in the esophagus, slowly force food from your mouth into your stomach.

Within Your Stomach

The muscle action of your esophagus slowly fills your stomach, where the next phase of digestion will take place.

Do you really know where your stomach is? Surprisingly, most people don't. Put your hand where you *think* your stomach is. Chances are your hand is right about where your navel is. Actually, your stomach is midway between your waist and your armpit, on the left side, at the base of your ribcage.

How do we know?

The Stomach Observed

Much of what we know about the actions of the stomach is based on an accident. In 1822, a young French Canadian fur trapper named Alexis St. Martin was shot in his left side. An army surgeon named William Beaumont successfully removed the bullet and saved Alexis's life. However, Dr. Beaumont could not close the wound completely, and Alexis was left with a hole in his side leading straight into his stomach.

Dr. Beaumont was a scientist as well as a physician. For a number of years, he observed the activity in Alexis's stomach under various conditions. For instance, he tied different kinds of foods on strings and lowered them into Alexis's stomach to observe the effect of stomach fluids on the different foods. Dr. Beaumont also removed samples of these fluids and had them analyzed. He identified hydrochloric acid in the fluid. More importantly, he discovered that although meats are chemically digested in the stomach, other types of food are not.

Dr. Beaumont published his observations in a book that is still referred to today. Alexis, by the way, lived to be 83.

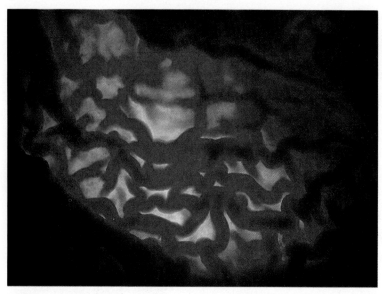

FIGURE 12-15. Folds on the inside of the stomach will smooth out as the stomach fills with food.

Your stomach is a sack with a thin wall of muscle. When empty, it's somewhat like a balloon that you've let the air out of. It is small, and its interior is wrinkled and folded, as shown in Figure 12-15. When full of food, however, the stomach expands, and the folds smooth out.

When the pizza you've been eating reaches your stomach, mechanical and chemical digestion continue. Your stomach muscles churn and mix the partially digested pizza. Meanwhile, the cells in your stomach wall produce substances that attack the pizza chemically. These substances are hydrochloric acid and enzymes.

 **FIND OUT!**

How do enzymes work?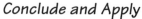
Your teacher will provide you with small samples of beef, water, and a commercial brand of meat tenderizer. Obtain two beef samples. Moisten each with water. Then sprinkle one generously with tenderizer. The other sample will not be treated. It is your control. After one half hour, examine the two samples. Look them over carefully. Feel the texture of each one.

Conclude and Apply
Do you detect any differences in the samples? If so, what?

Meat contains many different proteins. Meat tenderizer contains an enzyme that breaks down protein. Your stomach also contains enzymes to break down the protein in such foods as beef. But how is it that your stomach, which is also made of muscle, doesn't digest itself? Fortunately, your stomach wall produces a protective coating of slimy mucus that protects it from the action of hydrochloric acid and enzymes.

TRAVELING THROUGH THE SMALL INTESTINE

Your pizza will spend about four hours in your stomach being mechanically and chemically digested. During that time, your snack turns into a thin, watery liquid. Then, little by little, the muscles in your stomach push this liquid into your small intestine, where more breakdown takes place.

Most chemical digestion takes place in your small intestine. Your liver, gallbladder, and pancreas supply different digestive juices needed for chemical digestion to your small intestine. One kind of juice produced in your liver and stored in your gallbladder is a green liquid called bile. As shown in Figure 12-16, bile is added to the liquid nutrient mixture as it leaves the stomach. Bile physically breaks up large globs of fat. Enzymes made in the pancreas, a large gland behind your stomach, continue the chemical breakdown of carbohydrates, fats, and proteins as the liquid mass moves on through the intestine.

Your small intestine is less than an inch in diameter but is over six meters long! Imagine a garden hose coiled up inside your abdomen. Unlike a garden hose, however, your small intestine is not smooth and straight on the inside. It is lined with many ridges and folds, and the folds are covered with tiny finger-like projections called **villi**. Look at the piece of intestinal wall illustrated in Figure 12-17. Pay special attention to the villi. What do you suppose their function is?

All of the ridges, folds, and villi of your small intestine increase its surface area dramatically. In fact, the surface area of your small intestine could cover a tennis court! The surface area of your intestine is over 264 square meters.

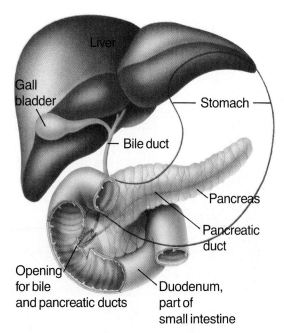

FIGURE 12-16. Bile produced in the liver aids in the digestion of fats.

FIGURE 12-17. Digested nutrients enter your body through finger-like projections called villi in your small intestine.

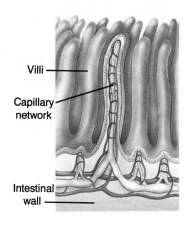

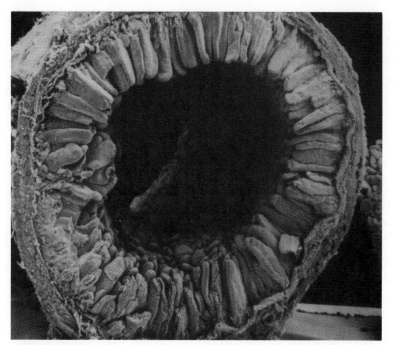

FIGURE 12-18. The surface of your small intestine could cover a tennis court.

Notice the many blood vessels in the villi. These are a clue to the villi's function. By the time your snack reaches your small intestine, its molecules have been broken down into a size small enough to pass through the walls of your villi and into your bloodstream. As the muscles of your small intestine move the liquid nutrient mixture along, the villi are completely bathed in the liquid, and nutrient molecules move from your digestive system into your circulatory system. From here, nutrients will be carried to cells throughout your body. The pizza you ate hours ago is finally going to get a chance to provide nutritional benefits.

THE END OF THE LINE: YOUR LARGE INTESTINE

By this time in the digestive process, you've probably long since forgotten about those delicious slices of pepperoni pizza. But your body hasn't. The last stage of digestion is about to take place.

The thin, watery liquid that's been moving through your small intestine is now pushed into your large intestine. This digestive organ is almost two meters long and six to seven centimeters in diameter. Muscle contractions here are much slower than they were in your small intestine. The large intestine absorbs large amounts of water. The liquid that isn't absorbed is concentrated into a somewhat solid mass of undigested material.

The solidified wastes also contain large numbers of bacteria. These bacteria are beneficial. They consume some of the last microscopic bits of food. As they do so, they produce vitamins—vitamin K and some of the B vitamins. Finally, the solidified wastes are eliminated from your body as feces.

SKILLBUILDER

SEQUENCING
Make a chart that shows the process of digestion in order from beginning to end. Your chart should include a description of each stage of digestion and the organs involved at each stage. If you need help, refer to the **Skill Handbook** on page 680.

THE NUTRITIONAL PAYOFF

The pizza you snacked on provided your body with starch, protein, fat, vitamins, and minerals. Once these nutrients have been distributed throughout your body by your circulatory system, how are they used? The nutrients you've taken in act as fuel for a variety of metabolic processes, including cell growth and repair. They provide your body with the energy it needs to function.

FIND OUT!

How much energy do you need?

You can calculate the rate at which your body uses energy. First you need to know that a Calorie is a unit of measurement of the energy available in food. Males use about 1.0 Calories per kilogram of body mass per hour. Females use less—about 0.9.

Now, convert your mass in pounds to kilograms by multiplying your weight by 0.453. Then multiply your mass in kilograms by 1.0 if you're a male and 0.9 if you're a female. The result is the energy in Calories you use per hour.

Calories Per Hour
Males use: 1C / kilg. body weight
Females use: .9c/kilg. body weight
Mass: 120 lbs.
Mass: 120 X .453 = 54.36 kg.
Energy in Calories per hour:
.9 X 54.36 = 48.92
or
.50 calories / Hour

Conclude and Apply

1. How many Calories of food energy do you use per day?
2. Compare the Calories needed per day by a 100 pound woman and a 150 pound man.
3. What factors would affect the calories you need on a given day?

These daily energy requirements are averages. If you're more active, you'll use more energy. If you take in more Calories of energy than you use in any given time period, the extra will be stored as fat. If you don't take in as many Calories as you require, your body will take them from your fat reserve, and you'll lose weight.

TABLE 12-3. Nutritional Values of Common Foods

Food	Portion	Calories
Apple, raw	1 large	125
Carrots, raw, grated	1 cup	45
Liver, beef, fried	3 ounces	185
Rice, white, enriched	1 cup	225
Sugar, white, granulated	1 tablespoon	45

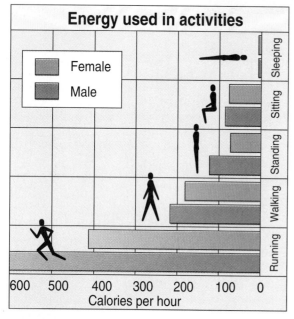

FIGURE 12-19. Which activity burns the most calories?

Have you ever seen or used a Calorie-counter book that lists the Calories in various foods? Such a list gives you a feel for the energy available in different types of foods. A sample listing of some foods and their Calories are given in Table 12-3.

Figure 12-19 shows the Calories used up during different physical activities, such as walking, running, swimming, sitting—even lying down. Calculate how long you would have to perform each activity to burn off the Calories in a bowl of ice cream.

Your digestive system is an incredible machine. It will process close to 100,000 pounds of food for you during your lifetime, chopping, mashing, and grinding whatever you put into it. It will break down the nutrients you need and send them off across the villi into your blood stream for transport throughout your body. What it can't use, it will efficiently eliminate. Supply it with useful nutrients, and your digestive system will help you remain healthy and strong.

Check Your Understanding

1. What is the difference between mechanical and chemical digestion?
2. How do enzymes work?
3. What do teeth have to do with increasing surface area?

4. **APPLY:** Suppose you ate a cheeseburger for lunch. Identify the various types of nutrients it contains and explain what is happening to them on the way from your mouth to your cells.

EXPANDING YOUR VIEW

CONTENTS

A CLOSER LOOK

EATING LIKE A BIRD

The expression "eats like a bird" describes someone who eats very little. Birds, however, eat a lot of food because flying requires a lot of energy.

Hummingbirds beat their wings up to 90 times a second when they are hovering at a flower. This activity burns energy so quickly that hummingbirds need to eat 70 percent of their body weight each day.

How much food an animal needs to eat depends on both the kind of animal and the kind of food. Animals that eat berries eat more than animals that eat nuts and seeds. Berries contain a lot of water, which has no nutritional value. Nuts and seeds are mostly dry and are packed full of nutrients.

Whether an animal eats plants or other animals also affects how much food is consumed. In general, animals that feed on plants eat larger quantities of food to get the nutrients they need than meat-eating animals do. Plants are harder to digest than meat. Plant cells contain cellulose, a rigid substance that gives support to stems and leaves.

A 6000-kilogram African bull elephant, for example, eats about 170 kilograms of plants a

day. Consequently, elephants spend a lot of time grazing —17 to 19 hours a day. Cows, deer, horses, and other grazing animals also spend almost all of the time they are awake eating.

Meat eaters, on the other hand, spend much less time eating. An adult male lion weighing between 150 and 250 kilograms eats about 32.5 kilograms of food each day.

YOU TRY IT!

Keep a record of all the food you eat in one day. Estimate the number of kilograms you consume. Prepackaged foods list the amount on the label. If possible, use a balance to measure food servings. How much of your total body mass do you consume in food each day?

Physics Connection

DO YOU ALWAYS HAVE A TEMPERATURE?

You might think that the only time you have a temperature is when you are sick. In fact, even when you are healthy, your body has a temperature of about 37°C. Where does that heat come from?

Remember that the process of respiration releases energy. Only a small amount of this energy is captured in a form that can be used by your body for daily activities. Most of the energy released from stored nutrients is in the form of heat. Some of this heat maintains a constant body temperature.

For birds and mammals, a constant body temperature makes it possible to live and be active in a wide range of habitats, no matter what the temperature of the environment is. Birds and mammals can live in the Arctic, where winter temperatures are below freezing. Amphibians and reptiles, which depend on heat from the environment to regulate their body temperature, cannot live in such a cold habitat.

Not all of the heat released by metabolism of food is

Metabolic rate

Body Weight (Kg)

used by an animal, however. Much is lost to the environment through the skin. Just how much heat is lost depends on an animal's size.

Small animals lose heat faster than larger ones do, because small animals have a large surface area-to-volume ratio. (Surface area is how much surface is exposed to the environment.) The larger the ratio, the more surface there is through which heat can be lost from the inside. Small animals that have a higher rate of metabolism than larger animals do lose heat more rapidly. The graph shows the relationship between body size and metabolism for several different species. As you can see, the smaller the animal, the faster its metabolism.

A higher rate of meta-

bolism in turn requires more food consumption. So small animals also eat more, relative to body size. For example, a mouse with a mass of 3 grams eats 30 times more food per gram of body mass than a 5000-kilogram elephant.

YOU TRY IT!

Freeze 1 L of water into a single block. Freeze another 1 L of water as small cubes. Place the large block in one pan and the small cubes in another pan. Allow all the ice to melt. Keep track of how long it takes. Which melts faster, the large block or the small cubes? Explain your answer in terms of surface area-to-volume ratio.

SCIENCE AND SOCIETY

ENVIRONMENTAL IMPACT OF MODERN AGRICULTURE

If you are like most people, you don't think much about where the food you eat comes from. You just buy it in the supermarket, or restaurants, or the school cafeteria.

The wide variety and large amounts of food that are available are mainly the result of modern agriculture. Modern agriculture came into wide use after World War II. It is a system of farming that relies heavily on the use of machinery and chemical fertilizers and pesticides to increase crop yields.

In the last 30 years, however, modern agriculture has become associated with a number of serious problems. For example, use of large heavy machines to manage

vast fields, combined with extended growing seasons, depletes soil fertility. Eventually, the soil breaks down and can no longer be farmed. When soil is severely damaged, nothing grows in it, and often it is carried away by wind and water.

CAREER CONNECTION

An agronomist is an agricultural scientist. Agronomists study biology. They work for corporations, government agencies, and colleges and universities.

The use of chemical fertilizers and pesticides is associated with environmental contamination and threats to human and animal health. In California's San Joaquin Valley, for example, about one million people have been exposed to the pesticide DBCP in their drinking water. This chemical, created to eliminate pests on the roots of farm crops, is known to cause cancer and sterility. Its use has been

banned. Other pesticides still being used have also contaminated water supplies in the valley. Water from 1500 wells in the region cannot be used for drinking, bathing, or cooking because of contamination with pesticides known to cause kidney and liver damage, cancer, sterility, and genetic damage. About half the states in the country have some contamination of water supplies from farm chemicals.

Critics of modern agricultural practices point out that many techniques are available to make agriculture sustainable. A sustainable farm is one that produces good quality food at a profit while keeping the soil fertile and healthy. To save energy, reduce pollution, and cut costs, farm chemicals and fuels are replaced whenever possible by resources found on the farm.

For example, some farmers use solar or wind power to generate electricity. Chemical pesticides are replaced by biological pest controls, such as insect predators and microorganisms that infect insect pests.

Animal and green manure are used instead of chemical fertilizers. Green manure is a crop such as grass or soybeans that is plowed into the soil at the end of the growing season. Green manure increases soil fertility and helps control weeds and insect pests. It is also a source of food for livestock.

Another important method in sustainable agriculture is crop rotation. Over the course of several growing seasons, a planned series of different crops is grown in a given field.

For example, a farmer might grow alfalfa for three seasons. The plants are plowed back into the soil at the end of each season to enrich the soil. Then crops that are harvested are grown for four seasons in a row — wheat, soybeans, wheat, and

then oats. Then the rotation is started again. Alfalfa and soybeans add nitrogen, an important plant nutrient, to the soil.

Diversity is another key characteristic of sustainable farms. Unlike standard farms, which grow huge fields of only one or a few kinds of crops, sustainable farms have a mixture of species and varieties of crops. They also have livestock and trees.

In case of a natural disaster or a sudden drop in prices for a single crop, farmers with more diverse crops are less likely to lose their entire yield for a season.

In 1980, there were between 20,000 and 30,000 farmers using sustainable agriculture methods, according to the U.S. Department of Agriculture. Farm experts estimate that today there may be two to three times that number. However, that is still just a tiny percent of the country's two million farmers.

Converting from standard farming to sustainable methods is not easy or quick. The more damaged the soil is and the more dependent on chemicals the farm is, the longer it takes the soil to be returned to a productive condition without the use of applied fertilizers.

Government policies have also worked to discourage farmers from using sustainable methods. For example, the federal government purchases a handful of crops and

sets prices for them. Wheat, cotton, soybeans, corn, and grains used as animal feed account for three-quarters of all crops supported by the government. So farmers who want to be certain of a profit are, in a way, trapped by a system of federal price supports. Because so many farmers are heavily in debt, they are unable to switch to sustainable methods. To do so would mean risking economic loss.

YOU TRY IT!

Should the federal government help farmers convert to sustainable methods? Explain your answer. How might the government help with this change?

*H*ealth
C O N N E C T I O N

EATING A BALANCED DIET

A healthy body needs proteins, fats, carbo-hydrates, vitamins, and minerals. But how much of each of these nutrients does your body need each day?

For many years, nutritional guides recommended eating food from four basic groups: fruits and vegetables, grains, meat, and milk. The average teenager was said to need two servings of meat a day and four servings from each of the other three groups. However, a diet based on these recommendations would be very high in fat and would contain more animal protein than is needed.

Scientists have long known that too much fat in the diet causes heart disease. A high level of dietary fat is also associated with breast and colon cancer. Current research now links too much protein from meat to heart disease and cancer as well.

Nutrition experts recommend that people pay more attention to the specific nutrients they eat. For example, no more than 20 percent of the calories in your daily food intake should be from fat. The average American has a diet that is about 48 percent fat.

Americans need to cut down on meat consumption as well. Just about 30 grams of protein are needed each day, but most people eat around 100 grams.

A healthful diet should be high in complex carbohydrates, fiber, vitamins, and minerals. To eat a healthful diet, there are certain guidelines you should follow. Think of your diet as a pyramid. At the bottom, which is the widest part, are grains. Grains include bread, cereal, rice, and pasta.

Your diet should also contain large amounts of fresh fruits and vegetables, the next layer in the pyramid.

A much smaller portion of your diet should be dairy products and meat because these foods are high in fat. Even lean meat and chicken can contribute too much fat to your diet. The protein they provide can be obtained as easily by eating grains and beans instead, which contain little fat.

YOU TRY IT!

Draw a diagram that shows the proportions of the different nutrients in your diet. How does your diet compare to what is recommended for a healthful diet?

HOW IT WORKS

HOW DOES A MICROWAVE OVEN COOK FOOD?

Suppose you come home from school one afternoon and want to have a snack. In the freezer, you find a frozen pizza that can be cooked in either a regular gas or electric oven. Or, the pizza can be cooked in a microwave oven instead. If you use the microwave, the pizza will be done in a fraction of the time it takes in the gas oven. How does the microwave oven work?

A microwave oven produces microwaves. Microwaves are a kind of electromagnetic radiation, like visible light and radio waves. Like radio waves, microwaves cannot be seen. They can, however, be reflected off metal surfaces. For this reason, the doors of microwave ovens have metal grids inserted in them. The microwaves bounce off the grid and back into the oven, where they cook the food. Without the grid, the microwaves would pass through the glass of the oven door and not be of much use

for cooking. The metal grid also acts as a protective shield that helps to prevent microwaves from striking you.

Only substances that contain water are affected by the microwave energy. That is why glass and ceramic containers stay cool in a microwave. They have no water molecules in them.

When the microwaves strike the food, however, they cause the water molecules in the food to vibrate very quickly. This rapid vibration produces heat, and the water in the food actually boils. Thus, the food literally cooks

YOU TRY IT!

Obtain some prepackaged microwave popcorn and prepare it according to the directions. When it is finished cooking, open the bag carefully. Notice that steam comes out when you open the package. Where does the steam come from? Explain your answer in terms of how a microwave works.

from the inside out. Conventional gas and electric ovens, on the other hand, cook food by raising the temperature — from the outside in.

Reviewing Main Ideas

1. Nutrients are the chemical substances in foods that your body uses as the material for growth and repair and as fuel to release the energy it needs. The six types of nutrients your body needs are carbohydrates, fats, proteins, vitamins, minerals, and water.

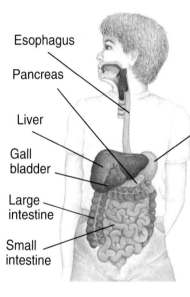

Esophagus

Pancreas

Liver

Gall bladder

Large intestine

Small intestine

Stomach

2. Your digestive system is a long, complex tube that begins at your mouth and ends at your anus. Along the way, nutrients are mechanically and chemically broken down.

3. Absorption is an important part of the digestive process. It is through the villi that nutrients pass into the bloodstream, to be delivered to individual cells throughout the body.

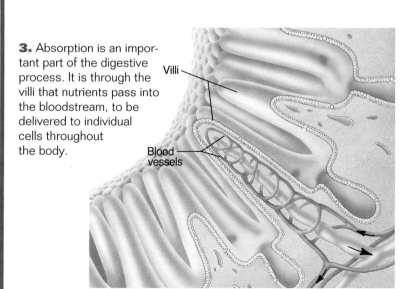

Villi

Blood vessels

4. Your body has a well-designed system for taking in food, digesting it, and removing waste efficiently. This balanced system keeps your body functioning healthfully. Improper amounts of particular nutrients in the diet can lead to diseases such as osteoporosis and goiter.

Chapter Review

USING KEY SCIENCE TERMS

digestion   peristalsis
enzymes   villi
minerals   vitamins
nutrients

For each set of terms below, explain the relationship that exists.

1. nutrients, vitamins, minerals
2. digestion, enzymes
3. nutrients, villi
4. digestion, peristalsis
5. enzymes, nutrients

UNDERSTANDING IDEAS

Choose the best answer to complete each sentence.

1. Which of the following is not a nutrient?
   a. carbohydrates   **c.** water
   b. enzymes   **d.** vitamins
2. Which of these is an inorganic molecule?
   a. carbohydrate   **c.** protein
   b. fat   **d.** mineral
3. Which of the following results in the body maintaining proper water balance?
   a. homeostasis   **c.** enzyme action
   b. peristalsis   **d.** digestion
4. Salt is an example of which of the following?
   a. protein   **c.** carbohydrate
   b. mineral   **d.** enzyme

5. As food moves through your digestive system, which of the following will it encounter first?
   a. villi   **c.** stomach
   b. small intestine   **d.** esophagus

Answer the following questions.

6. What three chemicals are largely responsible for chemical digestion?
7. What is peristalsis?
8. What happens to the starch in a slice of wheat bread as you begin to chew it?
9. What role do bacteria play in digestion?
10. Why are vitamins absorbed more readily by your body than are carbohydrates?

CRITICAL THINKING

Use your understanding of the concepts developed in the chapter to answer each of the following questions.

1. Describe the portions of the digestive process that take place in the mouth.
2. Sugar, in the form of glucose, is the essential form from which energy is released in your cells. Yet, you could survive without ever eating sugar itself. How is this possible?
3. Describe how the huge surface area of the villi are an advantage in the process of digestion.

4. Explain how people who are vegetarians can get the right amounts of protein in their diets without the use of meat.

5. Look at the chart. It gives some of the nutritional information on a box of frozen lasagna. Using this information, calculate what percentage of the calories in this dish comes from fat. Then explain whether or not this lasagna is a healthful food choice.

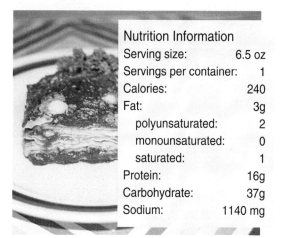

Nutrition Information	
Serving size:	6.5 oz
Servings per container:	1
Calories:	240
Fat:	3g
polyunsaturated:	2
monounsaturated:	0
saturated:	1
Protein:	16g
Carbohydrate:	37g
Sodium:	1140 mg

6. Vitamins B and C dissolve in water. How should vegetables containing these vitamins be cooked to preserve as much of the vitamins as possible?

PROBLEM SOLVING

Read the following problem and discuss your answers in a brief paragraph.

Imagine you're lost in Death Valley, California. All you can see for miles in any direction are cacti, ant hills, an occasional gopher hole, and the glare of the hot sun. It could be weeks before you're found. How will you survive? How will you meet your body's needs for energy, water, protein, minerals, and vitamins?

CONNECTING IDEAS

Discuss each of the following in a brief paragraph.

1. How do your muscles enable your digestive system to accomplish its job?

2. What role does your circulatory system play in the process of digestion?

3. What happens when nutrients obtained through digestion are delivered to individual cells?

4. PHYSICS CONNECTION Explain why a small animal might eat more food per gram of body mass than a large animal.

5. SCIENCE AND SOCIETY Describe how the agricultural method of crop rotation can protect the environment.

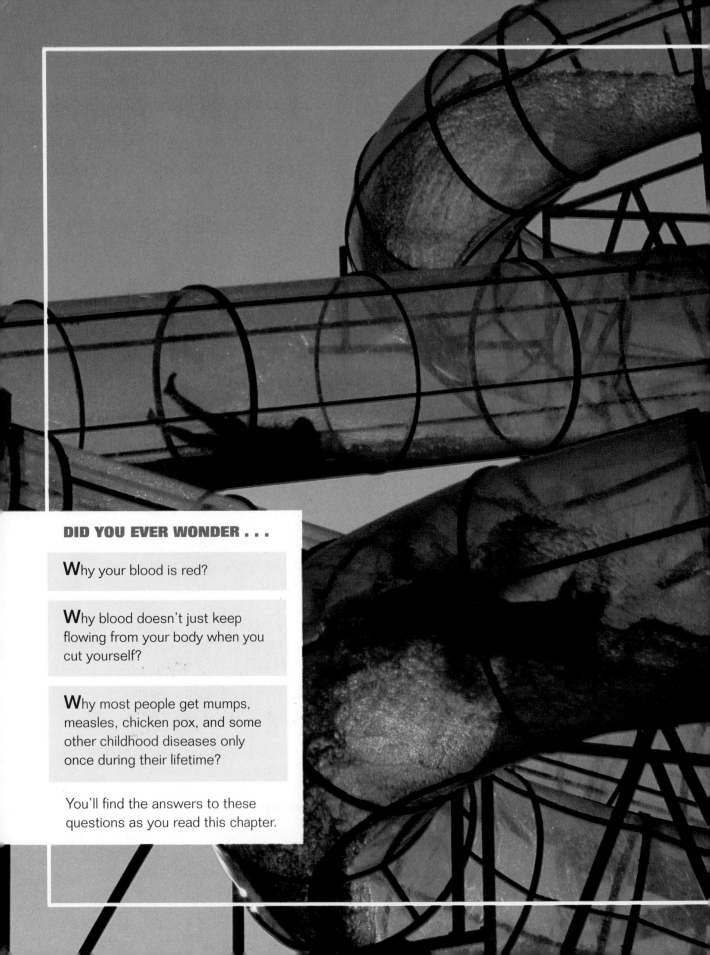

DID YOU EVER WONDER . . .

Why your blood is red?

Why blood doesn't just keep flowing from your body when you cut yourself?

Why most people get mumps, measles, chicken pox, and some other childhood diseases only once during their lifetime?

You'll find the answers to these questions as you read this chapter.

Blood: Transport and Protection

magine you could shrink yourself to the size of the period at the end of this sentence and go sailing through your body's blood vessels. Riding down a water slide is similar to the twisting and turning travels of a blood cell inside a blood vessel. At this very moment, blood pumping through your blood vessels behaves very much like the water that rapidly propels you through a narrow passageway in the waterslide. Just as rushing water surrounds and carries you along, solid particles move in a liquid through your arteries and veins propelled by the beating of your heart.

In this chapter, you will learn about the liquid and solid parts that make up your blood. You will also come to understand how your blood acts as a natural defense system to protect your body from disease.

EXPLORE!

How much blood is in your body right now?

Generally, blood makes up about eight percent of your body's total mass. Figure out your total body mass by multiplying your weight in pounds by 0.45. This will give you your body weight in kilograms. After you calculate your body weight, you will then have to find eight percent of that figure. The answer will be your body's mass of blood in kilograms.

13-1 Blood: Transporter of Life

OBJECTIVES

In this section, you will
- describe how blood transports substances within living organisms;
- describe plasma, red and white blood cells, and hemoglobin in the blood and explain their functions.

KEY SCIENCE TERMS

plasma
red blood cells
hemoglobin
white blood cells

BLOOD

In the Explore activity, you may have discovered that the amount of blood in a person's body depends on the size of the individual. Although we have varying amounts of blood in our bodies, we all need it to survive and to maintain good health. In fact, blood is one of the most accurate indicators of your health. That is why a blood test is a vital part of a good physical exam. It tells your doctor much about the condition of your body and its systems.

Blood, shown in Figure 13-1, is a tissue consisting of cells, cell fragments, and liquid. Blood has many impor-

FIGURE 13-1. Human blood has three main components: red and white cells, platelets, and plasma.

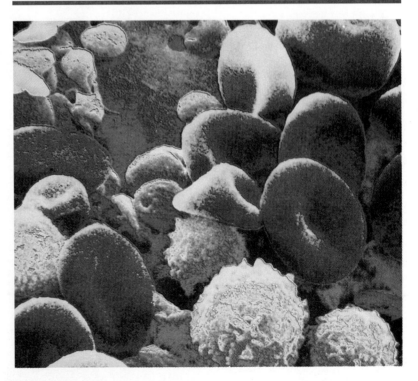

tant functions and plays a part in every major activity of your body. It functions like the highway system that nurtures your community. In the same way the highway system takes goods into, and transports wastes out of your community, blood supplies and renews the community of cells that work together to make up your body.

Just as water in a waterslide is continuously pumped to transport you through its chutes, you have a heart that recirculates blood to keep it moving throughout your body. If the amount of water and the pressure in the slide decreases, you may stop moving. Similarly, your blood is moved out of your heart in a continuous fashion so that the materials your body needs for survival can be transported to all parts of the body. This is critical to your health. If the heart, brain, and other vital organs do not receive oxygen that is carried by blood, they can become permanently damaged.

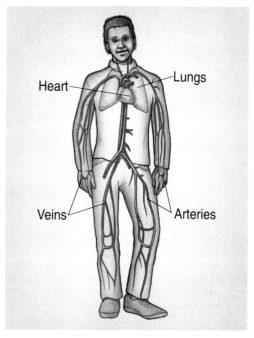

FIGURE 13-2. The heart is the pump that drives blood through a network of vessels to all the cells in the body.

THE FUNCTIONS OF BLOOD

You have learned that the cells of most organisms need nutrients and oxygen to release energy for work. One-celled organisms get nutrients and oxygen directly from their environment. Cytoplasm streams around inside of them so their bodies do not need an elaborate system to move nutrients and waste products. Certain many-celled organisms, such as jellyfish and sponges, do not have blood either. In these animals, food and oxygen diffuse directly from their watery environment through the outer cells and into their inner body layers. The majority of many-celled organisms, however, contain a complex circulatory system with blood that performs many of the same jobs as human blood.

As you just learned, many simple animals get their food and oxygen directly from their environment, such as the ocean. Our blood on the other hand, provides us with an inner ocean. Let's take a close look at the components that make up this vital fluid tissue.

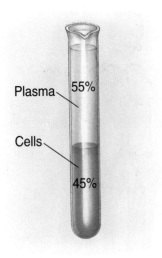

Plasma — 55%

Cells — 45%

FIGURE 13-3. Over half of your blood is made up of plasma.

Plasma

Blood is a tissue made of red and white blood cells, platelets, and plasma. As you see in Figure 13-3, about 55 percent of your blood is made up of plasma. **Plasma** is the liquid part of blood and consists mostly of water. The following Explore will give you an idea of how this complex fluid is constructed.

EXPLORE!

What substances make up your blood?
You can make a model of blood using cooking oil, water, and red food coloring. In a test tube, pour 5 mL of cooking oil into 5 mL of water. Then add a drop of red food coloring. Put a stopper in the tube and shake it. Allow the liquids to separate. How many layers do you see?

In the Explore activity, you made a red-colored liquid that settled into two distinctly different substances. Why did this happen? Think back to when you studied density. Remember that less dense substances float on more dense substances. The oil portion of the liquid you used in the Explore activity represents the plasma in your blood in that it floated to the top. From your observations, which of the materials that make up your blood is the least dense?

Just as droplets of food coloring were suspended in the oil, red and white blood cells and platelets are suspended in plasma as it moves through your circulatory system.

Dissolved nutrients, minerals, and oxygen are also contained in plasma. As you learned in Chapter 12, dissolved nutrients from the digestive system are transported to all body cells by blood. Blood flows in capillaries to body cells, where the oxygen, nutrients, and minerals diffuse through the capillary walls into the body cells. There, oxygen combines in mitochondria with nutrients, releasing energy that powers the cell. The energy is used by the cell for life processes, to repair itself, and in some cases, to reproduce itself. These processes produce waste products. Wastes diffuse from the cell through the capillary wall and back into the blood. There, they are carried away for disposal in the kidneys and lungs.

As you can see, a constantly flowing blood supply is important to all parts of the body. The force that moves the blood through the system is pressure produced by the pumping of the heart. In order for the heart's pressure to be transmitted throughout the circulatory system, the system must be completely filled. If injury or disease causes a major loss of blood, pressure is lost. Blood cannot move to where it is needed. As a result, cells throughout the body will begin to die. This is why emergency medical technicians inject plasma into a bleeding accident victim.

Plasma also carries various chemical substances called hormones from one part of the body to another. Hormones regulate a variety of body functions, such as growth or the way the body uses food.

Now that you've learned about some of the liquid portion of blood, let's look at some of the cells that are present.

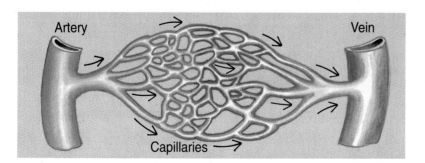

FIGURE 13-4. Nutrients and oxygen are exchanged for waste products as blood passes through capillaries in body tissues.

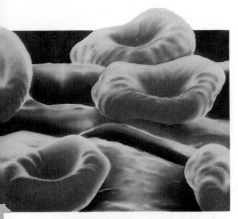

FIGURE 13-5. Red blood cells have a unique disk shape.

FIGURE 13-6. A cut vessel shows an escaping red blood cell.

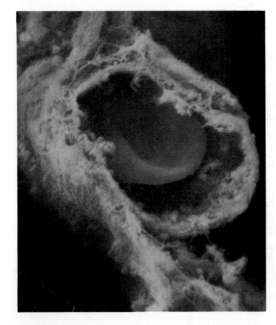

Red Blood Cells

While the liquid portion of the blood carries carbohydrates, fats, proteins, and amino acids and transmits the pressure that moves everything along, you could not live without the cell portion of blood.

The most numerous type of cell in whole blood is the red blood cell, pictured in Figure 13-5. One cubic millimeter of blood, a drop about the size of a dull pencil point, has more than five million red blood cells! The main function of **red blood cells** is to carry oxygen from the lungs to all body cells.

Red blood cells are formed in the marrow of long bones. When a red blood cell first forms, it contains a nucleus like other cells. However, as the cell develops in bone marrow, it fills with hemoglobin. The hemoglobin forces the nucleus and other cell structures out of the cell. As a result, mature red blood cells lack a nucleus.

Red blood cells are shaped somewhat like donuts without a hole but with a flat, thin area in the center. This adaptation makes a red blood cell quite flexible. This flexibility seems to enable the cell to squeeze through even the narrowest capillary.

Did you know that you have something in common with rusty old cans? Rust, which is iron oxide, forms when iron comes in contact with oxygen. Red blood cells contain **hemoglobin**, a red, iron-containing pigment that gives them their color. When blood moves through the lungs, oxygen attaches to the iron part of hemoglobin in red blood cells. The red blood cells then move to other parts of the body where hemoglobin releases the oxygen load and it diffuses into body cells. The body cells use the oxygen to release energy from nutrients such as carbohydrates and fats. What advantage might the lack of a nucleus give red blood cells?

Carbon dioxide, the resulting waste made by this activity, diffuses into the blood. Red blood cells and plasma then carry carbon dioxide on a pathway, first to the heart, then to the lungs. There, carbon dioxide diffuses into the alveoli and is exhaled.

White Blood Cells

In contrast to red blood cells, there are only about five to ten thousand white blood cells in a cubic millimeter of blood. This means that for every 500 red cells in your blood, you will find only one white cell! That is quite a difference, isn't it? Is their function different from red blood cells?

White blood cells, like the one you see in Figure 13-7, fight bacteria, viruses, and other foreign substances that constantly try to invade your body. Your body responds to infections by increasing its number of white blood cells. In the next section, you will learn more about how white blood cells destroy the invading bacteria, virus, or foreign substance.

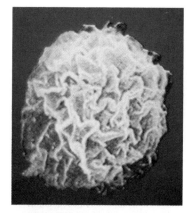

FIGURE 13-7. White blood cells defend your body against invading bacteria and viruses.

Platelets

Figure 13-8 shows what blood looks like under a microscope. You can see in this photo that blood contains tiny, irregularly shaped cell fragments called platelets. While a red blood cell may live up to 120 days, the life span of a platelet is only about 5 to 9 days. Yet, in this short time, platelets play an important role in healing wounds to keep your body free from disease. You will learn more about how platelets accomplish this later in this chapter.

In this section, you have learned that blood is made up of several different components. Do you think that blood from all vertebrates contains these same components? Investigate to find the answer to this question.

DID YOU KNOW?

In contrast to humans, the blood of insects does not contain an oxygen-carrying substance like hemoglobin. Insect blood may be green, yellow, or even colorless, but almost never red. If you smack a mosquito and see red, it's your own blood you're looking at!

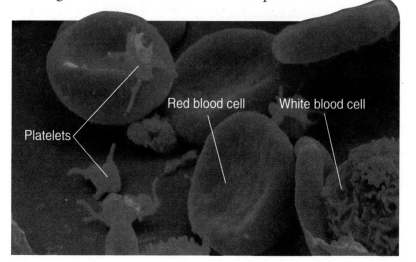

Platelets

Red blood cell   White blood cell

FIGURE 13-8. Platelets are cell fragments that play a role in healing wounds.

I N V E S T I G A T E !

Textbooks often include illustrations of human blood cells when describing blood tissue. For this reason, we usually think that all blood cells look alike. In this activity, you will compare and contrast blood cells from several different vertebrates.

PROBLEM
Do blood cells of vertebrates differ?

MATERIALS
prepared microscope slides of human blood and blood of two other vertebrates (fish, frog, bird, reptile)
microscope

PROCEDURE
1. Copy the data table .
2. Under low power, **observe** the prepared slide of human blood.
3. Locate and examine the red blood cells under high power.

DATA AND OBSERVATIONS

VERTEBRATE TYPE	BLOOD CELL TYPE	DESCRIPTION	NUMBER IN FIELD	DRAWING
HUMAN	Red			
	White			
	Platelets			
BIRD	Red			
	White			
	Platelets			
FROG	Red			
	White			
	Platelets			

4. Draw, count, and describe the red blood cells.
5. Move the slide to another position. Find one or two white blood cells. The nuclei will be blue or purple due to the stain.
6. Record the information about white cells in your data table.
7. Still using high power, examine the slide for very small fragments that are blue. These are platelets.
8. **Record** the information about platelets in your data table.
9. Follow Steps 2 through 8 for each of the other two slides of vertebrate blood.

ANALYZE
1. Which type of blood cells are present in the greatest number in your samples?
2. **Compare and contrast** the red blood cells, white blood cells, and platelets of the other vertebrates to the human cells.

CONCLUDE AND APPLY
3. **Interpret** your data to tell if each vertebrate has all three cell and cell fragment components.
4. **Going Further**: What might you **infer** about the ability of different red blood cells to carry oxygen? Explain your answer.

You can see from the results of the Investigate that blood in different vertebrates is similar in that it contains certain basic components. All of the vertebrate blood you examined contained red blood cells, white blood cells, and platelets.

You probably also noticed that the shape of each type of cell or fragment was similar. What do you think this tells you about how these parts function in other animals? These similarities may show an evolutionary relationship or that all vertebrates have similar needs. Birds, frogs, and other animals require oxygen, face disease and infection, and get injured, like yourself.

In this section, you have learned that the different components of blood have different functions. Plasma transports nutrients, minerals, and oxygen to all the cells in your body. It delivers waste products produced by the cells to other organs, such as the lungs or kidneys, where they are eliminated. Red blood cells transport oxygen that body cells use for energy release. They then deliver small amounts of carbon dioxide to the lungs where it is exhaled. White blood cells help the body to fight disease and infection, while platelets help to heal wounds.

In the next section, you will further understand how these different parts of blood help your body fight infections and heal wounds.

FIGURE 13-9. The blood of other vertebrates also contains structures to carry oxygen and fight disease.

SKILLBUILDER

COMPARING AND CONTRASTING
Compare and contrast red blood cells, white blood cells, and platelets in human blood. Consider the following about each type of cell: its size, its shape, and its function. Also, tell which type of cell is present in the greatest and least numbers in the blood. If you need help, refer to the **Skill Handbook** on page 685.

Check Your Understanding

1. Describe the characteristics and functions of red blood cells and plasma.
2. Explain how white blood cells differ from red blood cells.
3. **APPLY:** Predict what would happen to your tissues if red blood cells and plasma did not pick up and eliminate carbon dioxide from your cells.

13-2 Blood: The Body's Defense

SEALING THE LEAKS

Your skin is your body's first line of defense against potentially harmful invading bacteria. Because of this, your body works quickly to plug up and seal off cuts in your skin. Think back to the last time you cut your finger or scraped an elbow. The wound stopped bleeding after a short time didn't it? Later a scab formed over the wound. How did your cut stop bleeding? How did the scab form?

A cut stops bleeding due to the action of platelets in your blood. **Platelets** are cell fragments that stop the flow of blood from a broken blood vessel. When you cut yourself, you tear open numerous capillaries. Blood in these vessels begins to flow out through the opening in your skin, like water out of a leaking garden hose. But unlike a hose, you know from experience that the flow of blood usually stops fairly quickly. Platelets in your blood act to prevent serious bleeding. How do platelets stop the bleeding?

The process by which a broken blood vessel seals off is called **clotting**. Soon after a blood vessel is cut, platelets begin sticking to the vessel walls and to one another.

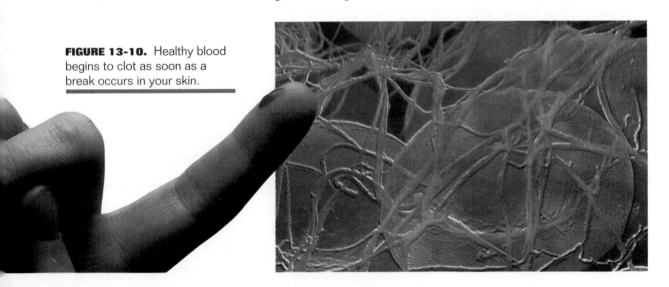

FIGURE 13-10. Healthy blood begins to clot as soon as a break occurs in your skin.

In the process, the platelets release chemicals. When these chemicals react with substances in the plasma, sticky fibers are produced that form a network of threads over the break. Escaping blood cells become trapped in the threads along with the platelets already in place. Over time, this mass of fibers, blood cells, and platelets thickens and dries to form a clot that permanently seals the break. Eventually, as it is exposed to air, the clot hardens into a scab. Soon the scab is lifted off by the growth of new cells under it.

NATURAL DEFENSES

In addition to your skin and your blood, other body systems maintain your health. The trachea, also called the wind pipe, in your respiratory system is lined with short, hairlike cilia and mucus that trap both harmful and harmless organisms. You expel bacteria that are trapped in the mucus when you cough to clear your throat. But sometimes, bacteria get swallowed. In Chapter 12, you learned that your digestive system contains chemicals that destroy some disease-causing organisms.

Luckily for you, your body is like a well-equipped fortress. Cells, blood, organs, and body systems all work together to fight bacteria. All of these structures are part of your immune system. The immune system, pictured in Figure 13-11, is a complex group of defenses that work to fight disease in your body.

Millions of helpful bacteria live on your skin and give you your first line of defense by killing many harmful types of bacteria. Nevertheless, disease-causing bacteria can enter your body through breaks in your skin. Even then, your body is not defenseless. Your body mobilizes a series of defenses against disease-causing intruders.

Let's find out what kind of challenge your immune system meets every day in a location where you spend quite a bit of time.

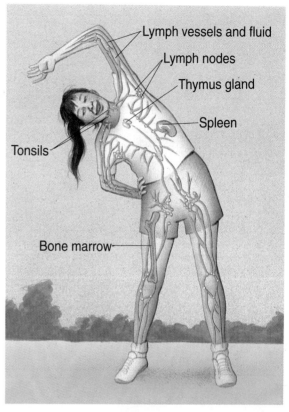

Lymph vessels and fluid
Lymph nodes
Thymus gland
Spleen
Tonsils
Bone marrow

FIGURE 13-11. The immune system is a group of organs and body structures that help fight disease.

What kinds of organisms
live in your classroom?

You share your classroom with thousands of organisms, some of which are bacteria and fungi. You can collect some of these organisms by placing an open petri dish of agar in the classroom. After one hour, place a lid on the dish and have your teacher incubate it in a warm, dark place for two days. After several days, inspect the unopened dish. **CAUTION**: *Do not open the petri dish.*

Conclude and Apply
1. Did the contents of the dish change at all?
2. Use a magnifying glass to get a closer look at the contents of the dish. Describe what you see on the agar.

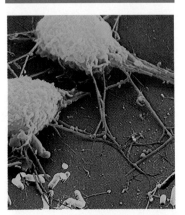

FIGURE 13-12. Invading bacteria are surrounded and destroyed by white blood cells.

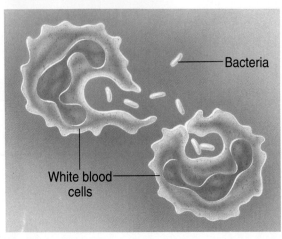

Bacteria

White blood cells

Most of the organisms that grew in your petri dish are not harmful. Humans and most bacteria have learned to peacefully coexist. However, there are a few bacteria that can be real trouble when they get inside your body. These disease-causing bacteria are a major focus of the immune system.

When disease-causing bacteria attack body cells, your immune system springs into action. Blood carries white blood cells to the site of the attack. Constantly on guard, white blood cells patrol the body, slipping between cells in the capillary wall when signaled chemically to attack bacteria and other invaders that threaten your health. White blood cells send out tendril-like extensions that surround and digest invading bacteria, as shown in Figure 13-12.

This is a real battle for survival and some white blood cells don't survive. Have you ever had pus ooze from a wound? If so, you saw the result of this battle. The pus was actually the remains of dead white blood cells, dead bacteria, and damaged body cells.

All of the functions of your immune system are general defenses that are on guard to keep you disease-free. But they don't always work, and you can get sick. Fortunately, your body has other lines of defense in the form of active and passive immunity.

SPECIFIC DEFENSES

When your body fights disease, it is really battling proteins or chemicals that don't belong in your system. Proteins and chemicals that are foreign to your body are called **antigens**. A healthy immune system responds to an antigen, by forming a specific substance to fight that antigen. The substance that forms to fight the antigen is called an antibody. **Antibodies** are substances produced in response to specific antigens. Antibodies are produced on the surface of certain kinds of white blood cells. Your blood carries these antibodies to the site of the antigens. Figure 13-13 shows in a simplified way how each antibody binds with an antigen, making it harmless.

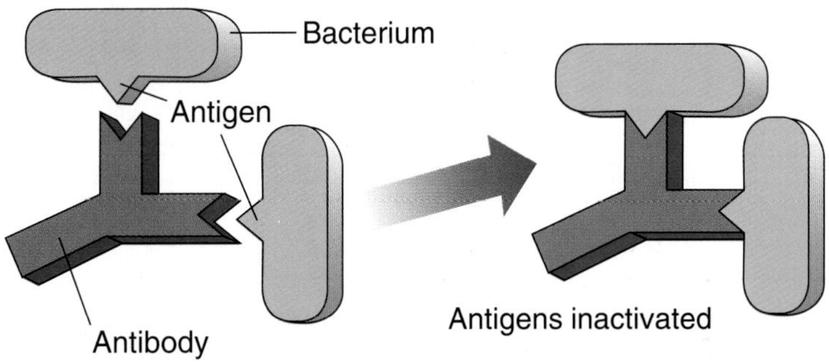

Once you produce a specific antibody to defend against a particular antigen, your body is said to be immune, or protected against the harmful effects of that disease-causing substance. When this happens, you have an **immunity** to that antigen.

FIGURE 13-13. Antibodies lock on to invading antigens and render them harmless.

Antibodies help build immunities that defend against diseases in two ways, actively and passively. Active immunity occurs when your body makes its own antibodies in response to an antigen. Passive immunity occurs when antibodies produced by another source are introduced into your body.

Active Immunity

The person in Figure 13-14 (a) has chicken pox. His body has been invaded by an antigen. You cannot see it, but his immune system has started to make antibodies. Once enough antibodies have formed to defeat the antigen, his health will be restored. These antibodies will stay in his blood long after the antigen has been destroyed. If the antigen enters his body again, the cells making antibodies

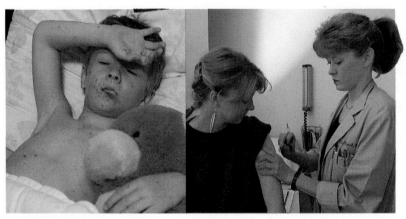

FIGURE 13-14. The body produces antibodies after an illness or in response to a vaccination.

again become active. In this way, his body has developed an active immunity to a particular disease such as chicken pox.

Another way to develop active immunity to a certain disease is to introduce a dead or weakened form of the antigen to the body. This causes the body to produce antibodies. The introduction of an antigen into the body by inoculation or through the mouth is called a vaccination. Figure 13-14 shows a vaccine being administered. A **vaccine** gives you active immunity against a specific disease without you having to get the disease first. For example, suppose you receive a vaccine for measles. The vaccine causes your body to form antibodies against the measles antigen. If the antigen later enters your body, antibodies that can destroy it are already available in your bloodstream. The antigens are destroyed before they have a chance to break down your body's immune system and cause illness.

However, a vaccine for measles will not protect you against the mumps. Mumps are caused by an antigen different from the antigen that causes measles. Even some diseases that are called by the same name, such as influenza (flu), change rapidly, and last year's flu antibodies will probably not protect you against this year's strain of the flu.

Passive Immunity

Passive immunity is similar to active immunity because both are the result of the work of antibodies in the body. However, in passive immunity, the body gets antibodies from another source. The body does not make these antibodies. Antibodies produced by another human or animal are injected into the body.

For example, when you were born, you were a bundle of passive immunity because you were born with all the antibodies that your mother had in her blood. These antibodies moved through the placenta from her blood to yours. However, they stayed with you only a few months. Passive immunity does not last as long as active immunity because the antibodies gradually disappear. Newborn babies lose their passive immunity in a few months. Then they are vaccinated to develop their own immunity, or they are injected with antibodies from another source.

You probably were once injected by a doctor or nurse with antibodies to a disease called tetanus. If the antibodies are still present in your body, you have a passive immunity. Tetanus toxin is produced by a bacterium in soil and can enter your body through a cut or puncture wound. The toxin paralyzes muscles and can cause death by suffocation if the muscles that control breathing become paralyzed. Figure 13-15 shows that tetanus antitoxin is produced in horses when they respond to injections of the tetanus antigen.

FIGURE 13-15. A horse produces antitoxin after being injected with the tetanus antigen. This antitoxin is then used to protect people against tetanus.

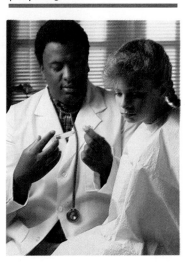

When you receive a tetanus shot, antibodies made by horses are injected into your body. These antibodies provide you with limited immunity. Throughout your life, periodic booster shots keep you immune to the tetanus antigen. Unfortunately, you cannot be immunized against some of the most common diseases such as the common cold. Let's find out why.

COMMUNICABLE DISEASES

The last time you had a cold or the flu, you probably felt miserable. Your symptoms very likely included body aches, watery eyes, congested lungs, and a runny nose. Eventually, after a few days of rest, your symptoms disappeared. Using what you have learned about antibodies and antigens, describe what was happening in your body the last time you got one of these diseases. Why did you get sick in the first place?

FIND OUT!

How do agents that cause disease spread?

Work with a partner. Place a drop of peppermint or lemon food flavoring on a cotton ball. Rub the cotton ball in the shape of an X over the palm of your right hand and let it dry. Can you smell the flavoring? Dry your hands on a towel. Now, shake hands with a classmate.

Conclude and Apply

1. How do you know if the flavoring has been passed to your classmate?
2. What does this tell you about how some diseases are spread?

As you found out in the Find Out, things in your environment can be picked up and passed very easily. Some of the more common things in your environment are viruses.

Colds are caused by viruses. Viruses are not bacteria. In fact there has been debate over whether they are alive or not. Viruses seem to be mostly DNA or RNA and must be inside a living cell to reproduce. When viruses reproduce, they produce thousands of copies of themselves and frequently destroy the host cell.

Viruses can be passed from person to person. When a person suffering with a cold coughs or sneezes, he or she releases small droplets containing the virus into the air. When you breathe in, you stand a good chance of inhaling some of these airborne problems. Some of the droplets also land on objects. If you don't wash your hands after they have come in contact with a contaminated object, you may also pick up the virus, which you can then pass with a handshake.

A cold is an example of a communicable disease, one that is spread, or transmitted, from one organism to another. Viruses are only one kind of agent that causes a communicable disease. Disease-causing bacteria, protists, and fungi also cause communicable diseases. Table 13-1 identifies some diseases caused by these agents.

Communicable diseases can be spread through water and air, on food, by contact with contaminated objects, and by animals such as mosquitoes and rats. Each time you turn a doorknob or press the button on a water fountain at school, your skin comes in contact with bacteria and viruses, most of which won't harm you. To help prevent the spread of disease-causing organisms, however, water systems and swimming pools are treated with chlorine.

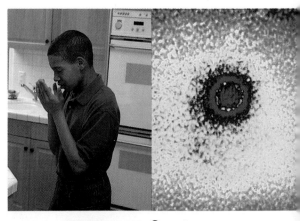

FIGURE 13-16. Sneezing or coughing can spread viruses through airborne particles.

TABLE 13-1. Diseases and Their Agents

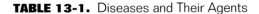

Bacteria	Protists	Fungi	Viruses
Tetanus	Malaria	Ringworm	Colds
Bacterial pneumonia	Sleeping sickness	Athlete's foot	Viral pneumonia
Typhoid fever			AIDS
Pink eye			Measles
Tuberculosis			Mumps
Plague			Influenza

13-2 STOPPING THE SPREAD OF COMMUNICABLE DISEASES

This activity will help you understand how simple measures of cleanliness can help prevent the spread of infection by microorganisms.

PROBLEM

What effect does cleaning have on the spread of disease?

MATERIALS

6 fresh apples
rotting apple
6 sealable plastic bags
labels and pencil
alcohol
paper towels
sandpaper
cotton ball
soap and water

PROCEDURE

1. Copy the data table.
2. Label the bags 1 through 6.
3. Seal a fresh apple in bag 1. Label it *Fresh.*
4. Rub the rotting apple over the entire surface of the remaining 5 apples. The rotting apple is your source of disease-causing organisms. **CAUTION:** *Always wash your hands*

DATA AND OBSERVATIONS

APPLE #	HYPOTHESIS	APPEARANCE OF APPLE AFTER 1 WEEK
1		
2		
3		
4		
5		
6		

after handling disease causing organisms.

5. Put one of the apples in bag 2 and label it *Contaminated.*
6. Drop one apple to the floor from a height of about 2 meters. Put this apple into bag 3 and label it *Contaminated—2 Meter Drop.*
7. Rub one of the apples with sandpaper. Place this apple in bag 4 and label it *Contaminated—Sandpaper.*
8. Wash one of the apples with soap and water. Dry the apple well with a paper towel. Put this apple in bag 5 and label it *Contaminated—Washed.*
9. Use a cotton ball to spread alcohol all over the last apple. Let the apple air-dry and place it in bag 6. Label it *Contaminated—Alcohol.*
10. Place the apples in a dark

place. Wash your hands. Leave the apples undisturbed for a week.
11. **Predict** what you think will happen to each apple.
12. At the end of the week, **compare** the apples. Record your observations in the data table. **CAUTION:** *Give all apples to your teacher for proper disposal.*

ANALYZE

1. **Observe** and **compare** any changes in the apples.
2. Share your findings with other students. What was the purpose of each apple?

CONCLUDE AND APPLY

3. What effect does cleaning have on the spread of disease?
4. **Going Further:** Why is it important that people who work in restaurants wash their hands before leaving a restroom?

Koch's Postulates

Discovering which particular virus or bacteria causes a particular disease can be difficult. It was a German doctor, Robert Koch, who developed a set of rules used for figuring out which organism caused a particular disease. These rules, called Koch's Postulates, stated that:

1. In every case of a particular disease, the organism thought to be the cause must be found to be present.

2. The organism has to be separated from all others and grown in a pure culture.

3. The organism from the pure culture must cause a healthy test subject to get the disease when it is injected into the subject.

4. The organism must be removed from the test subject and cultured again and compared with the original organism to see if they are identical. If they are, then the organism has been identified as the cause of the disease.

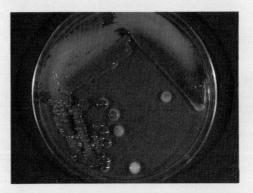

SEXUALLY TRANSMITTED DISEASES

You've seen how diseases can be passed from person to person by contact with contaminated objects. Some of the most serious diseases are those transmitted by sexual contact. Diseases transmitted from person to person during sexual contact are called sexually transmitted diseases, or STDs.

Genital herpes is an example of a STD. It causes small, painful blisters on the genitals. The herpes virus hides in the body for long periods and then reappears suddenly. There is no cure for herpes, and there is no vaccine to prevent it.

Gonorrhea and syphilis are two other common STDs. The main symptoms of gonorrhea are genital irritation and discharge. Figure 13-17 shows the bacteria that cause gonorrhea. The bacteria can be carried and transmitted by both men and women. If the disease is not treated with antibiotic drugs, it can lead to sterility. It can also cause blindness in babies born to an infected mother. Syphilis is a more serious disease that can cause death in later stages if left untreated.

FIGURE 13-17. Gonorrhea is caused by bacteria. Females may not know they are infected.

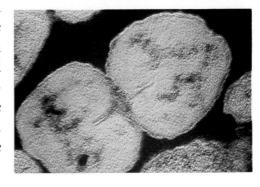

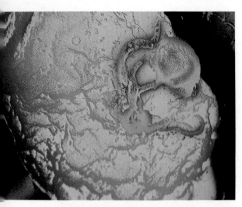

FIGURE 13-18. The AIDS virus destroys lymphocytes, white blood cells that normally protect the body against disease.

SKILLBUILDER

RECOGNIZING CAUSE AND EFFECT
How is not washing your hands, not covering your mouth when you cough, or not covering your nose when you sneeze related to the spread of disease? If you need help, refer to the **Skill Handbook** on page 685.

Sexually transmitted diseases are difficult to treat. For years, penicillin was used to treat syphilis. However, the organism that causes syphilis has become resistant to it.

AIDS AND YOUR IMMUNE SYSTEM

If you listen to the news or read newspapers or magazines, you've undoubtedly heard of AIDS. The abbreviation AIDS stands for Acquired Immune Deficiency Syndrome. It is a disease that was first identified in the early 1980s. Today, millions of people around the world are suffering from AIDS.

AIDS is caused by a virus that attacks cells in your immune system called lymphocytes (LIHM fuh sites). Lymphocytes, shown in Figure 13-18, are white blood cells that normally produce specific antibodies in the presence of antigens, thereby destroying invading antigens. Because the AIDS virus destroys lymphocytes, the body is left with no way to fight invading antigens that cause other diseases. For this reason, most people with AIDS die not from AIDS, but from diseases caused by other microorganisms.

Your immune system is a complex group of defenses that your body has to fight diseases. It is made up of cells, tissues, organs, and body systems that fight bacteria, viruses, and harmful chemicals. When your immune system recognizes a foreign protein or chemical, it forms antibodies that help your body build defenses. While there are many diseases that can be prevented by vaccinations and good health habits, some diseases, like AIDS, cannot. If the AIDS virus destroys the immune system, there is no defense left.

Check Your Understanding

1. What is the platelets' role in healing skin?
2. Explain how skin and blood protect your body from disease-causing organisms.
3. How are active and passive immunity alike? How do they differ?
4. Why is it hard to avoid communicable diseases?
5. **APPLY:** Some vaccinations require booster shots. What would happen if you failed to get your booster shots for a particular disease?

EXPANDING YOUR VIEW

CONTENTS

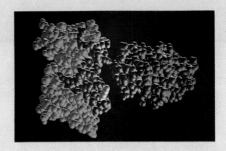

A **CLOSER** LOOK

PRODUCING ANTIBODIES

Disease-causing viruses, bacteria, and parasites are all around you and would be deadly were it not for your immune system. Antibodies, a key part of your immune system, are a group of proteins that circulate in the blood. They are also found in mucus and saliva. A computer-generated model of an antibody molecule is shown in the photograph.

Antibodies are produced in response to antigens — *anti*body *gen*erators. Just about any large molecule, from protein to complex carbohydrate, can be an antigen. For example, protein molecules on the surface of viruses act as antigens. Molecules on the surface of bacteria and parasites also act as antigens. Each kind of antibody recognizes and responds to only one kind of antigen. There are millions of different antigens in the world. How does your body know which antibodies to make? That is the work of B-cells—a type of white blood cell.

Each B-cell contains a different antibody on its surface. There are about two trillion different B-cells in your body at any one time, so the odds are very high that there is a B-cell

antibody to match any antigen you might encounter. When the antibody on the surface of the B-cell meets its matching antigen, it bonds to it. The two fit together perfectly, and antibody production begins.

The B-cell then forms either plasma cells or memory cells. A plasma cell can produce between 3000 and 30,000 antibodies per second and offers short-term protection. Memory cells give you lifelong immunity to certain diseases. Long after the infection is over and the plasma cells have died, memory cells continue to circulate. The next time the same antigen invades, the memory cells immediately start large-scale antibody production. There is no time for an infection to take hold.

WHAT DO YOU THINK?

What memory cells might you have in your blood? Make a list of sicknesses that you have had that you are unlikely to get again. Compare lists with your classmates.

Physics Connection

OXYGEN AND CARBON DIOXIDE TRANSPORT

The average red blood cell contains about 265 million hemoglobin molecules. Because each hemoglobin molecule can carry four oxygen atoms, each red blood cell can carry an enormous amount of oxygen. What makes hemoglobin such a good carrier of oxygen?

As you know, hemoglobin contains iron, which has a strong attraction for oxygen. Ordinarily, iron atoms exposed to the air grab and hold oxygen tightly. Within hemoglobin, however, oxygen attaches to iron very loosely. Under certain conditions, these loosely attached oxygen molecules can be released from the iron.

Whether oxygen is held or released by hemoglobin depends on a property called partial pressure. Partial pressure is the pressure caused by each gas within a mixture of gases.

The air you breathe is a mixture of gases that includes oxygen, nitrogen, and carbon dioxide. At sea level, air pressure is 760 millimeters of mercury. This means that the weight of a column of air will push a column of mercury up a height of 760 millimeters.

Air is only 21 percent oxygen, so only 21 percent of the air pressure—about 160 millimeters of mercury—is caused by oxygen. This amount is the partial pressure of oxygen (PO_2). How does

Blood from heart to lungs (Low PO_2 High PCO_2)

Air in lung (in alveolus)

Blood to heart from lungs (High PO_2 Low PCO_2)

CO_2

O_2

the partial pressure of oxygen affect oxygen transport by hemoglobin? Hemoglobin holds on to oxygen when the partial pressure of oxygen surrounding it is high. When the partial pressure of oxygen is low, hemoglobin lets go of oxygen.

More oxygen molecules are in the lungs than anywhere else in the body, so the partial pressure of oxygen is highest there. Blood passing through lung tissue picks up oxygen easily. As blood flows away from the lungs out to the body, the partial pressure of oxygen begins to decrease. When the blood reaches other parts of the body, where there is much less oxygen, hemoglobin releases the oxygen molecules to the cells.

The transport of carbon dioxide works somewhat differently. Hemoglobin carries only 11 percent of the carbon dioxide in the blood. The rest is carried by blood plasma. Whether the blood is picking up or letting go of carbon dioxide also depends on partial pressure.

In active tissues, the partial pressure of carbon dioxide (PCO_2) is high. Thus, carbon dioxide moves easily and quickly into the blood. In the lungs, the partial pressure of carbon dioxide is much lower, so the carbon dioxide diffuses out of the blood and is exhaled from the lungs.

WHAT DO YOU THINK?

At very high altitudes, the air is thinner, and the air pressure is much lower than at sea level. The lower air pressure can be dangerous for mountain climbers. Experienced climbers usually ascend a high peak over several days to give their bodies time to adjust to the change in air pressure by producing more red blood cells. How does this help the body survive?

SCIENCE AND SOCIETY

HEALTH WORKERS WITH AIDS

What would you do if your family doctor had AIDS? Would you find another doctor? Would you worry about becoming infected?

According to the Centers for Disease Control (CDC) in Atlanta, 6436 health-care workers in the United States have developed AIDS since the early 1980s. More than 46,000 others are estimated to be HIV positive. HIV is the virus that causes AIDS. Yet this is just 0.1 percent of this country's 4.5 million health-care professionals.

Medical experts generally agree that the risks of infection are very small for patients. Many routine procedures, like checkups or blood pressure reading, pose no risk at all because there is no exchange of blood or other body fluids involved in these procedures. Even in surgery, the chances of infection are estimated to be between 1 in 42,000, and 1 in 417,000 when proper precautions are taken.

Ordinary dental care is thought to be more of a concern because there is generally some bleeding in a patient's mouth. Even so, according to the CDC, the risk of being infected with HIV by a dentist is between 1 in 263,000 and 1 in 2,632,000.

However, despite the small risks, many citizens are pressuring politicians at different levels of government to pass laws to require HIV testing for all health-care professionals. Members of some professional medical associations have also supported mandatory testing. Most medical experts oppose such testing. They say that required testing is impractical and expensive. It can be six months from the time a person is infected until the time that he or she produces the antibodies to the virus that show a positive test result. To be reliable, then, workers would have to be tested every six months.

Civil rights groups also oppose mandatory testing. Involuntary testing, they say, violates a person's right to privacy.

The American Medical Association and the American Dental Association have urged members to tell patients if they are HIV positive or if they have AIDS. They also recommend that doctors and dentists should follow procedures that protect their patients from risk. Other experts suggest that health-care workers should discuss the matter privately with their patients.

WHAT DO YOU THINK?

Consider the pros and cons of determining whether health-care workers are HIV infected. Should these workers be required to tell their patients? Their employers? Do patients have an obligation to tell their doctors whether they are HIV infected?

*H*ealth
CONNECTION

VACCINES AND THE DEVELOPING WORLD

Three-quarters of the world's people live in developing countries—in Latin America, the Caribbean, Africa, and Asia. About 86 percent of all births and 96 percent of all infant and child deaths occur in these parts of the world. Many of these deaths are the result of childhood diseases that could be prevented through immunization.

Immunization is a relatively simple and inexpensive process. In developing countries, it is one of the most effective and inexpensive

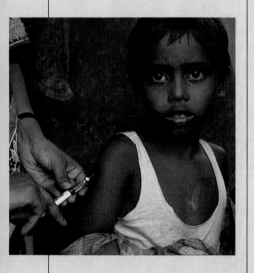

ways to prevent disease. About 60 million children in developing countries are now vaccinated each year against diphtheria, pertussis, tetanus, polio, tuberculosis, and measles. Yet millions more are not immunized. For example, measles alone still kills two million children in developing countries each year.

Part of the problem is the nature of the vaccines themselves. Some vaccines must be kept refrigerated at all times, and refrigeration often is not available. Some vaccines require a series of booster shots spread over several weeks or months. Getting to a clinic can be extremely difficult, so many children do not get completely immunized.

Some experts have recommended that new or improved vaccines be developed specifically for use in developing countries. Such vaccines should not require refrigeration, should be given as close to birth as possible, and should be given in just one dose. Because of the spread of AIDS, vaccines should be simple to give in a way that

YOU TRY IT!

Find out what vaccines you received as a child. Ask your doctor whether any new vaccines are given now that were not available when you were an infant.

does not require an injection.

Although it costs only about $10 per child for immunization, international agencies and health-care workers struggle to find funding for their programs. At the same time, the world's nations spend about $1 trillion a year, or about $200 per person, on defense.

CAREER CONNECTION

Immunologists study diseases of the immune system. They attend college and medical school. They work for hospitals and research institutions, and some are in private practice.

HOW IT WORKS

HOW DO ANTIBIOTICS FIGHT INFECTIONS?

Suppose you wake up one morning with a sore throat, swollen glands, and a fever. You go to the doctor, who prepares a throat culture. The following day the results come back positive—you have strep throat. Your doctor then prescribes an antibiotic. It's not long before you are feeling better, and the infection is gone.

Antibiotics are naturally occurring chemicals produced by microorganisms, like the bacteria in the picture. They kill or limit the growth of other microorganisms. This activity occurs without affecting human cells or tissues and makes these chemicals lifesavers. Until antibiotics came into widespread use, bacterial diseases were a leading cause of death.

The widespread use of antibiotics in medicine was not established until 1927. That's when British scientist Alexander Fleming accidentally discovered that a mold called *Penicillium* had killed some bacteria he was studying in his lab. As you may have guessed, *Penicillium* is responsible for the antibiotic that you might take for a sore throat.

Because antibiotics are produced by microorganisms, scientists can produce these drugs in large quantities by simply encouraging the growth of these organisms.

Antibiotics work in different ways. Some, like penicillin, interfere with a bacterium's ability to repair its cell wall—a rigid, supporting structure. The bacterium then bursts and dies. Other antibiotics prevent

WHAT DO YOU THINK?

You already know that Fleming discovered penicillin accidentally, but did you know that some of the more important antibiotics have been found in rather strange places? For example, the antibiotic *bacitracin* was originally isolated from a patient's skinned knee. Another antibiotic, *streptomycin*, was isolated from bacteria found in the throat of a chicken. Given these examples, where do you think scientists could look in order to develop new antibiotics?

proteins from being made in the bacterium. Proteins are important compounds in cell structures. They also act as enzymes that direct cell functions. A cell cannot survive if it is unable to make proteins.

*H*istory
C O N N E C T I O N

CHARLES RICHARD DREW: BLOOD BANK PIONEER

Many hospitals bear the name of Charles Richard Drew. Read on to find out why!

As a medical student at McGill University in Canada, Drew became interested in blood transfusion. His interest was sparked by the Nobel Prize-winning work of Dr. Karl Landsteiner, who showed that there are four blood types in humans (A, B, AB, or O) and that a transfusion cannot be successful if the recipient and the donor have different types.

Drew saw many patients die from blood loss. Delay was caused by typing a patient's blood, finding donors, and drawing and administering the blood. By then it was often too late. Drew saw the need for blood to be preserved, stored, and ready for use in emergency situations.

Four years after becoming a surgeon, Drew was given money to do research. Between 1938 and 1940, Drew studied how blood and transfusion relate to shock. During shock, a patient's blood pressure drops dramatically and the pulse grows weak. Drew found that patients given adequate amounts of blood during shock had a chance for survival. There was one obstacle—blood was difficult to preserve.

Drew studied the factors that made blood unfit for transfusion and made a pioneering discovery. He found that plasma, the liquid part of the blood without the cells, could be stored for a long time and could be given to any patient, regardless of blood type!

Drew's discovery became very important during World War II. With war raging in England and many wounded, blood supplies were short. Furthermore, hospitals were using different procedures to collect and process blood. As a result, much of the blood became contaminated—and completely useless.

Clearly, something had to be done. So Charles Drew organized what became known as the "Blood for Britain" project.

Drew's blood bank project was so successful that by the end of 1940, Britain no longer needed blood from the United States. So, in 1941, the American Red Cross turned its attention back to the United States. Its goal was to set up a program to collect blood for those American soldiers wounded in the war. Again, Drew led the way!

Throughout his career, Drew was recognized as a pioneer in blood transfusion. He was the first African-American to receive a Doctor of Science degree. In 1950, at the age of 46, Drew was killed in a tragic auto accident. His legacy continues, though, in every blood bank throughout the world—tributes to the brilliance of Dr. Charles Richard Drew.

WHAT DO YOU THINK?

How did Drew's discovery help the American armies during World War II?

Reviewing Main Ideas

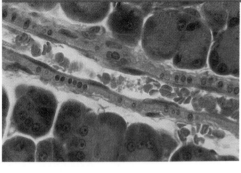

3. Your body can have active or passive immunity to some diseases.

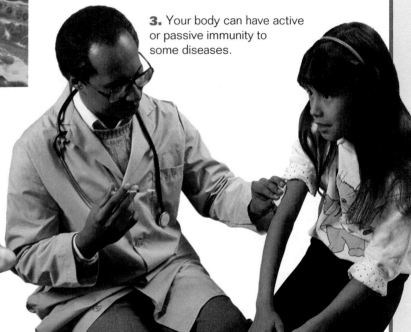

1. The cells and liquid in your blood carry oxygen and nutrients to all body cells and remove carbon dioxide and other wastes.

2. Your skin, blood, and organs work together in the immune system to defend your body from disease. For example, your skin acts as a natural barrier against intruding organisms and viruses.

4. Disease-causing organisms can invade your body, but cleanliness and good health can help fight many communicable diseases.

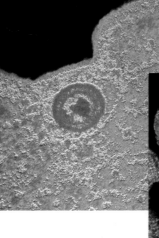

Virus

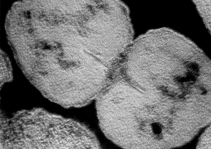

Bacteria

Chapter Review

USING KEY SCIENCE TERMS

antibodies   plasma
antigens   platelets
clotting   red blood cells
hemoglobin   vaccine
immunity   white blood cells

For each set of terms below, explain the relationship that exists.

1. red blood cells, hemoglobin
2. antibodies, antigens
3. clotting, platelets
4. plasma, red blood cells
5. vaccine, antibodies
6. white blood cells, antibodies
7. immunity, antigens

UNDERSTANDING IDEAS

Choose the best answer to complete each sentence.

1. The main job of platelets is to ____.
   a. carry oxygen
   b. clot blood
   c. carry carbon dioxide
   d. produce antibodies

2. Your body reacts to infection by increasing its number of ____.
   a. white blood cells   c. hemoglobin
   b. red blood cells   d. platelets

3. Hemoglobin is found in ____.
   a. platelets   c. white blood cells
   b. red blood cells   d. antibodies

4. Blood transports nutrients and oxygen to your cells and carries away ____.
   a. carbon dioxide
   b. antibodies
   c. platelets
   d. all of these

5. ____ first stick to the sides of a broken blood vessel.
   a. Antibodies
   b. White blood cells
   c. Platelets
   d. Red blood cells

6. One way to gain an active immunity against a certain disease is by ____.
   a. being vaccinated
   b. having the disease
   c. inheriting antibodies
   d. both a and b

7. The AIDS virus attacks ____.
   a. hemoglobin   c. platelets
   b. white blood cells   d. red blood cells

8. An example of an STD is ____.
   a. influenza   c. syphilis
   b. tetanus   d. measles

9. If you were to examine a sample of your blood under a microscope, the structure you would see the greatest number of is ____.
   a. red blood cells   c. white blood cells
   b. platelets   d. antigens

10. A complex group of defenses your body uses to fight disease is the ____.
    a. respiratory system
    b. circulatory system
    c. immune system
    d. digestive system

CRITICAL THINKING

Use your understanding of the concepts developed in the chapter to answer each of the following questions.

1. You had a cold last year. This year you got another cold. What does this indicate about your immune system?

2. If the number of white blood cells in your body increases, what might this mean?

3. Look at the following chart. Would a patient with this blood cell count show any symptoms of illnesses? Explain your answer.

BLOOD CELL COUNTS		
	Number in 1 Cubic Millimeter of Blood	Normal Amount in 1 Cubic Millimeter of Blood
Red Blood Cells	5,000,000	5,000,000
White Blood Cells	9,000	5-10,000

PROBLEM SOLVING

Read the following problem and discuss your answers in a brief paragraph.

You and your younger brother have been invited to a birthday cookout at a friend's house. Your friend's little sister has just come down with chicken pox. You had the disease four years ago but your younger brother has never had the disease. Should you both attend the party? What is likely to happen to you? To your brother?

CONNECTING IDEAS

Discuss each of the following in a brief paragraph.

1. You go to the doctor feeling very tired and run down. The doctor draws blood for tests and takes notes on your vital signs such as blood pressure, breathing, and pulse rates. Later, the doctor says you have a lung infection. What did the blood tests reveal about your white blood cells?

2. How is your diet important to the blood in your body?

3. Where in your body can you find bacteria that don't cause disease?

4. PHYSICS CONNECTION Briefly explain how the partial pressure of oxygen affects oxygen transport by red blood cells.

5. HEALTH CONNECTION Describe some of the reasons why measles kills two million children a year in some countries.

LOOKING BACK ▨▨▨▨▨

UNIT 3
OUR FLUID
ENVIRONMENT

CONTENTS

UNIT FOCUS

In this unit, you investigated how movements of air and water molecules are affected by differences in temperature and density, and by Earth's rotation.

You studied the chemistry of carbon compounds and the chemistry that occurs in your digestive system to break down some of these compounds. Finally, you saw how blood circulates these compounds to all other parts of your body.

Try the exercises and activity that follow—they will challenge you to use and apply some of the ideas you learned in this unit.

CONNECTING IDEAS

1. What is being measured when you obtain a reading of air pressure, water pressure, or blood pressure? How are these readings similar? In what way is a measurement of blood pressure different than the measurements of air or water pressure?

2. Organisms living in the oceans depend on sea water for certain things in order to survive. In a similar way, your cells depend on your blood for some of these same things. Make a list of those things that both sea water and blood provide.

EXPLORING FURTHER

Many people are affected by changes in the weather. Sometimes this is just the inconvenience of dealing with storms, but sometimes changes in weather affect their well-being. Design a research project to study the effects of dark, dreary, rainy days on the moods that people project as related to the moods of these same people on bright, sunny days.

UNIT 4
CHANGES IN LIFE AND EARTH OVER TIME

CONTENTS

UNIT FOCUS

In Unit 3, you learned about the movements of materials on Earth and in your body. In this unit, you will study the movements of continents and the forces that cause them. You will explore the dramatic changes that have occurred on Earth and in its living inhabitants over great spans of time. By studying reproduction and heredity, you'll investigate the processes that make many of the changes in living things possible.

TRY IT

Draw a calendar for the year. Simply use boxes for each month but don't bother with the exact dates. Just include four lines for each month to represent the weeks. Give January, June, September, and December five weeks. You could also use a calendar that has already been prepared. If the entire calendar represents the age of Earth, then each day is about 12.5 million years. Today is December 31st. Mark and label when you think these events took place on your calendar: when the Appalachian Mountains were formed, when dinosaurs first appeared, when the Grand Canyon started to form, and when the American Declaration of Independence was signed. After you have studied this unit, try this activity again and compare your calendars.

DID YOU EVER WONDER . . .

Why you resemble other members of your family?

Why insects, such as bees, are attracted to flowers?

How a single flower makes seeds?

You'll find the answers to these questions as you read this chapter.

Reproduction

A blur of buzzing yellow and black zips by Hector like a miniature B-52 bomber. Its destination? The zinnias beckoning with their bright red and yellow blooms from the Orozcos' flower garden.

Why do bees visit zinnias? They drink the nectar and collect the pollen that zinnias produce. Bees use nectar and pollen for food. While collecting pollen, bees also transfer pollen from one flower to another, helping flowers make seeds and reproduce. Both plants and animals, including human beings, need to reproduce if their species are to survive.

Plants and animals don't reproduce in exactly the same way, of course. But for both, the process almost always begins with the union of a female egg and a male sperm. How does this union take place? How are the egg and the sperm produced? How do insects help plants reproduce? In this chapter, you'll discover the answers as you learn about the life process called reproduction.

EXPLORE!

What's an egg?

An egg may be just breakfast to you, but it is much more to a chicken. Your teacher will provide you with a chicken egg. Look at the physical traits of the egg, such as its size, color, and presence of a shell. What do your observations indicate about the habitat of a chicken? (HINT: Think about where a chicken lives.) Now examine the internal structure of the egg. Break open the chicken egg and pour the contents into a dish. What does the membrane look like? Would this egg have grown into a chicken?

14-1 Sex Cells—A Different Story

THIS IS NOT MITOSIS

Your body contains billions and billions of cells, the basic unit of structure in all living things. Just as whole organisms grow and die, individual cells grow and die. In the short time it takes you to read this paragraph, millions of your cells will die!

How can your body continue to work properly even as millions of its cells are dying? Your body is constantly producing new cells. Even as cells are dying, new cells are being produced at a faster rate. Most of the cells that make up your body, your **body cells,** reproduce exact copies of themselves by mitosis. You may recall that in mitosis, one parent cell forms two identical new cells. The instructions that "tell" a cell how to develop, whether to be a blood cell or skin cell or some other kind of cell, are contained in the cell's chromosomes. All human body cells contain 46 chromosomes. Mitosis produces two new body cells, each with 46 chromosomes, just like the parent cell.

All species of organisms have a certain number of chromosomes in their body cells. This number is the same for all members of the species. For example, a body cell of a dog, whether it is a poodle or a collie, contains 78 chromosomes.

FIGURE 14-1. Human body cells, such as this white blood cell (a) and these skin cells (b), have 46 chromosomes.

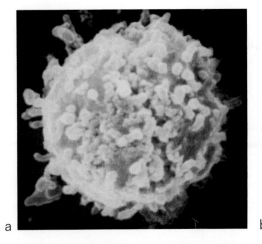

a

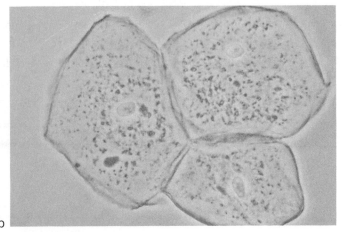

b

FIND OUT!

Does a relationship exist between chromosome number and the complexity of an organism?

In this activity, you will determine whether or not complexity of an organism is related to its chromosome number. List the following organisms according to chromosome number, beginning with the smallest number of chromosomes: grasshopper–24, giant sequoia–22, fruit fly–8, tomato–24, guinea pig–64, goldfish–94, spider plant–24, dog–78, human–46. Next to each, indicate the kingdom each organism is in. Which organisms listed have the same chromosome number? Are these organisms in the same kingdom?

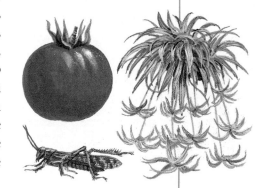

Conclude and Apply

What can you conclude about a relationship between chromosome number and type of organism?

As you saw in the previous activity, there is no relationship between the type of organism and chromosome number. Some plants, such as the spider plant, have the same number of chromosomes as an animal like the grasshopper. These organisms have very little in common. However, all the organisms you studied in the Find Out activity do have this in common—they all produce body cells through mitosis. Body cells are not the only kind of cell in your body, and mitosis is not the only kind of cell reproduction that occurs. In order for many organisms to produce offspring, they must produce special cells called **sex cells.** These cells are formed by a different process. If you are a male, the sex cells your body produces are called **sperm.** If you are a female, the sex cells your body produces are called **eggs.** Offspring may be produced only when a male sex cell and a female sex cell have united. Sex cells play an important role in reproduction. In the next section, you will learn about the process by which sex cells reproduce.

SPERM AND EGGS—
ALIKE AND DIFFERENT

Figures 14-2 and 14-3 show a human sperm and a human egg. As you can see, sex cells are quite different from each other. Look closely at the physical traits of these cells. Sperm have tails and can swim, like tadpoles; eggs cannot. Sperm are very tiny and can be seen only under a microscope; eggs are the only human cells that can be seen with the naked eye. A human egg is about the size of the point of a needle. Eggs contain a food supply in the form of a yolk. Tiny sperm do not.

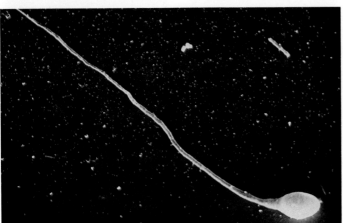

FIGURE 14-2. This human sperm is a male sex cell.

Another way that sperm and eggs differ is in the number produced. A bull can produce as many as five billion sperm at one time. But a cow usually produces only one egg at a time. This is the case with most mammals, including humans. Human males produce lots of sperm, while females produce relatively few eggs. Although the traits of sperm and eggs are quite different, the main job of these sex cells is the same: to join together to produce a new organism.

You have learned that a human body cell contains 46 chromosomes. You have also learned that body cells are produced through mitosis. Remember, through the process of mitosis, each new body cell contains 46 chromosomes, just like the parent body cell. This ensures that the new cells look and function exactly like the parent cell. Sex cells are formed by a different process. Do you think that a human sex cell contains 46 chromosomes like a body cell? You will discover the answer to this question in the following activity.

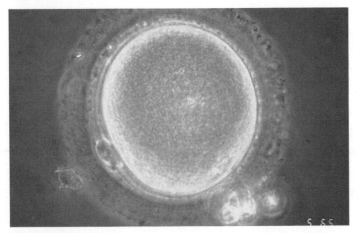

FIGURE 14-3. This human egg is a female sex cell. How does its appearance compare with that of the sperm?

EXPLORE!

How do the number of chromosomes in body cells and sex cells compare?

What relationship do you see between the number of chromosomes in body cells and sex cells of humans and peas? Predict the numbers that complete the table.

BODY CELLS AND SEX CELLS OF DIFFERENT ORGANISMS

Organism	Body Cell Chromosomes	Egg Chromosomes	Sperm Chromosomes
Human	46	23	23
Pea	14	7	7
Tomato	24		
Corn	20		
Rabbit	44		
Chicken	78		
Mouse	40		
Crayfish	200		

a

b

FIGURE 14-4. The body cells of the rabbit (a) each contain 44 chromosomes. The developing frogs (b) also contain a complete set of chromosomes. Half came from the sperm, and half came from the egg.

As you discovered in the Explore, there is a major difference in the number of chromosomes contained in a body cell and a sex cell. Sex cells, whether sperm or eggs, contain half the number of chromosomes contained in a body cell of the organism. In the next section, you will learn why these special cells contain half the number of chromosomes in body cells.

Check Your Understanding

1. Tell which of the following phrases describe sperm, eggs, both, or neither: relatively large, relatively small, tail present, stored food present, formed by mitosis, body cell, sex cell.
2. The muscle cells in a housefly's leg contain 24 chromosomes. If each of the following cell types came from a housefly, how many chromosomes does each contain: sperm, body cell, egg, eye cell?
3. **APPLY:** What do the physical traits of a human sperm indicate about the environment in which the cell lives?

14-2 Meiosis Makes Sex Cells

OBJECTIVES

In this section, you will
- describe the process of meiosis;
- determine the results of meiosis and why it is needed;
- determine where and when meiosis occurs.

KEY SCIENCE TERMS

meiosis
testis
ovary

THE PROCESS OF MEIOSIS

Body cells are formed by the process of mitosis. Mitosis is a process of body cell division in which a body cell makes an identical copy of itself. But as you learned in the last section, sex cells contain half the number of chromosomes found in body cells. Sex cells can't be formed by mitosis. They are produced in a different way.

Sex cells are formed by a process called **meiosis** (mi OH suhs). While the names of these two reproduction processes are similar, they occur in different kinds of cells and have different outcomes. In the following activity, you will make a model to give you a general idea of what occurs during meiosis.

EXPLORE!

How are sex cells formed?
In this activity, you will create an edible model of meiosis. Obtain a package of colored candies and five paper cups. Begin by placing two different-colored

pairs of candies, for a total of four candies, in a paper cup. Add four more identical candies to the cup. Divide the eight candies evenly between two other cups, so that each cup contains the same number of each color of candy. Finally, divide the contents of each cup evenly so that the end product is four cups that each contain one of each color candy. What is the relationship between the number of candies placed in the original cup and those contained in the final four cups?

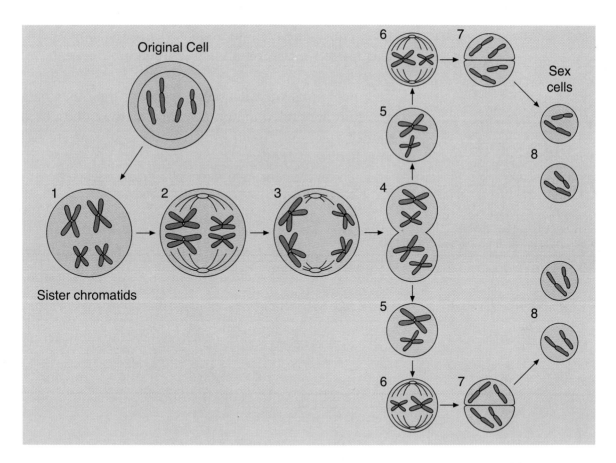

FIGURE 14-5. Meiosis is a process of cell reproduction that results in four sex cells.

In the Explore activity, you used candy and paper cups to make a model of meiosis. In your model, candy represented chromosomes, while the cups represented cells. The first cup was a body cell, but the final four cups were sex cells. What does this indicate about the relationship between the number of chromosomes found in a body cell and the number of chromosomes in cells that form by meiosis?

Now that you have a general idea of what occurs during meiosis, let's look at the process in detail. Figure 14-5 shows the steps that make this process. Meiosis begins in a cell in the reproductive organs of an organism. The number of chromosomes in the cell varies among different species of organisms. For this example, the cell in Figure 14-5 has two pairs of chromosomes for a total of four chromosomes.

1. Each chromosome makes a copy of itself. The copy and original chromosome are attached. They are now called sister chromatids.

SKILLBUILDER

**INTERPRETING SCIEN-
TIFIC ILLUSTRATIONS**
Make a diagram to illustrate meiosis in humans. At the top of your
diagram draw a circle around the
number 46. This represents an
original cell with its full number of
chromosomes. Continue the diagram by drawing additional circles
to represent each change the
original cell undergoes. Be sure
you write the number of chromosomes or chromatids each new
cell contains. If you need help,
refer to the **Skill Handbook** on
page 691.

2. Like chromatids come together in matching pairs. Groups of four chromatids line up along the center of the cell.

3. One pair of chromatids separates from the other pair, and they are pulled to opposite ends of the cell. In each pair of sister chromatids, the original and copy are still attached to each other.

4. The cell divides and two new cells form. Each cell contains sister chromatids that are not paired.

5. The chromatids line up again along the center of each new cell.

6. Sister chromatids separate and move to opposite ends of the cell. This particular stage of meiosis is very similar to mitosis.

7. The cells divide. Four new cells are formed. Each of the four new cells contains exactly half the number of chromosomes found in the original cell.

   Figure 14-6 shows a comparison of mitosis and meiosis. In the following Investigate, you will take a closer look at these two processes.

FIGURE 14-6. Compare the processes of mitosis and meiosis.

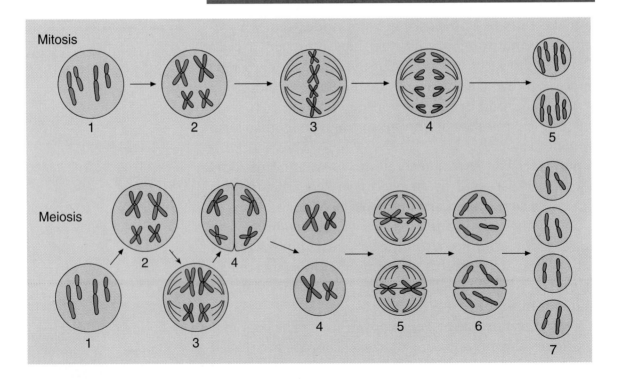

14-1
MITOSIS AND MEIOSIS

In this activity, you will make a model of the steps of meiosis and **compare** the end products of mitosis and meiosis.

PROBLEM
How is meiosis different from mitosis?

MATERIALS
cell outlines showing steps that occur during mitosis and meiosis
wool strands, two different colors
tape
scissors

PROCEDURE
1. Copy the data table.
2. Obtain copies of cell outlines from your teacher.

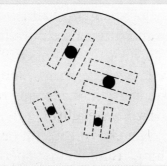
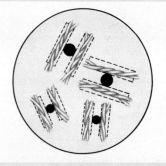

The actual steps that occur during mitosis and meiosis are shown in Figure 14-6. The appearance of cells before cell reproduction begins is shown in Steps 1 and 2.
3. Cut the strands of wool and tape them to the dashed outlines in the figure. These strands of wool represent chromosomes. Use one color of wool for all long chromosomes and the second color for all short chromosomes. The solid circles that connect the dashed outlines on the

diagram show the point at which original and copy chromosomes are attached.
4. Complete the table when your models are finished.

ANALYZE
1. **Compare** the location and arrangement of chromosomes in the cell during Step 3 of mitosis and meiosis.
2. **Compare** the location and arrangement of chromosomes in the cell during Step 4 of mitosis and meiosis.

CONCLUDE AND APPLY
3. How do the end products of each process differ?
4. **Going Further: Predict** what would occur if sex cells were produced by mitosis rather than meiosis.

DATA AND OBSERVATIONS

COMPARING MITOSIS AND MEIOSIS	MITOSIS	MEIOSIS
Type of cell undergoing division		
Number of chromosomes before cell begins to divide	4	4
Chromosome pairs in the original cell		
Final number of chromosomes in each new cell at the end of division		
Chromosome pairs in each new cell at conclusion of reproduction		

WHERE MEIOSIS OCCURS

As you saw in the Investigate activity, cells produced by meiosis contain half the number of chromosomes found in the original cell, while cells produced by mitosis contain the same number of chromosomes as in the original cell. Because sperm and eggs are produced by meiosis, they have half as many chromosomes as body cells from the same organism.

Meiosis can occur only in the sex organ of a living thing. In humans, sperm are produced in a male sex organ called a **testis**. A male usually has two testes. Eggs are produced in a female sex organ called an **ovary**. Females usually have two ovaries. Where does meiosis occur in your body?

WHEN MEIOSIS OCCURS

From the time you were an embryo, mitosis has been occurring in most of your body cells. This is not true of meiosis. For males, meiosis begins when the organism reaches sexual maturity. For females, meiosis begins before birth. Chromosomes duplicate themselves, but cells remain in this stage until the female is sexually mature. Then the process of meiosis continues. Cells divide to form eggs, usually one at a time.

The time of your own sexual maturity is marked by the production of sex cells by your sex organs. If you are a male, your testes will be producing sperm for the rest of your life. However, the number of sperm your body produces will decrease as you age. If you are a female, your ovaries will produce eggs until between the ages of 45 and 50.

The time of sexual maturity differs in all living things. For humans, sexual maturity usually occurs between the ages of 10 and 14. A mouse can reach sex-

FIGURE 14-7. Sexual maturity depends on the species. Humans become sexually mature between 10 years and 14 years; a corn plant becomes sexually mature between 3 and 4 months old.

ual maturity at the age of 2 months. Sexual maturity in a corn plant occurs when the plant is between 3 and 4 months old, while most dandelion plants reach sexual maturity when 4 to 5 weeks old.

WHY MEIOSIS IS NEEDED

Did you ever wonder why you resemble other members of your family? You probably share physical traits with each of your parents because you inherited genetic material from each of them. Half of the 46 chromosomes in each of your body cells resemble half of the chromosomes in your mother's body cells. The other half of the chromosomes in your body cells resemble half of the chromosomes in your father's body cells.

In order to understand why this happens, think again about meiosis. Meiosis produces sex cells that contain half the number of chromosomes found in a body cell. Human eggs contain 23 chromosomes. Human sperm also contain 23 chromosomes. During fertilization, an egg and a sperm join. The cell that results contains 46 chromosomes. You should now understand why sex cells must divide by meiosis rather than mitosis. If human sex cells formed by mitosis, they would each contain 46 chromosomes. The cell produced by fertilization would contain 92 chromosomes!

In this section, you have compared two methods of cell division that occur in your body. You have learned why it is important that sex cells divide by meiosis rather than mitosis. In the next section, you will discover how sex cells meet during fertilization.

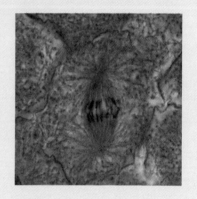
Check Your Understanding

1. How many times in meiosis do chromosomes make copies of themselves? How many times do identical chromosomes line up along the cell center in groups of four? How many times do a chromosome original and copy separate?

2. Why must an egg and sperm have half the number of chromosomes as the fertilized egg?

3. Where does meiosis occur in your body?

4. **APPLY:** A muscle cell of a cat contains 38 chromosomes. How many chromosomes does a cat sperm contain? Explain how you arrived at your answer.

14-3 Plant Reproduction

OBJECTIVES

In this section, you will

- diagram the structure of a typical flower;
- describe how flowering plants reproduce.

KEY SCIENCE TERMS

stamen
pistil

THE NEED FOR FERTILIZATION

On its own, a single egg or sperm cannot form a new offspring. An egg and sperm must come together. But the joining of an egg and a sperm is no easy task. In most plants and animals, a sizeable distance lies between the male and female sex organs. Most organisms have specialized structures that aid the fertilization process. In this section, you'll learn about fertilization in plants. In the next section, you'll read about fertilization in animals.

PLANT REPRODUCTION

Nearly all the plants you are familiar with are seed plants. Many people are surprised to learn that seed plants reproduce sexually—in other words, they reproduce with sex cells and the fertilization of an egg. Like animals, seed plants have both body cells and sex cells. A plant's body cells grow and divide by mitosis. The body cells develop into roots, stems, and leaves. A plant's sex cells are produced by meiosis in the reproductive organs of the plant. If a seed plant's male and female sex cells join, a new seed develops.

Seed plants are different from simple plants in that, appropriately enough, seed plants grow from a seed. You may remember that seed plants are divided into two major groups—conifers and flowering plants. Conifers such as pine, fir, and spruce trees, produce seeds on the scales of cones, like the one in Figure 14-8. Flowering plants produce seeds enclosed in a fruit.

Have you ever stopped to admire a flower in bloom? Flowers are the reproductive

FIGURE 14-8. Conifers produce seeds on the scales of pinecones.

organs of flowering plants. Figure 14-9 shows the anatomy of a flower. Study the figure as you read about each part below.

1. Sepals are the leaflike parts of a flower. They protect and cover a young flower.

2. Petals are the colored parts that protect the sex organs of a flower. The petals' color and scent attract insects, birds, and moths to the flower. You will discover later in the section how these organisms help fertilization occur.

3. The **stamen** is the male reproductive organ. Most flowers have several stamens.

4. The anther is the saclike top of a stamen. Anthers produce pollen, which contain sperm.

5. The filament is the long, stalklike part of the stamen that holds the anther up.

6. The **pistil** is the female reproductive organ. It is a long, stalklike structure with a round base. It is generally located in the center of the flower.

7. The round base of the pistil is the ovary. Female sex cells, or eggs, are produced in the ovary by meiosis.

8. The top end of the pistil is the stigma. The surface of the stigma is very sticky. This helps the stigma trap pollen formed by the male part of the flower.

9. The middle part of the pistil is called the style. The style supports the stigma, raising it toward the top of the flower, where pollen is most likely located.

All of these structures are found in flowers. Some flowers do contain both male and female structures, while others have only male or female parts. Whether an egg and sperm come from the same plant or different plants, pollination must occur for a new organism to develop. In the following Investigate activity, you will examine the parts of a flower to see how pollination occurs.

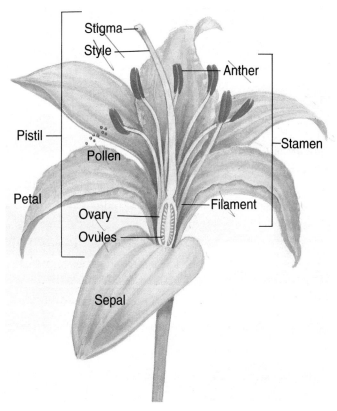

FIGURE 14-9. Some flowers have both male parts (the stamen) and female parts (the pistil).

I N V E S T I G A T E !

14-2 POLLINATION AND PARTS OF A FLOWER

Many plants are both male and female. In this activity, you will locate the male and female reproductive organs of a flower and hypothesize how pollination occurs.

PROBLEM
How does pollination occur?

MATERIALS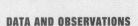
gladiolus, fresh or preserved
scalpel   water
hand lens   eyedropper
microscope   coverslip
microscope slide

PROCEDURE
1. Copy the data table.
2. Remove the flower's sepals. Record their number and color in your table.

3. Remove the flower's petals, and record their number and color.
4. Remove the stamens. Look at one with a hand lens. **Observe** its top part, or anther, and also its filament. Record the number and color of stamens.
5. Hold the anther over a drop of water on a microscope slide, and tap it gently. Add a coverslip. Observe the pollen grains under a microscope and make a drawing of them.

6. The structure that remains is the pistil, the female reproductive structure. Record the pistil's color.
7. The stigma is located at the top of the style. Touch the stigma. Describe how it feels.
8. The round base of the pistil is the ovary. Cut the ovary in half crosswise. **CAUTION:** *Always be careful with sharp instruments such as a scalpel.*
9. Examine the inside of the ovary with a hand lens. Make a drawing of what you see.

ANALYZE
1. **Compare and contrast** the numbers and sizes of the male and female reproductive organs.
2. How many compartments did you see in the cross-section of the ovary?
3. What did you observe inside the ovary?

CONCLUDE AND APPLY
4. What is the function of the petals?
5. How is the stigma adapted for attracting pollen?
6. **Going Further:** You probably have seen bees travel among flowers in a garden. **Hypothesize** how the movement of a bee might aid in pollination.

DATA AND OBSERVATIONS

FLOWER PART	NUMBER	COLOR
Sepals		
Petals		
Stamens		
Anthers		
Pollen grains		
Pistil		
Inside ovary		

GETTING SPERM AND EGG TOGETHER

Eggs are located inside the ovary of a flower. Sperm are found in pollen grains located in stamens above the pistils. The distance between the stamens and pistils makes the chance of their meeting seem difficult. How do sperm and egg get together?

The brightly colored petals and sweet scent of a flower attract insects. As the insect moves about the flower, pollen sticks to its body, and is carried on the body of the insect to the sticky surface of the stigma. Wind can also move pollen from the anther to the stigma. Without the help of both the living and nonliving parts of the flower's environment, pollination wouldn't occur!

Once pollen lands on the stigma, it still has a way to go before reaching the ovary. A series of events then begins that helps sperm and egg meet. Figure 14-10 shows this. First, the pollen forms a long tube that grows down through the pistil. The tube grows down to the ovary, reaching the egg. Sperm then move down the tube to meet an egg. Fertilization occurs when a sperm and egg join.

After fertilization, the ovary grows and develops into a fruit. The fertilized egg becomes a seed containing the developing plant embryo. An embryo, or new living thing, has formed due to fertilization, and this embryo will eventually develop into a new plant.

FIGURE 14-10. Fertilization in a flower

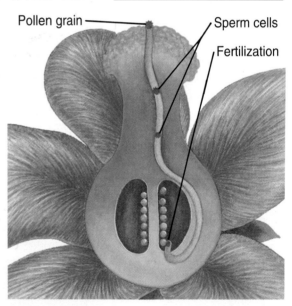

Pollen grain

Sperm cells

Fertilization

Check Your Understanding

1. Diagram and label all parts of a typical flower.
2. What is the role of stamens and pistils in plant reproduction?
3. Describe the process of reproduction in a flowering plant.
4. **APPLY:** Could pollination occur in an ecosystem that didn't contain any insect populations? Explain your answer.

14-4 Animal Reproduction

OBJECTIVES

In this section, you will
- compare and contrast external and internal fertilization in animals and where each occurs;
- demonstrate an understanding of how humans reproduce.

KEY SCIENCE TERMS

menstrual cycle
menstruation

ANIMAL REPRODUCTION

Unlike many plants, a frog does not have both male and female reproductive structures. A frog is either a male or a female. This is not the case, however, for all animals. Each earthworm, sponge, and flatworm contains both male and female parts in the same animal. But animals in most species are either male or female.

Because a frog is either male or female, certain actions are necessary for fertilization to occur. The joining of a sperm and an egg occurs outside the bodies of the two frogs. This type of fertilization is called external fertilization. *External* means outside.

How does external fertilization occur in frogs? The female frog releases her eggs into the water, as shown in Figure 14-11. The male frog then releases millions of sperm over the eggs into the water. Every egg does not join with a sperm. Some eggs and sperm are eaten by other organisms. Other sex cells float away in the water. However, some eggs usually are fertilized.

FIGURE 14-11. A female frog releases her eggs into the water.

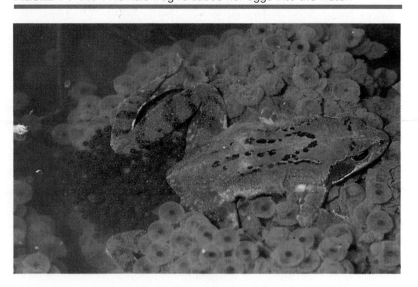

Your teacher can give you some preserved frog eggs. Do they resemble the chicken eggs you examined at the beginning of this chapter? Could they survive on land without drying out?

As you observed in the last activity, frog eggs are very delicate. They must be kept moist, or they will dry out. The same is true for frog sperm. In external fertilization, there is no guarantee that sperm will reach eggs because the sperm are released into the environment rather than into the female's reproductive system. The vast number of sperm the male releases, however, increases the likelihood of fertilization occurring.

HUMAN REPRODUCTION

Male Reproductive System

Like frogs, humans are either male or female. In humans, however, as in many other animals, fertilization occurs inside the body of the female. This is called internal fertilization because *internal* means inside. The male reproductive system consists of organs and tissues that produce sperm and move them out of the body. Figure 14-12 shows the parts of the male reproductive system. You already know that the testes are two oval organs that produce sperm. The testes are in a pouchlike sac called the scrotum that is suspended outside the body. The temperature in the scrotum is several degrees lower than body temperature. This difference is important because sperm would not form or survive at body temperature. Once formed, sperm leave the testes through a tube, or duct. The sperm move into the urethra in the penis, the organ through which they pass from the body. The penis allows the sperm to be deposited directly within the female's reproductive system.

FIGURE 14-12. The structures of the human male reproductive system are shown.

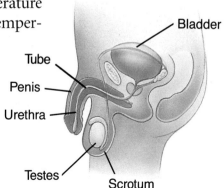

What is the pathway of sperm through the male reproductive system?

Trace the figure of the male reproductive system in Figure 14-12. Then use arrows to show the pathway that sperm follow through the system. List in order the structures sperm pass through to get to the female reproductive system.

FIGURE 14-13. The structures of the human female reproductive system are shown.

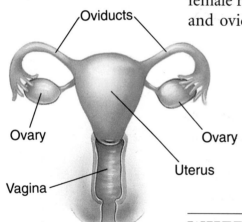

Oviducts

Ovary

Ovary

Uterus

Vagina

Female Reproductive System

The main job of the male reproductive system is to produce sex cells. The female reproductive system has two jobs—to produce sex cells and to provide a home to a developing embryo. Figure 14-13 shows the parts of the female reproductive system. It consists of a pair of ovaries and oviducts, a uterus, and a vagina. You already know that ovaries are oval-shaped organs that produce eggs. Oviducts are tubes through which the eggs pass from the ovaries to the uterus. The uterus is a hollow, thick-walled, muscular organ in which a fertilized egg develops. The uterus is connected to the vagina, a muscular tube that leads from the uterus to the outside of the female body.

WHERE DOES FERTILIZATION OCCUR?

You already know that fertilization in humans takes place internally. During mating, the male releases sperm directly into the female's vagina. Internal fertilization increases the chance that egg and sperm will meet. Millions of sperm are deposited into the female's reproductive system. A fertilized egg, or zygote, results only if a sperm joins with an egg and fertilizes it. It only takes one sperm to fertilize an egg. About every 28 days, the female reproductive system goes through a cycle that prepares an egg for fertilization.

Menstrual Cycle

When a human female is born, there are nearly half a million undeveloped eggs in her ovaries. Only about 500

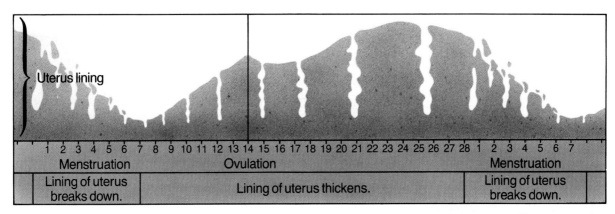

Uterus lining		
1 2 3 4 5 6 7 8 9 10 11 12 13 14 15 16 17 18 19 20 21 22 23 24 25 26 27 28 1 2 3 4 5 6 7		
Menstruation	Ovulation	Menstruation
Lining of uterus breaks down.	Lining of uterus thickens.	Lining of uterus breaks down.

FIGURE 14-14. The menstrual cycle begins on day 1 of menstruation. Ovulation occurs near day 14 of a regular 28-day cycle.

of these eggs will ever develop. Beginning between the ages of 10 and 14, the ovaries begin to release an egg about once every 28 days. The egg is either fertilized, or it is shed from the body in a monthly cycle called the menstrual cycle. The **menstrual cycle** is a cycle in which the ovary produces an egg and the uterus prepares to receive it, then discards it if the egg is not fertilized.

Figure 14-14 shows the changes that occur in the uterus during an average 28-day menstrual cycle. About midway through the cycle, a female ovulates; that is, an egg is released from the ovary and enters an oviduct. As the figure shows, ovulation occurs on approximately day 14. It is important to note, however, that ovulation does not always occur on day 14. Some females ovulate sooner; others later. It all depends on the individual female's menstrual cycle. The egg travels through the oviduct, remaining alive for about 24 to 48 hours. During this time, a female can become pregnant. The egg can be fertilized if live sperm are present in the oviduct beginning 48 hours before ovulation and up to 48 hours after it.

Meanwhile, the lining of the uterus has been thickening in preparation to receive a fertilized egg. If the egg is not fertilized by a sperm, it disintegrates. The lining of the uterus is shed and bleeding occurs. This monthly discharge of uterine lining and blood through the vagina is called **menstruation.** Menstruation occurs about 14 days after ovulation and usually lasts from four to six days. While menstruation is going on, a new egg is being prepared in one of the ovaries. In the following activity, you will trace the pathway of a mature egg through the uterus.

SKILLBUILDER

CLASSIFYING
Classify each structure as either male or female and internal or external in the body: ovary, testis, penis, vagina, uterus, scrotum. If you need help, refer to the **Skill Handbook** on page 680.

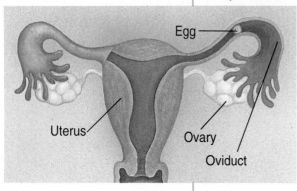

During the menstrual cycle, a mature egg moves through the female reproductive system. If the egg is not fertilized, menstruation occurs. Make a diagram that shows the movement of an egg through the female reproductive system from ovulation to menstruation.

Conclude and Apply

How would your diagram differ if the egg was fertilized?

FIGURE 14-15. Fertilization occurs when a sperm meets the egg in the oviduct.

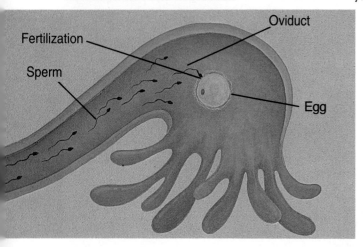

If sperm are deposited in the vagina, they move up into the oviducts. If sperm are already in an oviduct as an egg leaves the ovary, fertilization can take place. When these sex cells unite, the fertilized egg moves into the uterus and attaches itself to the lining, where an embryo then develops.

You've learned that reproduction using sex cells and fertilization of an egg is called sexual reproduction. Seed plants and most animals—including humans—reproduce sexually. In the next chapter, you will learn how offspring produced by sexual reproduction inherit the traits from both parents.

Check Your Understanding

1. What is the difference between internal and external fertilization?
2. Why can animals that reproduce through internal fertilization afford to produce so few eggs at a time?
3. **APPLY:** For each time period given below, indicate whether fertilization can occur and briefly explain why it can or can't occur. Assume sperm are present.
   a. 24 hours after ovulation;
   b. 48 hours after menstruation has ended;
   c. during menstruation.

EXPANDING YOUR VIEW

CONTENTS

A CLOSER LOOK

THE SHELLED EGG

Have you ever thought about which came first, the chicken or the egg? A shelled egg was the key to life on land for many of the animals you are familiar with.

The first group of vertebrates able to lay its eggs on dry land appeared around 310 million years ago. Those eggs were encased in leathery shells, similar to the shells found on eggs laid by modern reptiles, such as the snake pictured here. The first land vertebrates were successful in this new environment because the shell provided the egg with protection from predators and prevented it from drying out.

In animals that lay shelled eggs, the shell is deposited around the fertilized egg cell just before it leaves the animal's reproductive tract. Packaged along with the fertilized egg is a large food supply called the yolk. There is also a large amount of albumen, or egg white. Albumen, a protein in egg whites, provides water and additional nutrients.

WHAT DO YOU THINK?

In most animals that lay unshelled eggs in water, fertilization is external. What kind of fertilization occurs in animals that lay shelled eggs? What is the advantage of this kind of fertilization?

Another important characteristic of shelled eggs is their protective membranes. The first membrane to form encloses the yolk. The cells of this membrane digest the yolk, while membrane blood vessels carry the food nutrients to the embryo.

Another membrane surrounds the embryo with fluid. This liquid-filled space acts as a shock absorber, cushioning the developing embryo.

A third membrane lines the eggshell and allows the embryo to exchange oxygen and carbon dioxide with the air outside. The remaining membrane forms a sac into which the embryo excretes nitrogen wastes from metabolism.

Shelled eggs provide a developing embryo with everything it needs to survive. Why do you think they were such an important adaptation for the evolution of land vertebrates?

Chemistry Connection

CHEMICALS AND BIRTH DEFECTS

Although scientists do not know what causes the majority of birth defects in humans, they do know that certain chemicals and other substances pose a risk to a developing fetus. For example, if a pregnant woman is exposed to lead, it can move from her bloodstream through the umbilical cord and into the fetus. The fetus can then suffer damage to its nervous system.

Until recently, most attention to preventing birth defects focused on women while they were pregnant. Scientists had long assumed that most children born with birth defects had suffered some kind of damage while they were developing inside their mothers.

New research shows, however, that men's reproductive health also affects their children. For example, men exposed to lead may produce defective sperm. Defective sperm usually cannot fertilize an egg. If, however, fertilization does occur, the

result may be a deformed fetus.

Men who smoke cigarettes or drink alcohol heavily may also have fertility problems or may have children with birth defects that stem from these habits. It has long been

known, for example, that women who smoke during pregnancy risk having low birth weight babies. Research now indicates that low birth weight in babies can also result from fathers who smoke. Heavy drinking by men one month before fertilization can also cause low birth weight in babies.

Exactly how chemicals affect men's reproductive health is still mostly unknown. A toxin may directly damage sperm-producing cells in the testes,

so not enough sperm are produced and sterility results. Other times defective sperm are produced, which also may cause sterility. Or, the defective sperm might fertilize an egg and result in a damaged fetus. Men also might pass toxins in their semen to women. These toxins can then damage the egg.

WHAT DO YOU THINK?

A woman usually produces one egg each month, whereas a man produces millions of sperm. How might this difference make men more likely than women to produce deformed reproductive cells?

Some employers have fetal protection policies. These policies keep women of child-bearing age from working at jobs where they might be exposed to toxic chemicals. What is the problem with focusing only on women when it comes to toxins in the workplace?

SCIENCE
A N D
SOCIETY

CAREER CONNECTION

Nurse-midwives study biology, chemistry, and medicine. They work at hospitals, clinics, and at birthing centers assisting in childbirth.

CURING INFERTILITY

For a variety of reasons, one in twelve couples in the United States is experiencing infertility. They are unable to conceive a child. The number of people going to a doctor because of fertility problems recently exceeded one million.

But as the number of people dealing with infertility increases, new techniques are being developed for treatment. For example, one cause of infertility is that sperm are too weak or don't have the right enzymes to break through the egg's outer membrane. To overcome this problem, doctors can now use a needle and a powerful microscope to inject sperm directly into the egg.

When a woman does not release an egg through ovulation, which is another cause of infertility, she can be given hormones. Then she will produce many eggs, increasing her chances of getting pregnant.

Sometimes infertility occurs because the fertilized egg does not implant itself in the uterus. One-third of all pregnancies may end because implantation does not occur. To fix this problem, doctors pierce a tiny hole in the egg's protective outer layer. For some reason, eggs that are pierced attach better than those without the hole.

The use of technology to assist in reproduction has increased dramatically since the first test tube baby was born over a decade ago. At that time, *in vitro* fertilization (IVF — fertilization in a glass dish) was revolutionary. Since then, more than 10,000 babies in the

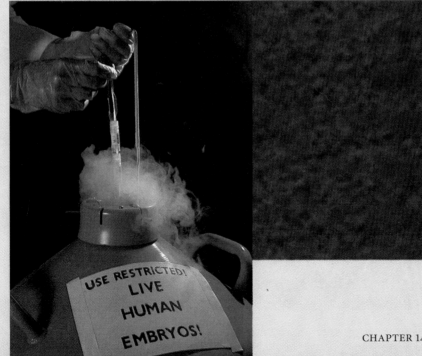

WHAT DO YOU THINK?

In 1980, the federal government cut funding for research on IVF. Do you think that the government should support research in reproductive technology? To what extent is society responsible for helping couples who are infertile?

United States have been produced through IVF.

IVF is used when a woman is unable to conceive naturally. It can also be used when a woman is infertile but still able to carry a child. Different combinations of egg and sperm are possible using IVF. The couple themselves may contribute eggs and sperm. Or the woman may give eggs that will be fertilized by sperm from a male donor. If the woman is infertile, her partner's sperm may be used to fertilize eggs donated by another woman.

As reproductive technology has become more complex and more widely used, it has raised many ethical questions. For example, more than one egg is fertilized during the IVF procedure because not all fertilized eggs will survive. So several eggs are used to ensure that there will be at least one embryo that can be placed into the mother's uterus. The remaining embryos are frozen.

But questions have come up concerning what to do with these extra embryos. In one court case, a divorced couple fought about whether the woman can have custody of the embryos that were created while the couple was still married.

Other questions relate to the cost of the treatment. IVF can cost from $6000 to $50,000 to produce one child. This means that only wealthy people or those with good health insurance have access to the procedure. Only nine states have laws that require insurance companies to pay for infertility treatments.

Still other concerns about the development of reproductive technology have to do with larger questions of world population growth. The world's population is currently 5.4 billion and is expected to double around the year 2030. There is growing concern that Earth cannot support such a large human population. Thus the use of scientific resources and millions of dollars to help certain people have children is seen by some as unwise.

TECHNOLOGY CONNECTION

SAVING ENDANGERED SPECIES

Every year numerous animal species edge closer to extinction because of human activities. Loss of habitat is a major threat, as is illegal hunting. For example, the number of black rhinoceroses has fallen from 60,000 in 1970 to just 3500 today. The animal is slaughtered for its horn, which some people believe can cure diseases.

To increase the populations of some rare and endangered animals, scientists are using new methods in reproductive technology. One method is embryo transfer.

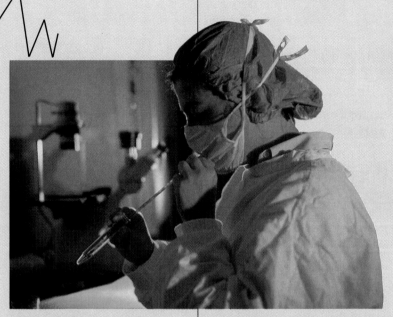

WHAT DO YOU THINK?

Why might embryo transfer and IVF be preferable to shipping live animals for zoo breeding programs?

Reproductive technologies are expensive and success is still limited. Do you think there might be better ways to save endangered species?

For example, a female rhino is injected with hormones that will allow her to produce about 30 eggs at one time. The animal is then allowed to mate naturally or is fertilized by artificial insemination. In artificial insemination, sperm are collected from a male animal and are then deposited in the female's reproductive tract using a special syringe. After fertilization, the embryos are collected and frozen in liquid nitrogen for later use.

An embryo from an endangered animal can be implanted into a surrogate, or substitute, mother. There it will complete its development. The surrogate is usually a member of a related species. The advantage of this process is that it allows more offspring to be born than would otherwise occur naturally. A rhino, for example, undergoes a 15-month pregnancy and delivers just a single calf. The rhino won't become pregnant again for at least four years.

Scientists have successfully used embryo transfer to produce Bengal tigers, African bongo antelope, and an endangered Indian desert cat. Producing the desert cat also involved the use of *in vitro* fertilization.

Some scientists expect that IVF and embryo transfer will replace more traditional breeding methods used by zoos. Live animals will no longer be shipped from one part of the world to another. Sperm, eggs, or embryos will be shipped to zoos trying to breed endangered species.

HOW IT WORKS

ADAPTATIONS FOR POLLINATION

When it comes to sexual reproduction, animals have a slight advantage over plants. Animals are able to move around in search of mates. Plants, on the other hand, must remain in one place. However, plants have adaptations that allow them to reproduce sexually in spite of being immobile.

In one of the largest groups of plants, the adaptation that makes sexual reproduction possible is the flower. Flowers are reproductive organs. They produce eggs and pollen, which contain sperm. Pollen must be transferred from one flower to another for fertilization to occur.

Each species of flowering plant generally depends on a particular kind of pollinator to carry out pollen transfer. In corn, for example, pollen is carried by the wind, while in roses, pollen is carried from one flower to another by bees.

If you examine a flower, you can determine how it is pollinated. Flowers pollinated by butterflies are usually long and narrow because these insects feed with a long, slender tongue. Because butterflies must land to feed, the flowers are upright and clustered to provide a landing platform. Butterflies seem to prefer white, cream, yellow, pink, and blue pastel-colored flowers.

Bees and wasps have short tongues, so the flowers they pollinate are usually open and shallow or have a broad tube shape with a landing platform. These insects are attracted to white, yellow, orange, blue, and violet flowers that have a sweet fragrance.

Birds also pollinate flowers. The most common bird pollinators are hummingbirds. Hummingbird flowers are often large and tube shaped to match the birds' long, thin beaks. These flowers contain abundant amounts of nectar deep within the flower that meet the birds' high metabolic needs. Anthers tend to stick out where they will brush against a hummingbird's head feathers and deposit pollen. Because hummingbirds see red and yellow well but have a poor sense of smell, they visit brightly colored flowers that are not very fragrant.

WHAT DO YOU THINK?

A plant has flowers that are dull-colored, unscented, and that produce little nectar. There are no petals and the anthers and stigmas hang out. How do you think this plant is pollinated? Considering how it is pollinated, do you think this plant would need to produce a little pollen or a lot for pollination to succeed? Why?

Reviewing Main Ideas

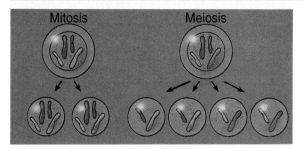

1. Mitosis produces body cells with the same number of chromosomes as the parent cell. Meiosis produces eggs and sperm that contain half the number of chromosomes as their parent cells.

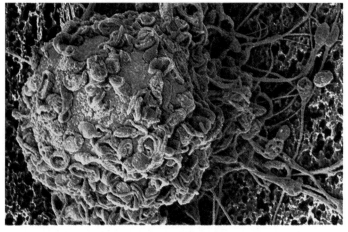

2. In animals that reproduce sexually, eggs are produced in the ovaries of females, and sperm are produced in the testes of males. When united, egg and sperm produce a new organism containing the original chromosome number.

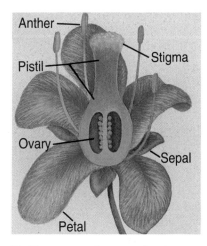

3. Flowers are the reproductive organs of some sexually reproducing seed plants.

4. The menstrual cycle is the monthly cycle of changes in the human female reproductive system. The menstrual cycle prepares the reproductive system for fertilization.

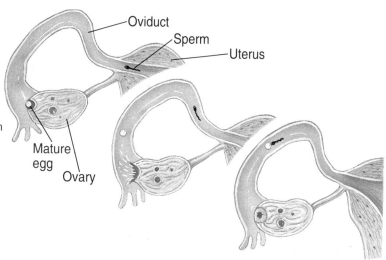

Chapter Review

USING KEY SCIENCE TERMS

body cells	pistil
eggs	sex cells
meiosis	sperm
menstrual cycle	stamen
menstruation	testis
ovary	

An analogy is a relationship between two pairs of words generally written in the following manner: a:b::c:d. The symbol : is read "is to," and the symbol :: is read "as." For example, cat:animal::rose:plant is read "cat is to animal as rose is to plant." In the analogies that follow, a word is missing. Complete each analogy by providing the missing word from the list above.

1. sperm:testis::_____:ovary
2. mitosis:body cells::_____:sex cells
3. ovulation:egg::_____:uterine lining and blood
4. vagina:human::_____:flower
5. testis:male lion::_____:male part of lily

UNDERSTANDING IDEAS

Answer the following questions.

1. How are a human egg and sperm alike?
2. A muscle cell of a frog contains 26 chromosomes. How many chromosomes does a frog's egg contain? Explain your answer.
3. In what organ(s) of the human body does meiosis occur?

4. Mitosis has been occurring in your body since you were an embryo. Is this true of meiosis? Explain your answer.
5. What role do insects play in plant pollination?
6. Can fertilization occur without ovulation? Explain your answer.
7. How does internal fertilization increase the likelihood of fertilization occurring?
8. What is menstruation?
9. Why do offspring produced by sexual reproduction resemble their parents?

CRITICAL THINKING

Use your understanding of the concepts developed in the chapter to answer each of the following questions.

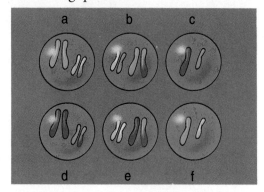

1. Study the six cells labeled (a) through (f) in the illustration. Which represent parents? Which represent offspring? Which represent sex cells? Explain your answers.
2. If only two fish can release millions of sperm and thousands of eggs, why aren't Earth's oceans choking with aquatic life?

3. Is fertilization likely to occur on day 1 of the menstrual cycle? Explain your answer.

4. Pollination can occur either between male and female parts of the same plant or between male and female parts of different plants of the same species. Which type of pollination would likely produce nearly identical offspring?

5. Sperm are extremely active cells. Located behind the head of each sperm is a packet of mitochondria. What function do the mitochondria serve in sperm?

PROBLEM SOLVING

Read the following problem and discuss your answers in a brief paragraph.

Steve's biology report was on a particular type of catfish. Steve chose this species of catfish because of some interesting facts about the fish's reproductive behavior. Interestingly enough, in this type of catfish, males are actively involved in the process of reproduction. Fertilized catfish eggs develop inside the mouth of the male parent. After reading more about the fish in general, Steve became perplexed. Steve found, in his research, that fish reproduce by external fertilization. What would you explain to Steve to help him understand the reproductive behavior of his catfish?

CONNECTING IDEAS

Discuss each of the following in a brief paragraph.

1. Use your knowledge of mitosis to explain how skin grows back after it has been scraped off during a fall.

2. Explain why a diet with the essential nutrients is essential for growth and repair of the body.

3. Sequence the events of fertilization in humans.

4. HOW IT WORKS Describe three adaptations to pollination found in flowers.

5. TECHNOLOGY CONNECTION Describe one method scientists use to increase the populations of rare and endangered animals.

DID YOU EVER WONDER . . .

Why certain features run in some families but not in others?

How features are passed from one generation to the next?

What your children could look like?

You'll find the answers to these questions as you read this chapter.

Heredity

Have you ever heard words similar to these: "You got your curly, red hair from Grandfather," or "You have bright blue eyes like Aunt Gina," or "You're going to be tall, just like all the Krols"?

The very features and traits that make you *you* first appeared in your parents or other ancestors, then were passed down to you. Each generation produces offspring that may or may not possess the same traits. When people go to their family reunion, they may notice that they share traits with some of their other relatives, not just brothers and sisters. They may even look like someone who is distantly related.

Sometimes a trait, such as curly, red hair, won't appear for several generations. Is such an occurrence an accident, or is there a pattern that can be predicted? In this chapter you will use your knowledge of reproduction to discover patterns of heredity—a process important not only to your appearance but also to your health.

EXPLORE!

Which of your features have you inherited?

Look at yourself in a mirror. Identify at least five of your features. For example, what color are your eyes? What color is your hair? Is it straight or curly? What is the shape of your nose or mouth? Who else in your family has each of your features?

15-1 How Organisms Get Their Traits

OBJECTIVES

In this section, you will

- define a trait;
- explain and draw pedigrees;
- describe how pedigrees are used to trace patterns of inheritance.

KEY SCIENCE TERMS

traits

pedigree

WHAT'S A TRAIT?

We share certain features with more than five million different kinds of organisms on Earth. Humans, like all living things, are made up of cells that require energy to do their work, to grow, and to reproduce.

You may want to know where your features came from. Every living thing has specific characteristics called **traits** that are unique. Even nonliving things such as rocks and minerals have traits. We can describe, identify, and classify each living or nonliving thing if we can recognize its traits.

EXPLORE!

How can traits help us to classify?
Look at the objects pictured. What trait is used to classify them in Method 1? Method 2? Method 3? The objects in each group have one trait in common. Are they identical? How do the objects in the first group differ? In the second group? In the third group?

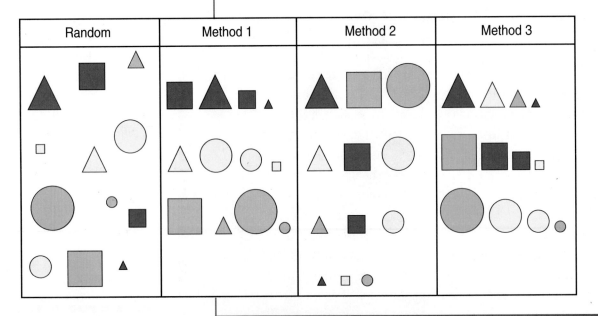

| Random | Method 1 | Method 2 | Method 3 |

As you've just observed, traits can be expressed in different ways. In humans, how many different hair colors are there? For each color, how many different shades exist? Can you think of other traits that are expressed in a variety of different ways? What about skin color or texture? What about the shape of your nose, ears, or mouth? Are all people the same height or weight?

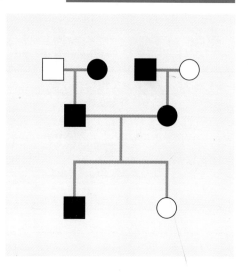

FIGURE 15-1. Notice the similarities and differences in the appearances of the three generations of this family.

FAMILY PEDIGREES

Can you tell which people are closely related from the family reunion picture at the beginning of the chapter? Some of the family members look very much alike. Others don't resemble each other at all. It is difficult to believe that some people are closely related when they look so different from one another.

To find out how family members can have such different features, we can use a tool called a pedigree to trace each trait in a family. A **pedigree** shows the history of a trait from one generation to the next. Imagine three generations of the Giuliano family—a brother and sister, Joseph and Anna, with their parents, Mr. and Mrs. Giuliano, and grandparents. To see how Anna could have straight hair, for example, while Joseph has curly hair like both his parents, we can draw a pedigree for the trait of hair form in three generations of the Giuliano family.

FIGURE 15-2. Giuliano family pedigree for hair form. Shading represents curly hair.

To draw a pedigree, we use shapes to represent the different members of the family and lines to connect them. Squares represent males, and circles represent females. Two parents are connected by a horizontal line. You can see Mr. Giuliano's parents as the two shapes on the left in the top row of shapes in Figure 15-2. To show a child, we draw a vertical line down from the parents' horizontal line to the shape for the child. Mr. Giuliano is represented by the square on the left in the middle row of shapes. If there are two or more children, we draw a horizontal line at the bottom of the vertical line and attach the children to it,

MAKING AND USING TABLES

Choose five physical traits such as curly hair, freckles, dimples, left-handedness, and the space between the top front teeth. Arrange the traits in a table. Survey five of your family members for each of the traits and arrange the data in your table. If you prefer, you may survey a friend's family. If you need help, refer to the **Skill Handbook** on page 681.

left to right, oldest to youngest. Joseph and Anna are represented by the two shapes in the bottom row. Is Anna older than Joseph?

How the trait of hair form is expressed in the family is shown by shading or not shading the shapes. In this pedigree, shaded shapes represent family members with curly hair. The shapes of family members with straight hair are not shaded. Does anyone in the family have straight hair besides Anna? If so, who? Do more members of the Giuliano family have straight hair or curly hair? What does this pedigree suggest about hair form? Does Anna have straight hair purely by chance, or did she inherit it even though both her parents have curly hair?

The inheritance of many traits in humans is not as simple and direct as this pedigree for hair form might lead you to believe. Hair color, for example, is much more complicated. Pedigrees are useful for tracing traits in a family, and are particularly important to tracing traits that can affect a person's health. You'll learn more about these traits in Section 3.

FIND OUT!

What can a pedigree tell you about a family?
Look back over the list of your features that you made at the beginning of this chapter. Choose one trait and draw a pedigree for your family. Decide what shaded shapes will represent, for example, blue versus brown eyes or curly versus straight hair. Include as many generations and as many of your relatives as you can. If you prefer, you can use a friend's family rather than your own.

Conclude and Apply

1. Who else in the family has the trait expressed in the same way you do or your friend does?
2. Do more family members have the trait expressed in one way than the other?
3. What might this suggest?

☐ = Male without trait

◼ = Male with trait

◯ = Female without trait

● = Female with trait

Parents

Do you or your friend have a feature that has not appeared in the family for two or three generations? If so, do you think it's something picked up from your environment? Or is it a trait that was somehow hidden in your or your friend's parents but came from grandparents? Do you see a pattern, or do traits appear and disappear at random? Random means that nothing is causing one trait to appear more often than another—neither trait is favored. It's like the lottery. Each number in the lottery has an equal chance of coming up because of randomness. No one number is favored over another. In the case of two traits, if the traits are appearing randomly, there is an equal chance that either trait will appear. In a large group of people, that would mean that about one-half of the people could have one trait, and one-half would have the other trait. To find out if traits appear in patterns or randomly, try the following activity.

FIND OUT!

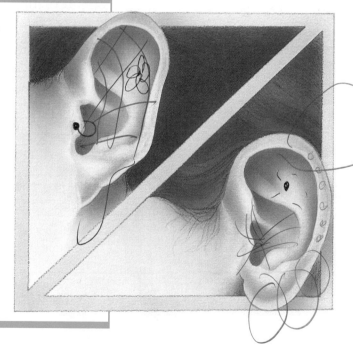

Do more students have attached or unattached earlobes?
Some people have earlobes that are attached like the one on the left in the illustration. Others have earlobes that hang free like the one on the right. Count the number of your classmates with each type of earlobe.

Conclude and Apply
1. How do the two numbers compare — are they nearly equal, or is one much larger than the other? If so, which?
2. What might this suggest about the occurrence of this trait?
3. Do you think it occurs randomly?

MENDEL'S WORK WITH PEAS

Gregor Mendel was the first to see that traits do not occur purely at random. He was the first to recognize that traits occur in family pedigrees according to certain patterns of inheritance. Although Mendel's parents were rather poor,

TRAITS COMPARED BY MENDEL						
Shape of seeds	Color of seeds	Color of seed coats	Color of pods	Shape of pods	Plant height	Position of flowers
Round	Yellow	Green	Green	Full	Tall	On side branches
Wrinkled	Green	White	Yellow	Flat or Constricted	Short	At tips of branches

FIGURE 15-3. Mendel's pea plant traits

FIGURE 15-4. Mendel's pea plant crosses

he was sent to a good school some distance from home. Mendel was a good student and loved nature and the out-of-doors. At the age of 20, he decided to enter a monastery, where he had no real distractions and lots of time for his nature experiments.

Mendel observed the variation in different plants. Variation is the occurrence of an inherited trait that makes a person or thing different from other members within the same species. He observed, for example, that pea plants varied in the shape and color of their seeds. Some were

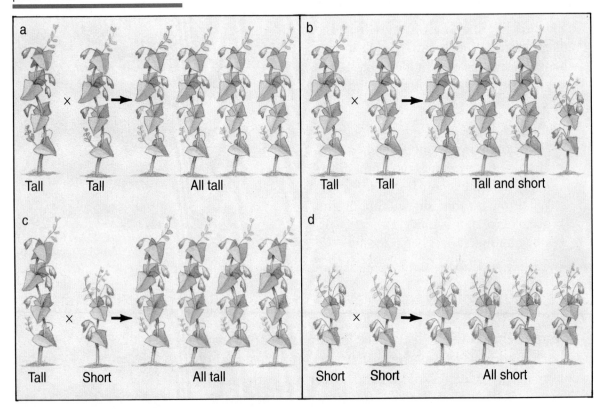

smooth, and others were wrinkled. Some seeds were green, and others were yellow. Some pea plants were tall, others short. Mendel noticed that some pea plants produced red flowers and others white flowers. Some of the many variations that Mendel observed in pea plants are shown in Figure 15-3.

Mendel hypothesized that the variation in the plants was controlled by something inherited from the parent plants because particular traits kept appearing across generations. He designed experiments in which he crossed pea plants with different traits and carefully recorded the results, generation after generation. He found that certain traits kept appearing again and again while others appeared only occasionally.

For example, Mendel crossed pea plants that varied in height as in Figure 15-4 (a–d). When he crossed certain tall plants, all the offspring were tall (a). When he crossed certain other tall plants, some offspring were tall and some were short (b). When he crossed tall with short, he got all tall offspring (c), and when he crossed short with short, he got only short (d). Was there a pattern in these results that supported Mendel's hypothesis that the traits of offspring come from their parents? Or were the results random?

Figure 15-4 (a) and (d) suggest that a pattern of inheritance exists and a trait, in this case pea plant height, is passed from parents to offspring.

FIGURE 15-5. Through experiments, Mendel discovered basic laws of inheritance.

FIGURE 15-6. Many people breed dogs for specific traits using the patterns of inheritance.

Check Your Understanding

1. What are traits, and how are they useful to scientists?
2. Draw a pedigree for a family with two brown-eyed parents, a brown-eyed son, and a blue-eyed daughter, who is the oldest child. What is the significance of the shading in the shapes in your pedigree?
3. How did Gregor Mendel use pedigrees to form his hypothesis that the traits of offspring come from their parents?
4. **APPLY:** If Joseph Giuliano grows up and marries a woman who has curly hair, can you say for sure that their children will have curly hair? Explain.

15-2 Mendel's Work Explained

OBJECTIVES

In this section, you will
- define a gene and tell where it is located;
- explain how the sorting of genes during meiosis demonstrates that traits are inherited;
- describe how dominant and recessive genes explain pedigrees and the results of Mendel's pea plant experiments.

KEY SCIENCE TERMS

dominant trait
recessive trait
gene
pure dominant
pure recessive
heterozygote

DID YOU KNOW?

Mendel's results from his plant breeding experiments were first ignored because they were published in an obscure scientific journal. In 1900, the time of Mendel's death, and 34 years after his original experiments, Mendel's papers were discovered and they became known around the world.

WHAT KINDS OF TRAITS ARE THERE?

When Mendel crossed tall pea plants and collected and planted the seeds that were produced, the offspring always grew into tall pea plants. Likewise, short pea plants crossed with short pea plants produced short pea plants time after time. Because the results of these crosses were always the same, he referred to these traits as pure. These crosses were shown in Figure 15-4(a) and (d), shown on page 452. As shown in Figure 15-4(c), when Mendel crossed pure tall with pure short peas, the offspring were always tall. The short trait seemed to disappear. Mendel called tallness, which was always expressed, a **dominant trait** because it seemed to dominate or cover up the short trait. He called shortness a **recessive trait** because it seemed to recede or disappear. What really happened to the recessive trait of shortness? Mendel crossed more pea plants to find out.

When tall offspring of one tall and one short parent were crossed with other tall offspring of one tall and one short parent, the next generation consisted of both tall and short plants. The short trait had reappeared! Mendel counted the offspring and found about three tall pea plants for every short one. The tall parent plants shown in Figure 15-4(b) were themselves the offspring of one tall and one short parent. This observation led Mendel to conclude that a trait must be controlled by factors inherited from both parents. These factors interact to determine how the trait is expressed in the offspring.

MENDEL'S FACTORS ARE GENES

We now know that the factors that Mendel used to explain his results are located on chromosomes within the cell. Each chromosome has many, many genes that are arranged along its length, like beads in a necklace. A **gene** is a specific location on a chromosome that controls a certain trait. Chromosomes normally occur in pairs; therefore, the genes they carry usually occur in pairs, too.

Gregor Mendel had been right. A trait is controlled by two factors, one from each parent, and the interaction of these two factors, now called genes, determines how the trait is expressed. As you learned in the last chapter on reproduction, when cells undergo meiosis, their chromosomes duplicate and pair up, then divide twice so that each egg or sperm has only one of each of the originally paired chromosomes. When a sperm fertilizes an egg, a chromosome from the egg pairs with the same kind of chromosome from the sperm. Each parent has contributed one chromosome per pair and a set of particular genes per trait in the offspring. Figure 15-7 shows how chromosome pairs that separate in the sex cells can recombine in the offspring.

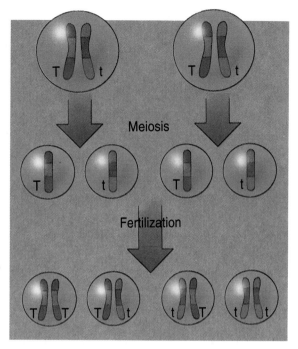

FIGURE 15-7. A pair of genes is labeled *T* and *t* in both parents. The chromosome pairs separate during meiosis and recombine during fertilization.

HOW ARE GENES EXPRESSED?

Figure 15-7 shows how different combinations of genes are possible when egg and sperm chromosomes form

How do we know?

Where are genes located on chromosomes?

Using a technique called gene splicing, scientists remove a section of a chromosome from one kind of organism and splice or insert it into a chromosome of a different kind of organism. The trait controlled by the transferred gene now appears in the second organism. This demonstrates that the gene or genes that control the trait must be located on the section of transferred chromosome. Pictured here are chromosome pieces being spliced into a bacterium's chromosome.

Mice can receive human genes that make them more likely to develop human cancers. These same mice can be used to test the

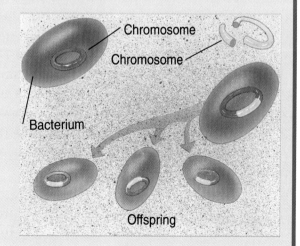

effectiveness of anticancer drugs before they are used on humans.

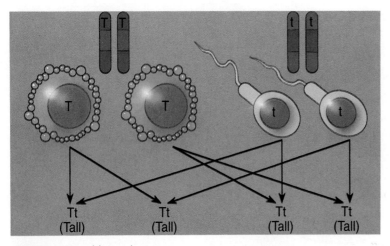

FIGURE 15-8. Notice how pea plant genes for pure tallness and pure shortness separate and recombine.

pairs. Geneticists use letters to represent the pair of genes that determines a certain trait such as pea plant height. A capital letter represents the dominant trait, *T* for tall, and a small letter represents the recessive trait, *t* for short. When Mendel crossed what he called pure-tall and pure-short pea plants, the offspring were all tall. Why did shortness disappear? The **pure dominant** trait of tallness is represented in Figure 15-8, by a double capital *TT*, and the **pure recessive** trait of shortness is represented by a double small *tt*. Pea plants with the gene pair *Tt* will grow to be tall plants because they have a gene for tallness, which is dominant. However, their tallness is not a pure trait. They also have recessive genes for shortness, which are not expressed. An organism with one dominant gene and one recessive gene for a trait is called a **heterozygote**. The offspring in Figure 15-8 are heterozygous for tallness.

EXPLORE!

Can you explain how Mendel got tall and short plants when he crossed tall heterozygotes?
Make a diagram similar to that in Figure 15-8 but start with two *Tt* parents. What genes did their sex cells carry? What gene pairs resulted in tall offspring? What gene pairs produced short offspring? What was the ratio of tall to short offspring? How does your ratio compare to Mendel's results?

The diagram you made in the Explore activity should look like Figure 15-9. Do you think Mendel could tell the difference between tall pea plants with *TT* genes and tall pea plants with *Tt* genes? It is impossible to tell by looking at a tall pea plant whether it is a pure dominant with *TT* genes or whether it is a heterozygote with *Tt* genes.

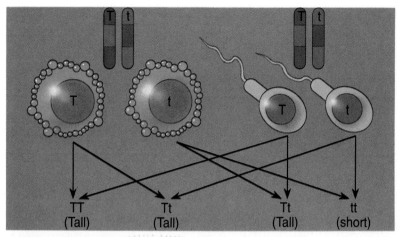

FIGURE 15-9. When the heterozygous offspring reproduce, it is impossible to tell the difference between **TT** and **Tt** genes.

PREDICTING OFFSPRING

When you counted earlobes earlier in this chapter, you probably found that many more of your classmates have unattached earlobes than attached. This is because the attached earlobe trait is recessive. It can be represented by a small letter *e* while a capital letter *E* represents the dominant trait of unattached earlobes. What combination of genes would be responsible for unattached earlobes? There are two possibilities, either the pure dominant *EE* or the heterozygous *Ee*. What combination of genes must a person with attached earlobes have? For attached earlobes to show up, the genes controlling the trait would have to be the pure recessive *ee*.

If you have unattached earlobes and marry someone with attached earlobes, can you predict what kind of earlobes your children will have? One way to do this is by using a tool called a Punnett square. A Punnett square shows the possible combinations of parental gene pairs for a given trait. It's a shortcut to the kind of diagram shown in Figures 15-8 and 15-9. To draw a Punnett square, first draw a large square, then divide it into four smaller squares. Write the letters representing a father's genes across the top of

FIGURE 15-10. This Punnett square shows the possible offspring of a *TT* tall parent and a *tt* short parent.

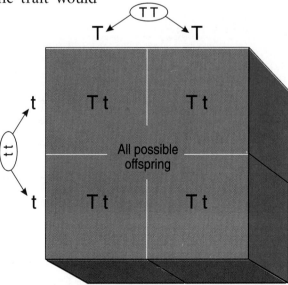

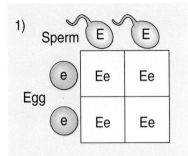

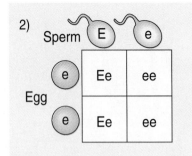

FIGURE 15-11. A Punnett square shows you all the possible combinations of parental genes in the offspring of a given cross.

SKILLBUILDER

OBSERVING AND INFERRING

The shape of your hairline is another inherited trait. Your hairline may be straight across the top of your forehead, or it may be V–shaped in the center. This is called a widow's peak. The widow's peak is the dominant trait. A straight hairline is the recessive trait. From what you've learned, infer how two parents with widow's peaks could have a child with a straight hairline. If you need help, refer to the **Skill Handbook** on page 684.

the large square, one above each of the two columns of small squares. Write the letters that represent the mother's genes down the left side next to the two rows of small squares. Then fill in the four possible gene pairs by carrying the individual gene letters down and across. How many Punnett squares are required to predict what kind of earlobes your children will have?

Figure 15-11 shows the two Punnett squares you would need to predict the likelihood of your children having attached or unattached earlobes. Two squares are required because your unattached earlobes may be the result of either of two gene pairs, *EE* or *Ee*. What kind of earlobes might your children have by square 1? By square 2?

Because a Punnett square shows all the possible combinations of parental genes in offspring of a given cross, it can be used to calculate the expected outcome of the cross. To do this, count the number of times a possible combination occurs in the square and compare it to 4. This is the chance that the combination will occur. For example, by square 1 in Figure 15-11, the chance that your first child will have unattached earlobes is 4 in 4 or 100 percent. By square 2, the chance is 2 in 4 or 50 percent. By square 2, what is the chance that your first child will have attached earlobes?

What about your second child? The chance of having a child with a certain trait is the same with each child, whether the child is your first, second, third, fourth, or fifth. Each time a sperm fertilizes an egg, the chances of genes combining in certain ways are the same.

You inherited the form and color of your hair and the shape of your hairline from your parents. You inherited your eye and skin colors and the basic size and shape of your body. You inherited thousands of other traits as well. There are inherited traits that are important to your well-being. These traits determine whether you are likely to have certain diseases or harmful conditions.

15-1 ALBINO OFFSPRING IN PLANTS

DATA AND OBSERVATIONS

SEED TYPE	YOUR TOTALS		CLASS TOTALS	
	GREEN	ALBINO	GREEN	ALBINO
A				
B				

Sometimes an inherited trait leads to serious health problems. Humans who show the albino trait have no skin pigment. These people get skin cancer more easily than people without the trait. Plants having the albino trait lack the green pigment called chlorophyll and cannot carry out photosynthesis. Now you will be a genetic detective and find out how genetic combinations are associated with albinism in plants.

PROBLEM
What kind of inheritance patterns are associated with the albino trait?

MATERIALS
petri dishes with covers
labels
paper towels
scissors
water
tobacco seeds A
tobacco seeds B

PROCEDURE
1. Copy the data table.
2. Label two petri dishes with your name; label one A and one B.
3. Cut out several thicknesses of paper towel to fit in the bottom of each of two petri dishes. Moisten the towels. **CAUTION:** *Scissors are very sharp. Please handle with care.*
4. Distribute 20 seeds of type A on the towels in dish A and 20 seeds of type B in dish B.
5. Cover the dishes, and place them where they will receive sunlight during the day.
6. Check the dishes daily, and add enough water to keep the towels moist.
7. After five days, count the number of green and white seedlings in each dish. Record your data and the class totals in the table.

ANALYZE
1. Using your data, calculate the percentage of albino seedlings from type A seeds. How does this **compare** to the class totals?

2. Using your data, calculate the percentage of albino seedlings from type B seeds. How did your result **compare** to the rest of the class?

CONCLUDE AND APPLY
3. If green pigment is the dominant trait and albinism is the recessive trait, use your own symbols to determine what different gene combinations the green seedlings could have.

4. **Predict** whether a cross of heterozygous and pure recessive parents gives you the results you observed in the type B seedlings. Draw a Punnett square to find the answer.

5. **Going Further: Infer** what different gene combinations the parents of the type B seeds must have had to produce the results you observed in their offspring? (HINT: Work a Punnett square backward.)

Albinism occurs in humans and other animals as well as in plants. If melanin, the protective dark-colored pigment in your skin and the iris of your eye, is missing, you would be an albino. When albinism occurs in plants, the seedlings cannot survive because they lack the green pigment chlorophyll for photosynthesis. However, albinism is not necessarily fatal in animals.

Mendel didn't know anything about genes or chromosomes when he began his work. Yet, he did reason out that there were factors in the plants that caused a certain trait to appear. He also reasoned that these factors separated when the plants reproduced. These factors are known as genes. Your traits are determined by genes on your chromosomes. Genes may be dominant or recessive. When the chromosome pairs separate during meiosis and recombine during fertilization, different gene combinations occur. You can use a Punnett square to determine these different gene combinations in future offspring. You will learn about other inherited traits in the next section.

FIGURE 15-12. This albino koala is missing the dark colored pigment found in normal koalas.

Check Your Understanding

1. If a chromosome has 1027 different genes on it, how many genes will be found on the other chromosome of the pair and why?
2. Explain how the sorting of genes during meiosis results in a child receiving blue eyes when both parents have brown eyes.
3. How did Mendel's pea plant crosses enable him to explain the appearance and disappearance of certain traits in pedigrees?
4. **APPLY:** Explain how it's possible for two parents who both have dimples, a dominant trait, to have a child without dimples, the recessive condition.

15-3 Mendel's Work Refined

SICKLE-CELL ANEMIA

When you studied circulation and blood, you learned that your red blood cells carry oxygen to all of the other cells throughout your body. The red blood cells are normally shaped like a round disc. In some people, however, the red blood cells may have a different shape.

EXPLORE!

What do red blood cells really look like?
Examine a prepared slide of normal red blood cells under the high power of a microscope. Sketch what you see. Now examine a slide of abnormal red blood cells. Again sketch what you see. How are the cells different?

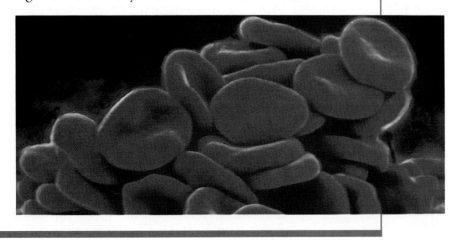

OBJECTIVES

In this section, you will
- describe what causes the genetic disease called sickle-cell anemia;
- explain how sickle-cell anemia illustrates a pattern of inheritance called incomplete dominance;
- recognize the usefulness of genetic counseling.

KEY SCIENCE TERMS

sickle-cell anemia

You may recall that a normal blood cell is like a donut without a hole. People who have a disease called **sickle-cell anemia** have misshapen red blood cells. Many of these red blood cells are shaped like curved sickles, as shown in Figure 15-13. These sickle cells can't carry as much oxygen as normal blood cells, and they don't move through the blood vessels as easily. Without enough oxygen, body tissues may be damaged. In severe cases, sickle-cell anemia can be fatal.

FIGURE 15-13. In sickle-cell
anemia, many red blood cells
are abnormally shaped.

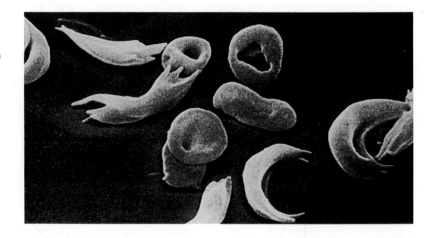

Red blood cell shape is an inherited trait and controls how much oxygen the cell can carry. Most people have all round cells. Some people have some round and some sickle-cells. They have slightly less oxygen delivered to their body tissues than normal. These people carry the sickle-cell trait. Fewer people have all sickle-cells, which prevent them from getting enough oxygen to their tissues. These people have sickle-cell anemia. In the United States sickle-cell anemia is more common in African Americans than in other population groups. About one out of every 12 African Americans has the sickle-cell trait, and one out of every 600 African Americans has sickle-cell anemia.

INCOMPLETE DOMINANCE

How can a person have both normal and sickle-cells? Which trait is dominant? Sickle-cell anemia is different from the inherited traits that Mendel studied because neither gene that determines red blood cell shape is dominant. We can indicate this lack of dominance by using two capital letters. A person with all normal blood cells is *AA*. A person with the sickle-cell trait is *AA'*, and a person with sickle-cell anemia is *A'A'*. A person can have both kinds of blood cells when both kinds of genes are present. The sickle-cell trait is not hidden like the recessive trait in a heterozygote, which occurs when traits are inherited through dominant and recessive genes. The Investigate activity will help you understand how genetic counselors might determine whether a child could have this inherited condition.

15-2 GENETIC COUNSELING

A genetic counselor advises couples on how probable it is that their children will have an inherited disease like sickle-cell anemia. We call diseases that are inherited genetic diseases. Imagine that you are a genetic counselor and that a couple has come to you for advice.

PROBLEM
What is the chance that the couple's children will inherit sickle-cell anemia?

PROCEDURE
1. Copy the data table.
2. Blood samples from the parents are illustrated. Study the cells in each sample as if you were observing them through a microscope. **Classify** the cells in your data table as all normal, half normal and half sickled, or all sickled.

DATA AND OBSERVATIONS

BLOOD SAMPLE	BLOOD CELLS	BLOOD CONDITION	GENE COMBINATION
Father			
Mother			

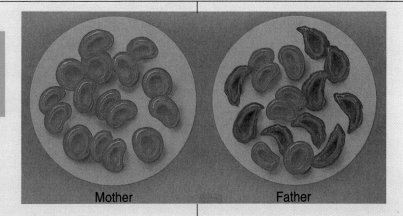

Mother   Father

3. What can you **infer** about the condition of each sample? Record your inferences in your table as normal, sickle-cell trait, or sickle-cell anemia.
4. What can you **infer** about the gene combination of each parent? Record your inferences in the table as *AA*, *AA'*, or *A'A'*.

ANALYZE
1. Draw a Punnett square to show the possible gene combinations in the couple's children. Can you **predict** what the chance might be of each gene combination occurring?

2. How would the possible gene combinations change if both the father and mother had the sickle-cell trait?

CONCLUDE AND APPLY
3. What would you tell the couple about their chances of having a child with sickle-cell anemia? What are their chances of having a child with sickle-cell trait?

4. **Going Further:** Two more parents come to you for advice. They both carry the sickle-cell trait. Because they already have one child with sickle-cell anemia, they are concerned that their next child is at increased risk of having sickle-cell anemia, too. What should you tell them?

FIGURE 15-14. Genetically engineered bacteria are being developed to consume oil spills.

Knowledge in the field of genetics has grown tremendously since the mid-1800s when Mendel was experimenting with pea plants. Present-day geneticists have extended Mendel's rules of inheritance. They have also found that many conditions are hereditary. Some, like sickle-cell anemia, are caused by specific genes. Others are caused by abnormal arrangements of chromosomes. In a condition called Down's syndrome, three chromosomes are present where only a pair should be. The extra chromosome causes changes in physical appearance and mental retardation. In addition to genetic counseling to prevent abnormalities, scientists have applied their knowledge of heredity in other useful ways. Careful breeding and selection of offspring with desired traits means better plant and animal varieties to improve the foods you eat.

Check Your Understanding

1. How do normal red blood cells differ from the red blood cells of someone with sickle-cell trait? With sickle-cell anemia?
2. Is the presence of sickled red blood cells a dominant or a recessive trait? Explain.
3. What kind of advice do families receive from genetic counseling?
4. **APPLY:** What would you need to know to advise a couple on the likelihood that their children will inherit cystic fibrosis, a disease in which mucus clogs the lungs and digestive system, starving the body of both oxygen and nutrients?

15-4 How Do Genes Control Traits?

WHAT IS DNA?

What do your chromosomes really look like? What are the genes that control your thousands of different traits actually made of? Figure 15-15 is a photograph of a chromosome taken through a powerful microscope. As depicted in Figure 15-15, the chromosomes in the nucleus of each of your cells are made of long threads of a material called **DNA**. Genes are short pieces of this DNA that make up your chromosomes. Each piece of DNA that corresponds to a gene determines a trait. How? To understand how a gene actually determines a trait, you need to understand more about the material called DNA.

OBJECTIVES

In this section, you will
- explain what DNA is and where it's found;
- model the structure of DNA;
- relate genes to the model of DNA.

KEY SCIENCE TERMS

DNA

EXPLORE!

How are airport codes similar to the DNA code?

The airline industry uses three-letter codes for the names of airports all over the world. The baggage tags in the photograph are three examples. Can you figure out what airports bags with these tags are going to? Why do you suppose airlines use these codes?

Have you ever sent a message to someone using a code? In order to read your message, the other person had to know or be able to figure out the meaning of the symbols in your code. Airline personnel quickly recognize the three-letter codes. Machines recognize codes, too. Super-

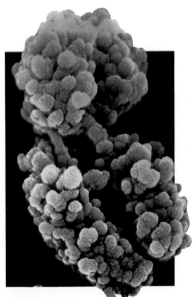

FIGURE 15-15.
Miles of thread-like DNA and protein condense to make up chromosomes.

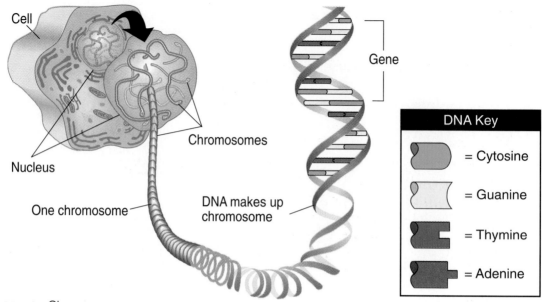

Cell

Nucleus

One chromosome

Chromosomes

DNA makes up
chromosome

Gene

DNA Key

= Cytosine

= Guanine

= Thymine

= Adenine

FIGURE 15-16. Chromosomes
are made of DNA.

market scanning machines are programmed to recognize the bar codes on things you buy. This makes checkout faster and reduces errors.

Chromosomes contain codes embedded in the chemical structure of DNA. Before your body cells divide, the DNA code of the parent cell is duplicated, and the copied DNA is passed on to the daughter cells. The new cells recognize the code of instructions that dictates what proteins to make, which in turn determine how each trait is expressed. For example, certain proteins produce curly hair, and slightly different proteins produce straight hair.

THE STRUCTURE OF DNA

Let's look more closely at a DNA molecule. The DNA molecule looks like a twisted ladder or a spiral staircase. The steps of the ladder are made of specific kinds of chemical compounds called bases. There are four bases in DNA called adenine, guanine, cytosine, and thymine. They are represented by the letters A, G, C, and T. They fit together like pieces of a jigsaw puzzle. A piece of DNA is shown on the right in Figure 15-17. This drawing shows how the bases occur in certain pairs. A always pairs with T, and G always pairs with C, never A with G or T with C. Scientists make models of DNA like the one on the right in Figure 15-17 to help them visualize what DNA looks like. You can do this, too.

FIND OUT!

Can you make a candy model of DNA?

Use two long pieces of licorice rope for the side rails of the ladder model of DNA. To make the steps of the ladder, use four different colors of gumdrops for the bases, and use toothpicks to connect them to each other and the licorice. Be sure the toothpicks stick out of the licorice on each side as far as possible to make your model secure. When you've assembled your model, carefully twist it a little to visualize how the DNA molecule spirals but not so much as to break it.

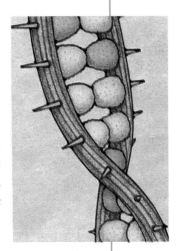

Conclude and Apply

1. How many gumdrops form each step of the ladder?
2. What do your four colors of gumdrops represent?
3. Can base A form a step with base C? Why or why not?

Different genes consist of different arrangements of A, G, C, and T bases. Just as four letters of the alphabet can be rearranged to make many different words, these four bases can be arranged in different ways to form different chemical messages. These messages control different traits. Some genes control the traits that determine how you look. Other genes control every way your body functions inside: how your blood cells carry oxygen, how you digest your food, how your reproductive organs produce eggs or sperm, and thousands of other details.

All of the characteristics that you have are affected by the DNA that you have in your cells. It controls the color of your eyes, the color of your hair, and whether or not you can digest certain foods. These characteristics are called traits, and the traits that appear in you depend on the kind of proteins your cells make.

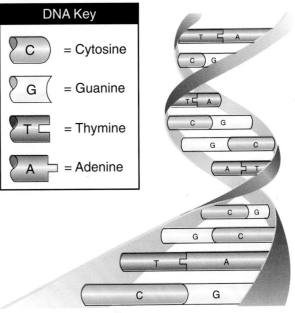

DNA Key	
C	= Cytosine
G	= Guanine
T	= Thymine
A	= Adenine

FIGURE 15-17. DNA controls the activities of cells with coded instructions.

FIGURE 15-18. Your traits make you different from everyone else.

Parents pass copies of parts of themselves on to their offspring. The way each individual develops depends on the instructions coded in the DNA an individual receives from both parents. You are like your parents in many ways but different too. Because so many different combinations are possible, you are different from your brothers and sisters, from other relatives, from your classmates, and from everyone else on Earth. You are unique.

Check Your Understanding

1. Explain how chromosomes and DNA are related. Describe where they are found.
2. To make a model of DNA, what must you know about its shape and the bases it contains?
3. How are genes related to the structure of DNA?
4. **APPLY:** Defend or reject this statement: "The functions of frog stomach cells are controlled by genes, but the growth of tree leaf cells is not."

CONTENTS

A **CLOSER** LOOK

LOOKING AT COLOR BLINDNESS

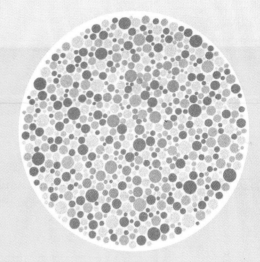

Colors do not appear the same to everyone. If you're color-blind, green may look grayish. Red may appear yellowish. A person with normal color vision will see a different number in the picture of the circle than a color-blind person will see. Color blindness is a sex-linked trait. So is hemophilia—a blood defect that causes delayed clotting. These and other sex-linked traits occur more often in males than females. To understand how sex-linked traits work, you have to be introduced to the chromosomes that determine sex. In humans, there are two types of sex chromosomes—X and Y. You learned that chromosomes come in pairs. Females have two X chromosomes and are designated as XX. Males have one of each type and are designated as XY.

Sex-linked traits are usually controlled by genes of the X chromosome. For a female to inherit a recessive sex-linked trait, the trait must be present in both of her X chromosomes. This fact has an effect on which sex will inherit the trait.

Although color blindness and other recessive sex-linked traits are found more often in males, females are usually carriers of the trait. Carriers are individuals who carry the gene for color blindness on an X chromosome but are not color-blind themselves.

YOU TRY IT!

Work out the different combinations of genes present in a mother and father of three families. N stands for normal trait, while C stands for color-blind trait.

Family	Father	Mother
1	$X^N Y$	$X^N X^C$
2	$X^C Y$	$X^N X^N$
3	$X^C Y$	$X^C X^N$

What are the possibilities of a son or a daughter inheriting color blindness in each instance? Can you explain why males are color-blind more often than females?

Physics Connection

PLANTS AND LIGHT

As you know, albinism is a mutation in which organisms are not able to produce pigments. Pigments are substances that absorb certain colors of the spectrum and reflect others. Organisms with albinism lack pigments, and their cells can't absorb colors. All colors are reflected, and the organ-

isms appear whitish in color. How does albinism affect organisms?

Albinism occurs in both plants and animals. Plants with albinism are completely unable to produce the pigment chlorophyll, which absorbs sunlight for the process of photosynthesis. Since it is a mutation of a gene, you know from the chapter that it can also be inherited. Try the following activity to understand how the inheritance of albino genes affects the corn plant.

Materials
- 20 corn seeds
- paper towels
- petri dish
- water
- wax pencil

Procedure
1. Copy the data table.
2. Look at the seeds carefully. Can you tell which seeds will produce green leaves, and which will produce white leaves?
3. Moisten a paper towel with water.
4. Place the moist towel in the petri dish.
5. Spread the seeds on the paper towel, cover with the petri dish lid, and write your name on the cover.
6. Place the petri dish under a light and check it every day, adding water if needed.
7. When the seeds sprout, record the leaf color in the Day 1 row of the table.
8. Check corn seeds for four more days. Record the numbers of new plants with green and white leaves each day.

WHAT DO YOU THINK?

Corn plants that remain white several days after sprouting have the albino trait. Do you think your albino seedlings will last very long? Explain your answer.

Data and Observations			
	Number of seeds sprouted	Number with green leaves	Number with white leaves
Day 1			
Day 2			
Day 3			
Day 4			
Day 5			
Total			

SCIENCE AND SOCIETY

GENETIC ENGINEERING: PRO AND CON

You're a diabetic. You have to take insulin every single day. Recently, you've had bad news. The insulin you take is produced from pigs, and you have developed an allergy to it.

A few years ago, this would have meant real trouble for you. Now, though, a new product—artificially produced human insulin—is available. The insulin is made by genetic engineering, and for you it's a real lifesaver. Literally.

DNA is the material that passes on genetic information in the cells of almost all living things. Genetic engineering is a new technology that allows scientists to separate a short string of DNA from one species and insert it into the DNA of another species.

Often the new host species is a bacterium, and the DNA carries the code for a desirable protein, such as a hormone. After the DNA is inserted into the DNA of the bacteria, the bacteria are allowed to reproduce. As they do so, they produce more of the desired protein—a protein that they would not produce normally.

Human insulin is produced in this way, but it is made in two parts. The human genes for the two different proteins that make up the insulin molecule are inserted into the DNA of two separate groups of bacteria. The bacteria grow, producing the proteins. The proteins are purified and then combined to form insulin. Other medicines produced by bacteria include human growth hormone for the treatment of dwarfism and a medicine that dissolves blood clots.

Genetic engineering has produced many products for use in agriculture. One makes plants resistant to frost damage. There is a species of bacteria that commonly grows on the leaves of plants. Normally, the bacteria produce a protein that enables ice to crystallize on the leaves. Scientists have removed the gene for this protein from the DNA of the bacteria, so the protein is no longer produced. If the altered bacteria are sprayed on plants, ice will not form on the plants' leaves.

Scientists have also inserted genes from other species into the DNA of plants. Genes from plants that are tolerant to weed killers can be introduced into plants that are normally intolerant to weed killers. When the newly tolerant plants reproduce, their offspring are tolerant.

In another development, a gene from a bacterium was introduced into tomato plants. The gene produces a protein that is poisonous to some insects. The tomato plants now produce this protein and are resistant to attack by those insects.

Genes from other species have even been introduced into the DNA of mammals. For instance, using a machine called a "gene gun," like the one shown below, the gene for human growth hormone has been inserted into the DNA of mice. In the picture at the right, one mouse now has the gene that produces human growth hormone in its DNA. Can you tell which mouse it is?

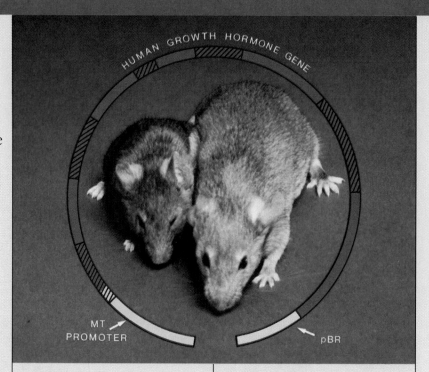

At first glance, genetic engineering seems wonderful. However, some groups are concerned that there may be problems associated with it.

One of the main concerns is that genetically-engineered organisms might accidentally escape from a laboratory. No one really knows if any harm would come from this, but scientists have developed guidelines to head off such accidents. Laboratories dealing with potentially harmful organisms have strict security procedures.

Another concern is that even beneficial organisms that are released intentionally may not be as good as we first thought. Bacteria released to help a crop could multiply and spread beyond the field where they're applied. They could harm the environment in ways that we can't even foresee. If plants are more resistant to weed killers, couldn't that eventually lead to more weed killers in the environment? If a plant contains a protein that makes it poisonous to insects, can we be sure that it is not harmful to humans?

Is genetic engineering a lifesaver, the farmer's friend, or a threat to the environment?

WHAT DO YOU THINK?

Some people think all genetic research should stop until we are able to see more clearly just what the risks are. Do you agree?

Do you think scientists should be allowed to do any research they want in genetic engineering? What exceptions, if any, would you make?

*H*istory
C O N N E C T I O N

HEREDITY AND THE AMISH

Ellis-van Creveld syndrome, a type of dwarfism, is much more common among the Amish who live in Lancaster County, Pennsylvania, than in the population of the United States as a whole. People born with this syndrome have short arms and legs. They may also have more than five fingers or toes. The syndrome is a recessive disorder.

Why is Ellis-van Creveld syndrome so common among the Amish? To answer this, one must know something about Amish life. The Amish are members of a small religious group in the United States. They chose to reject most of modern technology and follow a traditional way of life similar to that of the 1600s in Europe. Most Amish are farmers, and Amish boys and girls help with the farm work as soon as they are able to walk. They might feed animals or help plant and harvest food. After the boys and girls finish eighth grade, they enter a home work-study program to learn more about running a farm and household. Amish do not own cars or telephones, so the horse and buggy is their primary way of contacting others.

Amish families are large, and they keep thorough records of births, marriages, and deaths because family is important to them. Amish are expected to marry only within the Amish community. The Amish believe in helping others, so poverty is virtually unknown. Anyone in need receives help from others in the community. As a result of the good medical care they seek, several genetic conditions have been diagnosed. One of these is Ellis-van Creveld syndrome.

Records show that most of the 14,000 Lancaster County Amish are descendants of about 200 settlers who came to America before the Revolutionary War. One, or more, of the original settlers must have been a carrier of Ellis-van Creveld syndrome. Since the Amish marry only Amish, this makes it more likely for two recessive carriers of the syndrome to produce children who will have two recessive genes, and so have the actual syndrome.

These practices of the Amish, particularly their thorough record-keeping of family histories and their practice of marrying only Amish, make it easier to follow genetic disorders that have been passed on through generations. By allowing geneticists to study their medical records and geneologies, the Amish have helped them understand inherited disorders such as Ellis-van Creveld syndrome.

WHAT DO YOU THINK?

What differences can you see between your life and that of the Amish? Why is it hard for researchers to study human traits in the general population?

TECHNOLOGY CONNECTION

Suspects

Sample A in the figure is a DNA fingerprint taken from one strand of hair. The hair was found on the body of a murder victim at the crime scene. It does not belong to the victim. Samples B through G are DNA fingerprints from six suspects. Who is the murderer? Match the DNA from sample A to one of the other samples, and you'll find out!

If the owner of Sample A has an identical twin, how would that factor complicate your detective work?

DNA FINGERPRINTING

I t's almost as though each person has a specific product bar code. With the exception of identical twins, who have the same DNA, every person in the world has a different set of genes, and each person's DNA is unique. DNA is like a fingerprint.

The unique nature of DNA means that each person should be able to be identified by his or her DNA. This has an important application in crime solving.

Skin cells contain DNA. If a person is murdered, and the police find bits of the murderer's skin under the victim's fingernails, these bits can be used to identify the suspect. If the police have several suspects, how can they tell who is guilty? Cells of the skin contain DNA that belongs only to the murderer. The DNA of the skin left at the scene and the DNA of the guilty person will match exactly.

DNA fingerprinting helps identify criminals. Here is how it works: Scientists can remove the DNA from almost any kind of cell left behind by the criminal. The DNA is treated so that it produces an image of the chemicals that it contains, similar to those pictured at the left. This picture of DNA is compared with DNA images from other cell samples of the murder suspect.

Reviewing Main Ideas

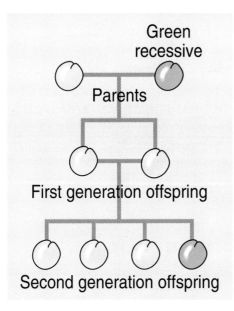

1. Gregor Mendel crossed different types of pea plants to discover the pattern of inheritance of dominant and recessive traits.

2. Traits are controlled by genes on the DNA molecules that make up chromosomes. A gene is a short sequence of bases that form a code.

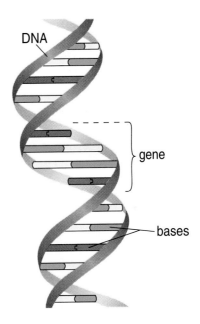

3. Understanding how genes are expressed enables couples and genetic counselors to estimate the chance that offspring will have a specific trait or genetic disease such as sickle-cell anemia.

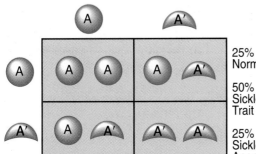

Chapter Review

USING KEY SCIENCE TERMS

DNA	pure dominant
dominant trait	pure recessive
gene	recessive trait
heterozygote	sickle-cell anemia
pedigree	traits

Choose the science term that best describes each of the codes below.

1. *TT*
2. *Tt*
3. *A-T-C-G-A-T*
4. *tt*
5. *A'A'*

UNDERSTANDING IDEAS

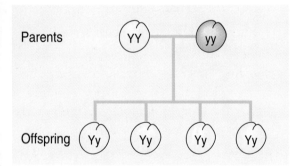

Complete each sentence. The questions are about the cross shown between a plant with yellow peas (*YY*) and one with green peas (*yy*).

1. The parent with the yellow peas was _____.
   a. a heterozygote
   b. a pure recessive
   c. a pure dominant
   d. lacked dominance

2. The genes in the sex cells of the parent with green peas were _____.
   a. *Yy*   c. *y*
   b. *YY*   d. *yy*

3. The trait of green pea color is _____.
   a. pure dominant   c. dominant
   b. pure recessive   d. heterozygous

4. The offspring for this cross will be _____.
   a. 25 percent green
   b. 50 percent yellow
   c. 100 percent yellow
   d. 100 percent green

5. The trait of the offspring is _____.
   a. pure dominant   c. pure recessive
   b. recessive   d. heterozygous

6. The illustration is a _____.
   a. Punnett square   c. gene map
   b. DNA molecule   d. pedigree

7. If two of the offspring shown are crossed, the chance of their offspring being green is _____.
   a. 25 percent   c. 75 percent
   b. 50 percent   d. 100 percent

CRITICAL THINKING

Use your understanding of the concepts developed in the chapter to answer each of the following questions.

1. Explain the difference between a pedigree and a Punnett square.

2. Explain how the cheeks of a person with *Dd* genes for dimples could look the same as the cheeks of a person with *DD* genes.

3. What is wrong with the DNA molecule in the drawing?

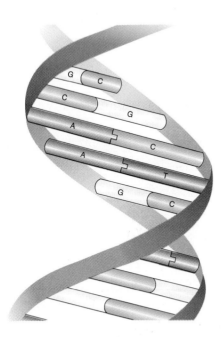

4. A pure black dog is crossed with a pure white dog. All the puppies produced from this mating are black. What are the gene combinations of both parents?

5. Explain how Mendel concluded that traits are controlled by two factors, which we now call genes.

PROBLEM SOLVING

Read the following problems and discuss your answers in a brief paragraph.

Drawing a Punnett square for one trait is fairly simple, but constructing a Punnett square for two traits is more challenging.

1. Draw a Punnett square for a cross between a pea plant that is pure dominant for green color *(GG)* and roundness *(RR)* and one that is pure recessive for these traits. These peas will appear yellow *(gg)* and wrinkled *(rr)*. Over each top box you will write **GR**. What gene pairs will you write next to each side box?

2. With two traits, you will have four letters instead of two when you fill in the four boxes of your Punnett square. What are they, and what would the peas from each offspring look like?

3. Now cross the heterozygotes *GgRr* to produce a second set of offspring. How would you draw this Punnett square?

4. Fill in all the squares of this Punnett, showing the genes of the second set of offspring. How many of these plants would have round, green peas? What other kinds of peas would this cross produce?

CONNECTING IDEAS

Discuss each of the following in a brief paragraph.

1. How do environmental factors complicate our understanding of heredity? Give an example.

2. How does meiosis enable pure recessive traits to be expressed?

3. In humans, sex is determined by a pair of chromosomes. Females are **XX**, and males are **XY**. Use a Punnett square to show why about equal numbers of males and females are born.

4. TECHNOLOGY CONNECTION Describe two benefits of genetic engineering research.

5. SCIENCE AND SOCIETY Explain how DNA can be used to solve crimes.

DID YOU EVER WONDER . . .

How deep the oceans are?

Why California has so many earthquakes?

How a dormant volcano could suddenly erupt after 600 years?

You'll find the answers to these questions as you read this chapter.

Moving Continents

You can hardly imagine how beautiful Earth must look from space. Then you see the satellite photo of Earth on the jigsaw puzzle you were given. The picture is spectacular! You can't wait to begin working on the puzzle.

For days, you fit pieces together, and ever so slowly the puzzle begins to take shape. You easily finish North America and Europe. They are now intact on the puzzle. You turn your attention to completing the African continent, and you make an interesting discovery. You notice that although the pieces you've placed all fit together well, the continent doesn't look like the picture on the puzzle box. You recheck your work and discover that some of the pieces you placed on the western coast of Africa actually belong on the eastern coast of South America. How could you have made this mistake? Is it possible that your puzzle pieces fit in two different places?

This chapter will help you understand the movement of continents and how the forces behind this movement can affect Earth's surface.

EXPLORE!

What clues are used to piece together puzzles?

Cut a picture out of an old magazine and paste it on lightweight cardboard. Then cut the picture into pieces of different sizes and shapes. Try to piece it back together again. What clues do you use to help you put the picture together?

16-1 The Moving Continents

OBJECTIVES

In this section, you will

- explain the hypothesis of continental drift;
- identify and discuss four pieces of evidence used to support the hypothesis of continental drift.

KEY SCIENCE TERMS

continental drift

CONTINENTAL DRIFT

Have you ever told your friends a true story that they would not believe? Maybe you gave them all kinds of specific details to support your story—and they still wouldn't believe you.

The same sort of thing happened to the people who first said that the continents move. No one would believe them.

Alfred Wegener observed the similarity in the shapes of continental coastlines. Wegener thought that the fit of the continents wasn't a coincidence. He believed that all the continents were once joined as one large supercontinent called Pangaea (pan JEE uh), which means "all Earth." Wegener believed that Pangaea broke apart about 200 million years ago, and that the continents had since moved. In 1915, Wegener announced his hypothesis known as **continental drift**.

Because of lack of proof, however, Wegener's hypothesis was not taken seriously by other scientists. One reason Wegener's ideas were scoffed at was because he was not a geologist. He had been trained as a meteorologist. After his hypothesis was rejected by other scientists, Wegener decided to gather more data to support his idea. You'll use some of these data in the Investigate activity.

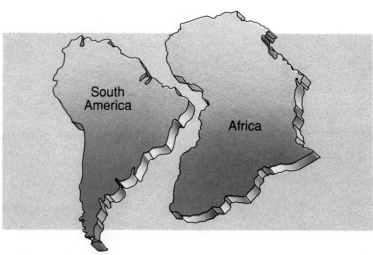

FIGURE 16-1. The coastlines of South America and Africa look as if they fit together as puzzle pieces.

16-1 RECONSTRUCT PANGAEA

You know that a scientist must have evidence to support a hypothesis. In this activity, you will examine evidence that Pangaea existed.

PROBLEM
What evidence is helpful in reconstructing Pangaea?

MATERIALS
world map
5 sheets unlined paper
large sheet of paper
scissors
glue

PROCEDURE
1. Trace the continents and Greenland from the world map onto the unlined paper. Label each landmass.

2. Cut out the landmasses.
3. The landmasses probably won't fit together exactly, but try to fit the shapes together as many ways as you can. Keep track of the number of ways you try.
4. **Use the table** below to add information to the pieces. Put the symbol found in parentheses for each type of evidence in the location listed in the table.
5. Using the new data, try again to fit the labeled landmasses together. **Compare** your first attempt with this one. Record the number of ways the continents fit together.
6. When you have the best fit, glue the assembled pieces to the large piece of paper. This is your reconstruction of Pangaea.

ANALYZE
1. Using only the shapes of the landmasses as evidence, how many ways did they fit together?
2. Using the shapes plus the evidence from the data table, how many ways did the landmasses fit?

CONCLUDE AND APPLY
3. How did the additional evidence help you reconstruct a model of Pangaea?
4. How does this reconstruction of Pangaea help explain the evidence of glaciers in Africa where no glaciers currently exist?
5. **Going Further:** From what evidence can you **infer** that India may once have been separated from Asia?

TYPE OF EVIDENCE	SYMBOL	LOCATION
Type A mountains	(**AAAA**):	eastern North America, western Europe, southern tip of Greenland
Type C mountains	(**CCCC**):	southern end of South America, southern end of Africa
Evidence of glaciers	(**XXXX**):	western Australia, southern tip of India, southern Africa, southeastern South America, Antarctica
Type G fossils	(**GGGG**):	western Australia, southern tip of India, southern Africa, southeastern South America, Antarctica
Type M fossils	(**MMMM**):	southern tip of Africa, southern tip of South America

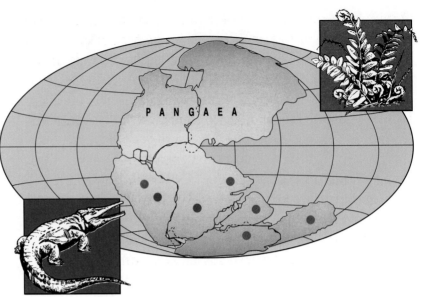

FIGURE 16-2. *Mesosaurus* and *Glossopteris* were a reptile and a fern that lived in warm parts of Pangaea. Red dots indicate where *Glossopteris* fossils have been found. Purple dots indicate where *Mesosaurus* fossils have been found.

FOSSIL AND CLIMATE CLUES

Think back to the Explore activity at the beginning of this chapter. How did you fit the magazine picture pieces together? One clue you used was their shapes. What other clues did you use to put the magazine picture back together?

To develop his supercontinent idea, Wegener also started with the puzzle-like fit of the continents, but then he gathered additional information to help in the reconstruction of Pangaea. One type of data he gathered was fossil information such as the information you used in the Investigate activity. The Type M fossil is from a reptile called *Mesosaurus*. The Type G fossil is from a fern called *Glossopteris*. *Mesosaurus* fossils are found in South America and Africa. *Glossopteris* fossils are found in Africa, South America, India, Australia, and Antarctica. Figure 16-2 shows how Pangaea might be reconstructed using the fossil information as well as the shapes of landmasses.

If *Mesosaurus* fossils are found in South America and Africa, which are not currently connected by land, how did *Mesosaurus* get from one continent to the other? *Mesosaurus* was a reptile that lived both on land and in water. You might hypothesize that *Mesosaurus* was able to swim between the continents. However, *Mesosaurus* lived only in fresh water. Even if swimming the entire Atlantic

FIGURE 16-3. Alfred Wegener developed the hypothesis of continental drift.

Ocean were possible for *Mesosaurus*, it would not have been able to survive in the salt water for long. At that time, there wasn't anything that could have transported *Mesosaurus* across the Atlantic Ocean. Therefore, the best explanation is that *Mesosaurus* was able to move across South America and Africa because the two continents were joined at one time.

The story of the *Glossopteris* fossils is similar. *Glossopteris* fossils are found on continents that have climates that are very different from one another. In what kind of climate would you expect to find a fern? If *Glossopteris* lived in a warm climate, what does this say about the places in which *Glossopteris* fossils are found? The part of Pangaea where *Glossopteris* lived must have had a warm climate. The fact that *Glossopteris* fossils are found today on continents with different climates is more evidence that the continents have moved.

Wegener gathered evidence of deposits of glacial sediment and grooved bedrock in the southern parts of South America, Africa, India, and Australia. Although these areas are now located in the middle and low latitudes, and their climates are different from one another, Wegener thought that these areas must have once been connected and covered with glaciers. Based on this glacial evidence, Wegener hypothesized that these areas were once in high latitudes near the South Pole, and that they had had very cold climates at one time. This led him to believe that these areas were once covered by glaciers. Using fossil and climate evidence such as that gathered by Wegener, computer models like those in Figure 16-4 can show how Pangaea broke apart.

FIGURE 16-4. These computer models show the probable course that continents have taken. On the far left is their position 200 million years ago, in the middle is their position 100 million years ago, and at right is their current position.

CLUES FROM ROCKS

If the continents were once all part of the same super-continent, shouldn't the rock structures of continents that were once joined be similar along the place they split apart? Of course, not all the rocks on a continent are the same. Rocks along the eastern coast of North America, for example, are not the same as the ones near the middle of the continent. However, you would expect to find similar types, ages, and structures of rocks along the coastal areas of two continents that were once joined.

In the Investigate activity, you used similar mountain chains to help reconstruct a model of Pangaea. The Type A mountains are like the Appalachian Mountains in the eastern United States. Similar rock structures and mountains are found in Greenland and western Europe. In southern Africa, the Cape Mountains extend to the edge of the Atlantic Ocean. These are the Type C mountains used in the activity. You would find similar mountains in South America. If the continents were put together to form Pangaea, you would find that the mountain ranges listed above would form two continuous mountain chains.

Unfortunately, Wegener was never able to explain how or why the continents move. As a result, other scientists of his time rejected his idea of continental drift. However, additional evidence found in the 1940s and 1950s revived the hypothesis. Today, the hypothesis of continental drift has been largely accepted. In the following section, you will read about the evidence that has helped support it.

Check Your Understanding

1. How did Wegener use four types of evidence to help support his hypothesis of continental drift?
2. Fossils indicate that tropical plants once lived on what is now Antarctica. What two explanations can you give for this?
3. **APPLY:** "Continental slopes, the parts of the ocean floor that dip steeply to the seafloor located next to the continental shelves, mark the true edges of the continents." How would this statement affect how you might reassemble traced outlines of continents into Pangaea?

16-2 Sea-Floor Spreading

THE LAYERED EARTH

If Wegener had possessed more information about what lay beneath the continents, he might have been better able to explain how continents can move. Figure 16-5 shows a model of Earth's inner structure. At the center is a very dense iron and nickel core. It can be compared to the seed of a peach. Above the solid inner core lies a liquid outer core, also made of iron and nickel. This layer has the same relationship as the peach pit surrounding the seed.

Directly above the outer core is the mantle. The rock material in the mantle, made mostly of silicon, oxygen, magnesium, and iron, has characteristics of a solid. However, it also flows like a liquid when under pressure. This layer can be compared to the juicy, fleshy part of a peach. Finally, the outermost layer is the crust. The crust is like the skin of a peach. It ranges in thickness from more than 70 kilometers in some mountainous regions to less than 5 kilometers under the ocean.

FIGURE 16-5. This wedge shows the layers inside Earth from the inner core. The inner core, outer core, and mantle are shown at the correct scale, but the crust is shown much thicker than it actually is.

OBJECTIVES

In this section, you will
- explain how sea-floor spreading supports the hypothesis of continental drift;
- explain how the age of rocks and magnetic clues confirm sea-floor spreading.

KEY SCIENCE TERMS

sea-floor spreading

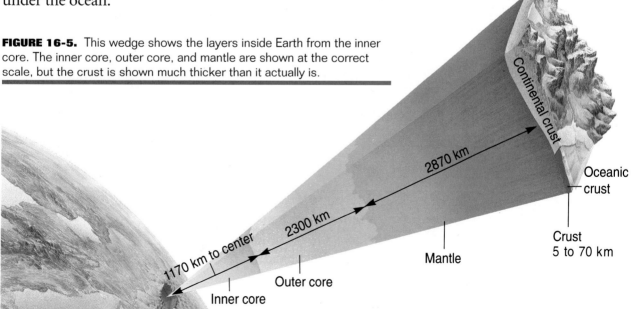

FIGURE 16-6. Echo sounding can make very accurate maps of the ocean floor like the one shown in this figure.

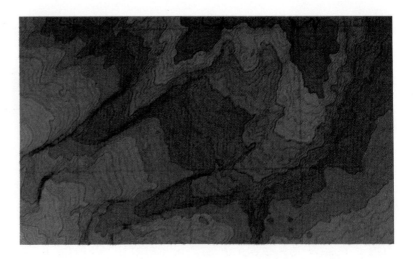

CLUES ON THE OCEAN FLOOR

During Wegener's lifetime, little was known about the ocean floor. However, by the late 1950s, research vessels had crisscrossed Earth's oceans, taking thousands of echo soundings. Echo sounding was made possible by sound wave technology. Scientists would send a sound wave to the seafloor, and the sound would echo back up to the ship. Scientists could time the returning sound and determine how far from the surface the seafloor was. The resulting maps showed mountains and valleys just like those on the continents. The most amazing discovery was mountain chains thousands of kilometers long. One chain runs down the middle of the Atlantic Ocean. These mountain chains are called mid-ocean ridges. Along the crests of these ridges are narrow regions called rift valleys.

The seafloor maps also showed the location of deep trenches. The deepest trench, the Marianas Trench, is over 11 kilometers deep in some parts.

AGE EVIDENCE

In the 1960s, scientists on board the research ship *Glomar Challenger* began gathering information about rocks in the ocean crust. The scientists used a hollow drill bit and drill pipe to drill into the seafloor and pull out samples, in the same way you could stick a straw into gelatin and pull out a sample. None of the ocean floor rock samples was older than 200 million years. This was surprising because some rocks have been found on the continents that are more than three billion years old! Rocks at the mid-ocean ridges were very young, but rocks became increasingly older farther away from the ridges. This was true in both directions from the mid-ocean ridges. Why were the rocks near the ridges younger?

Princeton University scientist Harry Hess proposed that molten material within Earth's mantle rises at a mid-ocean ridge. Between the crust and the outer core, part of the mantle is solid, and part is putty-like. Trace the motions of the molten materials at the mid-ocean ridge using Figure 16-7. Some of the molten material is lava, which cools when it reaches the surface of the crust to form new ocean crust. The rest of the material flows away from the mid-ocean ridge underneath the ocean crust. As the material moves away, it pulls the ocean crust away from the ridge, creating a valley. New crust is formed in this rift valley. Rock formed in the rift is carried farther from the mid-ocean ridge as time goes on. This explains why the youngest rock is found near the ridge, and the oldest rock is found farthest from the ridge.

Hess believed that crust pushed away from the mid-ocean ridge eventually gets destroyed when it comes in contact with another section of crust. When this occurs, a trench is formed. You'll find out more about trenches later in this chapter.

Hess's hypothesis, known as **sea-floor spreading**, states that molten material from Earth's mantle rises to the surface at mid-ocean ridges and cools to form new seafloor.

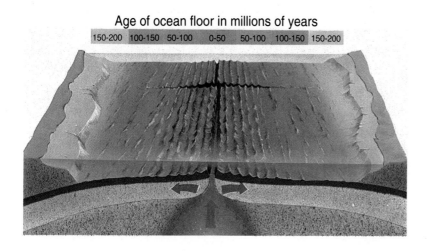

Age of ocean floor in millions of years

| 150-200 | 100-150 | 50-100 | 0-50 | 50-100 | 100-150 | 150-200 |

FIGURE 16-7. As magma rises at a mid-ocean ridge, the seafloor moves away from the ridge in opposite directions.

New magma slowly pushes this material away from the ridges. Like any hypothesis, sea-floor spreading had to be able to explain new information as it became available. The next information available, in this case, was magnetic information locked within the ocean floor rocks. The Explore activity will help you understand the magnetic nature of rocks.

EXPLORE!

How does a magnet affect iron filings?
Carefully place a small amount of iron filings on a section of stiff cardboard. Place a large bar magnet flat on a table. Note which way the north and south poles are facing. Place the cardboard and filings on top of the magnet. How do the filings align themselves? Carefully spray the iron filings with clear lacquer in a well-ventilated area so they retain their alignment. Allow the lacquer to dry. Change the position of the magnet by 90°. Place more iron filings on the cardboard, put the cardboard on top of the magnet, and observe. What happens to the alignment of the lacquered filings? To the filings you added?

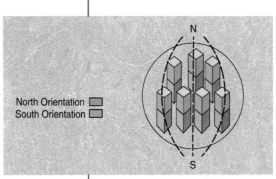

North Orientation
South Orientation

MAGNETIC CLUES

Earth has a magnetic field much like that of a bar magnet. While lava is still liquid, the iron in it is free to move and align itself with Earth's magnetic field. When the lava hardens into rock, the iron is no longer free to move. The hardened rock contains a record of how Earth's magnetic field was aligned at the time the lava cooled.

When Harry Hess first suggested sea-floor spreading as an explanation for the mid-ocean ridges, he did not know about the magnetic field data recorded in the seafloor rocks. As you will see in the Investigate activity, the magnetic record suggests how the seafloor has moved.

16-2 MAGNETIC DATA

Magnetic data can be used to support the hypothesis of sea-floor spreading. What other information do the magnetic data provide?

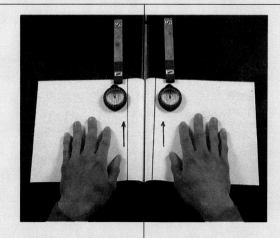

PROBLEM

How do rocks show locations of Earth's magnetic poles?

MATERIALS

metric ruler
paper
tape
2 small magnetic compasses
2 bar magnets
pen or marker

PROCEDURE

1. Tape several sheets of paper together, end to end, to produce a strip 40 to 60 cm long.

2. Fold the strip of paper in the middle as shown in the figure and place it between two desks or piles of books. The paper represents oceanic crust that forms as lava comes out of the mid-ocean ridge.

3. Place the two small magnets and the compasses on the paper as shown in the figure.

4. Draw lines on the paper along each side of the space to represent the edges of the mid-ocean ridge.

5. Beside each line, draw an arrow that shows the direction of north as shown on the compass needle.

6. Spread the seafloor by pulling paper up from the space and away from the center. Pull the paper out about 3 cm on each side.

7. Reverse the magnets by turning them 180°.

8. Move the compasses so that they are again aligned. Draw new arrows on the paper to represent the direction that the compass needles are now pointing.

9. Repeat Steps 6–8 several times, but vary the amount of paper you pull out each time. Be sure to move the same amount of paper on each side of the space.

10. Number the stripes you made when you drew the lines. Use 1 to represent the oldest stripe.

ANALYZE

1. Where are the oldest stripes on your paper?

2. **Compare** your paper to the patterns in Figure 16-8 on page 490. What are the similarities?

3. What do the arrows on the paper represent?

CONCLUDE AND APPLY

4. Why were you instructed to pull the same amount of paper out from both sides of the middle space?

5. **Going Further:** A rock that is 50 million years old is found 3000 km west of a mid-ocean ridge. What can you **infer** about a rock found 4000 km west of the ridge? 3000 km east?

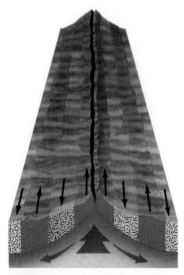

 Normal polarity   Reversed polarity

FIGURE 16-8. Changes in magnetic polarity of the rock on both sides of mid-ocean ridges reflect the past reversals of Earth's magnetic poles. This is evidence for sea-floor spreading.

Just as you found a pattern to the stripes in the Investigate activity, scientists examining seafloor rocks found an interesting pattern in the magnetic records of the rocks. This pattern is shown in Figure 16-8. The rocks show that Earth's magnetic field has reversed itself many times. Each time the magnetic field switched, the rocks recorded the new field. The magnetic properties of rocks aligned with the magnetic orientation at the time that they formed.

Using magnetometers, research ships took magnetic readings on ocean floor igneous rocks and plotted the data on maps. The maps revealed that stripes of magnetically similar rock run parallel to a mid-ocean ridge. The pattern of stripes on one side of a mid-ocean ridge was very similar to the pattern on the other side. Radiometric dating revealed that the age of the rocks on either side of a rift is also very similar. What do these findings suggest about what happens at a mid-ocean ridge?

The discovery of similar magnetic records and ages of rock on both sides of a mid-ocean ridge helped support Hess's hypothesis of sea-floor spreading. For one thing, the magnetic reversal showed that new rock was being formed at the mid-ocean ridges. For another, if the floor were not spreading, the ages and magnetic records of rocks on either side of a rift would probably not be the same.

While Wegener believed that the continents were moving, Hess believed that the seafloor was moving. Was it possible that both were correct? Like putting pieces of a puzzle together, scientists began to fit the two hypotheses together to show us the big picture of Earth in continual motion.

Check Your Understanding

1. How are the ideas of continental drift and sea-floor spreading related?
2. Discuss two pieces of data used to support the idea of sea-floor spreading.
3. What eventually happens to seafloor that is carried away from a mid-ocean ridge?
4. **APPLY:** How old would you expect igneous rock just outside a rift valley to be? Where would iron in this rock indicate the North Pole is?

16-3 Colliding Plates

TECTONIC PLATES

Do you enjoy reading mystery stories? Do you try to guess how the mystery will be solved by the story characters? Usually, the characters piece together clues or evidence. Think of the hypotheses of continental drift and sea-floor spreading as clues to a mystery. How can Wegener's and Hess's hypotheses be explained?

In the late 1960s, geologists developed a new theory to explain the apparent movement of the continents. The theory of **plate tectonics** suggests that Earth's crust and upper mantle are broken into sections called plates that move. But what are the plates made of, and why do they move?

You already know that Earth's crust is a layer of solid rock. The uppermost portion of the mantle is also solid. Together, these two areas are the **lithosphere.** The lithosphere is generally about 100 kilometers thick. A plate is a section of lithosphere that usually contains sections of both ocean and continental crust. Therefore, a moving plate usually carries a landmass and part of a seafloor. These sections of crust and mantle are diagrammed in Figure 16-9.

How are these solid plates able to move around? Below the lithosphere is a portion of the mantle that is less solid. It is near its melting point and is easily deformed. The material here behaves almost like putty; it's a solid that can flow. This putty-like layer is called the asthenosphere (as THEN uh sfihr). The plates can be thought of as rafts that slide around on the asthenosphere. Because they cover the entire planet, there are always places where the plates are in contact with each other. The place where two plates meet is called a plate boundary. In the following activity, you will explore the different types of plate boundaries.

OBJECTIVES

In this section, you will

- explain how plate tectonics accounts for the movement of continents;
- compare and contrast divergent, convergent, and transform plate boundaries;
- explain how convection currents inside Earth might be the cause of plate tectonics.

KEY SCIENCE TERMS

plate tectonics
lithosphere
divergent boundary
convergent boundary
transform fault boundary

FIGURE 16-9. Together, Earth's crust and solid mantle make up the lithosphere. The putty-like portion of the mantle is the asthenosphere.

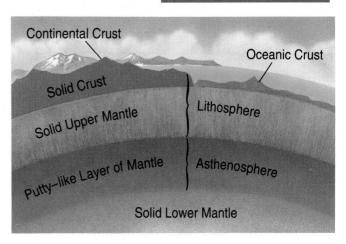

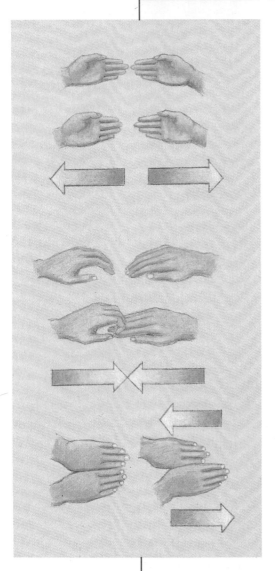

What happens when plates move?
Refer to the illustration and follow the directions to simulate the motions of plates with your hands.

1. Begin with the fingertips of both hands pressing against each other as shown. Slowly pull your hands apart. Notice the space between your hands as they spread apart.

2. Start with your hands facing end to end, about 15 cm apart. Bring your hands together so that one hand is forced under the other. As your fingertips meet, one hand curves under the other. The hand on top starts to curl and makes a fist.

3. Put your hands side by side and press them together. Continue pressing them together as you slide them slowly past each other. Notice that the motion is not even. The places where one hand bulges get locked into the places where the other hand dents. Eventually, you push hard enough that your hands come unlocked, and the sliding movement continues.

As you saw in the activity, the directions of plate movement determine what occurs at a plate boundary. Plates can move away from each other, they can move toward each other and collide, or they can simply slide past each other. Let's look at the basic types of plate boundaries.

Divergent Boundaries

The boundary between two plates that are moving away from each other and spreading apart is called a **divergent boundary.** You simulated this type of bound-

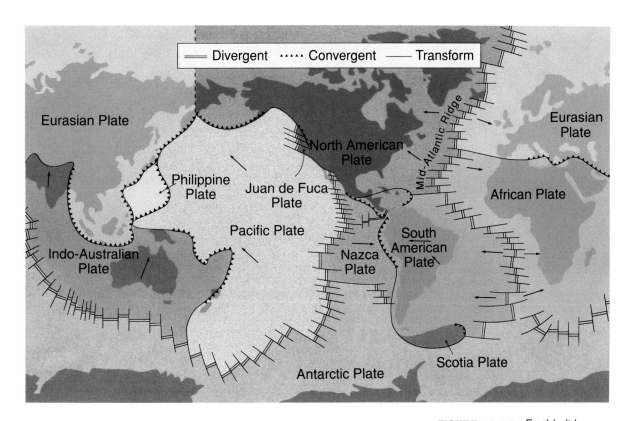

Divergent ····· Convergent —— Transform

Eurasian Plate

North American Plate

Philippine Plate

Juan de Fuca Plate

Pacific Plate

Indo-Australian Plate

Nazca Plate

South American Plate

Mid-Atlantic Ridge

Eurasian Plate

African Plate

Scotia Plate

Antarctic Plate

FIGURE 16-10. Earth's lithosphere is made up of nine major plates and several small ones. The arrows indicate directions of movement.

ary when you pulled your hands apart in the Explore activity. Magma rises to Earth's surface in the rift valley that forms between the two plates, creating new crust. Mid-ocean ridges are divergent boundaries. In the Atlantic Ocean, the North American Plate is moving away from the Eurasian and African plates. This divergent boundary is the Mid-Atlantic Ridge discussed earlier. This boundary is shown in Figure 16-10. The Atlantic Ocean formed when the North American Plate pulled apart from the Eurasian and African plates.

Convergent Boundaries

If new crust is being added at the divergent boundaries, why isn't Earth getting bigger? Think of the hypothesis of sea-floor spreading, where ocean floor crust is destroyed at the trenches. Earth doesn't get bigger because as new crust is added in one place, it sinks into Earth's interior at another. Crustal material can be destroyed where two plates meet head on. This type of plate boundary is called a **convergent boundary.**

DID YOU KNOW?

The Great Rift Valley in eastern Africa lies along a divergent plate boundary. Here, a valley has formed where two continental plates have started pulling apart. Millions of years from now, Africa will split into two landmasses at the valley.

With convergent boundaries, much of what happens when the two plates collide depends on the type of crust on the leading edge of each plate. Remember that a plate typically contains both continental crust and seafloor crust. Continental crust is thicker and less dense than oceanic crust. Ocean floor crust can meet continental crust, ocean floor crust can meet other ocean floor crust, or continental crust can meet other continental crust.

Trenches are formed when a plate containing ocean floor crust collides with a continental plate. Because the ocean crust is denser, it sinks under the continental crust. You simulated this event when you forced one of your hands under the other in the Explore activity. The area where one plate is pushed under another plate and down into the mantle is called a subduction zone, as shown in Figure 16-11.

Trenches and subduction zones also form when two plates containing ocean floor crust collide with one another. When two pieces of ocean floor crust collide, one plate is forced under the other.

What do you think happens when two plates containing continental crust collide? The two plates crumple, forming mountain ranges. The Himalaya Mountains formed when the Indian Plate collided with the southern part of the Eurasian Plate. Even now, the Indian Plate continues to move

FIGURE 16-11. As Earth's plates pull apart at some boundaries, they collide at others, forming mountains and volcanoes.

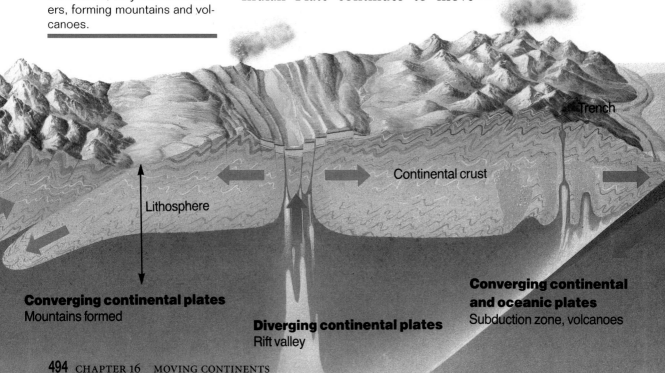

Lithosphere

Continental crust

Trench

Converging continental plates
Mountains formed

Diverging continental plates
Rift valley

Converging continental and oceanic plates
Subduction zone, volcanoes

north, and the crumpling effect raises the world's tallest mountains even higher.

Transform Fault Boundaries

A third type of plate boundary, called a **transform fault boundary,** is formed when two plates slide past one another in opposite directions or in the same direction at different rates. You simulated this type of boundary when you slid your hands past one another in the Explore activity. Look back at Figure 16-10. Find where the North American and Pacific plates meet in California. This is the San Andreas Fault. The San Andreas is a transform fault boundary. Along this boundary, the Pacific Plate moves northwest compared with the North American Plate. The part of California that is on the Pacific Plate is actually moving northward in relation to the North American Plate at an average rate of two centimeters per year.

CAUSES OF PLATE TECTONICS

How does the theory of plate tectonics explain the cause of plate movements? The driving force behind that movement is heat. A material that is hot is less dense than the same material that is cold. This is because the same mass takes up more volume when the material is heated.

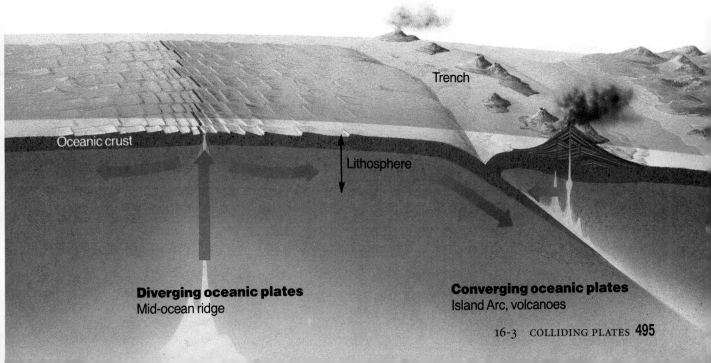

Oceanic crust

Lithosphere

Trench

Diverging oceanic plates
Mid-ocean ridge

Converging oceanic plates
Island Arc, volcanoes

16-3 COLLIDING PLATES **495**

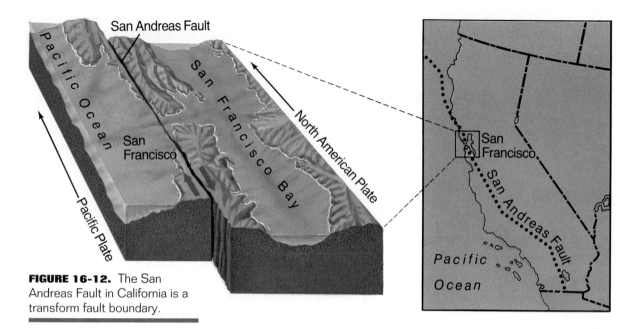

San Andreas Fault

Pacific Ocean

San Francisco

San Francisco Bay

North American Plate

Pacific Plate

San Francisco

San Andreas Fault

Pacific Ocean

FIGURE 16-12. The San Andreas Fault in California is a transform fault boundary.

FIGURE 16-13. An aerial view of the San Andreas Fault shows what happens when two plates move past each other.

Remember that less dense material is forced up by more dense material. Think about how a room is heated. A radiator heats air in the room. The heated air is forced upward by cool, denser surrounding air. As it loses heat, the air becomes cooler and more dense. The cooler air sinks to the floor, where it forces more warm air upward. This cycle of heating, being forced upward, cooling, and sinking is called a convection current.

Trace the following steps on Figure 16-14. Heating of the putty-like rock in the asthenosphere causes it to

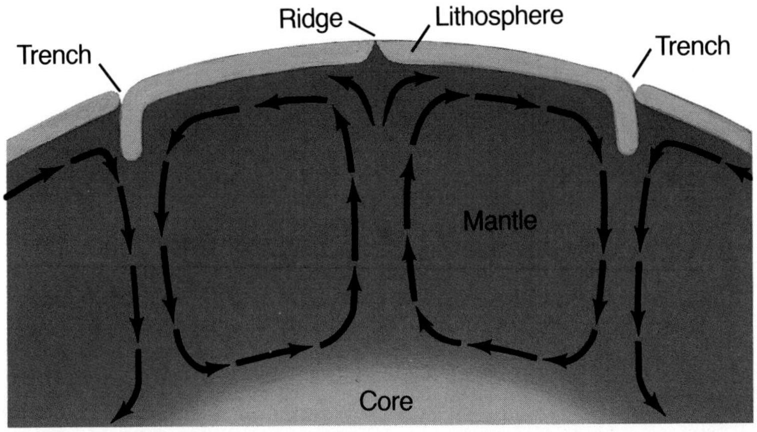

FIGURE 16-14. Convection currents in the asthenosphere result in movement of Earth's plates.

become less dense and be forced upward toward the lithosphere. When the rising material reaches the lithosphere, it moves sideways in opposite directions. This pulls the overlying plates apart and forms a divergent plate boundary. When the moving material cools and becomes more dense, it starts to sink under less dense crustal material and pulls the plate down along a subduction zone. This forms a convergent plate boundary. The sinking material is reheated within the asthenosphere and eventually is forced upward again, completing the convection current cycle.

The theory of plate tectonics explains the puzzle-like fit of the continents as well as how the seafloors change over time. As you'll see in Section 16-4, it also helps explain why some parts of Earth's surface can change at any moment, as Earth erupts to form a volcano or shakes with the power of an earthquake.

Check Your Understanding

1. Describe continental drift and relate it to plate tectonics.
2. Compare and contrast the types of movements that occur at divergent, convergent, and transform fault plate boundaries.
3. **APPLY:** Suppose that over millions of years a change takes place inside the asthenosphere. The areas beneath the mid-ocean ridges become cold; the areas beneath the trenches become hot. Draw a before-and-after diagram showing the direction of plate movement and the convection within the asthenosphere.

16-4 Dynamic Earth

OBJECTIVES

In this section, you will

- relate the occurrence of earthquakes and volcanoes to plate tectonics;
- compare and contrast the three types of regions where volcanoes occur.

KEY SCIENCE TERMS

hot spots

CHANGES IN EARTH'S SURFACE

When Earth's plates meet, mountains are formed, volcanoes erupt, and earthquakes rumble through the ground. Let's look at the connections between earthquakes, volcanoes, and plate boundaries.

FIND OUT!

How are plate boundaries related to earthquakes and volcanoes?
Review Figure 16-10, which shows the locations of known plate boundaries. Now look at Figure 16-15, which shows the locations of active volcanoes and areas of high earthquake activity. Are there similarities between the two diagrams? How do the locations of earthquake epicenters and active volcanoes relate to the location of plate boundaries?

Conclude and Apply
How might you explain the relationship between earthquakes, volcanoes, and plate boundaries?

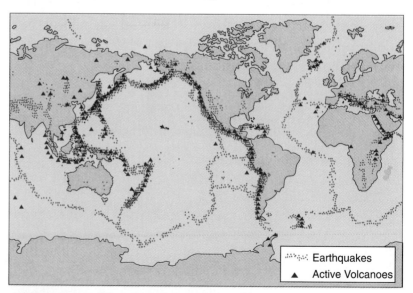

Earthquakes
▲ Active Volcanoes

FIGURE 16-15. The map indicates areas of frequent earthquake and volcanic activity.

WHERE DO EARTHQUAKES OCCUR?

As you saw in the Find Out activity, earthquakes are common at plate boundaries. Think about what you know about earthquakes. Rocks under pressure can break or snap suddenly along faults. Movement along the faults releases energy that shakes the ground.

How do we know where earthquakes occur? You know that the energy released by a quake is in the form of seismic waves. Primary seismic waves travel faster than secondary waves. The time that elapses between primary and secondary waves is used to determine an earthquake's distance from a given location. The farther away the earthquake is from you, the longer the lag time between the two kinds of waves.

Think of it this way: If Runner A is always faster than Runner B and both runners maintain their speed, you would expect Runner A to win by a greater margin at 100 meters than at 50 meters. Lag time is a primary wave's winning margin over a secondary wave.

Knowing the distance to an earthquake does not tell you exactly where it was located because the earthquake could have occurred that distance in any direction from you. Using your location as the center and the distance as the radius, you can draw a circle on a map to represent the circle on which the earthquake occurred. The earthquake's actual location can be determined by measuring the earthquake's distance from three locations, as shown in Figure 16-16. The point where all three circles meet would be the location of the earthquake's epicenter. The earthquake occurred somewhere beneath that spot at a point called the focus.

Plate boundaries aren't just lines on a map. They represent an entire surface along which two plates are in contact. If an earthquake occurs along a plate

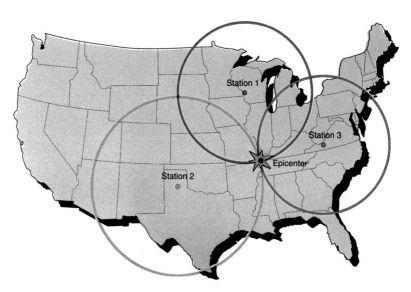

FIGURE 16-16. The radius of each circle is equal to the distance to the epicenter from each seismograph station. The intersection of the three circles is the location of the epicenter.

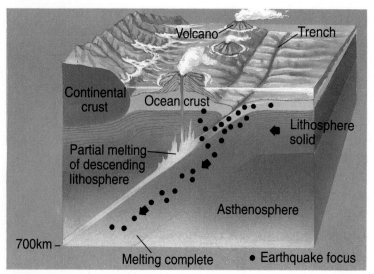

FIGURE 16-17. Deep earthquakes occur at subduction zones where crust descends into the asthenosphere.

boundary, its focus is located underground somewhere along the buried contact between the two plates. This is illustrated in Figure 16-17.

As plates slide past each other, such as at the San Andreas Fault, earthquakes can occur. Rising magma at mid-ocean ridges can also cause earthquakes.

Normally, earthquakes occur in the lithosphere. This means that earthquakes usually occur in the upper 100 kilometers of Earth's crust and mantle. But some earthquakes occur in the asthenosphere. These deep-focus earthquakes occur as deep as 700 kilometers. What does this imply about the causes of these earthquakes?

Earthquakes with deep foci are associated with subduction zones. Rock needs to be solid in order to break. Rocks in the lithosphere are solid and brittle; rocks in the asthenosphere are solid, but they flow under pressure similar to the way in which putty flows. Yet earthquakes below 100 kilometers do occur within the asthenosphere. How is this possible? Remember that the plate being forced down into Earth is about 100 kilometers thick. It takes a long time to melt something that big. The plate cannot fully melt until it reaches a depth of about 700 kilometers. Until that time, it is still solid, and earthquakes can occur within the plate as it sinks deeper into the asthenosphere.

WHERE DO VOLCANOES OCCUR?

Volcanoes form in three kinds of places related to plate tectonics: divergent plate boundaries, convergent plate boundaries, and locations called hot spots.

Divergent Boundaries

Find Iceland on a world map. Iceland is an island in the North Atlantic Ocean. From its name and its location near the Arctic Circle, you shouldn't be surprised to learn that Iceland has glaciers. But you might be surprised to learn that it also has many volcanoes. Iceland is sometimes called "the land of fire and ice." Why do you think there is volcanic activity in Iceland?

Look at Iceland's location in Figure 16-10. Iceland is on the Mid-Atlantic Ridge. Recall that the Mid-Atlantic Ridge is a divergent plate boundary. Where the plates pull apart, magma is forced upward to Earth's surface and erupts as lava. Lava that flows from underwater rifts cools quickly in the cold ocean water. As eruptions continue over time, layers of cooled lava accumulate. Iceland was formed when the layers of lava accumulated to form an island.

Convergent Boundaries

Earth's most well-known volcanoes are not found at divergent plate boundaries. Mount Saint Helens is one of several volcanoes that make up the Cascade Range in western Oregon and Washington. Mount Saint Helens and the other volcanic peaks in the Cascade Range formed at a convergent plate boundary. Look at Figure 16-10. Find the Juan de Fuca Plate. The Cascades were formed where the Juan de Fuca Plate converges with the North American Plate. Which plate is being subducted? Melting of the subducted plate creates magma, which is forced upward to the surface. When the magma reaches the surface, it erupts as lava, forming volcanoes.

Volcanoes also form at convergent boundaries where two pieces of ocean crust collide. A deep-sea trench is formed, and the magma produced by the melting plate is forced up to form an island arc. An island arc is a string of volcanic islands. The islands of the Philippines and Japan are volcanic island arcs. Today, the plates continue to collide and subduct. Find Japan and the Philippines on your map of plate boundaries. Which plates are colliding?

Hot Spots

The Hawaiian Islands are actually the tips of volcanoes that have risen from the ocean floor. However, unlike Iceland, these islands did not form at a divergent plate boundary. They did not form at any type of plate boundary. The Hawaiian Islands are in the middle of the Pacific

FIGURE 16-18. Iceland is known as "the land of fire and ice." The fire is the result of the island's many volcanoes.

SKILLBUILDER

FORMING A HYPOTHESIS
Mount Unzen in Japan and Mount Pinatubo in the Philippines both erupted in the spring of 1991. Use Figures 16-10 and 16-15 to hypothesize how these volcanoes may have formed. If you need help, refer to the **Skill Handbook** on page 689.

Plate. How then are these islands related to plate tectonics? Some areas of Earth's mantle are hotter than others. In these areas, magma is forced up by surrounding denser material. The magma is forced up through cracks in the solid lithosphere and spills out as lava. These areas are known as **hot spots.** The Hawaiian Islands were formed by a hot spot in the middle of the Pacific Ocean.

What happens to a volcano as its plate moves, and it moves off the hot spot? Look at Figure 16-19. If the Pacific Plate is moving toward the northwest, which island would you expect to be the oldest? The island of Kauai is

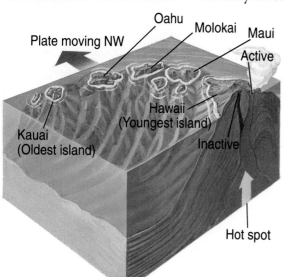

FIGURE 16-19. As the Pacific Plate continues to move, new Hawaiian islands will form over the hot spot.

Oahu
Molokai Maui
Plate moving NW
Active
Hawaii
(Youngest island)
Kauai
(Oldest island)
Inactive
Hot spot

the oldest. It was once located where the big island of Hawaii is today. As the Pacific Plate moved, Kauai was moved to the northwest, and a new volcanic island, Oahu, formed. Continued movement of the Pacific Plate formed Molokai, Maui, and Hawaii over a period of about five million years.

Another hot spot is located in the middle of the North American Plate, near Yellowstone National Park. This hot spot is responsible for the park's mud pots, hot springs, and geysers.

Plate tectonics is a story of energy transfer. The thermal energy from inside Earth is transferred to Earth's surface. Some is released as lava at volcanoes. Some is changed into energy of motion, causing the plates to move. Throughout geologic time, plate movements form and reform oceans, continents, and mountains.

Check Your Understanding

1. Both Japan and California are prone to earthquakes. Explain this fact using plate tectonics.
2. Where does lava come from that flows out of a rift? A convergent boundary?
3. In what three types of locations can volcanoes form?

4. **APPLY:** Today, a new Hawaiian volcano, Loihi Seamount, is forming. However, this new volcano has not reached the surface of the ocean. Look at Figure 16-19 and predict where it is forming.

EXPANDING YOUR VIEW

CONTENTS

A **CLOSER** LOOK

SEA-FLOOR SPREADING

You have learned that changes in Earth's magnetic field help support the idea of sea-floor spreading. In this activity, you'll use data from the magnetic field profile of the Mid-Atlantic Ridge to measure how fast the seafloor is spreading. You will work with six major peaks east and west of the Mid-Atlantic Ridge, for both normal and reversed polarity.

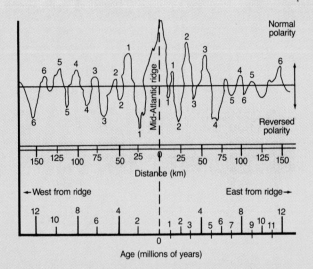

YOU TRY IT!

Materials
• paper • pencil • metric ruler

Procedure
1. Place the ruler through the first peak west of the Mid-Atlantic Ridge. This peak shows reverse polarity and extends downward on the profile. Determine and record the distance in kilometers to the Mid-Atlantic Ridge using the distance scale.

2. Repeat Step 1 for each of the six major peaks east and west of the main ridge, for both normal and reversed polarity.

3. Find the average distance from peak to ridge for each pair of peaks on either side of the ridge. Record these values.

4. Place the ruler through each of the normal polarity peaks and find the age of the rocks.

5. Using the normal polarity readings, calculate the rate of movement in centimeters per year. You will need to convert kilometers to centimeters. Use this formula:
   distance = rate × time.

6. Find the average rate of sea-floor spreading in both directions in one year, based on the rate of movement in one direction you determined in Step 5.

7. How many years would it take rock to move from the ridge to a trench 300 km away?

Physics Connection

MOVING FLUIDS AND MOVING PLATES

Convection currents deep inside Earth provide energy that moves plates in Earth's lithosphere.

In the familiar environment of your home, convection is one of the main ways in which thermal energy is transferred in fluids. You've seen water move in a current as it boiled, and you've experienced that air is warmer near the ceiling and cooler near the floor. These are examples of the movement of fluids due to their different densities. Let's build a model of convection in action.

YOU TRY IT!

Materials
- clear glass baking dish
- immersion heater
- plastic sandwich bag with wire tie
- ice cubes
- tape
- 2 eyedroppers
- red and blue food coloring
- water

Procedure
1. Fill the baking dish with cool water to about 2 cm from the top.
2. Put six ice cubes in the sandwich bag and close the bag with a wire tie.
3. Put the bag in the water at one end of the pan. Tape the top of the bag to the outside of the pan to hold the bag in place.
4. Place the immersion heater in the water at the other end of the pan and plug it in. Wait about a minute for the water to heat.
   CAUTION: *The heater is very hot. Do not touch it. Do not put any part of the heater in the water except the coil.*
5. While you're waiting for the water to heat, fill one eyedropper with red food coloring and the other with blue food coloring.
6. Squeeze two drops of red food coloring into the water near the heater, about halfway from the bottom. Observe what happens.
7. Squeeze two drops of blue food coloring just under the surface of the water near the ice. Observe what happens.

What causes the movement of the red-colored water? What causes the movement of the blue-colored water? Notice that a sideways movement occurs during the heating and cooling process in the water. Ongoing convection currents are produced as liquids are heated, are pushed up by cooler, denser liquids, then cool and once again sink. Use your knowledge of Earth's mantle and lithosphere to explain how convection currents could produce plate movement.

SCIENCE AND SOCIETY

VOLCANOES AND SAVING LIVES

Barry Voigt adjusts a sensitive scientific instrument. He's in the midst of a landscape so alien that it could be on another planet. The rocks have edges as sharp as razors. He has to wear a mask for protection against poisonous fumes. It is truly hostile territory.

Voigt is on Merapi, a dangerous, active volcano in Indonesia. Here, 5890 meters above sea level, he risks his life carrying out research that may someday save thousands of lives.

Voigt wants to reliably predict volcanic explosions weeks before they happen. That way, people in the path of a volcano's destruction would have plenty of time to get out of the way.

As recently as 1985, nearly 22,000 people died in the town of Armero in Colombia, South America, when a nearby volcano erupted. Authorities were hesitant to order an evacuation because they were not sure just when the volcano would erupt. Reliable prediction could have prevented this and many similar tragedies.

Voigt began studying volcanoes in 1980, when earthquakes started to shake Mount Saint Helens in Washington. A specialist in rockslides and avalanches, Voigt predicted that rockslides caused by the earthquakes could make Mount Saint Helens erupt sideways. And that's what happened.

In March of 1980, earthquakes began to shake the mountain, and the growing magma pocket produced a bulge on the north face of the mountain. The diagrams below show what happened then. Although it was hot enough inside the magma chamber to turn water into steam, the steam was kept in liquid form by the pressure of the rock on top of the magma. On May 18, 1980, a new earthquake produced a landslide on the north face of the mountain. This action reduced the pressure of the rock over the magma chamber. The

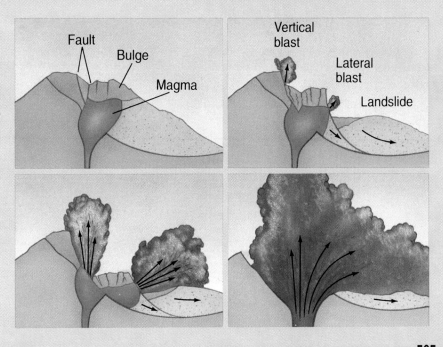

activity in the volcano, the light will take a slightly different amount of time to make the trip. This is how scientists knew that a bulge was developing on Mount Saint Helens.

When thick, slowly moving lava builds up over the central vent of a volcano, a lava dome develops. When the dome plugs the vent of the volcano, pressure builds up beneath the dome. This pressure may result in a future eruption. Scientists place an instrument known as a tiltmeter on the side of the dome. This device measures the inclination, or tilt, of the sides of the dome. If the tilt changes, it can be a sign that trouble is brewing.

Voigt also uses seismographs, which measure earthquakes occurring near the volcano.

If Voigt succeeds in working out a way to predict eruptions, he may save the lives of thousands of people. Inhabitants of volcanic regions all over the globe will live more securely.

water changed to steam and exploded from the summit and from a fissure farther down the mountain. Freed from its pocket, magma and ash then blasted horizontally from the fissure. This entire chain of events occurred in less than 30 seconds!

Voigt has developed new techniques for analyzing information from the special instruments he uses and for predicting when the rock in a volcano will give way and allow an eruption to take place.

To collect the data that he needs, Voigt uses an array of instruments. Laser measuring devices like the one illustrated are especially important. A laser beam—an intense beam of light—hits a reflecting instrument on the sides of the volcano and is reflected back to its source. A timer measures how long it takes the light to make the round-trip. If the ground under the reflector shifts because of

WHAT DO YOU THINK?

At times, government officials have forced the evacuation of an area when a volcanic eruption was predicted. The eruption may never have happened or may have been much less severe than predicted. The evacuation may have produced many hardships that some people would consider unnecessary.

At other times, government officials have waited too long, as was the case in Armero.

Imagine you're in the government of a country with many active volcanoes. What factors would you use to decide when to order evacuation?

Explain your choices.

TECHNOLOGY CONNECTION

GETTING A BETTER PICTURE

Scientists are always trying to improve their techniques and increase their knowledge of the natural world. Several new approaches have increased our understanding of Earth's structure and its plates.

Since the early 1900s, scientists have been using earthquakes to create models of the structure of Earth's interior. When an earthquake occurs, it generates an energy wave that travels through Earth. By measuring the speed of the wave, scientists constructed a model of Earth's interior. Scientists have

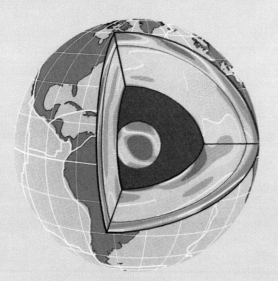

developed a new technique called travel-time tomography (TTT). With this technique, they have developed a new model of Earth's interior. TTT uses a computer that combines data from thousands of earthquakes around the world. The models from the computer have shown hot blobs of mantle material rising from the core-mantle boundary in some places and cooler blobs sinking from the

upper mantle in other places. This new model suggests that the boundaries between the layers aren't smooth, but have different thicknesses.

A second approach has allowed researchers to gather information about the deepest section of Earth's plates. Geophysicists have long used explosions to study what lies below Earth's surface. By sending seismic waves into the ground and measuring the reflected waves that return, they can see structures within Earth's lithospheric plates, which contain the crust and the uppermost section of the mantle.

Researchers, headed by Norwegian J. E. Lie, recently collected data from the research ship, *Mobil Search*. The ship towed hundreds of microphones strung out along a 4.5 kilometer-long streamer. Moving through the waters south of Norway, the ship shot off a large air gun and recorded the reflected waves.

Lie's group found several very reflective patches located at depths of 100 to 110 kilometers. The same sort of reflection in shallower portions of the plates usually indicates the presence of faults or borders between different types of rock.

If this proves to be true at greater depths, researchers will actually have evidence of how the lower portion of the lithosphere behaves when plates collide or stretch.

WHAT DO YOU THINK?

Some people suggest that scientists spend too much time and money trying to find out what went on in Earth's past and what is going on in inner regions of Earth. Is this work a waste of time and resources? What is the value of such research, other than simply a search for new knowledge?

*H*istory
C O N N E C T I O N

CHANGING SEA LEVELS

One branch of science may shed light on another. You've seen how fossil records contributed to the theory of plate tectonics. Knowledge from different fields may help explain changing sea levels.

Ocean levels have sometimes changed by as much as 150 feet. It has long been assumed that this change came from the melting and refreezing of polar ice caps. However, evidence from geologic and fossil records suggests that changes in the ice cap aren't large enough to account for it.

A new theory proposes that the sea's rise and fall may have been caused by changes in the ocean floor plates. Like the continents, the ocean bottoms are rocky plates adrift on a partly molten mantle. If the plates pulled apart, deep rifts and depressions would open in the seafloor. Ocean water would fill the depressions, creating a drop in levels around the world. Molten rock from the mantle would then slowly refill the rift, pushing sea levels back up.

Look at the map of the Atlantic Ocean basin. It is not too hard to imagine how changes in the topography of this vast area of the ocean floor might have a major effect on sea levels.

Fossil records suggest that this idea may have some merit. They indicate that during the time of sea level changes, huge numbers of sea creatures became extinct. Magma filling in a rift would combine with dissolved oxygen in the water. This would remove the oxygen from the water and cause widespread suffocation among marine life.

Once again, the sciences have worked together to improve our understanding of our world.

WHAT DO YOU THINK?

On a human time scale, changes in sea level take place slowly. However, what if a very dramatic shift in ocean levels took place? What do you think the effects would be of an extremely sharp rise or drop in sea level on coastal cities? What might the effects be on Earth's ecology?

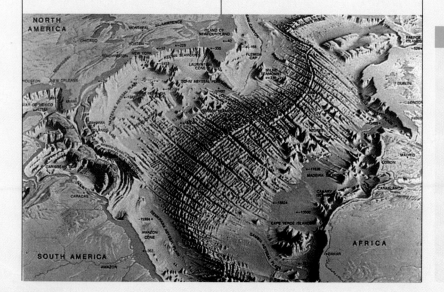

Reviewing Main Ideas

1. The first evidence for continental drift was the obvious fit of some continents.

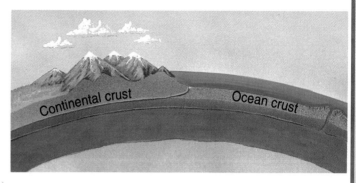

2. A plate is a piece of lithosphere that usually contains both seafloor and part of a continent.

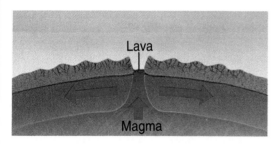

3. Lava pouring out of a rift valley forms new ocean crust. Oceans with sea-floor spreading at mid-ocean ridges get wider.

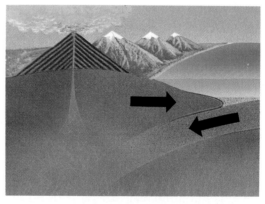

4. In subduction, one plate is forced beneath another. At a depth of 700 km, the subducted plate is mostly melted.

5. Most earthquakes and volcanoes occur near plate boundaries.

Chapter Review

USING KEY SCIENCE TERMS

continental drift
convergent boundary
divergent boundary
hot spots
lithosphere
plate tectonics
sea-floor spreading
transform fault boundary

An analogy is a relationship between two pairs of words generally written in the following manner: a:b::c:d. The symbol : is read "is to," and the symbol :: is read "as." For example, cat:animal::rose:plant is read "cat is to animal as rose is to plant." In the analogies that follow, a word is missing. Complete each analogy by providing the missing word from the list above.

1. hot spots:Hawaii:: ____ : Mount Pinatubo
2. Wegener:continental drift::Hess: ____
3. ____:solid::asthenosphere:putty-like
4. divergent boundary:rift:: ____ : trench
5. gasoline:automobiles:: convection ____

UNDERSTANDING IDEAS

Complete each sentence.

1. Wegener supported his ideas about moving continents by pointing to the fit of Africa and ____.
2. The San Andreas Fault is a ____.

3. The putty-like layer of Earth's interior in which convection occurs is called the ____.
4. The Philippines and Japan are examples of ____ formed at the convergent boundary of two plates.
5. Similar rocks and mountains are found in Greenland, the western part of Europe, and ____.
6. Because of convection, material in the asthenosphere is forced up beneath mid-ocean ridges and ____.
7. A moving plate usually carries part of a ____ and a seafloor.

CRITICAL THINKING

Use your understanding of the concepts developed in the chapter to answer each of the following questions.

1. Look at the world map on pages 676–677. Make predictions about how the size of the Atlantic and Pacific oceans will change in the next 200 million years. What will happen to the Gulf of California?
2. Projections of where the continents will be in 100 million years are based on what evidence?
3. If a sudden and tremendous increase in the temperature of rocks within the asthenosphere occurred, how would plate movement be affected?

4. The diagram shows convection currents in the upper mantle. Explain why the features labeled a and b occur at those positions.

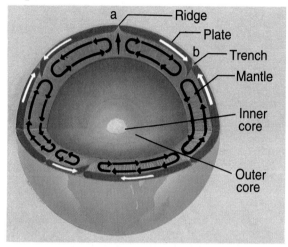

5. How did fossil data help support Wegener's hypothesis of continental drift? How did magnetic rock data help support Hess's hypothesis of sea-floor spreading?

PROBLEM SOLVING

Read the following problem and discuss your answers in a brief paragraph.

Mapmakers Shelly and Luis are updating a topographic map of the Banquo Valley. Shelly and Luis measure the distance from Smitty on the western side of the valley to Hazy on the eastern side of the valley. Oddly, they find the distance between places has changed since 1920.

Year	Distance from Smitty to Hazy	Angle from Smitty to Hazy
1920	1.0 km	50°
1992	1.4 km	45°

Draw two figures representing the data. One should represent the locations of Smitty and Hazy in 1920, and the other should represent the locations of these places in 1992.

1. Assume the measurements are accurate. What explanation can you give for the changes in location?

2. In which direction is Smitty moving relative to Hazy?

CONNECTING IDEAS

Discuss each of the following in a brief paragraph.

1. How does plate tectonics help explain continental drift and sea-floor spreading?

2. How would the thermal energy reaching the sea-floor surface at a mid-ocean ridge affect water temperature? Describe a possible density current set up over a rift valley.

3. Researchers find a rock on the seafloor that is 180 million years old. A magnetometer reading on the rock reveals a reversed pole. A piece of volcanic rock formed on land is also 180 million years old. What do you expect a magnetometer reading to show for the land rock?

4. TECHNOLOGY CONNECTION How have earthquakes helped scientists form a model of Earth's interior?

5. HISTORY CONNECTION How can sea-floor spreading help account for the periodic rise and fall of ocean water levels?

DID YOU EVER WONDER . . .

How old Earth is?

How fossils are formed?

How we know what dinosaurs looked like?

You'll find the answers to these questions as you read this chapter.

Geologic Time

magine you have built a machine that can take you back in time. You strap yourself in, set the controls, and away you go—traveling millions of years into Earth's past! Each minute by your watch takes you another million years back in time. The windows you installed in the time machine are useless; at this rate, all of Earth's past events are a blur.

Finally, after traveling for several hours, your time machine grinds to a halt. You've reached your time journey's end.

Outside your machine is lush, green vegetation. Suddenly, you see a large, fierce-looking animal with long, sharp teeth eyeing you. A *Tyrannosaurus!* You've traveled back in time to the age of dinosaurs! In this chapter, you'll see how scientists travel back in geologic time.

EXPLORE!

How can you discover and organize events that happened in the past?

Use a stack of last week's newspapers with the dates cut off. Most of the papers should be in the order in which they were read—oldest papers on the bottom, more recent toward the top. Some papers may be slightly out of order.

Make a time line of all the front page stories during the past week. Without the dates on the papers, how do you know the correct order in which the events occurred? What clues could you use to tell if one of your papers was out of order?

17-1 Fossils

OBJECTIVES

In this section, you will

- explain the conditions necessary for fossils to form;
- describe two processes of fossil formation.

KEY SCIENCE TERMS

fossil

mold

cast

TRACES FROM THE PAST

Using a stack of newspapers in the opening Explore, you modeled how scientists learn about events in Earth's past. One of the most fascinating events in Earth's history is the existence of dinosaurs. You've probably read about dinosaurs and other previous inhabitants of Earth. You've also probably seen them depicted, not always accurately, in science fiction movies. In fact, your imagined journey back in time at the beginning of this chapter may have reminded you of a science fiction movie.

But how do we know dinosaurs really did exist? What "newspaper stories" do scientists use as evidence of past life on Earth? The following Explore activity will help you begin to answer these questions.

EXPLORE!

How do organisms leave clues that they've been here?

Cut the top off a small milk carton and add enough plaster of paris to fill it halfway. Mix in enough water to make the plaster smooth and thick.

Coat a leaf, shell, bone, or other plant or animal part with petroleum jelly. Press the coated object into the plaster of paris. Allow the plaster to dry for at least 24 hours. Then remove the object.

Did the object leave a clue in the hardened plaster? That is, does its imprint look like the original object? Can others in your class guess what object you used to make your imprint? How do you think imprints of plants and animals are made in nature?

HOW FOSSILS FORM

In the Explore activity, you made plaster imprints of parts of organisms that were once alive. When such imprints occur in nature, we call them fossils. A **fossil** is

FIGURE 17-1. What clues about past life on Earth do you think these fossils offer?

the remains or trace of an organism that was once alive. A fossil can show us what an organism looked like when it was alive. It also can tell us when, where, and how an organism once lived. In fact, fossils have helped us determine approximately when life on Earth began and what types of plants and animals lived in the past.

But how are fossils formed? Usually, the remains of dead plants and animals disappear quickly. Scavengers may eat the dead organisms, or bacteria will cause them to decay. What makes the remains of some plants and animals stay around long enough to become fossils?

The body of a dead organism must be protected in some way from scavengers and bacteria in order to produce a fossil. One way this can happen is for the body to be covered quickly by sediments. For example, if a fish dies and sinks to the bottom of a pond, as shown in Figure 17-2, sediments carried into the pond by a stream can rapidly cover the fish's body. If this happens, scavengers and bacteria are less likely to get to it.

FIGURE 17-2. Why are chances good for fossilization of the dead fish in these sketches?

But it takes more than a quick burial to make a fossil. Organisms have a better chance of being at least partially preserved if they have hard parts, such as bones, shells, teeth, or wood. Such hard parts are less likely to be disturbed or eaten by other organisms and are less likely to be broken. Most of the fossils we see are remains or traces of the hard parts of organisms. The petrification of remains and the mold-and-cast process are two ways in which these hard parts of organisms eventually produce fossils.

Remains of organisms become petrified when groundwater containing dissolved minerals seeps into the tiny, natural openings of buried bones, wood, shells, or other porous parts of dead organisms. As the water evaporates or slowly passes through the organism, the minerals crystallize and settle out, filling the pores. The crystallization of minerals in dead organisms is similar to the crystallization of minerals in rocks.

Sometimes, the water partially or completely dissolves the original material of the organism, depositing minerals such as quartz in its place. A mineral like quartz is harder than the original calcium in a bone, for example, so the bone becomes hard like rock. Petrified remains are hard and rocklike because some or all of the original materials have been replaced by new, harder minerals.

FIGURE 17-3. A cast resembling the original organism forms when a mold fills with sediments that eventually harden into rock.

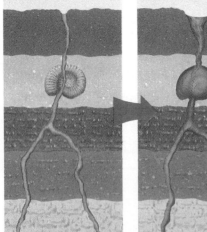
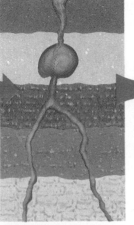
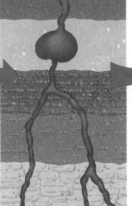

A cast is formed.

The organism begins to decompose as water moves through the rock layers.

The organism has been eroded away; the harder rocks once surrounding it form a mold.

Sediments are carried into the mold and deposited.

In the mold-and-cast process, the sediments around an object are compacted and cemented until they become rock. Next, cracks may form in this rock and allow water and air to reach the shell or hard part, and the object then decays and erodes. This leaves behind a cavity in the rock called a **mold**. Later, other sediments may fill the mold, harden into rock, and produce a **cast** of the original object, as shown in Figure 17-3.

FOSSILS AND GEOLOGIC TIME

In the opening Explore activity, you used clues from newspaper stories to put past events in order. One method that scientists use to learn about events for which there is no written history is to study fossils. They use fossils and other clues to organize the events in Earth's past into a time line.

In your imaginary journey at the beginning of this chapter, you pretended that you traveled back through time to the age of dinosaurs. You looked out the window of your time machine and observed the plants and animals in Earth's past. In a way, this is what scientists do when they dig into Earth and uncover fossils. They find fossils of dinosaurs and other organisms preserved in layers of rock. These rock layers provide a window to Earth's past.

In the next section, you'll see how fossils can help us separate the millions of years of geologic time into relative time periods by giving us clues to determine the relative dates of the rock layers in which they are found.

DID YOU KNOW?

When a dinosaur skeleton is discovered, pieces are usually missing. Bones may have been carried away by predators or scavengers. Teeth or other small parts may have been carried away by wind or water. When incomplete skeletons are found, molds can be made from similar parts or by hypothesizing about what the missing pieces look like. Casts of the missing parts are then attached to the actual bones in a museum's skeleton display.

Check Your Understanding

1. Identify the conditions necessary for fossil formation.
2. How can scavengers and bacteria make it difficult for fossils to form?
3. Compare and contrast petrified fossil formation with the mold-and-cast formation of fossils.
4. How can water both help and hinder fossil formation?
5. **APPLY:** A shallow pond dries in the summer heat, and a fish dies for lack of water. Is a fossil of the fish likely to be formed? Why or why not?

17-2 Dating Rock Layers

OBJECTIVES

In this section, you will
- describe two methods used to date rock layers relative to one another;
- explain how an unconformity may occur.

KEY SCIENCE TERMS

law of superposition
unconformity

USING FOSSILS TO DATE ROCK LAYERS

Think once more about your opening Explore activity. Just as you used clues in newspaper stories to figure out which events in the news came before others, scientists use fossils to help them figure out which events in Earth's past came before others. In fact, fossils can show us which rock layers in Earth's crust formed before other rock layers.

FIND OUT!

How can fossils be used to date rock layers?

Suppose that you find some layers of sedimentary rock containing fossils. You number the layers 1 through 5, from bottom to top. The bottom layer, layer 1, contains fossils A and C. Layer 2 contains fossils A, B, and C. Layer 3 contains fossils A, B, and D. Layer 4 contains fossils B and D. The top layer, layer 5, contains only fossil D.

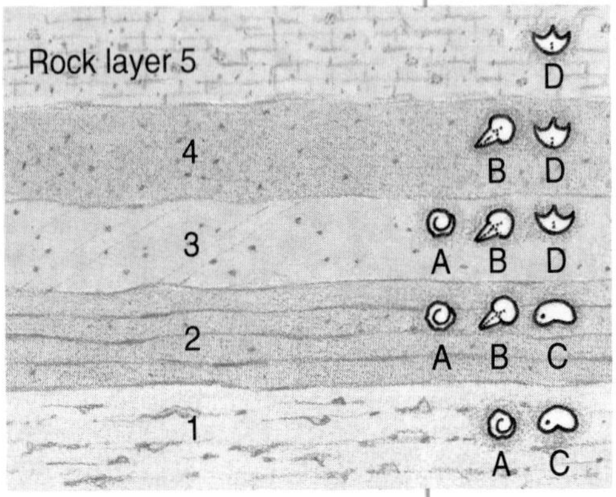

The organisms that produced these four types of fossils are known to have lived during seven different divisions of time in Earth's history. These divisions are shown in the table.

Rock layer 5

Ended Million Years Ago	Began Million Years Ago	Fossil Types of This Time		
225	280			D
280	320		B	D
320	345		B	D
345	400	A	B	D
400	425	A	B	
425	500	A	B	C
500	570	A		C

Construct a three-column table that shows rock layer numbers, fossil types found in each layer, and the range of possible ages for each rock layer. Use the illustration to help you complete columns 1 and 2. Use the information in the table to identify the earliest date at which the fossils in each layer could have appeared together, then identify the most recent date the fossils could have appeared.

Conclude and Apply

1. You can date only two layers to one specific time division. Which layers are they, and why is this so?
2. Why isn't it possible to determine during which specific period each of the other layers formed?

In the Find Out activity, you saw how fossils can be used to date rock layers in relation to one another. Now you'll learn about a geologic principle that also helps us date rock layers relative to one another.

You know that sediments may be deposited in layers, which can then form layers of sedimentary rock. Newer layers form on top of older layers. We also say that newer layers of rock are *super*imposed on older layers.

The **law of superposition** states that, in layers of rocks, the oldest rocks are generally on the bottom, and the youngest rocks are generally on top if the layers have not been disturbed. Sometimes, however, the law of superposition appears to be broken. Can you think of a situation that might appear to break the law of superposition? Does Figure 17-4 bring one to mind?

Remember what you learned in Chapter 16 about plate tectonics, as well as mountain building,

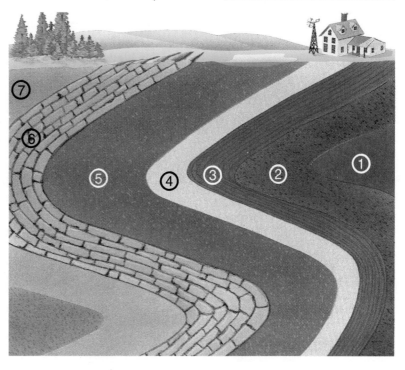

FIGURE 17-4. Starting with layer 1, can you tell if the layers become progressively older or younger?

volcanoes, and earthquakes? What do such activities do to rock layers—to the layered history of Earth? Also, how could erosion change the way scientists might interpret rock layers?

Violent conditions in Earth can disturb rock layers, producing arrangements of rocks that appear to break the law of superposition. When the plates of Earth's crust collide and form mountains, the rock layers are no longer neat and horizontal. Faults, earthquakes, and volcanic eruptions may also rearrange layers of rock, so that old rocks may come to rest beside or on top of newer rocks. However, these arrangements are misleading because younger rocks always form on top of older rocks.

Sometimes an entire layer or layers of sedimentary rock are completely missing from an area. Look at Figure 17-5(a). How many layers of rock do you see? Now pretend the middle layer of rock is missing, as in (b). The record of plants and animals that existed during that time would not have been preserved. How might the missing layer of Earth's history change our interpretation of when the top and bottom rock layers were formed? How would it affect our knowledge of when certain organisms lived?

When layers of rock that were there originally are missing, the gap in that particular area's geologic history is called an **unconformity.** Geologists can use unconformities to learn about Earth and its history. Unconformities can have various causes. One possible cause is that a

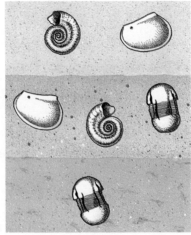
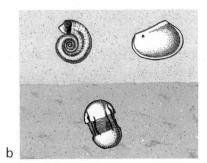

FIGURE 17-5. What might we think if the middle layer of the rock in (a) had disappeared, and all we had to go on was the remaining two layers (b)?

a   b

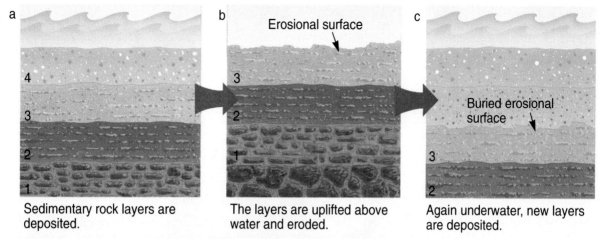

a — Sedimentary rock layers are deposited.

b — Erosional surface — The layers are uplifted above water and eroded.

c — Buried erosional surface — Again underwater, new layers are deposited.

FIGURE 17-6. Do the layers in (c) offer a complete record of Earth's history?

period of time went by when, for one reason or another, no new deposition occurred to form new layers of rock. In this case, a record of plants and animals that existed during this time period would not have been preserved.

What else could cause an unconformity? Look at Figure 17-6. In (a), sediments have hardened to form layers beneath water. In (b), plate tectonics or some other force has caused the layers to rise; layer 4 and part of 3 were exposed to weathering and erosion. In (c), eroded layer 3 is again under water, and sediments have formed two new layers on top of it. But the upper surface of layer 3 is now an incomplete record of this time in Earth's history. This surface is now an unconformity.

An unconformity created by lack of deposition, erosion, or other processes could be easily overlooked by an observer. At first glance, the rock layers may seem normal; they are all horizontal, and there is no sign of disturbance. But a closer look shows an uneven, eroded surface in one of the layers. An experienced scientist would realize that this layer may now contain an incomplete history of the years during which it was originally formed.

Now that you know about unconformities, the law of superposition, and other ways of determining the relative ages of rocks, do the Investigate activity on the next page to apply what you've learned.

INVESTIGATE!

DETERMINING RELATIVE AGES OF ROCK LAYERS

You have learned that certain clues in rock layers can be used to determine the relative ages of the rocks in those layers. In this activity, you will **observe and infer** the ages of rock layers.

PROBLEM
How do you determine the relative ages of rock layers?

MATERIALS
pen or pencil
paper

PROCEDURE
1. Study the figure at the bottom of this page. The key will help you **interpret the scientific illustration** of the different types of rock layers.

2. **Infer** the relative ages of the rock layers, unconformities, and the fault in the figure.

ANALYZE
1. Where can you **observe** an unconformity?
2. Determine which layer is incomplete because of the unconformity. Explain your answer.
3. Is it possible that there were originally more layers of rock between the top and bottom of the figure than are now shown? Explain your answer.

CONCLUDE AND APPLY
4. What can you **infer** caused the unconformity?
5. Assume that the layers have not been overturned. Based on the figure alone, do you know whether the shale was deposited before or after the fault occurred? Explain.
6. **Going Further: Predict** what may happen to the top limestone layer above the fault. Explain your prediction.

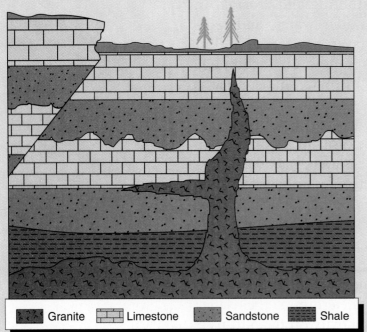

Granite   Limestone   Sandstone   Shale

ROCK LAYERS AND GEOLOGIC TIME

The Investigate activity gave you a chance to apply what you've learned about rock layers using a variety of skills, and it showed you how much you've already learned about rock layers and geologic time. The more people learn, however, the harder it becomes to keep information straight. Eventually, there are so many things we know and want to remember that we have to put all the pieces of information in some sort of order.

As scientists learned more and more about rock layers and geologic time, they too needed to get organized. In the next section, you'll learn about the system scientists use to organize the information they've learned about rock layers and geologic time, and you'll look at some of the discoveries they've made concerning these different spans of time.

FIGURE 17-7. Geologists can read Earth's history in exposed rock layers like these in the Grand Canyon.

Check Your Understanding

1. Describe how fossils may be used to determine the relative ages of rock layers.
2. Describe how the law of superposition is used to determine the relative ages of rock layers.
3. Give two examples of situations that can cause an unconformity.
4. **APPLY:** A geologist finds a series of rocks. The sandstone contains a fossil that is 400 million years old. The shale contains some fossils that are between 550 and 500 million years old. The limestone contains fossils that are between 500 and 400 million years old. Which rock bed is oldest? Which rock bed is most likely below the others? Explain. Draw an illustration if that will help you.

17-3 Early Earth History

OBJECTIVES

In this section, you will

- give examples of the different life-forms of the Precambrian and Paleozoic eras;
- describe the major geologic changes of the Precambrian and Paleozoic eras;
- explain the subdivisions of the Paleozoic Era.

KEY SCIENCE TERMS

era
Precambrian Era
Paleozoic Era
period

TIME BRINGS CHANGE

At one time, you may have thought that mountains existed forever. But based on what you learned in Chapter 16 and in Section 17-2 of this chapter, you now know that the geological features of Earth are continually changing. Today, Earth looks very different from the way it did billions, millions, or even thousands of years ago.

Have you ever heard the expression "If you don't like the weather, wait an hour. It will change!"? Not only the weather, but Earth's climates are also continually changing. At various times in the past, Earth has been both warmer and colder than it is now.

How do you think changes in Earth's geology and climate have affected the plants and animals on Earth? What happened to the dinosaur pictured at the beginning of this chapter? Where are its descendants?

As you've learned, we have a geologic record of Earth's past that helps us assign relative dates to objects and events. Geologists think of this record in terms of a geologic time scale that is similar to a calendar. The following Explore activity will help you see how geologists devised Earth's geologic time scale.

EXPLORE!

Can you make a time scale of your life?
On 3 × 5 cards, write important events that have happened in your lifetime, one event per card. Use the following list for ideas.

learned to ride a bike	learned to walk
spoke first words	went to first dance
learned to add	tried to swim
entered first grade	was born
attended seventh grade	

DID YOU KNOW?

Throughout geologic time, the average temperature of Earth has been from 1° to 3°C warmer than current average temperatures.

You can use more cards to write other events of your life.

Now arrange the cards in the order in which the events happened. Then cut two blank cards in half to make the following labels:

Preschool Years
Early Elementary Years
Middle School Years
Late Elementary Years

Place each label before the group of events that occurred during its time description.

THE GEOLOGIC TIME SCALE

In the activity, you made a time scale based on the events in your life. Geologists organize events in Earth's past using another kind of time scale, a geologic time scale.

The geologic time scale is organized into lengths of time based on events that happened within those times. And just as you labeled the lengths of time within your life, geologists label different lengths of time on the geologic time scale.

You organized your life history into four time divisions. The geologic time scale is also organized into four divisions, but they cover much longer time spans than your life time scale. Each of the four major divisions in the geologic time scale is called an **era**.

In your life time scale, you divided your early life history into two "eras": Preschool Years and Early Elementary Years. The geologic time scale similarly divides early Earth history into two eras: the Precambrian Era and the Paleozoic Era.

These geologic labels help us organize information so we can better understand and discuss it. When we put all the information together, we end up with a sequence of events in Earth's history. Figure 17-9 on the next page shows this geologic time scale with its eras and other labels.

FIGURE 17-8. Time brings changes to Earth's geology, climates, and life forms, such as *Tyrannosaurus.*

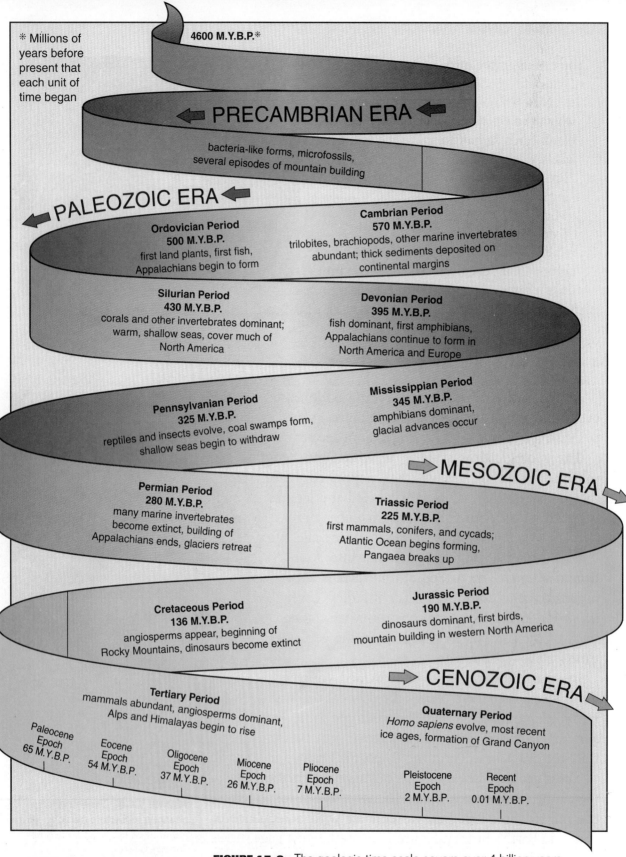

* Millions of years before present that each unit of time began

4600 M.Y.B.P.*

← PRECAMBRIAN ERA ←

bacteria-like forms, microfossils, several episodes of mountain building

← PALEOZOIC ERA ←

Cambrian Period
570 M.Y.B.P.
trilobites, brachiopods, other marine invertebrates abundant; thick sediments deposited on continental margins

Ordovician Period
500 M.Y.B.P.
first land plants, first fish, Appalachians begin to form

Silurian Period
430 M.Y.B.P.
corals and other invertebrates dominant; warm, shallow seas, cover much of North America

Devonian Period
395 M.Y.B.P.
fish dominant, first amphibians, Appalachians continue to form in North America and Europe

Pennsylvanian Period
325 M.Y.B.P.
reptiles and insects evolve, coal swamps form, shallow seas begin to withdraw

Mississippian Period
345 M.Y.B.P.
amphibians dominant, glacial advances occur

→ MESOZOIC ERA →

Permian Period
280 M.Y.B.P.
many marine invertebrates become extinct, building of Appalachians ends, glaciers retreat

Triassic Period
225 M.Y.B.P.
first mammals, conifers, and cycads; Atlantic Ocean begins forming, Pangaea breaks up

Cretaceous Period
136 M.Y.B.P.
angiosperms appear, beginning of Rocky Mountains, dinosaurs become extinct

Jurassic Period
190 M.Y.B.P.
dinosaurs dominant, first birds, mountain building in western North America

→ CENOZOIC ERA →

Tertiary Period
mammals abundant, angiosperms dominant, Alps and Himalayas begin to rise

Quaternary Period
Homo sapiens evolve, most recent ice ages, formation of Grand Canyon

Paleocene Epoch 65 M.Y.B.P.

Eocene Epoch 54 M.Y.B.P.

Oligocene Epoch 37 M.Y.B.P.

Miocene Epoch 26 M.Y.B.P.

Pliocene Epoch 7 M.Y.B.P.

Pleistocene Epoch 2 M.Y.B.P.

Recent Epoch 0.01 M.Y.B.P.

FIGURE 17-9. The geologic time scale covers over 4 billion years.

THE PRECAMBRIAN ERA

Let's begin at the beginning. Just as your life time scale began with your birth, the geologic time scale begins with Earth's birth, or beginning—about 4.6 billion years ago. However, unlike your lifetime scale, in which your first "era" was approximately six years long, the first geologic era was roughly 4 billion years long. In fact, this single era makes up about 90 percent of Earth's history to date. This is the **Precambrian Era**, and it lasted from about 4.6 billion years ago to about 570 million years ago.

How much do you remember about your preschool years compared with more recent years? Look around your room at home. Do you see more things related to your recent years or to your preschool years? Not much is known about Earth's climate or its organisms during the Precambrian Era. Can you guess why?

Precambrian rocks have been buried deep within Earth by processes such as plate tectonics and deposition, and they have been changed by heat and pressure. Few exist, and even fewer exist near Earth's surface, where they can be studied. And because they have been exposed to water, wind, and ice longer than younger rocks, Precambrian rocks have been eroded significantly. Most of the fossil record of the history of the Precambrian Era has been destroyed by the heat, pressure, and erosion that Precambrian rocks have experienced.

Another reason Precambrian fossils are less commonly found than those in later eras is that Precambrian life-forms were soft-bodied. What do you remember from Section 17-1 about the conditions necessary for fossil formation? Do soft-bodied organisms tend to fossilize?

THE PALEOZOIC ERA

When organisms have hard parts, fossil formation is easier. The appearance of fossils formed by organisms with hard parts marks the beginning of the second major geologic time scale division, the **Paleozoic** (pay lee uh ZOH ihk) **Era**. Look back to Figure 17-9. The Paleozoic Era began about 570 million years ago.

How do we know?

The Age of Earth

Scientists believe our planet is about 4.6 billion years old. Yet they have dated Earth rocks only as old as 3.9 billion years, using a method called radioactive dating that you will read about in Chapter 19. Scientists can, however, date the ages of meteorites—rocks from space that sometimes strike Earth. Meteorites are believed to have formed at the same time as the solar system, and therefore at the same time as Earth. By determining that meteorites are 4.6 billion years old, we can infer that Earth must be that old, too.

FIGURE 17-10. This model recreates a Paleozoic sea. Trilobites, brachiopods, mollusks, and other organisms were common marine animals of the time.

Warm, shallow seas covered much of Earth's surface during early Paleozoic time. Therefore, most life-forms during this era were marine. Examples of Paleozoic life forms include trilobites (TRI luh bites), brachiopods (BRAK ee uh pahdz), and crinoids (KRI noydz), which you can see in Figure 17-10. The first fish are also thought to have lived during the Paleozoic Era.

The lifetime scale you made for the Explore activity earlier in this section contained only four labels, similar to the four labels we call eras in the geologic time scale. However, if you had had too much information to organize easily under your "Middle School Years" label, you could have added subdivisions such as Sixth Grade, Seventh Grade, and Eighth Grade.

To better understand the Paleozoic Era, geologists have divided this era into seven subdivisions, as you can see in Figure 17-9. A subdivision of an era is called a **period**. Periods in geologic time are based on the life-forms that existed at approximately the same time and on geologic events, such as mountain building and plate movements.

Explore the Paleozoic Era to see what you can learn about its different periods.

In this section, you've learned about the organisms that lived during Earth's early history and about some of the geologic events that occurred. In the next section, you'll journey forward in time through 225 million years to the present. You'll look at the two eras that make up middle and recent Earth history.

Check Your Understanding

1. What life-forms existed in the Paleozoic Era that did not exist in the Precambrian Era?
2. What changes in Earth's geology during early Earth history can still be recognized now?
3. Why is the Paleozoic Era divided into periods, while the Precambrian Era is not?

4. **APPLY:** When were trilobites an abundant species? What does the presence of trilobite fossils in an area tell you about the geologic history of the area? Use Figure 17-9 to help you answer the questions.

17-4 Middle and Recent Earth History

OBJECTIVES

In this section, you will

- give examples of the different life-forms of the Mesozoic and Cenozoic eras;
- describe the major geologic changes of the Mesozoic and Cenozoic eras;
- explain the subdivisions of the Mesozoic and the Cenozoic eras.

KEY SCIENCE TERMS

Mesozoic Era
Cenozoic Era
epoch

SKILLBUILDER

INTERPRETING SCIENTIFIC ILLUSTRATIONS
Use Figure 17-9 to answer these questions. If you need help, refer to the **Skill Handbook** on page 691.
1. When did the first period of the Mesozoic Era begin?
2. When did the first epoch of the first period of the Cenozoic Era begin?
3. From Figure 17-9, can you tell when the Rocky Mountains began to form?

WHAT HAPPENED TO ANCIENT LIFE-FORMS?

Look closely at the Permian Period in Figure 17-9. You'll see that mass extinctions occurred near the end of the Paleozoic Era. Trilobites and other marine invertebrates died out.

What happened to these life-forms? We can't be sure, but scientists believe changes in the environment caused their extinction. You already know that Earth was both warmer and colder at certain times in its history than it is today. Changes in climate can cause mass extinctions. So, too, can the loss of a food source or the destruction of a species' habitat.

But if you look again at Figure 17-9, you'll find that new life-forms appeared during the next era of geologic time. In fact, one life-form became so abundant that it dominated much of this era. It is the life-form you met on your imaginary time travel at the beginning of this chapter.

THE MESOZOIC ERA

The **Mesozoic** (mehz uh ZOH ihk) **Era** began when the Paleozoic Era ended. This time is often called "the age of dinosaurs" because those creatures were so abundant. Can you tell from Figure 17-9 in which period of the Mesozoic Era dinosaurs were dominant?

Dinosaurs were not the only organisms that appeared during the Mesozoic Era. Fossil evidence suggests that the first mammals appeared as well, along with the first birds and the first flowering plants, or angiosperms.

Life-forms were not the only things changing during the Mesozoic Era. According to Figure 17-9, what was happening to Earth's geology during this time?

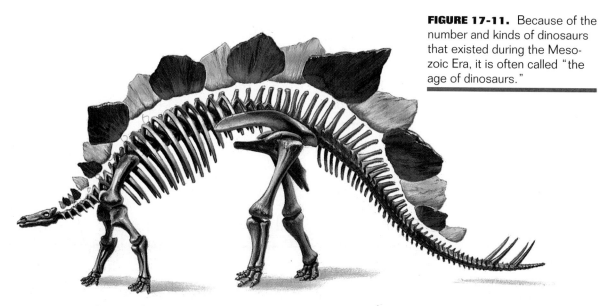

FIGURE 17-11. Because of the number and kinds of dinosaurs that existed during the Mesozoic Era, it is often called "the age of dinosaurs."

As you learned in Chapter 16, Earth's plates are continually moving. These plates brought all of Earth's landmasses together into one large continent toward the end of the Paleozoic Era. This ancient continent is called Pangaea.

At the beginning of the Mesozoic Era, Pangaea began separating into two large landmasses, Laurasia and Gondwanaland, as you can see in Figure 17-12. Later in the Mesozoic Era, Laurasia and Gondwanaland broke apart and drifted to form our present-day continents.

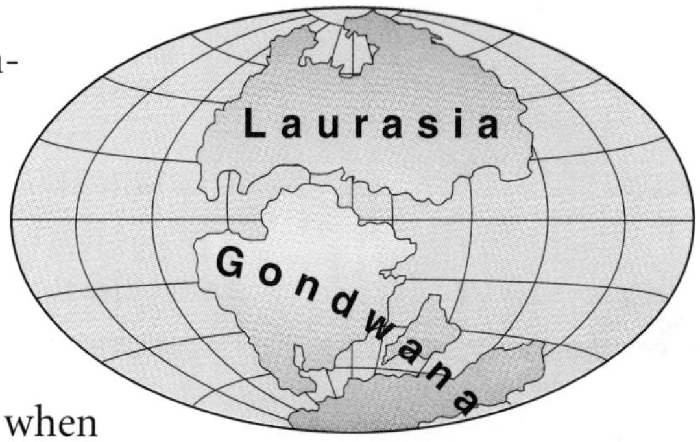

The end of the Mesozoic Era was a time when landmasses were breaking apart and seas were draining from the land into the ocean basins. There was also increased volcanic activity. What effect do you think these changes may have had on the life-forms of the era? Toward the end of the Mesozoic Era, many life-forms, including the dinosaurs, became extinct. The extinction of the dinosaurs was so sudden, in terms of geologic time, that many scientists believe it must have been the result of unusual environmental changes.

FIGURE 17-12. During the Mesozoic Era, Pangaea broke apart into Laurasia and Gondwanaland.

THE CENOZOIC ERA

The wide-scale extinctions and other physical and environmental changes at the end of the Mesozoic Era mark the beginning of the **Cenozoic Era**. You learned that the Paleozoic Era is subdivided into periods, while the Precambrian Era is not. Do you remember why? Into how many periods is the Cenozoic Era divided?

The periods of the Cenozoic Era are also subdivided. Why do you think this is so?

The geologic record is more complete in the Cenozoic Era than in previous eras because the rocks are newer. They therefore have been exposed to less erosion and other destructive geologic processes. Also, Earth's geology, climate, and life-forms have changed often during the Cenozoic Era. As a result, there is more geologic information for geologists to organize. Thus, the periods of the Cenozoic Era are further subdivided into **epochs.**

Let's take a closer look at some of the geologic changes that occurred during the Cenozoic Era. During this time, the African Plate collided with the Eurasian Plate, forming the Alps you see in Figure 17-13(a). When the Indian Plate began to collide with the Eurasian Plate, the Himalaya Mountains (b) started to form. Both mountain ranges are continuing to rise even now.

From Figure 17-9, you should be able to determine how the climate changed during the Cenozoic Era. Did it get warmer or colder?

In the cooler climate of the Cenozoic Era, the number of flowering plants increased. Also, the number of insects, plant-eating mammals, and meat-eating mammals increased. Most scientists think the human species, *Homo sapiens*, first appeared about 500,000 years ago but didn't become a dominant animal until about 10,000 years ago.

A period of 10,000 years may seem like a long time, but it is short compared with Earth's history, as you've seen. In the following activity, you will be able to relate this length of time more clearly to the long span of Earth's past.

FIGURE 17-13. The Alps (a) and the Himalayas (b) formed during the Cenozoic Era.

a

b

17-2 GEOLOGIC TIME SCALE

In this activity, you will see how an absolute time line is constructed.

PROBLEM

How can you arrange the geologic time scale on a proportional time line?

MATERIALS

adding machine paper
meterstick
pencil
scissors

PROCEDURE

1. Using a scale of 1 mm = 1,000,000 years, **measure** and cut a piece of adding machine paper equal to the approximate age of Earth (4.6 billion years).

2. Mark one end of the paper "Today" and the other end "4.6 billion years ago."

3. Using Figure 17-9, **measure** and mark the places on the paper that represent the time when each era began.

4. Choose ten events after examining the events and ages listed in the table. Measuring carefully, **sequence** each event on

your adding machine paper in the proper place in time. Note that the dates are provided in years B.P. (before the present).

ANALYZE

1. Identify which events were most difficult to plot.

2. **Compare** the length of time humans have existed on Earth with the total geologic time.

3. Approximately what percent of geologic time

EARTH HISTORY EVENTS	
EVENT	**APPROXIMATE YEARS B.P.**
1. today	0
2. astronauts land on moon	25
3. U.S. Civil War	135
4. Columbus lands in America	500
5. Pompeii destroyed	1900
6. Eratosthenes calculates Earth's circumference	2100
7. continental ice retreats from North America	10,000
8. beginning of most recent ice age	1 million
9. early human ancestors	5 million
10. first elephants	40 million
11. first horses	50 million
12. beginning of Paleocene	65 million
13. Rocky Mountains begin to rise	80 million
14. beginning of Cretaceous	136 million
15. first birds	150 million
16. beginning of Jurassic	190 million
17. first dinosaurs	225 million
18. beginning of Permian	280 million
19. first reptiles	325 million
20. Appalachian Mountains rise	330 million
21. beginning of Mississippian	345 million
22. first amphibians	390 million
23. beginning of Silurian	430 million
24. first land plants and vertebrates	480 million
25. beginning of Ordovician	500 million
26. animals evolve hard parts	570 million
27. early sponges	600 million
28. oldest microfossils (algae)	3300 million
29. oldest known rocks	3900 million

occurred during the Precambrian Era? Use this formula.

$$\frac{\text{Precambrian Era}}{\text{total geologic time}} \times 100\%$$

CONCLUDE AND APPLY

4. **Compare** your time line with the geologic time scale in Figure 17-9. Which time scale is easier to read information from? Which time line gives the better sense of the actual age of the world and of the relative time spans of the individual eras, periods, and epochs?

5. **Going Further:** Think of different data you might want to display graphically. What kinds of illustrations would best present your data effectively?

SEQUENCING
Arrange these organisms in sequence according to when they first appeared on Earth. If you need help, refer to the **Skill Handbook** on page 680.

mammals	reptiles
dinosaurs	humans
fish	amphibians
birds	insects
land plants	angiosperms
bacteria	

JOURNEY'S END AND RETURN

Your imaginary journey at the beginning of this chapter took you backward through time to the Mesozoic Era, in much the same way that digging deep into the ground takes geologists backward through older and older rock layers. As you delved deeper into the chapter, you also dug deeper into Earth's past, peering back into its beginnings in the Precambrian Era. In this section, you have returned through the Mesozoic Era and the Cenozoic Era to the present day.

In the following chapter, you will explore even further how life-forms have changed throughout the long history of Earth.

FIGURE 17-14. This woolly mammoth roamed Earth in the Cenozoic Era as recently as 10,000 years ago.

Check Your Understanding

1. Which life-forms existed in the Mesozoic Era that did not exist in the Paleozoic Era? Which life-forms existed in the Cenozoic Era that did not exist in the Mesozoic Era?

2. What changes did the movement of plates create in Earth's geology in the Mesozoic Era? What changes did this movement create in Earth's geology in the Cenozoic Era?

3. Why is the Cenozoic Era divided into epochs as well as periods?

4. **APPLY:** Mammals began to become abundant on Earth shortly before the dinosaurs became extinct. Suggest a way in which mammals may have contributed to the extinction of the dinosaurs.

EXPANDING YOUR VIEW

CONTENTS

A CLOSER LOOK

A TRIP THROUGH TIME

Earlier in this chapter, you saw Earth's history shown on a geologic time scale. Geologists have divided the two periods of the present geologic era—the Cenozoic—into seven smaller units of time called epochs. The chart here shows how life on Earth evolved during the seven epochs. It may be difficult for us to imagine a world without humans, but as you can see, we represent only a tiny portion of geologic time.

YOU TRY IT!

Many artists and science-fiction writers have imagined creatures of the future. Look at the geologic timetable below and think about some of the animals that have existed over the course of time. Then try drawing organisms that might exist in the next epoch.

CENOZOIC ERA

	Epoch	Beginning (years ago)	Development of Life During Epoch
Quaternary Period	Holocene	10 thousand	Human beings learned to use resources, developed agriculture.
Quaternary Period	Pleistocene	2 million	Modern human beings appeared. Mammoths, woolly rhinos, and others were present at first—then disappeared at end of epoch.
Tertiary Period	Pliocene	7 million	Humanlike animals appeared. Sea life, birds, and mammals more like today's.
Tertiary Period	Miocene	26 million	Bears and raccoons appeared. More modern flowering plants and trees.
Tertiary Period	Oligocene	37 million	Primitive apes appeared. Huge rhinoceros-like animals disappeared.
Tertiary Period	Eocene	54 million	Bats, camels, cats, horses, monkeys, rhinoceroses, and whales appeared.
Tertiary Period	Paleocene	65 million	Flowering plants, invertebrates, fish, amphibians, reptiles, and small mammals that had appeared earlier.

LIFE SCIENCE CONNECTION

A LIZARD WITH THE BENDS!

Divers take care to avoid the bends, a potentially fatal condition that can develop if they rise too rapidly from deep water to the surface. As divers ascend from a dive, the water pressure decreases. If the divers ascend too quickly, bubbles can form in their tissues and blood. These bubbles can cause breathing difficulties or paralysis, or they can prevent blood from flowing to various body parts.

Two University of Kansas scientists, Larry D. Martin and Bruce M. Rothschild, have discovered that these problems also existed for mosasaurs, which were sea reptiles that lived millions of years ago. Martin and Rothschild noticed that seven mosasaur vertebrae in a museum collection were fused together. Taking a closer look, they found a shark's tooth embedded in the bone, leading them to believe that infection caused by the shark bite had caused the vertebrae to fuse. Not only did this tell something about the dietary habits of sharks at the time, but it also showed that the mosasaur survived the attack.

Martin and Rothschild were fascinated by what they found, but being good scientists, they wanted to compare the fused vertebrae with normal vertebrae from the mosasaur. When they looked at normal vertebrae, they discovered areas of dead bone, resulting, they believe, from a lack of blood flow to the affected bone. Based on their years of study, they speculated that the mosasaur they examined had developed the bends by a rapid ascent to the water's surface. The bends, in turn, caused blood to stop flowing to some part of the spinal column, resulting in areas of bone death.

The studies of Martin and Rothschild, which are described in a scientific journal, are part of the growing field of paleopathology, the study of illnesses and injuries in ancient animals. Other paleopathologists have used modern medical techniques such as X rays and dental examination to diagnose illnesses and identify injuries of creatures that lived long ago.

As alien as mosasaurs and other ancient animals may seem to us, we know they suffered illnesses similar to those of modern animals. They probably responded to changes in their surroundings much as we would today. Sometimes the similarities between ancient and modern animals are more amazing than the differences.

YOU TRY IT!

Describe some ways that the jobs of physicians, paleopathologists, and detectives might be similar.

SCIENCE
A N D
SOCIETY

THE MYSTERIOUS END OF THE DINOSAUR AGE

The disappearance of the dinosaurs is a scientific mystery as fascinating as the best of detective stories! Dinosaurs of all shapes and sizes thrived on Earth for about 130 million years. There was usually enough food available, and the climate was tolerable.

But about 65 million years ago, the dinosaurs and many other animals disappeared. No one knows for sure why, but scientists are trying to find out. Present-day scientists — like all good detectives — have examined the evidence (fossils and rock layers) to find clues. The clues they've found have led to some amazing hypotheses.

Among the most popular hypotheses is that an enormous rocklike object called a meteorite collided with Earth. Dust from the collision may have filled the upper atmosphere and blocked the sunlight from the ground below.

Without sunlight, plants couldn't survive. Without plants, plant-eating dinosaurs would have starved. This, in turn, would have brought about the end of carnivorous dinosaurs that fed on plant-eating dinosaurs.

In support of the hypothesis, scientists say the dust gradually settled to Earth, where it formed a clay layer. Experts have tested the clay layer and determined that it is about 65 million years old! Therefore, the clay layer must have been deposited about the same time the dinosaurs became extinct.

In the same clay layer, scientists have found the chemical element iridium, which usually is not common near Earth's surface but is found in greater amounts in meteorites.

Even though the evidence for the impact hypothesis sounds good to some scientists, others disagree. For example, some think that the clay layer containing iridium can be explained by large numbers of volcanic eruptions. The eruptions, according to this hypothesis, brought iridium from deep within Earth to its surface. The volcanic ash could have blocked sunlight from Earth and led to the death of plant and animal species.

Another hypothesis suggests that there was nothing unusual about the extinction of dinosaurs and that they disappeared gradually because of slow changes in their environment. Experts who believe this hypothesis think that many animals besides the dinosaurs have become extinct because of gradual changes on Earth. No single disaster was necessary to kill the dinosaurs, they say.

As you can see, scientists often take the same evidence and come to remarkably different conclusions. Hypotheses often change or become more believable when more evidence is gathered. But sometimes new evidence simply raises new questions.

While scientists disagree about what caused the disappearance of dinosaurs, they usually do agree that changes in climate 65 million years ago brought about the end of the dinosaur age.

The fact that scientists have found evidence at all is pretty impressive, considering the evidence was buried more than 60 million years before the first human walked on Earth!

While some researchers try to determine what happened to the dinosaurs, others study the changes occurring right now on our

planet. Could present-day changes eventually bring an end to the plant and animal species that currently inhabit Earth? Which present-day changes are caused by humans, and which ones are not?

Many scientists fear that Earth's climate may eventually change, partly because of the large amounts of pollutants that human activities—such as burning of fossil fuels—release into the atmosphere. These scientists want to know how much and how quickly Earth's climate could change and how such changes could affect life on Earth. By examining climatic changes over millions of years, they can estimate how Earth's future climate may be affected by human activity. They also hope to discover ways to prevent significant changes in climate.

YOU TRY IT!

Read about a creature that lived during the Cretaceous period to learn about its lifestyle and environment. What did it eat, for example? Did it live in water? Was the climate tropical or cold?

Using what you learn from the reading, sketch the creature or sculpt it in clay.

TECHNOLOGY CONNECTION

BUILDING A DINOSAUR

Imagine yourself surrounded by hundreds of ancient bones. They were embedded in rock, retrieved by paleontologists, and carefully delivered to you for assembly. It's your responsibility to reconstruct the skeleton of a creature that lived millions of years ago.

It's like a giant, and very valuable, jigsaw puzzle—with an unknown number of pieces missing. It's your job to put them together for museum visitors. But how?

In many ways, the solution is much like working a jigsaw puzzle or constructing a plastic airplane model. For example, you would study diagrams drawn by other people who have already reconstructed similar skeletons. Then, by examining the skeletal parts, you could sort out the pieces and their relation to one another.

You would also have to build a support or framework to hold the bones together because the animal's tissues no longer exist to perform this function. And you'd have to replace missing pieces, combining your knowledge of prehistoric life with your sculpting ability.

The photograph below shows a reconstruction of *Mosasaurus maximus*, a giant reptile that lived in water about 90 million years ago. Can you imagine how many separate parts it has?

The tools paleontologists use

may include potter's clay, fiber glass, dental plaster, and sculpting knives. They also need patience and attention to detail.

For missing parts, they sometimes cast molds. If a rib is missing, a paleontologist might make a mold of the matching rib. The plaster rib could then be placed opposite the prehistoric animal's original rib.

A missing part or parts may need to be sculpted. To do this accurately, paleontologists draw on all available knowledge about the creature or similar creatures.

The paleontologist must be willing to put up with very slow progress because the reconstruction process can take years of work. So why do people spend their lives rebuilding such creatures?

Many paleontologists became fascinated with prehistoric animals as children and wanted to contribute to scientific knowledge about these animals as adults.

YOU TRY IT!

Find pictures of a dinosaur and its skeleton. Using the skeleton as a guide, write a description you could give an artist who could paint a detailed picture of the dinosaur.

TEENS
in
SCIENCE

DIG IT!

Y ou carefully scoop up a handful of dry, crumbly dirt. At first glance, you think the small gray object in your hand must be a stone. But as you gently work the dirt away with a toothbrush, your heart begins to beat faster. Could it be that you've just found an artifact from an ancient Native American people?

Jose Kubes, a 17-year-old senior at Manual Arts High School in Los Angeles, California, knows what it's like to hold history in his hands. In the summer of 1991, Jose received a scholarship to attend an archaeological expedition sponsored by Earthwatch.

"I joined an expedition in Nebraska. The dig is called the Hudson Meng Bison Kill Site. The name refers to the fact that the area was a popular spot for early North American hunters," Jose said, "We uncovered lots of pieces of arrowheads and chips of bison bones. It was really neat. I kept thinking about how I was working, sleeping, and eating in the same place where Native Americans had worked, slept, and ate 10,000 years ago."

Ten thousand years doesn't seem very long on the geologic time scale. But it is long enough to affect the quality of artifacts.The combination of weather and time can be very destructive. Many of the artifacts at the Hudson Meng Bison Kill Site have splintered into tiny pieces. To be certain that none of the evidence of life was overlooked, the expedition team searched the entire site—millimeter by millimeter. However, not everything

uncovered had historical value.

"Everything we found had to be sent to a lab to be identified and dated," Jose said, "You can't depend on your eyes. Once I thought I'd found a terrific specimen of a bison bone. It turned out to be a piece of bone from an old cow that happened to die in the same spot a few years back. Working on the dig taught me a lot about what archaeologists really do. They are detectives working on the mystery of time."

YOU TRY IT!

It is thousands of years into the future. An archaeological dig is in progress on the site of your school. Make a list of some of the artifacts that might be uncovered. For each artifact you've included, write a brief description about what the piece might tell the archaeologists about you and your classmates.

Reviewing Main Ideas

1. Fossils are the remains or traces of organisms that were once alive. Conditions that increase the likelihood of fossilization include having hard parts and being protected from scavengers, erosion, and decay.

2. Deposited sediments can be cemented or compacted into a layer of rock. Rock layers may be dated relative to each other, but erosion and other forces can create unconformities.

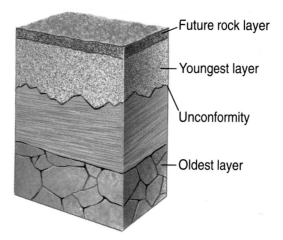

- Future rock layer
- Youngest layer
- Unconformity
- Oldest layer

3. Earth's history can be divided into units of time called eras.

Precambrian Era	Paleozoic Era							Mesozoic Era			Cenozoic Era
Almost 4 billion years	Cambrian Period (70 million years)	Ordovician Period (70 million years)	Silurian Period (35 million years)	Devonian Period (50 million years)	Mississippian Period (20 million years)	Pennsylvanian Period (45 million years)	Permian Period (55 million years)	Triassic Period (35 million years)	Jurassic Period (54 million years)	Cretaceous Period (71 million years)	Paleocene Epoch / Eocene Epoch / Oligocene Epoch / Miocene Epoch / Pliocene Epoch / Pleistocene Epoch / Recent Epoch

4. Geologic eras are further divided into periods and epochs based on the appearance of life-forms and geologic events.

Chapter Review

USING KEY SCIENCE TERMS

cast
Cenozoic Era
epoch
era
fossil
law of superposition
Mesozoic Era
mold
Paleozoic Era
period
Precambrian Era
unconformity

For each set of terms below, explain the relationship that exists.

1. fossil, mold, cast
2. fossil, unconformity, law of superposition
3. epoch, era, period
4. Mesozoic Era, Paleozoic Era, Cenozoic Era, Precambrian Era

UNDERSTANDING IDEAS

Choose the word or phrase in parentheses that makes each sentence true.

1. In one kind of fossil formation, (an epoch/a mold) is created.

2. A condition helpful in the formation of fossils is (soft body parts/hard body parts).
3. A concept used in the dating of rock layers is (the law of superposition/ petrification).
4. One division or subdivision of geologic time is a (period/cast).
5. One thing that helps mark and define a geologic era is (the development of certain life-forms/a definite number of years).
6. An example of an organism alive during the Cenozoic Era would be (a *Tyrannosaurus*/an angiosperm).
7. Life first appeared in the (Precambrian/Paleozoic) Era.
8. One geologic event that occurred in every era was (glacial advances/mountain building).
9. A possible cause of the Permian extinctions was (the arrival of humans/a climate change).
10. Older rocks are generally found (above/below) younger rocks.

CRITICAL THINKING

Use your understanding of the concepts developed in the chapter to answer each of the following questions.

1. What is the most significant difference between Precambrian and Paleozoic life-forms?
2. Compare and contrast a fossil cast and a fossil mold.

3. How does an unconformity affect our fossil record of life on Earth?

4. The pie graph represents geologic time. Determine which era of geologic time is represented by each portion of the graph.

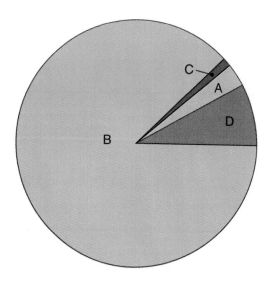

5. What kinds of information would we need to divide the Precambrian Era into periods? Why don't we have that kind of information?

PROBLEM SOLVING

Read the following paragraphs and answer the questions.

Neila enjoyed finding and collecting fossils. She had investigated many of the rock outcrops in her city and had begun an excellent collection of local fossil types. Her favorite fossil was a particular species of brachiopod known as *Mucrospirifer*. She identified her fossil using pictures and descriptions from a book on Paleozoic fossils.

While on a trip with her family to visit relatives in another state, Neila found what seemed like the same type of *Mucrospirifer* fossil in a rock formation on her aunt's farm.

1. What could Neila say about the rocks in which she found both fossils?

2. Could she say exactly how old the rocks were? Why or why not?

CONNECTING IDEAS

Discuss each of the following in a brief paragraph.

1. What relation does the ocean have to the development of life on Earth?

2. Rock layers disturbed by a fault must be older than the fault itself. Why is this so?

3. How might a mass extinction be reflected in the fossil record?

4. **A CLOSER LOOK** How does the length of time humans have been on Earth compare with the overall length of geologic time? With the length of the Cenozoic Era?

5. **SCIENCE AND SOCIETY** Compare and contrast the "rock from space" hypothesis and the "volcanic eruption" hypothesis, which have been suggested to explain the extinction of dinosaurs.

DID YOU EVER WONDER . . .

How a new species of animal evolves from a single ancestor?

What you can learn about how and where an organism lived from fossils?

How similar you might be to other animals or organisms?

You'll find the answers to these questions as you read this chapter.

Evolution of Life

A snake loops sideways over the desert sand. A camel munches noisily on a tall desert plant. A lizard perched atop a rock keeps watch like an armored guard. It's hot enough to fry eggs —sunny-side up! The snake, lizard, camel, and even the desert plant are adapted to the hot, dry desert climate. A sidewinder like the one in the photograph can move sideways over sand. However, many kinds of snakes exist — garter snakes, rattlesnakes, king snakes, and water snakes, just to name a few. These snakes display a variety of shapes, sizes, and colors, and they don't all live in the desert or move over sand. What accounts for these differences in snakes? What accounts for all the other different kinds of plants and animals? In this chapter, you will examine a process that offers an explanation—evolution.

EXPLORE!

Can you find any differences?
A quick walk around your school or neighborhood can introduce you to the variety of life. In this activity, you will explore how much variety you find in pine needles. First, collect about 20 pine needles. To the nearest millimeter, find the lengths of each pine needle. Record your findings. What did you find out about the lengths of the pine needles?

18-1 Raw Materials of Evolution

OBJECTIVES

In this section, you will
- explain how variation occurs in populations;
- give examples of how adaptations help organisms survive.

KEY SCIENCE TERMS

variation

VARIATIONS AND ADAPTATIONS

Have you ever gone into a pet store and watched the playful puppies? Even with puppies, you could find dogs of different sizes, colors, and shapes. Some had long, silky coats and others had short curly coats. Snakes and lizards, cacti and pine trees, poodles and cocker spaniels all have some differences in color, size, or shape that set them apart from other members of their own species. You discovered in the Explore activity that not all pine needles are the same size. The dogs in Figure 18-1 are all the same breed but they have different colored coats. The size of the pine needles and the colors of the dogs' coats are examples of variation. A **variation** is an appearance of an inherited trait or a behavior that makes one organism different from others of the same species. Remember from Chapter 15 how traits are passed from generation to generation. If

FIGURE 18-1. These puppies can be a variety of colors, whether their parents were the same colors or not.

you were able to see the parents of the puppies shown in the photograph, you would find that they were not the same color as all of their offspring. Traits such as coat color show variation even when the parents are the same.

The different colored coats of the dogs really don't make any difference in whether these animals will survive, but it can make a difference to other animals in nature. How do some variations help organisms survive in their environments? Try the following activity to find out.

FIND OUT!

Which beans are easier to find?
Work with a partner. Place one large sheet of dark red construction paper and one large sheet of white construction paper next to each other on your desk. Turn around. Have your partner scatter 25 white beans on the white paper. Turn back and see how many beans you can pick up one at a time in 20 seconds. Record your results. Then, turn your back again, and have your partner scatter the 25 white beans on the dark red paper. Turn around and see how many you can pick up in 20 seconds. Record your results. Use the dark red beans instead of white beans and repeat this activity.

Conclude and Apply
1. When was it easier to find the white beans?
2. When was it easier to find the red beans?
3. What variation were you working with?

The color of the dogs and the color of the beans are both variations. Sometimes a variation will be advantageous, or helpful, to an organism. That organism has a better chance of surviving because of the variation. Didn't you find it easier to pick out the white beans on the red construction paper than when they were on white paper? A variation that makes an organism better able to survive in its environment is called an adaptation. Look at the birds in Figure 18-2. The macaw spends a lot of time perched on tree branches and eating seeds or fruits. It uses its long feet to grasp branches or other objects. The duck spends a lot of time in water. It uses its webbed feet for swimming. Both the macaw's and the duck's feet are adaptations.

Let's examine more closely how adaptations help organisms survive in their environments. What happens when an organism with a certain adaptation is able to survive?

a   b

FIGURE 18-2. Macaws have feet adapted to perching on tree branches and grasping objects (a). Ducks have feet adapted to swimming (b).

AN EXAMPLE OF SURVIVAL

Wolves live in a cold wilderness area that has a large population of different species of rabbits. The rabbits are prey for wolves. One species of rabbit, the snowshoe rabbit, has big feet. Because of their big feet, these snowshoe rabbits are able to move more quickly over the snow. Thus, the snowshoe rabbits are better protected because wolves have smaller, heavier feet and sink into the snow. The snowshoe rabbits' big feet are an adaptation, a variation that helps them survive. Recall from Chapter 15 that organisms don't always pass a specific trait on to every offspring. So, some of the young snowshoe rabbits have smaller feet than others. Because of the size of their feet, smaller-footed, slower rabbits are usually found and eaten first. These rabbits are poorly adapted to their sur-

FIGURE 18-3. Snowshoe rabbits are adapted for fast movement across snow. This adaptation enables them to avoid predators, such as cougars.

roundings and few of them survive. As a result, few smaller-footed snowshoe rabbits reproduce, and the number of these rabbits in the population remains low. The snowshoe rabbits with large feet survive and reproduce. They continue to outnumber the smaller-footed rabbits.

Suppose something happens to allow the wolves to find the snowshoe rabbits more easily. Maybe the snow melts, and the large-footed snowshoe rabbits do not have the advantage of moving quickly across the snow anymore. As a result, the wolves can catch more large-footed snowshoe rabbits. Now the smaller-footed rabbits are better adapted to the environment because they can move more quickly across the solid ground. The balance between the two kinds of rabbits begins to change. Eventually the population will have more small-footed rabbits than large-footed rabbits.

Check Your Understanding

1. Most praying mantises are green in color. How can you explain the appearance of an all white one?
2. How would the white color of the praying mantis, in Question 1, affect its survival?
3. **APPLY:** Which of the following variations might be beneficial to an animal living in the Arctic; brown fur, thick fur, small feet? Why?

18-2 How Evolution Works

In this section, you will
- describe how natural selection operates to bring about change in living things;
- explain Darwin's theory of natural selection.

KEY SCIENCE TERMS

natural selection
evolution
mutation

FIGURE 18-4. The hot and dry conditions of the desert are selecting agents.

NATURAL SELECTION

In the last section, you learned about variations within populations. You learned that sometimes a variation can improve an animal's chances for survival. Now think about the Find Out activity you completed on page 547. Who or what was finding and picking up the colored beans in the activity? By selecting the beans that stood out from the background instead of those beans that blended with the background, you became a selecting agent.

Now think about the rabbits and wolves. What was the selecting agent in this example? In nature, predators are often a selecting agent. Bacteria and viruses can be selecting agents. Environmental conditions, such as the extremely dry and hot conditions of the desert, salt content of water, and acid levels in soil are also selecting agents. Only organisms that are adapted to these conditions can survive. These selecting agents are part of the process called natural selection. The process by which living things that are better adapted to their environment are more likely to survive and reproduce is known as **natural selection.** In our story, the population of rabbits changed from slow to fast mostly because of natural selection. The following activity will show how moths' chances of survival can be affected by a predator through natural selection.

I N V E S T I G A T E !

Moths are most active at night and spend their days resting on tree trunks. Birds feed on moths during the day. This activity represents a model of how birds feed on moths.

PROBLEM
How can an animal's color affect its chance of survival?

MATERIALS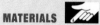
tape
scissors
thin cardboard
forceps
newspaper classified section
black construction paper
watch with second hand

PROCEDURE
1. Copy the data table.
2. Trace the outline of the moth shown onto a piece of thin cardboard and cut it out. Use the moth-shaped hole as a template.
3. Use the template to draw 20 moths on a piece of newspaper. Be sure it consists of uniform small print (no large ads). This will represent gray moths. Cut out the moths.
4. Repeat Step 3 using black construction paper.
5. Tape four pieces of black paper together to form a rectangle 43 x 56 cm. Tape only on one side. This will simulate a black tree trunk.

6. Cut out a piece of classified newspaper 43 x 56 cm. This will simulate a gray tree trunk.
7. Drop 40 moths, half gray and half black, onto the newspaper. Have your partner time you for 10 seconds while you use the forceps to pick up as many moths as you can. Record the number of gray moths and the number of black moths you were able to pick up.
8. Repeat Step 7 four more times, then average the results.
9. Repeat Steps 7 and 8 using the black background.

ANALYZE
1. Did you catch more gray or black moths on the gray tree trunk? On the black tree trunk?

CONCLUDE AND APPLY
2. **Determine** how the colors of the tree trunk affected the gray moths.
3. Where in this simulation did you **observe** variation?
4. **Going Further: Hypothesize** how this activity could be expanded to show what would happen to the moths if natural selection occurred?

DATA AND OBSERVATIONS

Sample data

TRIAL	GRAY TREE TRUNK		BLACK TREE TRUNK	
	GRAY MOTHS	BLACK MOTHS	GRAY MOTHS	BLACK MOTHS
1	5	1	2	6
2	4	1	1	5
3	5	2	3	4
4	4	3	1	3
5	3	1	1	4
TOTAL	21	8	8	22
AVG.	4.2	1.6	1.6	4.4

Natural selection occurs in nature

What you simulated in the Investigate actually happened in England. During the early 1800s, the speckled pepper moth shown in the figure was prominent. Around 1850, a rare black variety of the moth was found more often. By 1900, the black variety was prominent and the speckled variety was rare. The change was brought about by a change in the moth's environment. In the early 1800s, the speckled moth blended perfectly with lichens that grew on tree trunks.

The moth spent its days resting on the trunks. The Industrial Revolution of the 1800s resulted in many factories that billowed black smoke and soot into the air. This pollution killed the lichens and blackened the tree trunks. With each generation, fewer speckled moths survived and more black moths survived. In 1956, the British government passed a clean air act forcing factories to reduce air pollution. Since that time, the proportion of speckled pepper moths collected in industrialized areas has gradually increased.

CHARLES DARWIN

Much of what you have learned so far about variation, adaptation, and natural selection is not new. It was stated over 100 years ago by Charles Darwin. In 1831, Darwin began a job as ship's naturalist aboard a British ship. For five years he collected thousands of fossils and specimens of living plants and animals. He continuously made observations about the behavior of plants and animals and their relationships with each other.

One of the stops on the voyage was at the Galapagos Islands. Here he observed 14 species of finches. Each species had a different shaped beak and lived on a different island. The beaks ranged from stubby, parrotlike beaks to long, thin beaks. Each bird, therefore, could eat only a certain type of food. Remember, you learned earlier that all animals are adapted to live in their environment. Darwin

FIGURE 18-5. Organisms produce more offspring than can survive.

Sharp-beaked ground finch

Small insect-eating finch

Cactus ground finch

Vegetarian finch

Large cactus ground finch

Tool-using finch

Medium insect-eating finch

Small ground finch

Large insect-eating finch

Medium ground finch

Large ground finch

observed that the finches with parrotlike beaks ate nuts and seeds and lived on the islands where these foods were plentiful. Those with long, thin beaks lived on islands where they could pry insects out of the bark of trees.

FIGURE 18-6. The finches on the Galapagos Islands have beaks adapted to getting the types of foods they eat.

DARWIN'S THEORY OF NATURAL SELECTION

For 20 years after he returned to England, Darwin studied his collections and observations. The fossils, living specimens, and recorded observations were evidence of the variation in organisms. And while Darwin collected specimens of some organisms that could be found in only one location, he realized that these living things were similar to organisms present in other parts of the world. In 1859, he published a book explaining his theory of natural selection. This theory explains how organisms change over periods of time. His more important ideas are summarized for you in the list below.

1. *Organisms produce more offspring than can survive.* A single cottonwood tree produces thousands of seeds while one salmon can lay thousands of eggs.
2. *Variations exist within populations.* Each individual doesn't appear exactly like all the other members of its species.
3. *Some variations are more advantageous for survival and reproduction than others.* There is a struggle to survive

SKILLBUILDER

OBSERVING AND INFERRING

Frog eggs are commonly observed in ponds in spring. Can you infer from this why ponds are not overpopulated by frogs in the summer? Use the ideas of natural selection to help you. If you need help, refer to the **Skill Handbook** on page 684.

FIGURE 18-7. Natural selection operates on the variations in nature.

that results in competition. For example, young pine trees compete for light, water, and soil nutrients.

4. *Over time, offspring of survivors will make up a larger proportion of the population.* Individuals with less desirable traits are less fit and produce fewer offspring that survive. Individuals with more desirable traits are more fit and survive to produce more offspring.

The relationship between the rabbits and wolves, and the black and speckled pepper moths in England illustrate that species of organisms change. Darwin also realized that species are always changing. He knew that these changes didn't happen quickly. Darwin's observations and studies led him to form the theory of natural selection to explain evolution. **Evolution** is the change in the hereditary features of a population of organisms over time. When a species changes through time, scientists say that it has evolved. While earlier scientists may have recognized that change occurs in living things, Darwin was able to successfully explain the process involved in the change.

MUTATIONS

Variation is the key idea to the process of natural selection. But how does a variation come about? Remember that a variation is an inherited trait that makes an individual different from other individuals of its species. You learned in Chapter 15 that genes control the traits you

FIGURE 18-8. Mutations caused the change of color in both the deer (a) and praying mantis (b).

a

b

inherit. Sometimes a gene or chromo-some is changed. When that happens, the trait controlled by the gene is also changed. A permanent change in a gene or chromosome is called a **mutation**. Variations in color, size, shape, and so on are often caused by mutations. Most mutations have little effect on an organ-ism. Some mutations are harmful and some are helpful to an organism. You may recall from Chapter 15 the disease called sickle-cell anemia. Sickle-cell anemia is an example of a mutation harmful to organisms. Figure 18-9 shows an example of a mutation that is neither helpful nor harmful.

FIGURE 18-9. Extra toes on cats are examples of mutations that are neither helpful nor harmful.

Evolutionary change by natural selection is occurring all the time. The finches that Dar-win studied on the Galapagos Islands are one well-known example of the formation of new species. Remember that each species had a certain kind of beak that was adapted for eating specific foods. The different species began to develop when offspring of one ancestor spread out over the islands. As the finches became separated, each group developed different beaks because their environments were different. The groups became less like each other and eventually several different species evolved from the single ancestor.

Check Your Understanding

1. How did natural selection bring about a change in the population of the speckled pepper moth?
2. What are the four points to Darwin's theory of natural selection?
3. What causes new variations to appear in a population?
4. **APPLY:** Two kinds of trout inhabit a very popular fishing lake. One species of trout has more meat and tastes better, but it is more susceptible to the water pollution in the lake. The other species of trout is beginning to take over the lake because the pollution does not affect it as much. What may have occurred in the body of the other species that allows it to survive pollution?

18-3 Evidence of Evolution

OBJECTIVES

In this section, you will
- determine how fossils are evidence of evolution;
- compare the similarity in structure and chemical makeup of cells;
- determine how homologous structures are evidence of evolution.

KEY SCIENCE TERMS

homologous structure
primate

FOSSILS

Suppose you suspected that two organisms were related but didn't know for sure if they were or how they were. Scientists can find evidence of evolution in many different places. They are like detectives in search of clues to solve a mystery. Some evidence of evolution comes from fossils.

You learned in Chapter 17 that fossils are any remains of life from earlier times. While many fossils are imprints, some are petrified bone or wood, plants or animals frozen in ice, or organisms trapped in plant resin.

Recall from Chapter 17 that fossils are usually found within rock layers. If you could cut away a section of Earth, you would see the rock layers, almost like the layers of a cake. If the layers have not been disturbed, the older layers are on the bottom. The younger layers are on top. Fossils found in the older layers are earlier forms of life. Generally, fossils of earlier life forms show organisms with simpler body structures than fossils of later organisms. Sometimes more recent fossils show an organism that falls somewhere between the early simple organism and the more complex organism that lives today. These organisms are called intermediate forms. If a complete fossil record was available, you could trace the evolution of a species from its earliest ancestor to its present form. The following activity allows you to study an example of an intermediate form.

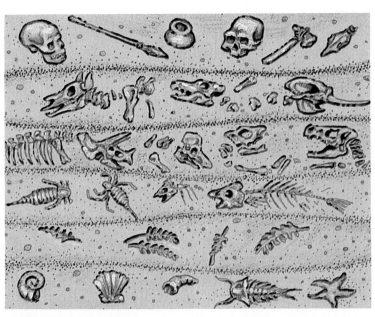

FIGURE 18-10. Fossils found in older layers are usually of earlier, simpler forms of life.

Peripatus—Is it an Annelid or Arthropod?

Study the pictures of these three different organisms. The earthworm belongs to the phylum Annelida, and the millipede belongs to the phylum Arthropoda. *Peripatus* has characteristics common to both of the other animals. Use the photos shown to observe how *Peripatus* is similar to each animal.

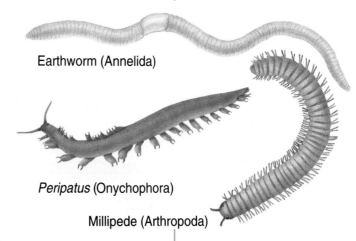

Earthworm (Annelida)

Peripatus (Onychophora)

Millipede (Arthropoda)

Conclude and Apply

1. How would you classify this animal?
2. Why could it be called an intermediate organism?

Sometimes fossils provide evidence about the climate or landscape of an area during earlier periods. Fossils of marine organisms have been found hundreds of kilometers from the nearest ocean. How did marine animals move inland? Remember the theory of plate tectonics and the breakup of Pangaea? As the continents slowly moved apart, areas that had been ocean became dry land. Mountains thrust up and new shorelines formed. The remains of ocean organisms were left high and dry on mountain tops.

CELL STRUCTURE

Let's return to the analogy of a scientist being a detective. Suppose the detective was trying to prove that an unidentified accident victim was a member of a certain family. One possible method could be comparing the physical characteristics of the victim with the characteristics of members of the family. Height, weight, color of hair, and structure of the face are some of the characteristics that might be compared. If many of the characteristics are similar, then a case could be made that the victim and family members were related. Scientists use the same methods for finding evidence of evolution. Try the following activity and see what similarities you can find in different cells.

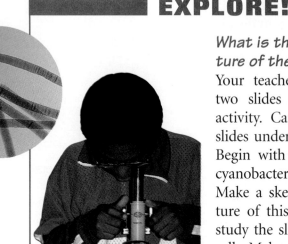

EXPLORE!

What is the basic structure of the cell?
Your teacher will give you two slides to use for this activity. Carefully study the slides under the microscope. Begin with the slide of the cyanobacterium *Oscillatoria*. Make a sketch of the structure of this moneran. Then study the slide of the *Elodea* cells. Make a simple sketch of the cell structure of this freshwater plant. Compare the two drawings. How are the cells similar?

Your drawings from the Explore activity probably included structures such as cell walls, nuclei, and chloroplasts. In addition, you may remember that all cells have a cell membrane and contain a gel-like material called cytoplasm. Cells also have other structures such as mitochondria and vacuoles in common.

Look at the cells in Figure 18-11. Compare these cells to the moneran and plant cells you saw in the activity. Are there more similarities or differences in the structure of the cells? Chances are you think the cells look very much alike. The structure of the cells from the activity look a lot like the structure of the animal cells shown here.

Because cells from modern organisms have some similar structures, you might suggest that these cells are also similar to those of ancient organisms. But how could this idea be proven? The oldest fossils show organisms that lived about 3.5 billion years ago. These organisms resemble some very simple bacteria that live today. These organisms are found in salt ponds and hot sulfur

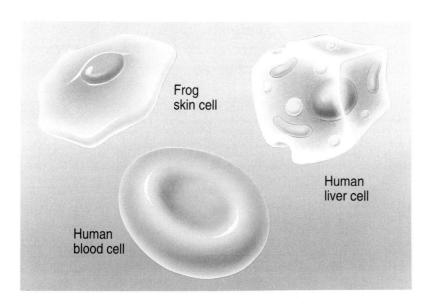

FIGURE 18-11. Cells from different kinds of organisms show many similarities of structure.

springs— the same kind of environment scientists believe existed on Earth millions of years ago. The resemblance suggests a relatedness between ancient and modern organisms.

CHEMICAL MAKEUP OF THE CELL

Just as cells have many common structures, their contents are chemically similar. All organisms have the same molecules that are building blocks of their cells: proteins, fats, and carbohydrates. All organisms also have similar kinds of enzymes to speed up chemical reactions within their cells.

Recall from Chapter 15 that the chemical DNA controls the characteristics, or traits, of all organisms. When new cells are formed, they receive the same DNA code as the original cell. Scientists know that the DNA of each species has a specific sequence for the four kinds of bases. The more closely related one species is to another, the more similar their DNA codes are. Scientists can use this information to genetically map out the relationships

FIGURE 18-12. Species have unique sequences of bases in their DNA.

among different organisms. Studies have shown the sequences of the nitrogen bases are very similar in humans, chimpanzees, gorillas, and the other African apes.

HOMOLOGOUS STRUCTURES

You learned that comparing cell structure and comparing cell chemistry are ways to determine relatedness among organisms. The comparison of other body structures can also show relatedness. Figure 18-13 shows body parts from different animals. The human arm, bird's wing, dolphin's flipper, and bat's wing all perform different functions. However, all of these body parts contain approximately the same number and types of bones and muscles. If you were able to trace the development of these animals from the embryo stage to adult, you would see that each limb developed from similar tissues in the embryos. Body parts of different organisms that are similar in origin and structure are called **homologous structures**. Homologous structures also provide evidence of evolution because they suggest that organisms evolve from a common ancestor.

FIGURE 18-13. Homologous structures have similar origins and structures. They are evidence of common ancestry.

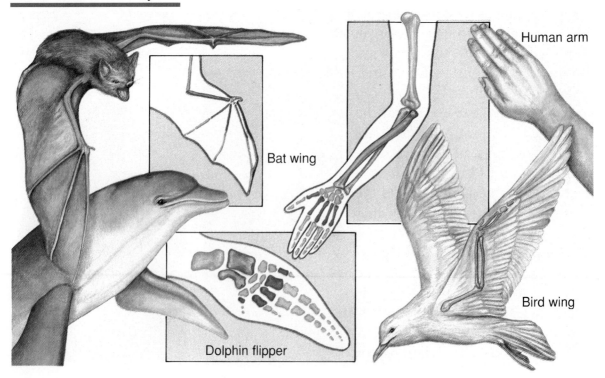

Bat wing

Human arm

Dolphin flipper

Bird wing

18-2
HOW ARE YOUR ARMS LIKE CHICKEN WINGS?

In this activity, you will find out if your arm and a chicken's wing are homologous structures.

PROBLEM
What are the similarities and differences between human arms and chicken wings?

MATERIALS
cooked chicken wing
forceps
scalpel
model of human arm and hand bones
paper towels
dissecting pan
drawing paper
pencil
colored pencils

PROCEDURE
1. Place a chicken wing in the dissecting pan. Use the scalpel to remove as much meat as possible from the wing. **CAUTION**: *Care should be used to prevent cutting yourself.*

2. Wrap the meat in a paper towel and follow your teacher's instructions for discarding it.

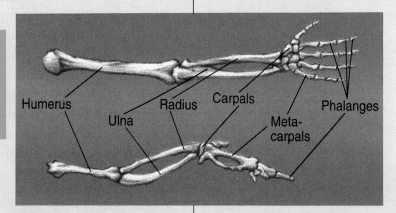

CAUTION:*Don't eat the meat.*

3. Examine the bones of the wing. Draw the bones separately and as they fit together.

4. **Hypothesize** how the bones in your arm and hand might be similar to the bones in a chicken wing.

5. Study the bones of the human arm and hand. Draw how the bones fit together.

6. **Compare** the bones of the wing and the human arm and hand. Color any structures you think are homologous the same color.

7. Wrap the chicken bones in a paper towel and follow your teacher's instructions for discarding them. Clean your scalpel, forceps, and dissecting pan. Be sure to wash your hands thoroughly with soapy water after this activity.

ANALYZE
1. How do the bones in the human arm compare to the bones in the chicken wing? Consider size, shape, and number.

2. **Compare** and **contrast** the bones in the human hand to the bones in the chicken wing. Again consider size, shape and number.

CONCLUDE AND APPLY
3. Do your observations support your original hypothesis? If not, formulate a new hypothesis.

4. Based on information gained from this activity, could you classify your arm and a chicken wing as homologous structures? Why or why not?

5. **Going Further:** What could you do to make sure both structures are homologous structures?

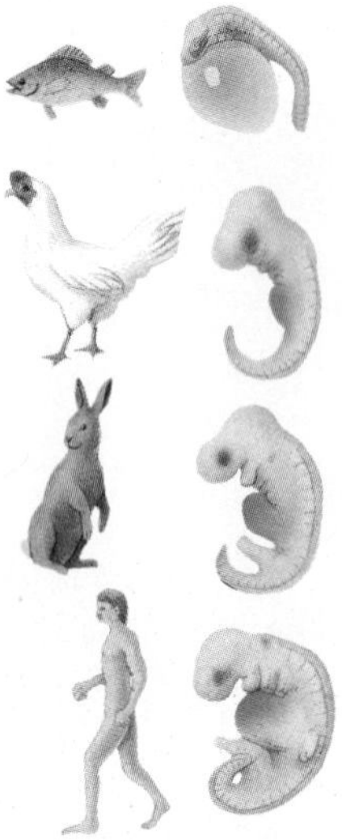

EVIDENCE FROM EMBRYOS

Study the embryos in Figure 18-14. In the early stages of development, all of these animals look similar. They all have tails and gills or gill slits. Fish, and many aquatic amphibians, such as mudpuppies and sirens, are the only vertebrates to keep the gills as adults. All other vertebrates develop lungs. The human tail disappears but fish, birds, and reptiles keep their tails as adults. These similarities suggest that there is a common ancestor for all of the vertebrates.

FIGURE 18-14. Similarities in the embryos of all vertebrates are evidence of a common ancestor for these animals.

FIGURE 18-15. Flexible shoulders and rotating forelimbs are characteristics humans share with other primates.

EVIDENCE OF HUMAN EVOLUTION

You know that the DNA of chimpanzees and gorillas has been found to be very similar to the DNA of humans. **Primates**, the group of mammals that includes monkeys, apes, and humans, share many characteristics. Opposable thumbs allow you and other primates to grasp and hold objects. Flexible shoulders allow the gymnast to swing on the bars as other primates swing through trees. Binocular vision allows you to judge depth with your eyes just like chimps, monkeys, and lemurs. Each piece of evidence suggests that all of the primates evolved from a common ancestor.

You have learned that change is normal. It's not surprising then that life has changed and is continuing to change on Earth.

Check Your Understanding

1. If you were digging on the side of a cliff, how might fossils at the bottom differ from those at the top?
2. What are some structures common to all cells?
3. Why are homologous structures considered evidence of evolution?
4. **APPLY:** Suppose a scientist had the DNA sequence of four organisms. How could he or she determine which two organisms belonged to the same species?

EXPANDING YOUR VIEW

CONTENTS

A CLOSER LOOK

LIVING LINKS

Scientists believe that the annelid phylum, which includes earthworms and leeches, is closely related to the arthropod phylum, which includes insects and millipedes. Yet, strangely enough, a rare animal called *Peripatus* (puh RIP uh tus) belongs to neither phylum and shares important traits of both.

YOU TRY IT!

Draw a chart like the one shown. Using the information given, put an X in the box in which each trait occurs. Use your chart to compare and contrast *Peripatus*, a grasshopper, and an earthworm. Do you see why scientists think that *Peripatus* evolved from the same ancestors as annelids and arthropods?

Look at this comparison:
P = *Peripatus*
G = grasshopper (an arthropod)
E = earthworm (an annelid)

1. G and E have segmented bodies (bodies in sections.)
2. G and P have antennae and eyes.
3. P and G have open circulation.
4. The heart is on the top of all three.
5. The nerve cord is on the bottom of all three.
6. E and P both have a thin outer skin.
7. Oxygen is taken into the body of P and G through small tubes, while E breathes through its skin.
8. P and E have kidneys that are similar.

	segmented body	antennae and eyes	open circulation	heart on top	nerve cord on bottom	thin outer skin	breathe through tubes	similar kidney structure
E								
G								
P								

Chemistry Connection

CHEMICAL BUILDING BLOCKS OF LIFE

All living organisms share many of the same elements. Their chemistry is rooted in the six elements of life — oxygen, nitrogen, hydrogen, sulfur, phosphorus, and most importantly, carbon. Atoms of these six elements combine and bond in various ways to become molecules. Simple molecules also combine and bond into larger, more complex molecules.

In all living things, the basic molecule of life is DNA (deoxyribonucleic acid). The DNA molecule is formed from six smaller molecules. In every plant and animal on Earth, these six molecules are the chemical foundation of life. The six molecules combine in different ways. These combinations form a code containing thousands of messages. Some of these messages determine heredity. Others run the day-to-day operations of the body. For instance, they give cells instructions for making protein molecules.

Proteins are absolutely vital to all life. They serve many different functions.

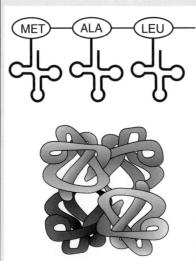

Hemoglobin molecule

Some are part of skin, hair, horns, and feathers. Others are parts of the body's defense system. The blood protein, hemoglobin (HEE mah globe en), carries oxygen from the lungs to the body tissues. Hormones, such as insulin (which controls sugar metabolism), are made of proteins. So are enzymes, which help chemical processes occur.

Protein molecules are formed of many amino (ah MEE no) acids linked together in a long sequence, like beads on a string or railroad cars in a train. The DNA code instructs the cell where to place each amino acid in the sequence. Only 20 types of amino acids form into proteins. However, those 20 can combine in hundreds of millions of different ways. The proteins formed are complicated, folded, and coiled shapes.

A single protein molecule could have as few as eight amino acid molecules or as many as 100,000! Hemoglobin, an average-sized protein, has a total of 600 amino acids in 19 different varieties. The tiny insulin molecule has a total of 51 amino acids in 17 different varieties.

WHAT DO YOU THINK?

Plants produce their own amino acids. They take the necessary elements from the soil, water, and air and convert them into the chemical building blocks of life. However, animals cannot manufacture many of their own amino acids. They must get them by eating plants. Because most plants contain small amounts of amino acids, animals must eat large quantities to get enough for their bodies' needs. Animals that eat other animals and animal products, such as milk and eggs, do not have this problem. Can you explain why?

SCIENCE AND SOCIETY

EVOLUTION ON THE FARM

In nature, species that are well adapted to their environment have a better chance of surviving and passing their genes on to the next generation than those that aren't. This process is known as natural selection because conditions in nature have selected which organisms will survive and which will not.

When people began to grow their own food, they developed a process called artificial selection, and thus influenced the evolution of many species of plants and animals. The earliest farmers saved seeds from their best plants — the biggest, strongest, or best tasting crops — to plant the next year. In this way, certain traits were nurtured while others were discouraged. People used this crude form of artificial selection for thousands of years.

During the past 100 years, scientists have become very sophisticated at artificial selection. After learning the laws of genetic inheritance, agricultural scientists began to breed plants scientifically. Working with farmers, they experimented with different species, trying to develop plants that would mature more quickly and produce more food, that could withstand hot and cold weather, and that could resist diseases and insects. Sometimes they even developed plants that were more nutritious than before.

Despite all the progress in plant breeding, farmers still must battle unwanted insect pests in their fields. Insect pests not only eat the plants, they carry the bacteria and viruses that cause plant diseases.

Some farmers spray their crops with insecticides to control harmful organisms. However, using the poisonous chemicals in insecticides has caused problems. First, chem-

icals that are dangerous to insects are often dangerous to humans, too. The chemical must be washed from harvested crops to prevent poisoning those who eat them. Second, insecticides can enter rivers and affect other wildlife in the environment. Third, without realizing it, the scientists and farmers who developed and used insecticides were also interfering with natural selection.

Many species of insects are now resistant to the chemicals in certain insecticides. When farmers originally used these insecticides, insects that had insecticide-resistant genes survived. These insects reproduced, passing the gene for resistance to their offspring. The insects that weren't resistant died, leaving no offspring. Because of this artificial selection, many types of insects are now resistant. The insecticides no longer kill any of them. As a result, new and stronger insecticides have been developed.

During the past decade or so, scientists have developed new techniques for fighting unwanted insects. Certain plants contain natural substances that repel insects. Using a new technology called genetic engineering, scientists can move genes from one organism to another. Many scientists feel that it may be possible to transfer genes that control the production of these insect-repelling substances from one kind of plant to another. The receiving plant would then have the genetic trait to repel insect pests. Natural plant chemicals would not endanger humans or harm the environment but only affect the insects that feed on that particular plant species.

Scientists have also been using artificial selection with insects as well as the plants they eat. For example, scientists have used genetic engineering to give certain insects genetic diseases that will spread in the insect population. They also have developed new kinds of insecticides that do not poison the insects but instead affect their growth hormones. These insects cannot mature into adulthood, so they cannot reproduce. Another technique is treating thousands of male insects so they cannot reproduce, then letting them go in the fields. These males mate with female insects but cannot fertilize their eggs. In this way, the insect population becomes reduced. This technique was very successful in helping to control the fruit flies, shown in the photo, that were destroying crops in California.

WHAT DO YOU THINK?

Before any plants are genetically engineered to repel insect pests, should effects on insect species be considered? It is possible that insect species might become extinct or that new insect species will evolve. Also, if scientists genetically alter insects, what might the effect be on other species of insects, or even animals—for example, the birds, reptiles, and other insects that eat the genetically altered insects? Perhaps species might be altered in a way that is not beneficial to humans and other animals. Are there other ways to solve the problems caused by insects? Instead of changing the DNA of plants or insects, should we consider other ways to grow crops?

TECHNOLOGY CONNECTION

WHEN WERE ROCK PICTURES PAINTED?

When scientists find a prehistoric site, they want to learn as much as they can about the people who lived there. They study the pots, spears, and other objects that are scattered around such places. They also study the paintings, called pictographs, on cave walls and other rocks.

Carbon-14 dating helps these scientists calculate just how long ago a basket was woven or a piece of horn was carved. However, until recently, they could not use carbon-14 dating to learn the age of pictographs. Carbon-14 dating was impossible

because of the similarity between the carbon in the paint and the carbon in the limestone rock the paint is on. Because of this problem, scientists had to use the carbon-14 dates of objects near the paintings and the style of the art to estimate the age of pictographs.

WHAT DO YOU THINK?

Notice the rock, brick, and concrete walls in your town that have something painted on them—perhaps a mural, an advertisement, or even graffiti. What could scientists thousands of years from now learn about our society from studying these pictures?

A few years ago, some scientists used a limestone chip from an ancient pictograph to invent a way to separate the two kinds of carbon. First, the scientists scraped paint from the rock and put it in a container. This container had a partial vacuum that caused the carbon dioxide inside it to evaporate. Next, they filled the contain-

er with a gas that changed the carbon from the paint into carbon dioxide but left the carbon from the rock alone. The scientists turned the carbon dioxide from the paint into dry ice. Then they converted it into graphite. Finally, they measured the carbon-14 in the graphite with a piece of equipment called an accelerated mass spectrometer.

Using the earlier method, the scientists would have estimated the age of the pictograph to be from 2000 to 6000 years old. Plus or minus 4000 years isn't a very precise measurement!

Using their new method, the scientists calculated that the paint was 3865 years old, plus or minus 100 years. This calculation is much more precise than the earlier estimate!

History
CONNECTION

ALFRED RUSSEL WALLACE

Charles Darwin was not the only scientist who developed the theory of natural selection to explain the evolution of species. A fellow scientist by the name of Alfred Russel Wallace came up with an almost identical theory at the same time as Darwin.

In 1848, when Wallace was 25 years old, he went on an expedition to the Amazon to study insects. Unfortunately, his ship sank on the return voyage to England, and with it almost all of his insects. From 1854 to 1862, Wallace traveled in Southeast Asia to collect more evidence that would show the process of evolution at work.

In 1855, Wallace wrote that for ten years "... the question of how changes of species could have been brought about was rarely out of my mind." Then in 1858, ill and feverish from a severe attack of malaria, he had an inspiration: "[T]here suddenly flashed upon me the idea of the survival of the fittest." Even though he was quite ill, Wallace spent the next three nights writing an essay explaining his idea of "the survival of the fittest" — the phrase he coined for his theory. He mailed his essay to Charles Darwin, who saw at once that the young naturalist had a theory like his own.

Wallace and Darwin presented their theories together to a meeting of scientists in 1858. They explained that animals that are healthy and strong survive, while those that are weaker do not. They also described how certain traits — such as camouflage coloring in insects — helped these animals survive longer than animals that do not have these traits. But Wallace and Darwin did not agree on everything. They both believed that the human body evolved to its present form by natural selection. But Wallace insisted that the human mind could not have resulted only from natural selection. He believed some spiritual power was responsible.

WHAT DO YOU THINK?

It is not uncommon for two scientists to develop similar discoveries at the same time. You've learned about the observations Darwin made in order to propose his theories of natural selection. What kinds of observation of the natural world do you think Wallace made? Do you think Wallace and Darwin had to have made similar observations to arrive at their theories independently?

Reviewing Main Ideas

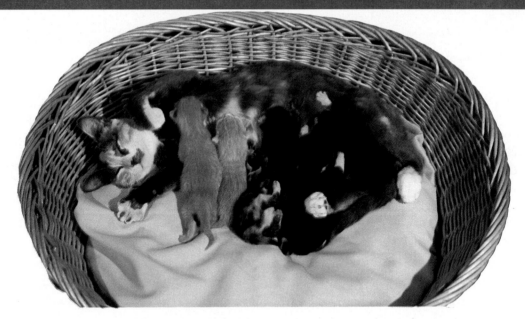

1. Variations are differences in inherited traits among members of the same species. Variations that allow an organism to be better suited to its environment are adaptations.

2. Charles Darwin is credited with developing the theory of natural selection. This theory states that natural selection is a process in which living things that are better adapted to their environment are more likely to survive and reproduce.

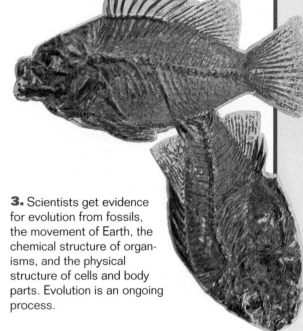

3. Scientists get evidence for evolution from fossils, the movement of Earth, the chemical structure of organisms, and the physical structure of cells and body parts. Evolution is an ongoing process.

Chapter Review

USING KEY SCIENCE TERMS

evolution
homologous structure
mutation
natural selection
primate
variation

Each phrase below describes a science term from the list. Write the term that matches the phrase describing it.

1. an appearance of an inherited trait that makes one individual different from others of the same species

2. a process in which living things that are better adapted to their environment are more likely to survive and reproduce

3. a permanent change in a gene or chromosome

4. the change in the hereditary features of an organism over time

5. the group of mammals that includes monkeys, apes, and humans

6. body parts that are similar in origin and structure

UNDERSTANDING IDEAS

Complete each sentence.

1. _____ is the change in the hereditary features of an organism over time.

2. The speckled pepper moth is a good example of how the theory of _____ works in nature.

3. The difference in height among your classmates is an example of human _____.

4. In nature, _____ such as wolves can be selecting agents because they often reduce the numbers of poorly adapted animals by feeding on them.

5. The chemical _____ controls the characteristics of all organisms.

6. The human's arm, bat's wing, and dolphin's flipper are _____ structures.

7. The _____ of all vertebrates have tails, and gills or gill slits.

8. _____ was the first to successfully explain the process that resulted in evolution.

CRITICAL THINKING

Use your understanding of the concepts developed in the chapter to answer each of the following questions.

1. Use what you've learned about evolution through natural selection to hypothesize how humans might evolve over time if our atmosphere keeps becoming more polluted.

2. An athlete breaks her leg in a high jump. Years later, she has a son who walks with a slight limp. Is this an example of evolution? Why or why not?

3. Explain how producing large numbers of offspring is an adaptation for survival of a species.

4. Study the sketches of the Arctic fox, red fox, and desert fox. How might the variations you observe have evolved?

Arctic fox

Red fox

Desert fox

5. Animal A and animal B share 89 percent of the DNA code. Animal A and animal C share 91 percent of the DNA code. Which animals are more closely related?

6. Why were Darwin's observations of the Galapagos finches important to his theory?

7. How does cell structure provide evidence of evolution?

8. Describe how mutations play a role in the evolution of organisms.

9. Why are homologous structures useful for understanding evolution?

PROBLEM SOLVING

Read the following problem and discuss your answers in a brief paragraph.

Rumors of a primitive humanlike animal have circulated in a remote wilderness area for over 100 years. An individual brings the remains of what appears to be a humanlike animal and claims that this is the mysterious beast. The remains consist of some long hairs and a partial skeleton. As a scientist, what could you do to prove that the beast was real or a hoax?

CONNECTING IDEAS

Discuss each of the following in a brief paragraph.

1. Fossils of two almost identical animals that lived millions of years ago were found in both Africa and South America. How do you explain this from what you have learned about evolution and plate tectonics?

2. Farmers often develop domestic animals and plants with certain characteristics. Give an example of this type of breeding and tell how it is different from natural selection.

3. How do the disciplines of life, earth, and physical science all contribute evidence for evolution?

4. TECHNOLOGY CONNECTION Describe the method of carbon-14 dating. How can carbon-14 dating help scientists learn about life in the past?

5. SCIENCE AND SOCIETY Scientists have discovered ways to modify the genes of some living organisms. Do you think human evolution will be affected by these techniques?

LOOKING BACK

UNIT 4
CHANGES IN LIFE AND EARTH OVER TIME

CONTENTS

UNIT FOCUS

In this unit, you learned that the face of Earth and the living things on it are very different today than they were in the distant past. In geologic time, measured in millions of years, continents have moved, mountains have appeared and disappeared, and many life-forms have flourished and then become extinct. Also, you explored in depth the processes that produce the genetic diversity on which natural selection works.

Try the exercises and activity that follow—they will challenge you to use and apply some of the ideas you learned in this unit.

CONNECTING IDEAS

1. Coal deposits are located in some very cold regions of the world near the Arctic Circle. Relate the appearance of coal in these areas to the climate that must have existed when the coal beds started forming and why the coal appears in these areas today.

2. Suppose that conditions in an area change so much that certain easily chewed and digested plants died off over a short period of time. The only plants remaining as a supply of food were enclosed in rather tough shells that could not be easily chewed. What characteristics would better prepare one organism to survive this sudden change in the environment better than another?

EXPLORING FURTHER

Write a letter to Charles Darwin. Provide him with evidence that he was not aware of at the time he wrote that would support his ideas on evolution and natural selection. Using what you know about heredity, evolution, and natural selection, how would you answer someone who claims that evolution could not be correct because we have never found an organism that is half of one species and half of another?

TRY IT

Icy objects called comets travel through the solar system and around the sun. You can see how a comet moves around the sun using a phenakisto-scope (fee nuh KIS toh scope). Use the diagram provided by your teacher. Make a circle about 8 inches in diameter on a piece of white cardboard. Divide the circle into 16 equally-sized pie sections. Cut out small, rectangular sections from the outer portion of the disk between each section. Now, draw a comet near the outer edge on one section. In each of the other sections, draw a comet a little further in its progression around the sun. Push a tack through the center of the disk and into a stick. While standing in front of a mirror, hold the disk in front of your face with the pictures facing the mirror. While looking through the slits, slowly spin the disk. You should be able to see the comet moving around the sun. After you've learned more about comets, see if you can explain why your comet moves the way it does.

UNIT FOCUS

In Unit 4, you learned how life-forms on Earth and Earth itself have changed over time. As you study Unit 5, you'll see how changes in elements occur because of fission and fusion reactions. You will see how fusion reactions produce the energy you receive from the sun each day. You will also study how the solar system and the universe itself have changed over time. You will learn that the structure of our solar system is related to the energy produced by fusion and the movement of molecules you learned about earlier.

DID YOU EVER WONDER . . .

How all the positive particles stay in an atom's nucleus even though they repel each other?

What causes radioactivity?

What happens in a nuclear reaction?

You'll find the answers to these questions as you read this chapter.

Chapter 19

Fission and Fusion

You're outdoors. The sun is providing you with the light and warmth that makes life possible, thanks to nuclear reactions. On your way to school, you pass by a woman out jogging. She could have died a year ago, but she's alive today thanks to medical breakthroughs made possible by nuclear science.

At school, some students are talking about a nearby power station that has been shut down for refueling. There has been much debate over the years about this station because it runs on nuclear reactions. You recall that several states in your part of the country have been discussing the best methods for storing and disposing of materials created by other nuclear power plants.

Just what are nuclear reactions?

How and why will they play an important role in your life and in the decisions you will be asked to make? In this chapter you'll learn about this important source of energy.

EXPLORE!

Is there a use for radioactive elements in your home?

Remove the outside cover of a smoke detector. Look for a small metal cover or cage. **CAUTION:** *Don't take this metal cage apart!*

Most home smoke detectors have a small identification label describing the material on this metal shield. It may also contain a symbol such as the one used above. This symbol indicates an area where radioactive materials are located. Look for this symbol inside the smoke detector. Describe it. What does it say?

19-1 Radioactivity, Natural and Artificial

OBJECTIVES

In this section, you will

- describe an artificial transmutation;
- compare artificial and natural transmutations.

KEY SCIENCE TERMS

transmutation
artificial transmutation

GETTING TO THE SOURCE OF NUCLEAR ENERGY

When you talk about nuclear energy, radioactivity, and nuclear reactions, you are talking about changes that are taking place in the nucleus of an atom. You may recall that we looked at the spontaneous decay of unstable nuclei, called radioactivity, in Chapter 5. Here, you are going to take a closer look at the forces inside the nucleus of an atom. You will see that changes occur in the nucleus naturally and that changes in the nucleus can also be caused to happen.

EXPLORE!

How do protons stick together in an atom's nucleus?
Place 10 BB pellets in a pile on a tray. Shoot one BB pellet along the tray toward the pile. What happens to the BBs in the pile when they are struck? Now lightly coat the 10 BB pellets with salad oil and shoot one BB pellet along the tray toward the pile. Regroup the BB pellets and roll another pellet towards the pile. Observe the behavior of the BBs when they are struck. Did each pile of BBs break apart in the same way? Why did they behave differently?

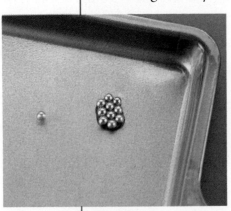

In the Explore activity, you observed a model for the behavior of nuclear particles. The BBs coated with oil behave in a similar manner to protons in the nuclei of atoms. A force, modeled by the oil, seems to be holding them together.

An atomic nucleus contains positively charged protons. Just like any objects with similar electric charge, the protons repel one another. Yet the protons in a nucleus are very close to each other. Some force must be holding the protons together.

There are neutrons in the nucleus as well. Neutrons aren't charged so they don't repel protons. Neutrons don't attract protons either. Neutrons do, however, help to hold the nucleus together. Protons and neutrons share a force that holds the nucleus together. It's an extremely strong force that holds neutrons to protons, protons to protons, and neutrons to neutrons. This force is very strong but it works only over extremely short distances. It's called the strong nuclear force. The protons and neutrons must be nearly touching or the strong force has no effect. As a result, this strong force can't hold every nucleus together.

The nucleus of a lighter element stays together if it has roughly equal numbers of protons and neutrons. For example, the most common isotopes of He, C, N, and O have exactly as many neutrons as protons. In a more massive element, more neutrons are needed so that the strong force can balance the repulsion between the protons. If there are too few or too many neutrons, something gives. The nucleus will expel a particle as it moves toward stability. When this happens, we say that the element decays. Some elements of light and medium mass are radioactive. Unlike the lighter elements, elements with more than 83 protons are always unstable, whatever the number of neutrons.

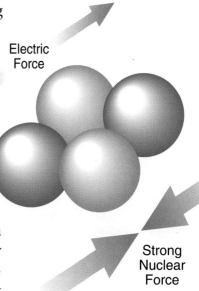

Electric Force

Strong Nuclear Force

FIGURE 19-1. Small nuclei tend to be stable if the number of protons and the number of neutrons is nearly the same.

DECAY CHANGES ELEMENTS

In the first Explore activity, you looked inside a smoke detector. The most common radioactive element used in smoke detectors is americium-241, element number 95. It decays by expelling an alpha particle. Alpha particles are helium nuclei—two protons and two neutrons. An element is defined by the number of protons in its nucleus, and americium has 95. If an americium atom loses two protons, it's not americium anymore. As shown in Figure

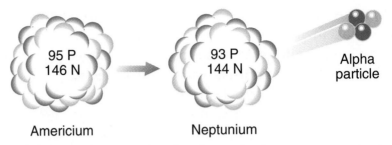

FIGURE 19-2. Americium-241, found in smoke detectors, transmutes to neptunium-237 plus an alpha particle.

19-2, it becomes an atom with 93 protons—an atom of the element neptunium. When a nucleus emits an alpha particle, it loses two protons, so it becomes a lighter element two numbers lower on the periodic table. Because the alpha particle has an atomic mass number 4, the nucleus must also lose two neutrons, and the new element has a mass number that is 4 smaller than the original. When an atom changes from one element to another by emitting particles, it's called **transmutation**.

Transmutation also occurs when a nucleus ejects an electron. But there are no electrons in a nucleus. How can a nucleus expel a particle it doesn't have? If there are too many neutrons in a nucleus, a neutron can become unstable. This neutron decays, turning into an electron and a proton. When this happens, the atom gains a proton. The atom turns into an atom of an element one number higher on the periodic table. Because the mass of the electron is so small, the atomic mass of the element doesn't change. For example, an isotope of bismuth (83) can either eject an alpha particle to become thallium (81), or decay a neutron and eject an electron to become polonium (84). These alternatives are illustrated in Figure 19-3.

The spontaneous radioactivity that occurs in certain isotopes of all elements is an example of natural transmutation. The time it takes for an element to transmute can be determined. A time interval known as half-life measures this length or period of time. In the next Investigate you will make a model of half-life.

FIGURE 19-3. Bismuth-213 can transmute to thallium-209 plus an alpha particle, or it can transmute to polonium-213 plus an electron.

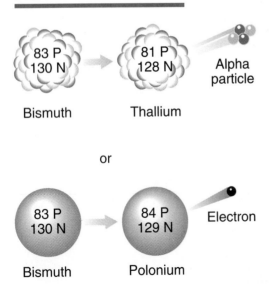

I N V E S T I G A T E !

All radioactive materials decay at a steady rate. The rate differs from element to element and from isotope to isotope. Radioactive decay is measured in terms of half-life.

PROBLEM

How do half-lives result in a steady rate of decay?

MATERIALS

rubber stoppers (one for each student in class)
graph paper
goggles

PROCEDURE

1. Copy the data table.
2. Hold a rubber stopper. Stand an equal distance from nearby classmates.
3. When the teacher says *go*, gently toss your stopper to a student on your right. Be ready to catch the stopper tossed to you.

4. If you drop a stopper, don't pick it up.
5. If you catch a stopper, immediately toss it to someone other than the person who threw it to you. Keep on throwing and catching the stoppers.
6. When your teacher says *stop*, hold your stopper up if you have one. Count the number of stoppers being held. Record the time and number of stoppers held on your data table.
7. Repeat Steps 3 through 6 four more times.
8. Plot the data from your table onto a graph. Connect the points with a smooth curve.

ANALYZE

1. Assume each stopper is an atom of a radioactive element. The stoppers that have fallen represent atoms that have transmuted. During which time period did most of the atoms change?
2. **Observe** your graph. How long did it take for half your atoms to change? How many atoms changed in twice that amount of time?
3. From your graph, **infer** how many seconds ago the class started the exercise if 20 atoms are unchanged.

CONCLUDE AND APPLY

4. How long would you **predict** it would take for all the atoms to change?
5. **Going Further:** The graph you made shows the half-life curve for your activity. **Predict** what the half-life curve would look like for a class of 40 students if the half-life time were the same as for your class?

DATA AND OBSERVATIONS

Sample data

INTERVAL	TOTAL TIME	ATOMS REMAINING
0	0	36
1	4	18
2	8	9
3	12	5
4	16	3

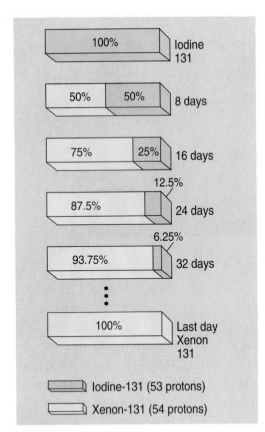

100%	Iodine 131
50%	50%	8 days
75%	25%	16 days
87.5%	12.5%	24 days
93.75%	6.25%	32 days
100%	Last day Xenon 131

Iodine-131 (53 protons)
Xenon-131 (54 protons)

FIGURE 19-4. How much Xenon is there on day 40?

In the Investigate, you found that your class dropped stoppers at a steady rate rather than dropping a certain number each time. It was a matter of dropping a certain fraction of stoppers each time you tossed. From that, you figured out that your class would lose half the stoppers every few seconds.

That's how radioactive materials decay. Half of their nuclei transmute in a certain amount of time. The period it takes for half of the nuclei to transmute is called the half-life of the element. If you had one gram of iodine-131 whose half-life is 8 days, in one week you would have one-half a gram of iodine-131 and one-half a gram of xenon, the element iodine transmutes to. After another week, you would have one-quarter gram of iodine-131 and three-quarters gram of xenon. What particle does an iodine-131 nucleus eject?

Elements with relatively short half-lives are useful in medicine to help physicians diagnose ailments. But some half-lives are as long as tens of thousands of years. These elements help geologists determine the age of the rocks they find. When uranium-238 decays, a series of decaying elements results. The last element in this series is lead-206, a stable element. The half-life of uranium-238 is 4,500,000,000 years—about the age of our solar system. Therefore, researchers can use the ratio of uranium-238 to lead-206 to determine the age of rocks that are as old as our solar system.

FIGURE 19-5. Using radioactive dating techniques, scientists calculate this lunar rock to be about 4.5 billion years old.

CHANGING STABLE ELEMENTS

You have seen that heavy, unstable elements transmute by way of radioactive decay. But what about lighter elements—

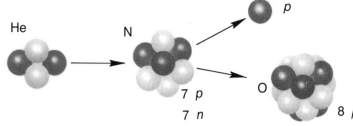

elements that are stable and not radioactive? Can these elements be made to transmute? Yes, they can, as physicist Ernest Rutherford first discovered in 1919.

Rutherford allowed alpha particles (helium nuclei) to move through nitrogen gas. As a result, some alpha particles collided with nitrogen nuclei. Rutherford was surprised to see that in some collisions, a particle left the nitrogen nuclei at a much higher speed than the incoming alpha. He identified the particle as a proton. Because the nitrogen nucleus gained two protons—from the alpha particle—and lost one, the result was that the nitrogen nucleus gained one proton. A nitrogen atom changed from nitrogen (element number 7) to oxygen (element number 8).

When a transmutation doesn't happen spontaneously but is caused in any way, the reaction is an **artificial transmutation**. An outside influence—usually a collision with a particle—caused it to happen.

FIGURE 19-6. In this reaction, an alpha particle hit a nucleus of nitrogen. The resulting products were an atom of oxygen and a free proton.

How do we know?

How could Rutherford tell what was happening in atomic nuclei?

He used a device known as a cloud chamber. It's a cylinder whose inside is free of all dust particles. The air in the cylinder contains more water or alcohol than it could normally hold at a given temperature. Like a dense fog that condenses on windshields and plant leaves, the vapor in the chamber will condense on any solid object. So any charged particle that travels through the chamber leaves a trail of condensation behind it. If a strong magnetic field surrounds the chamber, the magnetic field will attract charged particles causing them to curve as they travel. By examining a photograph of

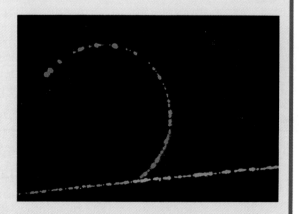

the curved tracks that particles leave behind them, you can tell how massive the particles are, whether they are positively or negatively charged, and how fast they travel.

FIGURE 19-7. With the periodic table, researchers could predict the properties of elements they had not studied.

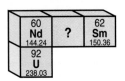

MAKING NEW ELEMENTS

Artificial transmutation was big news and created a lot of excitement among scientists when it was first described. It opened the way to finding elements that didn't exist on Earth. Some of them may have been part of the planet once, but all their nuclei had long ago decayed, transmuting into other elements. Now the door to true alchemy had been opened. Scientists could make one element out of another by sending particles toward it.

First, however, scientists had to find several alternate ways to bombard nuclei. Alpha particles from radioactive elements were adequate to bombard such light elements as nitrogen, neon, and sodium. But heavier elements contain more protons in their nuclei. These protons repel the protons in alpha particles and alpha particles ejected from decaying atoms don't have enough energy to overcome repulsion of the protons. Alpha particles would never reach the target nucleus.

One way to give a particle more energy is to increase its speed. For example, you could throw a BB, from the beginning of the chapter, at a window and the BB would bounce off the glass. If, however, you shot the BB from a BB gun, the BB would be moving fast enough to break the window. And so, particle accelerators were invented at this time. Particle accelerators speed up, or accelerate, subatomic particles such as protons, alpha particles, and electrons until they have enough energy to penetrate a large nucleus.

By 1930, nearly all the elements through uranium, element 92, had been studied. But four elements with numbers 43, 61, 85, and 87 eluded researchers. These elements had not been found in nature so researchers were eager to produce them in the laboratory. The problem was that nuclei of elements close to that of the missing elements were large enough to repel alpha particles.

Particle accelerators allowed scientists to find missing elements by creating them in the laboratory. Element 43 is now known as technetium, 61 is promethium, 85 is astatine, and 87 is francium. These elements have half-lives ranging from less than a second for astatine to six hours for technetium. As shown in Figure 19-9, not only

FIGURE 19-8. In this picture, the accelerator ring is just outside the dashed line. After several trips around the ring, particles are moving fast enough to break atoms apart.

did the particle accelerator allow scientists to fill gaps in the periodic table, it allowed them to make it larger. Increasingly powerful particle accelerators have made it possible for scientists to create atoms of elements beyond uranium. More than a dozen elements beyond uranium have been created in the laboratory. They are all radioactive and have half-lives of only a few seconds or less.

Artificial transmutation has also made it easy to manufacture radioactive isotopes of elements that are normally stable. You'll recall that isotopes are different forms of the same element. They're different only in the number of neutrons in their nuclei. Radioactive isotopes are especially useful because scientists can easily follow their

FIGURE 19-9. Elements heavier than uranium have been created in laboratories around the world.

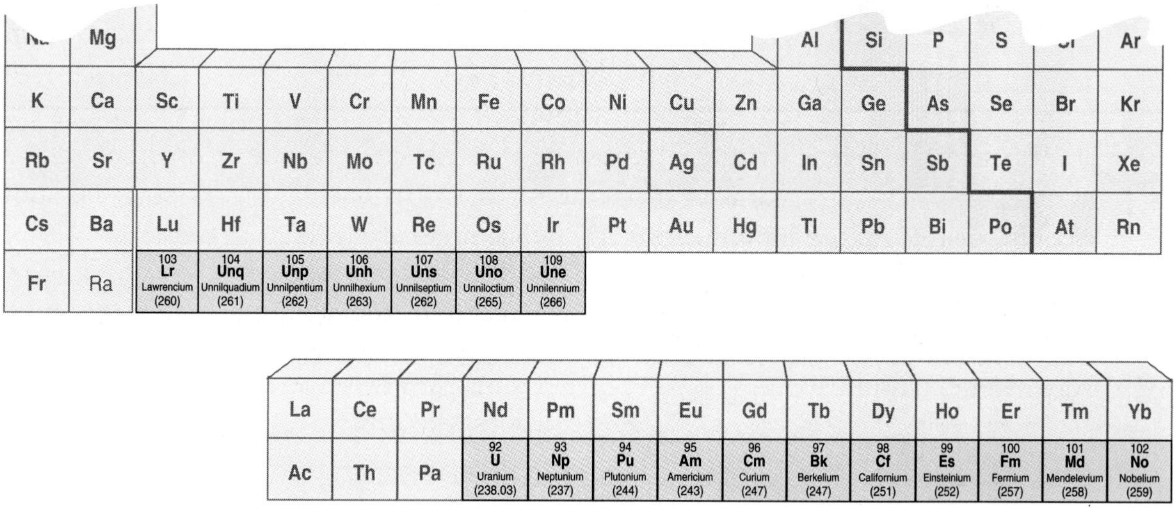

Na	Mg											Al	Si	P	S	Cl	Ar
K	Ca	Sc	Ti	V	Cr	Mn	Fe	Co	Ni	Cu	Zn	Ga	Ge	As	Se	Br	Kr
Rb	Sr	Y	Zr	Nb	Mo	Tc	Ru	Rh	Pd	Ag	Cd	In	Sn	Sb	Te	I	Xe
Cs	Ba	Lu	Hf	Ta	W	Re	Os	Ir	Pt	Au	Hg	Tl	Pb	Bi	Po	At	Rn
Fr	Ra	103 Lr Lawrencium (260)	104 Unq Unnilquadium (261)	105 Unp Unnilpentium (262)	106 Unh Unnilhexium (263)	107 Uns Unnilseptium (262)	108 Uno Unniloctium (265)	109 Une Unnilennium (266)									

La	Ce	Pr	Nd	Pm	Sm	Eu	Gd	Tb	Dy	Ho	Er	Tm	Yb
Ac	Th	Pa	92 U Uranium (238.03)	93 Np Neptunium (237)	94 Pu Plutonium (244)	95 Am Americium (243)	96 Cm Curium (247)	97 Bk Berkelium (247)	98 Cf Californium (251)	99 Es Einsteinium (252)	100 Fm Fermium (257)	101 Md Mendelevium (258)	102 No Nobelium (259)

FIGURE 19-10. Radioactive tracers give off radiation as they travel through objects such as this leaf.

progress as they move through a biological system. Isotopes used in this way are called tracers. Also, many of the artificial radioactive isotopes have extremely short half-lives. This allows them to be introduced into living things without the danger that is associated with long-term radioactivity. For years, physicians relied on iodine-131 as a radioactive tracer. Today, the majority of patients receive artificially-made technetium as a tracer. Technetium has proven valuable in diagnosing disorders of the heart, thyroid, brain, kidneys, and lungs.

People are not the only organisms studied with tracers. For example, at an agricultural lab, small amounts of radioactive isotopes are mixed with various fertilizers. By seeing how the radioactivity moves into plants, scientists can tell how well each fertilizer works. What they learn helps farmers do a better job of growing lettuce and tomatoes for your sandwich. The woman who was jogging is alive today because doctors could treat her thyroid cancer with a radioactive isotope of iodine. And thousands of lives have been saved from fires because of home smoke detectors with americium—a new element produced using artificial transmutation. In the next section, you'll discover other ways in which the atom and its nucleus are useful in everyday living.

Check Your Understanding

1. What happens to cause a transmutation when an alpha particle hits an atom's nucleus?
2. How is artificial transmutation different from natural transmutation?
3. Name a particle that can cause an artificial transmutation.
4. **APPLY:** An atom of nitrogen (element number 7) absorbs an alpha particle containing two protons. What element does it become?

19-2 Fission

SPLITTING THE ATOM

In 1938, scientists in laboratories around the world were studying nuclear transmutations. Among them were German physicists Otto Hahn and Fritz Strassman, who were bombarding uranium with neutrons. They expected to produce elements more massive than uranium. They were stunned to end up with atoms that acted as if they were atoms of barium. Could it possibly be barium, which was much lighter than uranium? Hahn wrote about the results to his former co-worker, Lise Meitner. She came up with an explanation.

A neutron hitting a uranium nucleus might not have the energy to split the nucleus in two, but it may have enough energy to knock it out of shape for an instant. Imagine poking a balloon, as in Figure 19-12. Your finger doesn't cut the balloon in half, but it does press the middle in and make the ends bulge out.

OBJECTIVES

In this section, you will
- describe nuclear fission;
- outline a nuclear fission reaction;
- model a chain reaction.

KEY SCIENCE TERMS

fission
chain reaction

FIGURE 19-11. When Hahn and Strassman bombarded uranium, they expected to get elements beyond uranium. Instead, they produced barium and krypton.

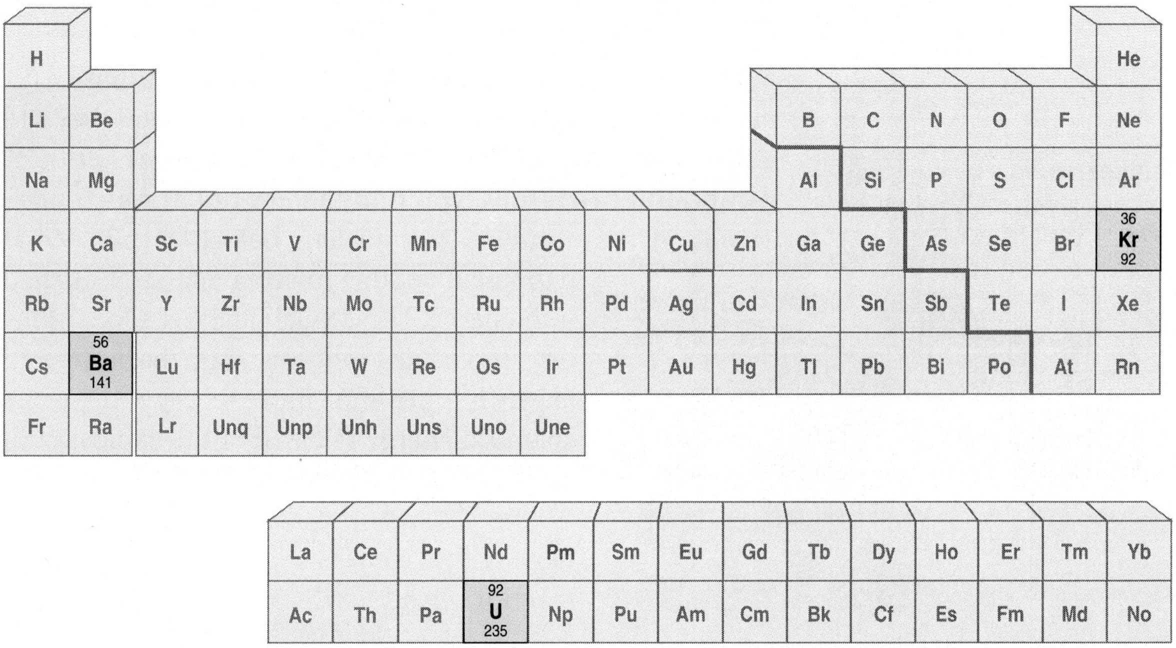

FIGURE 19-12. Pushing the balloon doesn't break it in half.

If the impact of a neutron has a similar effect on a large nucleus, such as uranium's, the nucleus might never go back to its original shape.

Remember that the electric forces between the protons in the nucleus make the protons repel each other while the neutrons are holding the protons together. But the strong nuclear force works only over a very short distance. Where the sides of the nucleus are squeezed together, there might not be enough force to hold the two bulges together any more. The repelling force among the protons is stronger than the attractive power of the strong force and the two bulges tear away from each other to form two smaller nuclei. Thinking of the way cells divide, Meitner named this process nuclear **fission**. A uranium-235 nucleus could therefore split into a barium-141 nucleus and a krypton-92 nucleus. That would leave three neutrons to go flying free. Two from the uranium-235 nucleus and one from the neutron fired into the U-235 nucleus. This reaction is diagramed in Figure 19-14.

There's no reason why uranium must split into barium and krypton rather than other elements. All that matters is that all the protons and neutrons are accounted for in the split. In fact, Hahn and Strassman found traces of lanthanum as well as barium in the products of their reaction.

THE POWER OF FISSION

However the nucleus splits, two important things happen. First, a great deal of energy is released. When you add up the mass of a barium-141 nucleus, a krypton-92 nucleus, and three neutrons, you find there is not as much mass as was in the uranium-235 nucleus before it split. What happened to the missing mass? It turned into energy. How much energy? One uranium molecule splitting into barium and krypton puts out more energy than the chemical energy released in the explosion of 6,600,000 molecules of TNT.

The second important thing that happens is that neutrons are produced by the reaction. And each of these neutrons is

FIGURE 19-13. Hahn and Meitner are among many scientists honored by their countries

available to bombard another uranium nucleus. What if the three neutrons emitted when the uranium nucleus split each hit another uranium nucleus and caused it to split? The result could be what's known as a chain reaction.

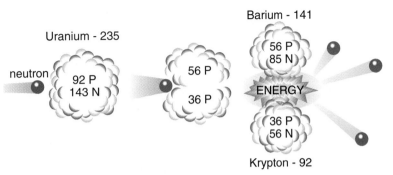

FIGURE 19-14. Enormous amounts of energy are released when an atom breaks apart.

FIND OUT!

What is a chain reaction?

When each reaction causes more reactions, energy released can grow at a fantastic rate. You can see how this works by making a model of the process known as a chain reaction, similar to the domino effect shown.

Your entire class should participate, making sure you all have plenty of room to move. Select one classmate to be the first free neutron. The rest of the class should divide into groups of three. Each group represents a radioactive nucleus. In each group, decide which two students will be neutrons. The third person represents both a proton and energy. When the teacher says to go, the first free neutron will collide with any nucleus. That nucleus then splits and the two neutrons rush off to collide with two other nuclei.

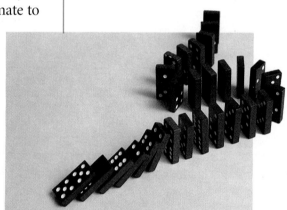

The proton should indicate the energy accompanied with this split by raising both arms above his/her head. Each time a neutron hits a nucleus, the student representing that neutron stays with the third student in the nucleus, the proton. Together, they'll represent the two nuclei and the energy resulting from the collision. Continue colliding and splitting until each nucleus has undergone fission. Be sure that you move in straight lines.

Conclude and Apply

1. How long were you able to keep track of who was going where?
2. How quickly did the process build?

When each reaction causes more reactions, energy released can grow at a fantastic rate. When the neutron released by one reaction creates the next reaction, and that reaction creates the reaction after that, you have a **chain reaction**. As shown in Figure 19-15, a chain reaction can occur at a steady rate if each reaction creates just one more reaction. But in your exercise, each reaction created two more reactions. In the case of uranium fission, each reaction can create three more. Why and how do we know this?

You saw how quickly the energy increased in your classroom. Imagine, then, what it would be like on the atomic scale. If only two neutrons from one reaction caused another reaction, there would be about 1000 fission reactions after only one millionth of a second. After just two milliseconds there would be a million reactions. After three there would be a billion. The reaction would be out of control. Remember, any single reaction releases tremendous amounts of energy. In a fraction of a second there would be an enormous amount of energy released—

FIGURE 19-15. A chain reaction occurs when neutrons produced by nuclear fission bombard other nuclei, releasing more neutrons, and so on. The control rods are used to absorb some of the neutrons to slow and control the reaction.

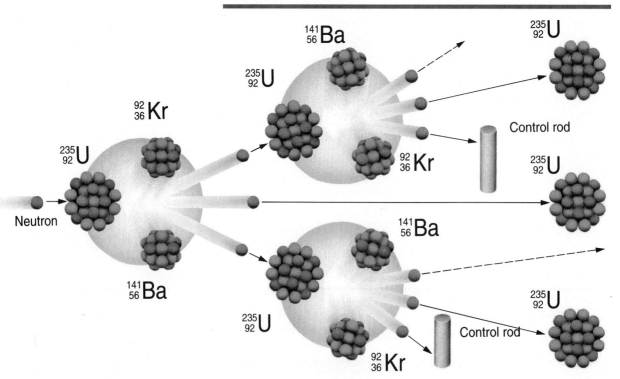

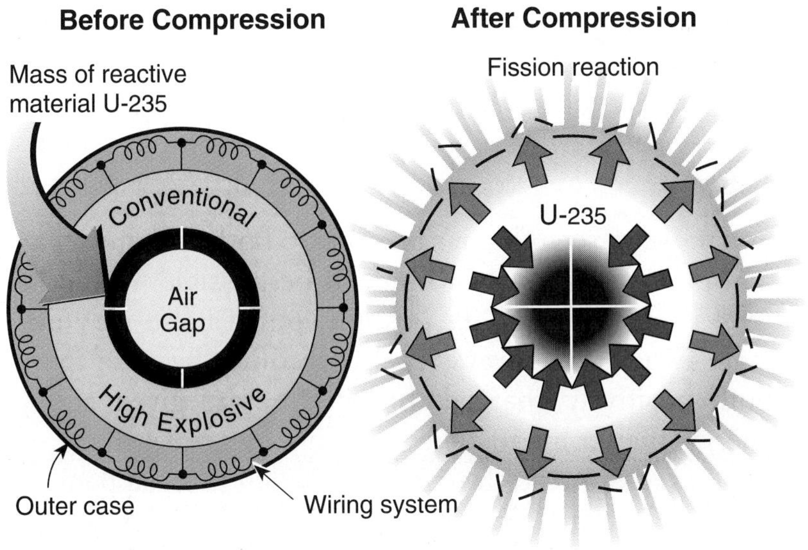

Before Compression　　　**After Compression**

Mass of reactive
material U-235

Conventional

Air
Gap

High Explosive

Outer case　　　　Wiring system

Fission reaction

U-235

FIGURE 19-16. A fission bomb has a hollow sphere of nuclear material surrounded by a hollow sphere of an ordinary explosive. When the outer sphere explodes, the explosion compresses the inner sphere, pushing the nuclear material into a small enough space to start a chain reaction.

an explosion. The first atomic bombs worked by causing just such a fission chain reaction. Fission chain reactions, however, can be controlled with neutron-absorbing material. By absorbing the neutrons before they can cause more fission, the rate of the reaction slows down. With the proper controls, a chain reaction can release as much energy as needed. The same fission reaction that is used to make extremely destructive atomic bombs is also used to generate electricity that you use every day.

Understanding fission reactions is an important part of living in the twentieth century. In the next century, there will be other, more impressive nuclear reactions available. You'll read about one of these reactions in the next section.

Check Your Understanding

1. What causes a fission reaction?
2. What is the sequence of events in fission reactions?
3. Where does the energy created by fission come from?

4. **APPLY:** If each uranium-235 releases three free neutrons in a fission reaction, how many free neutrons exist after four reactions?

19-3 Fusion

OBJECTIVES

In this section, you will

- explain nuclear fusion;
- distinguish between nuclear fusion and nuclear fission;
- outline a nuclear fusion reaction.

KEY SCIENCE TERMS

fusion

FIGURE 19-17. Fusion reactions provide the energy for sunshine.

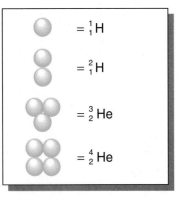

(sphere)	$= {}^{1}_{1}\text{H}$
(two spheres)	$= {}^{2}_{1}\text{H}$
(three spheres)	$= {}^{3}_{2}\text{He}$
(four spheres)	$= {}^{4}_{2}\text{He}$

JOINING NUCLEI TOGETHER

So far, we've seen that it's possible to both split nuclei and add particles to nuclei. Would it be possible to join two nuclei together? Yes, it's possible, but it's also very difficult. Two nuclei always repel each other because they're both positively charged. But if they are given enough energy, they come together close enough to let the strong force overcome the electric force. When that happens, the two nuclei can join into one. The joining of separate nuclei is called nuclear **fusion**.

Nuclear fusion is common in nature, but not on Earth. Fusion is what powers the stars, including our sun. Fusion occurs constantly inside the sun and provides an incredible amount of energy. Because of the extremely high temperatures involved, this process is known as thermonuclear fusion. The two hydrogen nuclei contain more mass than the resulting helium nucleus.

Because the sun has more than one isotope of hydrogen, there are several fusion reactions that occur in the sun. One common reaction is illustrated in Figure 19-17. To more easily describe these reactions, researchers use shorthand to identify the number of protons and the number of neutrons in a nucleus. An ordinary atom of hydrogen has one particle in the nucleus, a proton. The symbol for ordinary hydrogen is ${}^{1}_{1}\text{H}$. The isotope of hydrogen that also has a neutron is called deuterium. It has two particles in its nucleus, its symbol is ${}^{2}_{1}\text{H}$. In a fusion reaction, two hydrogen nuclei fuse to produce deuterium. You can use a clay model to represent what happens as nuclear fusion occurs.

Step 1: (sphere) + (sphere) ➡ (two spheres) + particles + energy

Step 2: (two spheres) + (sphere) ➡ (three spheres) + energy

Step 3: (three spheres) + (three spheres) ➡ (four spheres) + (sphere) + (sphere) + energy

19-2 NUCLEAR FUSION

In nuclear fusion the nuclei of one type of atom fuse with protons to form another type of atom. This process allows great amounts of energy to be released. In this Investigate, you will **use a model** to visualize fusion.

PROBLEM
Can you simulate fusion?

MATERIALS
6 balls of green clay
6 balls of white clay

PROCEDURE
1. Make six green balls (protons) and six white balls (neutrons) out of clay.
2. Refer to Step 1 of the data table and make two nuclei of deuterium.
3. When two hydrogen nuclei fuse, they form an isotope of hydrogen that has one proton and one neutron. What color clay

balls do you need for this model?
4. Refer to Step 2 of the data table and make two particles of $_2^3$He.
5. Refer to Step 3 of the data table and fuse a helium nucleus.

ANALYZE
1. What products do you have left over after making the helium nucleus, $_2^4$He?
2. How many total atoms of hydrogen does it take to make one helium atom?

CONCLUDE AND APPLY
3. What would you **predict** the leftover hydrogen could be used for?
4. Use the periodic table in Appendix E. **Compare** the mass of one helium atom to the mass of four hydrogen atoms. What can you **infer** about the relationship between this difference in mass and the energy produced on the sun?
5. **Going Further:** Gamma radiation is given off during this fusion reaction. What product produced in this series of steps might account for that radiation? How is this particle different from a proton?

DATA AND OBSERVATIONS

FUSION REACTIONS										
STEP 1	$_1^1$H	+	$_1^1$H	→	$_1^2$H	+	$_1^0$particle	+	energy	
STEP 2	$_1^2$H	+	$_1^1$H	→	$_2^3$He	+	energy			
STEP 3	$_2^3$He	+	$_2^3$He	→	$_2^4$He	+	2$_1^1$H	+	energy	

As you saw in the second Investigate, the particles resulting from a fusion reaction have less mass than the original particles. The clay-ball model does not show what happens to that mass, but you already know. The difference in mass becomes the energy for the sun's light and heat. In fact, the energy released is more than enough to cause two other nuclei to fuse. This may sound similar to what happened during fission reactions—the makings of another chain reaction. That's exactly what a star is—a gigantic thermonuclear fusion chain reaction.

While fission releases energy by splitting larger nuclei into smaller ones, fusion does just the opposite. It fuses smaller nuclei into larger ones. Fusion of hydrogen into helium releases vast amounts of energy. It's the source of energy in stars and the destructive forces in hydrogen bombs. Researchers are working on peaceful uses of nuclear fusion. Many believe that fusion, like fission, can be a clean, safe source of energy for the future. In the meantime, researchers also continue to study the thermonuclear fusion reactions that occur in the stars. In the last chapter of this book, you will learn more about the sun, the stars, and the other systems in outer space.

FIGURE 19-18. The sun—indeed all the stars—are enormous fusion chain reactions.

Check Your Understanding

1. Compare and contrast nuclear fusion with nuclear fission.
2. What happens to extra mass when hydrogen is fused into helium?
3. What is the sequence of events that must occur for fusion to take place?
4. **APPLY:** Would thorium (element number 90) be better suited for a fission or fusion reaction?

EXPANDING YOUR VIEW

CONTENTS

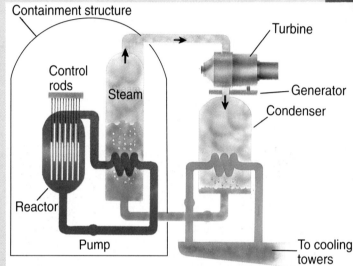

A **CLOSER** LOOK

NUCLEAR REACTORS

You probably already know that a nuclear reactor is a device that makes energy with a controlled nuclear chain reaction. A diagram of a reactor is shown in the figure.

Modern nuclear reactors vary in design, but they all work on the same principle. In the core of the reactor is fuel, usually pellets of uranium oxide. The fuel pellets are surrounded by water, which slows down the neutrons produced by the fission reaction. Only slow neutrons can cause U-235 to undergo fission. As soon as one nucleus undergoes fission, a chain reaction can start. Cadmium rods absorb enough neutrons to keep the reaction from going out of control. But how do we use the energy that the reactions release?

Most nuclear reactors make electricity. All the technology used to harness nuclear energy is used to boil water! Look at the diagram again. The fission taking place in the reactor makes the reactor intensely hot. The thermal energy heats the water surrounding the fuel rods. Because the water is pressurized, it doesn't boil. The superheated water passes through a heat exchanger where it heats other water, causing it to boil. The reactor water,

now much cooler, is then pumped back to the reactor. Steam from the boiling water in the heat exchanger turns the turbine that turns the generator that makes the electricity. Trace the flow. See if you can tell where nuclear energy becomes thermal energy, where thermal energy becomes mechanical energy, and where mechanical energy becomes electrical energy.

WHAT DO YOU THINK?

Trace the path of the water that is used inside the reactor. Is this the same water that goes to the cooling towers? Is it the same water that turns the turbines? Why do you think the water from the reactor core is contained in the core and not pumped through the turbines?

LIFE SCIENCE CONNECTION

HAS YOUR ORANGE BEEN IRRADIATED?

How often have you rummaged around the back of the refrigerator and found a green fuzzy ball? Was it once an orange? Or perhaps a grapefruit? You know not to eat that fruit. What about food that looks and smells all right but is contaminated with bacteria? If you were starving and nothing else were available, would you risk eating spoiled food? In most of the world, people do not have enough food to eat. Thousands of undernourished children go to bed hungry or eat food that is rotten or teeming with unhealthful bacteria. There are a variety of techniques to keep food fresh and healthful for an extended time. One of these techniques is irradiation—a process that exposes the food to small amounts of radiation.

This weak radiation kills bacteria such as salmonella. Salmonella poisoning is usually contracted by eating chicken contaminated with the salmonella bacteria. In the United States, salmonella affects two million people yearly — two thousand of whom do not recover. The low-dose radiation also kills most of the insect pests that feed on fresh produce.

Irradiation can be used to extend the shelf life of fruits and vegetables by slowing the ripening process. In this case, the radiation ionizes some of

the atoms and molecules in the produce. The ionized particles form gases not associated with ripening.

The Food and Drug Administration, the government agency charged with making sure that our food is safe to eat, has approved the irradiation process. In fact, governments of 37 countries have approved the process. Nevertheless, many people are opposed to the irradiation of food. Several states have banned irradiation plants and forbidden the sale of food treated in this manner. Although irradiated food is never radioactive, some people fear that irradiated food will spread radioactivity throughout the environment. Others argue that the process alters the molecular makeup of food.

Proper safeguards at processing plants should make the process less dangerous than using chemicals and pesticides during food processing. For some people, the risk of reaction to sulfites and nitrates is a far greater concern than eating irradiated food products.

Claims that irradiated food "might kill you" and "can lead to birth defects" have not been proven. Irradiated food is not radioactive. It can't spread radioactivity throughout the fruit stand or salad bar.

WHAT DO YOU THINK?

Find out if your state has banned the sale of irradiated food. Interview your family members and find out if they support or oppose irradiation of food. List the reasons they give. Are their reasons based on the risks involved with irradiated food or the fear of radiation? Decide if you support or oppose irradiation of food. Present your views to your class.

SCIENCE AND SOCIETY

NO NUCLEAR DUMPING

One of today's most hotly debated issues is the location of nuclear dump sites. Facilities have been producing nuclear waste for nearly 50 years. It has been put in drums, stored in warehouses, buried in landfills, and sunk underwater. As evidenced by a number of unpleasant incidents, this waste is coming back to haunt us.

A startling example of the effects of nuclear waste occurred near Oak Ridge National Laboratory in Tennessee. In the 1940s, Oak Ridge was a research center for atomic weapons. The research produced several highly radioactive materials.

The government and researchers in charge of the facility decided to sink the radioactive wastes under water. A 50-acre pond was created, and solid waste and drums of the liquid waste were placed at the bottom of the pond.

In the 1960s, scientists working near Oak Ridge noticed turtles had traveled as far as five miles from the pond. More amazing was the realization that these animals had high concentrations of radioactive cesium in their tissues and organs.

Despite the intentions of the original researchers, the radioactivity had spread. Small plants and organisms beneath the water and at the facility's edge had absorbed some of the products of radiation. The plants were eaten by the small animals, such as turtles, that lived at the storage pond. The plants that carried radioactivity had entered the food chain.

With further investigation, researchers found that tumbleweed absorbed radioactivity through its long root systems. When the tumbleweed dried and blew away, it carried radioactivity with it. Also, fish-eating birds would feed at the pond and then fly away, spreading radioactivity.

The problem was one not only of the spread of radioactivity, but also of its concentration. As an animal, such as a small fish, repeatedly eats contaminated food, the radioactive elements concentrate in its tissues and organs. If a larger fish or bird feeds on the small fish, the radioactive elements are concentrated further. Animals feeding on plants and other animals from the storage pond had cesium concentration levels a thousand times higher than the cesium concentration levels of the storage pond. The increase in concentration as a result of the natural feeding process is called biomagnification.

Exposure to radiation for prolonged periods of time is dangerous to humans, too. Radiation ionizes the atoms and tears apart molecules within the body. It leads to cancer, premature aging, and genetic alterations. As you learned in this chapter, the radioactivity can take a long time to disappear. The cesium-137 in the storage pond has a half-life of 30 years. Half the cesium remains after 30 years, a quarter of the cesium is still there after 60 years. Even after 90 years, there is more than ten percent of the original amount of cesium present. The pond was a storage site for dozens of elements, some of which have a half-life of 700 million years.

Oak Ridge is a single example of the problems that accompany high-level nuclear waste. High-level waste is a by-product of the operation of nuclear reactors. Each reactor produces solid wastes, usually from the fuel rods of the reactors. Liquid waste is an acid-based substance produced during the treatment of the rods. For years, there were fewer than a dozen of these reactors. They were used for research and all were under the control of the government. But, as the nation's demand for electricity increased, the number of nuclear reactors also increased. Today's reactors are scattered across the country and are owned and operated by a number of widespread commercial interests.

Government scientists have suggested that high-level waste be buried two or three thousand feet beneath Earth's surface, in a geologically stable rock formation. They think this will be safe, but they cannot be sure.

In addition to the high-level waste, reactors also produce low-level waste. Hospitals, too, produce low-level waste. The half-life of some of these materials is a few days, while other waste products have half-lives of 500 years.

Many of the medical facilities and power companies that produce waste employ waste management services to dispose of the waste—elsewhere. Transportation of nuclear waste has become as intense an issue as the actual disposal of waste.

Occasionally, metal drums filled with low-level radiation are dumped in shallow trenches. These sites are often affected by rainwater, and the containers may corrode, allowing the radioactive substances to leak into the ground and reach the groundwater supply. Drums stored in shuttered warehouses have leaked or corroded and contaminated the surrounding ground and water.

Authority over waste disposal can be a tangled web. The federal government has authority over the disposal of high-level nuclear waste, while the states have control of low-level radiation sites. If waste is transported across state lines, the federal government can be asked to intercede.

Leaders across the country are meeting intense opposition to nuclear disposal sites. At every proposed site, the community protests. Voters promise to turn the political leaders out of office for approving the site. Yet every voter is, in some sense, responsible for creating nuclear waste. The nuclear reactors exist to supply an increased demand for power. Nuclear medicine has flourished, employing technology to cure illness or prolong life. Each of us benefits in some way from nuclear technology.

WHAT DO YOU THINK?

In 1982, the federal government ordered that construction of a solid nuclear waste depository site should be completed by 1998. What would you do if a proposed site were three miles from your home?

HOW IT WORKS

HEALING RADIATION

Radiation and natural radioactive decay are useful for treating a variety of cancers. Cancers are a group of disorders involving cells that divide much more rapidly than normal cells. These abnormal cells form masses called tumors. Researchers have shown that cancer cells are more sensitive to radiation than are normal cells. This means that radiation can be used to kill cancer cells within a tumor and leave surrounding normal cells unharmed.

For instance, gamma radiation from cobalt-60 and cesium-137 are often directed at cancerous tumors. The beams of radiation are finely focused so that they are directed at only cancer cells and avoid healthy cells. This treatment requires expensive equipment, and the patient

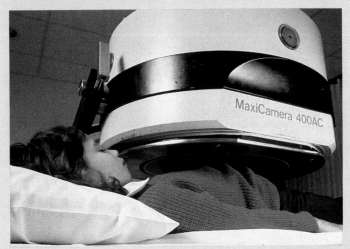

MaxiCamera 400AC

must go to the hospital every few days for another dose of radiation.

Another treatment uses the radioactive isotope sealed in a gold tube. The tube is implanted in the patient's tumor. The radiation kills the surrounding cancer cells, destroying the tumor from the inside out. This treatment is not dependent on expensive equipment and allows the patient some independence during treatment. Because the radioactive material is sealed in a capsule, materials with relatively long half-life may be used.

A third treatment involves the administration of a

radioactive isotope. For instance, radioactive iodine, iodine-131, collects in a patient's thyroid. From this location, the iodine can emit beta and gamma radiation to act upon a tumor in the thyroid gland. Because iodine does not collect in other parts of the body, other organs and organ systems remain relatively unaffected by the source of radioactivity.

WHAT DO YOU THINK?

Manganese is a trace element needed by the body. Manganese-56 emits a beta particle and has a half-life of 2.6 hours. After 10.4 hours, how much manganese would be in the patient's system? What other element would be in the patient's body as a result of treatment with manganese? Do you think manganese would be a good choice for radiation therapy?

TECHNOLOGY CONNECTION

FUSION REACTORS

As you have already learned, nuclear fusion does not pollute the air, and depends on Earth's most abundant element for fuel. If fusion power is so attractive, what keeps us from developing it? For one thing, nuclear fusion requires temperatures of more than 100 million degrees Celcius. No material can contain anything at such a temperature. However, scientists have been able to use a magnetic field to contain charged particles. When energy is added to hydrogen atoms, their electrons may be stripped away, forming a fluidlike material called a plasma that is comprised of electrons and ions. A design that might accomplish this is shown in the illustration.

A sudden increase in the magnetic field will compress the plasma, raising its temperature. This causes hydrogen nuclei to be fused into helium. The energy released by the reaction would be used to heat some other material, possibly liquified lithium, at 186°C. The lithium, in turn, would boil water, producing steam to turn electric generators. Unfortunately, more energy is used by the equipment than is produced by the reaction itself.

A technique that doesn't require a sustained reaction uses pellets of frozen hydrogen-2 and hydrogen-3 dropped into a chamber. Here they are blasted by several high-powered laser beams. The concentrated laser light compresses the hydrogen and heats the pellets to fusion point. Again, molten lithium is used to transfer the thermal energy and create steam for the turbines, just as in conventional power plants.

In late 1991, British researchers reported results of an experiment using tritium, an isotope of hydrogen that has two neutrons and one proton in its nucleus. They were able to produce a sustained fusion reaction for two seconds—a long time in nuclear circles. The reaction resulted in 2 million watts of power.

It is the promise of power like this that keeps researchers intent on meeting the challenges posed by fusion reactors.

WHAT DO YOU THINK?

More research is needed for a fusion reactor to become a reality. If a corporation funds a researcher who finds a solution, that corporation could make a huge profit from the discovery. If a government-funded researcher finds the solution, the government would share the development with all citizens. Do you think research should be funded by corporations or by the government? Why do you think as you do?

Reviewing Main Ideas

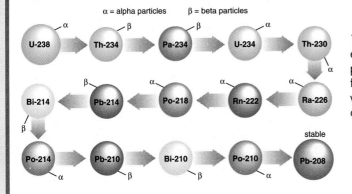

α = alpha particles   β = beta particles

1. One element can change into another by emitting particles and changing its number of protons. This is called transmutation. You can force nuclei to transmute by bombarding them with alpha particles. This is known as an artificial transmutation.

2. A collision with a neutron can cause a heavy nucleus to split into two lighter nuclei. This process is called nuclear fission. Fission generates a great deal of energy.

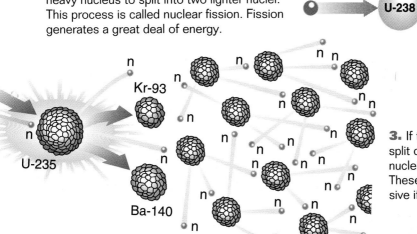

3. If the neutrons freed by one split can cause fission in other nuclei, a chain reaction can result. These can be devastatingly explosive if uncontrolled.

4. It's possible to fuse smaller nuclei into larger ones. Fusion of hydrogen into helium releases vast amounts of energy. It's the source of energy for stars.

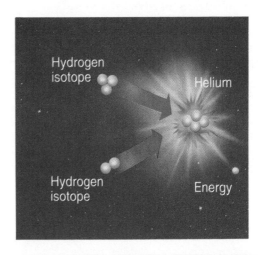

Chapter Review

USING KEY SCIENCE TERMS

artificial transmutation
chain reaction
fission
fusion
transmutation

Which science term describes each of the following processes?

1. Astatine-215 decays into bismuth-211.
2. Uranium-235 splits into lanthanum and rubidium.
3. Neutrons freed by the splitting of a plutonium nucleus cause other plutonium nuclei to split.
4. Two helium-3 nuclei combine to create helium-4 plus two free protons.
5. Molybdenum is bombarded with alpha particles to create technetium.

UNDERSTANDING IDEAS

Answer the following questions.

1. What do electrical forces have to do with nuclear fission?
2. How does one element turn into another element?
3. Which has more mass, a plutonium nucleus before it undergoes fission or the pieces remaining after it undergoes fission?
4. Which has more mass, two helium-3 nuclei or a helium-4 nucleus plus two protons?

5. What causes a chain reaction?
6. How can a chain reaction be slowed?
7. What happens to the mass lost in a fission or fusion reaction?
8. Why is it necessary to fire alpha particles at extremely high energies to cause heavier elements to transmute?
9. How can a nucleus decay into an element with more protons?
10. How can the rate of a chain reaction be controlled?

CRITICAL THINKING

Use your understanding of the concepts developed in the chapter to answer each of the following questions.

1. How is a fire similar to a nuclear chain reaction?
2. Actinium-227 has an atomic number of 89. If it transmutes by ejecting an alpha particle, what is the atomic number of the element it transmutes into?
3. If fission is splitting atoms and it releases energy, and fusion is joining atoms and it releases energy, might it be theoretically possible to keep joining and splitting nuclei to keep getting energy out of them?
4. Which decays more rapidly, an element with a long half-life or one with a short half-life?
5. Describe the role of particle accelerators in making new elements. Give some examples of these elements.

6. Write a nuclear equation to show how radon-222 decays to give off an alpha particle and another element. What is the other element?

7. Look closely at the table provided. Do you see any relation between mass number and half-life of the radioisotopes? Plot the mass numbers versus half-lives. Is it possible to predict the half-life of a radioisotope given its mass number?

Radioisotope	Mass Number	Half-life
Radium	222	4 days
Thorium	234	25 days
Iodine	131	8 days
Bismuth	210	5 days
Polonium	210	636 days

PROBLEM SOLVING

Read the following problem and discuss your answers in a brief paragraph.

Kristine found an old alarm clock in the attic and decided to put it next to her bed. During the night, Kristine was surprised by a greenish-white glow next to her bed. The glow was coming from the clock. She wondered what caused the glow.

The next day, Kristine did some library research and found that the numerals and the hands of the clock were coated with a paint containing radium and zinc sulfide. The zinc sulfide emits little flashes of light when excited by radiation. These tiny flashes of light make the hands of the clock appear to glow. Why does the zinc sulfide in the paint appear to glow? Why will the glow of the hands become dimmer over time?

CONNECTING IDEAS

Discuss each of the following in a brief paragraph.

1. How can Uranium-238 be used in the life and earth sciences? Why is it such an important tool?

2. Compare and contrast the benefits and disadvantages of using nuclear reactions.

3. A CLOSER LOOK Design an events chain for the generation of electricity in a nuclear fission reactor. Begin with the bombarding neutron and end with electric transmission lines.

4. LIFE SCIENCE CONNECTION How can irradiation help combat the problem of starvation in third-world countries?

5. SCIENCE AND SOCIETY Explain what effects biomagnification might have on society.

DID YOU EVER WONDER . . .

Where the solar system came from?

What it's like on other planets?

If there's life on other planets?

You'll find the answers to these questions as you read this chapter.

Chapter 20

The Solar System

Could it really happen to you? Probably not, but who doesn't like to dream about it? You suit up one day, board a spacecraft, and head out—way out. In a flash, you've left the atmosphere and entered the hushed, dark world of outer space.

After a while, you look back. There's the sun, shining steady and bright. Nine planets faithfully move around it. Some are huge, though not nearly as immense as the sun. Others are tiny and pretty unimpressive. There's Earth, the third planet out from the sun and one of the smaller ones.

Earth may be small by comparison, but it certainly is beautiful from space. It's a deep-blue color with white, wispy clouds hugging closely to the planet. Don't we Earthlings have a unique home in space? Yes, we do. Once you read this chapter

and its comparisons of things in the solar system, you'll understand how special Earth is.

EXPLORE!

How do the different bodies that travel around the sun compare with one another?
Using observable characteristics, compare Earth with the other planets shown in the opening photograph—Venus, Jupiter, Saturn, Uranus, and Neptune. How does Earth compare in color? In shape? In size?

20-1 The Solar System

A STAR-PLANET SYSTEM

How many times have you looked past the treetops, beyond the clouds, and wondered what's out there? What have you observed in the sky? The first objects most people think of are the sun and the moon. Next, of course, are the stars— there are so many of them that it's easy to overlook certain other points of light in the night sky. These other points of light are planets. A **planet** is a body of matter that travels around a star in a path called an orbit. Unlike stars, planets shed no light of their own. The planets we see in the night sky are reflecting sunlight.

Now suppose you reverse your position. You're in a spaceship looking back on Earth. As you continue to move farther and farther away from Earth, its features become less and less clear. Eventually it appears as a bright point of light like the other planets. Earth is one of nine planets that orbit the sun. The sun, the planets, and many smaller objects that travel around the sun make up the **solar system**.

FIGURE 20-1. According to a current hypothesis, a rotating cloud of dust and gases was the forerunner of the solar system.

FORMATION OF THE SOLAR SYSTEM

All throughout history, many explanations have been offered to account for how the solar system was formed. According to the most widely accepted hypothesis today, shown in Figure 20-1, the solar system formed more than 4.6 billion years ago from a slowly rotating cloud of dust and gas. Gravitational forces among particles within the cloud caused it to start contracting and so increase in density. During the contracting process, increased gravity pulled more gas and dust into the center of the cloud, causing it to rotate faster. Eventually, the cloud became a flattened disk rotating around its dense center.

Recent hypotheses suggest that a nearby star may have exploded, sending a shock wave through the cloud that was to become the solar system. The shock wave caused the particles in the cloud to condense, then gravity acted on the particles to pull them toward the center of the cloud.

A Central Star—Our Sun

At some point in time, the core of the cloud became so dense and so hot that hydrogen atoms began fusing to form helium atoms. And you know what a fusion reaction means—the release of tremendous amounts of energy. Energy from this central core began radiating into space, and a star—our sun—was born.

Planets Near to and Far from the Sun

While the core of the cloud was developing into the sun, dust and gases continued to revolve around the core. The larger particles attracted other particles to them and increased in size. Eventually, the planets you see in Figure 20-2 came into being. The planets are divided into two general groups—dense, Earthlike planets and huge, gaseous planets. If all planets formed in the same way, why did these differences occur?

In order for a hypothesis about the formation of the solar system to be accepted, it must be able to answer all such questions. The rotating cloud concept seems to do just that. As the planets near the sun were forming, intense heat from the newly formed sun allowed only the more massive materials to condense and remain solid. The common icy material in the inner solar system would have been vaporized by the high amounts of heat. The more massive elements that remained as solids were less abundant than the icy materials. This explains

Mercury

Venus

Earth

Mars

Jupiter

Sun

Saturn

Uranus

Neptune

Pluto

FIGURE 20-2. The sun dwarfs the planets in the solar system.

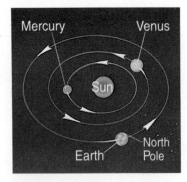

FIGURE 20-3. Planets orbit in the same direction as the rotating cloud did more than 4.6 billion years ago.

why the four planets nearest the sun are relatively small and are composed of dense, rocky material.

The material vaporized by the sun's heat would have been pushed outward by solar winds generated by the newly formed sun. Huge, gaseous planets formed farther from the sun, where the effects of solar heat and winds were less intense. Lighter gases and icy materials were able to condense along with some heavier materials, and so became parts of these planets.

MOTIONS OF THE PLANETS

In that early, pre–solar system cloud of dust and gas, the direction of rotation, as observed from above Earth's northern pole, was counterclockwise. You can see this direction of rotation in Figure 20-3. This is the direction in which the planets revolve around the sun today.

For much of history, people on Earth believed their planet was at the center of the universe. They were certain the sun, moon, and planets were embedded in the surface of a large sphere that revolved around Earth. After all, if you lie on your back and gaze up at the sky, do you feel Earth moving at more than 107,000 kilometers per hour? Of course not. Yet you do see the sun, moon, and planets change positions in the sky, as if they are moving around Earth. A Polish scientist, Copernicus, was the first to hypothesize that the planets, including Earth, orbit the sun. He published this revolutionary idea in 1543.

When Copernicus developed his sun-centered model of the solar system, he believed that the planets traveled around the sun in circular orbits. But later observers discovered that certain planetary motions could not easily be explained by circular orbits. In the early 1600s, Johannes Kepler, a German mathematician, determined that planetary orbits were ellipses, and that the sun is offset from the exact center of an orbit. Is there a way to get a true and accurate picture of the paths followed by the planets as they travel around the sun? The following Investigate activity will help you picture these planetary orbits.

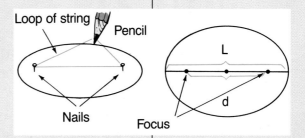

Loop of string — Pencil

Nails

Focus

L

d

20-1
ORBITS

You have learned that the planets travel around the sun along fixed paths called orbits. In this activity, you will construct a model of a planetary orbit.

PROBLEM
What is the shape of a planetary orbit?

MATERIALS
thumbtacks or pins
string
cardboard (21.5 cm x 28 cm)
metric ruler
pencil
paper

PROCEDURE
1. Copy the data table.
2. Place a blank sheet of paper on top of the cardboard and stick two thumbtacks or pins in the paper about 3 cm apart.
3. Tie a string into a circle with a circumference of 15–20 cm. Loop the string around the tacks. As someone holds the tacks in place, place the pencil inside the loop and pull it taut.
4. Keeping the string taut, move the pencil around the tacks until you have completed an elongated, closed curve, also known as an ellipse.
5. Repeat Steps 2 through 4 twice. First vary the distance between the tacks; then vary the circumference of the string. **Determine the effect** of each change on the size and shape of the ellipse.
6. Planetary orbits are usually described in terms of eccentricity (e). You drew the ellipse around the two thumbtacks. The two points around which an ellipse is drawn are called the foci. The eccentricity of any ellipse is determined by dividing the distance between the foci (f) by the length of the major axis (L). See the diagram above.
7. Refer to Appendix H on page 673 to find the eccentricities of the planetary orbits.
8. Construct an ellipse with the same eccentricity as Earth's orbit.

ANALYZE
1. What effect does a change in length of the string or distance between the tacks have on the ellipse?
2. What must be done to the string or placement of tacks to decrease the eccentricity of an ellipse?

CONCLUDE AND APPLY
3. Describe the shape of Earth's orbit. Where is the sun located within the orbit?
4. **Going Further: Hypothesize** what effect a change in Earth's orbit from elliptical to circular might have.

DATA AND OBSERVATIONS

CONSTRUCTED ELLIPSE	d (cm)	L (cm)	e (d/L)
1			
2			
3			
Earth's orbit			>.017

Except for the fact that planets all orbit the sun, do they have much else in common? To arrive at some answers, let's begin by comparing Earth with its nearest planetary neighbors. The three planets nearest Earth have one thing in common: their surfaces are made up of solid rock. With the proper equipment, you could travel across their surfaces collecting rock samples. Because of their size, they are classified as Earth-sized planets, or **terrestrial planets**.

VENUS

Venus, which orbits the sun at an average distance of 108 million kilometers, is the second planet out from the sun. This planet is sometimes called Earth's twin because it is similar in size and mass to Earth. If your space travels take you to Venus, your first encounter will be a thick blanket of dense clouds high up in the planet's atmosphere. These clouds contain sulfuric acid, which gives them a yellowish color.

Once past this cloud layer, you pass through an atmosphere made up mostly of carbon dioxide gas. This gas is much denser than the mixture of nitrogen and oxygen gases that makes up most of Earth's atmosphere. In fact, when you land on the surface of Venus, you discover that the pressure exerted by the atmosphere is 91 times greater than that exerted by Earth's atmosphere. You would have to dive down nearly one kilometer in the ocean to experience pressure this great on Earth.

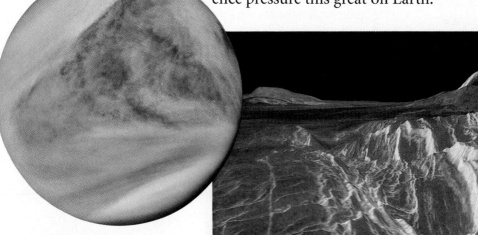

FIGURE 20-4. Similar in size to Earth, Venus is vastly different in atmosphere.

You notice the heat along with the pressure. The temperature on Venus's surface is 470°C! This temperature is high enough to melt lead! Compare this temperature with the highest temperature ever recorded on Earth, 58°C.

"Why is Venus so hot?" you ask. "Doesn't its cloud cover and dense atmosphere block out most of the sunlight?" You're right, but don't forget the high percentage of carbon dioxide gas in the atmosphere. It acts something like the glass in a greenhouse. Like the glass, carbon dioxide traps the heat from solar radiation and holds it near the planet's surface. Hence, the temperature of the atmosphere rises higher and higher. You know this process is called the greenhouse effect.

SKILLBUILDER

INTERPRETING DATA
Use the information in Appendix H to explain how Mars is like Earth. If you need help, refer to the **Skill Handbook** on page 691.

MARS

Mars is the fourth planet out from the sun, orbiting the sun at an average distance of 228 million kilometers. This means that Earth, which orbits the sun at an average distance of 150 million kilometers, is situated between Venus and Mars.

EXPLORE!

How do the atmospheres of Venus, Earth, and Mars compare?

Study the data in this table. Which planets have fairly similar atmospheres? Do all three planets have anything in common? Would you expect life as we know it to be present on Venus or Mars? Explain your answer.

Venus		Earth		Mars	
Gas	% of Total	Gas	% of Total	Gas	% of Total
CO_2	96.5	CO_2	0.03	CO_2	95.0
N_2	3.5	N_2	78.1	N_2	2.7
O_2	0.002	O_2	20.9	O_2	0.15
H_2O	0.01	H_2O	0.05-4.0	H_2O	0.03

You may have heard Mars called the red planet—and for good reason. The iron oxide in the weathered rocks on its surface actually gives it a reddish color. Because Mars has a very thin atmosphere with very few clouds, scientists have been able to view its surface through telescopes for centuries.

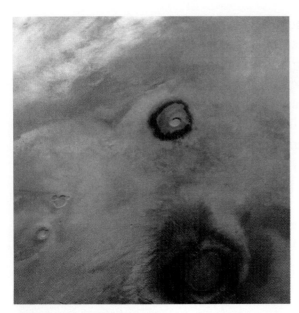

FIGURE 20-5. Space probes have given us good views of the surface of Mars.

Craggy, Barren Surface

Most of the information we now have about Mars came from the *Viking* probes. In 1976, *Viking 1* and *2* landed on Mars and changed our ideas about this planet completely. The *Viking* probes sent back pictures of a reddish-colored, barren, rocky, windswept surface with many craters.

The *Viking* probes also revealed long channels on the surface of Mars. These channels look as if they were carved by flowing water at some time in Mars's past. Other features revealed by the *Viking* probes included the largest known volcano in the solar system, Olympus Mons, and large rift zones. One rift, Valles Marineras, is more than 4000 kilometers long, up to 240 kilometers wide, and more than 6 kilometers deep. The rifts on the surface of Mars resemble those in the middle of Earth's oceans.

Polar Ice Caps

Have you ever used dry ice? People often put chunks of dry ice in water to make the foglike clouds that you see at concerts or plays. Dry ice is really frozen carbon dioxide. It is much colder than frozen water, and it is called dry ice

FIGURE 20-6. Like Earth, Mars has ice caps at both poles. One ice cap is shown directly below.

because it doesn't melt to form a liquid. It just changes back to carbon dioxide gas. Now imagine the ice sheet that covers Antarctica being made up of dry ice. This picture will give you an idea of what *Viking* reported about the ice cap that covers the Martian south pole. This polar cap changes very little throughout the Martian year. However, the northern polar ice cap on Mars is made up of frozen water and carbon dioxide. During the Martian summer, the carbon dioxide vaporizes, and the size of the polar cap decreases considerably.

It is very cold on the surface of Mars, mostly because the planet is so far from the sun. Actual temperatures range from a high of about 20°C to a low of −140°C.

Dead and Dusty

The surface of Mars appears to be completely lifeless, lacking even the simplest organic molecules. Lack of ozone in Mars's atmosphere could be one reason. Ozone absorbs harmful ultraviolet rays from the sun. Without this protection, organic molecules cannot survive ultraviolet radiation. Human activities are threatening to destroy the ozone layer in Earth's atmosphere. Such an event could endanger all life-forms on this planet.

MERCURY

Among the nine planets in the solar system, Mercury is the closest to the sun and the second smallest in diameter. Our first close look at Mercury came in 1974, when *Mariner 10* passed close to the planet and sent pictures back to Earth. As shown in Figure 20-7, the surface of Mercury looks much like that of our moon.

Mercury, Venus, Earth, and Mars make up the group of planets known as the terrestrial planets. Although Mercury is quite a bit smaller than the other members of this group, it is included because it has much more in common with Venus,

FIGURE 20-7. Mercury's surface, like the moon's, is covered with craters.

FIGURE 20-8. Conditions on Earth allow water to exist as solid, liquid, and gas.

Earth, and Mars than it does with the other planets of the solar system.

Because of its small size and mass, Mercury exerts a weak gravitational force. Thus, as you might expect, it has almost no atmosphere. And as you might also expect from its nearness to the sun, Mercury can get very hot. Daytime temperatures can reach as high as 450°C. Mercury's thin atmosphere, however, allows all this heat to radiate from the planet; nighttime temperatures fall as low as −170°C.

By now, Earth probably looks pretty good to you. It certainly has some impressive distinctions. First of all, Earth is situated between two planets that have very different conditions. Venus, closer to the sun, is very hot and has a dense atmosphere. Mars, farther from the sun, is very cold and has a thin atmosphere. Earth's location in the solar system has proved to be an especially fortunate one. Earth is the only planet where the range of surface temperatures allows water to exist in all three of its physical states. The presence of water, especially in the liquid state, is essential for the existence of life as we know it. Also, Earth has just the right mass to hold an atmosphere, which you know is also essential to life.

Check Your Understanding

1. How do scientists think the solar system formed?
2. In what ways are Venus, Earth, and Mars similar? In what ways are they different?
3. How has our study of Mars helped us understand the potential dangers of ozone depletion in our atmosphere?
4. Why are temperatures higher on Venus than on Mercury, which is much closer to the sun?
5. **APPLY:** Make a table showing the important characteristics of the Earth-sized planets.

20-2 The Gaseous Giants

THE OUTER PLANETS

Besides the four planets closest to the sun, there are five other planets in the solar system. How do these planets compare with the terrestrial planets?

It's time to put yourself back into the role of a space traveler. You have visited four planets so far. Now you will leave the terrestrial planets and travel to the next group of planets—the gaseous giants.

The **gaseous giant planets** are very large, low-density planets composed mainly of gases. Most of what we know about these planets was learned from the *Voyager* space probes. Launched in 1977, *Voyager 1* and *Voyager 2* provided a wealth of new information about Jupiter, Saturn, Uranus, and Neptune.

JUPITER

Jupiter is perhaps the most spectacular of all the planets in the solar system. It is one and a half times larger

FIGURE 20-9. Jupiter's cloud bands and Great Red Spot are its most visible features.

than all the other planets put together and contains more than twice their total mass. The planet is surrounded by very strong magnetic and gravitational fields.

Jupiter is composed mainly of gaseous and liquid hydrogen and helium, with lesser amounts of ammonia, methane, and water vapor. Because of its strong gravity, the atmosphere of hydrogen and helium gases probably changes to a liquid ocean as you travel deeper into the planet. Below this ocean is a solid rocky core about the size of Earth. The only part of Jupiter that has been seen is its outer covering of clouds. The *Voyager* probes provided vivid pictures of bands of red, white, tan, and brown clouds. Within these clouds are continuous storms of swirling gas; the most spectacular is visible as the Great Red Spot.

FIGURE 20-10. Of Jupiter's 16 moons, these are the 4 largest.

MOONS OF JUPITER

Io	Europa	Ganymede	Callisto

The most volcanically active object in the solar system. Sulfur lava gives it its distinctive red and orange color.	Rocky interior is covered by a 100 km thick ice crust, which has a network of cracks, indicating tectonic activity.	Has an ice crust about 100 km thick, covered with grooves. Crust surrounds a 900 km thick slushy mantle of water and ice. Has a rocky core.	Has a heavily cratered ice-rock crust several hundred km thick. Crust surrounds a water or ice mantle around a rocky core.

Sixteen moons revolve around Jupiter. Four of them are quite large. Io is the closest large moon to the surface of the planet. Ganymede, another moon, is the largest satellite in the solar system. It's larger than the planet Mercury.

SATURN

As you leave Jupiter and travel farther from the sun, the next planet you come to is Saturn, famous for its spectacular rings. Saturn is the second largest planet in the solar system, but it has the lowest density. If Saturn were placed in water, it would float. Saturn's structure is similar to that of Jupiter. Its atmosphere contains the same gases. Below the atmosphere is an ocean of liquid helium and hydrogen that surrounds a small rocky core.

Saturn is circled by several broad rings, each of which is made up of hundreds of smaller, narrower rings. Each ring is composed of millions of particles ranging in size from a speck of dust to chunks of rock several meters in diameter. Saturn also has at least 18 moons in orbit around it. The largest of these, Titan, is larger than the planet Mercury. Titan is surrounded by a dense atmosphere of nitrogen, argon, and methane, and it may have organic molecules on its surface.

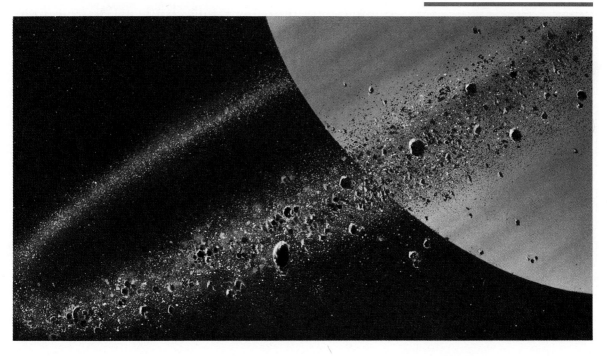

FIGURE 20-11. Saturn's rings are made of pieces of rock and ice.

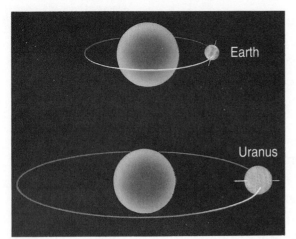

FIGURE 20-12. Earth's axis tilts at 23.5° from a line perpendicular to its plane of revolution. Uranus's axis lies almost parallel to its plane of revolution.

URANUS

The next stop on our space journey is Uranus, the seventh planet out from the sun. Uranus is a large, gaseous planet with 15 moons and a system of thin, dark rings. Its atmosphere is composed of hydrogen, helium, and methane. The methane gives the planet its blue-green color. Methane absorbs the red and yellow light from the sun, and the clouds in the atmosphere reflect back the green and blue light that reaches them. Beneath its atmosphere, Uranus probably has a liquid mantle surrounding a rocky core.

One of the most unusual features of Uranus is the degree of tilt of its axis of rotation. The axis is tilted so much that it is almost parallel to the plane of its orbit. Thus, the planet seems to be lying on its side as viewed from Earth.

NEPTUNE

The outermost member of the gaseous giant planets is Neptune. Neptune's atmosphere and structure are very much like those of Uranus. Therefore, Neptune also has a greenish-blue color. It has at least eight moons, of which Triton is the most interesting. Triton has a thin atmosphere composed mainly of nitrogen gas; large geysers have been observed on its surface. Neptune also has a system of rings that varies in thickness. From a distance, the thin portions of the rings are not visible, giving the impression that the rings are broken.

Neptune is considered the eighth planet from the sun. However, Pluto's orbit is so elliptical that it crosses Neptune's orbit. As a result, sometimes Pluto is actually closer to the sun than Neptune. In fact, Pluto is currently closer and will remain so until 1999.

At this point in your space travels, you have visited two groups of planets—the terrestrial planets and the gaseous giant planets. Each group has four members, leaving one more planet to be accounted for—Pluto, the exceptional planet. Before you go on to Pluto, take a moment to look back at the distances you have already traveled.

FIGURE 20-13. Methane gas surrounding both Uranus (above, top) and Neptune (bottom) gives them blue-green colors. Because Neptune is so far from the sun, most of the ammonia gas in its atmosphere is frozen.

I N V E S T I G A T E !

20-2 DISTANCES IN THE SOLAR SYSTEM

The distances between planets and between the planets and the sun vary considerably throughout the solar system. In this activity, you will make a scale model of the solar system and use it to discover how these distances are related.

PROBLEM
How can you construct a scale model of interplanetary distances?

MATERIALS
adding machine tape
meterstick
scissors
pencil

DATA AND OBSERVATIONS

PLANET	DISTANCE TO SUN (KM)	DISTANCE TO SUN (AU)	SCALE DISTANCE (1AU = 10CM)
Mercury	58×10^6		
Venus	108×10^6		
Earth	150×10^6		
Mars	228×10^6		
Jupiter	780×10^6		
Saturn	143×10^6		
Uranus	288×10^6		
Neptune	451×10^6		
Pluto	592×10^6		

PROCEDURE
1. Copy the data table.
2. Refer to Appendix H on page 673 to find the average distance in AUs from the sun to each planet. Record these data.
3. Using 10 cm as the distance between Earth and the sun (10 cm = 1 AU), determine the length of adding machine tape you will need to do this activity by calculating the scale distance between the sun and Pluto.
4. Calculate the scale distance of each planet from the sun. Record this data.
5. Cut the tape to the proper length. Mark one end of the tape to represent the position of the sun.
6. **Measure** and mark the tape to show the proper location of each planet if the planets were in a straight line outward from the sun.

ANALYZE
1. Explain how scale distance is determined.
2. On your model, **observe** the four planets closest to the sun, then the five farthest away. **Compare** the closeness of the planets in each group to each other.

CONCLUDE AND APPLY
3. Summarize distance in the solar system. How are distances within each group related to the group's distance from the sun?
4. In addition to scale distances, what other information would you need to construct an exact scale model of the solar system?
5. **Going Further:** Proxima Centauri, the closest star to the solar system, is about 40 trillion (40×10^{12}) km from the sun. Using a scale of 10 cm = 1 AU, what length of tape would you need to include this star on your scale model?

It's hard to imagine planets with moons that are themselves planet-sized. Is there a way to make the size differences among the planets more vivid?

EXPLORE!

How can you draw planets to scale?
Use the information on planet diameters found in Appendix H. Select a scale diameter for Earth and draw a circle with this diameter on a piece of paper. Using this diameter as 1.0, draw each of the other planets to scale.

PLUTO

No space probes have passed near Pluto. Scientists used Neptune's gravity to deflect *Voyager* away from Pluto and toward Triton. However, photographs from the Hubble Space Telescope have provided us with some information about the planet.

Pluto is not like any other planet. It doesn't have a thick, dense atmosphere like the gaseous giant planets. It's small, like the terrestrial planets, but it is composed of rock and ice. The only thing Pluto has in common with some other planets is that it has a moon, Charon. Charon's diameter is one half of Pluto's, and its orbit is so close to Pluto that the two bodies can be thought of as a double planet. Pluto is so different from any other planet that many scientists don't consider it to be a planet. It is more like other members of the solar system, which you will learn about in the next section.

Check Your Understanding

1. How are the gaseous giant planets different from the terrestrial planets? How are they similar?
2. How is Pluto different from other planets?

3. **APPLY:** If you had to stop during a space flight, which would make a better landing point, Saturn or its rings? Why?

20-3 Other Objects in the Solar System

COMETS

Imagine what you would think if you were studying the sky through a telescope and sighted a distant, unfamiliar object approaching Earth at great speed. For several nights, you watch as the object moves closer and closer and becomes ever brighter and larger. At some point, a glowing tail appears attached to the object. After a while, you don't even need a telescope to see it. Would you be frightened? People in ancient times often reacted with fear to the approach of such an object. However, as it always does, the object eventually disappears from the sky. You have witnessed the passing of a comet.

Except for the planets and their satellites, perhaps the best known objects in the solar system are comets. At one time, comets were greatly feared and the subjects of myth and legend. Today we know that a **comet** is a large chunk of ice, dust, frozen gases, and rock fragments that moves through space. In other words, a comet is like a large, dirty snowball.

As a comet approaches the sun, some of the frozen material becomes hot enough to vaporize and forms a bright cloud, called a coma, around the solid part of the comet. When the comet gets near enough to the sun, streams of charged particles from the sun, called a solar wind, push on the gases in the coma. The solar wind forces the gaseous coma out behind the comet into a bright tail, as shown in Figure 20-14. A comet's tail always points away from the sun. Most comets pass close to the sun and then journey on to the outer regions of the solar system or beyond. However, some comets actually crash into the sun. Regardless of what becomes of them, comets always display the same behavior as they approach the sun.

FIGURE 20-14. Some comets, like planets, orbit the sun.

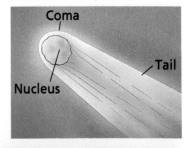

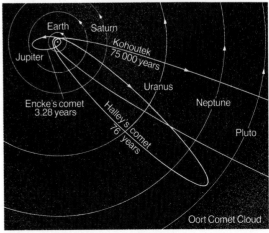

Where do comets come from? Most astronomers believe they originate in an icy cloud that surrounds the solar system out beyond the orbit of Pluto. This birthplace of comets is called the Oort cloud after the Dutch astronomer Jan Oort, who proposed the presence of this cloud. According to the latest theory, a chunk of icy material is pulled from the cloud by a passing star. The material is captured by the sun's gravity and pulled toward it, producing a comet.

Halley's Comet

Halley's comet is the best-known comet in the solar system. Halley's comet is a short-period comet. This means that it returns to the sun on a regular basis. In the case of Halley's comet, it takes about 76 years to complete one orbit of the sun. During its last passage close to the sun, in 1986, five space probes were launched by three different countries to study the comet. The probe *Giotto*, launched by the European Space Agency, passed within 600 kilometers of the comet's nucleus, sending back valuable information. For example, dust particles within the coma were found to be rich in the elements that combine to form organic molecules. This discovery has led to the speculation that comets at one time may have contributed some building blocks of organic material to the planets.

DID YOU KNOW?

The Italian artist, Giotto, may have been the first person to paint Halley's comet. The European spacecraft that probed Halley's comet in 1986 was named for this artist.

ASTEROIDS

An **asteroid** is a large chunk of rock traveling through space. Most asteroids are located in an area between the orbits of Mars and Jupiter known as the asteroid belt. Some astronomers believe that the asteroids in this belt represent material that might have combined into another planet were it not for the strong influence of Jupiter's gravity. It is likely that some of the larger asteroids have been thrown out of the belt and are now scattered throughout the solar system. It is also likely that many asteroids have been captured by planetary gravity to become moons of the planets.

Most asteroids in the asteroid belt are about 1 kilometer or less in diameter. The largest asteroid, Ceres, is 940 kilometers in diameter.

Not all asteroids are found in the asteroid belt. Large asteroids pass close to Earth from time to time. In 1972, an asteroid estimated to be about 10 meters in diameter and weighing more than 1000 tons passed within 60 kilometers of Earth's surface.

METEOROIDS, METEORS, AND METEORITES

While the space between planets is mostly empty, space does contain millions of solid particles. Many of these particles come from comet nuclei that have broken up. These small pieces of rock moving through space are then called meteoroids. Meteoroids range in size from grains of sand

FIGURE 20-16. This photo shows a meteor over the Grand Teton Mountains. It can be seen as a white streak near the top of the photograph.

FIGURE 20-17. This is Meteor Crater in Arizona. Such craters are not common on Earth's surface.

to huge fragments of rock. Astronomers also believe that many meteoroids come from the asteroid belt and are the result of collisions between asteroids. Sometimes a meteoroid enters Earth's gravitational field and is pulled toward Earth's surface. When a meteoroid enters the atmosphere, it becomes a **meteor**. Friction causes the meteor to glow as it streaks across the sky. People often call meteors shooting stars, although they have nothing to do with actual stars.

Most meteoroids burn up completely in Earth's atmosphere. However, occasionally a meteoroid survives and strikes Earth's surface. A meteoroid that strikes Earth's surface is called a **meteorite**. A few large meteorites have produced enormous craters on Earth's surface, such as the one shown in Figure 20-17.

Comets, meteoroids, and asteroids are probably all composed of material that formed early in the history of the solar system. As you have learned, some meteoroids are produced when comets disintegrate. Others are formed when asteroids collide. Thus, a study of meteorites is also a study of the materials in comets and asteroids. Scientists study the structure and composition of these space objects in order to learn what the solar system was like long ago. Such knowledge could help us understand the formation and development of Earth and its relationship to other objects in the solar system.

Check Your Understanding

1. How does a comet distant from the sun differ from one that is close to the sun?

2. Compare and contrast comets, meteoroids, and asteroids.

3. **APPLY:** Why is it unlikely that a comet would ever orbit a planet?

EXPANDING YOUR VIEW

CONTENTS

A CLOSER LOOK

REHEARSAL FOR MARS

The first crewed landing on Mars will follow years of planning and practice. Astronauts will practice their roles many times before the launch, much like actors preparing for a play. To do this, they will first need to know exactly where they will be landing and what the area looks like.

Robots with cameras and sensors will be sent to explore possible landing sites. These robots will be remotely controlled by people on Earth and will send back pictures of the Martian surface along with information about its atmosphere.

A mission specialist and assistant will operate remote controls that will enable the robot surface probe to move around on the Martian surface. A second mission specialist will operate the Remote Sample Retrieval (RSR) System and collect samples for study. A successful mission is one in which the lander explores all parts of the Martian surface within range, without colliding with boulders or falling into craters. A successful mission also involves retrieving rock samples from the planet's surface and returning them to Earth for study.

After the mission is complete, scientists and astronauts will study the photos and rock samples. This information will be used to help prepare a crewed launch to Mars.

WHAT DO YOU THINK?

Discuss the difficulties of exploring another planet. Talk about the steps needed to make sure everything is successful.

LIFE SCIENCE
CONNECTION

BIOSPHERE II

SPACE BIOSPHERES VENTURES

BIOSPHERE II
TEST MODULE

Can you imagine living in a world with only seven other people? In this world, you would have to rely on yourself, your companions, and the environment for food, water, and recreation.

Four women and four men live in such a world right now. Their world, an experiment called Biosphere II, is a huge glass building in Arizona that seals the eight people from the outside environment. For two years, they will live in this sealed-off world, where they'll recycle air, water, and wastes.

The experiment was designed as a model for similar buildings on the moon and on Mars. Ecological studies will be conducted that may yield valuable information we can use on Earth to help us to better conserve resources and protect rain forests. At the end of the Biosphere II experiment, scientists will know much more about surviving in a closed environment.

Biosphere II covers five acres and includes an ocean, desert, savannah, marsh, rain forest, and about 4000 animal species selected especially for the experiment. In addition to these environments, Biosphere II will include a farm with livestock, which will provide food for the scientists. All crops will be planted and grown in Biosphere II.

Scientists hope to learn how well the ecosystem provides air for the people to breathe and how well it regulates temperature. This will help to prevent problems that people would experience on other planets in a similar structure.

Scientists will learn other things about life in a sealed environment. For example, will the people get along? Will they argue? Will they be happy? And how will they feel when they leave Biosphere II to return to the real world?

YOU TRY IT!

Plant seeds or a small plant. Cut a 2-liter soft drink bottle in half. Carefully select and moisten planting soil and place it in the bottom of the bottle.

Plant the seeds or plant in the moist soil according to instructions from a library book or packet of seeds. Seal the top of the bottle with plastic wrap.

Watch the bottle for a few days. Try to determine ideal conditions for the plant. Does it need more water? Does it receive too much sunlight?

When you find the ideal environment for the plant, you may be able to leave the bottle sealed for many weeks without adding water or nutrients.

SCIENCE
AND
SOCIETY

WILL HUMANS OR ROBOTS EXPLORE MARS?

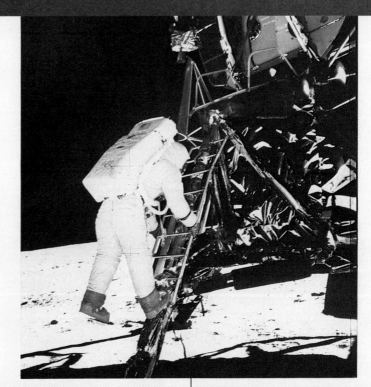

People who were lucky enough to watch astronauts land on the moon in the 1960s know how exciting crewed space travel can be. The first moon landing was televised to a world astounded by astronaut Neil Armstrong's step from the lunar lander to the moon's surface. "That's one small step for man, one giant leap for mankind," were his first words on the moon. It was indeed a giant step in history.

Space scientists today are beginning to talk about escaping Earth orbit and sending astronauts to the moon again—and to Mars. But talk of resuming crewed exploration has started a hot debate among those who believe humans should explore space and those who think space probes can do the job as well as humans.

Those in favor of using space probes say the cost of exploration would be much less than crewed exploration. They also point out that astronauts will not have to risk their lives if space probes are used.

Astronauts who survive a trip to another planet would suffer the health problems that have been suffered by astronauts in Earth orbit. For example, bones and muscles become weaker within a few days. Just imagine how weak they would be after a three-year trip to Mars!

Other health problems also result from prolonged weightlessness. The kidneys become confused by weightlessness and can eliminate too much fluid from the body. This could cause dehydration in an astronaut. Prolonged exposure to radiation from the sun could also cause problems.

You may also wonder how a machine could explore as well on another planet as a human could. Scientists who prefer robots have an answer for that question as well.

WHAT DO YOU THINK?

If robots can explore other planets more cheaply and as effectively as humans can, what reasons can you give for crewed exploration?

In the next few years, we should be able to launch probes with senses and intelligence. Cameras and other instruments on the probe could send information to Earth as they have in previous interplanetary visits.

But in the future, scientists on Earth will be able to wear goggles and data gloves that allow them to see what the probe sees and to feel what the probe feels. The Earth-bound scientists would be able to experience the probe's visit almost as though they were there themselves. Space scientists are already experi-menting with these techniques, which they call virtual reality because the experience seems real.

Also, the space probe will mimic the motions of the person wearing the special data gloves. In this way, the glove wearer could carefully control the probe millions of kilometers away.

and make intelligent decisions. This is called artificial intelligence and, if it becomes sophisticated enough, it could solve a major shortcoming of uncrewed exploration.

Despite all these arguments and the incredible expense of sending astronauts to other planets, many people firmly believe humans, not robots, should be the space travelers.

Dr. Carl Sagan, an astronomy professor, admits that robots could do the work of humans on Mars, but he feels that we should conduct crewed exploration if there is enough money to do so. One reason he favors this is because it would "provide an exciting, adventure-rich, and hopeful future for young people." And he believes we can afford crewed space travel if we share the adventure, planning, and cost with other countries.

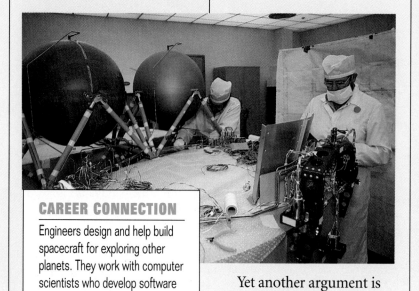

CAREER CONNECTION

Engineers design and help build spacecraft for exploring other planets. They work with computer scientists who develop software that guides the spacecraft and helps it conduct experiments.

Yet another argument is that space probes will be operated partly by computers that can analyze information

*L*iterature
C O N N E C T I O N

DESCRIBE YOUR TRIP TO MARS

Read part of *The Martian Chronicles*, a science fiction book by Ray Bradbury. Using his writing as a model, write your own short story about an adventure on Mars. Imagine life in a colony there.

Use your imagination to tell the story, but include accurate scientific information about Mars itself.

WHAT DO YOU THINK?

Do you think humans could live in the colony described in your short story?

TECHNOLOGY CONNECTION

SNAKE ON MARS!

American, French, and Russian scientists hope to get a feel of the Martian surface by using a device we're all familiar with—a balloon with a tail.

The balloon will be carried to Mars as part of a mission planned by Russian scientists for launch in 1996. The Russian spacecraft will drop the balloon to the Martian surface where it will inflate with helium, rise, and drag a long guide rope nicknamed "SNAKE."

The balloon will carry a camera and a number of scientific instruments and will be followed by SNAKE, which also will carry sensors to help map the Martian surface and measure wind speed.

The balloon and SNAKE will be powered by the Martian winds. During daytime, helium in the balloon will heat and expand, causing the balloon and SNAKE to rise. At night, colder temperatures will cause the balloon to descend closer to the surface. This will tell scientists something about wind movement on the planet while cameras and other instruments gather additional information.

George Powell, an engineer working on the project, says SNAKE is like a hand feeling its

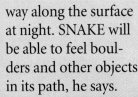

way along the surface at night. SNAKE will be able to feel boulders and other objects in its path, he says.

Although SNAKE will gather information for the mission, its primary purpose is to help stabilize the balloon, keeping it from tipping over and damaging the instruments it carries.

Scientists hope winds will not blow more than 30 kilometers per hour. There's also the worry that SNAKE will snag on the ground. That could spell disaster for the project because the balloon would be more likely to crash on the surface.

There are other concerns about the balloon and its instruments. "Our main concern is temperature," says Mr. Powell. "On a nice warm summer day on Mars, it might get up to −31°C. At night, it's probably around −124 °C." He points out that electronic instruments do not work well in such cold temperatures and that heaters might be sent along.

TEENS *in* SCIENCE

THE SPACE STATION PROJECT

Candace Kendrick was still in high school when she began working on NASA's space station project at Johnson Space Center. Although she was just 17 years old, she had already put in years of hard work in math and science, her favorite subjects.

Candace was one of only 17 students chosen to participate in the space center's eight-week summer program called SHARP (Summer High School Apprenticeship Program). The NASA program selects young people to work with engineers and scientists on a variety of projects at space research facilities in the United States. When she learned she had gotten the job, Candace turned her attention from the physics class she had just completed in high school and began to study a physics dictionary.

In her NASA job, Candace studied ways of calibrating electrical instruments on the Space Station *Freedom*. "The calibration devices at NASA are great," she says. "But they're too big and generate too much heat to put on the already crowded space station."

Her project was to find ways to overcome heat and size problems. She also had to find ways to prevent electromagnetic interference among instruments aboard the station.

From day to day, she calibrated electrical instruments, such as voltmeters and ohmmeters. She spent her lunch hour studying at the library. She also learned from NASA electrical engineers and electricians. Near the end of the SHARP program, Candace and the 16 other students at the space center prepared reports based on their research.

The effort paid off for Candace, who wrote a research paper recommending use of a diode to calibrate space station equipment. Her report was well received by NASA personnel, and she hopes to participate in future NASA programs for college students.

Candace's friends describe her as serious and meticulous, and Candace agrees. "I really hate surface learning. That's one thing about physics and math. If you don't understand one thing, it's hard to go on to the next thing. I know a lot of people who are having trouble with precalculus and calculus because they didn't learn the basics."

What advice does she offer junior-high students who want to follow in her footsteps? "Concentrate on math. If you really want to go into engineering, math is really important. It's probably important for anything you go into, but it's really important for engineering. And take the honors classes because they'll help you a lot, even if it's scary."

WHAT DO YOU THINK?

What specialized courses should you take to pursue the career of your dreams? In what ways can you use the courses you are taking now to help you in the future?

Reviewing Main Ideas

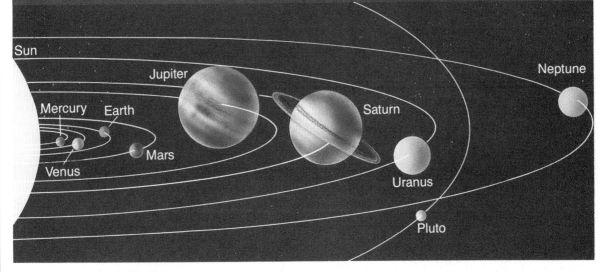

1. The major components of the solar system are the sun and the nine planets that revolve around the sun in elliptical orbits.

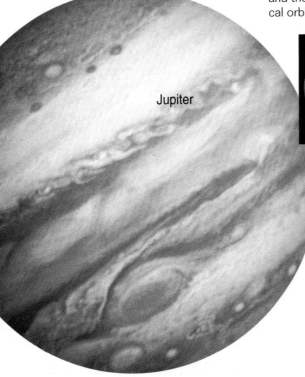

Jupiter

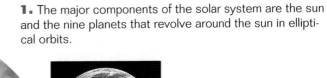

Earth

2. The planets are classified into two groups—Earth-sized, or terrestrial, planets and gaseous giant planets.

3. It is likely that the solar system was formed more than 4.6 billion years ago from a huge cloud of gas and dust that condensed to form the sun and planets.

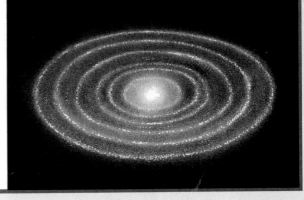

Chapter Review

USING KEY SCIENCE TERMS

asteroid
comet
gaseous giant planets
meteor

meteorite
planet
solar system
terrestrial planets

Read each statement. If the statement is true, write T. If false, replace the underlined term or terms with a term or terms that will make it true.

1. Earth is a <u>terrestrial planet</u>.
2. <u>Asteroids</u> originate in the Oort cloud.

3. The fifth through the eighth planets out from the sun are <u>terrestrial planets</u>.
4. A meteoroid that strikes Earth's surface is called a <u>meteorite</u>.
5. A large body that revolves around the sun in a fixed orbit is a(n) <u>asteroid</u>.

UNDERSTANDING IDEAS

Complete each sentence.

1. ____ is the planet with the most eccentric orbit.
2. ____ is the closest planet to the sun.
3. The region on the fringes of the solar system where comets originate is called the ____.
4. Among Saturn, Uranus, and Pluto, the planet that is not a gaseous giant is ____.
5. Most of the ____ in the solar system are found in a belt between Mars and Jupiter.
6. When a ____ enters Earth's atmosphere and begins to glow, it becomes a meteor.
7. Copernicus proposed a(n)____ model of the solar system.
8. The high percentage of carbon dioxide in the atmosphere of ____ keeps the planet very hot.
9. An unusual feature of ____ is the large tilt of its axis.
10. ____ have the most eccentric orbits of all members of the solar system.

CRITICAL THINKING

Use your understanding of the concepts developed in the chapter to answer each of the following questions.

1. What could happen if an object the size of Io were to pass relatively close to Earth?

2. At what point in the formation of the solar system did the core of the spinning disk become a star?

3. Why are scientists concerned about the possible destruction of the ozone layer of Earth's atmosphere?

4. We are able to see Mercury and Venus only in the early morning or early evening sky. Study the diagram. Then explain why we cannot see these two planets at midnight.

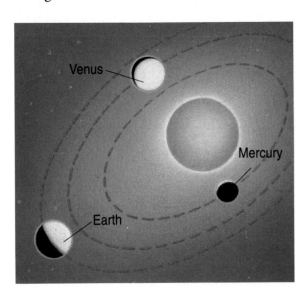

5. Why is the sun's gravity so much stronger than that of any of the planets?

6. What may have prevented the asteroids in the asteroid belt from becoming a planet?

7. If the sun were at the center of a planet's orbit, what shape would the orbit have?

PROBLEM SOLVING

Read the following problem and discuss your answers in a brief paragraph.

A new planet has been discovered and you have been asked to calculate information on its speed and orbit.

1. What factors do you need to know in order to calculate the average speed of the planet along its orbit?

2. If you knew the average orbital speed of the planet and its period of revolution, how could you calculate the length of its orbit?

CONNECTING IDEAS

Discuss each of the following in a brief paragraph.

1. Assuming the rotating cloud theory correctly describes the formation of the solar system, how might it relate to the Oort cloud?

2. How is it possible for a day to be longer than a year?

3. LIFE SCIENCE CONNECTION Do you think conflicts might arise between crew members on an extended planetary mission?

4. SCIENCE AND SOCIETY Do you think it will ever be possible to change the environment on Mars so that it can support a colony? How?

5. TECHNOLOGY CONNECTION Do you think airborne, helium filled balloons could be used to explore the surfaces of other planets besides Mars? Why or why not? Which ones, if any?

DID YOU EVER WONDER . . .

Why stars twinkle?

How long the sun will last?

Where you are in the universe?

You'll find the answers to these questions as you read this chapter.

Chapter 21

Stars and Galaxies

When you look up at the sky at night, what do you see? Perhaps the blinking red lights on a jumbo jet, or the thin trail of a meteor as it streaks across the sky. How many stars can you see?

On a dark, clear night, away from street lamps, headlights, and house lights, you might see over 3000 stars. Many more can be seen with a telescope. No one knows how many more there are that are too far away to be seen at all from Earth.

This chapter explores stars—the ones you can see and the ones you can't see. You will learn about the birth of stars, about the source of the energy that lights stars up, and about groups of billions of stars like the one shown here. From your exploration, you should begin to understand the immensity of the universe and Earth's place in it.

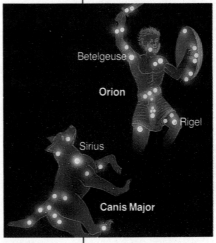
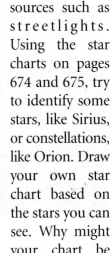
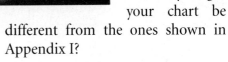

EXPLORE!

What stars can you identify?
Go outside on a clear night about two hours after sunset to observe stars. You'll be able to see more stars if you can get away from light sources such as streetlights. Using the star charts on pages 674 and 675, try to identify some stars, like Sirius, or constellations, like Orion. Draw your own star chart based on the stars you can see. Why might your chart be different from the ones shown in Appendix I?

21-1 Observing Stars

OBJECTIVES

In this section, you will

- compare and contrast a star's actual brightness with how bright it appears from Earth;
- explain the process by which a star produces energy;
- relate the temperature of a star to its color.

KEY SCIENCE TERMS

star
nebula
binary star system
star cluster
light-year

THE BRIGHTNESS OF STARS

If you've ever lain down in a field away from city lights and gazed at the night sky, you may have felt what it's like to be covered with a blanket of stars. Above you lie thousands of twinkling points of light. Some stars are bright, like holiday lights, while others are so faint they seem to disappear if you look directly at them. Have you ever wondered why some stars look brighter than others?

FIND OUT!

What factors affect the observable brightness of stars?

This activity has three parts. First, have a classmate stand at the back of the classroom holding one small and one large flashlight (for example, a penlight and a utility flashlight). Turn off the overhead lights and have your classmate turn on the flashlights. What do you notice about the brightness of the two lights?

Second, have two classmates stand at the back of the classroom holding identical flashlights with new batteries. Turn off the overhead lights. Have them turn on the flashlights. Compare the brightness of the two flashlights. Next, have one of your classmates approach you with a lighted flashlight. What do you notice about the comparative brightness of the two lights now?

Third, ask the student closest to you to exchange his or her flashlight for the penlight. Again, compare the brightness of the two lights.

Conclude and Apply

1. What are two factors that affect the brightness of light?
2. How might these factors relate to the brightness of stars?

FIGURE 21-1. The night sky is filled with stars of varying brightness.

In the Find Out activity, you discovered how size and distance can affect how bright an object appears. The same is true of stars. One star can appear brighter than another simply because it is larger than the other star. In the first step of this activity, for example, the large utility flashlight produced more light than the small penlight.

One star can also appear brighter than another because it is closer to Earth, just as in Step 2, when one of two identical flashlights looked brighter because it was moved closer to you. However, the closest stars aren't necessarily the brightest stars, as you observed in Step 3.

In order to understand the brightness of stars, you need to know what a star is. A **star** is a hot, glowing sphere of gas that produces energy by fusion, a process you learned about in Chapter 19. Some stars produce more energy and are therefore hotter than other stars of the same size. The hotter the star, the more light it produces, just as the light from a flashlight with new batteries is brighter than the light from a flashlight with weak batteries.

Actual vs. Apparent Brightness

Because of the variables of star size, distance, and temperature, astronomers talk about the brightness of stars in two ways: actual brightness and apparent brightness. The actual brightness of a star is the amount of light it gives off. A star's actual brightness depends on its size and temperature.

DID YOU KNOW?

A star twinkles because its light is bent and scattered by dust in Earth's atmosphere.

FIGURE 21-2. Sirius (a) appears much brighter than Rigel (b), but it is actually a smaller yet closer star.

The apparent brightness of a star is the amount of light received on Earth from the star. A star's apparent brightness is affected by its size and temperature as well as its distance from Earth. For example, a small, cool star can appear quite bright in the sky if it's close to Earth, while a large, hot star can appear dim if it's far away.

Look at Figure 21-2(a) and (b), for example. The star Sirius in the constellation Canis Major looks much brighter than Rigel in the constellation Orion. In other words, the apparent brightness of Sirius is greater than the apparent brightness of Rigel. Long ago, people thought Sirius must give off more light. In fact, Rigel is a much bigger and hotter star. But because it is farther away from Earth, it appears much dimmer than Sirius.

THE ORIGIN OF STARS

A star forms from a large cloud of gas and dust called a **nebula**. Every star begins like the nebula shown in Figure 21-3. The particles of gas and dust in a nebula exert a gravitational force on each other, causing the nebula to contract. As the particles move closer together, the temperature inside the nebula increases. The nebula continues to condense, and when the temperature reaches 10,000,000°C, fusion begins to take place. The energy released from fusion radiates outward through the condensing ball of gas. Once energy is released into space, a star is born.

FIGURE 21-3. Gases in the Horsehead Nebula may contract to form new stars sometime in the future.

The newborn star may continue producing energy for billions of years. Where does it get this energy?

HYDROGEN FUSION: ENERGY OF THE STARS

In 1905, Albert Einstein proposed the theory that mass could be converted into energy. This was exciting news to astronomers like A. S. Eddington. In 1920, Eddington used Einstein's theory to help explain where stars—including the sun—get their energy.

Eddington suggested that hydrogen atoms in the sun fuse, or combine, to form helium atoms. Fusion occurs in the cores of stars—the only place where temperature and pressure are high enough to cause atoms to fuse. In the core of a star, atoms are forced so close together that their nuclei attract.

During solar fusion, he explained, four hydrogen atoms combine to create one helium atom. The mass of one helium atom is less than the mass of four hydrogen atoms, which means that some mass is lost in the reaction. The mass

FIGURE 21-4. Albert Einstein (a) and A. S. Eddington (b) combined efforts to discover the source of stars' energy.

a

b

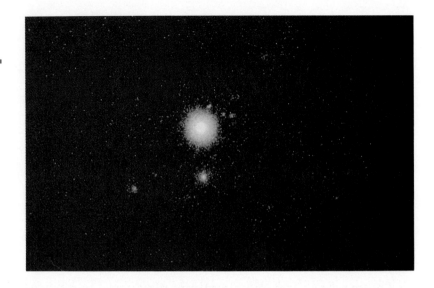

FIGURE 21-5. Many stars are part of a binary star system, like the two pictured here.

mass that is lost during fusion is converted to energy—an incredible amount of energy. Eddington concluded that this energy was what powered the sun and other stars.

STARS IN GROUPS

The sun, of course, is the star closest to Earth. You know now that the sun is so bright because it is so relatively close to us. In fact, it takes time for your eyes to adjust to outdoor light on a brilliant sunny day. Consider what it would be like to step outside some morning into the light of two suns! Yet astronomers have observed that most stars travel in groups of two or more. Our sun—a loner—is unlike most stars in this respect.

A **binary star system** is a two-star system in which the two stars orbit each other. Figure 21-5 shows you what a binary star system looks like.

In many cases, stars move through space together as a **star cluster**. Such a cluster usually contains hundreds or even thousands of stars. The stars are relatively close together and attract one another with their gravitational forces. Most star clusters lie far away from our solar system and appear only as fuzzy patches in the night sky.

FIGURE 21-6. The Pleiades is a cluster of stars gravitationally bound to each other. All the stars in this cluster have only recently begun fusing hydrogen.

The Pleiades (PLEE uh deez), shown in Figure 21-6, is an example of a star cluster. In this cluster, the stars are gravitationally bound to each other.

The Pleiades star cluster can be seen in the constellation of Taurus in the winter sky. On a clear night, you may be able to make out six or seven of the 400 stars of this cluster. The cluster may be harder to see if you are standing near an outdoor light. Street lamps, headlights, house lights, even the glow of a distant city at night can make stars appear to fade in the night sky. This effect is called light pollution, and it can prevent you from seeing many stars and planets.

LIGHT-YEARS

Distances to even the closest stars, aside from the sun, are very large, too large to measure in kilometers. For this reason, astronomers use an extremely large unit called a light-year to measure distances in space. A **light-year** is the distance light travels in one year.

Light travels faster than anything else in the universe, including sound. You may know this from watching lightning storms. Often, you see the flash of light before you hear the rumble of thunder. Astronomers use the speed of light as a form of measurement because it is so fast. In space, light travels at 300,000 kilometers per second, or about 9.5 trillion kilometers in one year. One light-year, then, is about 9.5 trillion kilometers. Look again at Figure 21-2. Sirius is 8.7 light-years from Earth. Rigel is more than 800 light-years away.

DETERMINING A STAR'S COMPOSITION

Astronomers learn about properties of stars by studying the colors in their spectra. They use spectroscopes to break visible light from a star into its component colors. Figure 21-7 shows how a spectroscope works. The next Investigate will show you how to use a star's colors to determine its composition.

SKILLBUILDER

MEASURING IN SI
Proxima Centauri, the star closest to our solar system, is about 40 trillion kilometers from Earth. How many light-years is this? How old were you when the light that you see left Proxima Centauri? Why might Proxima Centauri look dimmer than the star Betelgeuse (BEE tuhl jooz), a very large star 489 light-years away? If you need help, refer to the **Skill Handbook** on page 686.

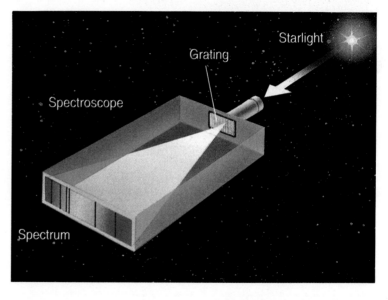

FIGURE 21-7. A spectroscope breaks starlight into a spectrum. By studying a star's spectrum, scientists can determine its composition.

Starlight

Grating

Spectroscope

Spectrum

21-1
ANALYZING
SPECTRA

Look closely at the spectrum of a star in Figure 21-7. Those lines are caused by elements in the star's atmosphere. As light emitted from a star passes through the star's atmosphere, some of it is absorbed by elements in the atmosphere. The wavelengths of the light that are absorbed appear as dark lines in the spectrum. Each element absorbs certain wavelengths, producing a certain pattern of dark lines. The pattern of lines can therefore be used to identify which elements are present in a star.

In this activity, you will **observe** spectra and determine the compositions of the sun and unknown objects by **comparing** the dark lines in their spectra with those in the spectra of known substances. The spectra have been greatly simplified for this activity so that line patterns can be easily identified. Actual spectral lines are much more complex.

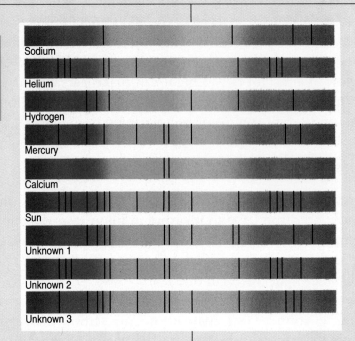

Sodium

Helium

Hydrogen

Mercury

Calcium

Sun

Unknown 1

Unknown 2

Unknown 3

PROBLEM

What do dark lines in the spectrum of light emitted from an object tell us?

MATERIALS

ruler or straightedge
pencil
paper

PROCEDURE

1. Look at the spectra on this page. Using a ruler or straightedge, try to match the vertical lines in the spectrum of the sun with lines in the spectra of the five known substances: hydrogen, helium, calcium, sodium, and mercury. A matching line indicates the presence of that element in the sun.

2. Record your findings.

3. Repeat Steps 1 and 2 for the spectra of the unknown objects.

ANALYZE

1. What elements are contained in the sun?

2. What elements can you **infer** are contained in the unknown objects?

CONCLUDE AND APPLY

3. How is a substance's spectrum like a fingerprint?

4. **Going Further:** How could scientists find out if stars within a newly discovered galaxy are composed of the same elements as stars within the Milky Way galaxy?

DETERMINING A STAR'S TEMPERATURE

The stars you see from your backyard or bedroom window probably look white. But if you examined those stars with a powerful telescope, you would see that they appear from bluish white to yellow, orange, and red.

Star color reveals the temperature of the star. Scientists have determined that very hot stars are bluish white. A relatively cool star looks orange or red. Stars the temperature of our sun have a yellow color.

How do we know that the color of a star indicates its temperature? A common example right here on Earth can help explain how. If you look at a nail as it is heated over a flame, it will begin to glow with a dull red color. As you heat the nail further, it will glow bright orange. If you can heat the nail long enough, it will glow white-hot and even bluish.

The same is true of any object that gives off its own thermal energy. The difference in temperature shows up as a gradual change in color in the spectrum of light coming from the glowing object—whether that object is a nail or a star. Figure 21-8 shows the progression of color in stars of progressively higher temperatures.

Now you know a lot more about the stars you see at night. You've learned what they are and how they form. You've discovered that their size, temperature, and distance from Earth affect how bright they appear. And you've seen how scientists determine the temperature and composition of a star by reading the colors as well as the gaps in its spectrum. In the next section, you will explore the most important star in your life—the sun.

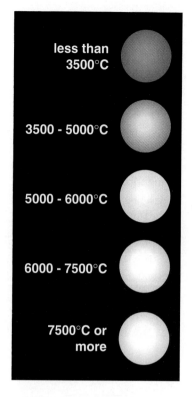

FIGURE 21-8. A star's color depends on its temperature.

less than 3500°C
3500 - 5000°C
5000 - 6000°C
6000 - 7500°C
7500°C or more

Check Your Understanding

1. How can two stars that have the same actual brightness look different to an observer on Earth?
2. Describe the process in which the sun produces energy.
3. What is true of the color of visible stars as you go from cooler to hotter?
4. **APPLY:** Suppose you observe the explosion tonight of an object in space that is 10 light-years away. When would the explosion have actually occurred?

21-2 The Sun

OBJECTIVES

In this section, you will

- describe phenomena on the sun's surface and recognize that sunspots, prominences, and solar flares are related;
- describe how phenomena on the sun's surface affect Earth.

KEY SCIENCE TERMS

sunspot

THE SUN AND YOU

The sun supplies Earth and the entire solar system with energy. Energy from the sun warms air and water masses, causing global wind patterns, changes in weather, and ocean currents. We can harness the energy from the sun for use in heating and lighting our homes, schools, and businesses. What are some other positive ways in which the sun affects your life?

Although the sun is extremely beneficial to us, solar radiation can be harmful. If you've ever gotten a blistering sunburn, you've felt the harmful effects of the sun's radiation on your body. Even a suntan can have long-range ill effects. Prolonged exposure to ultraviolet rays from the sun can cause skin cancer. About 27,000 Americans develop skin cancer each year, and about 6000 die from it. Think of some ways that the sun has had a negative effect on you.

AN AVERAGE STAR

You already learned that there are different types of stars. Some are brighter than others, while some just seem brighter. Stars also give off light in different colors. These differences in stars are due to the fact that stars evolve over time.

After a nebula forms a new star, it doesn't stay the same forever. Stars go through different phases of expansion and contraction as they use their hydrogen fuel. The temperature and size of a star change as it goes through these phases. When you look up at the sky at night, you are seeing stars that are in all different stages in their life cycles. Some stars are large and red, while others are smaller and yellow.

Our sun is just such a star. It is considered to be a star of average age and temperature. The actual brightness of our sun is also about average for a star of its fairly average size, though it is a bit on the small side.

DID YOU KNOW?

Compared with other stars, the sun may be average in size. But compared with other objects in our solar system, the sun is huge. It would take 109 Earths lined up side by side to equal the diameter of the sun.

One thing that sets the sun apart from other stars is its proximity to Earth. Because the sun is so close to Earth, we are affected by many of the phenomena that occur on its surface and in its atmosphere.

The cross section of the sun in Figure 21-9 shows you that the sun is an enormous ball of gas, fusing hydrogen into helium in its core. The corona is the halo of light around the sun that can be seen during a total solar eclipse. On the solar surface can be found sunspots, prominences, and flares. Let's take a look at some of these phenomena.

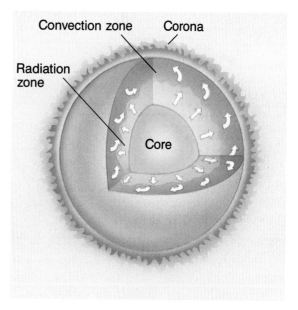

FIGURE 21-9. Energy produced by fusion in the sun's core travels outward by radiation and convection. The sun's atmosphere is illuminated by the energy produced in the core.

SUNSPOTS

From watching the sun rise on a very hazy day, you might think that the surface of the sun is perfectly smooth. It's not. There are many features that can be studied, including dark areas of the sun's surface that are cooler than surrounding areas. Such a cool, dark area on the sun's surface is called a **sunspot**. You can see examples of sunspots in Figure 21-10.

Galileo was the first to identify sunspots, and scientists have been fascinated by them ever since. One thing we've learned by studying sunspots is that the sun rotates. We can observe the movement of individual sunspots as they are carried by the sun's rotation. Unlike Earth, the sun doesn't rotate as a solid body. It rotates faster at its equator than at its poles. In fact, sunspots near the equator take about 25 days to go around the sun; at higher latitudes, they take a day or two longer. In the following Investigate activity, you will trace for yourself the movements of sunspots across the face of the sun.

FIGURE 21-10. Sunspots are much brighter than a full moon, but seen against the rest of the sun, they appear dark.

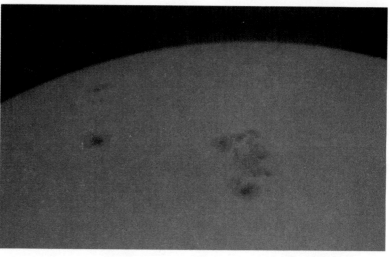

21-2 TRACKING SUNSPOTS

In this activity, you will **measure** the movement of sunspots and use your findings to determine the sun's period of rotation.

PROBLEM
How can you trace the movement of sunspots?

MATERIALS
several books cardboard
clipboard drawing paper
small tripod scissors
small refracting telescope

PROCEDURE
1. Copy the data table.
2. Find a spot where you can view the sun at the same time of day for 5 days. **CAUTION:** *Do not look directly at the sun. Do not look through the telescope at the sun. You could damage your eyes.*
3. Set up the telescope with the eyepiece facing away from the sun. Set up the clipboard with the drawing paper attached.

4. Use the books to prop the clipboard upright. Point the eyepiece at the drawing paper.
5. Cut a hole out of the center of the cardboard. Attach the cardboard to the telescope as shown. This shield will cast a shadow on your clipboard.
6. Move the clipboard back and forth until you have the largest possible image of the sun on the paper. Adjust the telescope to form a clear image.
7. Trace the outline of the sun on the paper.
8. Trace any sunspots that appear as dark areas on the sun's image. At the same time each day for a week, check the sun's image and trace the position of the sunspots.

9. The sun's diameter is approximately 1,400,000 kilometers. **Using this SI measure,** calculate the scale of your image. Estimate the size of the largest sunspots you observed.
10. Calculate and record how many kilometers any observed sunspots appear to move each day.
11. At the rate determined in Step 10, **predict** how many days it will take for the same sunspots to return to the same position in which you first saw them.

ANALYZE
1. Which part of the sun showed up in your image?
2. What was the average number of sunspots you observed each day?

CONCLUDE AND APPLY
3. How can the movement of sunspots be traced?
4. How can sunspots be used to prove that the sun is rotating?
5. **Going Further:** How can sunspots be used to determine that the sun's surface is not solid like Earth's?

DATA AND OBSERVATIONS

DATE OF OBSERVATION	NUMBER OF SUNSPOT GROUPS (APPROX.)		ESTIMATED AVERAGE SUNSPOT DIAM. (KM)	PREDICTED RETURN TIME (EARTH)

TABLE 21-1. Sunspot Activity

Date	Number of Sunspots	Date	Number of Sunspots	Date	Number of Sunspots
1964	11	1973	38	1982	116
1965	18	1974	35	1983	67
1966	53	1975	16	1984	46
1967	91	1976	13	1985	18
1968	106	1977	28	1986	14
1969	105	1978	93	1987	29
1970	104	1979	155	1988	100
1971	67	1980	155	1989	159
1972	69	1981	140		

SKILLBUILDER

MAKING AND USING GRAPHS

Using the data presented in Table 21-1, make a bar graph showing the number of sunspots that have occurred on the sun over the past three decades. Plot years on the horizontal axis and number of sunspots on the vertical axis. If you need help, refer to the **Skill Handbook** on page 682.

Sunspots are not permanent features on the sun. They may appear and disappear over a period of several days or several months. Look at Table 21-1. Sometimes there are many large sunspots—a period called a sunspot maximum—while at other times there are only a few small sunspots or none at all—a sunspot minimum. Sunspot maximums occur about every 11 years. The next is expected in 2001. This 11-year cycle of sunspot occurrences is often called the cycle of solar activity.

FIGURE 21-11. This photograph of a huge solar prominence was taken by astronauts on board Skylab in 1973. The prominence arches hundreds of thousands of kilometers into space and could contain several Earths.

PROMINENCES AND FLARES

Sunspots are related to other phenomena on the sun's surface—prominences and solar flares. A prominence is a huge arching column of gas. Some prominences are so eruptive that material from the sun is blasted into space at speeds approaching 1000 kilometers per second. Others form into loops through which matter flows into and out of the corona. These loops look like taffy in a giant taffy mixer.

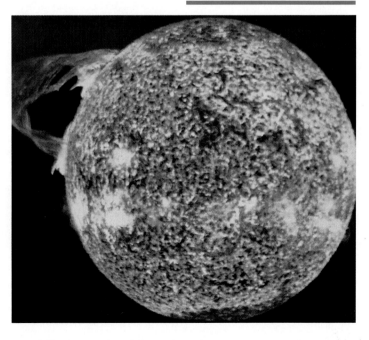

FIGURE 21-12. A solar flare ejects gas and radiation outward from the sun's surface, sometimes disrupting radio signals on Earth.

Gases near a sunspot sometimes brighten suddenly, shooting outward at high speed. These violent eruptions are called solar flares. Ultraviolet light and X rays from solar flares can reach Earth and disrupt radio signals, making communication by radio and telephone difficult. Figure 21-12 is a photograph of a solar flare.

Solar flares can also interact with Earth's magnetic field, producing a beautiful, eerie light show. This spectacular display of lights is called the aurora borealis, or northern lights, in the Northern Hemisphere, and the aurora australis in the Southern Hemisphere. In the next section, you will observe some more spectacular light displays that can be seen only through the lens of a powerful telescope.

FIGURE 21-13. The northern lights are a visual treat caused by radiation from solar flares.

Check Your Understanding

1. In what ways are sunspots, prominences, and solar flares related?
2. What effects do solar phenomena have on Earth?
3. **APPLY:** How does our sun differ from most other stars? In what ways is our sun average?

21-3 Galaxies

LOCATING EARTH

One reason to study astronomy is to learn about your place in the universe. Long ago, before the shapes and movements of the planets were understood, people thought they were living in the center of the universe and everything else revolved around them. Today, we know Earth is not at the center of the universe, nor even the center of our solar system!

Suppose you need to give directions to your house to a distant cousin who lives in another country. You could probably do it. But suppose your cousin lives in a galaxy millions of light-years away. Look at Figure 21-14. What other information would you need to give your cousin?

EARTH'S GALAXY—AND OTHERS

You are living on a planet in a giant galaxy called the Milky Way. A **galaxy** is a large group of stars, gas, and dust held together by gravity. Our galaxy contains about 200 billion stars. The sun is just one of those stars, and Earth revolves around it.

OBJECTIVES

In this section, you will

■ describe a galaxy and list three main types of galaxies;

■ identify several characteristics of the Milky Way galaxy.

KEY SCIENCE TERMS

galaxy

FIGURE 21-14. Earth is a tiny part of a vast universe.

Earth-moon system

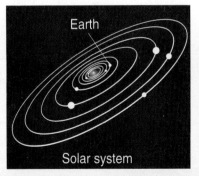
Earth

Solar system

Solar system

Milky Way galaxy

Many galaxies in universe

Just as stars are grouped together within galaxies, galaxies are grouped into clusters. Even so, the galaxies in a cluster are separated by huge distances—often millions of light-years. The cluster the Milky Way belongs to is called the Local Group. It contains about 25 galaxies of various shapes and sizes. However, there are three major types of galaxies: elliptical, spiral, and irregular.

Elliptical Galaxies

The most common type of galaxy is the elliptical galaxy. These galaxies are like large, three-dimensional ellipses. Many are football-shaped. Some elliptical galaxies are quite small, but others are so large that the entire Local Group of galaxies would fit inside them. Figure 21-15 shows an elliptical galaxy.

FIGURE 21-16. NGC 2997 is a spiral galaxy similar to our own. The scattered stars in the picture are in the foreground and belong to the Milky Way.

Spiral Galaxies

Spiral galaxies have arms that curve outward from a central hub, making them look something like a pinwheel. The spiral arms are made up of stars and dust. In between the arms are fewer stars. Figure 21-16 shows a typical spiral galaxy.

The fuzzy patch you can see in the constellation of Andromeda is actually a spiral galaxy. It's so far away that you can't see its individual stars. Instead, it appears as a hazy spot in the night sky.

The Andromeda galaxy is a member of the Local Group and is about 2 million light-years away from the Milky Way.

As you saw in Figure 21-16, arms in a typical spiral galaxy start close to the center of the galaxy. Barred spiral galaxies have two spiral arms extending from a large bar that passes through the center of the galaxy. Figure 21-17 shows a barred spiral galaxy.

Irregular Galaxies

The third type of galaxy includes all those galaxies that don't fit into the other two categories. Irregular galaxies come in many different shapes and are smaller and less common than ellipticals or spirals. The Large Magellanic Cloud, shown in Figure 21-18, is an irregular galaxy that orbits the Milky Way galaxy at a mere distance of about 170,000 light-years.

FIGURE 21-17. In a barred spiral, the spiral arms originate at the ends of a bar passing through the center. This galaxy is named NGC 1365.

THE MILKY WAY GALAXY

Our galaxy—the Milky Way—is about 100,000 light-years wide and contains more than 200 billion stars. These stars all orbit around a central hub. You're familiar with one of these stars—the sun. The sun is located about 30,000 light-years from the center of the Milky Way galaxy. It orbits around that center once every 200 million years.

FIGURE 21-18. The Large Magellanic Cloud is an irregular galaxy. It's a member of the Local Group, and it orbits our own galaxy.

The Milky Way is usually classified as a normal spiral galaxy. However, recent evidence suggests that it might be a barred spiral. It is difficult to know for sure because we have never seen our galaxy from the outside. We have an "insider's" view of the arrangement of the stars within the Milky Way. The next activity shows you why it is difficult to determine the shape of our galaxy while viewing it from inside.

Why is determining the shape of the Milky Way so difficult?

Place about 20 paper cups upside down on a table. Arrange them in the shape of a spiral galaxy. Look at the arrangement from above. Next, kneel down so that you are eye level with the cups. Look at the arrangement from this angle. From which view did the cups seem to be arranged in a pattern? Imagine that these cups are stars in the Milky Way galaxy. Which view represents what we see when we look at our galaxy from Earth?

As the activity showed, you can't see the normal spiral (or perhaps barred spiral) shape of the Milky Way because you are located within one of its spiral arms. What you can see of this galaxy is a faint band of light stretching across the sky.

Will we ever be able to travel into the center of the Milky Way and beyond? Probably not. It would take many generations of people to make a trip that long. What we can expect is to improve on the methods we now use to view it from Earth and from space. Astronomers are already doing this by using telescopes that examine the waves of radio and heat energy that come from the center of the Milky Way. And the more information that is gathered, the better you can understand your place in the universe.

How do we know?

The Position of the Solar System in the Galaxy

When plotting stars in the Milky Way, astronomers noted that there is a large concentration of stars about 30,000 light-years away. They believe this concentration of stars is the center of the galaxy.

Check Your Understanding

1. List the three major types of galaxies. What do they all have in common?
2. Name and describe the shape of the galaxy that you live in. How do the stars in this galaxy move?
3. Why is the Large Magellanic Cloud classified as an irregular galaxy?
4. **APPLY:** Specify Earth's location as much as possible by identifying, in order of size from smallest to largest, the systems of planets and stars to which it belongs.

EXPANDING YOUR VIEW

CONTENTS

A **CLOSER** LOOK

STELLAR EVOLUTION

You learned that stars begin as nebulas and eventually evolve. A massive star uses up its hydrogen supply rapidly, causing the star's core to contract. The temperature and pressure in the core rise, while the outer temperature slowly falls. The star expands and becomes a giant. In very large stars, the core heats up to a much higher temperature, elements heavier than helium can form by fusion, and the star expands into a supergiant.

As the core of a star about the size of our sun uses up its supply of helium and contracts, the outer layers escape into space. This leaves behind the hot, dense core, and the star becomes a white dwarf. White dwarfs were first observed in 1915. In 1939, researchers such as Subrahmanyan (sewb rah MAHN yahn) Chandrasekhar (chahn druh SAYK ar), an astrophysicist from India, offered an explanation about the evolution of very massive stars.

Chandrasekhar hypothesized that stars much more massive than the sun have cores so dense that fusion continues even when the supplies of hydrogen and helium have been used up. Elements as heavy as iron are produced. Once iron forms, no more fusion can occur, and the star explodes into a supernova. What remains may be a neutron star—a small, dense core of neutrons with an average radius of 15 kilometers.

The most massive stars, however, may collapse into black holes after the explosion, giving off large amounts of X rays. A black hole is so dense, nothing can escape its gravitational field. If you tried to shine a flashlight into a black hole, the light would simply disappear into it.

WHAT DO YOU THINK?

If black holes can't be seen, how do you think scientists could try to find them?

The sun

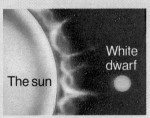
The sun
White dwarf

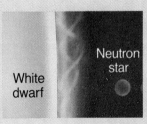
White dwarf
Neutron star

Neutron star
Black hole

Physics Connection

THE DOPPLER SHIFT

Have you ever heard the horn of a train or car as it approached you and then passed? If you have, you know the sound becomes louder and louder as it approaches and then becomes fainter as it leaves. But the volume is not all that changes. The sound also changes, from lower to higher, then back to lower pitches as the train moves away. The change in pitch is called the Doppler shift. Scientists have been able to associate the Doppler shift with sound waves and with light waves.

Astronomers understand that the change in wavelength on a light spectrum is similar to the change in pitch of the train's horn. The wavelength of light from an object becomes shorter as the object approaches, just as the sound waves did.

If a star were approaching, the dark lines of its spectrum, shown in (a), would move toward the blue-violet part of the spectrum (b). But if the star were traveling away, the lines would move toward the red part of the spectrum (c).

In 1924, Edward Hubble noticed that there is a red shift in the light from galaxies beyond the Local Group. What did this tell him about the universe? Because all galaxies beyond the Local Group show a red shift in their spectra, they must be moving away from Earth. Hubble then concluded that, for so many galaxies to be traveling away from Earth, the universe must be expanding.

YOU TRY IT!

You can get an idea of how distances between stars change by inflating a balloon slightly and then closing it with a clothespin to keep air from escaping. Use a felt-tipped pen to put dots in a number of places on the balloon. Next, inflate the balloon some more and watch how distances between dots change.

The dots move away from each other, just as scientists think galaxies in the universe are doing. Such reasoning led scientists to the "big bang" theory, which states that our expanding universe began with an incredibly large explosion. When the explosion occurred, matter was blown apart. With the universe, however, the particles are still continuing to travel away from the explosion.

Astronomers simply don't know whether the universe will expand forever or not. Some believe it could eventually reverse its expansion and contract.

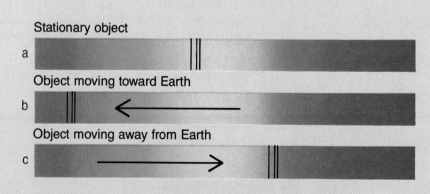

a   Stationary object

b   Object moving toward Earth

c   Object moving away from Earth

SCIENCE AND SOCIETY

A LOOK AT LIGHT POLLUTION

Some people love to visit rural areas where many stars can be seen against a dark, moonless night sky. They may travel for miles to reach a mountaintop for clear viewing.

Other people love to watch city lights from a distance. In their eyes, the nighttime view of Los Angeles from nearby hills is beautiful—much like a galaxy on Earth.

But the sky and city lights don't always mix. Urbanites must have lights for reading, safety, and thousands of other needs. And while the lights serve their purpose in the city, they also obscure the night sky.

That's a problem for astronomers and other star watchers who refer to the city's glow as light pollution. You can see a good example of light pollution while watching a nighttime baseball game in an outdoor stadium. The stars in the sky seem to disappear because of the glow of the lights.

It's obvious that cities can't do without light, and

that astronomers can't view the night sky through light pollution. Does this mean that scientific research must stop? Can compromise solve the problem for astronomers and city dwellers?

Some cities have taken measures to control light pollution. For example, one Arizona city near a mountaintop observatory has replaced its streetlights with lamps shining at wavelengths that can be filtered out by astronomers. The lamps are less expensive to operate, so the city is saving money while helping the pollution problem.

Light pollution might also be reduced by putting covers above some bright outdoor lights. This would allow the light to hit its target without illuminating the sky.

If such measures do not completely eliminate interference from light pollution, how can we solve the conflict between those who want to observe the stars and those

who need lights? Do you think the conflict could become as severe as disagreements over noise and air pollution?

To get a better idea of arguments that could be made about light pollution, pretend that your classroom is a courtroom. Some of your classmates are attorneys for a group of astronomers who say new lighting near their observatory has stopped their astronomy projects.

The attorneys also represent a neighborhood association that is upset over the new floodlights and neon lights near their homes. They say the lights keep them awake at night and make their neighborhood look cheap.

Defense attorneys should represent the businesses that added the new lighting. They say the businesses would lose business without all the bright signs. They also claim that the new lights have reduced the number of burglaries in the area.

Select classmates to serve as judge and jury to hear the arguments. Other classmates can be witnesses for the neighborhood association, while others can be owners of the well-lit businesses. Reporters from newspapers and TV should be present.

Both teams of attorneys should talk to their clients (the astronomers, neighborhood association, and business owners) before the trial begins. The attorneys and judge should know the local zoning laws that concern lighting.

After questioning their witnesses during the trial, the attorneys should make their closing arguments before the jury.

Remember that the news media should take notes for news coverage throughout the trial and when the jury announces its decision.

Remember also that some trials end when the plaintiffs and defendants finally reach an agreement outside of court.

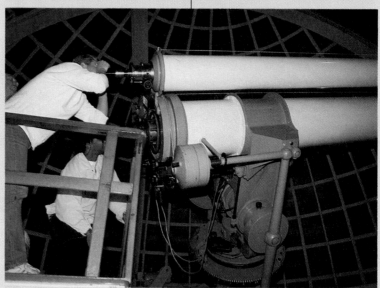

WHAT DO YOU THINK?

Did you agree with the outcome of the trial? What other viewpoints could you have added to the courtroom arguments? Were press reports of the trial accurate? Did they seem to support one side of the argument?

TECHNOLOGY CONNECTION

IN SEARCH OF THE TINY NEUTRINO

In "A Closer Look," you learned about the supernova. Now you will find out about something that plays a role in a star's evolution into a supernova.

Muons, pions, and neutrinos sound like the names of extraterrestrial creatures in a science fiction novel. But they are really the names of subatomic particles. These strangely named particles are of special interest to astronomers and physicists. They help scientists explore the universe.

The neutrino is a good example of a particle that helps scientists explore the universe. With almost no mass and no electric charge, neutrinos are not likely to react with other particles. This allows the neutrino to pass through the sun and other large objects almost as though those objects weren't there. They also travel at the speed of light.

These fascinating characteristics also mean the neutrino is hard to catch. How could you examine something that passes through walls at the speed of light? Scientists have figured out a way. When neutrinos hit protons, radiation is given off. So researchers decided to place large water-filled tanks, such as the one pictured above, underground with special instruments for sensing radiation.

By placing the tanks underground, the experimenters were able to avoid radiation

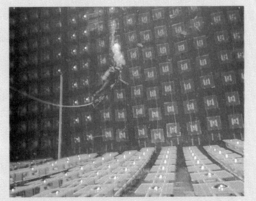

from sources other than the neutrino-proton collisions. When they measured radiation in the tank, they could assume they were measuring radiation caused by a neutrino's crash into a proton.

These experiments successfully measured radiation from the collisions. They also drew special attention from astronomers who suspected that neutrinos were thrown from stars transforming into supernovas.

In February 1987, astronomers in the Southern Hemisphere observed a supernova in the Large Magellanic Cloud. When checked later, instruments at tanks in both Ohio and Japan detected the presence of neutrinos at the time they should have arrived from this supernova. By showing that the birth of a supernova coincided with the increased numbers of neutrinos striking the underground tanks, scientists gained new evidence that exploding stars give off neutrinos.

WHAT DO YOU THINK?

Congress has approved the construction of the world's largest superconducting super collider. What will the superconductor tell us about subatomic particles like the neutrino? Do you think the research is worth the enormous cost? Or should the money be spent in other ways instead?

TEENS *in* SCIENCE

SPACE CAMP

Would you be interested in training the way a real astronaut does? Thousands of fourth to sixth graders who attend the Space Camp in Huntsville, Alabama, receive five days of this type of training. They learn about the development of the space program and even build and launch their own model rockets.

Space campers get to try many different kinds of simulators—devices that provide test conditions much like real experiences. The Microgravity Training Chair gives its occupant the feeling of walking on the moon. While in the chair, the occupant weighs only one-sixth of his or her normal weight. This seat, suspended from the ceiling with springs and pulleys, alters the results of average movements. Taking steps as we normally do simply causes the tester to bounce in place. "Moonwalking" requires slow, giant steps. The changes in weight and gravitational pull change the way your arms and legs work.

Further practice in moving without gravity comes with the Five Degrees of Freedom Simulator. In this activity, campers are strapped into a chair that floats on a cushion of air. This chair can swivel in any direction, so the slightest movement may bring surprising consequences, like a sudden tip upside down!

In Space Academy, a program for seventh through twelfth graders, the Multi-Axis Training Simulator is used. A camper sits in the center of a chamber surrounded by a system of large metal rings. When the simulator is activated, the camper-astronaut spins in three different directions at the same time. The student may lose sense of direction completely, in the same way that an astronaut might if a spaceship were spinning out of control in space.

The primary activity at both Space Camp and Space Academy is the team mission, shown here. Campers get specific assignments during this two-hour simulation of an actual space shuttle flight. They may direct take-off or landing, fly the shuttle, launch satellites, make repairs, or monitor life-support systems. Trainers radio changes and problems to campers from a computer as the campers follow a script of what to say and do in certain situations. Each crew member must think and follow directions carefully in order to complete a successful mission.

At the end of their five days, campers receive Space Camp diplomas and badges (a pair of wings) at a graduation ceremony. Many of them may return in future years for Space Academy I or II. One thing is sure—if any of them have dreams about becoming an astronaut, after Space Camp they have a much better idea of what it would be like!

WHAT DO YOU THINK?

Imagine that you are on a mission to explore the surface of the moon. What is your greatest thrill in doing this?

Reviewing Main Ideas

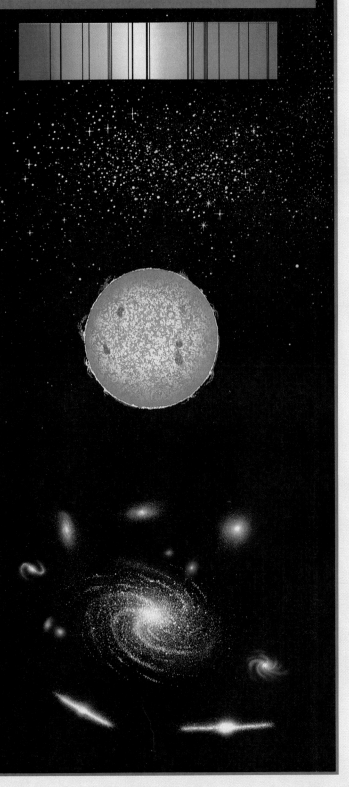

1. There are more stars in the universe than you could count in a lifetime. Some are brighter than others, depending on how big, how hot, and how far away from Earth they are. The temperature and composition of a star can be determined by its color and by examining the dark-line spectrum of the light it emits.

2. All life on Earth depends on one star—the sun. It is different from other stars in two ways. It is not a binary star, and it is the closest star to Earth. It is an average star in terms of its size and temperature. The surface of the sun contains sunspots, prominences, and solar flares.

3. Our solar system belongs to the Milky Way galaxy. The Milky Way is a spiral-shaped galaxy in a cluster of galaxies called the Local Group. Other galaxies are elliptical or irregularly shaped.

Chapter Review

USING KEY SCIENCE TERMS

binary star system   star
galaxy   star cluster
light-year   sunspot
nebula

For each set of terms below, explain the relationship that exists.

1. nebula, star
2. binary star system, galaxy, star cluster
3. star, sunspot
4. light-year, galaxy

UNDERSTANDING IDEAS

Choose the best answer to complete each sentence.

1. The apparent brightness of a star depends only on its ____.
   a. size, temperature, and distance from Earth
   b. size and distance from Earth
   c. actual brightness
   d. color and composition

2. A star's temperature can be determined by ____.
   a. measuring its size
   b. observing the color of the star
   c. calculating how far it is from Earth
   d. calculating how old it is

3. A star's composition can be determined by ____.
   a. examining its apparent brightness
   b. testing samples of its star dust

c. determining the galaxy to which it belongs
   d. examining the dark-line spectrum of its emitted light

4. Stars get their energy from ____.
   a. hydrogen fission
   b. helium fission
   c. hydrogen fusion
   d. gravitational forces

5. The sun began as a ____.
   a. cluster of sunspots
   b. cloud of gas and dust
   c. core of helium
   d. solar prominence

6. The sun is different from many stars in that it ____.
   a. belongs to a binary star system
   b. belongs to a star cluster
   c. belongs to a galaxy
   d. travels alone

7. The sun is an average star in that it ____.
   a. is of medium size and temperature
   b. supports life
   c. is so close to Earth
   d. belongs to the Milky Way galaxy

8. One thing we've learned by studying sunspots is that ____.
   a. the sun rotates
   b. the sun's surface is a perfectly smooth layer of gas
   c. the surface of the sun is evenly heated
   d. sunspots can be cancerous and are caused by overexposure to the sun

9. Galaxies look like fuzzy patches in the sky because ____.
   a. they are composed of hydrogen and helium gases

b. they are so far away we cannot see individual stars in them
c. they are moving so fast
d. they are so hot

10. The shape of the Milky Way galaxy is ____.
a. spiral   c. irregular
b. elliptical   d. a cluster

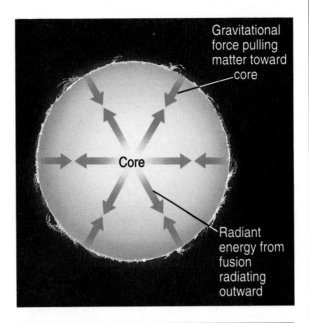

Gravitational force pulling matter toward core

Core

Radiant energy from fusion radiating outward

CRITICAL THINKING

Use your understanding of the concepts developed in the chapter to answer each of the following questions.

1. Explain why a hotter star might appear dimmer than a cooler star.

2. Explain why a small and a large star may appear to have the same brightness.

3. Describe the effects on life on Earth if the sun were to move one light-year away.

4. Suppose the sun were part of a binary system so that a second star was in close proximity to Earth. Describe some effects of this situation.

5. The diagram shows the forces that act within a star such as our sun. What do you think the overall effect of these forces is on the size of the star?

PROBLEM SOLVING

Read the following problem and discuss your answers in a brief paragraph.

Suppose you had a rocket that could travel at the speed of light.

1. How long would it take you to complete a round-trip journey to a galaxy that is 15 light-years from Earth?

2. Explain why you might make the mistake of taking off for the star without realizing that it no longer exists.

CONNECTING IDEAS

Discuss each of the following in a brief paragraph.

1. Explain the difference between fusion and fission. How do we know fusion and not fission occurs in the sun?

2. How does Earth's closest star affect its ocean currents?

3. How do we know that the sun contains hydrogen?

4. A CLOSER LOOK What kind of stars may become black holes? Why?

5. PHYSICS CONNECTION Why does a red shift in light spectra lead scientists to believe the universe is expanding?

UNIT 5
PLANETS, STARS, AND GALAXIES

CONTENTS

UNIT FOCUS

In this unit, you investigated how transmutations of elements occur by fission and fusion. You learned that during fission, atoms split apart and during fusion, they are forced together. You explored the idea that the solar system began as a huge rotating cloud of gas and dust, and that the universe is composed of small particles and huge galaxies of stars. You have investigated how humans are attempting to artificially cause and control nuclear processes to produce energy for human use.

Try the exercises and activity that follow — they will challenge you to use and apply some of the ideas you learned in this unit.

CONNECTING IDEAS

1. Why are the interiors of some planets molten while others are solid? What causes differences in temperatures in the interiors of planets? How might the cause of differing temperatures inside planets relate to fission or fusion reactions humans generate when producing nuclear energy?

2. When four hydrogen nuclei undergo fusion to form a helium nucleus, mass is lost. Explain what happens to account for the loss of mass and how this shows the conservation of mass and energy. How does this explain how stars produce energy?

EXPLORING FURTHER

Compare and contrast the diameters of the planets in the solar system. Obtain charts or tables to provide information on the diameters of the planets. Determine how many times bigger in diameter each planet is than Pluto, the smallest. Mix up some cookie dough and cut out cookies having diameters based on this scale. Decorate your planet cookies and bake them. **CAUTION**: *Be sure to have an adult help you with this activity.*

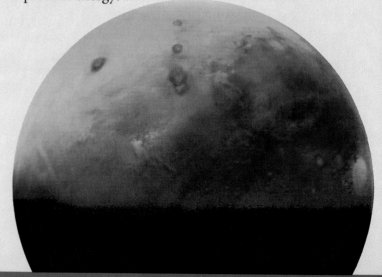

Appendices
Table of Contents

Appendix A

INTERNATIONAL SYSTEM OF UNITS

The International System (SI) of Measurement is accepted as the standard for measurement throughout most of the world. Three base units in SI are the meter, kilogram, and second. Frequently used SI units are listed below.

TABLE A-1

FREQUENTLY USED SI UNITS	
LENGTH	1 millimeter (mm) = 1000 micrometers (μm)
	1 centimeter (cm) = 10 millimeters (mm)
	1 meter (m) = 100 centimeters (cm)
	1 kilometer (km) = 1000 meters (m)
	1 light-year = 9,460,000,000,000 kilometers (km)
AREA	1 square meter (m^2) = 10,000 square centimeters (cm^2)
	1 square kilometer (km^2) = 1,000,000 square meters (m^2)
VOLUME	1 milliliter (mL) = 1 cubic centimeter (cm^3)
	1 liter (L) = 1000 milliliters (mL)
MASS	1 gram (g) = 1000 milligrams (mg)
	1 kilogram (kg) = 1000 grams (g)
	1 metric ton = 1000 kilograms (kg)
TIME	1 s = 1 second

Temperature measurements in SI are often made in degrees Celsius. Celsius temperature is a supplementary unit derived from the base unit kelvin. The Celsius scale (°C) has 100 equal graduations between the freezing temperature (0°C) and the boiling temperature of water (100°C). The following relationship exists between the Celsius and kelvin temperature scales:

$$K = °C + 273$$

Several other supplementary SI units are listed below.

TABLE A-2

SUPPLEMENTARY SI UNITS			
MEASUREMENT	**UNIT**	**SYMBOL**	**EXPRESSED IN BASE UNITS**
Energy	Joule	J	$kg \bullet m^2/s^2$ ($N \bullet m$)
Force	Newton	N	$kg \bullet m/s^2$
Power	Watt	W	$kg \bullet m^2/s^3$ (J/s)
Pressure	Pascal	Pa	$kg/m \bullet s^2$ N/m^2

Appendix B

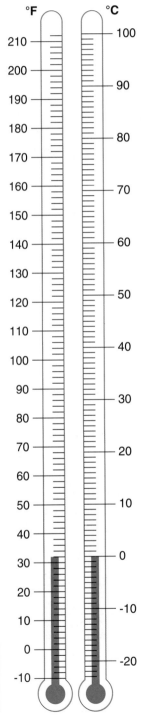

SI/METRIC TO ENGLISH CONVERSIONS			
	WHEN YOU WANT TO CONVERT:	**MULTIPLY BY:**	**TO FIND:**
LENGTH	inches	2.54	centimeters
	centimeters	0.39	inches
	feet	0.30	meters
	meters	3.28	feet
	yards	0.91	meters
	meters	1.09	yards
	miles	1.61	kilometers
	kilometers	0.62	miles
MASS AND WEIGHT*	ounces	28.41	grams
	grams	0.04	ounces
	pounds	0.45	kilograms
	kilograms	2.2	pounds
	tons	0.91	tonnes (metric tons)
	tonnes (metric tons)	1.10	tons
	pounds	4.45	newtons
	newtons	0.23	pounds
VOLUME	cubic inches	16.39	cubic centimeters
	cubic centimeters	0.06	cubic inches
	cubic feet	0.02	cubic meters
	cubic meters	35.3	cubic feet
	liters	1.06	quarts
	liters	0.26	gallons
	gallons	3.78	liters
AREA	square inches	6.45	square centimeters
	square centimeters	0.16	square inches
	square feet	0.09	square meters
	square meters	10.76	square feet
	square miles	2.59	square kilometers
	square kilometers	0.39	square miles
	hectares	2.47	acres
	acres	0.40	hectares
TEMPERATURE	Fahrenheit	5/9 (°F − 32)	Celsius
	Celsius	9/5 °C + 32	Fahrenheit

*Weight as measured in standard Earth gravity

Appendix C

SAFETY IN THE SCIENCE CLASSROOM

1. Always obtain your teacher's permission to begin an investigation.
2. Study the procedure. If you have questions, ask your teacher. Understand any safety symbols shown on the page.
3. Use the safety equipment provided for you. Goggles and a safety apron should be worn when any investigation calls for using chemicals.
4. Always slant test tubes away from yourself and others when heating them.
5. Never eat or drink in the lab, and never use lab glassware as food or drink containers. Never inhale chemicals. Do not taste any substances or draw any material into a tube with your mouth.
6. If you spill any chemical, wash it off immediately with water. Report the spill immediately to your teacher.
7. Know the location and proper use of the fire extinguisher, safety shower, fire blanket, first aid kit, and fire alarm.
8. Keep materials away from flames. Tie back hair and loose clothing.
9. If a fire should break out in the classroom, or if your clothing should catch fire, smother it with the fire blanket or a coat, or get under a safety shower. **NEVER RUN.**
10. Report any accident or injury, no matter how small, to your teacher.

Follow these procedures as you clean up your work area.

1. Turn off the water and gas. Disconnect electrical devices.
2. Return all materials to their proper places.
3. Dispose of chemicals and other materials as directed by your teacher. Place broken glass and solid substances in the proper containers. Never discard materials in the sink.
4. Clean your work area.
5. Wash your hands thoroughly after working in the laboratory.

TABLE C-1

FIRST AID	
INJURY	**SAFE RESPONSE**
Burns	Apply cold water. Call your teacher immediately.
Cuts and bruises	Stop any bleeding by applying direct pressure. Cover cuts with a clean dressing. Apply cold compresses to bruises. Call your teacher immediately.
Fainting	Leave the person lying down. Loosen any tight clothing and keep crowds away. Call your teacher immediately.
Foreign matter in eye	Flush with plenty of water. Use eyewash bottle or fountain.
Poisoning	Note the suspected poisoning agent and call your teacher immediately.
Any spills on skin	Flush with large amounts of water or use safety shower. Call your teacher immediately.

Appendix D

SAFETY SYMBOLS

	DISPOSAL ALERT This symbol appears when care must be taken to dispose of materials properly.		**ANIMAL SAFETY** This symbol appears whenever live animals are studied and the safety of the animals and the students must be ensured.
	BIOLOGICAL HAZARD This symbol appears when there is danger involving bacteria, fungi, or protists.		**RADIOACTIVE SAFETY** This symbol appears when radioactive materials are used.
	OPEN FLAME ALERT This symbol appears when use of an open flame could cause a fire or an explosion.		**CLOTHING PROTECTION SAFETY** This symbol appears when substances used could stain or burn clothing.
	THERMAL SAFETY This symbol appears as a reminder to use caution when handling hot objects.		**FIRE SAFETY** This symbol appears when care should be taken around open flames.
	SHARP OBJECT SAFETY This symbol appears when a danger of cuts or punctures caused by the use of sharp objects exists.		**EXPLOSION SAFETY** This symbol appears when the misuse of chemicals could cause an explosion.
	FUME SAFETY This symbol appears when chemicals or chemical reactions could cause dangerous fumes.		**EYE SAFETY** This symbol appears when a danger to the eyes exists. Safety goggles should be worn when this symbol appears.
	ELECTRICAL SAFETY This symbol appears when care should be taken when using electrical equipment.		**POISON SAFETY** This symbol appears when poisonous substances are used.
	PLANT SAFETY This symbol appears when poisonous plants or plants with thorns are handled.		**CHEMICAL SAFETY** This symbol appears when chemicals used can cause burns or are poisonous if absorbed through the skin.

Appendix E

PERIODIC TABLE

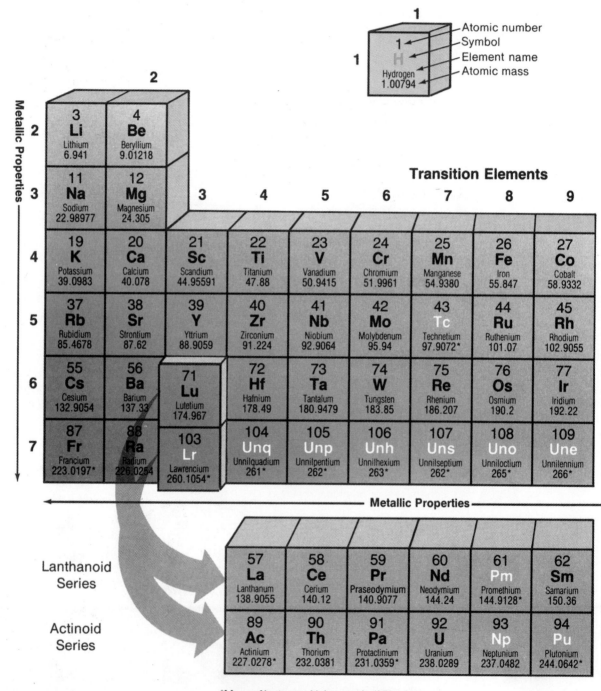

				Atomic number
			1	Symbol
1		1	H	Element name
			Hydrogen	Atomic mass
			1.00794	

Metallic Properties

	2								
2	3 **Li** Lithium 6.941	4 **Be** Beryllium 9.01218							
3	11 **Na** Sodium 22.98977	12 **Mg** Magnesium 24.305							

Transition Elements

	2		3	4	5	6	7	8	9
4	19 **K** Potassium 39.0983	20 **Ca** Calcium 40.078	21 **Sc** Scandium 44.95591	22 **Ti** Titanium 47.88	23 **V** Vanadium 50.9415	24 **Cr** Chromium 51.9961	25 **Mn** Manganese 54.9380	26 **Fe** Iron 55.847	27 **Co** Cobalt 58.9332
5	37 **Rb** Rubidium 85.4678	38 **Sr** Strontium 87.62	39 **Y** Yttrium 88.9059	40 **Zr** Zirconium 91.224	41 **Nb** Niobium 92.9064	42 **Mo** Molybdenum 95.94	43 **Tc** Technetium 97.9072*	44 **Ru** Ruthenium 101.07	45 **Rh** Rhodium 102.9055
6	55 **Cs** Cesium 132.9054	56 **Ba** Barium 137.33	71 **Lu** Lutetium 174.967	72 **Hf** Hafnium 178.49	73 **Ta** Tantalum 180.9479	74 **W** Tungsten 183.85	75 **Re** Rhenium 186.207	76 **Os** Osmium 190.2	77 **Ir** Iridium 192.22
7	87 **Fr** Francium 223.0197*	88 **Ra** Radium 226.0254	103 **Lr** Lawrencium 260.1054*	104 **Unq** Unnilquadium 261*	105 **Unp** Unnilpentium 262*	106 **Unh** Unnilhexium 263*	107 **Uns** Unnilseptium 262*	108 **Uno** Unniloctium 265*	109 **Une** Unnilennium 266*

Metallic Properties

Lanthanoid Series	57 **La** Lanthanum 138.9055	58 **Ce** Cerium 140.12	59 **Pr** Praseodymium 140.9077	60 **Nd** Neodymium 144.24	61 **Pm** Promethium 144.9128*	62 **Sm** Samarium 150.36
Actinoid Series	89 **Ac** Actinium 227.0278*	90 **Th** Thorium 232.0381	91 **Pa** Protactinium 231.0359*	92 **U** Uranium 238.0289	93 **Np** Neptunium 237.0482	94 **Pu** Plutonium 244.0642*

*Mass of isotope with longest half-life, that is, the most stable isotope of the element

Noble Gases

18

2	
He	
Helium	
4.002602	

13	14	15	16	17
5	6	7	8	9
B	**C**	N	O	F
Boron	Carbon	Nitrogen	Oxygen	Fluorine
10.811	12.011	14.0067	15.9994	18.998403

10	11	12						

			13	14	15	16	17	18
			Al	**Si**	**P**	**S**	Cl	Ar
			Aluminum	Silicon	Phosphorus	Sulfur	Chlorine	Argon
			26.98154	28.0855	30.97376	32.06	35.453	39.948
28	29	30	31	32	33	34	35	36
Ni	**Cu**	**Zn**	**Ga**	**Ge**	**As**	**Se**	Br	Kr
Nickel	Copper	Zinc	Gallium	Germanium	Arsenic	Selenium	Bromine	Krypton
58.69	63.546	65.39	69.723	72.59	74.9216	78.96	79.904	83.80
46	47	48	49	50	51	52	53	54
Pd	**Ag**	**Cd**	**In**	**Sn**	**Sb**	**Te**	**I**	Xe
Palladium	Silver	Cadmium	Indium	Tin	Antimony	Tellurium	Iodine	Xenon
106.42	107.8682	112.41	114.82	118.710	121.75	127.60	126.9045	131.29
78	79	80	81	82	83	84	85	86
Pt	**Au**	**Hg**	**Tl**	**Pb**	**Bi**	**Po**	**At**	Rn
Platinum	Gold	Mercury	Thallium	Lead	Bismuth	Polonium	Astatine	Radon
195.08	196.9665	200.59	204.383	207.2	208.9804	208.9824*	209.98712*	222.017*

Nonmetallic Properties

■ Metallic Properties   ■ Metalloids   State at Room Temperature:
■ Nonmetallic Properties □ Synthetic Elements   ■ and □ Solid ■ Liquid ■ Gas

63	64	65	66	67	68	69	70
Eu	**Gd**	**Tb**	**Dy**	**Ho**	**Er**	**Tm**	**Yb**
Europium	Gadolinium	Terbium	Dysprosium	Holmium	Erbium	Thulium	Ytterbium
151.96	157.25	158.9254	162.50	164.9304	167.26	168.9342	173.04
95	96	97	98	99	100	101	102
Am	**Cm**	**Bk**	**Cf**	**Es**	**Fm**	**Md**	**No**
Americium	Curium	Berkelium	Californium	Einsteinium	Fermium	Mendelevium	Nobelium
243.0614*	247.0703*	247.0703*	251.0796*	252.0828*	257.0951*	258.986*	259.1009*

Appendix F

CLASSIFICATION OF LIVING ORGANISMS

Scientists use a five kingdom system for the classification of organisms. In this system, there is one kingdom of organisms, Kingdom Monera, which contains organisms that lack a true nucleus and lack specialized structures in the cytoplasm of their cells. The members of the other four kingdoms have cells that contain a nucleus and structures in the cytoplasm that are surrounded by membranes. These kingdoms are Kingdom Protista, Kingdom Fungi, the Plant Kingdom, and the Animal Kingdom.

KINGDOM MONERA

Phylum Cyanobacteria: one-celled; make their own food, contain chlorophyll, some species form colonies, most are blue-green

Bacteria: one-celled; most absorb food from their surroundings, some are photosynthetic; many are parasites; round, spiral, or rod shaped

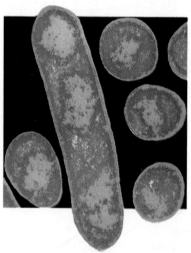

Clostridium botulinum
× 13,960

KINGDOM PROTISTA

Phylum Euglenophyta: one-celled; can photosynthesize or take in food; most have one flagellum

Phylum Crysophyta: most are one-celled; make their own food through photosynthesis; golden-brown pigments mask chlorophyll; diatoms

Phylum Pyrrophyta: one-celled; make their own food through photosynthesis; contain red pigments and have two flagella; dinoflagellates

Phylum Chlorophyta: one-celled, many-celled, or colonies; contain chlorophyll and make their own food; live on land, in fresh water or salt water; green algae

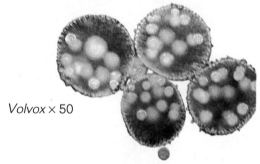

Volvox × 50

Phylum Rhodophyta: most are many-celled and photosynthetic; contain red pigments; most live in deep saltwater environments; red algae

Phylum Phaeophyta: most are many-celled and photosynthetic; contain brown pigments; most live in saltwater environments; brown algae

Phylum Sarcodina: one-celled; take in food; move by means of pseudopods; free-living or parasitic; sarcodines

Phylum Mastigophora: one-celled; take in food; have two or more flagella; free living or parasitic; flagellates

Phylum Ciliophora: one-celled; take in food; have large numbers of cilia; ciliates

Phylum Sporozoa: one-celled; take in food; no means of movement; parasites in animals; sporozoans

Phylum Myxomycetes, Phylum Acrasiomycota: one- or many-celled; absorb food; change form during life cycle; cellular and plasmodial slime molds

Pretzel Slime mold

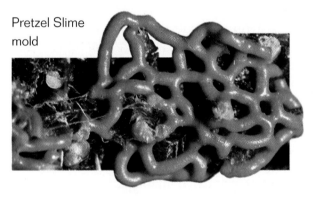

KINGDOM FUNGI

Division Zygomycota: many-celled; absorb food; spores are produced in sporangia; zygote fungi

Division Ascomycota: one- and many-celled; absorb food; spores produced in asci; sac fungi

Yeast × 7800

Division Basidiomycota: many-celled; absorb food; spores produced in basidia; club fungi

Division Deuteromycota: members with unknown reproductive structures; imperfect fungi

Lichens: organism formed by symbiotic relationship between an ascomycote or a basidiomycote and a green alga or a cyanobacterium

Old Man's Beard lichen

PLANT KINGDOM
Spore Plants

Division Bryophyta: nonvascular plants that reproduce by spores produced in capsules; many-celled; green; grow in moist land environments; mosses and liverworts

Liverwort

Division Lycophyta: many-celled vascular plants; spores produced in cones; live on land; are photosynthetic; club mosses

Division Sphenophyta: vascular plants with ribbed and jointed stems; scalelike leaves; spores produced in cones; horsetails

Division Pterophyta: vascular plants with feathery leaves called fronds; spores produced in clusters of sporangia called sori; live on land or in water; ferns

Seed Plants

Division Ginkgophyta: deciduous gymnosperms; only one living species called the maiden hair tree; fan-shaped leaves with branching veins; reproduces with seeds; ginkgos

Division Cycadophyta: palmlike gymnosperms; large compound leaves; produce seeds in cones; cycads

Division Coniferophyta: deciduous or evergreen gymnosperms; trees or shrubs; needlelike or scalelike leaves; seeds produced in cones; conifers

Slash Pine cones

Division Gnetophyta: shrubs or woody vines; seeds produced in cones; division contains only three genera; gnetum

Purple Coneflower

Oranges and blossoms

Division Anthophyta: dominant group of plants; ovules protected at fertilization by an ovary; sperm carried to ovules by pollen tube; produce flowers and seeds in fruits; flowering plants

ANIMAL KINGDOM

Phylum Porifera: aquatic organisms that lack true tissues and organs; they are asymmetrical and sessile; sponges

Phylum Cnidaria: radially symmetrical organisms with a digestive cavity with one opening; most have tentacles armed with stinging cells; live in aquatic environments singly or in colonies; includes jellyfish, corals, hydra, and sea anemones

Jellyfish

Phylum Platyhelminthes: bilaterally symmetrical worms with flattened bodies; digestive system has one opening; parasitic and free-living species; flatworms

Phylum Nematoda: round bilaterally symmetrical body; digestive system with two openings; some free-living forms but mostly parasitic; roundworms

Phylum Mollusca: soft-bodied animals, many with a hard shell; a mantle covers the soft body; aquatic and terrestrial species; includes clams, snails, squid, and octopuses

Phylum Annelida: bilaterally symmetrical worms with round segmented bodies; terrestrial and aquatic species; includes earthworms, leeches, and marine polychaetes

Christmas Tree worm

Phylum Arthropoda: very large phylum of organisms that have segmented bodies with pairs of jointed appendages, and a hard exoskeleton; terrestrial and aquatic species; includes insects, crustaceans, spiders, and horseshoe crabs

Seahorse

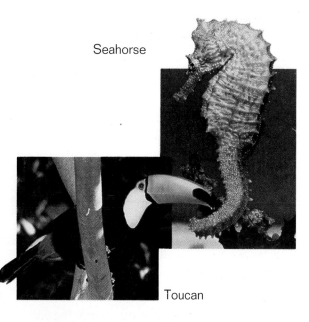

Toucan

Swallowtail butterfly

Sally Light-foot crab

Jumping spider

Phylum Chordata: organisms with internal skeletons, specialized body systems, and paired appendages; all at some time have a notochord, dorsal nerve cord, gill slits, and a tail; include fish, amphibians, reptiles, birds, and mammals

Peninsula turtles

Phylum Echinodermata: saltwater organisms with spiny or leathery skin; water-vascular system with tube feet; radial symmetry; includes starfish, sand dollars, and sea urchins

Brittle stars

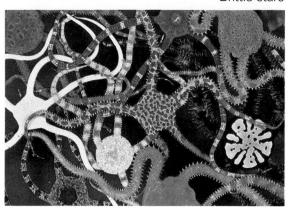

Mare and foal

Appendix G

CARE AND USE OF A MICROSCOPE

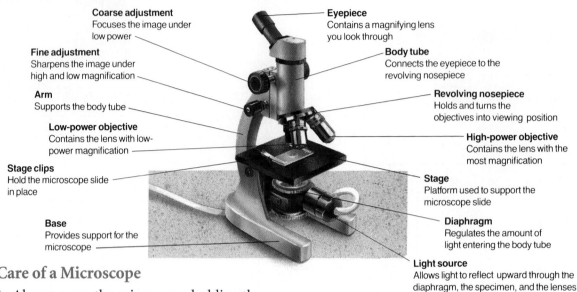

Coarse adjustment
Focuses the image under low power

Fine adjustment
Sharpens the image under high and low magnification

Arm
Supports the body tube

Low-power objective
Contains the lens with low-power magnification

Stage clips
Hold the microscope slide in place

Base
Provides support for the microscope

Eyepiece
Contains a magnifying lens you look through

Body tube
Connects the eyepiece to the revolving nosepiece

Revolving nosepiece
Holds and turns the objectives into viewing position

High-power objective
Contains the lens with the most magnification

Stage
Platform used to support the microscope slide

Diaphragm
Regulates the amount of light entering the body tube

Light source
Allows light to reflect upward through the diaphragm, the specimen, and the lenses

Care of a Microscope

1. Always carry the microscope holding the arm with one hand and supporting the base with the other hand.
2. Don't touch the lenses with your finger.
3. Never lower the coarse adjustment knob when looking through the eyepiece lens.
4. Always focus first with the low-power objective.
5. Don't use the coarse adjustment knob when the high-power objective is in place.
6. Store the microscope covered.

Using a Microscope

1. Place the microscope on a flat surface that is clear of objects. The arm should be toward you.
2. Look through the eyepiece. Adjust the diaphragm so that light comes through the opening in the stage.
3. Place a slide on the stage so that the specimen is in the field of view. Hold it firmly in place by using the stage clips.

4. Always focus first with the coarse adjustment and the low-power objective lens. Once the object is in focus on low power, turn the nosepiece until the high-power objective is in place. Use ONLY the fine adjustment to focus with this lens.

Making a Wet Mount Slide

1. Carefully place the item you want to look at in the center of a clean glass slide. Make sure the sample is thin enough for light to pass through.
2. Use a dropper to place one or two drops of water on the sample.
3. Hold a clean coverslip by the edges and place it at one edge of the drop of water. Slowly lower the coverslip onto the drop of water until it lies flat.
   If you have too much water or a lot of air bubbles, touch the edge of a paper towel to the edge of the coverslip to draw off extra water and force air out.

Appendix H

SOLAR SYSTEM INFORMATION

Planet	Mercury	Venus	Earth	Mars	Jupiter	Saturn	Uranus	Neptune	Pluto
Diameter (km)	4878	12104	12756	6794	142796	120660	51118	49528	2290
Diameter (E = 1.0)*	0.38	0.95	1.00	0.53	11.19	9.46	4.01	3.88	0.18
Mass (E = 1.0)*	0.06	0.82	1.00	0.11	317.83	95.15	14.54	17.23	0.002
Density (g/cm³)	5.42	5.24	5.50	3.94	1.31	0.70	1.30	1.66	2.03
Period of Rotation: days / hours / minutes (R = retrograde)	58 / 15 / 28	243 / 00 / 14$_R$	00 / 23 / 56	00 / 24 / 37	00 / 09 / 55	00 / 10 / 39	00 / 17 / 14$_R$	00 / 16 / 03	06 / 09 / 17
Surface gravity (E = 1.0)*	0.38	0.90	1.00	0.38	2.53	1.07	0.92	1.12	0.06
Average distance to sun (AU)	0.387	0.723	1.000	1.524	5.203	9.529	19.191	30.061	39.529
Period of revolution	87.97d	224.70d	365.26d	686.98d	11.86y	29.46y	84.04y	164.79y	248.53y
Eccentricity of orbit	0.206	0.007	0.017	0.093	0.048	0.056	0.046	0.010	0.248
Average orbital speed (km/s)	47.89	35.03	29.79	24.13	13.06	9.64	6.81	5.43	4.74
Number of known satellites	0	0	1	2	16	18	15	8	1
Known rings	0	0	0	0	1	thou-sands	11	4	0

*Earth = 1.0

Appendix I

STAR CHARTS

Shown here are star charts for viewing stars in the Northern Hemisphere during the four different seasons. These charts are drawn from the night sky at about 35° north latitude, but they can be used for most locations in the Northern Hemisphere. The lines on the charts outline major constellations. The dense band of stars is the Milky Way. To use, hold the chart vertically, with the direction you are facing at the bottom of the map.

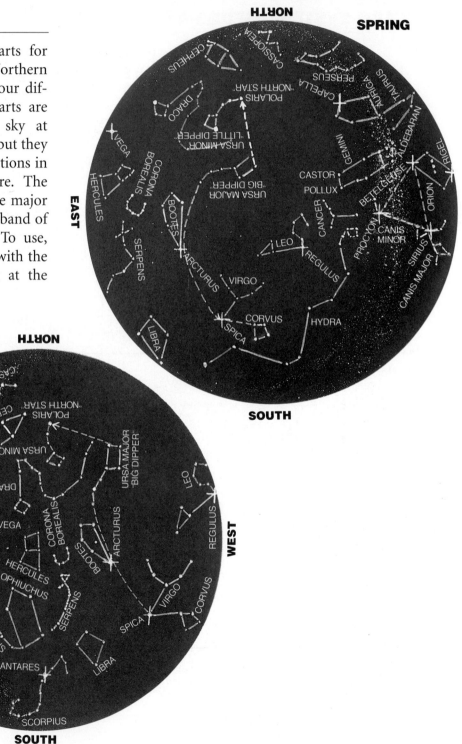

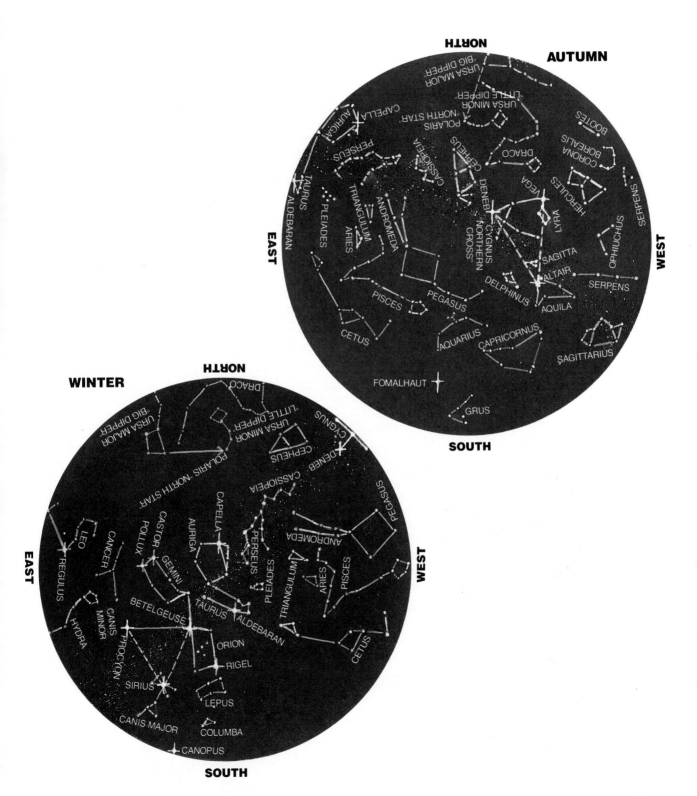

Appendix J

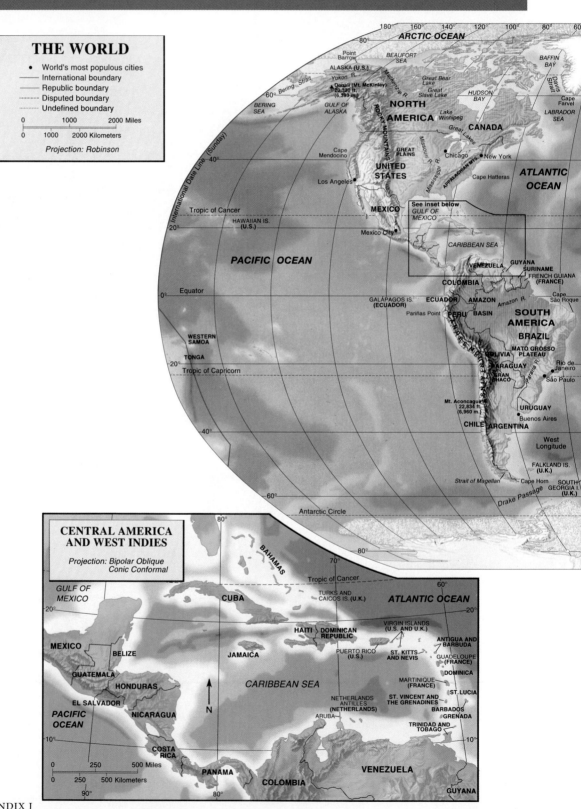

THE WORLD

- • World's most populous cities
- —— International boundary
- —— Republic boundary
- – – – Disputed boundary
- ········ Undefined boundary

0   1000   2000 Miles
0   1000   2000 Kilometers

Projection: Robinson

ARCTIC OCEAN
Point Barrow
BEAUFORT SEA
BAFFIN BAY
ALASKA (U.S.)
Yukon R.
Denali (Mt. McKinley) 20,320 ft. (6,193 m)
Great Bear Lake
Bering Strait
Great Slave Lake
HUDSON BAY
Davis Strait
Cape Farvel
BERING SEA
GULF OF ALASKA
NORTH AMERICA
Lake Winnipeg
Great Lakes
CANADA
LABRADOR SEA
ROCKY MOUNTAINS
Cape Mendocino
GREAT PLAINS
Missouri R.
Mississippi R.
Chicago
New York
APPALACHIAN MTS.
ATLANTIC OCEAN
UNITED STATES
Cape Hatteras
Los Angeles
International Date Line (Sunday)
Tropic of Cancer
MEXICO
See inset below
GULF OF MEXICO
HAWAIIAN IS. (U.S.)
Mexico City
CARIBBEAN SEA
GUYANA
SURINAME
VENEZUELA
FRENCH GUIANA (FRANCE)
COLOMBIA
PACIFIC OCEAN
Equator
GALÁPAGOS IS. (ECUADOR)
ECUADOR
AMAZON
Amazon R.
Cape São Roque
Pariñas Point
PERU
BASIN
SOUTH AMERICA
WESTERN SAMOA
BRAZIL
BOLIVIA
MATO GROSSO PLATEAU
TONGA
Tropic of Capricorn
PARAGUAY
Rio de Janeiro
GRAN CHACO
Paraná R.
São Paulo
Mt. Aconcagua 22,834 ft. (6,960 m)
URUGUAY
Buenos Aires
CHILE
ARGENTINA
West Longitude
FALKLAND IS. (U.K.)
Strait of Magellan
Cape Horn
SOUTH GEORGIA I. (U.K.)
Drake Passage
Antarctic Circle

CENTRAL AMERICA AND WEST INDIES

Projection: Bipolar Oblique Conic Conformal

BAHAMAS
GULF OF MEXICO
CUBA
TURKS AND CAICOS IS. (U.K.)
Tropic of Cancer
ATLANTIC OCEAN
HAITI
DOMINICAN REPUBLIC
VIRGIN ISLANDS (U.S. AND U.K.)
ANTIGUA AND BARBUDA
MEXICO
JAMAICA
PUERTO RICO (U.S.)
ST. KITTS AND NEVIS
GUADELOUPE (FRANCE)
BELIZE
DOMINICA
GUATEMALA
CARIBBEAN SEA
MARTINIQUE (FRANCE)
ST. LUCIA
HONDURAS
NETHERLANDS ANTILLES (NETHERLANDS)
ST. VINCENT AND THE GRENADINES
BARBADOS
EL SALVADOR
ARUBA
GRENADA
PACIFIC OCEAN
NICARAGUA
TRINIDAD AND TOBAGO
N
COSTA RICA
0   250   500 Miles
0   250   500 Kilometers
PANAMA
VENEZUELA
COLOMBIA
GUYANA

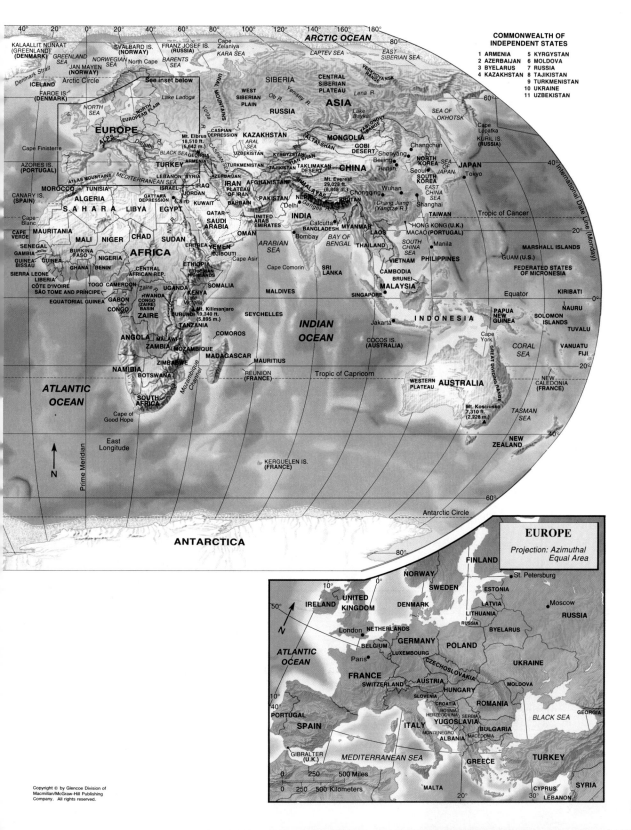

ARCTIC OCEAN

COMMONWEALTH OF INDEPENDENT STATES
1 ARMENIA
2 AZERBAIJAN
3 BYELARUS
4 KAZAKHSTAN
5 KYRGYSTAN
6 MOLDOVA
7 RUSSIA
8 TAJIKISTAN
9 TURKMENISTAN
10 UKRAINE
11 UZBEKISTAN

SIBERIA

ASIA

EUROPE

RUSSIA

KAZAKHSTAN

MONGOLIA

CHINA

AFRICA

INDIA

INDIAN OCEAN

ATLANTIC OCEAN

AUSTRALIA

ANTARCTICA

EUROPE
Projection: Azimuthal Equal Area

NORWAY
SWEDEN
FINLAND
RUSSIA
UNITED KINGDOM
IRELAND
GERMANY
POLAND
UKRAINE
FRANCE
SPAIN
ITALY
YUGOSLAVIA
TURKEY

MEDITERRANEAN SEA

0   250   500 Miles
0   250   500 Kilometers

Appendix K

WEATHER MAP SYMBOLS

SAMPLE PLOTTED REPORT AT EACH STATION

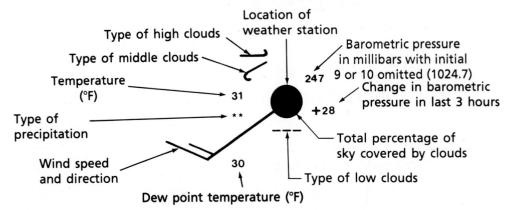

Location of weather station

Type of high clouds

Type of middle clouds

Temperature (°F)

Type of precipitation

Wind speed and direction

Dew point temperature (°F)

Barometric pressure in millibars with initial 9 or 10 omitted (1024.7)

Change in barometric pressure in last 3 hours

Total percentage of sky covered by clouds

Type of low clouds

247

31

**

30

+28

SYMBOLS USED IN PLOTTING REPORT

Precipitation	Wind speed and direction	Sky coverage	Some types of high clouds
≡ Fog	○ 0 calm	○ No cover	Scattered cirrus
* Snow	/ 1–2 knots	◑ 1/10 or less	Dense cirrus in patches
• Rain	∠ 3–7 knots	◕ 2/10 to 3/10	
Thunder-storm	∨ 8–12 knots	◔ 4/10	Veil of cirrus covering entire sky
⟩ Drizzle	∨ 13–17 knots	◐ ½	
∇ Showers	∨ 18–22 knots	⊖ 6/10	Cirrus not covering entire sky
	∨ 23-27 knots	◕ 7/10	
	∨ 48-52 knots	◑ Overcast with openings	
	1 knot = 1.852 km/h	● Complete overcast	

Some types of middle clouds	Some types of low clouds	Fronts and pressure systems	
∠ Thin altostratus layer	⌒ Cumulus of fair weather	(H) or High (L) or Low	Center of high or low pressure system
⫽ Thick altostratus layer	⊻ Stratocumulus	▲▲▲▲	Cold front
⟨ Thin altostratus in patches	--- Fractocumulus of bad weather	●●●●	Warm front
⟨ Thin altostratus in bands	___ Stratus of fair weather	▲●▲●	Occluded front
		⌒⌒⌒	Stationary front

Skill Handbook
Table of Contents

Skill Handbook

ORGANIZING INFORMATION

CLASSIFYING

You may not realize it, but you make things orderly in the world around you. If your shirts hang in the closet together, your socks take up a particular corner of a dresser drawer, or your favorite cassette tapes are stacked together, you have used the skill of classifying.

Classifying is the process of sorting objects or events into groups based on their common features. When classifying, you first make observations of the objects or events to be classified. Then, you select one feature that is shared by some members in the group but not by others. Those members that share the feature are placed in a subgroup. You can classify members into smaller and smaller subgroups based on characteristics.

How would you classify a collection of cassette tapes? You might classify cassettes you like to dance to in one subgroup and cassettes you like to listen to in another. The cassettes you like to dance to could be subdivided into a rap subgroup and a rock subgroup. Note that for each feature selected, each cassette only fits into one subgroup. Keep selecting features until all the cassettes are classified. The concept map in the next column shows one possible classification.

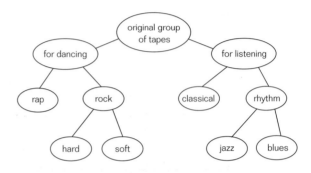

Remember when you classify, you are grouping objects or events for a purpose. Select common features to form groups and subgroups with your purpose in mind.

SEQUENCING

A sequence is an arrangement of things or events in a particular order. A sequence with which you are familiar is sitting in alphabetical order in a class. Another example of sequence would be the steps in a recipe. Think about baking chocolate chip cookies. The steps in the recipe have to be followed in order for the cookies to turn out right.

When you are asked to sequence objects or events, identify what comes first, then what should come second. Continue to choose objects or events until they are all in order. Then, go back over the sequence to make sure each thing or event in your sequence logically leads to the next.

Suppose you wanted to watch a movie that just came out on videotape. What sequence of events would you have to follow to watch the movie? You would first turn the television set to Channel 3 or 4. Then you would turn the videotape player on and insert the tape. Once the tape started playing, you would adjust the sound and picture. When the movie was over, you would rewind the tape and return it to the store.

MAKING AND USING TABLES

Browse through your textbook, and you will notice many tables both in the text and in the activities. Tables arrange data or information in such a way that makes it easier for you to understand. Activity tables help organize the data you collect during an activity so that results can be interpreted more easily.

Most tables have a title that tells what the table is about. The table then is divided into columns and rows. The first column lists items to be compared. In the table in the next column, different magnitudes of force are being compared. The rows across the top list the specific characteristics being compared. Within the grid of the table, the collected data is recorded. Look at the features in the following table.

EARTHQUAKE MAGNITUDE		
MAGNITUDE AT FOCUS	**DISTANCE FROM EPICENTERS THAT TREMORS ARE FELT**	**AVERAGE NUMBER EXPECTED PER YEAR**
1.0 to 3.9	24 km	> 100 000
4.0 to 4.9	48 km	6 200
5.0 to 5.9	112 km	800
6.0 to 6.9	200 km	120
7.0 to 7.9	400 km	20
8.0 to 8.9	720 km	< 1

What is the title of this table? The title is "Earthquake Magnitude." What is being compared? The distance away from the epicenter that tremors are felt and the average number of earthquakes expected per year are being compared for different magnitudes on the Richter scale.

What is the average number of earthquakes expected per year for an earthquake with a magnitude of 5.5 at the focus? Locate the column labeled "Average number expected per year" and the row "5.0 to 5.9." The data in the box where the column and row intersect is the answer. Did you answer "800"? What is the distance away from the epicenter for an earthquake with a magnitude of 8.1? If you answered "720 km," you understand how to use the table.

To make a table, you simply list the items compared in columns and the characteristics compared in rows. Make a table and record the data comparing the mass of recycled materials collected by a class. On Monday, students turned in 4 kg of paper, 2 kg of aluminum, and 0.5 kg of plastic. Wednesday, they turned in 3.5 kg of paper, 1.5 kg of aluminum, and 0.5 kg of plastic. On Friday, the totals were 3 kg of paper, 1 kg of aluminum, and 1.5 kg of plastic. If your table looks like the one shown, you should be able to make tables to organize data.

RECYCLED MATERIALS			
DAY OF WEEK	PAPER (KG)	ALUMINUM (KG)	PLASTIC (KG)
Mon.	4	2	0.5
Wed.	3.5	1.5	0.5
Fri.	3	1	1.5

MAKING AND USING GRAPHS

After scientists organize data in tables, they may display the data in a graph. A graph is a diagram that shows how variables compare. A graph makes interpretation and analysis of data easier. There are three basic types of graphs used in science, the line graph, bar graph, and pie graph.

A line graph is used to show the relationship between two variables. The variables being compared go on two axes of the graph. The independent variable always goes on the horizontal axis, called the *x*-axis. The dependent variable always goes on the vertical axis or *y*-axis.

Suppose a school started a peer study program with a class of students to see how science grades were affected.

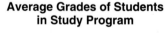

AVERAGE GRADES OF STUDENTS IN STUDY PROGRAM	
GRADING PERIOD	AVERAGE SCIENCE GRADE
First	81
Second	85
Third	86
Fourth	89

You could make a graph of the grades of students in the program over the four grading periods of the school year. The grading period is the independent variable and is placed on the *x*-axis of your graph. The average grade of the students in the program is the dependent variable and would go on the *y*-axis.

After drawing your axes, you would label each axis with a scale. The *x*-axis simply lists the four grading periods. To make a scale of grades on the *y*-axis, you must look at the data values. Since the lowest grade was 81 and the highest was 89, you know that you will have to start numbering at least at 81 and go through 89. You decide to start numbering at 80 and number by twos through 90.

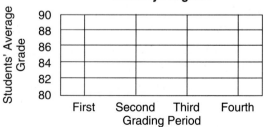

Next, you must plot the data points. The first pair of data you want to plot is the first grading period and 81. Locate "First" on the *x*-axis and locate "81" on the *y*-axis. Where an imaginary vertical line from the *x*-axis and an imaginary horizontal line from the *y*-axis would meet, place the first data point. Place the other data points the same way. After all the points are plotted, connect them with straight lines.

Mass Lifted by Electromagnets

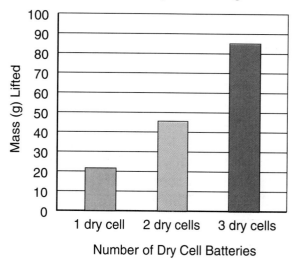

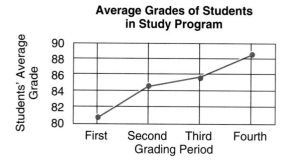

Average Grades of Students in Study Program

Bar graphs are similar to line graphs, except they compare or display data that do not continuously change. In a bar graph, thick bars show the relationships among data rather than data points.

To make a bar graph, set up the *x*-axis and *y*-axis as you did for the line graph. The data is plotted by drawing thick bars from the *x*-axis up to a point where the *y*-axis would intersect the bar if it was extended.

Look at the bar graph comparing the masses lifted by an electromagnet with different numbers of dry cell batteries. The *x*-axis is the number of dry cell batteries, and the *y*-axis is the mass lifted. The lifting power of the electromagnet as it changed with different numbers of dry cell batteries is being compared.

A pie graph uses a circle divided into sections to display data. Each section represents part of the whole. All the sections together equal 100 percent.

Suppose you wanted to make a pie graph to show the number of seeds that germinated in a package. You would have to count the total number of seeds and the number of seeds that germinated out of the total. You find that there are 143 seeds in the package. This represents 100 percent, the whole pie.

You plant the seeds, and 129 seeds germinate. The seeds that germinated will make up one section of the pie graph, and the seeds that did not germinate will make up the remaining section.

To find out how much of the pie each section should take, divide the number of seeds in each section by the total number of seeds. Then multiply your answer by 360, the number of degrees in a circle, and round to the nearest whole number. The number of seeds germinated as a measure of degrees is shown on the following page.

$$\frac{143}{129} \times 360 = 324.75 \text{ or } 325 \text{ degrees}$$

Plot this group on the pie graph, with a compass and a protractor. Use the compass to draw a circle. Then, draw a straight line from the center to the edge of the circle. Place your protractor on this line and use it to mark a point on the edge of the circle at 325 degrees. Connect this point with a straight line to the center of the circle. This is the section for the group of seeds that germinated. The other section represents the group of seeds that did not germinate. Label the sections of your graph and give the graph a title.

NUMBER OF SEEDS GERMINATED

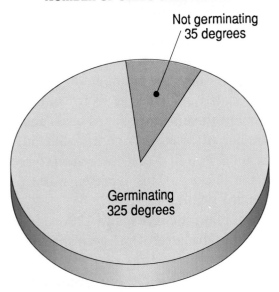

Not germinating
35 degrees

Germinating
325 degrees

THINKING CRITICALLY

OBSERVING AND INFERRING

Imagine that you have just finished a volleyball game. At home, you open the refrigerator and see a jug of orange juice on the back of the top shelf. The jug feels cold as you grasp it. "Ah, just what I need," you think. When you drink the juice, you smell the oranges and enjoy the tart taste in your mouth.

As you imagined yourself in the story, you used your senses to make observations. You used your sense of sight to find the jug in the refrigerator, your sense of touch to feel the coldness of the jug, your sense of hearing to listen as the liquid filled the glass, and your senses of smell and taste to enjoy the odor and tartness of the juice. The basis of all scientific investigation is observation.

Scientists try to make careful and accurate observations. When possible, they use instruments, like microscopes, to extend their senses. Other instruments, such as a thermometer or a pan balance, measure observations. Measurements provide numerical data, a concrete means of comparing collected data that can be checked and repeated.

When you make observations in science, you may find it helpful first to examine the entire object or situation. Then, look carefully for details. Write down everything you see before using other senses to make additional observations.

Scientists often make inferences based on their observations. An inference is an attempt to explain or interpret observations or to say what caused what you observed. For example, if you observed a CLOSED sign in a store window around noon, you might infer the owner is taking a lunch break. But, it's possible that the owner has a doctor's appointment or has taken the day off to go fishing. The only way to be sure your inference is correct is to investigate further.

When making an inference, be certain to make use of accurate data and observations. Analyze all of the data that you've collected. Then, based on everything you know, try to explain or interpret what you've observed. If possible, investigate further to determine if your inference is correct. What is there in the photo that you could use to check your inference?

COMPARING AND CONTRASTING

Observations can be analyzed by noting the similarities and differences between two or more objects or events that you observed. When you examine objects or events to see how they are similar, you are comparing them. Contrasting is looking for differences in similar objects or events.

Suppose you were asked to compare and contrast the planets Venus and Earth. You would start by looking at what is known about these planets. Then make two columns on a piece of paper. List ways the planets are similar in one column and ways they are different in the other. Then, report your findings in a table or in a paragraph.

COMPARISON OF VENUS AND EARTH		
PROPERTIES	**EARTH**	**VENUS**
Diameter (km)	12 742	12 112
Average density (g/cm^3)	5.5	5.3
Percentage of sunlight reflected	39	76
Daytime surface temperature	300	750
Number of satellites	1	0

Similarities you might point out are that both are similar in size, shape, and mass. Differences include Venus having hotter surface temperatures, a dense cloudy atmosphere, and an intense greenhouse effect.

RECOGNIZING CAUSE AND EFFECT

Have you ever watched something happen and then tried to figure out why

or how it happened? If so, you have observed an event and inferred a reason for its occurrence. The event is an effect, and the reason for the event is the cause.

Suppose that every time your teacher fed fish in a classroom aquarium, she or he tapped the food container on the edge of the aquarium. Then, one day your teacher just happened to tap the edge of the aquarium with a pencil while making a point about an ecology lesson. You observed the fish swim to the surface of the aquarium to feed. What is the effect, and what would you infer to be the cause? The effect is the fish swimming to the surface of the aquarium. You might infer the cause to be the teacher tapping on the edge of the aquarium. In determining cause and effect, you have made a logical inference based on your observations.

Perhaps the fish swam to the surface because they reacted to the teacher's waving hand or for some other reason. When scientists are unsure of the cause for a certain event, they design controlled experiments to determine what caused the event. Although you have made a logical conclusion about the fish's behavior, you would have to perform an experiment to be certain that it was the tapping that caused the effect you observed.

MEASURING IN SI

You're probably somewhat familiar with the metric system of measurement. The metric system is a system of measurement developed by a group of scientists in 1795. The development of the metric system helped scientists avoid problems by providing an international standard of comparison for measurements that all scientists around the world could understand. A modern form of the metric system called the International System, or SI, was adopted for worldwide use in 1960.

Your text uses metric units in many measurements. In the activities and experiments you will be doing, you will frequently use the metric system of measurement.

The metric system is convenient because it has a systematic way of naming units and a decimal base. For example, meter is a unit for measuring length, gram for measuring mass, and liter for measuring volume. Unit sizes vary by multiples of ten. When changing from smaller units to larger, you divide by ten. When changing from larger units to smaller, you multiply by ten. Prefixes are used to name units. Look at the following table for some common metric prefixes and their meanings.

METRIC PREFIXES

PREFIX	SYMBOL	MEANING	
kilo-	k	1000	thousand
hecto-	h	100	hundred
deka-	da	10	ten
deci-	d	0.1	tenth
centi-	c	0.01	hundreth
milli-	m	0.001	thousandth

Do you see how the prefix kilo-attached to the unit gram is kilogram, or 1000 grams? The prefix deci- attached to the unit meter is decimeter, or one-tenth (0.1) of a meter.

You have probably measured distance many times. The meter is the SI unit used to measure distance. To visualize the length of a meter, think of a baseball bat. A baseball bat is about one meter long. When measuring smaller distances, the meter is divided into smaller units called centimeters and millimeters. A centimeter is one-hundredth (0.01) of a meter, which is about the size of the width of the fingernail on your ring finger. A millimeter is one-thousandth of a meter (0.001), about the thickness of a dime.

Most metric rulers have lines indicating centimeters and millimeters. The centimeter lines are the longer numbered lines, and the shorter lines are millimeter lines.

When using a metric ruler, first decide on a unit of measurement. You then line up the zero centimeter mark with the end of the object being measured and read the number where the object ends.

Units of length are also used to measure surface area. The standard unit of area is the square meter (m^2). A square that's one meter long on each side has a surface area of one square meter. Similarly, a square centimeter (cm^2) is a square one centimeter long on each side. The surface area of an object is determined by multiplying the number of units in length times the number of units in width.

The volume of rectangular solids is also calculated using units of length. The cubic meter (m^3) is the standard SI unit of volume. A cubic meter is a cube one meter on a side. You can determine the volume of rectangular solids by multiplying length times width times height.

Liquid volume is measured using a unit called a liter. A liter has the volume of 1000 cubic centimeters. Since the prefix milli- means thousandth (0.001), a milliliter equals one cubic centimeter. One milliliter of liquid would completely fill a cube measuring one centimeter on each side.

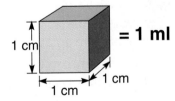

During science activities, you will measure liquids using beakers and graduated cylinders marked in milliliters. A graduated cylinder is a tall cylindrical container marked with lines from bottom to top.

Scientists use a balance to find the mass of an object in grams. You will likely use a beam balance similar to the one illustrated. Notice that on one side of the beam balance is a pan and on the other side is a set of beams. Each beam has an object of a known mass called a rider that slides on the beam.

Before you find the mass of an object, set the balance to zero by sliding all the riders back to zero point. Check the pointer on the right to make sure it swings an equal distance above and below the zero point on the scale. If the swing is unequal, find and turn the adjusting screw until you have an equal swing.

You are now ready to use the balance to find the mass of the object. Place the object on the pan. Slide the rider with the largest mass along its beam until the pointer drops below the zero point. Then move it back one notch. Repeat the process on each beam until the pointer swings an equal distance above and below the zero point. Read the masses indicated on each beam. The sum of these masses is the mass of the object.

You should never place a hot object or pour chemicals directly on the pan. Instead,

find the mass of a clean container, such as a beaker or a glass jar. Place into the container the dry or liquid chemicals you want to measure. Next, you need to find the combined mass of the container and the chemicals. Calculate the mass of the chemicals by subtracting the mass of the empty container from the combined mass.

PRACTICING SCIENTIFIC METHODS

You might say that the work of a scientist is to solve problems. But when you decide how to dress on a particular day, you are doing problem solving, too. You may observe what the weather looks like through a window. You may go outside and see if what you are wearing is warm or cool enough.

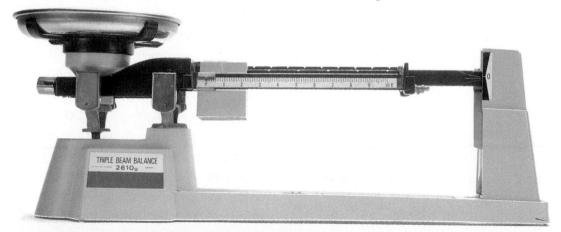

Scientists use an orderly approach to learn new information and to solve problems. The methods scientists use include observing, forming a hypothesis, testing a hypothesis, separating and controlling variables, and interpreting data.

OBSERVING

You observe all the time. Anytime you smell wood burning, touch a pet, see lightning, taste food, or hear your favorite music, you are observing. Observation gives you information about events or things. Scientists must try to observe as much as possible about the things and events they study.

Some observations describe something using only words. These observations are called qualitative observations. If you were making qualitative observations of a dog, you might use words such as cute, furry, brown, short-haired, or short-eared.

Other observations describe how much of something there is. These are quantitative observations and use numbers as well as words in the description. Tools or equipment are used to measure the characteristic being described. Quantitative observations of a dog might include a mass of 459 g, a height of 27 cm, ear length of 14 mm, and an age of 283 days.

FORMING A HYPOTHESIS

Suppose you wanted to make a perfect score on a spelling test. You think of several ways to accomplish a perfect score. You base these possibilities on past observations. If you put these possibilities into a sentence using the words *if* and *then*, you have formed a hypothesis. All of the following are hypotheses you might consider to explain how you could score 100% on your test:

If the test is easy, then I will get a good grade.

If I am intelligent, then I will get a good grade.

If I study hard, then I will get a good grade.

Scientists use hypotheses that they can test to explain the observations they have made. Perhaps a scientist has observed that plants that receive fertilizer grow taller than plants that do not. A scientist may form a hypothesis that says: If you fertilize plants, their growth will increase.

DESIGNING AN EXPERIMENT TO TEST A HYPOTHESIS

Once you have stated a hypothesis, you probably want to find out if it explains an event or an observation or not. This requires a test. A hypothesis *must* be something you can test. To test a hypothesis, you have to design and carry out an experiment. An experiment involves planning and materials. Let's figure out how you would conduct an experiment to test the hypothesis stated before about the effects of fertilizer on plants.

First, you need to lay out a procedure. A procedure is the plan that you will follow in your experiment. A procedure tells you what materials to use and how you will use them. In this experiment, your plan may involve using ten bean plants that are 15-cm tall in two groups, Groups A and B. You will water the five bean plants in Group A with 200 mL of plain water and no fertilizer once a week for three weeks. You will treat the five bean plants in Group B with 200 mL of fertilizer solution once a week for three weeks.

You will need to measure all the plants in both groups at the beginning of the experiment and again at the end of the three-week test period. These measurements will be the data that you record in a table. For instance, look at the data in the table for this experiment. From the data you recorded, you will draw a conclusion and make a statement about your results. If your conclusion supports your hypothesis, then you can say that your hypothesis is reliable. If it did not support your hypothesis, then you would have to make new observations and state a new hypothesis, one that you could also test.

GROWING BEAN PLANTS		
PLANTS	**TREATMENT**	**HEIGHT 3 WEEKS LATER**
Group A	no fertilizer added to soil	17 cm
Group B	3 g fertilizer added to soil	31 cm

SEPARATING AND CONTROLLING VARIABLES

In the experiment above with the bean plants, you made everything the same except for treating one group (Group B) with fertilizer. By doing so, you've controlled as many things as possible. The type of plants, their beginning heights, the soil, the frequency with which you watered them—all these things were kept the same, or constant. By doing this, you made sure that at the end of three weeks any change you saw depended on whether or not the plants had been fertilized. The only thing that you changed, or varied, was the use of fertilizer. The one factor that you change in an experiment—in this case, the fertilizer—is called the *independent* variable. The factor that changes as a result of the independent variable is called the *dependent* variable—in this case, growth. Always make sure that there is only one independent variable. If you allow more than one, you will not know what causes any change you observe in the dependent variable.

Experiments also need a control, a treatment that you can compare with the results of your experiment. In this case, Group A was the control because it was not treated with fertilizer. Group B was the test group. At the end of three weeks, you were able to compare Group A with Group B and draw a conclusion.

INTERPRETING DATA

The word *interpret* means to explain the meaning of something. Information, or data, needs to mean something. Look at the problem originally being explored and find out what the data is trying to show. Perhaps you are looking at a table from an experiment designed to answer the question: does fertilizer affect plant growth and leaf color? Look back to the table showing the results of the bean plant experiment.

Identify the control group and the experimental group so you can see whether or not the variable has had an effect. In this example, Group A was the control and Group B was the experimental group. Now you need to check differences between the control and experimental groups. These differences may be qualitative or quantitative. A qualitative difference would be if the leaf colors of plants in Groups A and B were different. A quantitative difference would be the difference in number of centimeters of height among the plants in each group. Group B was in fact taller than Group A after three weeks.

If there are differences, the variable being tested may have had an effect. If there is no difference between the control and the experimental groups, the variable being tested probably had no effect. From the data table in this experiment, it appears that fertilizer does have an effect on plant growth.

REPRESENTING AND APPLYING DATA

INTERPRETING SCIENTIFIC ILLUSTRATIONS

Most of the textbooks you use in school have illustrations. Illustrations help you to understand what you read. As you read this textbook, you will see many drawings, diagrams, and photographs. Some are included to help you understand an idea that you can't see by yourself. For instance, we can't see atoms, but we can look at a diagram of an atom and that helps us to understand what atoms are and how they work. Seeing something often helps you remember more easily. The text may describe the surface of Jupiter in detail, but seeing a photograph of it may help you to remember that it has cloud bands. Illustrations also provide examples that clarify something you have read or give additional information about the topic you are

studying. Maps, for example, help you to locate places that may be described in the text.

Most illustrations have captions. A caption is a brief comment that identifies or explains the illustration. Diagrams often have labels to identify parts of the item shown or the order of steps in a process.

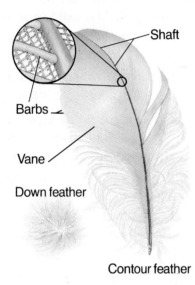

Down feather

Contour feather

An illustration of an organism shows that organism from a particular view or orientation. In order to understand the illustration, you need to identify the front (anterior) end, tail (posterior) end, the underside (ventral), and the back (dorsal) side of the organism shown.

You might also check for symmetry so you know how many sides the organism

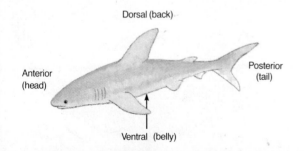

has. A shark has bilateral symmetry. This means that drawing an imaginary line through the center of the animal from the anterior to posterior end forms two mirror images. If you can draw a second imaginary line at right angles to the first and divide the organism into four equal parts, the organism has radial symmetry.

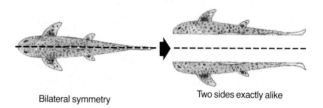

Bilateral symmetry   Two sides exactly alike

Some illustrations give an internal view of an organism or object. These illustrations are called sections.

Look at all illustrations carefully and read captions and labels so that you understand exactly what the illustration is showing you.

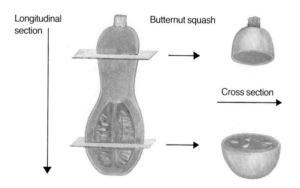

Longitudinal section   Butternut squash

Cross section

MAKING MODELS

You or your friends may have worked on a model car or plane or rocket. These models look, and sometimes work, just like the real thing, but they are usually much smaller than the real thing. In science, models are used to help simplify processes or structures that may be difficult to understand.

Often, everyday objects are used to make scientific principles and ideas simpler.

In order to make a model, you first have to learn about the structure or process involved. You decide to make a model showing the differences in size of arteries, veins, and capillaries. First, you must read about these structures. All three are hollow tubes. Arteries are round and thick. Veins are flat and thinner than arteries. Capillaries are very small.

Now you will need to decide what you can use for your model. Different kinds and sizes of pasta might work. Different sizes of rubber tubing might do just as well. Cut and glue the different noodles or tubing onto thick paper so the openings can be seen. Then label each. Now you have a model showing the differences in size of arteries, veins, and capillaries.

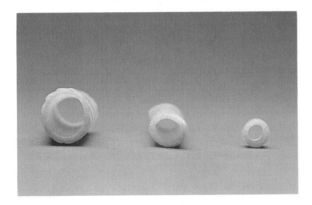

What other scientific ideas might a model help you to understand? A model of a compound can be made from gumdrops (using different colors for the different elements present) and toothpicks (to show different chemical bonds). A working model of a volcano can be made from clay, a small amount of baking soda, vinegar, and a bottle cap.

PREDICTING

When you apply a hypothesis, or general explanation, to a specific situation, you predict something about that situation. First, you must identify which hypothesis fits the situation you are considering. Maybe you want to predict whether or not eating a chocolate candy bar will increase your pulse rate. You've read that chocolate contains caffeine. So you could hypothesize that: if you consume caffeine in some form, then your pulse rate will increase. Next, you must figure out how the hypothesis affects the question you are asking. Since chocolate candy bars have caffeine and you think caffeine increases your pulse rate, you would predict that eating a chocolate candy bar would make your pulse rate faster.

We use predicting to make everyday decisions. Based on your previous observations and experiences, you may form a hypothesis that if it is wintertime, then temperatures will be lower. You may then use this hypothesis to predict specific temperatures and weather for four or five days in advance. You may use these predictions to plan what your activities will be for that time period.

Glossary

This glossary defines each key term that appears in **bold type** in the text. It also shows the page number where you can find the word used.

A

absolute zero: temperature (−273°C) at which the kinetic energy of molecules would have decreased to zero (239)

air mass: large body of air whose properties are determined by the part of Earth's surface over which it develops (263)

alcohol: family of compounds formed when a hydroxyl (-OH) group replaces one or more hydrogen atoms in a hydrocarbon (330)

alkali metals: Column 1 elements in the periodic table that have one electron in their outer energy level (169)

alkaline earth metals: Column 2 elements in the periodic table that have two electrons in their outer energy level (170)

alpha particles: positively charged particles given off by a radioactive substance; helium nucleus (132)

amines: organic compounds formed when an amine group ($-NH_2$) replaces hydrogen in a hydrocarbon (331)

antibodies: substances produced by some white blood cells in response to specific antigens such as those on invading bacteria or viruses (397)

antigens: proteins and chemicals that are foreign to the body (397)

artificial transmutation: the changing of one element into another by radioactive decay resulting from outside influence (581)

asteroid: large chunk of rock traveling through space (620)

atomic mass: average mass of isotopes of an element found in nature (163)

atomic number: number of protons in an atom (161)

B

balanced chemical equation: equation having the same number of atoms of each element on each side (204)

beta particle: high speed electron given off by a radioactive substance (132)

binary compound: compound composed of two elements (198)

binary star system: two-star system in which the two stars orbit each other (638)

body cells: cells in the body that reproduce by mitosis (418)

boiling: process during which vapor bubbles form throughout a liquid and rise to the surface (233)

C

carbohydrates: class of nutrient containing sugars and starches that provides fuel for cells (337)

carboxylic acid: substance formed when a $-CH_3$ group is displaced by a carboxyl (-COOH) group in a hydrocarbon molecule (330)

cast: fossil formed when sediment fills in a mold and hardens into rock (517)

Cenozoic Era: era that began about 65 million years ago, when mammals became abundant (532)

chain reaction: continuous reaction in which the neutrons released by nuclear reactions initiate further nuclear reactions (588)

circuit: complete path through which a charge flows (14)

circuit breaker: device designed to break the circuit to prevent an overload (70)

clotting: process by which platelets help seal a broken blood vessel (394)

comet: large chunk of ice, dust, frozen gases, and rock fragments that moves through space (619)

condensation: process of a gas becoming a liquid (234)

conductor: material through which an electrical charge moves freely (9)

continental drift: hypothesis that all the continents were once joined but split and moved apart (480)

convergent boundary: boundary formed as two of Earth's plates meet (493)

covalent bond: bond that forms between atoms when they share electrons (192)

current: rate at which charges flow through a circuit (14)

D

density current: movement of water that occurs when dense seawater moves toward an area of less dense seawater (306)

dew point: temperature at which air is saturated with water vapor and the water vapor condenses (259)

diffraction: bending of light around a barrier (105)

diffraction grating: device having many rows of equally-spaced grooves that produce a light spectrum by interference (111)

digestion: process that breaks down carbohydrates, fats, and proteins into smaller and simpler molecules that can be absorbed and used by cells in the body (365)

diode: a semiconductor device that allows electric current to flow only in one direction (73)

divergent boundary: boundary formed between two of Earth's plates that are moving away from each other and spreading apart (492)

DNA: molecule found in the chromosomes of cells that determines the traits of organisms (465)

dominant trait: trait that covers up or masks another form of the same trait (454)

E

eggs: sex cells produced by female organisms (419)

electrical charge: a property of matter that gives rise to a force between two charged objects (5)

electric generator: device that changes mechanical energy into electric energy (51)

electric motor: device that uses an electromagnet to change electric energy into mechanical energy (49)

electromagnet: magnet made of a current-carrying wire (43)

electromagnetic spectrum: entire range of electromagnetic waves, from lowest to highest frequencies (100)

electromagnetic wave: alternating electrical and magnetic wave produced by moving charges (96)

electron: tiny negatively charged particle (128)

enzyme: protein molecule that controls the rate of different processes in the body (368)

epoch: subdivision of periods on the geologic time scale (532)

era: one of the four major divisions in the geologic time scale (525)

evaporation: process of surface particles of a liquid changing to a gas or vapor (232)

evolution: change in the hereditary features of a population of organisms over time (554)

F

family of elements: elements with similar properties that are in the same column on the periodic table (167)

fission: splitting of an atomic nucleus with the release of energy (586)

fossil: remains or trace of an organism that was once alive (514)

front: boundary that forms when one air mass moves and collides with another air mass (264)

fusion: process of two atomic nuclei joining into one (590)

G

galaxy: massive group of stars, gas, and dust held together by gravity (647)

gamma rays: high-energy electromagnetic radiation emitted by radioactive nuclei (132)

gaseous giant planets: very large, low-density planets composed mainly of gases; also the five planets farthest from the sun (613)

gene: specific location on a chromosome that controls a specific trait (454)

H

hemoglobin: red, iron-containing pigment that binds with oxygen molecules and gives red blood cells their color (390)

heterozygote: organism with one dominant gene and one recessive gene for a trait (456)

homologous structures: body parts of different organisms that are similar in origin and structure (560)

hot spots: areas where magma is forced up through cracks in the solid lithosphere (502)

hurricane: very large, swirling, low pressure system that forms over tropical oceans (274)

hydrocarbon: compound formed between carbon and hydrogen atoms (322)

I

immunity: production of a specific antibody to defend the body against a particular antigen (397)

induced current: electric current produced in a conductor by a changing magnetic field (51)

induced magnetism: magnetism that occurs only in the presence of an outside magnetic field (39)

insulator: material through which an electrical charge does not move freely (8)

intertidal zone: area of a coastline between high and low tide (295)

ion: charged atom or group of atoms (189)

ionic bond: attraction between positive ions and negative ions (190)

isomers: compounds that have identical chemical formulas, but different molecular structures or shapes (326)

isotopes: atoms of the same element with different numbers of neutrons (163)

K

kilowatt: unit of power equal to 1000 watts (79)

kilowatt-hour: large unit of electrical energy used by utility companies (81)

kinetic-molecular theory: the theory that states that all matter is made up of tiny particles in constant, random motion (223)

L

law of superposition: undisturbed layers of rocks in which the oldest rocks are generally on the bottom and the youngest rocks are generally on top (519)

light-year: distance light travels in one year, about 9.5 trillion kilometers (639)

like charges: electrical charges that repel one another (5)

lipids: organic compounds that feel greasy and will not dissolve in water (337)

lithosphere: Earth's crust and uppermost portion of the mantle together (491)

loudspeaker: instrument that changes variations in electric current into sound waves (47)

M

magnetic field: region around a magnet where the magnetic force acts (37)

magnetic poles: two ends of the magnet that point north-south when a magnet is allowed to turn freely (35)

manganese nodule: rounded rock that forms when minerals collect around a small object in the ocean (299)

mass number: total number of protons and neutrons in the nucleus (161)

meiosis: reproductive process of sex cells in which new cells contain half the number of chromosomes as the parent cell (422)

menstrual cycle: monthly cycle in which the ovary produces an egg and the uterus prepares for fertilization (435)

menstruation: monthly discharge of uterine lining and blood through the vagina (435)

Mesozoic Era: era that began about 225 million years ago, often called the age of dinosaurs (530)

meteor: meteoroid that has entered Earth's atmosphere (622)

meteorite: meteoroid that strikes Earth's surface (622)

minerals: inorganic compounds that regulate many of the chemical reactions that take place in the body (356)

mold: the cavity left in rock by a decaying and eroding object (517)

molecules: neutral particles formed as a result of atoms sharing electrons (192)

mutation: permanent change in a gene or chromosome (555)

N

natural selection: process in which living things that are better adapted to their environment are more likely to survive and reproduce (550)

nebula: large cloud of gas and dust that can form a star (636)

nekton: swimming forms of fish and other animals (306)

neutron: particle in the nucleus of an atom having no charge (141)

nonpolar molecules: molecules that have evenly distributed charges (195)

nucleus: dense, positively charged center of an atom (138)

nutrients: substances in food that provide energy and materials for the development, growth, and repair of cells (353)

O

organic compound: substance that contains carbon (320)

ovary: female sex organ that produces eggs (426)

oxidation number: number of electrons that an atom gains, loses, or shares when bonding with another atom (198)

P

Paleozoic Era: second major geologic time scale division, which began about 570 million years ago (527)

parallel circuit: circuit that has several paths (67)

pedigree: chart showing the passing of a trait from one generation to the next (449)

period: a row of elements in the periodic table (173); subdivision of a geologic era (528)

periodic table: table of elements arranged according to increasing atomic number and physical and chemical properties (160)

peristalsis: wave-like action of the smooth muscle of the esophagus that pushes bites of food to the stomach (369)

permanent magnet: magnet that can retain its magnetism over a long period of time (41)

pistil: female reproductive organ of a flower (429)

planet: body of matter that travels around a star in a path called an orbit (604)

plankton: drifting protists and animals (305)

plasma: liquid part of blood that consists mostly of water (388)

platelets: cell fragments that stop the flow of blood from a broken blood vessel (394)

plate tectonics: theory that Earth's crust and upper mantle are broken into sections called plates that move (491)

polar molecule: molecule that has a slightly positive end and a slightly negative end (195)

polyatomic ions: positively or negatively charged group of covalently-bonded atoms (200)

polymers: huge molecules made of many smaller organic molecules linked together (334)

potential difference: change in total potential energy divided by the total charge (13)

Precambrian Era: first major geologic time scale division, which began about 4.6 billion years ago and ended 570 million years ago (527)

primates: group of mammals that includes monkeys, apes, and humans (562)

proteins: polymers formed by linking together various amino acids (335)

proton: positively charged particle in the nucleus of an atom (138)

pure dominant: trait characterized by two dominant genes (456)

pure recessive: trait characterized by two recessive genes (456)

R

radiation: transfer of energy by electromagnetic waves (101)

radioactivity: release of high-energy particles by radioactive elements (131)

recessive trait: trait that appears least often in offspring; trait masked by the dominant form of the same trait (454)

red blood cells: cells, formed in the marrow of long bones, that carry oxygen from the lungs to all body cells (390)

relative humidity: measure of the amount of water vapor in the air at a particular temperature, compared with the total amount of water vapor the air can hold at that temperature (256)

resistance: measure of how much potential a charge loses when moving through a material (14)

S

salinity: measure of the amount of solids, primarily salts, dissolved in ocean water (297)

saturated: describing air when its relative humidity reaches 100 percent (259)

sea-floor spreading: hypothesis which states that molten material from Earth's mantle rises to the surface at mid-ocean ridges and cools to form new seafloor (487)

semiconductor: material that conducts current better than an insulator, but not as well as a conductor (71)

series circuit: circuit that has only one path (64)

sex cells: special cells of organisms that, when united, produce offspring (419)

sickle-cell anemia: disease in which the red blood cells are shaped like curved sickles (461)

solar system: sun, the planets, and many smaller objects that travel around the sun (604)

sperm: sex cells produced by male organisms (419)

stamen: male reproductive organ of a flower (429)

star: hot, glowing sphere of gas that produces energy by fusion (635)

star cluster: large group of stars that moves through space together (638)

sublimation: process of a solid changing to a gas or a gas to a solid without first becoming a liquid (234)

sunspot: cool, dark area on the sun's surface (643)

surface current: movement of water that affects only the upper few hundred meters of seawater (303)

T

terrestrial planets: the four rocky, Earth-sized planets nearest the sun (608)

testis: male sex organ that produces sperm (426)

thermal expansion: expansion that occurs as a material is heated (225)

thin films: very thin layers of material that produce a rainbow effect when light strikes them (107)

tornado: violent, funnel-shaped storm whose whirling winds move in a narrow path over land (273)

traits: specific characteristics in living things (448)

transformer: device used to change the voltage in circuits (52)

transform fault boundary: boundary formed when two plates slide past one another in opposite directions or in the same direction at different rates (495)

transistor: a device with a region of one type of doped semiconductor sandwiched between layers of the opposite type (75)

transmutation: the changing of an atom of one element to another by emitting particles from its nucleus (578)

U, V, W

unconformity: gap in a particular area's geologic history caused by missing original layers of rock (520)

unlike charges: electrical charges that attract one another (5)

upwelling: upward movement of cold water in the ocean (308)

vaccine: substance that, when injected into the body, produces an immune response against a specific disease (398)

variation: appearance of an inherited trait or behavior that makes one organism different from others of the same species (546)

villi: finger like projections in the small intestine that help absorb digested food into the circulatory system (371)

viscosity: liquid's resistance to changing shape (229)

vitamins: organic nutrients necessary for continued good health (361)

white blood cells: cells that fight bacteria, viruses, and other foreign substances that invade the body (391)

Index

The Index for *Science Interactions* will help you locate major topics in the book quickly and easily. Each entry in the Index is followed by the numbers of the pages on which the entry is discussed. A page number given in **boldface type** indicates the page on which that entry is defined. A page number given in *italic type* indicates a page on which the entry is used in an illustration or photograph. The abbreviation *act.* indicates a page on which the entry is used in an activity.

eating balanced, 379
fats in, 359, *359, act.* 360
minerals in, 356-357, *357*
nutrients in, 352-353, *353, act.* 354
proteins in, 360-361, *361*
variety in, *act.* 352
vitamins in, 361-362, *362, act.* 362,
364
water in, 354-356, *act.* 355
Diffraction, 105-106, **105,** *105, 106*
Diffraction gratings, 108-109, *act.* 109,
111-112, **111**
Digestion, **365,** *act.* 366
chemical, 365, *act.* 367
enzymes in, *act.* 367, 368, *368,*
370-371
in large intestine, 372
organs in, 365-366, *365,* 368-369
in small intestine, 371-372, *371,*
372
in stomach, 369-370, *370*
Dihydrogen monoxide, 202
Dinosaurs, 530-531, *531*
disappearance of, 537-538, *537,*
538
reconstruction of, 539, *539*
Diode, **73,** *73, act.* 74
Direct current (DC), 49
converting to alternating current,
73
Disease, and production of antibodies, 405, *405*
Displacement reactions, 208
double, *act.* 209, 210
Divergent boundary, 492-493, **492**
volcanoes in, 500-501
DNA, **465,** *465, act.* 465, 466, 471,
564, *564*
and cell structure, 559-560, *559*
discovery of, 341, *341*
structure of, 466-468, *466, 467, act.*
467
DNA fingerprinting, 474, *474*
Dominant trait, **454**
Doppler shift, 652, *652*
Dot diagrams, for elements, 167-168,
168, 169
Double displacement reaction, *act.*
209, 210
Double-slit diffraction, *act.* 110
Drew, Charles Richard, 410
Du Fay, Charles, 7

Earth
age of, 527
atmosphere of, *act.* 609, 612, *612*
convection currents inside, 504
inner structure of, 485, *485*
magnetic field of, 37, 38, 488
rotation of, 303
Van Allen belt of, 54, *54*
Earthquakes
geographic locations of, 499-500
relation to plate boundaries, *act.*
498
use of, in studying interior of
Earth, 507
Echo sounding, 486, *486*
Eddington, A. S., 637-638, *637*
Edison, Thomas, 69
Eggs, *act.* 417, **419,** 420-421, *420*
external fertilization, 432-433, *act.*
433
shelled, 437, *437*
Einstein, Albert, 637-638, *637*
Electrical appliances, 79
power rating of, 77-78, *78*
Electrical charge, **5,** *5,* 7, 8-11, *act.* 8
identifying, *act.* 6
interaction of, *act.* 4-5
types of, 7, 8
Electrical circuits, *act.* 63, 64
parallel, *act.* 66, 67-68, *67*
series, 64-65, *65, act.* 66
Electrical current
changing, 51-52, *52*
generating, 51, *51*
and magnetism, 45-46, *act.* 46, 50-
51, *act.* 50
and resistance, *act.* 15
turning into sound, 46-47, *act.* 47
using, 47, 49
Electrical energy, 12-16, *12, act.* 13
Electrical power, 77-80
calculating, *act.* 80
calculating individual use of, 85
measurement of, 77, *act.* 77-78
using, 81, *81*
Electric generator, **51,** *51*
Electricity, 3
potential difference and current,
17, *17, act.* 18, 19-22
static, *act.* 3, 4-5, 7, 10-11

Electric meter, 81, *81*
Electric motor, **49**
making, *act.* 48
Electric potential energy, 12-13
Electromagnet(s), **43**
at work, 43-44, *43, 44*
Electromagnetic radiation, 117, *117*
Electromagnetic spectrum, 99-100,
100, *100*
ownership of, 115-116, *115, 116*
Electromagnetic wave, 55, **96**
characteristics of, 97-99, *98*
frequencies of, *act.* 98-99
types of, 97, *97*
uses of, 99-101, *100, 101,* 103
Electron, **128,** *141,* 271
energy levels of, 142-143, *act.* 142,
143
Electron cloud, 138-139, *138, 139,* 143
Electronics
converting AC to DC, 73, 75
and integrated circuits, 75-76, *76*
and semiconductors, 71-73, *71, 72*
transistors, 75, *75*
Elements
atoms of, 143-144, *144,* 146
in binary compounds, *199*
changing stable, 581
dot diagrams, 167-168, *168, 169*
effect of decay on, 577-578, *578*
making new, 582-584
synthetic, 179-180, *179*
ELF fields, as health hazard, 87-88, *87,*
88
Elliptical galaxies, 648
Embryos, evidence on evolution
from, 562, *562*
Embryo transfer, 441
Endangered species, saving, 441
Environment
and disposal of nuclear wastes, 180
impact of modern agriculture on,
377-378, *377, 378*
Enzymes, 336, **368**
in digestion, *act.* 367, 368, *368,*
370-371
Epicenter, 499, *499*
Epochs, **532**
Era, **525**
Cenozoic, *526,* 531-532, *532*
Mesozoic, *526,* 530-531, *531*
Paleozoic, *526,* 527-529, *528, act.*
529

Precambrian, *526, 527*
Esophagus, 369
    peristalsis in, 369, *369*
Ethane, 323, *323*
Ethanol, 330, *330, act.* 332, 345
Ethene, 325, *325*
Ethylene, 325
Evaporation, 231-233, **232,** *232*
Evolution, 554, **554**
    cell structure as evidence of, 557-
        560, *act.* 557, *559, 560*
    embryo as evidence of, 562, *562*
    fossils as evidence of, 556-557, *556*
External, fertilization, 432-433, *act.*
    433

relative, 256, *256, act.* 257, 258-259
Hurricane, 274-276, **274,** *275, 276,*
    281
Hydrocarbon(s), 322-325, **322,** *324*
    saturated, 323-324, *act.* 325
    substituted, 329-331, *act.* 329, *330,*
        331, 333, 333
Hydrofluorocarbons, 244
Hydrogen fusion, 637-638

I

Icebergs, melting, 309, *309*
Immune system, 395, *395*
    and AIDs, 404, *404*
    blood in, 394-395
    and communicable diseases, 400-
        401, *act.* 402
    natural defenses in, 395-397, *396,*
        act. 396
    and sexually transmitted diseases,
        403-404, *403*
    specific defenses in, 397-400, *397,*
        398, 399
Immunity, **397**
    active, 397-398
Incomplete dominance, 462, 464
Induced current, **51**
Induced magnetism, **39**
Infections, role of antibiotics in fight-
        ing, 409, *409*
Infertility, curing, 439-440, *439, 440*
Infrared photography, *101*
Infrared radiation, 101, *act.* 102, 103,
        103
Insects, blood in, 391
Insulator, 8-9, **8**
Integrated circuits, 75-76, *76*
Interference, 106-108, *106, 107, act.*
        106-107, *108*
Internal fertilization, 433
Intertidal zone, **295**
    life in, 294-295, *294, 295*
Intestine, digestion in, 372
In vitro fertilization, 439-440, 441
Iodine-131, 580, 584
Ion, **189**
Ionic bond, 190-192, **190,** *act.* 190,
        191, 195
Irradiation, 594
Irregular galaxies, 649

Island arc, 501
Isobutane, 326, *326, 327*
Isomers, 326-328, **326**
Isotopes, 162-163, *163, act.* 164, 165

J

Jenner, Edward, 399
Joule, James Prescott, 222
Jupiter, 614-615, *614*

K

Kelvin scale, 239-240, *240*
Kepler, Johannes, 606
Kilowatt, **79**
Kilowatt-hour, **81,** *81*
Kinetic-molecular theory, 222-223,
        223
    boiling, 233, *233*
    condensation, 234-235, *234*
    evaporation and condensation,
        231-233
    freezing and melting in, 229-231
    liquids in, 226, *act.* 227, 228-229
    solids in, 223, *223,* 225-226
    sublimation, 234, *234*
    and thermal expansion, *act.* 224,
        225-226
Kinetic theory, of gases, 236-240, *act.*
        236-237, *237, 238, 239, 240*
Kirchoff, Gustav, 113
Koch, Robert, 403
Krypton, 26
Krypton-92 nucleus, 586

L

Large Magellanic Cloud, 649, *649,* 655
Latimer, Lewis, 26
Law enforcement
    and DNA fingerprinting, 474, *474*
    and forensic chemistry, 213-214,
        213, 214
Law of superposition, **519**
Levitation, 149-150, *149*

Libavius, Andreas, 241
Lie, J. E., 507
Light
    differences in sources of, *act.* 111-
        112
    diffraction of, 105-106, *105, 106*
    and interference, 106-108, *107*
    and plants, 470, *470*
    properties of, 104, *act.* 104, *105*
Light bulb, improving, 26, *26*
Light emitting diode, *act.* 74
Lightning, 4, 10-11, *10, 27,* 271, *271,*
        272
    causes of, 23, *23*
    safety during, 9
Lightning rod, 23, 27
Light pollution, 115, 653-654, *653,*
        654
Light-year, **639**
Like charges, **5**
Lind, James, 361
Lipids, 337-338, **337,** *act.* 339, 340
Liquid
    molecular forces within, *act.* 228
    properties of, 226, *act.* 227, 228
    viscosity of, 229, *229*
Lithosphere, **491,** *491, 493,* 500
Longitudinal waves, 97, *97*
Loudspeaker, **47,** *act.* 48
Lucretius, 245
Lymphocytes, 404, *404*

M

MagLev trains, 58, *58*
MagLev transportations, 43
Magnesium, 170
Magnesium chloride, 191-192, *191*
Magnesium oxide, 190-191, *191*
Magnetic atoms, 40
Magnetic clues, for sea-floor spread-
        ing, 488, *act.* 489, 490
Magnetic domains, theory of, 44, *44*
Magnetic field, **37**
Magnetic force, *act.* 36
    revealing, 36-38
Magnetic poles, **35**
    interaction of, *act.* 35
Magnetic resonance imaging (MRI),
        55-56, *55,* 86
Magnetism, 33, *act.* 33

R

Photo Credits